CULTURAL HISTORY
FROM THE
VĀYU PURĀNA

DEVENDRAKUMAR RAJARAM PATIL
M. A., L.L. B., PH. D.
Assistant Director of Archaeology, Gwalior, Research Scholar Deccan College, Postgraduate & Research Institute, Poona

MOTILAL BANARSIDASS
DELHI :: PATNA :: VARANASI

Indological Publishers & Booksellers

Head Office : BUNGALOW ROAD, JAWAHARNAGAR, DELHI-7
Branches : 1. CHOWK, VARANASI (U.P.)
2. ASHOK RAJPATH (OPP. PATNA COLLEGE), PATNA-4 (BIHAR)

By arrangement with The Deccan College, Postgraduate & Research Institute, Poona

First Edition : Poona 1946
Reprint : Delhi 1973

Printed in India

BY JAYYAD PRESS, DELHI AND PUBLISHED BY SUNDARLAL JAIN FOR MOTILAL BANARSIDASS, BUNGALOW ROAD, JAWAHARNAGAR. DELHI-7

Most Respectfully Dedicated

To

His Highness, Maharaja, Mukhtar-ul-Mulk, Azim-ul-Iqtidar,

Rafi-us-Shan, Wala-Shikoh, Mohatashim-ud-Dauran,

Umdat-ul-Umra, Maharajadhiraja, Hisam-us-Saltanat,

Major General

MAHARAJA SIR JIWAJIRAO SCINDIA, G.C.S.I., G.C.I.E.,

Alijah Bahadur, Shrinath, Mansur-i-Zaman,

Fidwi Hazarat Malik Mauzzam, Rafi-ud-Darjat Inglistan

MAHARAJA OF GWALIOR

Patron of

HIGHER LEARNING AND LIBERAL EDUCATION

By

His Highness' Most Humble Servant

The Author

With Deepest Feelings of Gratitude and Reverence.

FOREWORD

The present volume forms the second issue in the Dissertation Series inaugurated this year to mark the 125th anniversary of the original foundation of the Institute, and represents the first contribution by the Department of Proto- and Ancient Indian History of the Deccan College Postgraduate and Research Institute. Dr. D. R. PATIL has thus the distinction of not only being one of the first scholars carrying on research in this Department, but also of being the first in contributing his valuable study for inclusion in this Series. Dr. PATIL's work was accepted for the degree of Doctor of Philosophy by the University of Bombay in 1944, and it is presented here with a few alterations necessitated by further research.

The field of pre-history is confined primarily to archaeology, while that of proto-history is considerably vaster. It may include sources which at a given time cannot be regarded as historical, but the information from which, if gathered objectively, may throw light on the prehistoric and historic periods. The evolution of material culture in India can, therefore, be best understood if both these subjects are studied simultaneously and their results compared and mutually checked. With this object in view the Department of Proto- and Ancient Indian History at the Institute organized its programme in 1939, and the present work represents one of the earliest fruits of that programme connected with the preparation of regional archaeological studies in conjunction with strictly objective analytical studies of literary sources like the Purāṇas, the Jaina Āgamas and the Epics.

While political or dynastic history has been reconstructed from the Purāṇic tradition, and a number of works have been published on various aspects of religious or social life in India, this is the first systematic attempt at collecting and interpreting "cultural history" from the rich Purāṇic sources, and for the purposes of this study, the oldest Purāṇa, according to generally accepted standards, has been subjected to a scientific analysis. The book is valuable not only for Indian Culture, but also for a critical edition of the *Vāyu*, and consequently of other Purāṇa material.

26th June 1946. S. M. K.

PREFACE

With the publication of PARGITER's famous works on the Purāṇic researches an altogether new vision has been presented to the world of scholarship regarding the early history of India. They have opened up a possibility that the vast mine of information contained in the traditional lore of the Purāṇas—which was formerly regarded useless for historical purposes—may, to a certain extent, be relied upon for unfolding the hoary Indian past where other sources fail to guide us. PARGITER, however, concerned himself mainly with the genealogical portion of the Purāṇic texts which forms but a small part of this whole range of literature. The remaining bulk of the Purāṇas is really staggering both in its volume and in the difficulty of its interpretation ; but in it (as also in the genealogical lists) are found the various items of information very valuable for building up the cultural history of our ancient past. The present work represents a modest effort in this direction only in so far as the Vāyu—an admittedly ancient Purāṇa is concerned. It attempts to supplement the work of PARGITER on the cultural plane taking for granted that his works are a sure basis in the interpretation of the ancient Indian political tradition. How far it has succeeded in doing so it is for the world of scholars to judge.

I must at the outset pay my humble homage to His Highness Sir JIWAJIRAO SCINDIA, Alijah Bahadur, Maharaja of Gwalior, the gracious blessings of whose patronage and whose love of India's ancient heritage have enabled me to bring this work to the light of the day.

Like all those students who are first introduced to the world of scholarship by their teachers I am deeply indebted to Dr. H. D. SANKALIA whose valuable guidance and sympathetic attitude have greatly helped me in the completion of this work. I must, however, here express that without the paternal care and help of the Deccan College Research Institute particularly of its Director, Dr. S. M. KATRE, I would not have been able to complete it. I thus owe a great debt to this celebrated Institution. Lastly I must thank Dr. R. G. HARSHE, the Registrar of the Institute, for going through the troublesome task of correcting the proofs and of editing the press-copy especially when I was far removed from the press in Poona.

I have also to thank the University of Bombay for the substantial financial help towards the cost of publication of this work, and the Deccan College Research Institute for including it in its Dissertation Series. Without the active co-operation of Mr. S. R. SARDESAI and his Samarth Bharat Press it would not have been possible to give the present appearance to this work, for which my best thanks are due to them.

Department of Archaeology, Gwalior,
26th June 1946. D. R. PATIL.

BIBLIOGRAPHY

(The topics dealt with in this work are, it will be clear from a glance at the contents, many and varied ; and thus in tracing the historical sketch of matters covered by these topics we have in some cases relied on previous researches carried out by others and to a certain extent we have not gone to the original sources utilized by them. In other cases, however, we have referred to the original sources themselves.)

Original Sanskrit and Prakrit Works and Translations

Aitareya Brāhmaṇa, Edited by Haug, 1863.

Atharvaveda, Translated into English by Bloomfield, Sacred Books of the East, Vol. 42.

Bhagavad-gītā, Translated into English by K. T. Telang, Sacred Books of the East, Vol. 8.

Bhagavata Purāṇa, Bombay Edition of Ganapat Krishnaji, 1887.

Bhagavatī Sūtra, Agamodaya Samiti Edition, Surat.

Brahma Purāṇa, Published in the Ānandāśrama Sanskrit Series.

Brahmāṇḍa Purāṇa, Venkateśvara Press Edition.

Bṛhadāraṇyaka Upaniṣad, Published in Ānandāśrama Sanskrit Series, 1888.

Bṛhannāradīya Purāṇa, Bibliotheca Indica Edition.

Bṛhatsaṁhitā of Varāhamihira, Text edited by Kern, Bibliotheca Indica Edition.

Chāndogya Upaniṣad, Published in Āandāśrama Sanskrit Series, 1890.

Gopatha Brāhmaṇa, Edited by R. Mitra and H. Vidyābhūṣaṇa, Bibliotheca Indica Edition, 1872.

Gṛhya Sūtras, Translated into English, Sacred Books of the East, Vols. 29–30.

Kalpa-Sūtra, English Translation, Sacred Books of the East, Vol. 22.

Kauṣītakī Brahmaṇa.

Kauṭilīya Arthaśāstra, Edited by Shama Sastri.

" " English Translation by Shama Sastri.

" " Index Verborum to the published Texts —by Shama Sastri.

Kumārasambhava of Kālidāsa, Nirṇaya Sāgara Edition.

Kūrma Purāṇa, Bibliotheca Indica Edition, 1890

Liṅga Purāṇa.

Mahābhārata, Critical Edition published by the Bhandarkar Oriental Research Institute, Poona.

Mahābhārata, Published by the Royal Asiatic Society of Bengal.

Manu-Smṛti, Nirnaya Sāgara Press Edition.

" —English translation by Bühler, Sacred Books of the East, Vol. 25.

Matsya Purāṇa, Published in Ānandāśrama Sanskrit Series.
Mārkaṇḍeya Purāṇa, Edited and Translated into English by F. E. Pargiter, Bibliotheca Indica Edition.
Meghadūta of Kālidāsa, Edited by Stenzler.
Padma Purāṇa, Published in Ānandāśrāma Sanskrit Series.
Questions of King Milinda, English Translation, Sacred Books of the East, Vols. 35–6.
Raghuvaṁśam of Kālidāsa, Nirṇaya Sāgara Press Edition
Rāmāyaṇa, Nirṇaya Sagara Press Edition.
Ṛgveda, English Translation by Wilson.
Śatapatha Brāhmaṇa, Translated into English by Eggeling, Sacred Books of the East, Vols. 12, 26, 41, 43, 44.
Skanda Purāṇa.
Suśruta-Saṁhitā, Calcutta Edition.
Sutta-Nipāta, English Translation, Sacred Books of the East, Vol. 10.
Śvetāśvatara Upaniṣad, Published in Ānandāśrama Sanskrit Series.
Taittirīya Saṁhitā.
Uttarādhyāyana, English Translation, Sacred Books of the East, Vol. 45.
Vājasaneyi Saṁhitā.
Varāha Purāṇa, Bibliotheca Indica Edition.
Vasiṣṭha Dharma Sūtra, Edited by Führer.
Vāyu Purāṇa, Published in Ānandāśrama Sanskrit Series, 1905.
,, ,, Edited by R. Mitra, Bibliotheca Indica Edition.
Viṣṇu, Institutes of, English Translation by Julius Jolly, Sacred Books of the East.
Viṣṇu Purāṇa, English Translation by Wilson

GENERAL WORKS

Acharya, P. K., *History of Indian Architecture.*
,, *Architecture of the Mānasāra*, English Translation.
Altekar, A. S., *Position of Women in Hindu Civilization.*
,, *Education in Ancient India.*
,, *History of Benares.*
,, *History of Towns and Cities in Gujarat and Kathiawad.*
,, *"Can We Reconstruct Pre-Bhārata-War History?"* Presidential Address, Archaic Section, Indian History Congress 1939.
Apte, V. M., *Social and Religious Life in the Gṛhya Sūtras*, Bombay, 1939.
Ayyar, C. V. N., *Origin and Early History of Śaivism in South India* Published by the Madras University, 1936.
Bacchoffer, *Early Indian Sculpture.*
Bagchi, Presidential Address, Indian History Congress, December, 1943.
Banerjea, P. N. *Public Administration in Ancient India.*

Banerji, R. D., *Age of the Imperial Guptas* (Mahindra Chandra Nandy Lectures, 1924) Published by the Benares Hindu University, 1933

Barua, B. M., *Old Brahmi Inscriptions.*
Barhut Sculptures.

Barua and Sinha, *Barhut Inscriptions.*

Bhandarkar, D R., *Some Aspects of Ancient Hindu Polity* Charmicael Lectures, 1918.

Bhandharkar, R. G., *Early History of the Dekhan.*
,, *Vaiṣṇavism, Śaivism and Minor Religious Systems,* Strassburg, 1913.

Bhandharkar, R. G., Collected Works of, published by the Bhandarkar Oriental Research Institute, Poona.

Bombay Gazetteers, Vols. I and XV.

Bose, G., "*Reconstruction of Andhra Chronology*", Published separately in the Journal of the Royal Asiatic Society of Bengal, 1939.

Calcutta Review, 1927

Calcutta Weekly Notes, Vol. 15.

Cambridge History of India, Vol. 1, Edited by E. J. Rapson.

Chakravarty, P. C., *Art of War in Ancient India*, published by the Dacca University, 1942.

Chanda, Rama Prasad, *Archaeology and Vaiṣṇava Tradition.* (Memoirs of the Archaeological Survey of India, No. 5).

Childe, V. C., *Aryans*, History of Civilization Series.

Coomaraswamy, A. K., *Elements of Buddhist Iconography.*

Crooke, *The Castes and Tribes of North-West Provinces and Audh.*

Cultural Heritage of India, Vol. 3 Ramakrishna Centenary Vols.

Cunningham, *Ancient Geography of India*, Edited by S. N. Majumdar.

Das, A. C., *Ṛgvedic Culture.*

Davids, Rhys, *Buddhist India.*
,, *Dialogues of Buddha.*

Davids and Williams, *Pāli-English Dictionary.*

Dawson, *Age of the Gods.*

De, Nandalal, *Geographical Dictionary of Ancient India* (Second Edition).

Deussen, *System des Vedanta*, 1883.

Dharma, Miss, *Rāmāyaṇa Polity.*

Dikshitar, V. R. R, *Some Aspects of the Vāyu Purāṇa.*
,, *Matsya Purāṇa, A Study.*
,, *Hindu Administrative Institutions.*
,, *Mauryan Polity.*
,, *War in Ancient India.*

Early History of Bengal, Edited by R. C. Majumdar, 1943.

Encyclopaedia of Social Sciences.

Enthoven, R. E., *The Castes and Tribes of the Bombay Presidency*, 1920.

Fick, R., *Social Organisation in North-East India in Buddha's Time* (Translated into English by K. L. Maitra).

Fleet, *Gupta Inscriptions*, *Corpus Inscriptionum Indicarum*, Vol. 3.

Getty, *Gaṇeśa*.

Ghoshal, U. N., *History of Hindu Political Theories*.

,, *A History of Hindu Public Life*.

Ghurye, *Caste and Race in India*.

Gopalachari, *Early History of the Andhra Country*.

Hall, H. R., *Ancient History of the Near East*.

Hazra, R. C., *Studies in the Purāṇic Records of Hindu Rites and Customs*, Published by the Dacca University.

Hastings, *Encyclopaedia of Religion and Ethics*.

Hocart, A. M., *Kingship*.

Hopkins, E. W., *Epic Mythology*.

,, *The Great Epic of India*.

Hultzsch, *Aśokan Inscriptions*, *Corpus Inscriptionum Indicarum*, Vol. 1.

Jayaswal, *Hindu Polity* (Two volumes).

,, *Manu and Yājñavalkya*, Tagore Law Lectures, 1917.

Jolly, J., *Hindu Law and Custom* (English Translation by Batakrishna Gosh).

Kane, P. V., *History of Dharmaśāstra*, Vol. 2.

Keith, *Religion and Philosophy of the Veda*, Harvard Oriental Series, Vols. 31-2).

Kirfel, *Das Purāṇa Pañcalakṣaṇa*.

Kramrisch St., *Indian Sculpture* (Heritage of India Series).

Law, B. C., *Ancient Indian Tribes*.

,, *Ancient Indian Tribes*, Second Volume.

,, *Geography of Early Buddhism*.

,, *India as Described in Early Texts of Buddhism and Jainism*, 1941.

,, *Śrāvasti in Indian Literature* (Memoirs of the Archaeological Survey of India, No. 50).

,, *Rājagṛha in Ancient Literature* (Memoirs of the Archaeological Survey of India, No. 58).

,, *Kauśāmbi in Ancient Indian Literature* (Memoirs of the Archaeological Survey of India, No. 60).

,, *Women in Buddhist Literature*.

Law, N. N., *Studies in Ancient Hindu Polity*.

Macdonell, A. A., *History of Sanskrit Literature*.

,, *Vedic Mythology*.

Majumdar, G. P., *Vanaspati*. Published by the Calcutta University.

,, R. C., *Corporate Life in Ancient India*.

Malalasekhara, *Dictionary of Pali Proper Names*, 2 Vols.

McCrindle, *Ancient India*.

Mehta, Ratilal, *Pre-Buddhist India.*

Mohenjodaro and the Indus Civilization, 3 Vols. Edited by John Marshall.

Mookerji, R. K., *Hindu Civilization.*

Morgan, Jacques de, *Prehistoric Man.*

Muir, *Original Sanskrit Texts*, Vol. 4.

Nilakantha Sastri, K. A., *Colas.*

Oldenberg, *Buddha.*

Panikkar, *Origin and Evolution of Kingship in India.*

Pargiter, F. E., *Ancient Indian Historical Tradition.*

,, *Purāṇic Text of the Dynasties of the Kali Age.*

Periplus of the Eurythrean Sea.

Perry, *Children of the Sun.*

Petrie, F., *Tools and Weapons.*

Pillay, *Tamils, 1800 Years Ago.*

Popley, *Music of India*, Heritage of India Series.

Pradhan, S. N., *Chronology of Ancient India.*

Radhakrishnan, *Philosophy of the Upaniṣads.*

,, *Indian Philosophy*, Vols. 1–2.

Raychaudhari, *Political History of Ancient India* (4th Edition).

,, *Materials for the Study of the Early History of the Vaiṣṇava Sect.*

,, *Studies in Indian Antiquities.*

Saletore, B. A., *Wild Tribes in Indian History.*

Saletore, R. N., *Life in the Gupta Age.*

Sankalia, H. D., *Archaeology of Gujarat.*

Schrader, F. O., *Prehistoric Antiquities of the Aryan Peoples.*

,, *Introduction to the Pāñcaratra System.*

Seal, B. N., *Positive Sciences of the Ancient Hindus.*

Sen Gupta, *Sources of Law and Society in Ancient India.*

Smith, *Early History of India* (4th Edition).

Sollas, *Ancient Hunters and their Modern Representatives.*

Sörensen, S., *Index to Names in the Mahābhārata.*

Sukthankar, V. S., *Collected Works of Sukthankar Memorial Edition.* Published by Bhandarkar Oriental Research Institute, 1944.

Sydney Smith, *Early History of Assyria.*

Tagore, *Hindu Musical Instruments.*

Tarn, *Greeks in Bactria and India.*

Vedic Index compiled by Macdonell and Keith (Two Volumes).

Venkataramanayya, *Rudra-Śiva*, (Dr. S. Subrahmanya Aiyar Lectures, 1939–40). Published by the Madras University, 1941.

Winternitz, *History of Indian Literature*, Vol. 1.

,, *Some Problems of Indian Literature.*

Volume of Eastern and Iranian Studies presented in honour of F. W. Thomas, New Indian Antiquary, Vol. III.

ABBREVIATIONS

ABORI	Annals of the Bhandarkar Oriental Research Institute, Poona.
AIHT	F. E. Pargiter, Ancient Indian Historical Tradition.
Ait. Br.	Aitareya Brāhmaṇa.
Altekar	A. S. Altekar, Position of Women in Hindu Civilization.
ASWI	Archaeological Survey of Western India.
AV	Atharva-Veda.
BDCRI	Bulletin of the Deccan College Research Institute, Poona.
Bhandarkar	R. G. Bhandarkar, Vaiṣṇavism, Śaivism and Minor Religious Systems.
Bṛ. Up.	Bṛhadāraṇyaka Upaniṣad.
Chakravarty	P. C. Chakravarty, Art of War in Ancient India.
CHI	Cambridge History of India.
Ch. Up	Chāndogya Upaniṣad.
Davids	Rhys Davids, Buddhist India.
De	De, Nandalal, Geographical Dictionary of Ancient India (2nd Edition).
EI	Epigraphia Indica.
ERE	Hastings, Encyclopaedia of Religion and Ethics.
Fick	Fick, Social Organisation in North-East India in Buddha's time.
Ghoshal	U. N. Ghoshal, History of Hindu Political Theories.
Hazra	Studies in the Purāṇic Records on Hindu Rites and Customs.
HOS	Harvard Oriental Series.
IA	Indian Antiquary.
IC	Indian Culture.
IHQ	Indian Historical Quarterly.
Ind. Verb.	Index Verborum to the published texts of the Kauṭilīya Arthaśāstra prepared by R. Shama Sastry.
JAOS	Journal of the American Oriental Society.
JASB	Journal of the Asiatic Society of Bengal.
Jayaswal	K. P. Jayaswal, Hindu Polity.
JBBRAS	Journal of the Bombay Branch of the Royal Asiatic Society.
JBORS	Journal of the Bihar and Orissa Research Society.
JDL	Journal of Department of Letters, Calcutta.
JIH	Journal of Indian History.
JOSIA	Journal of the Oriental Society of Indian Art.
JRAS	Journal of the Royal Asiatic Society.
Kane	P. V. Kane, History of Dharmaśāstra.
Mac., *HSL*	A. A. Macdonell, History of Sanskrit Literature.
MASI	Memoirs of the Archaeological Survey of India.
Mbh.	Mahābhārata.
Mehta	Ratilal Mehta, Pre-Buddhist India.
Mohenjodaro	Mohenjodaro and the Indus Civilization, edited by Sir John Marshall
Muir, *OST*	Muir, Original Sanskrit Texts.
PHAI	H. C. Raychaudhari, Political History of Ancient India.
Popley	Popley, Music of India.
QJMS	Quarterly Journal of Mythic Society.
Rudra-Śiva	Venkataramanayya, Rudra-Śiva.
RV	Ṛgveda.
SBE	Sacred Books of the East.
Ś. Br.	Śatapatha Brāhmaṇa.
Seal	B. N. Seal, Positive Sciences of the Ancient Hindus.
Sörensen	S. Sörensen, Index to Names in the Mahābhārata.
Trans.	Translation of the Arthaśāstra of Kauṭilya by R. Shama Sastry.
Ups.	Upaniṣads.
Vā.	Vāyu Purāṇa.
Ved. Ind.	Macdonell and Keith, Vedic Index.
VOJ	Vienna Oriental Journal.
Vsp.	G. P. Majumdar, Vanaspati.
YV	Yajurveda.

CONTENTS

Chapter III.—POLITICAL INSTITUTIONS

Chapter IV.—RELIGION

Chapter V.—YUGAS AND THE SYSTEM OF CHRONOLOGY

Chapter VI.—TOWNS, VILLAGES AND DWELLINGS

Chapter VII.—DRESS AND ORNAMENTS, FOOD AND DRINK

INTRODUCTION

The history of Purāṇic researches[1] ranges over a period of nearly a century. WILSON is generally regarded as a pioneer in the field. His heavy volume containing a lengthy preface and introduction on the *Viṣṇu Purāṇa* with its translation and learned notes thereon is too well-known to need mention here. He also wrote many essays on Purāṇas especially on their religious aspects. But to him the Purāṇas were only pious frauds written in subservience to sectarian imposture. He was not much interested in historical facts lying embedded in them. He greatly underrated the antiquity of the compilation of the extant texts and some of his views are now considered as being only of academic interest. Col. Vans KENNEDY, WILSON's contemporary, no doubt regarded the Purāṇas as a class of ancient literature, but he also did not contribute much from the historian's point of view. There were also minor attempts made by BURNOUF, Col. WILFORD and by the compilers of the catalogues of manuscripts like AUFRECHT and EGGELLING but they too did not concern themselves with their historical aspect. This was the condition of Purāṇic researches upto about the beginning of this century.

The dawn of this century heralded an era of awakening in India in all aspects of her national life. There has been an unprecedented interest in her ancient history and culture. Researches on Indian history have been growing apace both in their volume and quality. Naturally the Purāṇas received some attention as "sources" of ancient Indian history.[2] But the old prejudice that these works are mainly mythological had not died down all of a sudden. Historians generally treated their evidence with indifference and cold formality and that too only for the purposes of 'corroboration'. It was, however, PARGITER who put the Purāṇic studies on a sound basis and the credit of rescuing the Purāṇas from the morass of mythology and of convincing the learned world of their historical value must essentially go to him. His two works *The Purāṇa Text of the Dynasties of the Kali Age* and *Ancient Indian Historical Tradition* are epoch-making in the history of Purāṇic researches. He began with a tirade against those scholars who attempted to reconstruct India's most ancient past from the evidence of the Vedic literature. He called such attempts as absurd when there already existed the more reliable evidence of the Purāṇic and Epic traditions. But PARGITER was concerned more with political history. There is another important

1. For a survey of studies on Purāṇas so far carried out by scholars, see DIKSHITAR *Purāṇas, A Study, IHQ* 8. 747; and A. D. PUSALKAR, *Progress of Indic Studies* (published by Bhandarkar Oriental Research Institute, 1942, 139 ff.) and for the attitude of modern scholarship towards them, cf. *CHI* 1. 299.

2. SMITH, *Early History of India*, 11-2; *JRAS* 1914, 267 ff. etc.

work of S. N. PRADHAN, viz., *Chronology of Ancient India*, on the subject which too makes considerable use of the Purāṇic material. RAYCHAUDHARI in his *Political History of Ancient India* has also taken into account the evidence furnished by the Purāṇic tradition. DIKSHITAR, too, has contributed much to the field of Purāṇic researches especially by his works on individual Purāṇas such as the *Matsya* and the *Vāyu* and has, to a certain extent, dealt with the cultural aspect of their evidence. There is another important work of HAZRA which has traced the Smṛti material in the Purāṇas and has attempted to fix the chronology of the Purāṇic chapters containing that material. Recently ALTEKAR in his presidential address to the Indian History Congress, 1939, has tried to show how the pre-Bhārata-war history of India can be reconstructed from the evidence of Purāṇas and Epics with the help of the Vedic evidence. But in this second phase of Purāṇic studies much attention is devoted to the genealogies and their political history with the exception of DIKSHITAR and HAZRA.

The old idea of history mainly signifying political history is now no longer accepted by historians all over the civilised world. The scope of history has been considerably widened by the newly born sciences of archaeology and anthropology. In their synthesis of reconstitution historians have adopted two very different attitudes: that of political history and that of cultural history. To the idea that the state plays a preponderant rôle in the life of peoples, that the acts of governments, the facts of internal policy, of diplomacy and of war constitute the core of history, there has been opposed the thesis that the object of history is civilization, that is, a collection of facts on very different planes among which material and intellectual facts are of prime importance. History tends to embrace life in the entirety of its aspect, or to quote Henri PIRENNE, "the object of the study of history is the development of human societies in space and time." Due to this opposing thesis political history which is orientated towards political action has lost some of its prestige in the West, though the old claims of political history have not still lost their hold on the promoters of historical researches in India. Cultural history as such has not received due attention from scholars of ancient Indian history.[3] The present work attempts to fill in this want so far as it concerns the Vāyu Purāṇa. Thus it is obvious that only the *Kulturgeschichte* as can be gleaned from that Purāṇa has been the subject of this investigation, political history being relegated to a subsidiary position.

Originally the idea was to take up the *Vāyu*, *Viṣṇu*, *Mārkaṇḍeya* and *Matsya* Purāṇas for the purposes of this investigation as these Purāṇas are generally considered by scholars to be the "ancient" Purāṇas. But it was soon evident that the work could not have been completed within

3. *Progress of Indic Studies*, 237. (pub. by BORI, 1942).

the stipulated period and consequently the Vāyu was selected for reasons which are stated below :

Out of the four Purāṇas mentioned the *Viṣṇu* and the *Mārkaṇḍeya Purāṇas* have been translated into English by WILSON and PARGITER respectively and the geographical material of the latter has been considerably made use of by B.C. LAW in his articles pertaining to geography.[4] The *Matsya* too is generally referred to by scholars occasionally and there exists a study of the *Matsya Purāṇa* by DIKSHITAR which, as compared with his earlier work on the *Vāyu Purāṇa*, is more exhaustive. Thus the selection of the *Vāyu Purāṇa* was made not only because it is perhaps the earliest of the Purāṇas, as is often assumed, but also because it has not still received that attention which it really deserves.

There is most common agreement amongst scholars about the opinion that the *Vāyu* is one of the very few of the ancient Purāṇas, though they differ about their relative chronology. Long ago R. G. BHANDARKAR opined that the compilation of the *Vāyu Purāṇa* is older than that of the *Matsya*,[5] and that it is the earliest work of that class (i. e. the Purāṇas),[6] but PARGITER differs from him though he says that the *Vāyu* is older than the *Viṣṇu*.[7] He, however, quotes the evidence of *Vāyu* as accurate and as one having the best text on many occasions in the course of his investigations and they have been referred to in our work.[8] WINTERNITZ says that "there certainly existed an ancient Purāṇa under this name and undoubtedly there is still preserved in our texts much of the ancient work which is probably not later than the 5th century A. D.[9] The *Vāyu* is perhaps the only Purāṇa the existence of which is expressly indicated in the *Mbh.* and its supplement the *Harivaṁśa*.[10] We cannot do better than quote the remarks of V. S. ṢUKTHANKAR on this point : "The reference in our parvan to Vāyu, '*Vāyuproktam anusmṛtya*' (3.189.14), is worth considering in this connection. Nothing corresponding to the general contents of the passage where it occurs is to be found in the extant *Vāyu Purāṇa* as is remarked by HOPKINS,[11] or for the matter of that in any other Purāṇa proclaimed by *Vāyu*. There are, however, a few stanzas in the *Vāyu* describing the dissolution of the world where verbal similarity with some stanzas of this passage are pronounced, even though they are introduced in the *Vāyu*

---

4. See *ABORI* 17.217 ff. 319 ff.
5. *Early History of the Dekkan*, 1895, 162.
6. *Vaiṣṇavism, Śaivism*, etc.
7. *Purāṇa Text of the Dynasties of the Kali Age*, 14, and fn. 4; cf. also C.V. VAIDYA, *JBBRAS*, 1925, 155 ff. where he tries to ascribe it to the 8th century but his arguments are not convincing.
8. *Ibid.*, cf. also *AIHT*, 77 f.
9. *History of Indian Literature*, 1.554.
10. Cf. DIKSHITAR, *Some Aspects of the Vāyu Purāṇa*, 47.
11. *The Great Epic of India*, 48 ff.

in a different context. The Mbh...... draws upon a Purāṇa of *Vāyu*—and indeed the topic narrated belongs properly to a Purāṇa in its right, a Purāṇa which is older than the extant Purāṇas and which must be presumed to have been irretrievably lost. The evidence for establishing a relationship between the extant Vāyu and its old namesake to which the epic is indebted is lacking, barring these few stray stanzas."[12] But, as will be clear below, our Purāṇa shows at places a material definitely older than that of the Mbh., and though we do not claim to have discovered the truth that the *Vāyu* quoted in the Mbh. is the same as our text, we only wish to stress the fact that since it has preserved for us a material which in some cases is older than that of the great epic we may be allowed to infer that it has preserved for us a material which originally belonged to the Purāṇa of the same name known to the Mbh.

The other evidence for the date of this Purāṇa has been fully discussed by DIKSHITAR[13] and it is unnecessary for us to repeat his conclusions here. According to him the earliest portion of the Purāṇa goes to the 5th cent. B.C. and the latest to 500 A.D. On the ground of the evidence of the Smrti material in the *Vāyu* HAZRA too thinks that it is "perhaps the oldest of the extant Purāṇas", though the expression "oldest" is, according to him, "applicable only to the main skeleton of the work."[14]

DIKSHITAR's work, already referred to above, is the only independent treatise on the Purāṇa. In this work the author has dealt mainly with textual matter such as its name, its place in the Mahāpurāṇas, the classification of its contents, the literature known to it and its date both from external and internal evidence. He has also discussed, though not in full, the data of the Purāṇa on matters such as religion and philosophy, geography, music, sculpture and painting. The astronomical and other data and the genuineness of the historical tradition contained in it are also considered. And so far, we have to acknowledge that our investigation has been simplified. The material of the Purāṇa has been sparsely utilized by some scholars for which we may better refer to A. D. PUSALKAR's survey of Purāṇic studies.[15]

There exist two printed editions of the *Vāyu*. The earlier one was edited by Rajendralal MITRA and was published by the Asiatic Society of Bengal in 1880.[16] The second is that published by the Ānandāśrama, Poona, in 1905. The latter being the better one and since it also

12. Introduction to the Āraṇyaka parvan, published in *Sukthankar Memorial Edition* (1944) 1.156.

13. *Op. cit.*, 46 ff.

14. *Purāṇic Records on Hindu Rites and Customs*, 13 and fn. 9.

15. *Op. cit.*, 145.

16. In *Bibliotheca Indica*, New Series Nos. 420, 424, 428, 434, 437 and 445.

utilizes the earlier edition (as Ka) we have followed its text for our investigation. Again PARGITER also used the same edition in his works.[17] We have, however, noted, whenever necessary, the important variants substantially affecting the source material of the text.

(*a*) The Gayāmāhātmya (chapters 105-112) has been omitted in *toto* as there is no doubt as to its being an interpolation.[18] It is omitted in four of the five manuscripts utilized in the Ānandāśrama edition. "On the other hand, it is often found to appear as an independent text in MSS. as well as in printed editions."[19]

(*b*) Chapters 103-4 also are omitted in two MSS. and, as in the case of (*a*), are considered to be interpolations.[20]

(*c*) The material of the Purāṇa on astronomy (chapters 50-53) and its technical details on music have been omitted as it was not possible for us to do full justice to them, for the present. The chapters on music (Vā 86.29 ff. and 87) are also omitted in MSS. Kha and Gha and perhaps they did not originally belong to the *Vāyu Purāṇa*. The context also suggests that their place in the Purāṇa is liable to be suspect. DIKSHITAR appears to have overlooked this fact in his discussion of the contents of the Purāṇa and of the material on music contained in it.[21]

We have deliberately arranged the whole work into two parts and the Appendix. The first part embodies the facts as they have been collected from the Purāṇa. No attempt is here made either at a comment or gloss. Whenever remarks are made they are simply to explain the context in which the facts stand in the Purāṇa so as to make their position understandable in the interpretation. The first five chapters contain facts of intellectual culture and the last five of material culture.

The second part presents the *interpretation* of the facts collected from the Purāṇa in the first part. This interpretation is primarily 'chronological'.

It will be obvious that this arrangement has been responsible for increasing the bulk of our work. But it has a decided advantage inasmuch as it ensures clarity of expression. We have again an added advantage in this arrangement—i.e. of checking the source-material easily whenever a critical edition of the work is undertaken; and lastly, we have a hope that this arrangement will be considerably useful in the preparation of a critical edition of the text itself.

The first part essentially involves a great deal of translation of the material of the Purāṇa and in this we have tried our utmost to cling more to the sense of words than to the words themselves. Thus the

---

17. Cf. *The Purāṇa Text of the Dynasties of Kali Age*, v, and AIHT 78.
18. Cf. WINTERNITZ, *op. cit.*, cf. also DIKSHITAR, *op. cit.*, 5 and fn. 1.
19. HAZRA, *op.cit.*, 17.
20. *Ibid.*, *cf.* also DIKSHITAR, *op. cit.*
21. *Ibid.*, pp. 3-7; 33 ff.

English presentation of the material is *litera sensu* rather than *litera scriptu*. Wherever necessary the text of the material of the Purāṇa is also quoted immediately after it.

A Brief Outline of the Political History as Found in the Vāyu

Though political history is not the prime concern of this work still we cannot do away with it altogether. Occasionally we have had to deal with incidents that pertain to political history; and thus it will not be out of place if we narrate here a brief outline of the political history of the most ancient past of India as it has been handed down by the Purāṇa.

In its chapters 85-99 the Purāṇa sums up, in the form of genealogical lists, the account of the various ancient dynasties ruling in North India and occasionally narrates the incidents connected with these kings.

The account begins with the Primeval king Vaivasvata Manu, son of Vivasvat (i.e. the son-god). This Manu had nine sons. (But our Purāṇa actually mentions ten names, that of Nahuṣa being inserted wrongly in the list).[22] It is further stated that Manu offered a sacrifice to Mitra and Varuṇa to obtain a son but a daughter Ilā was born. Ilā, through cohabitation with Budha, son of Soma, had a son Purūravas and afterwards she became a man named Sudyumna.[23] Sudyumna had three sons viz. Utkala, Caya and Vinatāśva.

The account then starts with the different sons of Manu. Manu divided the earth into ten portions of which he gave nine to his nine sons and the tenth went to Purūravas, son of Ilā, who, being a female, had no share assigned to her. The story of the nine sons is stated thus:—

(1) *Pṛṣadhra:* He killed his preceptor's cow and was condemned to be a Śūdra. Nothing is then said of his descendants.

(2) *Karūṣa:* His descendants are said to have been determined fighters. This is the only tradition about them.

(3) *Nabhāga:* He is simply alluded to.

(4) *Ariṣṭa:*[24] His genealogy is given for a few generations and the last king of this line, named Marutta, is said to have been a *cakravartin*.

---

22. See *AIHT* 255. Pargiter does not expressly refer to this fact. Cf. also *ibid.*, 84 fn. 2.

23. For other versions of the same story in the other Purāṇas, cf. *ibid.*, 253 ff.

24. There is some confusion about this name in the Purāṇic tradition in general, cf. *AIHT* 255 fn. 13. We have mainly followed the *Vāyu* account only.

(5) *Narişyanta:* His descendants ruled at Vaiśālī.[25] The Vaiśālī dynasty came to an end with its last king Pramati (or Pramiti) who, according to synchronisms established by PARGITER,[26] was a contemporary of Daśaratha, father of Rāma and king of Ayodhyā.

(6) *Śaryāti:* He ruled in Ānarta (cf. No. 38 App.). After the mention of a few descendants there occurs a long passage on music narrated in connection with Revatī, daughter of king Reva of the line. And we are later told that after Raivata Kakudmin had died, the city of Kuśasthalī was besieged by the Puṇyajana Rākṣasas. The hundred brothers of Raivata—probably his kinsmen—fled at the attack and thus the line came to an end.

(7) *Dhṛṣṭa:* He is simply mentioned, no reference being made to his descendants.

(8) *Nabhāga:* A few descendants of his line are mentioned and with Rathītara, the last of the names mentioned, the line seems to have closed, probably because the descendants of Rathītara became Brahmins.[27]

(9) *Ikṣvāku:* The genealogy of his line is fully treated by the Purāṇa. He is said to have had hundred sons of whom the three viz. Vikukṣi, Nimi and Daṇḍa were the most important. Of them it is further stated that fifty ruled in the north, forty-eight in the south—[and twenty of those forty-eight (?) ruled in the Dakṣiṇāpatha]—Nimi in Videha and Vikukṣi succeeded to his father's kingdom of Ayodhyā. Of these branches of the line of Ikṣvāku only those of Vikukṣi and Nimi are treated fully in the Purāṇa ; the genealogies of the others are nowhere mentioned.

The important kings of the dynasty at Ayodhyā, of whom the Purāṇa tells more than merely alluding to their names, are : (in chronological order) Vikukṣi, Bṛhadaśva and his son Kuvalāśva Māṁdhātṛ, Satyavrata Triśaṅku, Hariścandra, Sagara, Bhagīratha, Aśmaka, Rāma, etc.

Nimi had set up an independent line in Videha. His son was Mithi or Janaka after whom the city of Mithilā was so-called (cf. No. 837 App.). The only other important king of this dynasty was Sīradhvaja Janaka who was probably the father-in-law of Dāśarathī Rāma.[28]

---

25. According to PARGITER Nābhānediṣṭa founded the Vaiśālī dynasty. Nābhānediṣṭa is mentioned in other Purāṇas and is the same as Asriṣṭa of the *Vāyu*. Cf. *AIHT* 96-7.

26. Pp. 97, 147.

27. There are thus two Nabhāgas whose descendants appear to be in the Purāṇa ; but the confusion is really about the first Nabhāga. (Cf. *AIHT* 255 fn. 13.)

28. Cf. *AIHT* 95. 147.

After this the Purāṇa proceeds to narrate the dynasties of the "lunar race" (Soma-Vaṁśa).

The history of the lunar race begins with the story of the birth of Soma. Soma's son, through his connection with Tārā, was Budha. Budha's son was Purūravas born of Ilā, daughter of Vaivasvata Manu. About the relation of Purūravas with Urvaśī we have an interesting legend in the Purāṇa. Purūravas ruled at Pratiṣṭhāna or Prayāga and appears to have been a powerful monarch who met his ruin, it is alleged, through his greed of the sacrificial wealth of the sages. He had six[29] sons of whom only two viz. Āyu and Amāvasu, are important.

Leaving aside the main line,[30] continued by Āyu, the Purāṇa first takes up the genealogy of Amāvasu who had established a separate kingdom in Kānyakubja. After Amāvasu, Jahnu was a very important king of the line and an incident is narrated about him by which the river Ganges was called Jāhnavī (cf. No. 298 App.). Jahnu was probably related to Māṁdhātā, king of Ayodhyā, who was his father-in-law. Jahnu's seventh successor was Gādhi about whom the text has a tale to tell. He was the father-in-law of the Bhārgava Ṛcīka, grandfather of Jāmadagnya Rāma. A story is here told of the birth of Jamadagni and of Viśvaratha who became the Brahmin Viśvāmitra and is, as such, famous in the Purāṇic tradition. He figures elsewhere in connection with Satyavrata Triśaṅku. Viśvaratha was succeeded by Aṣṭaka, after whom the dynasty seems to have come to a close.

The Purāṇa now commences the account of the *main line* of Āyu who succeeded his father at Pratiṣṭhāna. He had five sons through Prabhā, daughter of Svarbhānu. Of these five, only two, viz. Nahuṣa and Putradharma, are mentioned by the *Vāyu*.[31] As usual the Purāṇa leaves the main line of Nahuṣa and proceeds to narrate the genealogy of Putradharma (or Dharmavṛddha ?)[32] who founded a separate line at Kāśī, the name of this city having been derived from Kāśa, grandson of Putradharma. Of Dhanvantari, a few generations later, it is said that he was the Divine Physician Dhanvantari born on this earth as the son of Dīrghatapas (who had practised penance to obtain a son and had pleased Dhanvantari). About three generations later was born in this dynasty the famous king Divodāsa I about whom the incident of the destruction of his capital, the city of Vārāṇasī, is narrated (see No. 1403 App.). With king Divodāsa I begins a long contest between the kings of Kāśī and the Haihayas.[33] Bhadraśreṇya, the Haihaya

29. Seven according to some Purāṇas (cf. *AIHT* 85).

30. This is usually the method followed in the Purāṇa.

31. Cf. *AIHT*, 85 fn. 6, 101 fn. 3.

32. Cf. *ibid.*

33. The *Vāyu* account is somewhat confusing and instead of two Divodāsas of the dynasty it mentions only one. For a better account collected from the various texts of the Purāṇas cf. *AIHT* 153-5, 163. Cf. also ALTEKAR, *History of Benares*, 9 ff.

king, was successful against Divodāsa and had taken possession of his capital Vārāṇasī, but Divodāsa later recovered his territory and capital from the sons of Bhadraśreṇya, all of whom were killed in the war that ensued, except one Durdama whose life was spared on account of his tender age. The contest, however, continued for a long period afterwards in which the descendants of Divodāsa suffered a great deal. Pratardana, son of Divodāsa II of this dynasty was a great and powerful king who defeated the Haihayas but still it appears that he could not get possession of the city of Vārāṇasī, which had been occupied in the meanwhile by the Rākṣasas. His grandson Alarka was a great king and the Purāṇa has handed down two stanzas which sing of his glory according to the ancient tradition. He drove away the Rākṣasas and re-established himself in the ancestral capital of Kāśī and had a long and prosperous reign. After naming some descendants of Alarka the *Purāṇa* then closes the account of this Kāśī dynasty.

The genealogy of Raji, another of the five sons of Āyu,[34] is then narrated. He was a powerful king and a legend is told of him that he helped the gods in their war against the Dānavas and later on usurped the place of Indra, who in vengeance retaliated on his sons, and thus his line ended in disaster.

The descendants of Kṣatradharman are then mentioned. This Kṣatradharman, according to PARGITER, was a descendant of Anenas[35] son of Āyu[36] and the kings of the line were known afterwards as Kṣatradharman and nothing more is said of them.

The *Purāṇa* now begins with Nahuṣa who continued the main line of king Āyu at Pratiṣṭhāna. Nahuṣa had six sons amongst whom Yati was the eldest and Yayāti second to him. Yati became a *muni* and Yayāti then succeeded his father. Yayāti was a great king according to the Purāṇic tradition and much is said of him by way of legends. He had two wives, Devayānī, daughter of the Bhārgava Uśanas Śukra, and Śarmiṣṭhā, daughter of the Asura Vṛṣaparvan.[37] He seems to have ruled for a long period and later on relinquished his kingdom to his sons and embraced forest-life. Puru was a favourite of his father and he continued the main line of his ancestors. Yayāti had divided his kingdom into five portions; Puru ruled at Pratiṣṭhana, Yadu in the south, Turvasu in the south-east, Druhyu in the west and Anu in the north.

34. The *Vāyu* does not say so explicitly, but in other Purāṇas he is said to be a son of Āyu, cf. *AIHT* 85-8.

35. Cf. *AIHT* 85.

36. In the case of Raji, the *Vāyu* does not say explicitly of him that he was a son of Āyu, but other Purāṇas imply this, cf. *ibid* 86-8.

37. It should be noted that the *Vāyu* does not narrate nor even allude to the story of the rivalry between Śarmiṣṭhā and Devayānī which is found elsewhere, cf. *Matsya* 25-32; *Mbh.* 1·78-83; *Rāmāyaṇa* 58-9.

As usual the *Purāṇa* defers the account of the main line of Puru to later consideration and takes up the sub-line of *Yadu* first. Yadu had five sons amongst whom Sahasrajit and Kroṣṭu are the most important. Sahasrajit had a son Śatajit whose son was Haihaya, the ancestor of the Haihayas. Bhadraśreṇa was a descendant of Haihaya, born some four or five generations after him. It was he who started the contest with the kings of Kāśī and occupied the city of Vārāṇasī. Some generations after him the *Purāṇa* narrates the story of Kārtavīrya Arjuna who was the most famous and powerful king of the Haihayas. It should be noted that our *Purāṇa* depicts him as a great and virtuous king and not as in the *Mbh.* a vicious creature who misbehaved with the Bhārgavas. Kārtavīrya Arjuna is said to have had hundred sons but only five are mentioned by name, amongst whom Jayadhvaja succeeded his father. Jayadhvaja's successor was Tālajaṅgha who, in turn, was succeeded by Vīrahotra[38] and after naming a few of his descendants the *Purāṇa* closes the line of the Haihayas.

The genealogy of Kroṣṭu, who continued the main line of Yadu, is then narrated. The sixth successor of Kroṣṭu was the great king Śaśabindu who was a *cakravartin*. He had a hundred sons[39] amongst whom six are named. Of these six Pṛthuśravas, a few generations after him, was Rukmakavaca. Rukmakavaca had five sons. The *Purāṇa* here leaves the line of his eldest son and does not treat it anywhere else. It, however, continues the genealogy of Jyāmagha, a younger son of Rukmakavaca, who had founded his own line in Vidarbha. Jyāmagha was a great king and his son was Vidarbha after whom the territory, over which Jyāmagha ruled, was probably called afterwards. Vidarbha had three sons viz., Kratha, Kai(Kau)śika, and Lomapāda. The first son apparently continued the main līne in Vidarbha; while the second son Kaiśika established a separate line in Cedi, the name of this region probably having been derived from Cedi, son of Kaiśika. All kings after Cedi are summed up by the *Purāṇa* by merely stating that they were Caidyas. Lomapāda had founded a dynasty but only two of his descendants are mentioned in the *Purāṇa* and it does not add anything more about them.[40]

The account of the *dynasty ruling in Vidarbha*—i.e. the genealogy of the descendants of Kratha—is then given. After naming about fifteen descendants of Kratha the account comes to Sātvata. Sātvata had four sons viz. Bhajamāna, Devāvṛdha, Andhaka and Vṛṣṇi. Only the sons of Bhajamāna and Devāvṛdha are mentioned by their names in the *Purāṇa* and their genealogies are not further treated. The genea-

38. Cf. *AIHT* 146.

39. 'Hundred sons' appears to be merely a formal expression and may not be taken literally.

40. Cf. *AIHT* 102-3.

logies of the last two are narrated but the lists are very confusing and it is unnecessary to discuss them fully here.[41] The only important event in connection with these families is the one about the *symantaka* jewel. The story of Kṛṣṇa's conflict with Kaṁsa is also narrated in brief and in the same connection is told a detailed account of the incarnations of Viṣṇu of whom Kṛṣṇa was one.

The *Purāṇa* then proceeds to narrate the genealogy of Turvasu. It enumerates some of his successors, the last and the most notable amongst whom was king Marutta. Marutta had no son and it is stated that he adopted Duṣyanta as his son and that his line merged into that of the Pauravas as a result of this adoption.[42] In spite of this we find the *Purāṇa* further stating that from this line, or from Duṣyanta, there was a branch which founded the kingdoms of Pāṇḍya, Cola, Kerala and Kulya in the south. It appears Janāpīḍa was a grandson of Duṣyanta and he or his four sons migrated to the south and founded the four kingdoms so called after them. Nothing more is said of them in our text.

We have now a short account of the *line established by Druhyu*. After naming his seven descendants, the last of whom was Pracetas, the account closes by merely stating that Pracetas had hundred sons who were all kings and ruled over the countries of the Mlecchas in the north.

The *Purāṇa* then proceeds with *Anu's descendants*. The seventh king after Anu was Mahāmanas who had two sons viz. Uśīnara and Titikṣu. *Uśīnara* had five sons all of whom had carved separate principalities for themselves (cf. No. 891 App.). Śibi was one of these five and he had four sons whose separate *janapadas* are mentioned (No. 705 App.) and with this the account of Uśīnara's descendants ends. In the *line of Titikṣu* was born the king Bali of whom the *Purāṇa* has handed down a legend to us. He had five sons Aṅga, Vaṅga, Kaliṅga, Suhma and Puṇḍra. The line of Aṅga, the eldest son, is then narrated, but the text here has some omissions.[43] Campa was a notable descendant of Aṅga and the city of Campāvatī or Mālinī was founded by him (cf. No. 170 App.). The tenth successor after Campa was Karṇa of the *Mbh.* fame. The *Purāṇa* attempts to explain why he was called Sūta but the explanation does not appear to be satisfactory.

The last to be treated is the *main line of Puru*, who probably succeeded the ancestral kingdom of Yayāti at Pratiṣṭhāna. After enumerating some of his descendants the account comes to Bharata, son of Duṣyanta.[44] Bharata had three wives and also sons by them but it is

---

41. Cf. *ibid* 103 ff. for details.
42. Cf. *ibid* 108 ; the *Vāyu* mentions Duṣkṛta (or Duṣkanta) and not Duṣyanta.
43. Cf. *AIHT* 109.
44. Cf. *AIHT* 110 ff. for details.

alleged that they killed their sons because he was disappointed in them. Thus Bharata was left without an heir and later adopted Bharadvāja as his son. The fifth descendant of Bharata was Hastin who founded the city of Hastināpura (cf. No. 363 App.). Hastin had three sons viz. Ajamīḍha, Dvijāmīḍha (or Dvimīḍha) and Purumīḍha. Ajamīḍha had three wives. About Ajamīḍha there is some confusion in the *Purāṇa*. It appears he had four sons viz. Kaṇṭha,[45] Ṛkṣa, Bṛhadvasu and Nīla. Of these four Nīla's great-grandson was Ṛkṣa (No. 927 App.) who had five sons[46] after whom the name Pāñcāla of the region occupied by them became known. This is a very noteworthy dynasty because many of its kings play an important part in the *RV*.[47] The king Divodāsa who is referred to in the *RV*. belonged to this line.

Some of the descendants of Bṛhadvasu are also mentioned by the *Purāṇa* and PARGITER calls them as forming the south Pañcāla dynasty.[48]

The descendants of Dvijāmīḍha (or Dvimīḍha) are then treated in brief; but where this dynasty ruled is not clear. The only notable king in this line was Kṛta.

Ṛkṣa continued the main line at Hastināpura. His grandson was Kuru who probably founded the city of Kurukṣetra (No. 667). Kuru had three sons viz. Parīkṣit, Sudhanvan and Jahnu. Parīkṣit continued his father's line. *Sudhanvan* founded a separate line and Vasu, one of his descendants, conquered and founded anew the kingdoms of Cedi and Magadha probably by overcoming the Yādavas who were formerly ruling in that territory. Vasu had seven[49] sons, the oldest amongst whom was Bṛhadratha. Bṛhadratha's descendants were known as the Bārhadrathas amongst whom was born Jarāsaṁdha who was a powerful king. The account of this dynasty here stops for a while and is resumed afterwards.

The account then returns to the main line continued by Parīkṣit. His son was Janamejaya II and his son was Suratha.[50] The *Purāṇa* does not say anything further about the descendants of Janamejaya and passes on to Jahnu and gives his genealogy and it appears that the line of Jahnu became the main Paurava line.[51] It was in this line that Devāpi and his brother Śaṁtanu were. Śaṁtanu continued the main line at Hastināpura. Vicitravīrya succeeded Śaṁtanu and the subsequent

45. PARGITER does not refer to him in this connection, cf. *AIHT* 110 ff.

46. According to *Vāyu*, but cf. *AIHT* table on p. 116.

47. See *AIHT* 117 for details.

48. *Ibid*.

49. Five according to some Purāṇas, cf. *AIHT* 118.

50. The *Vāyu* account is here confusing; for according to the collated account by PARGITER Suratha was the son of Jahnu and the *Vāyu* also says so immediately. It should be noted that some Mss. omit the stanza relating Janamejaya with Suratha.

51. *Ibid* 114.

genealogy is too well-known to be treated here. Parīkṣit, son of Abhimanyu, had a son Janamejaya of whom we have a story in the *Purāṇa*. The son and successor of Janamejaya was Śatānīka whose grandson was Adhisāmà-Kṛṣṇa in whose reign this *Vāyu Purāṇa* is said to have been narrated by the Sūta to the sages who had assembled for the sacrificial session in the Naimiṣa forest.

The dynasties that ruled after this king are treated by the *Purāṇa* as those belonging to the "future". Adhisāma-Kṛṣṇa had a son Nirvaktra and it is stated that while he was ruling in Hastināpura the city was flooded by the Ganges and that he shifted his capital to Kauśāmbī.[52] The text then refers to the names of sixteen descendants of this king the last of whom was Kṣemaka. With Kṣemaka the line of the Pauravas ends and, it is stated, the Kali age begins.

The *Purāṇa* now returns to the dynasty that had been ruling in Ayodhyā. We are told that king Divākara was ruling in Ayodhyā, as a contemporary of Adhisāma-Kṛṣṇa, when the *Vāyu Purāṇa* was being narrated by the Sūta to the sages. The successors of Divākara apparently belong to the "future". We have twenty-five descendants of this king mentioned by their names the last of whom was Sumitra. Sumitra is stated to be the contemporary of Kṣemaka of the Paurava line. The *Purāṇa* thus states that both the line of the Pauravas and the Aikṣvākus of Ayodhyā came to an end at about the same time and that the Kali age began since then.

The *Purāṇa* now resumes the account of the dynasty ruling in Magadha. At the time when the sacrificial session was in progress in the Naimiṣa forest Senājit Bārhadratha was ruling in Magadha. After him nearly fifteen kings of the dynasty held the territory and the Pradyotas came into power. The Pradyotas were, in turn, supplanted by the Śaiśunakas. Next came Mahāpadma Nanda, a Śūdra who destroyed all the small kingdoms around Magadha and held sway over all those territories. We need not give details of the subsequent dynasties ruling in Magadha. The Purāṇa comes down upto the line of the Guptas who, according to it, were ruling in Anugaṅga, Sāketa, Prayāga and Magadha, thus suggesting that it is not aware of the great empire of Saṁudragupta and his successors.

---

52. The reference to Nāgas in the context suggests that their presence in the vicinity forced this king to retreat to the south and to establish himself there. Cf. *AIHT* 285. According to Pargiter Nirvaktra ruled about 820 B.C.

CONCLUSIONS

The results that have been obtained from the investigation may now be stated in brief.

For want of space it is not possible to summarize here the chronological discussion in the second part. What the whole of this chronological discussion tends to indicate is that the source material of the *Vāyu Purāṇa* may be assigned to three broad categories such as : (i) *The Archaic Survivals* which are coeval in point of time and contents with the similar material found in the Vedic Literature. 500 B. C. may be safely considered to be the lowest time-limit of this material ; (ii) *The Ancient Material* of the *Purāṇa* alligning itself with the early Dharmasūtras, the early Buddhist and Jain canonical literature, the *Arthaśāstra* of Kauṭalya, the *Manu-Smṛti*, and the earlier portions of the Great Epic *Mahābhārata*. Broadly speaking, the beginning of the Christian era may be supposed to be the lowest chronological *terminus* of the material ; (iii) *The Accretions* or the mass of material that has been incorporated into the body of the text. Most of this material falls in line with the Smṛti works, the later portions of the Great Epic, etc. It should be noted that this material does not generally cross the chronological line demarcated by the date 500 A.D.

The important facts of the material that has been so assigned may now be stated accordingly :

(*i*) *Archaic Survivals :*

(*a*) Some of the stories of the Kṣatriya–Brāhmaṇa conflicts, such as between Vasiṣṭha and Satyavrata Triśaṅku and Viśvāmitra; Brāhmaṇas and king Janamejaya, and between king Kārtavīrya Arjuna and the Bhṛgus. (*b*) Kṣatriya-Brāhmaṇa relations such as a few instances of Kṣatriya–Brāhmaṇa marriages, and the case of the Kṣatriya Bharata adopting a Brāhmaṇa as his son; and the references to Kṣatriya Brāhmaṇas (Kṣātropetāḥ Dvijātayaḥ). (*c*) The references to 'Dasyus' in the dynastic lists which indicate that the term does not there mean 'slaves' but signifies 'enemies'. (*d*) The few references indicative of slavery particularly in the case of Viśvāmitra's child sold for 100 cows. (*e*) The crude facts of the incidents suggestive of the primitive institution of marriage not essentially based on the conception of sexual morality and the peculiar cult of Godharma advocating sexual license. (*f*) The few instances of the custom of Niyoga or levirate, particularly the odd procedure followed in one of them, traces of which have been observed in one of the early *Dharma-sūtras*. (*g*) References to the use of chariots, the plough (Hala), and the bow in war, particularly in connection with the dynastic lists. (*h*) Cow as means of exchange.

It should be noted that this is the class of material that exclusively belongs to that portion of the Purāṇa which contains the dynastic lists.

(ii) Ancient Material:

(*a*) Some of the references to the term Vārtā reminding of similar references in Kauṭalīya *Arthaśāstra* and the *Manu-smṛti*, signifying 'a branch of learning', such as probably the science of economics. (*b*) Incidents indicating the influence of Brahmins, particularly of the Purohita in political matters. (*c*) References suggesting that women could proceed to higher studies and could move freely in society as is evidenced by the ealier portions of the Great Epic. (*d*) The theories regarding the origin of kingship, one of which is probably earlier than a similar one found in the *Mahābhārata*. (*e*) The references to 'Daṇḍa' and 'Daṇḍanīti' similarly found in the *Arthaśāstra*, the *Mahābhārata* and the *Manu-smṛti*. (*f*) The instances indicative of the existence of oligarchies for which evidence has been found in the *Jātakas*, in the *Arthaśāstra*, in the notices on India by the early Greek writers and in the Great Epic. (*g*) The references suggesting existence of popular institutions such as the 'Sabhā', 'Saṁsad' and the 'Paura-Jānapada', evidence for which has been found as in the case of oligarchies. The same can be said regarding the Purāṇic use of the expression 'Gaṇa'. (*h*) One of its 'table' of units of measurements of distance which as compared with the one found in Kauṭalya's *Arthaśāstra* is rudimentary. (*i*) Its cruder references suggestive of town-planning less systematic as compared with Kauṭalya. (*j*) Part of its information on the non-vegetarian diet which begins to appear as a taboo in the *Manu-smṛti*. (*k*) One of its conceptions regarding classification of plants which is cruder and more elementary than the one suggested by the *Manu-smṛti* and Caraka. (*l*) Two out of the three modes of classification of the animal world suggested in the *Purāṇa*, that are ancient as compared with Caraka who flourished in the first century A. D.

(iii) The Accretions:

These make the real bulk of the Purāṇa. It is here that the Brahmin redactor has made his influence felt. Most of the Purāṇa information on social organisation, excepting that already noted above, belongs to this category. Our *Purāṇa*, however, is comparatively more moderate in regard to its claims for the Brahmins than the Smṛtis and some of the other Purāṇas. This *Purāṇa* has much more to say with regard to religion, particularly Śaivism which it openly favours more than it does Vaiṣṇavism on which too it has something to say. It should be noted that our text throws a good deal of light on the early history of the Lakulīśa Pāśupata sect. The table of the twenty-eight incarnations of Śiva may help us to bring into limelight some of the ancient propounders of the sect of whom probably Kapila, Akṣapāda Kaṇāda and Lakulin were the notable ones. That the *Purāṇa* has no direct evidence on the actual worship of Liṅga is also interesting as is also the fact that the god Gaṇeśa is completely absent in the *Purāṇa*. This would suggest that even on matters of religion our text is earlier than many of the other Purāṇas, and the later portions of the Great Epic. The same can be stated with regard to the information on Yugas and the system of chronology on which our text is less schematic than the works referred to above. That the standard ten *avatāras* of Viṣṇu that are known to the later epic and to many of the other Purṇās are not found in the *Vāyu* is also a significant fact. These are only some of the salient facts that suggest that on the whole even this mass of accretions would not push the *Purāṇa* down to a period later than the approximate date of 500 A. D.

We have so far dealt with the positive evidence of the *Purāṇa*: but certain aspects of its negative evidence, particularly on its facts of material culture deserve to be noticed. It should be noted that it is this material of the text the value of the evidence of which must be deemed to be more reliable; for with regard to this kind of facts the hand of the tamperer is least likely to be felt. No redactor would unnecessarily fill in or insert facts of this kind in the accounts of ancient tradition as there would be no purpose for him to do so. This is apparently one of the reasons why we do not find facts of the material culture of a later age at all associated with the ancient dynastic lists. It is this portion of the text that contains the least information on the facts of material culture and wherever they contain them they only indicate their hoary antiquity. The only plant mentioned in connection with ancient kings is the *Aśvattha*, the most celebrated of the plants known to the Ṛgveda; the only animals referred to in the incidents about them are the cows, horses and goats, the most favourite animals of the Vedic sacrificers and their ancestors; and it has to be further noted that in these dynastic lists no indication of the use of cavalry in war is found and instances suggesting horse-riding are too few as compared with the employment of horses for war chariots. It is, again, in connection with this portion of the *Purāṇa* that the buffalo appears as a wild beast still to be domesticated.

Thus the earliest conditions of culture, or the archaic survivals, as we have called them, that have been traced in the *Purāṇa* are intimately connected with its genealogical lists and with the incidents narrated therein. This is a finding which is striking in itself for it confirms, to a certain extent, the authenticity of the information contained in them so far as the facts of material culture are concerned; and there is reason to believe that to that extent the *Purāṇa* has handed down to us the political history of the ancient dynasties in their true cultural setting. The case is, however, different when we examine the facts of intellectual culture. It is in this connection that the lists have suffered a great deal from the subsequent handling of their material. The references to the great kings of the past who are stated to have protected the *Varṇāśrama-dharma* and went along the traditional path of Dharma and their glorification as givers *par excellence* are the points in instance.

It appears that the dynastic lists have also suffered from omissions. For example, it is reasonable to expect that the original tradition as was handed down by the ancient bards must have contained picturesque descriptions of war that were fought by the kings of yore, in the manner in which we find them in the Greek poems of Homer and in our Epics, the *Mahābhārata* and the *Rāmāyaṇa*. It is this topic that has always inspired and nursed bardic poetry of ancient times; but our *Purāṇa* has not handed down to us any of such picturesque scenes of war; and the descriptions of 'war' found in it are too fanciful and scanty for comparison with the Greek poems of Homer and the Epics.

In some cases, it appears, that the *Purāṇa* has confounded the lists. According to PARGITER there were various reasons that caused this confusion; the cultural aspect of the lists indicates that one of these reasons might be that some of the ruling families probably converted themselves into oligarchic or republican clans and their 'genealogies' it would no longer be possible to narrate. It is probably for this very reason that real difficulties occur in tracing the genealogies of the *Vṛṣṇis* and the *Andhakas*. The same observation may probably be made as to why, in a few cases, the *Purāṇa* stops narrating further the 'genealogies' of certain kings, as in the case of king Uśīnara.

The negative evidence of the rest of the *Purāṇa* (i. e. the portion other than the dynastic lists) is likewise instructive. None of the "archaic survivals" noted above are to be found here. This is an additional proof with regard to the authenticity and antiquity of the material of the dynastic lists.

It must be stated here that our observations on relative chronology are bound, in the nature of things, to remain tentative. Still their value for the purposes of cultural history need not be overlooked. We often hear of the palaeographical evidence in the dating of an undated inscription and its value in the absence of a contrary evidence has rarely been denied. Such is the case also of the typological evidence of pre-historians. Our findings have been made in that manner and should be judged from that point of view.

The Purāṇas, in general, contain a good deal of information of value on ancient geography of India and some of them devote a number of chapters to this topic. Our *Vāyu Purāṇa* is one of them. One of the appendices gives an exhaustive and descriptive list of the tribal and place-names in the *Purāṇa* arranged alphabetically. There are certain of such names which on general assumption belong purely to the domain of mythology but some scholars have tried to identify even these names. It would be prejudging an issue to exclude them for the present and they are thus included in the Appendix.

The names of tribes and places in the Appendix are too numerous (about 1500) for discussion of the identification of all of them in the present work, which is not a treatise mainly on geography. It is clear that such a discussion should form a separate enquiry altogether and we hope to undertake it in the near future. The identifications of some names are, however, attempted in the present work only to see how far the *Vāyu* information admits of verification in the light of similar information available from other sources.

On the institution of pilgrimage too most of the *Purāṇas* offer valuable information as does also the *Vāyu Purāṇa*. This information also has been presented in a separate Appendix. As compared with the later portions of the *Great Epic*, the Smṛtis and some of the Purāṇas our text is less enthusiastic and elaborate in the matter. There is only one reference to a holy place of pilgrimage in the dynastic lists in connection with the king Gādhi and that too in a mythological setting, a fact which further attests our conclusion regarding the lists already noted above. Though the idea of the sanctity of water was known to the Vedic people it appears that the institution of pilgrimage, as such, was first started by the Buddhists or Jains and later on it became common to all the faiths in India. The Brahmins took it over probably in the early centuries of the Christian era and by the time of the *Institutes of Viṣṇu* it had become an established institution.

The terms 'cosmological', 'geographical', 'śrāddha' and 'genealogical' portions of the *Purāṇa* are often used in this investigation and they should be taken to imply the chapters 3–10, 34–49, 71–84 ai 35–99 respectively of the *Purāṇa*.

As regards the dates of various ancient and Pāli works, such as the Vedas, Jātakas etc. we have followed the views which are generally accepted by scholars. There is some conflict of opinion regarding the age of the compilations of the Jātakas. But scholars generally take the society and culture represented by them as belonging to the age of Buddha himself, if not earlier. Caraka is said to have flourished in the 1st cent. A.D. and Suśruta probably in the 5th cent. A.D.[53]

53. Mac. HSL. 455-6.

CHAPTER I

SOCIAL ORGANIZATION

SOCIAL THEORY

Cosmic origin : From the mouth of Brahmā arose the Brahmins, from his breast (*Pūrvabhāga*) the Kṣatriyas, from his belly the Vaiśyas and from his two feet the Śūdras.[1]

Mythic origin : In a prayer to Śiva by Dakṣa the former is glorified as being the originator of the *varṇāśrama*.[2] Manu and other sages are also credited with its propagation in every *yuga*,[3] and the same is said of the seven sages in the beginning of the Tretā age[4]. Brahmā once granted a boon to king Bali, a descendant of Yayāti, that he would be the founder of the four *varṇas* duly regulated.[5]

The terms *varṇa*, *āśrama* and *dharma* are often related to each other and are sometimes used conjointly. The compound word *varṇāśrama* is, however, a very common expression, and the four āśramas are said to have been set up by Brahmā immediately after the creation of the four varṇas.[6] The connection of these two terms with dharma is obvious from the following statements in the Purāna :—

"Brahmā had created the four varṇas but a spell of delusion (*moha*) swept over the people who defied the rules of varṇadharma which consequently led to mutual conflicts. Brahmā brooded over the matter again and set up proper limits to the respective functions of the four varṇas, and at the same time inaugurated the four āśramas."[7] The same information is cast in a different mould thus : In the Tretā age Brahmā planned the varṇāśrama but delusion (*moha*) disturbed the people and chaos ensued. The people approached Svāyaṁbhuva Manu... This led to the origin of Kingship with protection of dharma as its main function.[8] In the very first chapter of the Purāṇa we find it stated that varṇas and āśramas were set up according to dharma.[9]

Dharma, again, is either *śrauta* or *smārta*, the former being primarily concerned with the ritual and the Vedas and the latter with the various rules of varṇāśrama.[10] The smārta-dharma is based mainly on tradition (*paraṁparā*) as is stated by Svāyaṁbhuva Manu.[11] There is also a statement that whatever is enjoined by the *Śruti* and the *Smṛti* is the varṇāśramadharma though it must not, at the same time, be opposed to *śiṣṭācāra*.[12]

---

1. Cf. 6. 77 ; 9. 121. 2. Cf. 30. 218 3. Cf. 59. 35-36. 4. Cf. 61. 98.
5. Cf. 99. 32. 6. Cf. 8. 176. ff. 7. Cf. 8. 167. ff. 8. Cf. 57. 55-9.
9. Cf. 1. 110. omitted in Kha, Gha and Na.
10. Cf. 57. 39 ; 59. 31-9 ; 59. 106. 11. Cf. 57. 41. 12. Cf. 59. 51.

The descriptions of the four yugas and the one especially of the conditions obtaining at the end of the Kali age offer good instances of the linking up of these three terms. For instance, in the Kṛta age dharma did not exist nor did the varṇāśrama, but all of them originated in the Tretā age. Theoretically every King was duty-bound to follow dharma and to promote the varṇāśrama and wherever the varṇāśrama prevailed dharma was bound to be observed.

A gloomy and frightful picture of the state of *varṇasaṁkara* is found in the narrations of the conditions that were supposed to be prevalent at the end of the Kali age that was in the past or that will be in future.

The possibility of the modification of varṇas (cf. varṇavaikṛtam) arises in the fusion of the high and the low (*adharottaracāreṇa*). This is said in reference to the origin of the Sūta.[13] It is not clear, however, whether here *varṇasaṁkara* is also meant. The *Ājīvas*, who were regarded as being the products of the contamination of the varṇas and who belonged to the class of artisans, were supposed to have *Piśācas* as their deities[14] and the *Mlecchas* of similar origin are referred to as offering oblations to *Pitṛs*, i.e., they too performed *śrāddha* along with the four varṇas.[15]

Varṇāśrama and Vārtā :—Brahmā created the vegetable kingdom and set up *vārtās* for the sustenance of his creatures. After this had been achieved he regulated the various limits to the functions of the four varṇas.[16] Elsewhere it is mentioned that after the establishment of the vārtās the plan of the varṇāśrama was taken up and the *saṁhitās* (of the Vedas) were compiled.[17]

The mention of Tretā age in this connection is worthy of notice. In the first chapter we find an allusion to the fact that vārtās had their origin in the Tretā age[18] and we are informed elsewhere that the Creator ordained the setting up of vārtās in the middle of the Tretā age.[19] Śiva is also credited with the creation of vārtās.[20]

At the end of the Kali age the people will be giving up their vārtās and will become miserable.[21]

Of Manu and the other sages it is said that they promulgate the three (Vedas), *vārtā*, *daṇḍanīti*, *ijyā* and the *varṇāśrama* in every Yuga.[22]

II. The Brahmins

The Brahmins' claim for superiority : This claim is implicit in the cosmic account of the origin of the four varṇas. It is said that one who

---

13. Cf. 62.139–41 ; also 1.36. 14. Cf No. 15, App. 15. 63. 110–2.
16. Cf. *saṁsiddhāyāṁ tu vārtāyāṁ...maryādāḥ sthāpayāmāsa...*; 8.159 also 8.128–34.
17. 57. 89–90. 18. Cf. 1 109. 19. 8. 200–2. 20. 24. 103.
21. Cf. *vārtām utsṛjya duḥkhitāḥ* ; 58. 96 ; 99. 399 ; also 58. 32.
22. Cf. 59. 35–6 ; also No. 1027 in App.

makes others listen to the story of the birth of Pṛthu "after paying homage to Brahmins"[23] need not worry for whatever is done by him.

The sages are often shown in the company of gods, thus elevating their status. They lived with Devas on the peaks of the Meru mountain,[24] on the Kailāsa[25] in the hermitage of Śukra,[26] in Brahmakṣetra[27] and on the Mandara mountain in Malayadvīpa.[28] They even appear in the heaven (*svarga*) with Devas, Gandharvas etc.[29] In the ***amṛta-manthana*** incident we find them included in the party of Indra which led a deputation to Brahmā.[30] Their association with Viṣṇu is indicated by the fact that they attended upon that god in his abode on the Niṣadha mountain.[31] They had also the company of the thirty-three gods in the Puṣkaradvīpa.[32] In the descriptions of the various mountain-tops we often find references to sages associated with Devas, Gandharvas and other supernatural beings.[33]

The incident which led to the origin of the *avatāra* of Viṣṇu should be noted in this connection. It so transpired that Viṣṇu killed the mother of Śukra. Incensed at this outrage, which amounted to the murder of a woman, the sage Bhṛgu cursed Viṣṇu that he would be born as man seven times on the earth. But there is nothing in the narration of the story that Bhṛgu cursed the god because the Brahmin in him was roused to fury ; on the other hand, we find it expressly stated that Bhṛgu was enraged at the fact of the murder of a woman, which was considered as one of the most heinous offences.[34] But in the actual enumeration of these incarnations we find each incarnation of Viṣṇu having a Brahmin promoter (***puraḥsara***).[35]

Corresponding to this claim there was equally an assumption that the welfare of the society rested on their behaviour. Any defects in their ***karman*** may make the whole society suffer.[36]

Kinds of Sages[37] : There is reference to the three categories of sages (*ṛṣiprakṛtayaḥ*) viz., *Brahmarṣis*, *Devarṣis* and *Rājarṣis*. Their characteristics are also mentioned.[38] But elsewhere we find five *jātis* (classes) of sages enumerated thus : (1) the mind-born sons of Brahmā, (2) *Maharṣis*, (3) *Ṛṣis*, (4) *Ṛṣīkas* and (5) *Mantravādins*. It is not clear whether the group of seven sages formed a separate class.[39] Most probably they were the same as the mind-born sons of Brahmā, also referred to as *Prajāpatis*.[40] They are also mentioned as Maharṣis[41] and

---

23. *Brāhmaṇebhyo namaskṛtya*...cf. 62. 106.
24. Cf. 34. 74 ; 49. 48. 25. Cf. 41. 48. 26. Cf. 38. 62 ff. 27. Cf. 59. 107.
28. Cf. 48. 23. 29. Cf. 34. 93. 30. Cf. 54. 66 ff. 31. Cf. 41. 49.
32. Cf. 49. 135. 33. Cf. 42. 61 ; 41. 62 ; 41. 68 etc., and also App.
34. Cf. 99. 127–42. 35. Cf 98. 88–105.
36. Cf. *viprāṇāṁ karma doṣais taiḥ prajānāṁ jāyate bhayam* 58. 36.
37. The term *ṛṣi* is explained thus : *ṛṣiḥ sarvagatatvāc ca*. Cf. 5. 35.
38. Cf. 61. 80–90. 39. Cf. 61. 93 ff ; 100. 49 ff. 40. 100. 34–5 ; 65. 16 ff.
41. Cf. 7. 72–5 ; 65. 31 ff ; 100. 49 ff ; 62. 113–5.

probably were the same as Brahmarṣis, who were the first in the three categories of sages mentioned above.[42]

The Maharṣis, who were seven in number, do not seem to have been affected by the great catastrophe of the Deluge, for during that period they retire to the region called *Maharloka* whence they watch the slumbering Kāla in the darkness of the night.[43] Their origin is attributed to the sacrifice into which Brahmā offered his semen as an oblation.[44] It is said that they are called *maharṣis* because they see (*ṛṣanti mahat*).[45] They are also shown as practising the *Pāśupata yoga.*[46] At one place we find them questioning the propriety of killing animals in sacrifices and advocating the cause of non-violence. According to them *hiṁsā* cannot be dharma[47] nor do they think highly of *dāna* and *yajña.*[48]

The Brahmarṣis, as we have seen above, might probably be the same as Maharṣis. They are so called because they 'see' Brahman and it is stated that only in the five *gotras*, viz., Kaśyapa, Vasiṣṭha, Bhṛgu, Aṅgiras and Atri, are the Brahmarṣis born. It is for their knowledge of the Vedas, their birth and *tapas* that they are well-known. They are superior to Devarṣis and Rājarṣis and their ultimate goal is the *Brahmaloka.*[49] Sometimes the term *viprarṣi* is used.[50] Viśvāmitra is mentioned as a viprarṣi.[51] Terms such as *śrutarṣis* and *paramarṣis* are also used but it is difficult to say whether they are merely descriptive terms or signify different classes of sages denoted by these names.[52]

The Devarṣis were inferior to Brahmarṣis but were superior to Rājarṣis. They 'see' Devas : hence their name. The descendants of Dharma, Pulastya, Kratu, Pulaha, Prabhāsa and Kaśyapa were known as Devarṣis. Their ultimate goal was the *Devaloka.* Nara, Nārāyaṇa, Parvata and Nārada etc., are mentioned as Devarṣis.[53]

The Rājarṣis were so called because they 'see' their people through their (peoples') happiness. They are inferior both to Brahmarṣis and Devarṣis. They are mostly born in the *vaṁśas* or families of Mānava and Aiḍa. Their ultimate goal is the *Indraloka.*[54] A list of the names of Rājarṣis is also given.[55] Kings such as Damaghoṣa,[56] Janamejaya,[57] Aṅga,[58] Riveyu,[59] Somādhi,[60] Jahnu,[61] Divodāsa,[62] Lohagandha (?),[63] Yayāti,[64] Kārtavīrya Arjuna,[65] Kroṣṭu,[66] Bṛhadaśva,[67] Gaya,[68] and

42. Cf. 61. 10-2 ; 54. 8 ; 62. 113-5.
43. Cf. 7. 72-5 ; also 100. 188-92, which, however, mentioned *Janaloka* instead of Maharloka.
44. Cf. 65. 31 ff. 45. Cf. 59. 88 ; omitted in Gha. 46. Cf. 16. 24.
47. *Na hiṁsā dharma ucyate*—cf. 57. 99 ; 57. 97 ff. 48. Cf. 57. 115.
49. Cf. 61. 80-90. 50. Cf. 73. 17. 51. Cf. 41. 44-5.
52. Cf. 58. 13-4 ; 61. 12-3. etc. 53. Cf. 61. 80-88.
54. Cf. 61. 80-87. 55. Cf 57. 122-3. 56. Cf. 96. 158. 57. Cf. 99. 15.
58. Cf. 99. 100. 59. Cf. 99. 128. 60. Cf. 99. 296. 61. Cf. 91. 57.
62. Cf. 99. 201; 92. 25-6. 63. Cf. 93. 22-5. 64. Cf. 93. 102. 65. Cf. 94. 19 ; 95. 2.
66. Cf. 95. 14-9. 67. Cf. 88. 45-6. 68. Cf. 85. 19.

Janaka[69] are called Rājarṣis. Two verses, said to have been recited by Rājarṣis about king Alarka, are quoted in the Purāṇa.[70] Names of Kṣatriyas who are said to have achieved the status of sages through their efforts of penance are also mentioned. They are styled as *Kṣātropetāḥ dvijātayaḥ* (i.e. probably Kṣatriya Brahmins).[71]

The Munis are mentioned as if they are different from the Ṛṣis[72] and at one place we find Maharṣis styled as Munis who questioned Indra regarding the propriety of killing animals at sacrifices.[73] The sages of the Naimiṣa forest are also called Munis.[74] But the most frequent mention of the word Muni occurs in connection with the various incarnations of Maheśvara and with the description of the Pāśupata Yoga. God Maheśvara had revealed five dharmas and the *gaṇas* of Munis appear to have observed them ; and of them it is said that forsaking the human forms they can wander about like god.[75] They can see *Prakṛti* through their inward eye.[76] They are said to be indifferent both to insult and flattery.[77] Śiva in his different incarnations is also called Muni[78] and in his thirteenth incarnation he will be a great Muni named Vāli who will be born in the Vāli(la)khilyāśrama on the Gandhamādana mountain.[79] In the same context we find Bharadvāja[80] and Ṛtañjaya[81] called great munis. The story of the birth of Mahādeva is said to have been told by munis.[82] The munis also figure in the Purāṇa as worshippers of Śiva with dance and music, with the mystic *oṁkāra* and *huṁkāra* at *tīrthas* and temples in the north of the Himavat mountain.[83] Eighty-eight thousand Vālakhilya munis are said to have waited on the god Vāyu to listen to the latter's account of how Śiva came to be called Nīlakaṇṭha.[84] The god Vāyu, who many times appears as a narrator in the Purāṇa, is himself called a *mahāmuni*.[85] The munis also appear to be advocating the cause of non-violence and they have set up certain rules for *yatis* and *bhikṣus* (mendicants) regarding abstinence from animal food.[86] *Vaikhānasa-munis* who are mentioned here appear to have some connection with Rudra (?).[87] The Vālakhilyas (i.e., probably munis) were born of Śiva.[88] Vasiṣṭha is many times called a muni.[89] Aurva is also called muni[90] and similarly Ṛcīka,[91] Śaunaka,[92] Bṛhaspati, Uśanas, are also called munis.[93] Even Kṣatriyas such as Saṁyāti (brother of Yayāti)[94] and Devāpi, son of king Pratipa[95] had become munis.

---

69. Cf. 60. 35. 70. Cf. 92. 66. 71. Cf. 91. 114-8.
72. Cf. *ṛṣayo munibhis saha*—5. 4 ; also 60. 60 ; 60. 4°. 73. Cf. 56. 94-102.
74. Cf. 1. 28 ; 2. 45 ; 1. 48 ; 86. 35. 75. Cf. 10. 73-6.
76. Cf. *yuktāḥ paśyanti cetasā*—14. 12. 77. Cf. 16. 2-4.
78. Cf. 23. 115 ; 23. 198 ; 23. 206. 79. Cf. 23. 159. 80. Cf. 23. 185.
81. Cf. 23. 181. 82. Cf. 27. 1. 83. Cf. 54. 4-5. 84. Cf. 54. 8-10.
85. Cf. 22. 1. 86. Cf. 18. 9-17. 87. Cf. 65. 56-61. 88. Cf. 55. 41-3.
89. Cf. 88. 94-6 ; 88. 112 ; 88. 138. 90. Cf. 88. 158. 91. Cf. 91. 81.
92. Cf. 93. 25. 93. Cf. 3. 5. 94. Cf. 93. 14. 95. Cf. 99. 236.

Brahmins and the Ritual : To officiate as priest in sacrifices was one of the three duties of a Brahmin as ordained by Brahmā.[96] Many instances of great ritual performances are cited in the Purāṇa. The *Vāyu Purāṇa* itself was narrated at a sacrificial session.[97] Indra and Soma performed *yajñas.*[98] It was at this sacrifice performed by Indra that the maharṣis, also called munis, had raised a protest against killing of animals in yajña. The story of the Dakṣa-yajña covers a whole chapter.[99]

With Akrūra it appears to have been almost a habit to perform sacrifices so much so that Akrūra-yajñas are well-known.[100] King Raśādu and his son Citraratha performed great sacrifices and distributed ample wealth as *dakṣiṇā.*[101] King Rukmakavaca had performed an *aśvamedha* and bestowed wealth on Brahmins.[102] There is also an allusion to the performance of hundred aśvamedhas by king Sagara which led to the incident of the descent of the river Gaṅgā on the earth.[103] Sīradhvaja Janaka had also performed an aśvamedha and while the *agnikṣetra* was ploughed in the course of this sacrifice, it is said that Sītā was discovered from the clods of earth.[104] King Janamejaya performed an aśvamedha in which Indrota Śaunaka officiated as priest.[105] It is said that no one can be compared with king Kārtavīrya Arjuna in his performance of yajñas etc.[106] King Dharmaratha had the privilege of sharing Soma with Śakra in a sacrifice performed on the Viṣṇupada mountain.[107] *Rājasūya* was performed by Hariścandra.[108] A story of how Devamitra Śākalya was vanquished by Yājñavalkya in a debate at Janaka's aśvamedha is also narrated in the Purāṇa.[109] Of the kings of the 'future' we find an instance of king Pravīra who 'will be' performing many *vājapeya yajñas* in his city of Kāñcanakā accompanied by a generous distribution of wealth by way of daksiṇā.[110]

King Vena held ideas against the performance of sacrifices and in his reign gods did not partake of Soma at all. The sages offered a successful fight against him and installed Pṛthu in his place.[111] King Purūravas also tried to fall in line with Vena in this regard and coveted the wealth of the sages but he too met with a similar fate.

But ideas opposed to the performance of rituals, connected with the killing of animals are expressed, as we have seen, by the great sages themselves. They disliked both *dāna* and *yajña* on this very point.[112] Attempts are made to elevate dāna at the cost of actual performance of the ritual. One who gives his all to the Brahmins

---

96. Cf. 8. 169–70. 97. Cf. 1. 1 ff. 99. 257–60. 98. Cf. 57. 96 ff.; 90 22–4.
99. Cf. Chapt. 30. 100. Cf. 96. 81–2. 101. Cf. 95. .6–9 102. Cf. 95. 26.
103. Cf. 88. 143ff. 104. Cf. 89. 16–8. 105. Cf. 93. 25. 106. Cf. 94. 20.
107. Cf. 99. 102 ; Ga omits this. 108. Cf. 88. 118. 109. Cf. 60. 35 ff.
110. Cf. 99. 371–2. 111. Cf. 62. 109. ff.
112. *tasmān na dānaṁ yajñaṁ va praśaṁsanti maharṣayaḥ.* Cf. 57. 115.

is said to be capable of achieving the merits, of the performance of all sacrifices.[113] In attempts to evaluate the respective merits of *dāna*, *yajña*, *tapas*, *saṁnyāsa* and *jñāna* we find yajña standing far below in the grade[114] and we have also a discourse by Śiva to Brahmā that yajña, dāna, the Vedas, etc., are not sufficient for the comprehension of his real greatness.[115] The origin and the flourishing state of yajña particularly in the Tretā and Dvāpara ages are equally deserving of notice. It is said that the Kali is the age of *dāna*, i. e., of making gifts only.

Acceptance of gifts (*pratigraha*) is also one of the three primary duties of a Brahmin. In a passage on *dānalakṣaṇa* (characteristics of making gifts) we find a definition of dāna and its kinds. A gift, to be proper, must be made only of a property acquired by lawful means and to a person (i. e., a Brahmin) who is virtuous.[116] Such a gift can be of three kinds: the best, the intermediate and the worst. Gift of the first kind is made without any ulterior motive of a return. The second type of gift is what is made through pity (*kāruṇyāt*). The worst kind of gift is made in view of a selfish end.[117] It is emphasized that the Brahmins to whom gifts are made must be virtuous.[118] Contrary to this, however, we find an exhortation that while feeding Brahmins in Gayā one should not inquire about their birth, conduct and learning, etc.[119]

Subject-matter of Gifts: Feeding Brahmins seems to have been regarded as the most appropriate dāna.[120] It is stated that feeding Brahmins in Gayā makes gods and ancestors pleased.[122] Vipras should be offered food even if they come in thousands, for it is said that the blessed ones (*siddhāḥ...yogeśvarāḥ*) wander on this earth in the guise of vipras and protect the people according to dharma and that is why Brahmin guests should be offered food and hospitality with due respect.[123] Bṛhaspati particularly points out to Śaṁyu that at the time of *śrāddha* the ancestors are in the form of wind and become identified with Brahmins and that is why they should be served with food, clothes, cows, horses and villages.[121] Cows are also regarded as good gifts. Of Gāndinī (daughter of Śvaphalka, king of Kāśi) it is said that her father daily gave a cow to a Brahmin for she had insisted on this procedure as a condition precedent to her birth.[124] A thousand cows, gold, villages, jewels and slaves were the objects of prize offered by king Janaka to the most learned Brahmin amongst those assembled at his aśvamedha.[125] In the chapter on *dānaphala*[126] we find food, clothes, house-furniture (especially cots, bedding and cooking utensils) and foodstuffs as good gifts in śrāddha. We do not know from the Purāṇa

113. Cf. 79. 12. 114. Cf. 91. 113-4 115. Cf. 23. 101.
116. Cf 59. 49. 117. Cf. 59. 48-50. 118. Cf. 80. 28. 119. Cf. 82. 24-7.
120. Cf. *annadānāt paraṁ dānaṁ neha kiṁcana vidyate*—Cf. 80. 55.
121. Cf. 82. 25-6. 122. Cf. 71. 64-75. 123. Cf. 75. 13-4.
124. Cf. 96. 104-8. 125. Cf. 60. 37. 126. Cf. Chapt. 80.

as to what objects were offered as gifts in the various sacrifices performed by kings. There is a story of how Citrabhānu (the Sun-god in disguise) demanded of the king Kārtavīrya Arjuna a gift of the whole earth and of how the king granted it.[127]

Glorificatory statements regarding making of gifts are found in the Purāṇa at many places. We have seen above how the blessed ones and the spirits of the ancestors were capable of being represented in the Brahmins. Gods, Manes and Fire receive what is offered to dvijas.[128] In the *śrāddha-phala* chapters we find the merits of making gifts in śrāddha compared with those obtainable by performance of various sacrifices.[129] If respects are duly paid in a śrāddha to a yogin led by a thousand Brahmins it is certain that he will lead his host and his entourage (*bhoktṛn*) in crossing (the sea of life ?) as a boat afloat on the sea.[130] The story of the gift of silver (*rajata-dāna*) is without an end and virtuous sons enable their ancestors to cross (the ocean of life ?) with the help of this kind of gift.[131] There is also a general statement that those who give, go to the world of gods and those who do not, go to hell.[132]

As in the case of rituals we find statements in the Purāṇa indicating a low estimation of the spiritual value of dāna.

Brahmins at Tīrthas : We find many *tīrthas* mentioned in the Purāṇa as being holy for the purpose of śrāddha. At one of such tīrthas we are told of the existence of a sort of merito-metre (*dharmādharma-pradarśinī tulā*) with which Brahmins are said to have measured the merits of a tīrtha.[133] At the holy place of Vāyupura 18000 Brahmins—one-third of its total population—are said to have resided under the leadership of Mātariśvan. These Brahmins belonged to eleven gotras. This tīrtha, it is asserted, is famous throughout the world.[134]

Brahmins and Recitations of Kathās, Gāthās, etc. : There is an allusion in the Purāṇa to recitation of a *gāthā* by Brahmins on the family of king Devāvṛdha.[135] Their connection with the recitations of *Kathās* and *Purāṇa* are, however, mentioned many times. He who listens and makes others listen to the story of the origin of creation from Brahmins, especially from *yatis*, at places of pilgrimage and temples, enjoys a long life and is, in due course, glorified in heaven due to *purāṇānukīrtana* (i.e. recitation of a purāṇa ?).[136] One attains happiness by a regular attendance at a recitation of a purāṇa.[137] Women, Śūdras and Vaiśyas are recommended to listen to the story of Dakṣa-Śiva conflict from the Brahmins for securing a place in *Rudra-loka*.[138] Various merits are promised to the members of different varṇas if they listen to the

127. Cf. 94. 39-40 ; 95. 3. 128. Cf. 79. 14. 129. Cf. Chapters 79-80.
130. Cf. 76. 28. 131. Cf. 74. 1-2. 132. Cf. 81. 9. 133. Cf. 77. 73.
134. Cf. No. 1422, App. 135. Cf. 96. 13. 136. Cf. 4. 5-8.
137. Cf. 4. 92. 138. Cf. 30. 320-1.

story of how Śiva came to be called Nīlakaṇṭha (blue-necked).[139] Similarly, one who listens to and repeats the account of the birth of Maruts is said to enjoy a long life.[140] It is also meritorious and beneficial to listen to the account of the progeny of Kaśyapa in the assembly of learned Brahmins.[141] The Brahmin who repeats the account of Kṛṣṇa's birth is also expected to be happy if he makes others listen to the same.[142]

Brahmins and Politics : The *Purohita* was one of the seven jewels of a paramount sovereign (*cakravartin*). The other six were : the Queen, the Commander-in-Chief, the Charioteer, *Mantrin*, Horse and *Kalabha*. These jewels were the very breathing spirit of kingship.[143]

The influence of the Purohita in matters of state apparent from the following instances. In the absence of the king, who had retired to the forest, the sage Vasiṣṭha—who is here called *yājyopādhyāya*—looked after the kingdom of Ayodhyā and the royal seraglio. The enemies of Sagara repaired to Vasiṣṭha for protection and king Sagara allowed them their freedom on Vasiṣṭha's advice.[144]

The Brahmins as a class also appear in the Purāṇa as wielding some influence in political affairs. King Yayāti had decided to consecrate his youngest son Puru as the next ruler of the realm. This was, however, against ancient usage. The (representatives ? of the) people headed by Brahmins (*Brāhmaṇa-pramukhā varṇāḥ*) lodged a formal protest against this to the king and advised him to follow the dharma by installing any of the elder sons on the throne. To this the king replied rather calmly, "All my elder sons have behaved disrespectfully towards me, while only the youngest son Puru had proved himself to be respectful and obedient. Besides there is the boon of the sage Śukra that only an obedient son should succeed me. There is also the consideration that Puru is acceptable to you (*bhavato 'numato*) and being your favourite prince he shall certainly be benevolent to you.[145] Since the venerable sage Śukra had already ordained the matter through the boon, I am almost helpless to add any further explanation." The Paura-jānapadas were apparently satisfied and approved of the king's choice.[146]

Brahmins *versus* Kṣatriyas : King Trayyāruṇa of Ayodhyā expelled his son Satyavrata at the instigation of his priest Vasiṣṭha and feeling disgust at his son's behaviour retired to forest life. Satyavrata being thus in exile, Vasiṣṭha now looked after the affairs of state and also supervised over the royal seraglio. In the meanwhile famine stalked over the kingdom and it lasted for twelve years. During the period of this famine Satyavrata supported the family of Viśvāmitra who was

---

139. Cf. 54. 111-6. 140. Cf. 67. 135. 141. Cf. 69. 355.
142. Cf. 96. 191. This stanza is omitted in Gha. 143. Cf. 57. 70.
144. Cf. 88. 136-8. 145. Cf. *yaḥ priyaḥ priyakṛt tava*. 146. Cf. 93. 15. ff.

engaged in severe austerities. Though Vasiṣṭha was the *de facto* ruler of the kingdom still he felt insecure in his position and appears to have had an inclination to instal Satyavrata on the throne.[147] But it so happened that Satyavrata, partly through a spirit of revenge and partly because he could not get food elsewhere, killed the cow of Vasiṣṭha. The enraged sage condemned him to be called Triśaṅku (a man of three sins or stains). Viśvāmitra, after he had finished his penance, came to know of how Satyavrata had supported his family; and it appears that he helped Satyavrata in his restoration.[148] Triśanku is then stated to have been elevated to heaven by Viśvāmitra.[149]

The following factors in the narrative of Vena and Pṛthu should be noted :—

(1) The Prajāpati Aṅga was born in the family of Atri. His son was Vena born of Sunīthā, a daughter of Mṛtyu whose vices seem to have tainted the character of Vena.

(2) When Vena came to the throne he transgressed the injunctions of the Vedas and followed the path of adharma. In his reign sacrifices ceased to be performed and gods were without their drink of Soma in yajñas. He was even fanatically determined[150] to offer active resistance to the performance of rituals. He arrogantly asserted that he himself should be worshipped and offered oblations in sacrifices.

(3) The sages, with Marīci as their leader, approached him saying, "Vena, do not follow adharma; this is not the eternal law. It has been promised by you that you would protect the people".[151] But Vena replied in scorn, "Who else is the creator of dharma? ...Who can equal me in power, penance, knowledge and truth? ... I am the sole master and disposer of the earth ..."

(4) The great sages could not now control their anger. They seized him and 'churned' his left arm.[152] They then 'churned' his right arm and Pṛthu was born to the joy of all beings. The rivers and seas brought him jewels. The lord Pitāmaha, with gods, Aṅgirasas, and the creatures of the world, consecrated Pṛthu as the first king (*ādirājā*) of the world. An explanation of the word *rājan* (king) is then given. The king is called as such through the affection (*anurāga*) of his people.

(5) Then comes the incident of the birth of Sūta and Māgadha in the yajña. The sages called upon them to sing of the glory of Pṛthu.[153]

---

147. Cf. *abhiṣekṣyāmyahaṁ rājye......* .

148. But here the text is not clear. There is also no clue as to how the restoration was effected.

149. Ka, Ga, Gha and Ṅa omit this. There is, again, no description of the conflict between Viśvāmitra and Vasiṣṭha. Cf. 88. 80-116. But it is only alluded to elsewhere (2. 11) without any reference to Satyavrata Triśaṅku.

150. Cf. *krūrā pratijñā.* 151. Cf. *pālayiṣye prajāśca iti tvayā pūrvaṁ pratiśrutam.*
152. For further details cf. No. 576 in App. 153. Cf. *Pṛthos stavārthaṁ samāhūtau.*

They, however, replied, "We are accustomed to sing of gods and sages according to their achievements. Of the deeds of this king (i.e. Pṛthu) we know nothing that will enable us to praise him in suitable terms nor have we any indication (*lakṣaṇa*) of the same." The sages, however, asked them to sing of such deeds of the king as he was destined to perform in future. The Sūta and Māgadha praised the king according to the wishes of the sages. The king was pleased and offered the Anūpa-deśa to Sūta and the Magadha-deśa to Māgadha. Thenceforward are kings praised by Sūtas and Māgadhas.

(6) This is then followed by the speech of sages in words such as "Let this king Vainya be our sustainer," followed by an acclamation of the people in words: "Sustain us, our lord."

(7) The king now proceeds to vanquish the earth, which in the form of a cow, pleads mercy. The king commands her to always sustain his people which[154] the earth agrees to do. Henceforward is the earth known as Pṛthu's daughter.

(8) Last comes the incident of the 'milching of the earth' (*pṛthvīdohana*) in which the earth is symbolized as the cow. The king, gods, sages, yakṣas, etc. partake in this 'milching' of the earth.[155]

The facts about the Janamejaya and Gārgya episode are as follows:–

(*a*) He was the son of Parīkṣit and is also called Kaurava (i.e. a descendant of Kuru).

(*b*) He hurt the son of Gārgya.[156] Gārgya seems to have cursed Janamejaya and as a result of this curse the famous chariot which Janamejaya had inherited from his ancestor Yayāti was destroyed. The unfortunate king was also forsaken by the Paura-jānapadas and thus he was never at rest.[157]

(*c*) The sage Indrota Śaunaka purified him by officiating as a priest in a horse-sacrifice performed by him.[158]

We find another account of the same king elsewhere :—

(i) He supported the Vājasaneyika Brahmins.

(ii) According to some versions of the Purāṇa,[159] Vaiśampāyana is said to have cursed him, but the reason for this is not stated.

(iii) He performed aśvamedha twice.

(iv) He is here called the lord (? *kharva*) of the Aśvakamukhyas, the Aṅgas and of Madhyadeśa.

(v) It is further stated that he met his ruin through his quarrels with the Brahmins who installed his son Śatānīka on the throne.[160]

---

154. Cf. *saṁjīvaya prajā nityaṁ*. 155. Cf. 62. 103 ff.
156. The name of this son might be Lohagandha, but the text here is very confusing.
157. Cf. *Paurajānapadais tyakto no lebhe śarma karhicit*.
158. Cf. 93. 21-7. 159. As in Kha, Gha and Ṅa. 160. 99. 250-6.

While king Purūravas was ruling, the sages of the Naimiṣa forest had started a sacrificial session which was to last for twelve years. It is said that even the jewels of the eighteen seas did not satisfy his greed. He came to know of the wealth of the sages when he happened to come to the place of the sacrifice in the course of his hunting expedition. He tried to force it away but the sages opposed him and killed him with the blades of Kuśa grass. They then installed his son on the throne.[161]

Once upon a time the Sun-god in the guise of a Brahmin named Citrabhānu demanded from the king Kārtavīrya Arjuna the whole earth for alms. To effect this gift the king shot arrows which consumed with fire cities, villages etc., and also the hermitage of the sage Vasiṣṭha Āpava, probably son of Varuṇa. The sage was enraged and cursed the king that the Brahmin Rāma would annihilate him.[162]

Brahmins and Education: Teaching (*adhyāpana*)[163] was one of the three primary functions of a Brahmin as had been ordained by Brahmā.[164] The Sūta says that the story of the birth of Pṛthu is not to be narrated to a person, i. e., a Brahmin, without a disciple.[165] A Brahmin without the knowledge of the Vedas was not to be invited for *śrāddha*.[166]

There is an instance in the Purāṇa of how the Vedic lore was transmitted from father to son. Jaimini was entrusted with the compilation of the Sāmaveda Saṁhitā by his preceptor Vyāsa. He taught it to his son Sumantu, who in return transmitted the same to his son Sutvāna. Sutvāna further transmitted it to his son Sukarman.[167]

Some glimpses of the intellectual activities of the Brahmins are offered from the following story of Janaka's *aśvamedha*: Thousands of sages had assembled for this sacrifice. The king desired to know as to who was the most learned amongst them and announced a highly covetable prize for the most successful contestant in the debate. Yājñavalkya came forward to claim the prize but had an opponent in Devamitra Śākalya. The other sages had asked him many questions but he answered them easily. After some wordy warfare Śākalya asked Yājñavalkya some questions on *kāma* and the latter answered them quite satisfactorily. Yājñavalkya in turn now asked his rival only one question on *kāma* (*kāmikaṁ praśnam*) and warned him that death was waiting for him if he did not answer it. Śākalya was unable to answer and thus he courted death.[168]

There is a quaint reference to Brahmins preaching principles of atheism in the holy place of Gokarṇa.[169]

---

161. Cf. 2. 13–24 ; 1. 190–3.

162. Some versions do not read the name Apava; Ka omits it altogether. Cf. 94. 39. ff.; 95. 1-13. It should be noted that the patronymic Jāmadagnya is not mentioned in connection with Rāma.

163. Kha, Ga, Gha and Ṅa read *adhyayana*. 164. Cf. 8. 169. 165. Cf. 62. 104.

166. Cf. 82. 64. 167. Cf. 61. 27. Kha and Gha omit this. 168. Cf. 60. 35–60.

169. Cf. 77. 21 *Gokarṇe varṇitaṁ viprair nāstikānāṁ nidarśanam.*

III. THE KṢATRIYAS

The term Kṣattra is very often used in the Purāṇa to denote the whole order of the Kṣatriyas. King Hariścandra is referred to as the conqueror of the whole Kṣattra.[170] Rāma Jāmadagnya is styled as the 'annihilator of the whole Kṣattra'.[171] Mahāpadma conquered the whole Kṣattra.[172] Manu, a descendant of Ikṣvāku, is called the promoter of the Kṣattra (*Kṣattra-pravartaka*),[173] and the same is said of Devāpi and Suvarcas elsewhere.[174] Besides, we have expressions such as *Mānava Kṣattra*, *Aila Kṣattra*,[175] *Bāleya Kṣattra*,[176] *Rājeya Kṣattra*,[177] *Dhārṣṭaka Kṣattra*,[178] etc., meaning the descendants of Manu, Ilā, Bali, Raji, Dhṛṣṭa, etc., respectively. The compound word Brahma-Kṣattra is also mentioned sometimes.[179] The Kṣattra of Iksvāku is said to have come to a close with Sumitra and that of Aila with Kṣemaka.[180]

The word Kṣatriya meant a member of the order of Kṣattra. Vasudeva reminds Kaṁsa that a Kṣatriya should not kill a woman.[181] The word Kṣatriya is used in this sense in the Purāṇa many times. But in the account of the origin of the varṇas we find the word 'Kṣatriya' as signifying the class or order of Kṣatriyas and the use of the word in this sense is equally observable in the Purāṇa as in the case of Kṣattra.[182]

There is, however, an interesting instance of Kārtavīrya Arjuna who is called *Viśāṁ patiḥ*, i. e., "lord of *viś* or people",[183] and the term *rājanya* is very rarely used in the Purāṇa.[184] Even Śakas, Yavanas, Kāmbojas, Palhavas, Pāradas, Kalisparśas, Māhiṣikas, Darvas, Colas and Khasas are mentioned as Kṣatriya-gaṇas.[185]

Functions of the Kṣatriya Order: To protect others was the primary duty of Kṣatriyas.[186] But to be more explicit Brahmā had ordained the following as their chief functions: (i) *bala* (soldiery ?), (ii) *daṇḍa* (government ?) and (iii) war.[187]

After Brahmā had set up the vārtās he proceeded to regulate the limits of the functions of the varṇas. To protect others was the function he assigned to Kṣatriyas and then functions of other varṇas are mentioned. When this did not work well he reiterated the same though more explicitly. Here too the functions of the Kṣatriya order are mentioned *first*.[188]

---

170. Cf. 88. 120. 171. Cf. 98. 91. Omitted in Cha. Cf. also. 99. 449.
172. Cf. 99. 328. Kha has Kṣetra instead. 173. Cf. 88. 210. 174. Cf. 99. 438-40. Cf. also 28. 27-9. 175. Cf. 99. 293. 176. Cf. 99. 28. 177. Cf. 92. 75.
178. Cf. 88. 4. 179. Cf. 99. 116 ; 99. 2·8 ; 99. 246. etc. 180. Cf. 99. 431-3.
181. Cf. 96. ?24. 182. Cf. 99. 433; 99. 442; 99. 449; 91. 69; 91. 75; 91. 91 etc. etc.
183. Cf. 94, 39.
184. Cf. 28. 37, where Ketumat is called *rājanya* but Gha and Ṅa read *rājan*.
185. Cf. 88. 142-3. 83. 126. ff. 186. Cf. 8. 162. 187. Cf. 8. 169.
188. Cf. 8. 162-70.

INTELLECTUAL ACTIVITIES OF THE KṢATRIYAS

(i) The following kings are mentioned as being Brahmavādins in the Purāṇa :

(a) King Purūravas was Brahmavādin and Satyavādin.[189]

(b) Malina was the son of king Trasu and is called Brahmavādin. He had four sons of whom Duṣmanta or Duṣyanta was one.[190] This Duṣyanta was the father of Bharata born of Śakuntalā.[191]

(c) King Mitrajyoti's[192] sons gave up the life of a householder and embraced the life of renunciation and having followed the life of yatis they finally achieved the *brahmabhūya* (i.e., unity with Brahman).[193]

(ii) Kings who retired to forest life and practised penance and yoga :

(a) Bṛhadaśva installed his son Kuvalāśva on the throne and entered forest-life. Once it so happened that the sage Uttaṅka was disturbed by a demon Dhundhu (who also was practising penance) in the course of his austerities. Uttaṅka approached Bṛhadaśva (who had now embraced forest-life) for redress of his grievances. Bṛhadaśva replied, "I had already given up my arms[194] but my son Kuvalāśva will see to the matter". He is also called a rājarṣi.[195]

(b) Trayyāruṇa and (c) Viṣvāmitra are already mentioned.

(d) Vasudeva had two sons : Puṇḍra and Kapila. Of these, Puṇḍra became king and Kapila retired to forest-life.[196]

(e) Brahmā once granted some boons to king Bali according to which he was expected to be a great *yogin* and a master of the principles of dharma and artha.[197]

(f) Manu was the son of Śīghra of the Ikṣvāku line.[198] In the 19th *prayuga* (?) he is said to have resorted to yoga.[199]

(g) King Nahuṣa had five sons of whom Saṁyāti was one. He became a muni and having desired for emancipation became finally united with Brahman.[200]

(h) After installing his youngest son Puru on the throne Yayāti entered forest-life and practised penance on the Bhṛgutuṅga. He is styled as rājarṣi.[201]

---

189. Cf. 91. 4 ; 91. 2, 190. Cf. Kha and Gha have Duṣkanta.
191. Cf. 99. 132-5. 192. Cf. according to Ga *Mitradyoti*. 193. Cf. 93. 5-6.
194. Cf. *rājā saṁnyastaśastro 'haṁ*. 195. Cf. 88 32-45.
196. Cf. 96. 183. 197. Cf. 99. 30-2.
198. Cf. Kha and Gha call him Maru at one place. 199. Cf. 88. 210.
200. Cf. *Saṁyātir mokṣam āsthāya brahmabhūto 'bhavan muniḥ* ; 93. 14.
201. Cf. 93. 102.

(i) King Pratīpa had three sons, viz., Devāpi, Śaṁtanu and Vāhlīka. Devāpi entered forest-life as he was in earnest about dharma (*dharma-parīpsayā*). He became a muni, and the *upādhyāya* of Devas.[202]

There is another reference to Paurava King Devāpi who is said to have resorted to *yoga*. He is here called the promoter of Kṣattra (*Kṣattra-prāvartaka*).[203]

(iii) The Rājarṣi Kings: Two lists of Rājarṣi kings occur in the Purāṇa. The first list, which does not profess to be exhaustive, gives the following names of Rājarṣi kings:—Priyavrata, Uttānapāda, Dhruva, Medhātithi, Sumedhas, Virajas, Śaṅkhapāda, Prācīnabarhis, Parjanya and Havirdhāna, etc. They are said to have practised penance.[204] The second list, which too does not purport to be exhaustive, mentions the following royal sages:—Viśvāmitra, Māṁdhātā, Saṁkṛti, Kapi, Purukutsa, Satya, Ṛthu (?), Ārṣṭiṣeṇa, Ajamīḍha, Kakṣīva, Sṛñjaya, Rathītara, Rundha and Viṣṇuvṛddha, etc. They are said to have accomplished sage-hood through austerities. They are also styled as *Kṣātropetā dvijātayaḥ*.[205] The names of the royal sages scattered about in the Purāṇa are already mentioned.

Some of these kings, of whom we have more information from the Purāṇa, have been noted below:—

(1) Ambarīṣa: The Vāyu Purāṇa mentions two Ambarīṣas of whom one was a son of Nābhāga[206] and the other that of Māṁdhātā.[207] In these references to the king we do not find the epithets rājarṣi used, though the name occurs in one of the above lists.

(2) Ajamīḍha: There are two Ajamīḍhas mentioned in the Purāṇa. One of them was a son of Somaka. He was probably the grandfather of Drupada. His wife, by name Dhūminī, is said to have practised severe austerities for a hundred years! Here Ajamīḍha is not called rājarṣi.[208] The other Ajamīḍha was a son of Hastin, who founded the city of Hastināpura. This Ajamīḍha had three wives. One of them, Keśinī, gave birth to Kaṇṭha whose descendants were the Kāṇṭhāyana dvijas. His other wife, Nīlinī, gave birth to Nīla. Mudgala was a great-great-grandson of this Nīla. The descendants of Mudgala were known as the Maudgalya Brahmins who were Kṣatriya Brahmins.[209] This Ajamīḍha also is not mentioned as a rājarṣi. But his name occurs in the list of rājarṣi sages.

(3) Divodāsa: Divodāsa is mentioned as a son of Badhyaśva.[210] He is mentioned at another place as the king of Vārāṇasī. He was the

202. Cf. 99. 234-6. 203. Cf. 99. 437-40. 204. Cf. 57. 121-3.
205. Cf. 91. 114-18. 206. Cf. 88. 6. 207. Cf. 88. 71-2. 208. Cf. 99. 209-12.
209. Cf. 99. 166-200. But Ṅa omits this piece of information about the Maudgalyas.
210. Cf. 99. 200-1.

son of Ketumat. A story is narrated of the destruction of the city of Vārāṇasī and of the founding of another city by Divodāsa on the river Gomatī.[211] Here Divodāsa is mentioned as rājarṣi.

(4) Kakṣīvat: He is said to have been born of Dīrghatamas through a Śūdra maid-servant of king Bali. He is called a Brahmavādin. He practised severe austerities and through these achieved brahminhood.[212] But nowhere in this account is Kakṣīvat called a rājarṣi though his name occurs in the above lists.

(5) Māṁdhātā: He was the son of Yuvanāśva. He is said to have been bearing a *corpus* (*tanuḥ*) of Viṣṇu. He had three sons, viz., Purukutsa, Ambarīṣa and Mucukunda. The grandson of Ambarīṣa was Harita after whom the Hārita Brahmins—who were Kṣatriya Brahmins—were known.[213] Viṣṇuvṛddha was a descendant of Purukutsa. The Viṣṇuvṛddha Brahmins (?)—who too were Kṣatriya Brahmins—were known after this Viṣṇuvṛddha. The term rājarṣi, however, does not occur in the narration. Another reference makes Maṁdhātā an incarnation of Viṣṇu.[214]

(6) Pṛthu Vainya and (7) Purukutsa are already mentioned.

(8) Rathītara: Rathītara was a great-grandson of Ambarīṣa, son of Nābhāga. After him the Rathītaras, who were Kṣatriya Brahmins, came to be so called.[215] The epithet rājarṣi does not occur in connection with Rathītara.

(9) Saṁkṛti, (10) Janaka, (11) Bṛhadaśva and (12) Yayāti are mentioned above.

(13) Janamejaya: Rājarṣi Janamejaya was the son of Puraṁjaya.[216]

(14) Kapi: The ancestor of Kāpeya Brahmins.

(15) Viśvāmitra: In these accounts he is not called a rājarṣi, though his name occurs first in the list of rājarṣis.

(iv) Kṣatriyas and Vedic Learning: Sagara had his education in the hermitage of the sage Aurva who taught him the Vedas and the *śastras*.[217] King Kuśa had four sons who were well-versed in the Vedas.[218] Vaśiṣṭha, a descendant of Ikṣvāku, was a disciple of a grandson of Jaimini. He was well-versed in 105 *saṁhitās*. Yājñavalkya learnt *yoga* from him (?).[219] King Kṛta, a descendant of Puru, was a disciple of Hiraṇyanābhi Kauthuma. He compiled the twenty-four Sāmans which are known as the prācya sāmans of Kṛta.[220] The same fact is referred to in the account of the compilation of the Sāma-veda.[221]

---

211. Cf. No. 1403 in App.; 92. 20 ff. 212. Cf. 99. 67–94. 213. Cf. 88. 65–75.
214. Cf. 98. 90. Gha omits this. 215. Cf. 88. 6–7.
216. Cf. 99. 15. Ga omits this. 217. *Adhyāpya veda-śāstrāṇi*: 88. 134.
218. *Vedavarcasaḥ*: 91. 62. Gha reads differently. 219. Cf. 88. 206–8.
220. *Smṛtās te prācyanāmānaḥ Kārtā Sāmnāṁ tu Sāmagāḥ*: 99. 189–91.
221. Cf. 61. 44.

The following names of persons, who are known as kings elsewhere in the Purāṇa, occur in the list of *mantravādin* sages : Vītahavya, Pṛthu Vainya and Divodāsa.[222]

The names of Purukutsa, Māṁdhātā, Aṁbarīṣa, Yuvanāśva Paurukutsa, Trasadasyu, Ajamīḍha, Ṛṣabha, Bali and Pṛṣadaśva occur in the list of *mantrakṛt* sages.[223] Most of the kings who bore these names have already been noted above.

A *gāthā* which purports to have been sung by the great king Yayāti is actually handed down to us by the Purāṇa.[224]

Kṣatriya-Brahmin Relations

(A) Kṣatriya Brahmins : The expression 'Kṣātropetā dvijātayaḥ' occurs many times in the genealogical lists of the Purāṇa in connection with kings after whom these twice-born (dvijātayaḥ) were named.

Of such Brahmins the following are mentioned in the Purāṇa :

(a) Kaṇṭhāyana-dvijas. They belonged to the *pakṣa* of Aṅgirasas.

(b) Maudgalyas, (c) Hāritas and (d) Viṣṇuvṛddhas. They are included in the list of the fifteen pakṣas of the Aṅgirasas.[225]

(e) Rathītaras : They were known as Aṅgirasas and are also included in the list of the fifteen pakṣas of Aṅgirasas.[226]

(f) Gāgras, (g) Kapis and (h) Sāṁkritis : Vitatha Bharadvāja had a son Bhuvamanyu who had four sons, viz., Bṛhatkṣattra, Mahāvīrya, Nara and Gāgra.[227] The descendants of Gāgra were known after him as the Gāgra Kṣatriya Brahmins. Mahāvīrya had a great-grandson named Kapi whose descendants also were known as Kṣatriya Brahmins. Nara's son was Sāṁkṛti after whom the Sāṁkṛti Kṣatriya Brahmins were so called. All of these Kṣatriya Brahmins belonged to the pakṣas of Aṅgirasas.[228] The Gārgyakas and Sāṁkṛtikas are mentioned elsewhere as pakṣas of the Aṅgirasas.[229]

(i) Śāradvatas : Śatānanda, a great sage, had a son named Kṛpa through an apsaras. Kṛpa seems to have been brought up by the king Śaṁtanu. Śatānanda was a descendant of Mudgala referred to in connection with king Ajamīḍha. The descendants of Kṛpa, son of Śatānanda, were probably known as Śāradvatas. It appears that they were called also Ṛtathyas and Gautamas. They embraced the stock of the Bhārgavas.[230]

(j) Maitreyas : Mitrayu was a son of King Divodāsa. His descendants were the Maitreyas who were also Kṣatriya Brahmins following the stock of the Bhārgavas.[231]

---

222. Cf. 59. 96–7. 223. Cf. 59. 99. 224. Cf. 93. 94–101. 225. Cf. 65. 107.
226. 65. 106. 227. Ṅa Gārga. 228. Cf. 99. 157–64. 229. Cf. 65. 106.
230. 99. 204–8. 231. 99. 206–8.

(k) Ārṣṭiṣeṇas and Śaunakas. (l) King Sutahotra had three sons, viz., Kāśa, Śala and Gṛtsamada. Śala had a son Ārṣṭiṣeṇa after whom the Ārṣṭiṣeṇas—who were Kṣatriya Brahmins—were so called. Gṛtsamada had a son Śunaka after whom the Śaunakas—who too were Kṣatriya Brahmins—were so called.[232]

(m) Kauśikas: They were known after Viśvāmitra, son of king Gādhi. Many *gotras* of the Kauśikas are mentioned in the Purāṇa. It is stated that Viśvāmitra was also known by the name of Viśvaratha.[233]

(B) Kṣatriya-Brahmin Marriages: In the following references we find the Kṣatriyas related to Brahmins through matrimonial ties:

(a) Devayānī, wife of king Yayāti, was a daughter of the sage Śukra.[234]

(b) The wife of Jamadagni was Reṇukā, also called Kāmalī. She was a daughter of the king Suveṇu, a descendant of Ikṣvāku.[235]

(c) The Bhārgava Ṛcīka had a wife named Satyavatī who was the daughter of king Gādhi.[236]

(d) Ahalyā was a daughter of the king Badhyasva, whose son was Divodāsa. This Ahalyā was the wife of the sage Śatānanda whose descendants were known as the Śāradvatas.[237]

(e) Kāmyā was a daughter of the Prajāpati Kardama. She was given in marriage to king Priyavrata. She gave birth to sons who promoted the order of Kṣattra.[238]

(f) Vasiṣṭha had a daughter Puṇḍarīkā who was the queen of Pāṇḍu.[239]

The last two instances occur in genealogical narrations of the sages.

(C) Brahmins appointed to raise issues for Kṣatriyas: This question has been treated at length in the following chapter.

(D) Kṣatriya adopting a Brahmin as Son: Bharadvāja was born of an illicit connection of Bṛhaspati with Mamatā, wife of Aśija,[240] Bṛhaspati's brother. The new-born child was exposed to the care of nature by the parents. The Maruts are said to have brought up the child.[241] When king Bharata performed the Marut-Soma sacrifice for a son, the Maruts were pleased and gave Bharadvāja to the king (probably by way of adoption?). This Bharadvāja was known as Vitatha Bharadvāja. He was known as having two fathers and was called *dvimukhyāyana*.[242] Being first a Brahmin he later became a Kṣatriya.[243] He continued the royal line of Bharata.[244]

---

232. Cf. 92. 3-6. 233. Cf. 91. 93 ff. 234. Cf. 93. 77. 235. Cf. 91. 89-90.
236. Cf. 91. 65 ff. 237. Cf. 99. 201-6. 238. Cf. 28. 27-9.
239. Cf. 28. 34-5. 240. Kha. *Uśija*. 241. This is omitted in Ṅa.
242. Cf. *dvimukhyāyananāmā sa smṛto dvi-pitara(tṛka)s tu vai*.
243. Cf. *Brāhmaṇyāt Kṣatriyo 'bhavat*. 244. Cf. 99. 142-58.

IV. The Vaiśyas

The Purāṇa does not give much information on the Vaiśyas. In the cosmic account of the origin of the varṇas they are represented as being born of Brahmā's belly. They are said to be without any means of protection (*abalāḥ*) following agricultural pursuits.[245] The important functions assigned to them by the Creator are : cattle-breeding (*pāsupālya*), trade (*vāṇijya*) and agriculture (*kṛṣi*).[246] In the Tretā age the Vaiśyas (or Viś) followed the Kṣatriyas[247] which was expected of them in an ideal state of varṇāśrama.

Their relation with the king was that they expected protection from the latter. King Yayāti served them with protection.[248] King Pṛthu, who was revered by them, is called their sustainer (*vṛttidātā*).[249] King Kārtavīrya Arjuna is called the lord of the Vaiśyas (i.e. the people ?) (cf. *viśāṁ patiḥ*) and the same is the description of his son Jayadhvaja in the Avantis (?).[250] The expression *viśāṁ patiḥ* is also used elsewhere but there it means a vaiśya leader and not a king.[251]

A benedictory stanza shows that their attention was mainly focussed on wealth and profit.[252] Dealers in liquor, milk, flesh, lac, perfumes, etc., are condemned to hell[253] and the same lot is assigned to a dealer in horses.[254] Uncomplimentary references about them occur in the description of the conditions at the end of the Kali age. All will be like traders (*vāṇijakāḥ*) in this age.[255] But it is also asserted that during this period they will be extinct along with the Kṣatriyas.[256] The Dvāpara age is called as their age (*vaiśya-yuga*).[257] They are recommended with Śūdras and women to attend a recitation of the story of Dakṣa-Śiva conflict for a place in Rudraloka.[258] They are also mentioned as residing in the city of Campāvatī with the Brahmins and Kṣatriyas engaged in the worship of Viṣṇu.[259]

V. The Śūdras

In the cosmic account of the origin of the four orders of society the Śūdras are represented as having arisen out of the two feet of the Creator. In the first account of their origin elsewhere, they are described as a powerless, miserable and timid people always engaged in servile occupations.[260] But when the Creator revised the whole scheme of social functions he assigned them craftmanship and manual

---

245. *kīnāśā vṛttisādhakāḥ.* 246. Cf. 8. 164–70. 247. Cf. 57. 51–2.
248. Cf. 93. 66. 249. Cf. 63. 10. 250. Cf. 94. 39 ; 94 50.
251. Cf. 57. 50. 252. Cf. 100. 246 ; only in kh cf. also 54. 111.
253. Cf. 101. 162. 254. Cf. 101. 154. 255. Cf. 58. 51.
256. Cf. 58. 38. 257. Cf. 78. 36. 258. Cf. 30. 320–1.
259. Cf. 99. 106–7 but this information is not found in Gha and Ṅa.
260. Cf. *śocantaś ca dravantaś ca paricaryāsu ye ratāḥ nistejasolpavīryāś ca śūdrāṁs tān abravīt tu saḥ.*

labour as their chief functions.[261] Elsewhere they are treated as dependents of the first three classes.[262]

In the story of Pṛthu in which the first three varṇas are recommended to pay homage to the king Pṛthu they are not referred to at all;[263] but in connection with the king Yayāti they are mentioned as being distinct from the Dasyus. The king entertained the Śūdras with favour and the Dasyus with proper supervision.[264] These two references are probably indicative of their place in politics. But we have the instance of Mahāpadma in the Purāṇa to show how a Śūdra can raise himself in political sphere. King Mahānandin had a son Mahāpadma through a Śūdra (maid-servant or wife ?). This Mahāpadma destroyed the power of all the Kṣatriyas and was the sole ruler of the world. After him all the kings were Śūdras.[265]

The sage Dīrghatamas had two sons, viz., Kakṣīvat and Cakṣus through a Śūdra maid servant of king Bali. Kakṣīvat practised severe austerities and achieved the status of a Brahmin (*brāhmaṇyaṁ prāptavān*). The king Bali at first claimed both the sons of this maid-servant as his sons but Dīrghatamas set the claim aside.[266] Pṛsadhra, son of Vaivasvata Manu, ate the flesh of his preceptor's cow. The sage Cyavana cursed him to become a Śūdra.[267] These two accounts are suggestive of the social position of the Śūdras. In the description of the city of Vāyupura they number twice as much as the Brahmins in the composition of the city's population.[268] They are also mentioned with Vaiśyas and women who were recommended to listen to the story of Dakṣa-Śiva conflict from the Brahmins for a place in the Rudraloka.[269] In the Tretā age they were supposed to have behaved in the footsteps of the Vaiśyas.[270]

In the picturesque description of the conditions prevailing at the end of the Kali age many uncomplimentary remarks are passed about them. The Kali age is the age of Śūdras.[271]

A reference to Ājīvas, who were a class of artisans, is found in the Purāṇa. They are said to have their origin in the contamination of the varṇas and Piśācas were regarded as their deities. Are they to be included in the order of the Śūdras ?[272] There is again a story of the destruction of the city of Vārāṇasī in which a barber named Maṅkana is shown to be installing an image of Gaṇeśa Kṣemaka, an attendant of Śiva, at the city-gates. This deity Gaṇeśvara became a favourite object of worship especially for women who desired male progeny.[273]

Śūdra also occurs as a name of a country in northern Bhāratavarṣa.

261. Cf. 8. 165–71. 262. Cf. 7. 27. 263. Cf. 63. 6–10. 264 Cf. 93. 66.
265. Cf. 99. 326–9. 266. Cf. 99. 67–94. 267. Cf. 86. 1–2.
268. Cf. No. 1422 in App. 269. Cf. 30. 320–1. 270. Cf. 57. 51–3.
271. Cf. 78. 36. 272. Cf. No. 15 in App. 273. Cf. No. 1403 in App.

VI. The Dasyus or Dāsas

Words such as Dasyus or Dāsas occur sometimes in the Purāṇa. We have seen above in connection with king Yayāti how the Dasyus were regarded as distinct from the Śūdras. That king Yayāti 'entertained' (*anurañjan*) them with due control and supervision indicates that probably they were a people of wild habits. When Satyavrata killed the cow of Vasiṣṭha the latter took it that the exiled prince had followed the *dharma* of the Dasyus.[274] This leads us to infer that the Dasyus were a people who were accustomed to steal cows. There is another important fact which should be noted in this connection. This Satyavrata was condemned by his father to follow the ways of a *Śvapāka*, i. e. the life of a tribe who ate the flesh of dogs (?)[275] and it is said that Satyavrata did follow the ways of these people as was commanded by his father.[276] Budha, father of Purūravas, is thrice mentioned as "the best amongst the annihilators of the Dasyus".[277]

The Dasyus were also regarded as distinct from the various *jātis* of Mlecchas. In the Kuśadvīpa there were no Dasyus nor the various Jātis of Mlecchas.[278]

Satyavati, the daughter of a fisherman, is called *Dāseyī*. The sage Parāśara had a son born of her. This son was none else than the famous viprarṣi Vyāsa who is said to have arranged the four Vedas in the 28th Dvāpara age. Satyavatī later became the wife of King Śaṁtanu and had two sons.[279] She is also referred to in the genealogical lists as *dāseyī*.[280]

Slavery and Slave-trade : A reference to the twelve-year famine has been made above in connection with the story of Satyavrata Triśaṅku. At this time, Viśvāmitra was practising severe penance. Being severely affected by the famine, the wife of Viśvamitra tied a string (?) to the neck of her middle-most son and sold him for a price of hundred cows so as to enable her to support the rest of her children.[281] Satyavrata, the exiled prince, appears to have been present at the transaction and he effected the emancipation of the child and himself undertook to look after the family of Viśvāmitra. He did this partly with a view to please Viśvāmitra and partly through pity.[282]

The prize which king Janaka announced to the learned winner in his *Aśvamedha* included, among other things, such as cows, gold, etc., slaves also.[283]

---

274. Cf. *Dasyudharmaṁ gato dṛṣtvā :* 88. 104-5. 275. Cf. 88. 82.
276. Cf. 88. 84. 277. Cf. *Dasyuhantama* : 89. 37-42.
278. Cf. 49. 55. 279. Cf. 73. 16-20. 280. Cf. 99. 241.
281. Cf. *tasya patnī gale baddhvā madhyamaṁ putram aurasam śiṣṭānāṁ bharaṇārthāya vyakrīṇāt gośatena vai.* 282. Cf. 88.85-9.
283. According to readings in Ka and Gha they were male slaves while Kha, Ga and Na mention female slaves. Cf. 60. 37.

CHAPTER II

WOMAN AND MARRIAGE

I. Woman

Estimation of Women : It is prophesied that at the end of the Kali age—which is pictured as a repository of all vices—women will outnumber men.[1] It should be noted in this connection that this age is described as being essentially an age of Śūdra influence. Women are classed with Vaiśyas and Śūdras and are advised to listen to the story of Dakṣa-Śiva conflict for a place in Rudra-loka.[2]

When king Yayāti requested his son Druhya to accept his old age the latter replied, "Not an elephant, not a horse, not a chariot nor a woman does an old man enjoy."[3] Yayāti himself later expressed a similar sentiment mentioning women with food, gold and cattle to show as if they were articles of enjoyment.[4] The queen of a cakravartin is considered as being one of his seven select jewels (*atiśaya-ratnāni*), the other six being chariot, discus, jewel (maṇi), treasury, horses and elephant.[5] Vasudeva (father of Kṛṣṇa) had thirteen wives of whom two are mentioned as *paricārikās*.[6] A reciter of the prayer to Śiva, it is expected, goes to heaven, after his death, being surrounded by a thousand damsels,[7] and the meritorious return for a generous donor in śrāddha is that many beautiful maid-servants (*nāryaḥ*) will be at his command.[8]

King Jyāmagha had captured a girl in a victorious war and when he went home he told his wife that he had brought her a daughter-in-law. But Jyāmagha had no son and his wife reminded him of that. The king however retorted that a son that would be born would marry her.[9]

Her Status as Wife : Statements in praise of sexual purity occur in the Purāṇa. Men in the Uttara-Kuru land did not associate themselves with the wives of others.[10] One of the evil features of the future Kali-age is that men will be addicted to others' wives.[11] But cases of 'illicit' sexual intercourse occur in the Purāṇa.

It is said that the wives of Nārāyaṇa, Indra, Viṣṇu (?), Sūrya, and Vasiṣṭha never forsake them. They follow their husbands in all their rebirths in the different *Kalpas*.[12] By listening to the story of how

1. Cf. *puruṣālpaṁ bahustrīkaṁ yugānte paryupasthite* : 58. 52. 2. Cf. 30. 320–1.
3. Cf. *na gajaṁ na rathaṁ nāśvaṁ jīrṇo bhuṅkte na ca striyam* : 93. 48.
4. Cf. 93. 95–6. 5. Cf. 57. 68
6. Cf. 96. 161. Kha, Ga and Gha : *paricārakās*. 7. Cf. 30. 316.
8. Cf. 80. 36. 9. Cf. 95. 33–5. 10. Cf. 45. 20.
11. 58. 51 ; 58. 57. 12. Cf. 30. 72–3.

Śiva came to be known as Nīlakaṇṭha a wife is said to secure a male child and a girl a virtuous husband.[13] This was probably an ideal held out to women. Without the knowledge of her husband, Saṁjñā, the wife of Vivasvat, had gone to her father's place but he advised her to go home and be dutiful.[14]

There are, however, certain incidents which suggest that wives were loved and respected. Satī, wife of Śiva, was dearer to him than life,[15] and it is at her instigation that Śiva effected the destruction of Dakṣa's sacrifice.[16] In the genealogical lists we have an instance of king Jyāmagha who had no son but still he did not marry again for one.[17]

Her Status as Mother : Vivasvat had two wives of whom the first gave birth to Manu and Yama. The second wife, Savarṇā, ill-treated Manu and Yama. Manu suffered all the insults with patience but Yama did not bear them and once he kicked his step-mother who being enraged at this rude behaviour cursed him. Yama complained against this to his father Vivasvat but was told that there was no remedy against a mother's curse.[18]

The story of how Garutmat forced away *amṛta* from the custody of gods for the sake of his mother is also alluded to in the geographical chapters of the Purāṇa.[19]

Immunity from Capital Punishment : Once it so happened that Viṣṇu killed the mother of Kāvya. Bhṛgu became so angry at this outrageous act of Viṣṇu that he cursed him that he would be born seven times as a mortal on the earth. The expression *strīvadha* is here used to signify heinous crime which particularly upset the temper of Bhṛgu.[20] When king Pṛthu proceeded to vanquish the Earth, the latter, in the form of a cow, pleaded ; "In all the ages of mankind, women are deemed to be free from infliction of death."[21] But the dutiful king set aside the plea on the ground that for many, one may be allowed to suffer.[22] When Kaṁsa drew his sword and was about to kill his sister Devakī, Vasudeva intervened and reminded him that it was improper for him, as a Kṣatriya, to kill a woman.[23] King Mūlaka was afraid of Rāma and that is why he always kept himself surrounded by women.[24] This suggests that women were free from molestation. The same appears to have been the reason why the Asuras fled to the

13. Cf. *gurviṇī labhate putraṁ kanyā vindati satpatim* : 52. 112.

14. Cf. 84. 44-8. 15. Cf. *prāṇair api priyām* : 39. 122.

16. Cf. (30. 120 ff. ; cf. also No. 1403 App.) 17. Cf. 95. 32.

18. Cf. *no śakyam etanmithyā tu kartuṁ mātur vacas tava* : 84. 53-60.

19. Cf. No. 989 App. 20. Cf. 97. 137-42.

21. Cf. *avadhyāś ca striyaḥ prāhus tiryag-yoni-śateṣvapi*. 22. Cf. 62. 159-61.

23. Cf. 98. 224. According to Kha : improper for a Kṣatriya to kill his sister and according to Gha : to kill a woman unnecessarily.

24. Cf. 88. 178-9.

protection of the mother of Kāvya which led to the incident of her murder by Viṣṇu and subsequently to the curse of Bhṛgu mentioned above.[25] One of the evil features of the Kali age is that strīvadha will be very common during this period.

Women and Higher Studies : There are many instances of women practising penance and *yoga*. The sister of Bṛhaspati, though a married woman—being the wife of Prabhāsa,—is called brahmacāriṇī[26] and had accomplished *yoga*.[27] Saṁjñā, the wife of Vivasvat, practised austerities in the Śāḍvala forest.[28] Śatarūpā, the female portion of Brahmā, practised severe penance and secured a husband in Svāyaṁbhuva Manu, the male portion of Brahmā.[29] In the geographical chapters, we find a reference to penance being practised by Umā, the wife of Śiva, on the Kailāsa mountain.[30] Diti, too, practised severe austerities in a forest to secure a son who would be the annihilator of Indra[31] and all the wives of Kaśyapa are called brahma-vādinīs.[32]

Similar instances occur in the genealogical lists. The unfortunate king Bāhu, who had lost his kingdom, entered a forest and practised austerities with his wife. This Bāhu was the father of Sagara.[33] The two wives of king Sagara pleased the sage Aurva[34] through their penance.[35] Dhūminī, the wife of king Ajamīḍha, had practised severe austerities for a hundred years.[36]

Seclusion of Women : When queen Keśinī, the wife of Sagara, was asked by the sage Aurva to select a boon she did so in the assembly of kings (*nṛpa-saṁsadi*).[37] The wives of gods were present at the sacrifice performed by Dakṣa and received sound drubbing from the Rudras who raided the sacrifice.[38] On another occasion of a sacrificial performance Brahmā happened to lose his self-control at the beauty of the wives and daughters of gods, who were then present, and his semen fell on the earth.[39] Soma had seduced Tārā, the wife of Bṛhaspati. During this period Tārā was pregnant and later gave birth to a son. The gods asked her as to who was the father of the child. But Tārā did not reply through bashfulness.[40] All these instances suggest that women could move freely in society.

But in a passage on the construction of forts we have a reference to Kumārīpura as the fort of an artificial kind (*kṛtrima durga*).[41] From this bare mention of Kumārīpura it is difficult to say whether seclusion of women is implied.

---

25. Cf. 97. 127 ff.
26. Kha, Ga, Gha and Ṅa : *brahmavādinī*.
27. *Yoga-siddhā* 66. 27-8.
28. Cf. No. 1083 in App.
29. Cf. 10. 9-12.
30. Cf. No. 469 in App.
31. Cf. 67. 88-95.
32. Cf. 65. 118.
33. Cf. 88. 129.
34. Kha and Gha : Ūrva.
35. Cf. 88. 155-8.
36. Cf. 99. 212.
37. Cf. 88. 155-8.
38. Cf. 30. 154.
39. Cf. 65. 29-31.
40. Cf. 90. 39-40.
41. Cf. 8. 109.

The Suttee : King Bāhu who had lost his kingdom and was practising austerities in a forest died of old age and his wife, a Yādava princess (*Yādavī*),—who was at that time pregnant—made preparations for the funeral pyre and set fire to it. While proceeding to ascend it, the Bhārgava Aurva dissuaded her from this act of self-immolation "through pity".[42] It appears that Aurva arrived at the place just at the time when she was about to enter the fire. The fact of her pregnancy and her husband's death in unfortunate circumstances are the points to be noted in this connection. The sage Aurva might have had these considerations in his mind when he "through pity" dissuaded her from her act of self-immolation. Assuming that this was so, one has to admit that the sage Aurva would not have acted in the manner he did but for the considerations referred to above.

Matronymics and the Matriarchate : There are many instances of matronymical names in the Purāṇa. Siṁhikā was a wife of the Asura Vipracitti and had fourteen sons who were called Saiṁhikeya Asuras.[43] They hated the Brahmins.[44] The Paulomas and the Kālakeyas, who were Dānavas, were known after their mothers Pulomā and Kālakā respectively.[45] Ālambā, Utkacā, Kṛṣṇā, Nirṛtā, Kapilā, Śivā, and Keśinī were the seven sisters after whom the gaṇas of Rākṣasas, viz., Ālambeyas, Autkaceyas, Kārṣṇeyas, Nairṛtas, Kāpileyas, Śaiveyas, (and Keśinīs ?) were respectively called.[46] Irāvatī was a Rākṣasī being the daughter of Krodhā. She gave birth to a son who was called after her name.[47] Agnikā, Kambalā, and Vasumatī were the three sisters after whom the three classes of Gandharvas, viz., Āgneyas, Kāmbaleyas and Vasumatī-sutas were so called.[48] Viśāla, a Yakṣa, had four Apsaras as wives, viz., Loheyī, Bharatā, Kṛśāṅgī[49] and Viśālā whose descendants were respectively known as Loheyas, Bharateyas, Kṛśāṅgeyas and Viśāleyas. Thus are these four gaṇas of Yakṣas well-known in the Purāṇa.[50] The Sauparṇeyas were the descendants of Suparṇā, the Kādraveyas of Kadrū, and the Khaśāyas of Khaśā.[51] Garuḍa is mentioned as Vainateya[52] and Takṣaka as Kādraveya.[53]

The other instances of matronymics are : Viśve Devas after Viśvā, the wife of Dharma;[54] Śādhyas, a class of Devas, after Sādhyā;[55] Sāvarṇa Manu after Savarṇā.[56] Aiḍa (or Aila) Purūravas is the only matronymic found in the genealogical lists.[57]

The sage Kaśyapa said to his wife Khaśā, a Rākṣasī, about her newly-born sons, "A son is devoted to his maternal uncle and a

---

42. *Cf. Sā tu bhartuś citāṁ kṛtvā vahniṁ taṁ samārohayat Aurvas tāṁ bhārgavo dṛṣṭvā kāruṇyād vinyavartayat* ; for "*vahniṁ taṁ*" Ka has "*vahnitaṁ*" ; 88. 129-33.

43. Cf. 68. 17-9. 44. *Cf. sarve brahma-dviṣaś ca te* 68. 21. 45. Cf. 68. 23-7.

46. Cf. 69. 170 ff. 47. Cf. *Irāvatyāḥ suto yasmāt tasmad Airāvato smṛtaḥ* 69. 210-1.

48. Cf. 69. 20-3. 49. Kha, Gha and Ṅa': *Kṛṣṇāṅgī*. 50. Cf. 69. 14-7.

51. Cf. 69. 67-79. 52. Cf. 1. 137. 53. Cf. 39. 54. 54. Cf. 76. 3.

55. Cf. 66. 3-4. 56. Cf. 88. 52. 57 Cf. 91. 10 ; 91. 22 ; also 2. 20.

daughter to her paternal ancestors; a son generally inherits the character of his mother......your sons have followed the conduct and disposition of their maternal uncle."[58]

II. Marriage

Promiscuity: The following episodes in the Purāṇa should be noted in this connection:

(a) After performing a rājasūya sacrifice, Soma, the eponymous ancestor of the lunar race, had become too much possessed of his power and glory. Lost to all sense of modesty, he seduced Tārā, wife of the Aṅgiras Bṛhaspati, inspite of the opposition of the Aṅgirasas.[59] The gods and sages requested Soma to allow Tārā to go to her husband but Soma did not yield. This eventually resulted in a terrible war in which Rudra took sides with Bṛhaspati. The Dānavas, too, took part in the battle, which is mentioned as being *Tārakāmayaṁ*.[60] Brahmā, however, effected a compromise and he himself led Tārā to her husband Bṛhaspati. Tārā was pregnant at this time and gave birth to a son. The Suras asked her as to whose child it was and after many entreaties she told Brahmā that Soma was the father of the child.

(b) Budha, son of Soma, invited Ilā for cohabitation and their issue was Purūravas.[61]

(c) Before entering into conjugal relations with king Purūravas, the Apsaras Urvaśī had made an agreement with him that he should not be seen naked except at the time of intercourse.[62] She expressly laid it down that any breach of this condition meant her immediate separation from him. She also used to keep two goats—her pets—at her bedside......The Gandharvas, however, became very uneasy about her long absence from the *svarga*. They commissioned Viśvāvasu to effect her separation from Purūravas. At the night-time, Viśvāvasu went to Pratiṣṭhāna, where the king resided with his beloved, and stole away one of the goats. Urvaśī told the king of what had happened but the king, who was then naked, did not do anything for fear of breaking the agreement. The Gandharvas came a second time and took away the second goat. Urvaśī again raised an alarm and said to the king that her two pets were forced away from her. At this Purūravas could not but hunt after the intruders even though he was naked and ran in search of the goats. Thus the agreement came to an end and Urvaśī disappeared.[63]

---

58. Cf. *Mātulaṁ bhajate putraḥ pitṝn bhajati kanyakā Yathāśīlā bhaven mātā tathā śīlo bhavet sutaḥ......Mātulaṁ tu anuyātās te putrakā guṇavṛttibhiḥ* 69. 88-97.

59. *sarvān avamatya Aṅgiraḥ-sutān.*

60. There is some confusion here about the Dānavas and about the Asura Tāraka and it is difficult to understand the sudden and unwarrantable entry of the Dānavas into the story.

61. *maithunyāya upamantritā*, 85. 17.

62. Cf. *anagnadarśanaṁ caiva akāmāt sahamaithunam.*

63. Cf. 91. 10 ff.

(d) The story regarding the birth of Bharadvāja who continued the line of king Bharata, the son of Duṣyanta, may be given here at length for its interesting details :

Bṛhaspati once asked his brother's wife, Mamatā, to get ready for cohabitation with him.[64] She, however, replied that she was pregnant and that compliance with his request would amount to violation of dharma.[65] But Bṛhaspati,[66] cutting short her remonstrance with an angry rebuff, proceeded to gratify his passion forcibly. The child in the womb, however, protested against Bṛhaspati's action which enraged the sage who at once cursed the child that it would be born blind. This union of Bṛhaspati with Mamatā led to the birth of Bharadvāja who later on was adopted by Bharata.[67]

Earlier in the same chapter we find the same story repeated to account for the birth of Dīrghatamas. Here Bṛhaspati is mentioned as the preceptor of the gods (*purodhā yo divaukasām*) and instead of Mamatā Ka reads Samatā.[68]

The Cult of Godharma : The sage Dīrghatamas, whose birth is referred to above, once came by a bull and played with it by firmly holding its horns. His grip was so tight that the bull could not move. The bull, who was really the vehicle of Śiva, was astonished at the unusual strength of Dīrghatamas. He informed the sage that he had come on this earth as a carrier of Tryambaka and that if he were allowed his freedom he would grant him a boon. Still Dīrghatamas was not convinced. The bull then said to him, "We (i.e. bulls) are sinless creatures who do not know the difference between good and bad ; nor do we observe any restrictions regarding sexual behaviour. This is known as the cult of the bulls".[69] Dīrghatamas went home profoundly impressed by this new teaching. He approached his younger (brother's ?) wife to practise this new cult himself upon her but was expelled for this very reason. It appears that he had to undergo many persecutions and was later on thrown into the river Ganges. The stream of the river brought him to the territory of king Bali who happened to see him and saved his life.[70]

Niyoga : There are two accounts in the Purāṇa which clearly testify to the custom of Niyoga : —

(a) We have already seen how king Bali rescued Dīrghatamas from being drowned. The king later on offered him an assylum

---

64. Cf. *alaṁkṛtya tanuṁ svāṁ tu maithunaṁ dehi me śubhe.*

65. Cf. *dharmaś caiva vigarhitaḥ.*

66. Cf. *vinayo nopadeṣṭavyas tvayā mama kathaṁcana.*

67. 99. 140 ff. 68. Cf. 99. 36. ff.

69. Cf. *kāryākāryaṁ na vai vidmo gamyāgamyaṁ tathaiva ca na pāpmāno vayaṁ vipra dharmo hyeṣa gavāṁ smṛtaḥ.* Kha, Ga and Gha and Ṅa give readings which are difficult to be construed. 70. Cf. 99. 35 ff.

in his own harem with all kinds of enjoyments.[71] Here the king is mentioned as Vairocana Bali, but really speaking this Bali was a descendant of Turvasu whose genealogical narration is the subject-matter of the chapter.

King Bali once requested Dīrghatamas to beget an issue for him[72] from his wife Sudeṣṇā and instructed his queen to that effect. Sudeṣṇā, however, felt repulsion at the appearance of the sage, as he was aged and blind, and sent her maid-servant as her substitute. The maid-servant gave birth to two sons whom king Bali claimed as his own but Dīrghatamas set aside his claim and disclosed the truth of the matter to the king. Bali rebuked his queen for her action and again sent her to the sage. Dīrghatamas now told her that if she, with an unperturbed mind, licked his naked frame after anointing it with curds and salt, from top to toe, her desire for sons would be fulfilled. She first hesitated to do so, but the impulse for a son prevailed upon her and she did likewise......Later on Sudeṣṇā gave birth to five sons, viz., Aṅga, Vaṅga, Kaliṅga, Puṇḍra and Brahma.[73] They are mentioned as the Kṣetraja sons of Bali.[74]

(b) Vasiṣṭha raised an issue on the Kṣetra of king Kalmāṣapāda to continue the line of Ikṣvāku[75]. This issue was Aśmaka.

(c) Vyāsa too raised issue on the Kṣetra of Vicitravīrya.[76]

Polygamy: Many instances of polygamy are observable in the Purāṇa. Bhṛgu had two wives.[77] Dakṣa gave his ten daughters to Dharma, thirteen to Kaśayapa, four to Ariṣṭanemi, twenty-seven to Indu, etc.[78] Atharvan had three wives.[79] The third Prajāpati Atri had ten beautiful wives[80] and Viśravas had four.[81] The ten wives of Pulaha were sisters.[82] Diti and Aditi were the two wives of Kaśyapa.[83]

There is a reference to the 16,000 wives of Kṛṣṇa.[84] His father was the lord of thirteen wives of whom seven were the daughters of Devaka.[85] Satrājit had ten wives all of whom were sisters.[86] Prabhākara married the ten daughters of King Raudrāśva[87] and Gāndhārī and Mādrī were the two wives of Vṛṣṇi.[88] Dauṣyanti Bharata had three wives[89]. Bṛhanmanas, Yayātī, Sagara and Bhajamāna had two each[90] while king Ajamīḍha had three.[91]

---

71. Cf *antaḥpure jugopainaṁ bhakṣyair bhojyaiś ca tarpayan.*
72. Cf. *santānārthaṁ mahābhāga.*
73. Cf. 99. 67 ff. 74. Cf. 99. 35.
75. *Ikṣvāku-kula-vṛddhaye.* Cf. 88. 177, 76. Cf. 99. 235 ff.
77. Cf. 65. 72-3. 78. Cf. 65. 39-42; 10. 26; 65. 118; 99. 21. 79. Cf. 65. 88.
80. Cf. 70. 67. 81. Cf. 70. 32. 82. Cf. 69. 204. 83. Cf. 67. 43. 50.
84. Cf. 96. 233 ff. 85. Cf. 96. 159. 86. Cf. 96. 53. 87. Cf. 99. 127.
88. Cf. 96. 17. 89. Cf. 99. 137. 90. Cf. 99. 114; 88. 155; 93. 15-6; 96. 3-4.
91. Cf. 99. 167. Ka omits the śloka which refers to the wives of Ajamīḍha.

CHAPTER III

POLITICAL INSTITUTIONS

I. Kingship

In the Tretā age, an ideal state of varṇāśrama existed. The four varṇas worked in perfect social harmony. This is how Brahmā had then ordained the constitution of the four varṇas.

But somehow or other—(the reason is not stated)—delusion 'again' swayed over the minds of the people who consequently ceased to observe the rules of dharma.[1] There was thus a state of turmoil and mutual conflicts. The people 'again' approached the Prajāpati Svāyaṁbhuva Manu. Manu pondered over the *pros* and *cons* of the matter and brooded over Śatarūpā who gave birth to two sons, viz., Priyavrata and Uttānapāda. They were the first to be called kings.[2] From this time onwards are the kings bearers of the royal sceptre and because they please their people they are known as *rājānaḥ*.[3] They are also enjoined to promulgate dharma.[4]

Conception of King's Divinity ; In all the manvantaras of the past and the future, the paramount sovereigns are born on this earth bearing a portion of Viṣṇu's personality.[5] Those versed in the Purāṇic tradition say that king Māṁdhātā bore the *corpus* of Viṣṇu.[6] The sage Uttaṅka complemented the king Bṛhadaśva that he possessed the lustre of Viṣṇu[7] and when Kuvalāśva (son of Bṛhadaśva) proceeded to annihilate Dhundhu, Lord Viṣṇu entered his body with all his lustre at the direction of Uttaṅka.[8]

King Raji fought on the side of the gods who had promised him the place of Indra in exchange for his help. He did achieve that honour. Indra, however, afterwards annihilated the sons of Raji and regained his position.[9] King Dharmaratha had an opportunity to drink *soma* in the company of Indra on the occasion of a sacrifice performed on the Viṣṇupada mountain.[10] We have already seen in connection with the Rājarṣis that their ultimate goal is the world of Indra. It is said that

---

1. Cf. *punaḥ prajās tu tā mohāt tān dharmān na hy apālayan.*
2. Cf. *prathamaṁ tau mahīpatī.*
3. Cf. *tataḥ prabhṛti rājāna utpannā daṇḍadhāriṇaḥ prajānāṁ rañjanāt caiva rājānas tv abhavan nṛpāḥ.* 4. 57. 51–0.
5. Cf. *Viṣṇor aṁśena jāyante pṛthivyāṁ cakravartinaḥ manvantareṣu sarveṣu atītān āgateṣu vai,* 57. 72.
6. Cf. *Māṁdhātā tu tanur Viṣṇoh Purāṇajñāḥ pracakṣate,* 88. 69.
7. Cf. *tejas te sumahā-Viṣṇus,* 88. 41.
8. Cf. *tam āviśat tato Viṣṇur bhagavān svena tejasā Uttaṅkasya niyogāt tu,* 88. 49.
9. 92. 76 ff.
10. Omitted in Ga ; Gha reads Śukra instead of Śakra, Cf. 99. 102.

Dāśarathi Rāma fulfilled the desire of gods in the course of his career in Janasthāna.[11] We also find a recommendation that Pṛthu, the first king (*ādirāja*), should be revered and worshipped by all beings alike.[12] The learned Brahmins, the warriors and the common people should pay homage to the king.[13]

Functions of a King: We have seen above how the great sages in their conflict against king Vena reminded him of his words that he would 'protect' the people. We have also a verse sung by the knowers of ancient genealogies,[14] pertaining to the king Ambarīṣa, who protected the earth with the force of his two arms and relieved her of the "three pains".[15] There is no indication whatsoever about the exact significance of these "three pains".[16] The successors of Yayāti protected the earth according to dharma.[17] In the reign of king Durjaya there was no loss or theft of property and the people were well protected.[18] The same was the case with Kārtavīrya Arjuna who protected his subjects according to dharma. He is again styled as the "protector of cattle and agriculture"(?).[19] The *janapadas* of Kaliṅga, etc. "will be protected" by Guha.[20]

An expression like "pleasing the people" is also used in connection with the origin of kingship and what is implied in this expression is probably indicated in the statement regarding Yayāti which runs thus: "King Yayāti" pleased (*atarpayat*) the gods with sacrifices, the ancestors with performance of śrāddha, the poor with favour (*anugraha*), the Brahmins with what they desired, the guests with food and drink, the Vaiśyas with protection, the Śūdras with equity (*ānṛśaṁsa*) and the Dasyus with due control (*saṁnigraheṇa*). Thus did he entertain (*anurañjayat*) his people according to dharma as a second Indra himself.[21] Of the great and wise kings it is said that they see their subjects through their happiness.[22]

Side by side with the protection of the people, there was also the duty to protect or to observe the rules of dharma. King Pṛthu was the protector of dharma.[23] Rathavara of Kroṣṭu line always followed dharma[24] and similar was the case with Nābhāga, grandson of Bhagīratha.[25] The great *sattra*, at which the Purāṇa was recited, was performed by the sages in the reign of the king Adhisāma-Kṛṣṇa who was ruling on this earth according to dharma.[26] King Sagara is styled as "victorious in dharma".[27] Brahmā had conferred a boon on king Bali

---

11. Cf. 88. 194. 12. Cf. *namasyaś caiva pūjyaś ca bhūtagrāmeṇa sarvaśaḥ*.
13. Cf. 63. 5-10. 14. Cf. *vaṁśa-purāṇajñāḥ*. 15. Cf. *tāpa-traya-vivarjitā*.
16. Cf. 88. 171-2. 17. Cf. 93. 91. 18. Cf. 94. 53-4.
19. Cf. *sa eṣa paśupālo' bhūt kṣetra-pālas tathaiva ca*. 94. 22-4. 20. Cf. 99. 386.
21. Cf. 93. 65-7. 22. Cf. *ṛṣanti rañjanād yasmāt prajā rājarṣayaḥ smṛtāḥ* 61. 87.
23. Cf. *dharmasya goptā* : 62. 106. 24. Cf. *dātā dharmarato nityaṁ* : 95. 42.
25. Cf. 88. 170. 26. Cf. 99. 258-9. 27. Cf. *dharma-vijayī* : 88. 144.

that he would be adept in matters of dharma and artha.[28] Dharma is one of the four striking features of a king in the Tretā age.[29] Attributes such as *dharmātmā*, *dharmajña*, *dharmārthakovida*, *dhārmika*, *parama-dhārmika*, *sudharmātmā*, *dharmaśīla*, etc., occur frequently in the description of kings in the genealogical lists.[30]

We have seen that King Yayāti deviated from the rules of dharma by appointing his youngest son Puru as his successor; but he had to convince the people about the propriety of his action. Similarly, Trayyāruṇa expelled his son Satyavrata because he followed adharma.[31] Vena arrogantly asserted that he was above dharma and he met his ruin on that very account.

Kings and Daṇḍa: The connection of the king with *Daṇḍa* has already been indicated in the account of the origin of kingship. Daṇḍa is also the most important function of the Kṣatriyas. King Dama is called 'Wielder of daṇḍa'.[32] In the Śākadvīpa, it is stated, there is no daṇḍa, nor any one to wield it. The people who knew well the dharma, protected each other by virtue of their own dharma. They had also no taxes to pay.[33] In the Puṣkara-dvīpa Brahmā himself wields the daṇḍa.[34]

The *daṇḍa-nīti* was brought into existence in the Tretā age—in which kingship originated for the establishment of (peace and?) order.[35] Promulgation of the daṇḍa-nīti along with *vārtā* etc. by Manu and the seven sages is already referred to. Śukra (or Kāvya) told the vanquished Asuras that he would evolve a *nīti* for them and that he would go to Mahādeva for certain mantras which would procure them victory.[36] It is not clear, however, whether nīti here means daṇḍa-nīti or any other nīti connected with the affairs of orderly government.

Devolution of Kingship: There is no reference to election of a king in the Vāyu Purāṇa. Hereditary succession was the general rule and the office of the king devolved on his eldest heir after his demise. This means that the rule of primogeniture was followed. In the genealogical lists, if many sons of a particular king are mentioned, we find only the genealogy of the eldest son further traced. For example, Kuvalāśva had three sons of whom Dṛḍhāśva was the eldest whose genealogy is then continued.[37] Kakudmin was the eldest amongst the

---

28. Cf. 99. 29–31. 29. Cf. 57. 74.

30. 86. 9; 88. 77; 88. 65–6; 88. 48; 88. 120–1; 88. 165–7; 88. 201–5; 99. 219; 99. 189–91; 99. 84; 99. 18; 95. 23–5: 95. 36–9; 93. 9–11; 92; 68–72; 91. 1–4; 89. 116; 88. 180–4; 89. 94. 3. etc.; cf. also 2. 24; 33. 53. etc.

31. Cf. 88. 81–4. 32. Cf. *rājā daṇḍadharo Damaḥ*: 86. 12.

33. Cf. *Karotpattir na teṣv asti na daṇḍo na ca daṇḍakāḥ sva-dharmeṇa-iva dharmajñās te rakṣanti parasparam*: 49. 103. 34. Cf. 49. 140; cf. also 49. 115–8.

35. Cf. *maryādā-sthāpanārthaṁ ca daṇḍa-nītiḥ pravartate*: 57. 82.

36. Cf. *nītiṁ vo hi vidhāsyāmi...yāsyāmy ahaṁ Mahādevaṁ mantrārthe vijayāya vaḥ*: 97. 105–6. 37. Cf. 88. 60 ff.

hundred sons of Reva whose line he continued.[38] That the rule of primogeniture was probably a settled law or usage regarding the succession to the throne becomes obvious from the nature of the objection raised by the people against king Yayāti's selection of his youngest son as his consecrated heir.

But there are also numerous instances suggesting a division of the kingdom. From the nature of their contents these instances have been presented in three separate categories:

(a) Manu had ten sons amongst whom he divided the earth. The share of Sudyumna—(who had once been a female)—went to Purūravas, his (or her) son.[39] The four sons of Daśaratha had their own shares in the kingdom of their father and their descendants established separate lines in their respective territories.[40] Even though consecration of Puru had taken place we find king Yayāti actually assigning portions of his kingdom to his other four sons too.[41] King Rukmakavaca had five sons of whom the eldest son Rukmeṣu (or Brahmeṣu) became king with the second son as his protégé.[42] To the youngest two was assigned the territory of Videha by their father. The third son Jyāmagha was probably without a share and was expelled by his brothers. He passed some period in exile and later carved a kingdom for himself in the region about the river Narmadā and the mountain Ṛkṣa.[43]

(b) King Bali had five sons all of whom were consecrated by him The janapadas of these five sons, (viz., Aṅga, Vaṅga, Kaliṅga, Puṇḍra and Brahma) are also mentioned.[44] Janāpīḍa had four sons, viz. Pāṇḍya, Cola, Kerala and Kulya, whose respective janapadas were called after them.[45] It should be noted that the genealogies of these four sons are not further stated. In the same manner the janapadas of the four sons of Auśīnara Śibi,[46] as well as of the five sons of Ṛkṣa are mentioned.[47]

Pracetas had hundred sons all of whom were kings.[48] They were the lords of the countries of the Mlecchas and ruled in the north.[49] Nīpa had hundred sons all of whom were kings known as Nīpas.[50]

(c) Agnīdhra consecrated his nine sons as kings and then retired to the forest life.[51] Priyavrata had ten sons amongst whom he divided the earth of the seven dvīpas.[52] The hundred sons of Śatajit were all of them kings[53] and the same is the description about the hundred sons of Vairocana Bali.[54]

---

38. Cf. 86. 25. 39. Cf. 85. 20-3. 40. Cf. 88. 187-200. 41. Cf. 93. 88-90.
42. Cf. *tad-āśrayaḥ*; but Kha, Gha and Ṅa read *taṭāśrayaḥ*. 43. Cf. 95. 27-32.
44. Cf. 99. 33-4; cf. also 99. 98. 103. 45. Cf. 99. 5-6.
46. Cf. No. 705 in App. 47. Cf. No. 927 in App.
48. Cf. *rājānaḥ sarva eva te*. 49. Cf. 99. 11-2. 50. Cf. 99. 175.
51. Cf. 33. 46. 52. Cf. No. 433 in App.
53. Cf. *rājānaḥ sarva eva te* 33. 60. 54. Cf. 67. 82.

The Consecration of a King and its Importance : It is stated of king Pṛthu, that the sprinkling ceremony was performed for him in the *rājasūya* according to Vedic injunctions.[55] Pṛthu's connection with the origin of kingship and the details of his consecration ceremony have already been noted. There is also a passage showing how the various beings and things have their respective "consecrated lords".[56] It should be noted that Puru is said to have been consecrated to *Svārājya*.[57] Stray references to consecrations of individual kings occur occasionally in the Purāṇa. Bṛhadaśva consecrated his son Kuvalāśva to his kingdom.[58] Bali performed the ceremony for all his five sons.[59] It is said that Munika (i.e. Pradyota ?) "will kill" his master and consecrate his son to the throne.[60] The Brahmins who had brought about the ruin of king Janamejaya consecrated his son Śatānīka. Here consecrations by kings or Brahmins should be noted. There are also references to performance of the *rājasūya* ceremony by Soma and Hariścandra.[61]

It is said that the kings of the Kali age "will be" like the Yavanas in matters of dharma, artha and kāma and "will not be sprinkled on their heads".[62] But the instance of Munika's son should be noted in this connection.

Aśvamedha : The aśvamedha was a sacrifice specially meant for a king and instances of the kings who had performed this sacrifice have already been mentioned.

Vājapeya : The Vājapeya sacrifice was also performed by kings of whom we have only a few instances in our Purāṇa.

The following statements about these three rituals are significant : A donor of cots, lands and vehicles in śrāddha is said to obtain the merits of the performance of an aśvamedha.[63] By muttering the syllables of *Oṁ* one achieves more merit than a king who performs aśvamedha every month.[64] By making a gift of a beautiful homestead (*āvasatha*) to a Brahmin in śrāddha the donor gets the merits of the performance of a rājasūya[65] and a gift of woollen and linen clothes together with golden ornaments is equal in sanctity to the performance of a vājapeya.[66]

II. Popular Institutions

Samiti : There is only a solitary reference to Samiti in our text. Bṛhatī was a daughter of Bṛhaduktha. Her three sons are styled as "ornaments of the assembly" (?).[67]

---

55. Cf. *Rājasūye'bhiṣiktaś ca Pṛthur......Veda-dṛṣṭena vidhinā kṛto rājā pratāpavān*, 70. 21. 56. Cf. 70. 1. ff. 57. Cf. 93. 88. Ka : *Svarāṣṭra*.
58. Cf. 88. 32. *raṣṭre* ; Gha : *rājye*. 59. Cf. 99. 98–100. 60. Cf. 99. 310.
61. Cf. 90. 25 ; 88. 118. 62. Cf. *naiva mūrdhābhiṣiktās te bhaviṣyanti*, 99. 389.
63. Cf. 80. 26–7. 64. Cf. 20. 16–7. 65. Cf. 80. 30. 66. Cf. 80. 34–5.
67. Cf. *samiti-śobhanāḥ* : 96. 246–7.

Sabhā : The expression '*sabhā*' occurs frequently in a variety of senses and the following references are classified accordingly :

(a) The sabhā of Kubera on the Kailāsa mountain is called Vipulā (i.e. literally 'spacious').[68] In the description of the Meru mountain sabhās of many gods are mentioned.[69] The sabhās of Mahendra and others were situated to the north of the Mānasa lake.[70] Here sabhā probably means a temple or a mansion.

(b) The merit of listening to the story of Dakṣa-Śiva conflict is that one is able to secure an admission to the sabhā of a king.[71] Here sabhā probably signifies the royal court.

(c) In the course of Dakṣa's prayer to Śiva, there is a reference to sabhā.[72]

(d) In the midst of the sabhā, Janārdana (i.e. Kṛṣṇa) addressed Akrūra thus : "Venerable sir, please hand over to me the jewel (i.e. the *syamantaka*) which is in your possession." Without any hesitation Babhru (i.e. Akrūra) acceded to the request of Kṛṣṇa and passed the jewel on to him "in the assembly of the Sātvatas" (*sarva-Sātvata-saṁsadi*).[73] Sabhā here has a synonym in *saṁsad* which meant an 'assembly'.

(e) King Kārtavīrya Arjuna conquered the Karkoṭaka-sabhā in the city of Māhiṣmatī (together with) the thousand Nāgas.[74] The sabhā of Karkoṭaka was, it appears, a representative institution of the Nāgas.

Gaṇa :—As in the case of sabhā, "gaṇa" also has different shades of meaning and hence references to it have been presented here in the same manner :

(a) *Gaṇas* of Kinnaras, Vidyādharas, Yakṣas and Gandharvas are enumerated and their names are mentioned in the narration of the progeny of Kaśyapa.[75] Similarly *gaṇas* of Devas are described and named.[76] Here 'gaṇa' is used in a general and collective sense.

(b) There is a reference to Saiṁhikeya gaṇa of Daityas which was ten thousand strong.[77] They were the descendants of the fourteen sons of Siṁhikā, who was a wife of the Daitya Vipracitti.[78] Hālāhala was a name of a gaṇa which comprised of a hundred thousand descendants of Vāyu and Sinīvālī (grandsons of Hiraṇyakaśipu).[79] Yātudhānas, Brahmadhānas and Vārtas were the three gaṇas of Rākṣasas who were active in the day time (divācarāḥ) and those who wandered about in the night time (niśācarāḥ) were known by the four gaṇas of Paulastyas, Nairṛtas,

---

68. Cf. No. 469, App. 69. Cf. No. 818 in App. 70. Cf. 1. 92.
71. Cf. *yāti sabhāyāṁ pārthivasya ca* : 54. 105.
72. 30. 279. 73. Cf. 96. 90-5. 74. Cf. 94. 26.
75. Cf. 69. 15 ff. 76. Cf. 64. 2-4 ; 100. 13-20 ; 100. 111.
77. Cf. *daśāyutāni sahasrāṇi Saiṁhikeyo gaṇaḥ smṛtaḥ*.
78. Cf. 68. 17-21. 79. Cf. 67. 74-5.

Āgastyas and Kauśikas. Thus, in all, there were seven *jātis* of Rākṣasas. Here jāti is equivalent to a gaṇa.[80] Hiraṇyākṣa had five sons whose descendants were known as the Bāḍeya gaṇa.[81] Rāma annihilated Rāvaṇa together with his gaṇas.[82] In almost all these instances "gaṇa" appears to denote a sort of organization based on the hereditary principle.

(c) The Aṅga, Śaṅkha and Varāha dvīpas are said to have been inhabited by numerous gaṇas of Mlecchas. These dvīpas are the subdivisions of the Jambūdvīpa.[83] Various gaṇas of Mlecchas occupy the Ketumāladvīpa[84] and the same is said of the Śaravaṇa.[85] Here the association of gaṇa with Mlecchas should be noted.

(d) In the chapters on śrāddha occurs a statement that one who regularly performs śrāddha on the seventh day of every pakṣa is sure to become a lord of gaṇas.[86] This 'gaṇa' apparently indicates a kind of organisation.

(e) Once upon a time the sages had some business to be transacted. After having assembled on the Meru mount for that very purpose they resolved thus : "This is our resolution[87] that whosoever does not turn up here within a period of seven nights from today shall be deemed to have incurred the sin of the murder of a Brahmin." According to the requirements of this resolution all the sages—with the exception of Vaiśampāyana—were present "with their gaṇas" (*sagaṇāḥ*) on that occasion when the transaction of the notified business had been arranged (*yatra saṁdhiḥ kṛto 'bhavat*). Vaiśampāyana had thus become subjected to the sin and later he tried to be purified of it.[88] The terms *samaya* and *saṁdhi* should be noted. Here gaṇa is certainly indicative of an organization of some kind.

(f) The Dhārṣṭaka[89] Kṣattra was composed of a gaṇa of three thousand Kṣatriyas. Nābhāga is said to be powerful as he was backed by a gaṇa of a thousand Kṣatriyas.[90] King Sagara annihilated a number of gaṇas of Kṣatriyas, viz., the Śakas, Yavanas, Pāradas, etc.[91] Of the Haihayas there were five gaṇas, viz., Vīrahotras, Bhojas, Āvartis, Tuṇḍikeras and Tālajaṅghas.[92] Here the association of the Kṣatriyas with 'gaṇa' should be noted.

Janapadas :—The expression 'janapada' is used sometimes as a geographical term and sometimes in the sense of a tribe or people occupy-

80. Cf. 70. 55–6.

81. Cf. *teṣāṁ putrāś ca pautrāś ca Bāḍeyaḥ sa gaṇaḥ mṛtaḥ*, 67. 67–9, Ga : Vāleya.

82. Cf. 70. 48, 88. 197.

83. No. 437, App. 84. No. 27, App. 85. Cf. 41. 46.

86. Cf. *gaṇānām adhipo bhavet*, 81. 14.

87. Cf. *samoyo naḥ prakīrtitaḥ*. 88. 61. 12 ff.

89. Kha, Gha and Ṅa : Dhārṣṭyaka ; Cf. 88. 4–5. (Here the text is confusing and the above rendering is liable to be doubtful.)

90. Cf. *sahasra-Kṣatriya-gaṇa-vikrānto...Nābhāgo*, 86. 3.

91. No. 345 App. 92. Cf. 94. 51–2.

ing a particular region called after them. We have also some information on the Paura-Jānapadas. The following references have been arranged accordingly :

(a) Janapada as a Geographical Term : The earth is described as including many janapadas.[93] The extent of several janapadas is also described.[94] The janapada in the centre of Tāmravarṇa mountain covers an area of a hundred yojanas.[95] At the end of the Kali age, people will be flying from their janapadas and will be seeking refuge in the outlying territories (*pratyantān*).[96] The janapadas that "will be ruled" by the Guptas are also mentioned.[97] The janapada is also a synonym for '*deśa*'.[98]

(b) Janapada Signifying a Tribe or People : We have an allusion to cities and "jubilant" janapadas.[99] Again janapadas 'drinking' the waters of rivers are alluded to.[100] At the end of the Kali age, the janapadas will be following the customs of the Mlecchas.[101] It is not certain, however, whether the janapadas mentioned in the genealogical lists signified peoples or tribes or they merely indicated the regions of those names.

(c) The Paura-Jānapadas : The Paura-Jānapadas are mentioned in connection with the selection of Puru by Yayāti. Similarly, king Janamejaya is said to have been forsaken by the Paura-Jānapadas and he was never at rest. We have one instance in which only the *Pauras* are mentioned. King Sagara, it is stated, expelled his son Asamañja because the latter was engaged in activities prejudicial to the Pauras.[102]

---

93. Cf. *nānā-jana-padākīrṇā*, 50. 2. 94. Cf. 44. 3 ; 46. 73–4 etc.
95. No. 1302 App. 96. Cf. 58. 96. 97. No. 708 App.
98. See Nos. 608, 524 App.
99. Cf. 9. 113. 100. Cf. 45. 93. 101. No. 844 App.
102. Cf. *Paurāṇām hite yuktaḥ pitrā nirvāsitaḥ purā*, 88. 166.

CHAPTER IV

RELIGION

I. Śaivism

Maheśvara, the Supreme God : Śiva is called Mahādeva because he excels all the gods, sages and Asuras in point of *tejas*.[1] As Hara is the greatest (*variṣṭha*) of all the gods so is his prayer, which is compiled by Brahmā himself, the greatest of all the prayers.[2] He is also called the god of gods[3] and as the greatest amongst the best of Suras and Asuras.[4] Again he is the senior-most amongst the Devas.[5] The gods, sages, Pitṛs and Dānavas worship Īśa because they are afraid of *Kāla* (i.e., the same as Mahādeva).[6]

Śiva also figures as the great creator of the universe. He is the real creator, supporter and the destroyer of the world.[7] From him are born the seven sages, gods and manes.[8] He is the source of the mountains, seas, etc.[9] He is called *Sthāṇu* because after creating this world he stood motionless till the time of deluge.[10] He himself asserts that he is the creator of the Yugas and of Kāla.[11] He is frequently mentioned as the lord of the universe, and of the three worlds.[12]

The status of Śiva amongst the deities of the Vāyu Purāṇa is best realized from his relation to the other great gods, viz., Viṣṇu and Brahmā. The gods and sages were afraid of the four-faced Kāla and approached Mahādeva for relief. The latter explained to them the true nature of Kāla and asserted that Brahmā was worshipped in the Kṛta-yuga, Yajña in Tretā, Viṣṇu in Dvāpara and he himself in all the ages.[13] Brahmā and Viṣṇu jointly offer a prayer to Śiva who is consequently pleased and confers upon them a boon. Here Śiva himself says that Brahmā is his right arm and Viṣṇu the left. The real creator is Śiva, the two gods being only his functionaries.[14] Dakṣa, in the course of his prayer to Śiva, says that Brahmā, Govinda and the ancient sages are unable to measure his greatness.[15] Viṣṇu once proposed to Brahmā that both of them should adore Maheśvara with a *stotra*. But the latter angrily spurned the idea and demanded as to who this Śaṁkara was, excelling both of them. Viṣṇu, however, pacified Brahmā and explained to him how Śiva was the real creator and Viṣṇu, the field of creation and Brahmā, the seed of it.[16] This was enough to reconcile Brahmā and

---

1. Cf. 10. 66–7. 2. Cf. 30. 307.
3. Cf. *deva-deveśa* : 23. 98–9 ; *deva-deva* : 54. 3. 4. Cf. 55. 65–8.
5. Cf *Devānāṁ jyeṣṭha* : 15. 10. 6. Cf. 32. 35.
7. Cf. 55. 37 ff. 3. 1 ; 1. 205. 8. Cf. 32. 4–5. 9. Cf. 24. 96–100.
10. Cf. 10. 64. 11. Cf. 32 7–26. 12. Cf. 1, 3-4 ; 69. 44 ; Cf. also 30. 289.
13. Cf. 32. 7–26. 14. Cf. *hetumātrā* : 55. 51–65. 15. Cf. 30. 26–9.
16. Cf. *eṣa bījī bhavān bījam ahaṁ yoniḥ sanātanaḥ*.

then both of them offered the prayer to Śiva.[17] Viṣṇu, though he is prayed to by all the gods, himself adores Śiva.[18] Viṣṇu vanquished Bali and was congratulated by gods and sages. But Viṣṇu attributed his greatness to Śiva.[19] It is stated that in the 22nd Kalpa, Viṣṇu, in the form of Meghin, was a carrier of Maheśvara for the period of a thousand divine years. · Once, being too much hard-pressed by the burden of Śiva, Viṣṇu heaved out a breath from which arose Kāla.[20]

There is, however, a solitary statement that all the three gods are merely manifestations of the one Supreme God.[21]

Rudra, the Malevolent : He is called the god of death as well as the destroyer of death itself.[22] He has always a fascination for the cremation-ground[23] and loves the funeral ashes.[24] He wanders naked with skulls in the hands.[25] In the Kṛṣṇa-Kalpa he was the terror itself but to those who knew him he was benevolent.[26] He is also identified with the terrible Kāla of whom the gods and sages were afraid.[27] Epithets such as *su-ghora*,[28] *naraka* (hell),[29] *kuṭila* (crooked),[30] *bhīma*, *ugra* (terrible),[31] *krūra* (cruel), *vikṛta*, *bībhatsa*, *bhīṣaṇa*, *kapāla*, *mṛtyu*,[32] *duḥsaha*, *durvāraṇa*,[33] frequently occur in connection with the god. He is called the bearer of terrible forms.[34] Śiva is also called Vāma-deva as he had attained vāmadevatva through *vāmatva yoga*.[35]

Names of Śiva : Śiva is referred to by many names in the Purāṇa and only the important amongst them have been noted.[36]

Maheśvara,[37] *Śaṁkara*,[38] *Mahādeva*,[39] *Hara*,[40] *Rudra*,[41] *Śarva*,[42] *Bhava*.[43] *Śaṁbhu*,[44] *Sthāṇu*,[45] *Īśāna*,[46]. *Vāmadeva*,[47] *Paśupati*,[48] *Bhūta-pati*,[49] *Kapardin*,[50] *Vṛṣabhadhvaja*.[51] *Tripuraghna*,[52] *Tri-netra*,[53] and *Nīlakaṇṭha*, etc. etc.

The story of the eight names of Śiva also occurs in the Purāṇa. These names, which were given by Brahmā to the eight sons of Śiva, i.e., the various forms of Śiva himself, are : Rudra, Bhava, Śiva, Paśupati, Īśa, Bhīma, Ugra and Mahādeva.[54]

---

17. The prayer is known as "*Śārvastava*." Omitted in Kha, Gha and Ṅa : Cf. 24. 60 ff. ; cf. also 1. 72-3.
18. Cf. 1. 105. 19. Cf. 55. 1-10. 20 Cf. 21. 50-2, 21. Cf. 1. 132.
22. Cf. 24. 128. 23. Cf. *śmaśāna-ratinityāya* : 24. 140.
24. Cf. *citā-bhasmapriya* : 30. 201. 25. Omitted in Ka, Cf. 24. 129.
26. Cf. *aghora* 23. 74-6. 27. Cf. 32. 8. ff. 28. Cf. 24. 120-3. 29. Cf. 24. 116.
30. Cf. 30. 196-8. 31. Cf. 97. 166-71. 32. Cf. 97. 172-81. 33. Cf. 30. 263.
34. Cf. *ghora-rūpa-dhṛk* : 55. 51-5 ; Cf. also No. 1403 App. 35. Cf. 23. 69-71.
36. The references are only illustrative and not exhaustive.
37. Cf. 34. 38-9 ; 55. 51-5 ; 55. 65-8. 38. Cf. 39. 42 ; 55. 65-8.
39. Cf. 40. 20-6 ; 34. 38-9 ; 69. 44. 40. Cf. 30. 307. 41. Cf. 21. 71 ; 10. 70.
42. Cf. 47. 27 ; 97. 166-71 ; 1. 152. 43. Cf. 47. 29-31 ; 92. 28-37.
44. Cf. 30. 211-2. 45. Cf. 10. 64. 46. Cf. 97. 182-90. 47. Cf. 23. 69-71.
48. Cf. 30. 89 ; 24. 105-7 ; 97. 191-202. 49. Cf. 50. 30 ff. ; 40. 20-6 ; 39. 42.
50. Cf. 97. 162-5 ; 24. 129. 51. Cf. 70. 7-8. 52. Cf. 97. 182-90.
53. Cf. 97. 172-81. 54. Cf. 27. 1-16.

Important Myths about Śiva :

(1) The story of Dakṣa's sacrifice : In the Svāyaṁbhuva manvantara Dakṣa had eight daughters of whom Satī, the wife of Śiva, was the eldest. Maheśvara had no respect for his father-in-law. Once Dakṣa invited his daughters (excluding Satī) to his place. Satī came to know that she was not invited but still she went to her father, who, however, showed her scant courtesy. She expressed her resentment at the treatment meted out to her. Dakṣa, however, replied that Bhava was inimical towards him[55] and that was the reason which prompted him to treat her like that. He further added that his other sons-in-law were, as compared with Tryambaka, more deserving of honour and respect. This was adding insult to injury and Satī, enraged as she was, said to her father that she would thenceforward cease to be his daughter. She informed her husband about what had happened and consigned herself to flames. God Maheśvara was now angry and he cursed Dakṣa that he would be born again.

As a result of this curse Dakṣa was reborn as Prācetasa Dakṣa. Once, at the source of the river Gaṅgā, Dakṣa started a sacrificial session. It is said[56] that the gods went to the place of the sacrifice with their own vehicles. All the beings were invited and attended the session. Dadhīci, however, felt uneasy at the whole affair and exclaimed, "This man (i.e. Dakṣa) is certainly committing a heinous sin in adoring the undeserved and in neglecting the deserved."[57] Turning towards Dakṣa he said, "Why don't you invite the venerable lord of the *paśus*?" Dakṣa replied that he did not know the god Maheśvara any more than the Rudras of whom he had seen many. Dadhīci reminded him that he was following an improper policy but Dakṣa neglected his advice and offered oblations to Viṣṇu as his favourite deity.

In the meanwhile, Umā, the wife of Śiva, had seen the gods going to attend the sacrifice and asked her husband as to why he was not invited. Śiva replied that under the arrangement made by the Suras there was no provision for his portion in the oblations offered in all the sacrifices.[58] Umā was pained to hear this and took the whole affair as a mark of disrespect towards her husband. Śiva tried to convince her that this was not so but Umā was not impressed and rebuked her husband that he knew well only to praise himself in the assembly of women. The taunt had its effect on Śiva who from his wrath created Vīrabhadra and commissioned him to destroy the sacrifice of Dakṣa. Vīrabhadra, with his host of Rudras, raided the sacrifice and played havoc at that place.

---

55. Cf. *pratikūlo hi me Bhavaḥ.* 56. *iti śrutiḥ.*

57. Cf. *apūjya-pūjane caiva pūjyānāṁ cāpyapūjane narah pāpam avāpnoti mahad vai nātra saṁśayaḥ.*

58. Cf. *Surair eva mahābhāge sarvam etad anuṣṭhitaṁ yajñeṣu mama sarveṣu na bhāga upakalpitaḥ.*

The gods and Dakṣa beseeched Vīrabhadra but he directed them to appeal to lord Śiva. Dakṣa then prayed to Śiva who appeared before him, after having arisen from the sacrificial fire......Here we find the text of the lengthy prayer addressed by Dakṣa to Maheśvara.[59]

(2) The story of how Śiva come to be known as Nīlakaṇṭha: In former times, the gods and the demons had started "churning of the ocean" for *amṛta* but at first a deadly poison issued out of it. All of them went to Brahmā but the latter told them that he was helpless and that only Śiva would be able to help them. Brahmā then prayed to Śiva and requested him to drink the poison. Śiva acceeded to the request and thenceforward he came to be known as "blue-necked".[60]

(3) Story of the origin of Liṅga is given in the following pages in another context.

(4) The story of the destruction of Vārāṇasī is given elsewhere.[61]

Śiva's Associates:

(i) The Bhūtas: Śiva and Umā enjoyed their stay in the Umāvana in the company of the Bhūtas.[62] The Bhūtas entertain Śiva with dance and music by playing on various instruments.[63] The Bhūtas, residing at Bhūta-vaṭa, a mansion of Śiva, have faces of various animals and hairy skin.[64] They adore Śiva in various forms.[65] Bhūtī (or Bhūtā), the wife of Kaśyapa, gave birth to the Bhūtas who were the followers of Rudra. They had various forms, mostly hideous, and are called terrible like the Rākṣasas, with skulls in their hands, horrible and crooked. They have neither wives nor children and are always *ūrdhvaretasaḥ*.[66] Śiva is called the "consecrated lord" of the Bhūtas and Piśācas.[67]

(ii) The Rudras: They are born of Śiva.[68] At the time of their birth they began to weep and run away, that is why they are called Rudras.[69] They figure more in the story of the sacrifice of Dakṣa than elsewhere. They helped Vīrabhadra in his raid on the sacrifice.

(iii) The Asuras, Rākṣasas, Daityas, etc.: Śiva is called the lord of the Rākṣasas.[70] He is worshipped by Suras and Asuras alike[71] and is called the best amongst the Suras and Asuras.[72] Hundreds of the gaṇas of the Rākṣasas follow (*anucaranti*) Śaṁkara, the lord of the world.[73] The Nairṛta-Rākṣasas adore Tryambaka.[74] In the story of the destruction of Vārāṇasī we find Kṣemaka, an attendant of Śiva, mentioned as a Rākṣasa.[75] In a mantra addressed to Śiva he is styled as Asura.[76]

---

59. Cf. Chapt. 30. 60. Cf. Chapt. 54 61. Cf. No. 1403 App.
62. Cf. 41. 32–6. 63. Cf. 40. 24–5. 64. Cf. 40. 21–3. 65. Cf. 3?. 89.
66. Cf. 69. 242–56. 67. Cf. 70. ?–8.
68. Cf. 55. 40–41. 69. Cf. 9. 75–80; 10. 43–60.
70. Cf. *Rakṣodhipati*: 24. 109. 71. Cf. 30. 317. 72. Cf. 55. 65–8.
73. Cf. 69. 175. 74. Cf. 69. 173. 75. Cf. 92. 68.
76. Cf. "*tvam agne rudro asuro ma o divas tvaṁ śardho mārutaṁ pṛkṣa īśiṣe*", etc. 21. 71.

(iv) Munis: Besides these, the Piśācas, Vināyakas, Nāgas, Yakṣas, Gandharvas, etc., are also associated with Śiva. Kubera, the lord of the Yakṣas, was a friend of Mahādeva.[77] In the house where Śiva is prayed, there shall be no danger from the Vināyakas, Piśācas, Nāgas, Yakṣas, etc.[78] The Nāgas and the others worship Śiva[79]. Śiva, in his future avatāras, will have four sons in each avatāra. They are often mentioned as Kumārakas.[80]

The Ādityas, Siddhas, Vasus, etc., are also associated with Śiva but there is nothing striking in this association.

Śiva, Tapas and Yoga: Śiva says to Brahmā that those who see through tapas the *Śivatva* as pervading everything are sure to be one with Śiva. For them rebirth is not possible.[81] To the same god he elsewhere states that since he has known Śiva as being on the *guhya-pada* by means of his own penance, those who do likewise shall achieve unity with Śiva without any fear of rebirth.[82] Śiva is 'hunted after' (*mṛgyate*) by Yatis who are afflicted with misery.[83] In his prayer to Śiva, Dakṣa addresses the god simply as Tapas.[84] The god himself practised severe austerities in the mansion of Devī (*devyālaye*), on the Umā-tuṅga standing on one foot for a whole heavenly yuga without taking any food.[85] He did the same by the side of (the river) Kauśikī by placing his one foot on the *muṇḍa-pṛṣṭha* for many yugas of gods.[86] Rudra practised severe penance on Sapta-Godāvara in the Gokarṇa-tapovana.[87] In the various stotras of Śiva he is often addressed as *Yatin*, *ūrdhvaretas*,[88] *tapo-nitya*,[89] etc. The explanation of the name Sthāṇu given above should be noted in this connection. The Devas and Dānavas practised severe austerities as a result of which Śiva created the Pāśupatavrata which enables one to be free from the *Paśu-pāśas*.[90] Śukra Kāvya who desired a mantra from lord Mahādeva to bring about the defeat of the Devas at the hands of the Asuras asked that god as to what he ought to do. Śiva advised him to practise a vrata by concentrating on him as a *brahmacārin* for a thousand years. Kāvya had already advised the Asuras to practise penance till the time he secured the necessary mantras from Mahādeva, and now he himself proceeded to practise austerities as advised by Śiva.[91] Umā is said to have practised penance on the southern side of the Himavat mountain.[92] Aparṇā practised austerities without having even leaves of trees for food, while Ekaparṇā had only one leaf and Ekapāṭalā only fruits and flowers of Pāṭalā trees as food.[93] The four

77. Cf. *Mahādeva sakhaḥ* : 41. 1-8. 78. Cf. 30. 311. 79. Cf. 40. 26.
80. Cf. Chapt. 23. 81. Cf. 23. 95-7. 82. Cf. 23. 66-7. 83. Cf. 24. 65-6.
84. Cf. 30. 256; also 24. 115. 85. Cf. 77. 81. 86. Cf. 77. 102.
87. Cf. 77. 20. 88. Cf. 97. 162 ff. 89. Cf. 30. 224.
90. Cf. *paśu-pāśa-vimokṣaṇa* : 30. 293-5. 91. Cf. 97. 105 ff. 92. Cf. 41. 31.
93. Aparṇā, Ekaparṇā and Ekapāṭalā are merely the other names of Durgā: Cf. 72. 7-11.

sons of Śiva in his different future avatāras are also credited with having performed tapas. One of such sons in the fourteenth avatāra will have a name *Ugra-tapas.*[94] They are also at times mentioned as Ūrdhva-retasaḥ.[95] King Bhagīratha practised severe penance and pleased Śiva for the sake of the river Gaṅgā.[96] All the twice-borns who practise tapas become free from rajas and tamas and having abandoned the human form merge into the god-head of Śiva.[97] They are similarly advised to please the god through penance and obtain high merits.

The stomach of Śiva is the home of *siddha-yogas.*[98] There is a lengthy chapter (23) on *Māheśvarāvatāra-yoga* in which are detailed the different future avatāras of Śiva. In each of these avatāras, Śiva "will have" four sons (or disciples) who are often mentioned either as *yogātmānaḥ* or are connected with yoga. After fulfilling their mission by practising yoga they "will" achieve the highest goal, viz., Rudra-loka. They are often said to have achieved the *Māheśvara-yoga* before their entry into the Rudra-loka or before they return to the presence of Śiva.[99] We are also told about the Kumārakas issuing from Kumāra (i. e. Maheśvara) in the various Kalpas. They too preach the gospel either of dharma or yoga and again merge into Śiva.[100] Śiva practised yoga on this earth in the Haimaka-vana.[101] Whenever a kalpa comes to a close, Rudra destroys the world through his *yoga-māyā.*[102] Śiva pervades everything because of his yoga.[103] Maheśvara goaded the *pradhāna-puruṣa* to action through his yoga and then entered the Egg.[104] Śiva says to Brahmā that he and Viṣṇu "will be" stunned at the power of Maheśvara's yoga.[105] Śiva's yoga is the cause which led to the origin of the lotus whence arose Brahmā who created the world.[106] There is also a reference to *tatva-yoga.*[107] Mahādeva created this universe by resorting to yoga.[108] A yogin is said to be elevated to the Rudra-loka after transcending the prakṛti.[109] Śiva achieved Vāmadevatva due to his *vāmatva-yoga.*[110] Śiva tells Dakṣa that he created the Pāśupata-vrata in support of Yoga, Sāṁkhya, the Vedas, etc.[111] "Lord of Yoga" is a very common attribute of Śiva in the Purāṇa.

Every Yogin is advised to know the Maheśvara of six *aṅgas* and also the seven *sūkṣmas*, to achieve final beatitude.[112] *Prāṇāyāma*, *dhyāna*, *pratyāhāra*, *dhāraṇā* and *smaraṇa* are the five dharmas enjoined by Rudra himself about the *Pāśupata yoga.*[113]

---

94. Cf. 23. 163–4. 95. Cf. 23. 159–61 : 23. 169–70. 96. Cf. 47. 36.
97. Cf. 23. 95–6.
98. Cf. *sarveṣāṁ siddha-yogānāṁ adhiṣṭhānaṁ tavodaram* : 24. 151.
99. Cf. *Śiva-sāmīpyatā* : 23. 140–2 ; 23. 209–13. 100. Cf. Chapt. 22.
101. Cf. 23. 155–7. 102. Cf. 66. 145. 103. Cf. 24. 39. 104. Cf. 5. 10–12.
105. Cf. 23. 111–3. 106. Cf. 34. 41–4 : Kha omits this. 107. Cf. 23. 98–9.
108. Cf. 1. 7. 109. Cf. 12. 38. 110. Cf. 23. 70. 111. Cf. 30. 293–5.
112. Cf. 12. 32. 113. Cf. 10. 70–6.

The Avatāras of Śiva: The following table gives the necessary details regarding the 'future' avatāras of Śiva and his sons (or disciples).[114]

	Name of the Avatāra.	Names of his sons or disciples.
1.	Śveta	Śveta, Śikha,[115] Śvetāśva, Śvetalohita.
2.	Sutāra	Dundubhi, Śatarūpa,[116] Ṛcīka, Ketumat.
3.	Damana[117]	Viśoka, Vikeśa, Viśāpa, Śāpanāśana.
4.	Suhotrin	Sumukha, Durmukha, Durdama,[118] Duratikrama.
5.	Kaṅka	Sana, Sanandana, Ṛtu,[119] Sanatkumāra.
6.	Lokākṣi	Sudhāman, Viraja, Śaṅkhapādrava (?).
7.	Jaigīṣavya	Sārasvata, Sumedha,[120] Vasuvāha, Suvāhana.
8.	Vasiṣṭha	Kapila, Āsuri, Pañcaśikha, Vāgvali.[121]
9.	Ṛṣabha	Parāśara, Gārgya, Bhārgava, Aṅgiras.
10.	Tridhāman	Balavandhu, Nirā(ra)mitra, Ketuśṛṅga, Tapodhana (?).
11.	Ugras (?)	Lambodara, Lamba, Lambākṣa, Lambakeśaka.
12.	Atri	Sarvajña, Samabuddhi, Sādhya, Sarva.
13	Vāli[122]	Sudhāman, Kaśyapa, Vasiṣṭha, Virajas.
14.	Gautama	Atri, Ugratapas, Śrāvaṇa, Sraviṣṭa(ṣṭha)ka.[123]
15.	Vedaśiras	Kuṇi, Kuṇibāhu, Kuśarīra, Kunetraka.
16.	Gokarṇa	Kāśyapa,[124] Uśanas, Cyavana, Bṛhaspati.
17.	Guhāvāsin[125]	Utathya, Vāmadeva, Mahākāla, Mahālaya.
18.	Śikhaṇḍin	Vācasravas, Ṛtti(cī)ka, Śāvāsa,[126] Dṛḍhavrata (?).
19.	Jaṭāmālin	Hiraṇyanāman, Kauśilya, Kākṣīva,[127] Kuthumi.
20.	Aṭṭahāsa	Sumantu, Barbari, Subandhu, Kuśikandhara.
21.	Dāruka	Plakṣa, Dākṣāyaṇi,[128] Ketumālin, Vaka.[129]
22.	Lāṅgalin	Tulyārcis, Madhupiṅgākṣa, Śvetaketu (?).[130]
23.	Śveta (2nd)	Ūsija,[131] Vṛhadukthya,[132] Devala, Kavi.
24.	Śūlin	Śālihotra, Agniveśya, Yuvanāśva, Saradvasu.
25.	Daṇḍin	Chagala, Kumbhakarṣāsya,[133] Kumbha, Pravāhuka.
26.	Sahiṣṇu	Ulūka, Vaidyuta, Śarvaka,[134] Āsvalāyana.
27.	Somaśarman	Akṣapāda, Kaṇāda, Ulūka, Vatsa.
28.	Nakulin[135]	Kuṣika, Gārgya, Mitraka, Ruṣṭa.

The sons (or disciples) are often mentioned as being Brahmins learned in the Vedas. The common description about them is that they practise austerities and after having achieved the Māheśvara yoga repair to the Rudraloka. Of the last incarnation of Śiva (Nakulin) it is stated

114. Cf. 23. 115 ff. 115. Kha, Ṅa : *Śveta*. 116. Kha, Ga and Ṅa : *Śatarūpā*. 117. Gha : *Madana*. 118. Ṅa : *Durmada*. 119. Kha and Ga : *Kratu*. 120. Kha : *Sumedhas*. 121. Ga omits these names. 122. Gha : *Vali*. 123. Kha, Ga and Ṅa : *Śraviṣṭa(ṣṭha)ka*. 124. Ka : *Kaśyapa*. 125. Ga and Ṅa : *Guhyavāsin*. 126. Kha, Ga, Gha and Ṅa : *Vāśvāsa*. 127. Ṅa : *Kāṅkṣiva*. 128. Ṅa : *Dālbhāyani*. 129. Kha and Ṅa : *Naka*. 130. Gha : *Citraketu*. 131. Ṅa : *Ausija*. 132. Kha, Ga : *Vṛhadutthi*. 133. Kha, Ga, Gha and Ṅa : *Kumbhakarṇa*. 134. Ka : *Sarvaka*. 135. Ga, Gha and Ṅa : *Lakulin*.

that Śiva "will be" entering a dead body lying uncared for in a cremation ground through the power of his *yoga-māyā* for the sake of the Brahmins; he "will" then be a brahmacārin.[137] This incarnation of Śiva will take place in the *siddhakṣetra* named Kāyārohana.[138]

Śiva and Liṅga: The Purāṇa has one chapter (55) entirely devoted to the origin of Liṅga. It runs thus:

Viṣṇu had vanquished Bali and was congratulated by gods and sages upon this act. But Viṣṇu attributed this success to the greatness of Śiva but for whose favour he would not have achieved *siddhatva* in former days.[139] Viṣṇu then narrates a tale with regard to this:

"In former times, I had absorbed all the three worlds. Everywhere there was darkness and with all the creatures in my bowels I slept. After some time, I happened to see something shining at a distance which was none else than the person of Brahmā. Brahmā came towards me and after asserting that he is the self-born (*svayaṁbhū*) and the creator of the world he questioned me as to who I was. I replied to him that I (too) was the creator and destroyer of the world. While we were thus engaged in a wordy warfare about our part in the creation we saw, at a distance, a blazing flame which appeared to envelop the whole world above and below. We were bewildered at this glaring sight and hastened towards it, and lo! we saw, in the midst of flames, a liṅga, terrible in appearance.[140] We felt a curiosity about its magnitude and Brahmā said to me, "Let us try to trace out its limits. I am going towards its upper extremity." He proceeded to do likewise and I went towards the bottom. But all our exploration was in vain. We were overtaken by *māyā* and could not find out our way. I was really very much afraid. We then offered prayers to Maheśvara who appeared before us to relieve us of our anxieties."

In the first chapter of contents an allusion is made to this meritorious story.[141] Stray references to liṅga also occur. Viṣṇu tells Brahmā: "Formerly (Śiva?) inserted the liṅga and your seed in me (i.e. the yoni) which in course of time developed into the golden egg".[142] Śiva is elsewhere called the subtle liṅga.[143] He is also called the lord of the kṣetra (*kṣetrādhipati*), bījin and ūrdhvameḍhra.[144]

---

136. For places where these avatāras 'will be' taking place see Nos. 385, 386, 387, 560A, 814, 995, 1155 in App.

137. Kha and Gha omit these details. 138. Cf. 30. 219-24.

139. Cf. *tasya eva prasādena ādau siddhatvam āgatam* : 55. 10.

140. Cf. *jvālā-mālāyataṁ nyastaṁ sarva-bhūta-bhayaṁkaram* : 55. 22.

141. Cf. 1. 105.

142. Cf. *purā liṅgaṁ bhavadbījaṁ prathamaṁ tv ādisargikam mayi yonau samāyuktaṁ tad-bījaṁ kālaparyayāt hiraṇmayam apāraṁ tad yonyām aṇḍam ajāyata* : 24. 72-3.

143. Cf. 97. 200-202. 144. Cf. 24. 91-2; also 24. 55-60.

Skanda-Kārtikeya : In the chapters on Śrāddha we find a story narrated about the birth of this god : Indra had fears about the issue arising out of the union of Śiva with Rudrāṇī.[145] He commissioned Agni to disturb them in their intercourse. Agni did his duty well and the semen of Śiva fell on the earth. Umā, with her passions thus ungratified, angrily cursed Agni to bear the *garbha* himself. After carrying the garbha for many years Agni requested the river Gaṅgā to bear it for him. Gaṅgā, though with great hesitation, agreed to do so and, in course of time, delivered it on the Śaravaṇa. Thus was born Kumāra, the child conjointly of Rudra, Agni and Gaṅgā. The wives of the seven sages (excluding Arundhatī) came to see the child as if they were its mothers.[146] Each of them in turn saw the child and that is why Kumāra has six faces. Since he vanquished the Dānavas, he is called Skanda[147] and since the Kṛttikās nursed him, he is called Kārtikeya. Various gods then brought him presents mostly in the form of animals. Skanda had many sports on the Krauñca-giri where he killed Tārakāsura. This son of Agni was later consecrated as the Commander-in-Chief of the gods. He is surrounded by the *Mātṛs* and the gaṇas of Vināyakas and Bhūtas.[148]

Skanda's birth in Śaravaṇa is alluded to in the geographical chapters. It was on the Krauñcaśaila that lions were yoked to the chariot of Kārtikeya and Guha (i.e. Skanda) was consecrated to the generalship of the gods.[149]

In the description of the city of Śiva (Śivapura) we find Skanda mentioned as Śikhivāhana (i.e. having peacock as his vehicle) with Śākha, Viśākha and others as his followers.[150] The sage Vasiṣṭha, who professes to be his devotee, also calls the god as *Śikhivāhana* and *Śaktihasta* (i.e. having Śakti as his weapon) in the course of his prayer.[151]

Skanda also figures as a leader of the Nairṛta Rākṣasas who were in the habit of kidnapping children.[152] The Vaināyakas and others are the classes of *Bhūmi-Rākṣasakas*. They wander unseen on the earth in various forms ; there are eight classes of them, viz., Bhadrakas, Nikaras, Pūtanas with Mātṛs (amongst them ?), etc. They have their eyes always on children.[153] They have Skandagraha in their train.[154] The Kaumāras amongst them have a particular tendency to kidnap children. Thus there are numerous gaṇas of Skandagrahas, Loka-Vināyakas, etc.[155]

145. Cf. *tābhyāṁ maithunasaktābhyām apatyodbhava-bhīruṇa......Indreṇa.*

146. Cf. *svakābhir iva mātṛbhiḥ.*

147. Cf. *Skanditā Dānavagaṇās tasmāt skandaḥ pratāpavan.* 148. Cf. 72. 21 ff.

149. No 469 App. 150. Cf. 101. 279-81. 151. Cf. 54. 22-6.

152. Cf. *Nairṛtā nāmatah smṛtā grahās te rākṣasāḥ sarve bālānaṁ tu viśeṣataḥ* : 84. 13-4.

153. Cf. *bālānāṁ mānuṣe loke grahāḥ.* 154. *Skanda-grahādayaś caiva.*

155. Cf. *Kaumāras te tu vijñeyā bālānāṁ grahavṛttayaḥ skandagrahaviśeṣāṇāṁ..... ye ca loka-vināyakāḥ.* They appear to have some connection with the Guhyakas : 69. 184-94.

Gaṇeśa : Sudyumna is said to have been turned into a female and achieved the status of *gāṇapatya* through the favour of Mahādeva.[157] A Śūdra devotee of Śiva is promised the same status of Gāṇapatya if he is not a drunkard.[158]

II. Vaiṣṇavism and the other sects

Vaiṣṇavism : Viṣṇu as the supreme god does not figure much in the Purāṇa. The only important account about him is the story of his avatāras brought into the genealogical portions of the Purāṇa in connection with the 'history' of Vāsudeva Kṛṣṇa. But here too we find the greatness of Śiva pervading the story. The sages asked Sūta as to who were Vasudeva, Devakī, Nandagopa, etc., amongst whom the god Viṣṇu was born and the latter elucidates the point by narrating the story of Bhṛgu's curse to Viṣṇu for killing his wife as the result of which Viṣṇu was born seven times on the earth.

Though Śiva is the supreme god of the Purāṇa, we find Viṣṇu too as a great god next to him. Nārāyaṇa creates the universe and pervades it, though he himself is created by Maheśvara.[159] He is the best amongst the Suras[160] and is the "consecrated lord" of the Ādityas and Sādhyas.[161] All the gods are pervaded by Viṣṇu (*Viṣṇumayāḥ*) and there is no goal better than the world of Viṣṇu.[162] This is what the gods sing. But still Hari adores Bhava.[163] When the period of destruction arrives, he absorbs the three worlds and goes to sleep. References to Viṣṇu reclining on his ocean-bed occur frequently[164] and there he is described as holding the *śaṅkha*, *cakra* and *gadā* in his hands,[165] as having eight arms and wearing the *kirīṭa*.[166] The mark of *cakra* on the feet and of *saṅkha* on the palm of the hands are some of the indications of a *cakravartin* in the Tretā age.[167] This cakravartin is animated by the spirit of Viṣṇu. Caṇḍa, the lord of Nāgas, was also marked with the discus of Viṣṇu.[168]

In the accounts of creation, Viṣṇu often figures with Brahmā and is sometimes identified with him. Brahmā is called Nārāyaṇa many times and the name Nārāyaṇa is explained in that connection.[169] When Viṣṇu asks Brahmā as to who he is, Brahmā answers that he is known as Nārāyaṇa, the creator of the world.[170] In the act of creation Brahmā himself assumes the form of a boar.[171]

---

156. For details of the story of the destruction of the city of Vārāṇasī through a curse of Gaṇeṣa Kṣemaka : Cf. No. 143 App.

157. 85. 28. 158. 101. 351–5.

159. Cf. 1. 204. 160. Cf. 69. 43. 161. Cf. 70. 5–6.

162. Cf. *na ca Viṣṇu-samā kācid gatiranyā vidhīyate.* 163. Cf. 21. 6–7.

164. Cf. 1. 56 ; 24. 10 ff. ; 55. 12, etc. 165. Cf. 55. 12 ; 24. 9.

166. Cf. 24. 9–10. 167. Cf. 57. 79. 168. *Viṣṇucakrāṅkita-cihna* Cf. 41. 73.

169. Cf. 6. 3 ; 3. 38 ; 7. 63–5 ; 7. 69–71. 170. Cf. 24. 21.

171. *Vārāha-rūpa* : Cf. 6. 10 ff.

The avatāras of Viṣṇu, referred to in the Purāṇa, are as follows :

Name of the avatāra	Details about the avatāra
1. Nārāyaṇa	He started the Institution of Sacrifice.
2. Narasiṁha	He killed Hiraṇyakaśipu.
3. Vāmana	As a Brahmin he begged of Vairocana Bali the portion of earth traversed by his "three steps" and vanquished Bali.
4. Dattātreya	Mārkaṇḍeya was his promoter (*puraḥsara*).
5. Māṁdhātā	He was a cakra-vartin and had[173] a promoter in Utathya.[174]
6. Jāmadagnya	He was the annihilator of all the Kṣatriyas and had Viśvāmitra as his promoter.[175]
7. Rāma	He was the son of Daśaratha with Vasiṣṭha as his promoter. He was born specially for the purpose of killing Rāvaṇa.
8. Vedavyāsa	He was the son of Parāśara with Jātūkarṇa as his promoter.
9. Kṛṣṇa	Son of Vasudeva by Devakī. Brahmargārgya (?) was his promoter.[176] Viṣṇu was born in the family of the Vṛṣṇis in order to promulgate dharma. He killed Kaṁsa, Śālva, Pūtanā, Keśin, Nāga Kuvalayāpīḍa, etc., who were really Daityas in different garbs. Here Sāndīpani is mentioned as his promoter.
10. Kalki	When this age will come to a close, Viṣṇuyaśas Kalki, belonging to the Parāśara (gotra ?) will be born with Yājñāvalkya as his promoter.[177]

The first three avataras are called *divya-saṁbhūtis* (i.e. incarnations in heaven) and the rest are the incarnations amongst men.[178]

Some of the above avatāras are mentioned elsewhere in the text. Hiraṇyakaśipu, the lord of Daityas, was killed by Narasiṁha Viṣṇu.[179] With reference to Vāmana the name of Viṣṇu is explained thus : "*tasmāt sa vai smṛto Viṣṇur viśer dhātoḥ praveśanāt.*[180] The knowers of Purāṇa say that Atri's son Dattātreya had the *corpus* of Viṣṇu.[181] Kārtavīrya Arjuna propitiated Datta, son of Atri, through practice of severe austerities and the latter granted him four boons.[182] Vyāsa, as an *aṁśa* (i.e. portion) of Viṣṇu, is also mentioned at some places.[183] We have also a narration about the future exploits of Kalki.[184]

---

172. Cf. 98. 70 ff. ; also 1. 148-50.
173. According to Ṅa only.
174. Gha does not mention him.
175. Gha omits his name.
176. Gha and Ṅa omit this.
177. For details see No. 842 App.
178. Cf. 98. 88.
179. Cf. 67. 66.
180. Cf. 66. 136.
181. Cf. 70. 77.
182. Cf. 94. 10-15.
183. Cf. 60. 11-2 ; 23. 217-8.
184. Cf. 99. 396.

The *Varāhāvatāra* of Viṣṇu is not included in the above list but the following references indicate that it was probably recognised as an avatāra. The people of Varāha-dvīpa worshipped Viṣṇu in his form of Varāha.[185] Pramiti, as an aṁśa of Mādhava, is also mentioned[186] but he is not included in the above list because he was an avatāra (?) of Viṣṇu in the Svāyambhuva Manvantara. The above list apparently refers to the avatāras of Viṣṇu in the Vaivasvata manvantara.[187]

Viṣṇu as a Sectarian God : There are some indications in the Purāṇa about Viṣṇu as a sectarian god. The Brahmins, Ksatriyas and Vaiśyas of the city of Campāvatī were worshippers of Viṣṇu.[188] Worship of Datta[189] by Kārtavīrya Arjuna has already been noted above. In the story of Dakṣa-sacrifice we find Dakṣa offering oblations to Viṣṇu as his favourite deity. There is also a statement[190] that Nārāyaṇa is the sole resort for emancipation.

We have a reference to Saṁkarṣaṇa, Vāsudeva, Pradyumna, Sāmba and Aniruddha as the five great men of his family (*vaṁśa-vīrāḥ*). This reference occurs in the context of the narration of the avatāras of Viṣṇu and is probably suggestive of the theology of the Bhāgavata sect.[191]

The Conception of the Triad : In the accounts of creation Brahmā is called both Nārāyaṇa and Maheśvara.[192] Lord Nārāyaṇa divides himself into three and performs the functions of creation, preservation and destruction.[193] In the first chapter which gives the contents of the Purāṇas, we find a provision made for the elucidation of the unity and diversity of the three gods.[194] We have already referred to the exposition made by Viṣṇu to Brahmā as to how Śiva is the generator (*bijin*), he himself the field of creation (*yoni*) and Brahmā the germ (*bījam*). Brahmā is the *Rajas*, Agni (i.e. Rudra) the *Tamas* and Viṣṇu the *Sattva*.[195] In the prayer to Śiva the god is also addressed as Viṣṇu and Brahmā.[196] The abode of Nārāyaṇa is to the east, of Śiva to the west and of Brahmā in the middle. These are the principal gods (*deva-mukhyāḥ*).[197] It is said that in the Puṣkaradvīpa Brahmā wields the daṇḍa with Śiva and Viṣṇu[198] and in the śrāddha chapters we find a recommendation that the Brahmin worshippers of Viṣṇu, Śiva and Brahmā should be invited on that occasion.[199]

---

185. Cf. 48. 40 ; also 97. 16 ; 97. 74. 186. Cf. 58 85. 187. Cf. 98. 71.
188. *Viṣṇuparāyaṇāḥ* : Cf. 99. 105-7. 189. Gha and Ṅa omit this.
190. It occurs only in Kha. 191 Cf 97. 1-2. 192 Cf 5. 38-42.
193. Cf. *Nārāyaṇaḥ......tridhā vibhajya svātmānaṁ......sṛjate grasate caiva vīkṣate ca tribhis tu yat* : 5. 38-9.
194. Cf. *ata ūrdhvaṁ brahmaṇaś ca viṣṇoś caiva bhavasya ca ekatvaṁ ca pṛthaktvaṁ ca......kīrtyate* : 1. 132.
195. Cf. 5. 15-6. 196. Cf. 54. 68-76 ; 54. 98 etc. 197. Cf. 41. 63.
198. Cf. 49. 140. 199. Cf. 82, 57-9. Gha omits this.

The Cult of the Sun-god : In the description of the Vāyupura there appears an allusion to the setting up of (an image of ?) Vāḍāditya by the god Vāyu. This Vāḍāditya is none else but the Sun-god or Sūrya. The people of the place were called Vāḍavas whose customs, it is stated, were many and varied.[200] Yājñavalkya and his pupils had become inflicted with the sin of *Brahma-hatyā*. On the advice of Brahmā they worshipped the god Vālukeśvara of twelve beams (*dvādaśārka*, i.e. the Sun-god) in the city of Vāyupura and had their baths in the tanks at that place and were thus rid of their sins. Then they adored Vāḍava, the lord of the north, and merged themselves into the world of Sūrya (*Sūrya-maṇḍalam*).[201] Of Yājñavalkya it is again stated that he returned what he had learnt about the Vedas to his teacher and concentrated his mind on the Sun-god. As a result of these efforts the god, in the form of a horse, gave a new *saṁhitā* to Yājñavalkya. This saṁhitā is known by the name Vājasaneya. The name of this Yājñavalkya was probably Brahmarāti.[202] The Rākṣasas named Yātudhānas—who were ten in number—were the followers of Sūrya and wandered with the deity.[203] Bhauvana who appears to be a Daitya, offered a prayer to the Sun-god with the *Rathantara sāman* and was immediately turned into an elephant.[204] In the Kiṁśuka forest, the Siddhas pay homage to *Āditya*[205] and we have already had a reference to the story of how Sūrya in the guise of a Brahmin begged of the king Kārtavīrya Arjuna the whole earth for alms. Śakrajit[206] was a friend (i.e. a devotee ?) of the Sun-god[207] who, as a token of his friendship (or devotion ?), presented a jewel to the former called *Syamantaka* which involved Vāsudeva Kṛṣṇa in many incidents.[208]

Buddhism and Jainism : In the genealogical narration of the Ikṣvākus, Śākya is mentioned as a son of Saṁjaya. His son was Śuddhodana.[209] The Vairājas are said to have achieved *ānanda-brahman* and become 'awakened'.[210] Of the conditions obtaining in the Kali age we are told that there is neither happiness nor *nirvāṇa* (emancipation).[211] In a prayer to Śiva by Dakṣa the god is addressed as *buddha*.[212]

In connection with the āśrama of the forest-dweller there is a reference to the five vratas and five upavratas. Such is the ten-fold dharma with regard to them as is enjoined by Svayaṁbhu.[113] In con-

200. Cf. No. 1422 App. 201. Cf. No. 1423 App.

202. Ka, Brahmarīti : Cf. 61. 20-2.

203. Cf. *Sūryasya anucarā hyete saha tena bhramanti ca* : 69. 128.

204. Gha omits the name Bhauvana ; Cf. 69. 209-10. 205. Cf. 38. 31-2.

206. Gha : Satrājit. 207. Cf. *Śakrajitaḥ Sūryaḥ sakhā*. 208. Cf. 96. 20 ff.

209. Cf. 99. 288-9. 210. Cf. *buddhāvasthāḥ* : 101. 81-5.

211. Cf. *na sukhaṁ nāpi nirvāṇaṁ tasmin bhavati vai yuge* : 32. 20.

212. Cf. *namaḥ śuddhāya buddhāya* : 30. 216 ; cf. also 97. 172.

213. Cf. *bhikṣor vratāni pañcātra pañcaivopavratāni ca daśa-lakṣano hyeṣa dharmaḥ proktaḥ Svayaṁbhuvā*.

tinuation of the same occurs an explanation of the *Parivraja-dharma*. The stanza which explains this dharma is in a different metre and may probably be a quotation. The dharma enjoins the following things : *dhyāna*, *samādhi*, *bhaikṣya*, *mauna and vimukti*.[214] This was the state of things in the Tretā age.[215] At another place there is a reference that the *bhikṣus* should observe *ahiṁsā*.[216]

A reference to bhikṣus and yatis has already been made in connection with munis. With reference to ś ādha it is enjoined that in the absence of *dhyāni-bhikṣus* (two ?) brahmacarins may be fed on the occasion.[217] This shows that the bhikṣus were more deserving of respect than the brahmacārins. It is not certain whether by these bhikṣus we should understand the monks of either the Buddhist or the Jaina faith. It is more in the fitness of things if we take them to be the *Śaivite yogins*.

The manner in which the *Vṛṣalas*, *Yatis* and *Pāṣaṇḍas* are described in the sketch of the state of things at the end of the Kali age may make us rightly infer that they belonged to some hostile faith such as that of the Jainas or the Buddhists.[218] Condemnatory remarks about the *Nirgranthas* occur in the same context. In connection with the rules regarding śrāddha, the Nagnas (i.e. naked ones) and others are mentioned as taboo and here we find a digression describing the Nagnas. The Nagnas, it is stated, have forsaken the Vedas and follow other ways for their emancipation (mokṣa). They consider the āśramas and the Vedas as useless, and (thus) do not comprehend the ultimate reality. Formerly, there took place a war between gods and demons in which the latter were defeated. (After this ?) the Brahmins, Kṣatriyas, Vaiśyas and Vṛsalas[219] were spoiled by the Pāṣaṇḍas. Here occurs a reference to Nirgranthas, *Karpaṭas*,[220] but the text here is very confusing. These Nagnas do not follow dharma and go by wrong ways.[221] The irreligious *Ājivas*, so called by the Suras, also figure in the Purāṇa in its accounts of the Piśācas,[222] who are said to be haunting the *Caityavṛkṣas*.[223]

---

214. Cf. *Dhyānaṁ samādhir manasendriyāṇāṁ saśāgarṇir bhaikṣyam athopagamya maunaṁ paritropacitair vimuktiḥ parivrajo dharmam idaṁ vadanti*

215. Cf. 8. 184–8. 216. Cf. *bhikṣūṇāṁ ahiṁsā paramārthitā* : 16. 18.

217. Cf. 71. 71–2. 218. Cf. Nos. 955–7, 1480 in App.

219. Gha : *Vṛsabhas* ; Ka reads it differently. 220. According to Ka, *Śākyas*.

221. Cf. 78. 24–33. 222. For details, see No. 15 App. 223. Cf. 69. 284.

CHAPTER V

YUGAS AND THE SYSTEM OF CHRONOLOGY

I. KALPAS

Of Kalpas in General : The first chapter dealing with the summary of contents provides for the narration of Kalpas.[1] Immediately after enumerating the five characteristics of a Purāṇa, the Sūta refers to Kalpa, that being involved in the topic of immediate narration.[2] A *Kalpa* is so called because Brahmā ordained it.[3] The sages request the god Vāyu to unfold to them the wonder and mystery about the Kalpas.[4]

Kalpa closely Connected with Cosmology : In the beginning of each Kalpa Viśvakarmā fashions the earth with its seas, mountains and islands.[5] In every Kalpa lord Mahādeva creates the universe.[6] When a Kalpa comes to a close, the time for the great fire, which causes the periodical destruction, arrives.[7] Creation and destruction of former Kalpas are occasionally mentioned.[8] Brahmā assumed different forms to lift up the earth from out of the waters "as in the former Kalpas".[9]

Duration of a Kalpa : The Kalpa immediately preceding the present Kalpa passed away at the end of a thousand *caturyugas* together with its days and *manvantaras*.[10] A half Kalpa is said to cover a period of 2862 *koṭis* and 70 *niyutas* (of years ?).[11] Other calculations are also given but they are complicated ; and again it is not necessary to work them out here.[12] There is, however, a statement that a thousand Kalpas make a year of Brahmā and that one thousand such years make his Yuga.[13]

Number and Names of Kalpas : The following Kalpas are mentioned in their order : Bhava, Bhuva, Tapas, Bhava (?), Rambha, Ṛtukalpa, Kratu, Vahni, Havyavāhana, Sāvitra, Bhuva (?), Uśika, Kuśika, Gandharva, Ṛsabha, Ṣaḍja,[14] Mārjālīya, Madhyama, Vairājaka, Niṣāda, Pañcama, Meghavāhana, Cintaka, Ākūti, Vijñāti, Manas, Bhāva and Bṛhat.[15] But in the next chapter[16] the list is further continued : Śvetalohita, Rakta. Pītavāsas,[17] Sita and Viśvarūpa. Thus the list includes 3. Kalpas. The Vāraha Kalpa, which is often mentioned elsewhere,[18] is not included in the above list. Again Padmakalpa is mentioned as the seventh Kalpa but that too is not found in the list. There is one statement which mentions the number of Kalpas as being ten.[19]

---

1. Cf. 1. 53-5 ; 1. 62 ; 1. 65 ; 1. 168. 2. Cf 4. 10-13.
3. Cf. *Kalpayāmāsa vai Brahmā tasmāt kalpo nirucyate* ; Gha has *Kāla* for *Kalpa* : 7. 77. 4. Cf. 22. 1. 5. Cf. 6. 33. 6. Cf. 7. 78. 7. Cf. 7. 15.
8. Cf. 6. 35 ; 7. 68-9 etc. 9. Cf. 8. 6 ; 6. 8-9. 10. Cf. 7. 14.
11. Cf. 21. 13-4. 12. Cf. 21. 15 ff. 13. Cf 22 4-5.
14. ha Ga and Ṅa : *Saḍga*. 15. Cf. 21 26 ff. 16. Cf. 22. 9 ff.
17. Kha, Ga, Gha and Ṅa : *Pītavāsa*. 18. Cf. 7. 5 ; 5. 49-50 ; 21. 11-2.
19. Cf. 7. 30.

II. Manvantaras

Of Manvantaras in General : The first chapter mentions the Manvantaras as a topic for narration in the Purāṇas.[20] In fact, description of Manvantaras is one of the five characteristics of a Purāṇa as such.[21] Every Manvantara has a Manu who is its lord[22] and it appears that a particular Manvantara bears the same name as that of the Manu who presides over it. Thus, in the Vaivasvata Manvantara, Vaivasvata was the "lord of men".[23] Every Manvantara, again, has its own set of Devas[24] and of the seven sages[25] and probably its own Indra also.[26] Viṣṇu too had different names in different Manvantaras.[27]

Duration of a Manvantara : Seventy-one caturyugas make a Manvantara.[28] There are seventy-one *padas* (steps) of Kāla. When it moves to cover one pada there is an end of one Yuga and seventy-one such movements bring the Manvantara to a close.[29]

Number of Manvantaras: The number of Manvantaras is fourteen.[30] There are fourteen Manus (i.e. Manvantaras also) in the Vārāha Kalpa.[31] From the fourteen *Svaras* arose the fourteen Manus who were the lords of the celestial Manvantaras.[32] Seven Manvantaras have passed already and seven more are still to pass.[33] The names of the Manvantaras that have passed are: Svāyaṁbhuva, Svārociṣa, Auttama, Cāriṣṇava,[34] Tāmasa, Cākṣuṣa and Vaivasvata, the last being the current Manvantara.[35] It is to Vaivasvata Manu that the royal genealogies owe their origin.[36] We have also a reference to Sāvarṇa Manu who is the same as Vaivasvata Manu.[37]

Excepting the Vaivasvata, the Svāyaṁbhuva and the Cākṣuṣa Manvantaras have received more attention in the Purāṇa. It was in the Svāyaṁbhuva, the first of the Manvantaras,[38] that the great sages questioned Indra regarding the utility of killing animals in sacrifices.[39] The Sūta narrates what Brahmā said to Manu in regard to the divisions of the Veda in the Dvāpara of the Svāyaṁbhuva Manvantara.[40] The Svāyaṁbhuva Manu had ten grandsons[41] who occupied this whole earth of the seven dvīpas. These ten sons or grandsons are also referred to elsewhere.[42] In the Cākṣuṣa which was the sixth of the Manvantaras immediately preceding the present Manvantara, the gods were called Sādhyas[43] whose leader was Nārāyaṇa.[44] The importance of this

---

20. Cf. 1. 53 ; 1. 120-1. 21. Cf. 4. 10-11. 22. Cf. 26. 30 ; 63. 12-9 ; 73. 49.
23. Cf. 70. 18. 24. Cf. 66. 64-5. 25. Cf. 100. 10 ff. 26. Cf. 64. 6.
27. Cf. 66. 128-35. 28. Cf. 57. 33 ; 10. 12. 29. Cf. 32. 31-2.
30. Cf. 7 17-21 ; 45. 69-70. 31. Cf. 5. 50. 32. Cf. 26. 30.
33. Cf. 100. 10 ff. 34. At one place we have *Raivata* instead : cf. 62. 3.
35. Cf. 66. 128-35 ; 63. 12-9 ; cf. also 85. 2. 36. Cf. 85. 1 ff.
37. Cf. 100. 9 ; 84. 38 ff. 38. Cf. 30. 5 ; 21. 22-3 ; 63. 12-9 ; 66. 128.
39. Cf. 57. 119. 40. Cf. 60. 1-2. 41. According to Gha : sons : Cf. 33. 4.
42. Cf. 31. 17-8. 43. Cf. 66. 8-10. 44. Cf. 70. 6 ; 66. 133-4 ; 70. 1.

Manvantara is brought out by the fact that the story of Pṛthu is narrated with reference to this Manvantara.[45] In the same context it is stated that in the Cākṣuṣa and in the Manvantaras preceding it, the earth was uneven[46] and there were no cities and villages; neither did agriculture, trade, pasture and cattle-breeding exist then. But all these things had their place in the Vaivasvata Manvantara from the time of Vainya.[47] This amounts to a suggestion that the reign of Vainya formed an interregnum between the Cākṣuṣa and the Vaivasvata Manvantaras.

One chapter[48] is entirely devoted to the description of the Vaivasvata Manvantara and the *vaṁśa* portion[49] of the Purāṇa begins with the story of Vaivasvata Manu.

III. The Yuga System of Chronology

Of Yugas in General: As in the case of Kalpas and Manvantaras, we find narration of Yugas also provided for in the first chapter of contents[50] The connection between Manvantaras and Yugas in point of calculations has already been noted above in connection with the duration of a Manvantara.

The concept of time is closely connected with Yugas—a fact which is significant in itself. Kāla appears as a deity identified with Śiva[51] Its four faces are the four Yugas.[52] The Yuga is the soul of time[53] and Kāla is known through the Yuga.[54] We have not found such explanations in connection with either the Kalpas or the Manvantaras.

The Yugas are again associated with the concept of dharma, as will be obvious from the description of the four Yugas below. When the Yuga-dharma is not followed god Viṣṇu appears on the earth in the form of an incarnation to put matters aright in point of dharma.[55] He acts according to the ways appropriate to Yugas.[56] Similarly, when the future incarnations of Śiva are mentioned, we find the corresponding Yugas too mentioned. There are six facts about the Yuga of which Yuga-dharma is one.[57]

Methods of Computation of a Yuga: The learned say that a *yuga* is comprised of five years.[58] The year (*saṁvatsara*) again is said to be five-souled (*pañcadhātmā*) but another view of Madhvādīnṛtapa (i.e. ?) that it is six-fold (*ṣaṭka*) is also quoted. This may probably refer to the number of seasons as it appears from the immediate reference to

---

45. Cf. 62. 88 ff. 46. Cf *viṣamā āsīd vasuṁdharā.* 47. Cf. 62. 170-4.
48. Chapter 64. 49. Chapters 85-99. 50 Cf. 1 109-13.
51. Cf. *uvāca devo bhagavān svayaṁ kālaḥ.* 52. Cf. 32 12-4.
53. Cf. *yugābhimānī kālātmā* : 3:. 5:. 54. Cf. *Kālas tu yuga saṁjñitaḥ* : 32. 6.
55. Cf. *yuga-dharme parāvṛtte kāle ca śithile prabhuḥ kartuṁ dharma-vyavasthānaṁ jāyate mānuṣeṣu iha* : 97. 65-6.
56. Cf. *yugānurūpaṁ yaḥ kṛtvā* : 97. 30. 57. Cf. 57. 3-4.
58. Cf. *iti etat pañcavarṣaṁ hi yugaṁ proktaṁ manīṣibhiḥ* 31. 49.

ṛtus (seasons).[59] A reference to five divisions of Kāla[60] is also made elsewhere and here Kāla appears to mean Yuga. These five divisions are : (1) Saṃvatsara, (2) Parivatsara, (3) Idvatsara, (4) Anuvatsara and Vatsara.[61]

There are in all six *prakāras* of Yugas, viz., Yuga, Yugabheda, Yugadharma, Yugasaṁdhyaṁśaka, Yugasaṁdhāna and (Yuga-saṁkhyā ?)[62] but they have no bearing on the method of computation of Yuga.

Divisions of Time and the Computation of Yuga : A *nimeṣa* forms the lowest unit in the measurement of time. The time required by a nimeṣa is equal to that taken in (pronouncing ?) the shortest letter (*akṣara*).[63]

15 Nimeṣas = Kāṣṭhā ; 30 Kāṣṭhās = Kalā ; 30 Kalās = Muhūrta ; 30 Muhūrtas = Day and Night.

The further divisions of time upto the year are taken to be understood.

The four Yugas cover a period of 12000 years in the following manner :—

1. Kṛta-yuga —4800 years with Saṁdhyā and Saṁdhyāṁsa.
2. Tretā-yuga —3600 ,, ,, ,,
3. Dvāpara-yuga—2400 ,, ,, ,,
4. Kali-yuga —1200 ,, ,, ,,

Calculations regarding the 'days', 'years', etc., of the Pitṛs, Devas and Saptarṣis are also given but it is unnecessary to give details about them here. There is also a calculation of the 'Krauñca year'.[64]

The divisions of time mentioned elsewhere are as follows :—

(1) Kāṣṭhā, Kalā, Parvan, Muhūrta, Vipakṣa, Pakṣa, etc.[65]

(2) Nimeṣa, Kāṣṭhā, Kalā, half-month, month, etc.[66]

(3) Lava, Kāṣṭhā, Kalā, Muhūrta, day, night, etc.[67]

(4) Nimeṣa, Kalā, Kāṣṭhā, Muhūrta, day and night.[68]

Description of Yugas

The Kṛta-yuga : The people lived without malice towards each other and faced no mutual conflicts. There were no houses for them to reside and they resorted to mountains and sea-shores for shelter. Ever gay, they wandered aimlessly. The animal kingdom did not exist nor

59. Cf. 31. 50. 60. Cf. *pañcānāṁ pravibhaktānāṁ kālāvasthāṁ.*

61. Cf. 31. 26-8 ; and 32. 65 where, however, we find it difficult to make out the exact sense ; cf. also 53. 116.

62. Cf. 57. 3-4.

63. Cf. *nimeṣa-kāla-tulyaṁ hi vidyāl laghvakṣaraṁ ca yat* : 57. 6.

64. Cf. 57. 6 ff.

65. The reference to *saṁvatsara* as "lord of Gaṇita-Yoga" should be noted : Cf. 70. 15.

66. Cf. 30. 233. 67. Cf. 8. 20. 68. Cf. 30. 15 omitted in Ka.

the vegetable world. The time was conducive to fulfilment of all desires and the climate was temperate.[69] The people were ever young[70] and did not observe any sacraments.[71] They were all equal in matters of birth, beauty and of various virtues. Things took shape of their own accord.[72] Virtuous or sinful deeds had no place in this Yuga.[73] The institution of the varṇāśrama, and consequently its saṁkaras, did not exist then.[74]

The Tretā-yuga : The coming of the Tretā age was heralded by a rain-fall and there was luxuriant vegetation.[75] The people became used to clothes and ornaments. Thus were they living happily. But after some period, greed (*lobha*) 'again' overtook them and because of their misdeeds (*apacāra*) the plant world failed to supply their needs. The climate appears to have become extreme and it brought upon them many sufferings. Formerly, people were of nomadic habits[76] and had no fixed dwellings; but now, 'again' they raised structures amidst the mountains and along the rivers. It was in this state of things that villages, towns, cities, etc. had their origin and units of measurement of distance were devised to make a suitable town-planning. It appears that there was again a crisis followed by a rainfall. This meant a rich vegetation which enabled the people to sustain themselves. The four varṇas were born and acted up to their respective functions. But "the same evil" again affected the plant world which consequently was unable to support the people. The hungry (*Kṣudhāviṣṭāḥ*) people approached the Creator who then 'milched' the earth and made the vegetation grow again. Brahmā then regulated the functions of the four varṇas. But 'again' the people became subject to delusion and Brahmā having scrutinized all the details of the problem framed clear-cut distinctions about the functions of the four varṇas. The *āśramas* were then set up.[77]

The origin of kingship in this age and the conception of Viṣṇu being represented in the person of a paramount sovereign have already been described. It was in the Tretā age that the *Daṇḍa-nīti* was promulgated[78] and the one Veda became four-fold.[79] Sacrifice, making of gifts, penance and truth constituted dharma in the Tretā age.[80] Thus, the Institution of Sacrifice originated in this age.[81] In the beginning of the Tretā, the seven sages are said to have promulgated the two-fold dharma, viz., *Śrauta* and *Smārta*.[82]

69. Cf. *nātyartham hi uṣṇa-śītatā*. 70. Cf. *sthira-yauvanāḥ*.

71. Cf. *asaṁskāryaiḥ*. 72. Cf. *abuddhi-pūrvakaṁ vṛttam*.

73. Cf. *apravṛttiḥ kṛta-yuge karmaṇo śubhapāpayoḥ*. 74. Cf. 8. 50 ff.

75. There is here a reference to the period of menstruation but we are unable to make out its significance.

76. Cf. *nikāmacārās te*. 77. Cf. 8. 77 ff.

78. Cf. 57. 82. 79. Cf. 57. 83. 80. Cf. 57. 81. 81. Cf. 57. 89 ff.

82. Cf. 57. 39. 83. Cf. 3. 21.

The Dvāpara-yuga: This Yuga is referred to in the Purāṇa very often in connection with the future incarnations of Śiva. It is said that the 2nd, 3rd, 4th, 5th, 10th, 11th and 15th incarnations of Śiva will be taking place in the 2nd, 3rd, 4th, 5th, 10th, 11th and 15th Dvāparas respectively. In the Dvāparas (*Dvāpareṣu*), the Vyāsas (*Vyāsāḥ*) extol the Vedas and compile them.[83] The Sūta quotes a speech of Brahmā to Manu in the Dvāpara of the Svāyaṁbhuva Manvantara regarding the compilation of the Vedas.[84] The *Śrutarṣis* are said to have arranged the Veda in the Dvāparas again and again.[85] But we also find a statement that though the Vedas were compiled in the Tretā they suffered a change in the Dvāparas.[86] The plural of Dvāpara in the cases cited above should be noted.[87]

The Kali-yuga: Instead of Kali, at some places, Tiṣya is mentioned.[88] Śiva tells the gods that in this fierce age there will be neither happiness nor emancipation and the people will be devoured by Kāla. But he further adds, "When this age arrives, I will be born for the sake of the world and be worshipped. So you need not be afraid".[89] The Sūta explains to his audience how Śiva, forsaking the former Yugas, has avatāras only in the Kali age.[90] But we have already seen that some of the future incarnations of Śiva were to take place in various Dvāpara ages. The 1st, 13th, 14th, 17th, 22nd and 26th incarnations will, however, take place in the Kali age.[91]

It is stated that in this age the Brahmins and the Kṣatriyas will be exterminated for the sake of the twice-born.[92] It is also said that the people of this Yuga have a longevity of only a hundred years.[93]

The conditions obtaining at the end of this Yuga have, however, received more attention in the Purāṇa. In this Yuga, the character of the people is dominated by vices, such as, violence, hatred, falsehood, etc. Dharma is on the decline and famine and pestilence take their toll. The authority of the *Smṛti* is neglected[94] and untimely deaths are common. The people, impious and addicted to bad customs as they are, do not study the Vedas nor do they perform sacrifices. The Kṣatriyas and the Vaiśyas become exterminated gradually and the Śūdras and the low-born (*antya yones tu*) are befriending the Brahmins in matters such as eating, drinking and merry-making'.[95] Society is topsy-turvy, the Śūdras acting as Brahmins and *vice versa*. Kings and

---

84. Ka suggests that the Dvāpara had passed away when the speech was made; cf. 60. 2.

85. Cf. 61. 124. 86. Cf. 57. 47. 87. Cf. also 57. 48, 58. 15.

88. Cf. 24. 1; 58. 30 ff. 89. Cf. 32. 18 ff. 90. Cf. 26. 2-3.

91. Vide. Chapter: Avatāras of Śiva.

92. Omitted in Ka. The exact significance of this statement is not clear. Cf. 32. 42-3. 93. Cf. 59. 4.

94. Cf. *na pramāṇaṁ smṛter asti*. 95. Cf. *śayanāsanabhojanaiḥ*.

thieves exchange their functions and the kings, Śūdras as they are, propagate the faiths of the impious.[96] The women, with no virtues or vows to bother, will turn out to be drunkards. Beasts will wax strong in number while the number of the cows will go diminishing. The earth is barren of vegetation. The Śūdras "will be" practising penance and the kings, instead of protecting the people, "will" bother only about their own protection. Everywhere, Śūdras are respected[97] and in this Kali-yuga there "will be" many yatis with the impious and useless *Pāṣaṇḍas*[98] multiplying fast. There will be more women than men. The Cūlikas "will be" stealing away the valuable property of others and will indulge in all kinds of vices. The Kauśikas will be deserting their countries being affected by famine. Alas ![99] nowhere are the Vedas seen nor the sacrifices performed. The Nirgranthas, the Kāpālins, the dealers in the Vedas and tīrthas and the Pāṣaṇḍas who have spoiled the varṇāśrama order will dominate the picture. The Vedas are not studied nor the *aśvamedha* performed by kings while the murder of women and cows becomes a common occurrence. While this is the state of things, there *was* born Pramiti, of Candramas gotra—an incarnation (*aṁśa*) of god Mādhava in the Svāyaṁbhuva Manvantara—who proceeded to bring about the destruction of the Bhṛgus.[100] He raised an army of armed Brahmins and commenced annihilating the various peoples such as the Mlecchas, Vṛṣalas, etc. After achieving this, he gave up his life at the confluence (?) of the rivers Gaṅgā and Yamunā. This is then followed by anarchy and social disorders and after some period the Kṛta age dawned.[101]

In the description of the tenth avatāra—i.e. Kalki—of Viṣṇu, we find a similar state of things sketched briefly. Kalki too will bring about the annihilation of the various peoples, such as, the Mlecchas and others,[102] and will end his life in the same manner as Pramiti did. After him again there will be anarchy and disruption and the Kṛta age will dawn.[103]

The same state of things is described a third time in the form of an epilogue to the genealogical lists.[104]

The fire that is said to work destruction at the end of a Yuga is a subject for simile to express fierceness.[105] The heat and light of the sun at the end of a Yuga is equally used metaphorically.[106] Śiva says to

---

96. Cf. *Pāṣaṇḍānāṁ pravartakāḥ.*
97. Cf *Śūdrābhivādinas sarve.*
98. Cf. *vṛthārūpaiḥ pāṣaṇḍaiḥ.*
99. Cf. *dṛśyante na ca dṛśyante.*
100. Cf. *Bhṛgūṇāṁ nidhanotthitaḥ.* This abrupt reference to Bhṛgus appears strange in the context.
101. In the whole of the above description confusion of tenses should be noted.
102. Cf. No. 842 of App. for details.
103. Cf 98. 103 ff.
104. For details see No. 844 App.
105. Cf. 30. 128; 94. 37 etc.
106. Cf. 54. 85–6; 54. 58 etc.

Viṣṇu that in the decline of the Yuga, excepting both of them, people have no other resort.[107] When the end of a Yuga draws near Śiva devours all the *bhūtas* (i.e. creatures).[108]

Yugas in Relation to Events and Personalities .

A. Kṛta-yuga

(1) King Bāhu, the father of Sagara, was deprived of his kingdom by the Haihayas, etc.,[109] in the *dharmya Satya-yuga.*[110] It is not certain whether we should take this *Satya* or *Dharma yuga* as meaning Kṛta-yuga.[111]

(2) Jāmadagnya Rāma annihilated the Kṣatriyas in the Kṛta-yuga.[112]

B. Tretā-yuga

(1) In the *ādya* (i.e. first ?) Tretā age of the Vaivasvata Manvantara, Bhṛgu and the other sages were born.[113]

(2) The 3rd, 4th, 5th, 6th and 7th avatāras of Viṣṇu took place in the 7th, 10th, 15th, 19th and 24th Tretā-yugas respectively.[114]

(3) King Karandhama, a descendant of Nābhāga, flourished in the beginning of the Tretā age.[115]

(4) Tṛṇabindu, a descendant of Karandhama—13 generations removed from him—also flourished in the beginning of the third Tretā age.[116]

(5) In the beginning of the third Tretā age king Tṛṇabindu (the same king as above ?) had a beautiful daughter who was married to the sage Pulastya.[117]

(6) Rāma killed Rāvaṇa in the 24th Tretā age.[118]

(7) King Purūravas flourished in the Tretā age.[119]

C. Dvāpara-yuga

(1) The 8th and 9th avatāras of Viṣṇu took place in the 28th Dvāpara age.

(2) It is said that in the 28th Dvāpara, Acchodā, an Apsaras, was born as a daughter of a fisherman. Her name was Satyavatī. She gave birth, through her cohabitation with Parāśara, to the great sage (Vyāsa) who arranged the Vedas.[120]

(3) In the second Dvāpara, king Dīrghatapas practised penance and pleased Dhanvantari who was then born as a son of the king.[121]

---

107. Cf. 25. 23. 108. Cf. 30. 74. 109. Cf. No. 345 App.

110. Kha, Ga, Gha and Ṅa read *dharme sati yuge* which probably means *dharma-yuga.* The expression, it appears, is incorrect Sanskrit.

111. Cf. 88. 123. 112. Cf. 99. 449. 113. Cf. 30. 76.

114. Gha omits the information regarding the 5th and the 6th incarnations.

115. Cf. *Tretā-yuga-mukhe bhavet* 86. 3-7

116. Cf. *Tretā-yuga-mukhe rājā tṛtīye sambabhūva ha* : 86. 15.

117. 70. 31. 118. 70. 48. 119. 91. 48. 120. 73. 16 ff. 121. 92. 17-22.

D. Kali-yuga

(1) The tenth avatāra of Viṣṇu will take place at the end of the Kali age.

(2) It appears that the destruction of the city of Vārāṇasī, at the hands of Gaṇeśa Kṣemaka, took place in the Kali age.[122] King Divodāsa was ruling at that time.[123]

(3) Kali-yuga commenced on the very day when Kṛṣṇa died.[124]

(4) The experts on ancient tradition say that at the time of king Kṣemaka, the last of the Paurava line, the Kali age will begin.[125]

(5) The knowers of the future cite a stanza that the Kali age will commence from the time of Sumitra, the last king of the Ikṣvākus.[126]

The following stanza is cited regarding the terminating point between the Kali and the next Kṛta-yuga :

yadā candraś ca sūryaś ca tathā tiṣya-bṛhaspatī
eka-rātre bhaviṣyanti tadā kṛta-yugaṁ bhavet.[127]

Schematic References to Yugas : Brahmā is adored in the Kṛta, Sacrifice in the Tretā, Viṣṇu in the Dvāpara and Śiva in all the ages.[128] The Vedas are revered in the Kṛta, the Suras in the Tretā, wars in the Dvāpara and Pāṣaṇḍas in the Kali.[129] The four Yugas are the four pādas of Viṣṇu in his Vārāha form.[130] The Kṛta is associated with Brahmins, the Tretā with Kṣatriyas, the Dvāpara with Vaiśyas and the Kali with Śūdras.[131] Dhyāna in Kṛta, Jñāna in Tretā, Yajña in Dvāpara and Dāna in Kali are the best things.[132] There is also a gradual morphological deterioration in men and animals in the different yugas.[133] Happiness, life, strength, beauty, dharma, artha, and kāma—all these suffer in degrees in the different Yugas.[134] In the Kṛta age dharma did not exist ; it was promulgated in the Tretā and was on the decline[135] in Dvāpara and finally destroyed in the Kali.[136] In the Tretā dharma is 'yearly', in the Dvāpara 'monthly' and in the Kali 'daily'.[137]

---

122. 92. 60. 123. Cf. No. 1403 App. 124. 99 428. 125. Cf. 99. 279.
126. Cf. 99 292. 127. For *rātre* Kha has *rāśau* ; cf. 99. 413.
128. Cf. 32. 21. 129. Cf. 78. 37. 130. Cf. 23. 105. 131. Cf. 78. 36.
132. Cf. 8. 65. 133. Cf. 59. 5 ff. 134. Cf. 58. 111–3.
135. Cf. *vyākulī-bhūtvā*. 136. Cf. 58. 5. 137. Cf. 58. 72.

CHAPTER VI

TOWNS, VILLAGES AND DWELLINGS

I. TOWNS AND VILLAGES

The Origin of the Communal Settlements : In the Cākṣuṣa and: in the Manvantaras preceding it, the face of the earth was uneven and there were neither cities nor villages. It was in the Vaivasvata Manvantara that they had their origin. In the Kṛta age, too, people probably had no communal settlements, such as villages or hamlets. In the Tretāyuga, however, there was a climatic crisis. The climate became extreme which brought many sufferings upon the people. Formerly the people were of nomadic habits and had no fixed dwellings[1] but now, due to the change in climate, they felt the necessity of resorting to some sort of shelter.[2] They raised artificial structures amidst hills and dales, in the wilds and lowlands and along the river-banks, according to their requirements and tastes.[3] Such is the origin of the dwellings of men which were primarily meant for protection against heat and cold.[4]

Different Terms used for Communal Settlements : Durga, i.e., Fort : A fort or *durga* is perhaps surrounded by a ditch, always filled with water.[5] There are four kinds of durgas. The first three kinds of durgas, names of which are not mentioned, are protected by hills and ditches.[6] The fourth kind of durga is called the *Kṛtrima*, i.e., artificial. It is distinguished by a rampart that runs round it. It has only one gate known as the *svastika* and has a *Kumārīpura* in it.[7] The ditch in front of the gate is about 8 × 10 *hastas* deep and wide (according to some 8 × 9 hastas[8]). River-fort (*nadī-durga*) is also mentioned.

Puras, Kheṭas, and Grāmas, etc. : A *nagara* or *pura* covers an area of a yojana, a *kheṭa*, of half a yojana and a *grāma*, of one-fourth yojana. (?)[9] Thus these terms are probably equivalent to the modern terms such as city, town and village. King Purūravas is said to have passed by *Kūlas*, kheṭas, *kharvaṭas*, *Vāṭīs* and Nagaras in the search of his beloved Urvaśī.[10] King Kārtavīrya Arjuna shot arrows which set fire to

---

1. Cf *pūrvaṁ nikāmacārās te aniketāśrayā bhṛśam.* 2. Cf. *cakrur āvaraṇāni ca.*

3. Cf. *yathā-yogyaṁ yathā-prīti niketeṣv avasan punaḥ marudhanvasu nimneṣu parvateṣu nadīṣu ca.*

4. Cf. *ārabdhās te niketān vai kartuṁ śītoṣṇa-vāraṇam.* Note the omission of reference to rainfall : 8. 95-100.

5. Cf. *saṁśrayanti ca durgāṇi dhanvānaṁ śāśvatodakam* : 8. 98.

6. Cf. *trividhānāṁ ca durgāṇaṁ p.rvatodaka-bandhanam* : 8. 111.

7. What this *Kumārīpura* signifies it is difficult to say.

8. This rendering is liable to be doubtful ; cf. *srotasīsaṁhatadvāraṁ nikhātaṁ punar eva ca hastāṣṭau ca daśa śreṣṭhā navāṣṭau vā' pare matāḥ* : 8. 110.

9. Cf. 9. 116-7. 10. Cf. 91. 29-30 Kha omits this.

puras, *ghoṣas*, grāmas and *pattanas*.[11] Gift of grāmas or villages to Brahmins in śrāddha and in the aśvamedha of Janaka has already been referred to

Town-planning and Units of Measurement of Distance: Before proceeding to explain the plans of the various kinds of towns or villages in the Tretā age, we have, in the Purāṇa, a brief information on the various units of measurements of distances. They are: Aṅgula, Hasta, Kiṣku, Dhanus,[12] Prādeśa, Tāla, Gokarṇa, Vitasti, Ratni,[13] Gavyūti and Yojana. The following table gives some idea about their relations to each other:[14]

8 Aṅgulas = Prādeśa (?);	12 Aṅgulas = Vitasti;
21 Aṅgulas = Ratni;	2 Ratnis or 42 Aṅgulas = Kiṣku;
24 Aṅgulas = Hasta;	4 Hastas = Dhanus;
2000 Dhanus = Gavyūti;	8000 Dhanus = Yojana.

It is not clear whether *Nālikā-yuga*[15] was also a unit.

Elsewhere the following appear as the units of measurement of distance:

Mahāsthūla,[16] Bhūtādi-Sthūla, Paramāṇu,[17] Trasareṇu (or Padmarajas), Rathareṇu,[18] Balāgra,[19] Likṣā, Yūkā, Yava, Aṅgula, Vitasti, Ratni, Hasta, Kiṣku, Dhanus, Daṇḍa, Yuga, Nālī, Gavyūti, Nalva, Yojana and Krośa.

The table is as follows:

10 Mahāsthūlas = Bhūtādisthūla;	10 Bhūtādisthūlas = Paramāṇu.
8 Paramāṇus = Trasareṇu;	8 Trasareṇus = Rathareṇu.
8 Rathareṇus = Balāgra;	8 Balāgras = Likṣā.
8 Likṣās = Yūkā;	8 Yūkās = Yava.
8 Yavas = Aṅguli.	

The table following Aṅgula agrees with the one given above but the following additional details are to be noted: Dhanus, Daṇḍa, Yuga and Nālī are equal.

300 Dhanus = Nalva.
1000 Yojanas = Śakra-Krośa (i.e. Krośa of Indra).

It should be noted that in this connection we find a reference to experts on the knowledge of Saṁkhyā.[20] Reference to Yojanas is very common in the geographical chapters of the Purāṇa.

---

11. Cf. 94. 40; cf. also 95. 9–10.
12. The last three are omitted in Ka. 13. From *Prādeśa* to *Ratni* omitted in Gha.
14. Cf. 8. 100–7. 15. 8. 106. 16 The shortest visible distance.
17. The shortest particle of dust visible in the sun-beam.
18. The particle of dust caused by the movement of a chariot.
19. Kha, Gha and Ṅa: *Bālāgra*.
20 Cf. *Saṁkhyājñāna-viśāradaiḥ*: 101. 115–198.

TOWN-PLANNING

Site for the Town and Village : Every communal settlement should be situated near mountains and water-sheds.[21] The case of the artificial durga was probably an exception.

Cities situated on the "tops of hills" or at "the foot of mountains" are often mentioned in the geographical chapters.[22] Most of these cities belonged to the Daityas, Dānavas, Gandharvas, Vidyādharas, etc. The city of Laṅkā was situated on the Trikūṭa mountain and was inaccessible.[23] Cities or tīrthas situated on the banks of rivers are also mentioned. There is again an allusion to a river-fort (*nadī-durga*) in a prayer by Dakṣa to Śiva.[24]

We have also a reference to the city of Guha which was situated in a cave on the Viśākha mountain.[25]

It is not clear whether the plan of a town or village is to be triangular in shape.[26] A city (*nagara*) is probably required to be 1 × 1 yojana in its area, a town (*kheṭa*) covering half its area and a village (*grāma*) half the area of the town.[27]

But in the case of the cities of the geogrphical chapters, we find references to their area being more or less fanciful. For example, the spacious city of Laṅkā was 100 × 30 yojanas in extent.[28] The cities of Gandharvas on the Kailāsa occupied 1000 × 30 yojanas of area.[29]

Of Village Boundaries : The boundary (of a village or town) should extend to two Krośas around it and the boundaries of the fields in this area should be four dhanus.[30]

Village Roads and Streets in the Town : The roads leading to various directions from a village or town should be twenty dhanus wide and the road across the boundary-line should be ten dhanus wide.[31] The street leading to the king's palace (i. e., *rājapathaḥ*) should be ten dhanus wide and it should provide easy passage for men, horses, chariots and elephants.[32] The other streets should be four dhanus wide. The lanes and bylanes (*uparathyāḥ and uparathyakāḥ*) and the paths joining the buildings with the streets (?) (*gṛha-rathyāḥ*) should also be four dhanus wide.[33] There is a reference to *Ghaṇṭā-patha* which probably refers to a village high-way or a main road passing through a

---

21. Cf. *Kheṭānāṁ nagarāṇāṁ ca grāmāṇāṁ caiva sarvaśaḥ trividhānāṁ ca durgāṇāṁ parvatodaka-bandhanam* : 8. 111.

22. Cf. Nos. 229, 437, 469, 727, 826, 905, 935, 1048, 1085, 1285, 1302, 1323, etc. App.

23. Cf. No. 437 App. 24. Cf. 30. 278. 25. Cf. 39. 55.

26. Cf. *chinna-karṇaṁ vikarṇaṁ tu vyañjanaṁ Kṛta-saṁsthitam* : 8. 115.

27. Cf. 8. 116–7. 28. No. 437 App. 29. No. 469 App.

30. Cf. *dvikrośaṁ paramā sīmā kṣetra-sīmā catur-dhanuḥ* : 8. 117.

31. Cf. *viṁśad-dhanur grāma-mārgaḥ sīmā-mārgo daśa eva tu* : 8. 118.

32. Cf. *nṛvāji-ratha-nāgānām asambādhaḥ susaṁcaraḥ* : 8. 119. 33. Cf. 8. 120.

village.[34] It should be four pādas wide being separated from the buildings by three pādas.[35] The *vṛtti-mārgas* should be one half pāda wide and the *prāg-vaṁśa* one pāda.[36]

Elsewhere we find it stated that a yogin ought not to perform *dhyānas* (i. e. feats of concentration) at the *catuṣpathas* (i. e. where four roads meet).[37] The god Śiva, however, is addressed as having a fascination for catuṣpatha and is also called *rathya*, *virathya*.[38] In connection with the Piśācas we are told that they haunt the *rāja-mārgas*, *uparathyas*, etc.[39] The cities of Rākṣasas, Daityas, etc., are said to have hundreds of *pratolīs* (i. e. broad-ways or main roads).[40] The city of Kālakeya Asuras on the Devakūṭa mountain had broad streets.[41]

City-gates and Ramparts : The svastika-gate of the artificial kind of durga has been described above. The main-gate of a town or city should be, it is stated, 800 *kiṣkus*.[42] The city of Dvāravatī had many gates.[43] That there was some reverence or awe inspired by a gate of a city appears from the story of the destruction of the city of Vārāṇasī.[44]

The cities of Kinnaras situated on the Mahānīla mountain are said to have had *bila-praveśas*.[45] The city of the Daityas on the southern side of the Niṣadha mountain had a cave entrance.[46] Gates and ramparts are often mentioned in connection with the description of the cities of the Daityas, Asuras, Gandharvas, etc. The city of Vidyādharas had *mahāprākāra-toraṇa*, a big gate and a wide rampart[47] and such was also the case with the city of the Saiṁhikeya Daityas.[48] The city of Laṅkā had 'golden' gates and ramparts[49] that being also the feature of the city of the Autkaca Rākṣasas.[50] It should be noted that most of these cities were supposed to have been situated in the midst of hills (or on the hills) and are described to be "difficult of access". Thus they were taken to be well protected because of their natural situation as well as of the construction of their enclosures. Ditches around the durga have been already noted above. They probably ran along the

---

34. The name is probably derived from its being frequented by elephants end cattle, adorned with tinkling ornaments such as bells, etc.

35. Cf. *ghaṇṭā-pathaś catuṣ-pādas tripādaṁ ca gṛhāntaram.* The three pādas may also refer to the distance between two buildings : 8. 121.

36. We are unable to bring out the exact significance of the information about the last two : cf. 8. 121.

37. Cf. 11. 33–4.

38. Cf. name *rathya-virathyāya catuṣpatha-ratāya ca.* Ṅa : *catuṣpatharathyāya* ; and Ga : *catuṣpatharathāya* : 30. 220.

39. Cf. *rāja-mārgoparathyāś ca......Piśācā viniviṣṭā vai sthāneṣv eteṣu sarvaśaḥ* : 69. 283.

40. Cf. 41. 50–4 and Nos. in App. quoted above for references in the text.

41. Cf. *viśālarathyaṁ* : 40. 11–5.

42. Cf. *atha kiṣku-śatāni aṣṭau prāhur mukhyaṁ niveśanam* : 8. 116.

43. *Bahu-dvārā* ; cf. 86. 26–1.

44. No. 1403 App.

45. Cf. 39. 34.

46. *Guhāpraveśa* : cf. 41. 55.

47. Cf. 39. 60.

48. Cf. 40. 9–11.

49. *Hema-prākāra-toraṇā* : cf. 48. 27–9.

50. Cf. 40. 16–7.

rampart with a large opening in front of the main gate. Nine durgas are said to have protected the *kṣetra* (circuit) of the Vāyu-pura.[51]

Drainage and Gutters : In connection with the planning of a town we are told that the *āvaskara* (i. e. gutters ?) and *parīvāha*[52] should be one pāda wide.[53]

Buildings, Parks, Gardens, etc. : Tall buildings lined in rows in the cities of Daityas, etc. are often mentioned. The city of Laṅkā was *harmya-prāsāda-mālinī*.[54] The seven cities of Gandharvas were graced with lines of spacious mansions,[55] the same being the description of the city of the Saiṁhikeyas.[56] The mansion in the city of Kālakeya Asuras almost pierced the clouds.[57]

In the same cities we occasionally find references to the existence of gardens. The city of Ulaṅghin, a Rākṣasa, had many gardens,[58] similar being the description of the city of the Saiṁhikeya Daityas.[59]

There is only one instance of a *dharma-śālā* (resting house or a charitable institution) in the Vāyupura which was a holy place.[60]

Regarding the Composition of the Population : From the description of the population of Vāyupura[61] we learn that it consisted of 18000 twice-borns and 36000 Śūdras.

II. Houses and Dwellings

Origin of a Fixed Dwelling : While explaining the word *śālā* (building) an attempt is made to connect its origin with the tree and its overspreading branches which, in former times, offered shelter and protection to men.[62] This may probably make us infer that the early dwelling was merely a hut for the construction of which branches of trees (primarily of *śāla* trees ?) were used. The emphasis on this point of connection between the śālā and the śākhās is interesting.

Cave-dwellings : Śiva is associated with habitation in a cave. He is called *guhā-priya*[63] and *guhāvāsin*.[64] Dakṣa, in his prayer to Śiva', offers salutations to those who dwell in caves.[65] Śiva says to Brahmā about his 28th incarnation as Nakulin that he will then be born with Viṣṇu in a cave of the Meru mountain.[66] The same god is called *sa-guha* (i. e. " with a cave " ?).[67]

---

51. Cf. 59. 123 omitted in Ka, Ga and Ṅa. 52. Kha, Ga, Ṅa : *parivāra*.
53. Cf. 8. 122. 54. Cf. 48. 27–9. 55. Cf. 40. 6–7. 56. Cf. 40. 9–11.
57. Cf. 40. 11–5. 58. Cf. 41. 54. 59. Cf. 40. 9–11. 60. Cf. 59. 126–7.
61. Cf. No. 1422 App.
62. *Te pūrvam āsan vai vṛkṣās tu gṛhasaṁsthitāḥ......evaṁ prasiddhāḥ śākhābhyaḥ śālāś caiva gṛhāṇi ca* : 8. 123–6 ; cf. also 8. 89.
63. Cf. 54. 116.
64. Cf. 24. 156. The name of Śiva in his 17th incarnation was *Guhāvāsin*.
65. Cf. 30. 278. 66. Cf. 23. 221 cf. App. No. 814. 67. Cf. 30. 315.

Caves were suitable for those of the last stage (āśrama) of life for purposes of meditation.[68] It is said that in the Kali age Śūdras and Yatins will be *gūḍha-vāsāḥ*.[69] One who goes to the cave of Vāmana is purified of his sin.[70]

The habitation of Ṛkṣarāja Jāmbavat was a huge cave where Kṛṣṇa fought against him for twenty-one days.[71]

Kinds of Dwellings : With the explanation of *śālā*, reference to *prāsāda* also occurs in the same context. Since it pleases the mind it is called *prāsāda*.[72] This is apparently an attempt at etymology. Anyway it suggests that *prāsāda* was regarded as more attractive and imposing in appearance than the śālā and probably it means a palatial building.

References to spacious buildings are noted above. We have an instance of the *bhavana* (mansion) of Yakṣa which measured 80 × 40 yojanas.[73]

Dakṣa, in the course of his prayer to god Śiva, offers salutations to those who are gone to *hastyaśvarathaśālās*, i. e. to stables for elephants, horses and chariots[74] and *goṣṭhas* of cows are also referred to in a simile.[75] A stable which was not used (*jīrṇa-goṣṭha*) was a taboo for a yogin for the purpose of meditation.[76]

It is said that the Piśācas haunt places such as *sūtikāgṛhas* (i. e. maternity homes ?), *śmaśānāyatanas* (i. e. shelters raised in cremation ground) and *śūnyāgāras* (i. e. desolate houses).[77]

Of Construction of Buildings : Viśvakarman was an architect of the gods.[78] He is the presiding deity of architecture (*śilpi-prajāpati*) and is also mentioned as Tvaṣṭṛ. His wife was a daughter of Prahlāda. His son was Maya.[79] He is also mentioned elsewhere in the same capacity as a *śilpi-prajāpati*. He is the founder of the science of architecture of the gods.[80] He is also the maker of their ornaments and *vimānas*.[81] Śiva too is credited with being the originator of the science of architecture, he being the best architect himself.[82] Siddhas are also referred to as builders of the gods' dwellings.[83]

It appears that certain rites were performed when a house was first inhabited or its construction was first undertaken. The Piśācas

68. Cf. 17, 5. 69. Cf. 58. 51.
70. Cf. 77. 82–3. The exact significance of this statement is not clear.
71. Cf. 96. 32–45.
72. Cf. *prasīdati manas tāsu prasādyanti tāḥ* : 8. 127 ; omitted in Ṅa.
73. Cf. 41. 22–3. 74. Cf. 30. 278–9. 75. Cf. 30. 186, 76. Cf. 11. 33–4.
77. Cf. 69. 271 Ka omits reference to the last.
78. *Tridaśānāṁ vāstukṛt*.
79. Cf. *Viśvakarmātmajaś caiva viśvakarmā mayaḥ smṛtaḥ* : 84. 16–20.
80. Cf. *sa kartā sarva-śilpānāṁ tridaśānāṁ ca*. 81. Cf. 66. 28–30.
82. Cf. *śilpīśaḥ śilpināṁ śreṣṭhaḥ sarva-śilpapravartakaḥ* : 30. 253. 83. Cf. 39. 50.

were supposed to haunt houses with regard to which saṁskāras are not observed and which are inhabited without the observation of ācāras.[84]

The mention of following terms in connection with the description of buildings shows that they formed part of their structures :—Sopāna (stair-case), *Śilātala* (pavement ?),[85] *Toraṇa* (gate),[86] *Valabhī* (roof, wooden thatchet), *Kūṭa* (projection), *Nirvyūha* (door, gate or turret),[87] *Gavākṣa* (window).[88] It should be noted that such terms are used only in connection with the description of the cities of Daityas, etc., mentioned above.

Houses appear to have been frequently exposed to dangers from fire. Kṣāma is the name of the fire which sets ablaze the dwellings of men.[89]

---

84. Cf. ......*anācāroṣitāni......saṁskārair varjitāni ca* : 69. 281-2.

85. Cf. 54. 30-1. 86. Cf. 34. 67. 87. Cf. 38. 14-5. 88. Cf. 45. 32-9.

89. Cf. 29. 34.

CHAPTER VII

DRESS AND ORNAMENTS, FOOD AND DRINK

I. Dress and Ornaments

(i) *Dress.*

Nudity : In the narration of the progeny of Kaśyapa we find the Piśācas described as naked (*nagnakāḥ*).[1] Śiva had by Satī thousands of sons who were not used to dress.[2] In prayers to Śiva he is often addressed as being "naked".[3]

Origin of Clothing and its Development : We have no evidence regarding dress in the sketch of the Kṛta age. Like houses and dwellings dress too had its origin in the Tretā age. This was an age of luxuriant vegetation and the trees offered man his requirements of clothes and ornaments.[4]

When we come to the chapters on śrāddha we find clothes as a primary necessity of man. It is stated that without clothes there can be no activity, no sacrifices, no knowledge of the Vedas, nay (not even) penance ; so should clothes be given particularly at the time of śrāddha.[5] We find gift of clothes to Brahmans on the occasion of śrāddha as a highly commendable act.[6]

Materials for Dress : *Leaves of Trees and Bark :* In connection with the origin of dress we have seen above how trees offered man the materials for his clothing. Whether this material consisted mainly of bark or leaves of trees it is difficult to say. The use of both the materials for the purposes of clothing is, however, often indicated. A brahmacārin of the Tretā age was expected to wear clothes of bark and leaves of trees.[7] There is a reference to suggest that this was the dress peculiar to the munis who prepared it themselves. With reference to the conditions at the end of the Kali age it is said that the dress of the people at that time "will be" of bark and leaves of trees and that they "will" prepare it themselves "just as the munis do".[8] When the Asuras commenced practising austerities at the advice of their preceptor, Śukra Kāvya, they used *valkalas ;* and when the Devas

---

1. Cf. 69. 279.

2. Cf. *vivāsān* : Kha, Ga and Na *Viṣāśān* i. e. swallowers of poison ; cf. also 10. 45–6.

3. Cf. *digvāsāya* or *digvastrāya* : 24. 132 ; 24. 129 ; 54. 72 ; 54. 77 ; 97. 192 etc.

4. Cf. *vṛkṣās te gṛha-saṁsthitāḥ vastrāṇi ca prasūyante phalāny ābharaṇāni ca* : 8. 89.

5. Cf. *vastrābhāve kriyā nāsti yajñā Vedās tapāṁsi ca tasmād vastrāṇi deyāni śrāddha-kāle viśeṣataḥ* : 80. 39–40.

6. Cf. 80. 4–6.

7. Cf. *cīrapatrājināni ca* : 8. 183.

8. Cf. *cīraṁ parṇaṁ ca vividhaṁ valkalāny ajināni ca svayaṁ kṛtvā vivatsyanti yathā muni-janās tatha.* Khs, Ga and Ṅa read *muni-janais* for *munijanās* : 99. 405.

attacked them in this condition which made them flee to the shelter of Kāvya's mother, the Asuras pleaded to the latter that the Devas had done an improper thing in attacking them while they were engaged in penance, "with the clothes of bark and leaves on them".[9] This may make us infer that these were not the clothes of the ordinary people. The Piśācas too are mentioned as wearing clothes of bark.[10] In prayers to the god Śiva he is often addressed as wearing these clothes.[11]

It is said that at the end of the Kali age people will be making use of clothes of this kind after the disruption of the society and the state had set in.[12]

Skin-garments : References to skin-garments occur mostly in connection with gods, particularly Śiva and with the Pitṛs. Śiva is called *Kṛttivāsas*.[13] Vīrabhadra is mentioned as *mṛgendra-Kṛtti-vāsas*[14] and as wearing the clothes made of tiger-skin.[15] The sons of Satī, the wife of Śiva, wore skin-garments.[16] *Kṛṣṇājina* is the dress for Brahmā,[17] Śiva[18] and Hari[19] likewise. The Pitṛs, too, love the *Kṛṣṇājina*.[20] It is stated that this will also be the dress of the people at the end of the Kali age.[21]

Use of Cotton, Silk, Wool and Linen : References to clothes and blankets made of these materials appear mostly in connection with gifts to Brahmins in śrāddha. Clothes and blankets made of wool and silk fetch for the giver the merit of the performance of a hundred *vājapeya* sacrifices[23] and to make a gift of garments of linen, silk and cotton is also highly meritorious.[23] The Sūdras and *Cūlikas* at the end of the Kali age "will be" *Kāṣāya-vāsasaḥ*.[24]

Shape of Garments : Expressions such as *nānā-veṣadharāḥ* (i. e. wearing different kinds of garments), *citraveṣa-dharāḥ* or *vicitra-vastrā-dharaṇāḥ* (i. e. using various kinds of garments) are frequently used in the description of the Rākṣasas, Vidyādharas, etc.[25] But they do not make us infer anything. *Prāvaraṇa* (i. e. upper garment) is mentioned in connection with evil forebodings in dreams.[26] *Upavīta* and *ācchādana* are mentioned as good gifts in śrāddha.[27] Śiva is called *Yajñopavītin*.[28] The wife of god Śaṁkara used one garment.[29]

Hair-dressing : The Piśācas are described as *lamba-keśāḥ* (i. e. long-haired).[30] One of the sons of Śiva in his eleventh incarnation had

---

9. Cf. 97. 108-25. 10. Cf. *cīra-vāsasaḥ* : 69. 273.

11. Cf. *cīra-vāsase* : 97. 164 ; cf. *hiraṇyacīra* : 55. 48 ; cf. also *valkalājinadhāriṇe*, *valkalājinavāsase* : 30. 224 ; cf. also 24. 93 etc.

12. Cf. 58. 98 ; 98. 121.

13. Cf. 97. 192 ; 21. 50-1 etc. 14. Cf. 30. 123-4. 15. Cf. 30. 125.

16. Cf. 10. 45-6. 17. Cf. 25. 80 ; 55. 14. 18. Cf. 30. 221.

19. Cf. 25. 34. 20. Cf. 74. 4. 21. Cf. 99. 410.

22. Cf. 80. 34. 23. Cf. 80. 37 ; cf. also 75. 29. 24. Cf. 58. 58-9.

25. Cf. 38. 16-7 ; 70. 62 etc. 26. Cf. 19. 33. 27. Cf. 80. 4-5.

28. Cf. 30. 221. 29. Cf. *eka-vāsasī* ; Ga : *eka vāsasā* : 9. 91.

30. Cf. 69. 279. Ga, Gha and Ṅa have a different reading.

a name Lambakeśaka. The Cūlikas who will flourish at the end of the Kali-yuga are mentioned as *mukta-keśāḥ* (i. e. with hair dishavelled).[31] Śiva too is called '*mukta-keśa*'.[32]

The *jaṭā* of Śiva is, however, a matter for much description and epithets. He is called *eka-jaṭa*,[33] *tri-jaṭin*,[34] *cūḍāla* (i. e. having a top-knot),[35] *jaṭāmālin*,[36] etc. The Kumārakas, who were regarded as the sons of Śiva, too, are described to have jaṭās.[37] The Bhūtas are also *jaṭilāḥ*.[38]

A brahmacārin, in the Tretā age, was also a *jaṭin*.[39] '*Śikhin*', '*Śikhaṇḍin*', '*Śikhā-yukta*' are also epithets of Śiva.[40] The name *Pañca-śikha* of one of the four sons of Śiva in his eighth incarnation is also mentioned. The origin of the name might have some connection with the fashion of five knots of hair. Apsarasas also are called *pañca-cūḍāḥ* (i. e. having five braids of hair ?).[41]

Growth of the Beard : Śiva is called *haricchmaśruḥ* (i. e. wearing grey beard)[42] and the Piśācas are mentioned as *śmaśrulāḥ* (i. e. bearded).[43]

When king Yayāti requested his son Yadu to exchange his youth for his own old age, the latter replied, "I do not wish to become a decrepit old man with a grey beard".[44]

Following are the indignities which king Sagara inflicted upon his enemies before he allowed them their freedom. The Śakas had their heads half-shaved while the Yavanas and Kāmbojas had clean-shaving. The Pāradas were allowed to go with their hair dishavelled and the Palhavas were allowed (only) to retain their beards.[45]

Uṣṇīṣa : References to uṣṇīṣa are often noted in the description of Śiva's appearance. He is called *uṣṇīṣa*,[46] *śvetoṣṇīṣa*,[47] *pītoṣṇīṣa*,[48] *kṛṣṇoṣṇīṣa*,[49] etc. Brahmā too is adorned with *śvetoṣṇīṣa*.[50] The Rākṣasas are mentioned as wearing crowns and uṣṇīṣa.[51]

ORNAMENTS

Of Ornaments in General : General references to ornaments, as in the case of different kinds of garments, are common in the Purāṇa and all such references need not be noted here. For example, Śiva is mentioned as being adorned with various kinds of ornaments.[52]

---

31. Cf. 58. 58-9. 32. Cf. 97. 165. 33. Cf. 55. 51-5. 34. Cf. 30. 189.
35. Cf. 30. 250. 36. Cf. 23. 186-8. 37. Cf. 23. 59. 38. Cf. 69. 245 ff.
39. Cf. 8. 182. 40. Cf. 22. 10 ; 30. 250 ; 97. 162 ff. ; 23. 115 etc.
41. Cf. 69. 49. 42. Cf. 30. 24. 43. Cf. 69. 273.
44. Cf. *sitaśmaśru-dharo dīno jarayā śithilī-kṛtaḥ* : 92. 33.
45. Cf. *ardhaṁ śakānāṁ śiraso muṇḍayitvā vyasarjayat yavanānāṁ śiraḥ sarvaṁ kāmbojānāṁ tathaiva ca pāradā mukta-keśāś ca pahlavā śmaśru-dhāriṇaḥ* : 88. 140-1
46. Cf. 97. 162 ff. 47. Cf. 22. 10. 48. Cf. 23. 2-3 ; 23. 17. 49. Cf. 23. 63-4.
50. Cf. *śvetoṣṇīṣa-bhūṣaṇaḥ* : 24. 52. 51. Cf. *mukuṭoṣṇīṣa-dhāriṇaḥ* : 70. 62.
52. Cf. *nānā-bhūṣaṇabhūṣitaḥ* : 55. 53.

Heavenly ornaments enhanced the beauty of Chāyā, the wife of Puṣṭi.[53] The name of Viśvakarman, the goldsmith of the gods,[54] is already noted above in connection with the construction of buildings.

For the sake of convenience, the references to ornaments together with the relevant details about them are given below in an alphabetical order :—

Akṣamālā	In the seventh Rasātala (i. e. Pātāla) rules king Bali adorned with an akṣamālā.[55]
Aṅgada	It was used as an ornament by the people of the Kuru land,[56] by Śiva[57] and by the Rākṣasas.[58]
Dāman	Vīrabhadra wore a jewelled necklace.[59]
Ghaṇṭā	(It is not certain whether it was an ornament). Śiva is often associated with its use. He loved a garland of bells.[60] He is called *ghaṇṭā-priya*[61] and *ghaṇṭīka*.[62]
Hāra	Used by the people of the Kuru land.[63] The Śūras are called *hārakāḥ*.[64]
Kāñcana-paṭṭa:	Belt made of gold. It was recommended as a gift to a Brahmin in śrāddha.[65]
Keyūra	It was an ornament used by the people of the Kuru land[66] and by Śiva.[67]
Kiṅkiṇī	Its use is associated with Skanda (?)[68] and also with Śiva.[69]
Kirīṭa	Hari or Viṣṇu is called *Kirīṭin*.[70]
Kuṇḍala	Used by the Rākṣasas[71] and by the people of the Kuru country.[72] Bali, lord of Pātāla, is called *Kuṇḍalin*.[73]
Mekhalā	A brahmacārin in the Tretā age was expected to use mekhalā.[74] Śiva is called *muñja-mekhalin* (i. e. having a girdle made of *muñja* grass).[75]
Mukuṭa	Used by the Rākṣasas[76] and by the people of the Kuru country.[77]
Śrīvatsa	Śrīvatsa is called the *lakṣaṇa* (distinguishing ornament ?) of Viṣṇu.[78]

53. Cf. *divyābharaṇa-bhūṣitā* : 62. 83. 54. Cf. *bhūṣaṇānaṁ......kartā.*
55. Cf. 50. 50. 56. Cf. No. 660 App. 57. Cf. 24. 153. 58. Cf. 70. 62.
59. Cf. *muktādāmavibhūṣita* · 30. 127. 60. Cf. *ghaṇṭā-mālā-priyāya* : 30. 209-10.
61. Cf. 24. 159. 62. Cf. 30. 250. 63. Cf. No. 660 App.
64. Cf. 69. 183, 65. Cf. 80. 34. 66. Cf. No. 660 App.
67. Cf. 24, 153. 68. Cf. *kiṅkiṇījāla-mālin* : 41. 38.
69. Cf. 24. 148 ; cf. also 73. 73. 70. Cf. 24. 9 ; 24. 53. 71. 70. 62.
72. Cf. No. 660 App. 73. Cf. 50. 47. 74. Cf. 8, 182. 75. Cf. 24. 56.
76. Cf. 70. 62. 77. Cf. No. 660 App. 78. Cf. 25. 25.

Śroṇī-bandha The kings of Aiḍa-vaṁśa are mentioned as being *Śroṇi-bandhāḥ* (i. e. having girdles round their waist ?:).[79]

Sūtra The neck of Śiva, after he had swallowed the poison, shone as if it was adorned with a golden thread.[80]

Valaya Its use is associated with the people of the Kuru land.[81]

Use of Garlands : Śiva is called *sragvin* (i. e. bearer of garland),[82] the same being the description of the Yakṣas,[83] of the people of the Kuru country[84] and of Puloma, the lord of the Vidyādharas.[85] The Rākṣasas too decorated themselves with garlands.[86] Śiva used the garland of lotus-flowers for his uṣṇīṣa.[87] He is also called *dhava-mālā-dhara* (i. e. decorated with garlands of white flowers).[88] Again he is mentioned as *pañca-mālārcitāṅga* (i. e. having his body decorated with five garlands).[89]

Cosmetics : The expression *mālyānulepana* occurs very frequently in connection with Śiva and the Kumārakas.[90] Śiva used various kinds of ointments.[91] The Rākṣasas too used garlands and ointments of various kinds.[92]

Śiva was fond of applying to his body the ashes from the cremation ground.[93]

Śiva used *gandha* also (for purposes of decoration).[94] Elsewhere he is called *Sugandhin*.[95] *Mālyas*, perfumes, *Gandha*, *dhūpa* and *guggula* were required for use in the performance of the śrāddha ceremony.[96] It was advised, however, that strong perfumes should not be used on the occasion.[97] *Turuṣka* was equally recommended for use in śrāddha.[98]

Reference to *añjana* (i. e. soot or kohl) also occurs. In connection with śrāddha we are informed that *trikakudañjana* is the best.[99] The wives of Mahiṣāsura, whom Kārtikeya annihilated, are also credited with the use of añjana for their eyes.[100]

---

79. Cf. 32. 47. 80. Cf. *hema-sūtra-vibhūṣita* : 24. 154. 81. Cf. No. 660 App.
82. Cf. 24. 120. 83. Cf. 69. 162. 84. Cf. 45. 44–5.
85. Cf. 38. 16-7. 86. Cf. 70. 62. 87. Cf. 24. 155.
88. Cf. 24. 140. Kha, Ga, Gha and Ṅa have *dhana* for *dhava*. 89. Cf. 30. 209.
90. Cf. 22. 10 ; 22. 23–31 ; 23. 2–3 ; 23. 17 ; 23. 26–31 etc. Also 30. 123–4.
91. Cf. *nānā-mālyānulepana* : 55. 51–5. 92. Cf. *citra-sraganulepanāḥ* : 70. 62.
93. Cf. 30. 205 ; cf. also 55. 45–6. 94. Cf. 30. 205.
95. Cf. 24. 120. 96. Cf. 75. 5 ff.
97. Cf. *varjanīyāni......ugra-gandhāni yāni ca* : 75. 35. Ka has *upagandhāni* for *ugragandhāni*. 98. Cf. 75. 32
99. Cf. *śreṣṭham āhus tri-kakudaṁ añjanaṁ nityam eva ca* : 75. 31.
100. Cf. 54. 19.

II. Food and Drink

On Food in General: In the first chapter of contents we find food also included as a topic for narration in the Purāṇa.[101]

That the plant world was considered to be the main source of sustenance of the people in the Tretā age is obvious from its description already given. The story of the Pṛthvī-dohana (i. e. "milching of the earth" by the king Pṛthu) is notable in this connection. In the Cākṣuṣa and in the Manvantaras preceding it, there were no food-grains, no cattle-breeding, etc.[102] But from the time of Vainya onwards, in the Vaivasvata Manvantara, all these came into being for the sake of man. The king Vainya "milched" the Earth in the form of a cow who yielded the milk in the form of food-grains. It is this food that enables the people to sustain themselves.[103] Elsewhere we find the self-born Creator "milching" the earth himself as a starting point for his creation of the plant world.[104] Reference to food being regarded as the best form of gift in śrāddha is already noted and we find here food elevated to the status of Prajāpati himself.[105]

Food-grains: With regard to the origin of the vegetable kingdom we have a reference to *grāmyauṣadhis*. They probably mean cultivated grains and some of them might have been used as food-grains. In the śrāddha chapters we find nine kinds of grains mentioned as being good gifts in śrāddha[106] but they are not enumerated. The Purāṇa has for us a *gāthā* said to have been sung by king Yayāti himself. It refers, amongst other things, to *vrīhi* and *yava* and the context of the reference suggests that they were regarded as food-grains.[107]

The list of food-preparations, given below, suggests that *masūra*, *saktu*, rice (i. e. *vrīhi*), *tila* and *yava* were used as food-grains. As to what food-grains were employed in the food-preparations such as *pūpa*, *piṇyāka*, *karambha* and *kardama* it is difficult to state definitely.

Food Preparations: For the sake of convenience, references to food-preparations together with relevant details have been given below in an alphabetical order:

Guḍakulya[108]	Used in Dakṣa-yajña.[109]
Guḍaudana	Mentioned in connection with Piśācas.[110]

101. Cf. *annādīnāṁ ca......sṛjanaṁ tyajanaṁ tathā* : 1. 60.

102. Cf. *na sasyāni na gorakṣā.......*

103. Cf. *sasyāni tena dugdhāni vainyena tu vasuṁdharā......tena annena tadā tā vai vartayante prajāḥ sadā* : 62. 176.

104. Cf. 8. 147-50 : This happened in the Tretā age.

105. Cf. *annaṁ Prajāpatiḥ sākṣāt* : 80. 57.

106. Cf. *navasasyāni yo dadyāc chrāddhe......* cf. 80. 49.

107. Cf. *yat pṛthivyāṁ vrīhi-yavaṁ hiraṇyaṁ paśavaḥ striyaḥ* : 93. 96.

108. Kha and Gha : *Guḍatulya*. 109. Cf. 30. 152. 110. Cf. 69. 287.

Karambha	Recommended as a gift in śrāddha.[111]
Kardama	Used in Dakṣa-yajña.[112]
Khaṇḍa-śarkara-vālukā	Used in Dakṣa-yajña.[113]
Kṛśara	In connection with the Piśācas we find *Hāridra-Kṛśara* mentioned.[114] *Kṛśara* in which *Masūra* was used, is referred to as a gift in śrāddha.[115]
Kulmāṣa	Mentioned with *vyañjana* as a good gift in śrāddha.[116]
Madhu-maṇḍodaka	Used in Dakṣa-yajña.[117]
Odana	Mentioned in connection with Piśācas[118] and re-recommended as gift in śrāddha.[119]
Piṇyāka	Recommended as food for yogins.[120]
Piṣṭaka	Recommended as gift in śrāddha.[121]
Pṛthuka	Pṛthuka, in the preparation of which sugar and milk were used, is recommended as a good gift in śrāddha.[122]
Pūpa	It was regarded as a good gift in śrāddha.[123] Oily (?) *pūpas* are mentioned in the same connection.[124]
Śaktu	Recommended as gift in śrāddha.[125]
Saktulāja	Recommended as gift in śrāddha.[126]
Sarpistila	Used for the *piṇḍi* in the śrāddha.[127]
Tilacūrṇa	Mentioned in connection with the Piśācas.[128] *Tila* mixed with *guḍa* is mentioned as a good gift in śrāddha.[129] *Tailabhadra* is also mentioned in connection with the Piśācas.[130]
Vyañjana	Cf. Kulmāṣa above.
Yavāgū	Yogins are advised to eat it with curds as a cure against *gudāvarta*, a kind of disease.[131] Also recommended as food for yogins.[132]
Yāvaka	Recommended as food for yogins.[133]

111. Cf. 80. 42. 112. Cf. 30. 151. 113. Cf. 30. 151. 114. Cf. 69. 287.
115. Cf. 80. 43–7. 116. Cf. *Kulmāṣa-vyañjanais tathā* : 80. 47.
117. Cf. 30. 151. 118. Cf. 69. 287. 119. Cf. 80. 46. 120. Cf. 16. 14.
121. Cf. 80. 42 Kha, Gha and Ṅa : *Piṣṭikā*.
122. Cf. *śarkara-kṣīra-saṁyuktaṁ pṛthukaṁ* : 80. 47.
123. Cf. 80. 48, 124. Cf. *snigdhāṁś ca pūpān yo dadyād* : 80. 43 ; cf. also 81. 3.
125. Cf. 80. 48. Kha, Gha and Ṅa have an altogether different reading.
126. Cf. 80. 48. 127. Cf. 75. 22. 128. Cf. 69. 287.
129. Cf. 82. 50. Gha omits this.
130. Cf. 69. 287. Kha, Ga and Ṅa : *Taila-bhakṣa*.
131. Cf. *bhuktvā dadhi yavāgūṁ vā* : 11. 42. 132. Cf. 16. 13. 133. Cf. 16. 13.

Other food-stuffs, such as *guḍa*, *śarkarā*, *hāridra* and *taila*, have been noted in connection with the above food-preparations. In the account of creation we find taila extracted from tila mentioned in a simile[134] and a reference to *Tailika* (i. e. a dealer in oil) as a person unfit for invitation at a śrāddha also occurs.[135] There is a reference to *lavaṇa* (i. e. salt) which was a taboo for yatis.[136]

Milk and its Products: Milk is recommended as a food for the yogins.[137] Śiva is called *Kṣīrapa* (i. e. he was fond of milk).[138] Its use in śrāddha is common.[139] Milk figures as an important factor in the story of "the milching of the earth".[140]

Vessels filled with butter are good gifts in śrāddha.[141] Urvaśī is stated to have lived only on the food of *ghṛta* during her stay with king Purūravas.[142] *Dadhi* (curds) is frequently mentioned in connection with śrāddha[143] and is considered as good food for yogins troubled with gastric disorders.[144] *Takra* too is recommended as good food for yogins.[145]

In the geographical chapters we find *Dadhimaṇḍodaka*, *Ghṛtodaka*, *Kṣīroda* and *Kṣīravāhinī* as proper names for rivers or seas.

Soma: Soma is usually referred to as a drink of the gods. Śiva is called *Somapa*.[146] In the reign of Vena, sacrifices ceased to be performed and gods were without their drink of Soma.[147] It was one of the most important objects created by Brahmā along with the Vedas[148] and in his boar form the Lord Brahmā is mentioned as *soma-śoṇita* (i. e. having Soma as his blood).[149] Its connection with Indra is also borne out. King Dharmaratha drank Soma with Śakra in a sacrifice performed on the Viṣṇupada mountain.[150] Inspite of the opposition of Indra, Tvaṣṭā drank Soma and in consequence was hurled down on the earth by the latter.[151] The Pitṛs too drink Soma. After enjoying Soma-drink offered in śrāddha they commenced their yogic practices.[152]

Soma also figures in the story of the "milching of the earth" as the "milk" which Bṛhaspati "milched" with gāyatrī as the vessel.[153] Offering of Soma in śrāddha, particularly on the *amāvāsyā* day is recommended as a meritorious act.[154] A dealer in Soma (*soma-vikrayin*) is not to be invited for a śrāddha.[155]

---

134. Cf. *tileṣu vā yathā tailaṁ* : 5. 9. 135. Cf. 83. 62.
136. Cf. *abhojyāṇi yatīnāṁ ca pratykṣalavaṇāni ca* : 18. 20 ; omitted in Gha.
137. Cf. 16. 13. 138. Cf. 30. 266. 139. Cf. 80. 46–8 etc.
140. Cf. 62. 151 ff. ; cf. also 1. 124 ; 8. 148 ff. 141. Cf. 80. 28.
142. Cf. *ghṛta-mātraṁ tathā'hāraḥ* : 91. 11. 143. Cf. 80. 42–4.
144. Cf. 11. 41–2 : *vāta-gulma*. 145. Cf. 16. 13.
146. Cf. 97. 179–80 ; 30. 266–7 etc. 147. Cf. 62. 110; cf. also 30. 100 ; 30. 10. etc.
148. Cf. 3. 16. 149. Cf. 6. 19. 150. Cf. 99. 102. 151. Cf. 78. 6.
152. Cf. 71. 65–6 ; cf. also 73. 14 ; 73. 26 ; 73. 52 ; 30. 7 etc.
153. Cf. 62. 176–7. 154. Cf. 81. 20–2. 155. Cf. 83. 62.

The story of the birth of Soma, the eponymous ancestor of the lunar race, is narrated in the Purāṇa. The sage Atri was practising severe austerities as a result of which Soma (the drink) began to flow from his eyes to all the ten directions. It was ordained that ten goddesses should bear this *garbha* (i. e. Soma) but they could not do it and Soma rushed down towards the earth along with them. For the sake of the world Brahmā yoked his chariot (but why he did so is not clear). The mind-born sons of Brahmā then recited hymns from the Vedas and Soma was born together with the plant-world.[156]

Amṛta : The celestial drink amṛta is mentioned many times. Fruits as sweet as amṛta is a common expression.[157] Amṛta is often mentioned in similes, e.g. *māna* (pride) is compared to amṛta and *avamāna* (insult) to poison.[158] The Vāyu Purāṇa itself is called *vāṅmayaṁ amṛtam.*[159]

The connection of amṛta with the moon is borne out by the statement that Soma (i. e. the moon) is called the mine of amṛta among the gods.[160] The gods had stocked amṛta on the Somaka mountain but Garutmat forcibly took it away from their custody for the sake of his mother.[161] The Aśvins cultivated certain plants on the mountain named Candra in the Plakṣa-dvīpa for obtaining amṛta.[162]

Śiva is called *amṛtapa* and *amṛtāṅga.*[163] The sea which forms the bed of Viṣṇu is called *amṛtodadhi.*[164] Amṛta also figures in the story of the "milching of the earth" as the "milk" of the earth.[165] With reference to the story of Śiva's name Nīlakaṇṭha we have already mentioned the story of the "churning of the ocean" for amṛta.

Honey : Honey is mentioned as food of the people in the Tretā age[166] and the people at the end of the Kali age will be living on honey, fruits and roots of trees.[167] We have a reference to honey of the *Kalpavṛkṣa* tree[168] and *Plakṣa-Khaṇḍa* is called *madhu-vaha.*[169] With Śiva honey was a favourite drink[170] and one of his sons in his future 22nd incarnation "will be" called *Madhu-piṅgākṣa.* A Brahmin guest, it is advised, should be offered honey[171] but a yati or bhikṣu must not even taste it.[172] Honey was also a good gift in śrāddha.[173] In the land of the Kurus there is a river named (?) *Madhumaireyavāhinī.*[174]

Surā : Śiva is called *surāpa*[175] and *surāsavas* (i. e. wine and other intoxicants) are mentioned in connection with the Piśācas.[176] *Kaśya* is a kind of *madya* (wine) and hence we have the name of Kaśyapa, the sage, apparently because he was addicted to that kind of drink.[177]

---

156. Cf. 90. 1–20. 157. Cf. 45. 28; 38. 21; 35. 28 etc. 158. Cf. 16. 5.
159. Cf. 1. 2. 160. Cf. *Devānāṁ amṛtâkara* : 42. 2. 161. Cf. 49. 10.
162. Cf. No. 989. App. 163. Cf. 30. 266-7; 97. 179–80. 164. Cf. 97. 22
165. Cf. 62. 179. 166. Cf. 8. 92. 167. Cf. 58. 97; 99. 404.
168. Cf. 8. 128. 169. Cf. 46. 7. 170. Cf. 39. 266-7.
171. Cf. 79. 11-2. 172. Cf. 18. 20-1. 173. Cf. 80. 50.
174. Cf. 45. 26-8. 175. Cf. 30. 266-7. 176. Cf. 69. 287.
177. Cf. *Kaśyaṁ madyaṁ smṛtaṁ vipraiḥ kaśyapānāt tu kaśyapaḥ* : 65. 116; omitted in Ṅa.

The following references suggest that drinking of wine was condemned as a sin. A drunkard (*surāpa*) is as bad as a murderer of a Brahmin and is a great sinner.[178] He is not to be invited for the śrāddha.[179] In the Dvāpara age, people were addicted to *mada* (wine ?) and here mada is mentioned with murder, begging and gambling as an evil.[180] It is stated that in the Kali age (even) women will be fond of wine and similar vices.[181]

But a drunkard can get rid of his sin if he pays his respects to the god Vāḍāditya.[182]

Other intoxicants such as *Meḍhra* and *Dhūma* (?) are also mentioned in connection with Śiva.[183]

Juices of Fruits : The sugar-cane juice (*Ikṣurasa*) was a favourite drink with the people of Harivarṣa.[184] In the land of the Kurus, there were *Kṣīrin* trees dripping with six kinds of *rasas*, sweet as amṛta. The people enjoy it and live a life of 13500 years.[185] The people of Hiraṇvata-varṣa drink the juice of *Lakuca* tree which is a reservoir of six rasas and live a life of 12500 years.[186] The people of Ramaṇaka-varṣa enjoy the juice of the fruits of a big *Nyagrodha* tree and live for 11500 years.[197] The juice of *Jambu* fruits is the food for the people of Ilāvṛta-varṣa and hence they do not know of old age.[188] In the Jambudvīpa, the Gandharvas, Devas, Dānavas, etc., enjoy the same, it being sweet as amṛta.[189] Īśvara, son of Brahmā, drinks the juice of the fruits of a heavenly *Panasa* tree—a fountain of six rasas on the Gandhamādana mountain.[190] The Siddhas drink the juice of *Parūṣaka* fruits.[191]

Non-vegetarian Diet : Eating of meat is regarded as a characteristic of the Piśācas.[192] Śiva is said to be greedy of both cooked and uncooked flesh[193] and his sons were equally fond of it.[194] The Rākṣasas and the Bhūtas are called flesh-eaters.[195] It is said that at the end of the Kali age people "will" live on honey, roots of trees and meat.[196] A yogin, however, was advised not to touch animal food.[197]

References to the use of meat in śrāddha occur frequently. The Viśvadeva offering in śrāddha primarily consisted of meat.[198] An offering of food-grains, such as *māṣa*, etc., in śrāddha, offers a month's satisfaction to the ancestors but the case is different in the case of offerings of the flesh of various animals. The flesh of fish offers them a satisfaction for two months, of deer, for three months, of hare, for four

178. *Mahā-pātakin* : cf. 82. 36–7. 179. Cf. 82. 61–3. 180. Cf. 58. 4.
181. Cf. 58. 43. 182. Cf. 60. 75. 183. Cf. 10. 49 ; 30. 100.
184. Cf. 46. 9. 185. Cf. 45. 14–20. 186. Cf. 45. 6–9. 187. Cf. 45. 3–5.
188. Cf. 46. 12–29. 189. Cf. 35. 30–1. 190. Cf. 43. 4–5. 191. Cf. 38. 65.
192. Cf. *Piśācāḥ piśitāśanāt* : 9. 39 ; 69. 257.
193. Cf. *pakvānnamāṁsa-lubdha* : 30. 203. 194. Cf. 10. 49.
195. Cf. 70. 63 ; 69. 254. 196. Cf. 58. 97. 197. Cf. 18. 20–1.
198. Cf. *bahu-māṁsa-paraṁ haviḥ* : 78. 5 ; 81. 3.

months, of *śakuna*, five months, of *Varāha*, six months, of *Chagala*, seven months, of *Pārṣata*, eight months, of *Ruru* (a kind of deer), nine months, of *Gavaya*, ten months, of *Kūrma*, eleven months, of *Gavya*, for a whole year, of *Gavya* and *Vadhrīṇasa* with honey and ghee, for twelve years and of *Kṛṣṇa-cchāga*, *Godha*[199] and *Khāḍmayāṁsa*, for ever.[200] Flesh of various kinds was also served in the sacrifice of Dakṣa.[201]

There is an interesting incident in the genealogical accounts regarding the use of meat in śrāddha. King Ikṣvāku once asked his son Vikukṣi to fetch flesh for the śrāddha ceremony which he intended to perform. Vikukṣi accordingly went to the forest and hunted many beasts (mṛgān) and as he was tired he ate part of the flesh particularly of śaśa (hare). When he returned home with the remaining portion, the king directed Vasiṣṭha to cleanse it (so as to make it ready for the ceremony). In the course of cleansing Vasiṣṭha came to know that a part of it had already been eaten by Vikukṣi. This meat was meant for the śrāddha and thus was *abhojya*. The priest informed the king of what had happened and the king being enraged at this unwise act of his son expelled him.[202] After recounting the tale (*ākhyāna*) that one should not eat in a manner opposed to *vidhi* (Vedic injunction) the word *māṁsa* is explained thus, "He to whom the flesh which I now eat belongs, will eat the flesh which belongs to me in the next world"—so say the learned.[203] Vikukṣi is thenceforward known also as *Śaśāda* (hare-eater).[204]

Pṛṣadhra was a son of Vaivasvata Manu. He ate the flesh of the cow belonging to his preceptor Cyavana who, for that act of his, cursed him to be a Śūdra.[205] There is also the note-worthy instance of Satyavrata Triśaṅku who was condemned by his father to live by *śva-pāka* (i. e. in the manner in which the dog-eaters—one of the outcaste tribes, such as the *Cāṇḍālas*, etc.—live).

Cannibalism: Gods, manes, men and Asuras were created by Brahmā but the creatures who issued out of the *rajas* and *tamas* portion of his body proceeded to devour the gods, etc. These creatures are called the Rākṣasas.[206] The Yakṣas are described as eating human flesh and drinking human blood.[207] The Piśācas[208] and the Rākṣasas[209] are also similarly described. It is stated that at the end of the Kali age people will be following carnivorous habits.[210]

---

199. Kha, Ga, Gha and Ṅa : *Loha*. 200. Cf. 83. 2–12. 201. Cf. 30. 150–2.

202. Here an attempt is made to explain, apparently etymologically, the word *māṁsa*.

203. Cf. *māṁsa bhakṣayitā'mutra yasya mamsam iha admy aham etan māṁsasya māṁsatvaṁ pravadanti manīṣiṇaḥ*. 204. Cf. 88. 12–24.

205. Cf. 86. 1–2. 206. Cf. 9. 29–31. 207. Cf. 69. 197.

208. Cf. 69. 114; 69. 267–79. 209. Cf. 70. 63. 210. Cf. *Kravyādanaḥ* : 58. 53.

CHAPTER VIII

MUSIC AND DANCING

On Music in General : The *Gāndharva-vidyā* (i.e. the Science of Music) is included in the list of eighteen *vidyās* such as the Vedas, their aṅgas, Mīmāṁsā, Nyāya, Dharmaśāstra, Purāṇa, Āyurveda, Dhanurveda, Gāndharva and Arthaśāstra.[1] We have already seen that the names Gandharva, Ṛṣabha, Ṣaḍja, Madhyama, Vairājaka, Niṣāda and Pañcama are mentioned as being the names of Kalpas and there they are directly associated with the *svaras* such as Gāndhāra, Ṛṣabha, Ṣaḍja, Madhyama or Dhaivata, (?), Snigdha (?), Niṣāda and Pañcama respectively. As to why these svaras, which are seven in number, should have been so associated with the corresponding names of Kalpas it is difficult to guess for the present. The connection of the Madhyama Kalpa with the Madhyama or Dhaivata svara should, however, be noted.[2] Elsewhere we find a lengthy passage[3] devoted entirely to the Science of Music. It has been brought in, in this Purāṇa, with reference to Revatī, the daughter of king Reva, who was given in marriage to Baladeva (i.e. brother of Vāsudeva Kṛṣṇa). The whole passage appears to be a digression deliberately made and its absence in the MSS. Kha and Gha also suggests that this is so. Here we are informed about the *svara-maṇḍala* according to which there are seven *svaras*, three *grāmas*, twenty-one *mūrcchanās*, and forty-nine *tālas*.[4] The explanatory details about these are too technical to be noted here. We find, however, that a musician or music is tabooed in śrāddha.[5]

Music in Relation to Sacrifice : The gods (?) had commenced the performance of a yajña which is famous for the fact that the seven sages had their origin from it. On this occasion all the gods, the various aṅgas of sacrifice itself and the Vedas had come to attend.[6] It is said that the Sāmaveda was here "attended upon"[7] by the Gandharvas such as Viśvāvasu and others. Again, the Sāmaveda is here styled as *sarva-geya-puraḥsaraḥ* (i.e. foremost amongst those to be sung).[8] The Gandharvas are also stated to be chanting Sāman hymns at the sacrificial session (*satra*) performed by the sages in the Naimiṣa forest.[9]

We have already referred to the origin of the Sūta and Māgadha narrated in the story of Pṛthu. It is not clear whether the yajña

---

1. Cf. 61. 78-0.
2. Cf. *yasmiṁs tu madhyamo nāma svaro ḍaivata-pūjitaḥ.*
3. Cf. 86. 29 to the end of chapter 87. 4. Cf. 86. 36. 5. Cf. 82. 61.
6. Cf. *samāgatāḥ.* 7. Cf. *saṁbhṛto'bhavat.*
8. Cf. *Śāmavedas' ca vṛttāḍhyaḥ sarva-geyapuraḥsaraḥ Viśvāvasvādibhiḥ sārdhaṁ Gandharvaiḥ saṃbhṛto'bhavat* : 65. 22-6.
9. Cf. 2. 31.

referred to there was performed by Pitāmaha (i.e. Brahmā) or by king Pṛthu.[10] It is in this yajña that while the Sāman hymns were being chanted that Māgadha was born in the utensil called *srug* which was meant for the Vaiśvadeva offering.[11] The context suggests that the function of the Māgadha here is that of a bard in the royal court.

With reference to the narration of the progeny of Kaśyapa we are told that Prabāhī (a Dānavī ?) gave birth to sons who proved to be the best singers in yajña.[12]

In the narration of an asvamedha performed by Indra we have an allusion to the recitation of *āgamas* with good *svaras*.[13]

Music Associated with Śiva : Śiva is frequently described in the Purāṇa as being fond of music and dance.[14] He is mentioned as *mukha-vāditrakārin* (i.e. maker of wind-instruments).[15] It is in his nature to sing[16] and epithets associating him, in general terms, with music and dance are too numerous to be quoted here. The *Tumba-Vīṇā* is his favourite instrument.[17] That he is called *Kiṅkiṇika* suggests that he used trinklets for the purposes of his dance and music.[18] He is also said to be using *ghaṇṭā* perhaps for the same reason.

The munis are said to worship the god Maheśvara with dance and music, with the mystic *oṁkāra* and *huṁkāra* at tīrthas and temples in the north of the Himavat mountain. The Bhūtas too worship the god with dance and music playing on various instruments.[19] He is also attended upon by Siddhas with the accompaniment of music.[20]

In the story of Dakṣa-yajña we find Śiva telling his wife that even though he is not assigned any portion of offerings in sacrifices, he is prayed by the stray travellers with the *Rathaṁtara Sāman*—a hymn which is worth singing.[21]

Music Associated with Gandharvas, Apsarasas and Kinnaras: The Deva-Gandharvas are said to be experts in music and dance.[22] It is stated that the Gandharvas and the Apsarasas sing and play with musical instruments[23] in honour of illustrious donors in śrāddha.[24] Siddhas,

---

10. Cf. *yajñe Paitāmahe* : 62. 137 Kha. apparently refers to the king Pṛthu.

11. Cf. *Sāmageṣu tu gāyatsu srug-bhāṇḍe Vaisvadevake Sāmagāne samutpannas tasmān Māgadha ucyate* : 62. 137-8 Ka omits this information.

12. Cf. *yajñe vai gāyanottamān* : 68. 37.

13. Cf. *saṁpragīteṣu teṣu āgameṣv atha susvaram* : 57. 93 Ka. has *sattvaram* for *susvaram*.

14. Cf. *gītavādyarata* : 30. 198 ff. 15. Cf. 30. 198 ff.

16. Cf. *gīta-śīla* : 24. 142-3. 17. Cf. *Tumba-Vīṇā-priya* : 30. 203.

18. Cf 24. 148. 19. 40. 24-5. 20. Cf. 24. 144.

21. Cf. *mām adhvare śaṁsitāraḥ stuvanti Rathaṁtare(raṁ) Sāma gāyanti geyam* : 30. 119.

22. Cf. *nṛtya-gīta-viśāradāḥ......nipuṇā gīta-vādinaḥ* : 69. 44-5.

23. Cf. *vādayanti ca.* 24. Cf. 80. 10-15.

Devas and Cāraṇas also figure as singers with Gandharvas and Apsarasas.[25] Hundreds of the gaṇas of Kinnaras are described as being adept in dance and music.[26]

Musical Instruments: Vādya, Vāditra or Vādanaka appear to be the terms signifying a musical instrument in general.[27] The following musical instruments have been noted in the Purāṇa and they are here arranged in an alphabetical order:

Bherī	The Bhūtas played upon the Bherīs to pay their respects to Śiva.[28]
Diṇḍima	Played upon by the Bhūtas as above.[29]
Dundubhi	Its use is associated with Śiva.[30] There is a mountain named Dundubhi in the Plakṣadvīpa so called because in former times the Suras beat the drums (i.e. Dundubhis) there and created a deadly noise.[31]
Gomukhas	The Bhūtas played upon the Gomukhas and paid their respects to Śiva.[32]
Jharjharas or Jhallaras	Played by the Bhūtas as above.[33]
Mṛdaṅga	Used by the people of the Kuru land.[34]
Mukhavāditra or Mukhamardalavāditra	Śiva is called the maker of the *Mukha-vāditras*.[35] The Bhūtas are said to be beating with force the *Mukha-mardala-vāditras* in the course of their worship of Śiva.[36]
Paṇava	Associated with the people of the Kuru land.[37]
Paṭaha	The Bhūtas played upon the Paṭahas to pay their respects to Śiva.[38]
Raṇi-tālasita (?)	The Bhūtas are associated with it.[39]
Śaṅkha	The Bhūtas blow the white conches. Viṣṇu is described as holding a Śaṅkha.
Tumba	Śiva loved this instrument.
Veṇu	Its use is associated with the people of Kuru.[40]
Vīṇā	Śiva loved this instrument. The Bhūtas who lived with Śiva played upon this instrument. When

25. Cf. 81. 21-4. 26. Cf. *nṛtya-gītapragalbha* : 69. 37.
27. Cf. 81. 21-4 ; 30. 248 etc. 28. Cf. 40. 24-5.
29. Cf. 40. 24-5. 30. Cf. 55. 55.
31. Cf. *śabda-mṛtyuḥ purā tasmin Dundubhis tāḍitaḥ Suraiḥ* : 49. 9.
32. Cf. 40. 24-5. 33. Cf. 40. 24-5.
34. Cf. No. 660 App. 35. Cf. 30. 198 ff.
36. Cf. *mukha-mardala-vāditrair balināṁ' sphoṭitais tathā* : 54. 35-7 Gha and Ṅa : *valgitāsphoṭanaih*, suggesting that they created all sorts of noises at that time.
37. Cf. No. 660 App. 38. Cf. 40. 24-5. 39. Cf. 40. 24-5.
40. Cf. No. 660 App.

Skanda was born, Sarasvatī presented him with a great Vīṇā.[41] It is also associated with the people of the Kuru country.[42]

Dancing : In references to Śiva's connection with music we have already noted his association with dance also. The munis and the Bhūtas worshipped the god Śiva with dance and music. There is a picturesque description of Vīrabhadra, created by Śiva to destroy the sacrifice of Dakṣa, which may be noted here : "He sometimes danced with various movements of his body and at the same time sang (in the accompaniment of his dance)".[43] It should be noted that this was the manner in which Vīrabhadra raided the sacrifice of Dakṣa. We find a similar description of Śiva also.[44] He is said to have a peculiar fascination for dancing.[45]

Gandharvas, Apsarasas and Kinnaras also are associated with dance. The gaṇas of Apsarasas danced on the occasion of the sacrificial session performed by the sages in the Naimiṣa forest at Kurukṣetra.[46]

The daughter of the Vṛṣṇi-chief Bṛhaduktha, named Bṛhatī, is called *nārtakonneyī*[47] but it is not clear whether this reference has anything to do with dancing.[48]

---

41. Cf. *mahāsvanā mahāvīṇā* : 72. 46. 42. No. 660 App.
43. Cf. *Kvacin nṛtyati citrāṅgaṁ kvacid vadati susvaram......kvacid gāyati*: 30. 134-5.
44. Cf. *nadate kūrdate caiva* i.e. dances and makes loud noise ? : 24. 145.
45. Cf. *nāṭyopahāra-lubdha* : 30. 199. 46. Cf. 2. 31. 47. Gha : *nārtakoneyī*.
48. Cf. 96. 246.

CHAPTER IX

WAR AND WEAPONS

Of War in General : In connection with the Kṣatriyas it has already been stated that war is the concern primarily of the Kṣatriyas to whom that function has been assigned by divine ordination. Of Bhāratavarṣa it is said that there the Kṣatriyas live on warfare.[1] The expression *Kṣāttravidhi* may be noted in this connection. This entire earth of the seven *dvīpas* and surrounded by seven seas was subjugated by king Kārtavīrya Arjuna in accordance with *Kṣāttra-vidhi*.[2] We have again an interesting reference that trade-war (*vaṇig-yuddha*) was the feature of the Dvāpara age.[3]

The warrior who pays his respects to king Pṛthu before proceeding to the scene of battle is sure to achieve victory.[4] It is said that by listening to the story of Nīlakaṇṭha Śiva one can aspire to display bravery in war[5] and such is the merit of the syllables of *oṁ* that the brave who utter them do not think of retreat in war.[6] Similarly, it is stated that a gift of fuel in a śrāddha performed in winter enables the donor to be always victorious.[7]

We have no picturesque descriptions of any long-drawn wars such as we meet with in the epics. The Devas and Asuras fought twelve wars but the details described about them do not reflect anything on the modes of actual warfare.[8] We have a graphic description of the raid of Dakṣa's sacrifice carried by Vīrabhadra but that too does not lead us to infer anything. King Raji is said to have helped the gods in their war against the Asuras but we have no details about the way in which he fought. The numerous references to the performance of aśvamedha suggest that wars had probably taken place before the sacrifice was actually performed but, except in the instance of Sagara's aśvamedha, we find none of them described, or even alluded to, in the Purāṇa and even in case of Sagara, the details are not at all connected with the practice of warfare.[9] We have, again, the instance of king Kuvalāśva fighting the water-demon (*udaka-Rākṣasa*) Dhundhu but the details are too fanciful to offer us any useful information.[10]

Some glimpses regarding the practice of warfare and facts incidental to it are, however, available from the following references :

---

1. Cf. 45. 83.

2. Cf. *tena iyaṁ pṛthivī Kṛtsnā sapta-dvīpā sapattanā saptodadhiparikṣiptā Kṣāttreṇa vidhinā jitā* : 94. 14.

3. Cf. 58. 3. 4. Cf. 63. 9. 5. Cf. 54. 106. 6. Cf. 20. 19

7. Cf. 80. 23-4. 8. Cf. 97. 87 ff.

9. Cf. 88. 144. Here we find the incident of Kapila being offended by the sons of Sagara as the subject of narration. 10. Cf. 88. 34-60.

In the battle between Bhoja Śatadhanvan and Kṛṣṇa the former was riding a mare capable of covering hundred yojanas at a stretch.[11] This mare had a name *Vijñāta-hṛdayā* (i.e. clever enough to read the master's mind). The animal, however, died through fatigue (and Śatadhanvan seems to have fled on foot). Kṛṣṇa, who was pursuing Śatadhanvan, came to know of the fate of the mare. He got down from the chariot and continued his pursuit on foot and afterwards killed Śatadhanvan.[12] We have another reference regarding Kṛṣṇa's fight against Ṛkṣarāja Jāmbavat. Here we do not find them using weapons and it appears that this is an instance of *muṣṭi-yuddha* which took place continuously for twenty-one days. Of king Kārtavīrya it is said that he invaded the city of Laṅkā, brought Rāvaṇa as a captive to his city of Māhiṣmatī and then set him free at the request of Pulastya.[13] King Sagara too vanquished his enemies and allowed them their freedom after inflicting certain indignities upon them. King Jyāmagha was victorious in a war and had brought home a girl (as a captive ?).

Composition of the Army : The only information directly pertaining to the composition of the army is obtained from the description of the end of the Kali age. Here it is stated that Kalki raised an army composed of horses, elephants and chariots and with the help of armed *Vipras* carried out his mission which took him twenty years.[14] Of the 'future' Kalki we have practically the same information.[15] These references imply that employment of cavalry, elephants and chariots in war was known. Of cavalry we have no other references in the Purāṇa. Horse-riding is, however, indicated in two cases of which the one of Śatadhanvan is already noted above and the other instance is hinted at in the story of Prasena who rode on horse-back when he went out for hunting and subsequently lost his life.[16] There is only one additional reference regarding the employment of elephants in war wherein names of elephants employed in the war between gods and Asuras are mentioned.[17]

We have many references, in addition to the one quoted above, in our text regarding the use of chariots in war. King Jyāmagha used a chariot in his victorious campaign.[18] There is a mysterious reference to the chariot of king Kārtavīrya that it appeared before him whenever he wished.[19] We have a history of the chariot of king Yayāti narrated in the Purāṇa. Rudra was pleased with Yayāti and gave him a shining golden chariot together with two inexhaustive quivers.

---

11. Cf. *śata-yojana-gāminī*. 12. Cf. 96. 68–74. 13. Cf. 94. 35–6.
14. Cf. *samāḥ sa viṁśatiṁ pūrṇāḥ......ācakarṣa sa vai senāṁ sa-vāji-ratha-kuñjarāṁ pragṛhītāyudhair Viprair* : 58. 76–8.
15. Cf. 98. 104–5. 16. Cf. *sāśvaṁ hataṁ Prasenaṁ taṁ* : 96. 39
17. Cf. 69. 230–1. 18. Cf. 95. 30.
19. Cf. *rathaś caiva prādurbhavati māyayā* : 94. 15.

It was with the help of this chariot that the king made conquests all over the world. It was the cherished possession of the Pauravas till the time of Janamejaya who lost it, because of a curse of Gārgya to king Vasu of the Cedi dynasty. From him it passed to Bṛhadratha and when Jarāsaṁdha, descendant of Bṛhadratha, was killed by Bhīma, Kṛṣṇa got it from him.[20] Expressions such as *rathin*,[21] *mahāratha*[22] are the epithets used for kings in the genealogical lists. Vidūratha, son of Bhajamāna is called *Rathi(tha)mukhya* (i.e. chief amongst *rathins*).[23] Śiva and his sons too are called *rathin*.[24] In the story of the birth of Soma we find Brahmā also yoking his chariot. Along with the above epithets we find the expression *dhvajin* too used,[25] probably suggesting that kings had their distinctive standards or flags fixed conspicuously their chariots.

A number of horses yoked to chariots are referred to only in one case. Brahmā's chariot was drawn by a thousand horses.[26] Skanda, however, had lions yoked to his chariot.[27] It is said that if one sees in a dream chariots yoked with bears, monkeys, donkeys or buffaloes going to the south that means a sign of impending death.[28]

About the size of the chariot we have almost no information. The fact that Kṛṣṇa and Balarāma were the only two persons in the chariot in which Kṛṣṇa pursued Śatadhanvan suggests that it was a small-sized vehicle.[29]

Weapons : The following is an alphabetical list of weapons compiled in the same manner as in the case of musical instruments.

Aṅkuśa — The fact that men control elephants with an Aṅkuśa is mentioned in a simile.[30] (Here Aṅkuśa is not a weapon of war.)

Asi — In his raid of the Dakṣa-yajña Vīrabhadra used *asi*.[31] Its use is also associated with Śiva[32] and his followers, the Bhūtas.[33]

Astras — Virocana, son of Prahlāda, is said to have obtained special astras from Bhava and had thus no fear of death. But Viṣṇu entered Śakra's body and killed Virocana in the sixth Asura-Deva war.[34] Śukra saw the Asuras wounded by Devas with astras[35] and then thought of

---

20. Cf. 93. 18–27. 21. Cf. 96. 21 ; 96. 175.
22. Cf. 96. 16 ; 94. 48 ; 92. 70 *Ratheśvara* according Gha only : 99. 109.
23. Cf. 96. 135. 24. Cf. 97. 191 ; 54. 78 ; 10–4 etc.
25. Cf. 94. 15 ; 95. 30–1 ; 96. 121–2 etc. 26. Cf. 90. 9–11.
27. Cf. No. 469 App. 28. Cf. 19. 13–27. 29. Cf. 96. 66–73.
30. Cf. 16. 20. 31. Cf. 30. 124. 32. Cf. 101. 272. 33. Cf. 69. 253.
34. Cf. *Bhavād avadhyatāṁ prāpya viśeṣāstrādibhis tu yaḥ saṁgrāme nihataḥ ṣaṣṭhe Śakrāviṣṭeṇa Viṣṇunā* : 97. 81.
35. Cf. *astrakṣatārtās* ; Kha, Ga, Gha and Ṅa read *śastra* instead.

some measure to procure victory for them.[36] Rudra used a great astra (*paramāstra*) in the war that broke out on the issue of the seduction of Tārā by Soma.[37] We have also a mention of *Vedaśiras* astra used by Vedaśiras, the 15th incarnation of Śiva.[38] The sons of Kārtavīrya Arjuna are called *Kṛtāstrāḥ* (i.e. accomplished in the use of astras).[39] King Sagara is said to have secured the *Āgneyāstra* from Jāmadagnya with which he annihilated the usurpers of his father's kingdom. This astra was terrible "even" to the Asuras.[40] In the description of his fight against Śatadhanvan Kṛṣṇa is called *paramāstravit*.[41] Cārudeṣṇa and Sāmba are called *kṛtāstrau*.[42]

Bhurbhura — Associated with Śiva.[43]

Cakra — It is mainly associated with Viṣṇu who meditated upon his *cakra* when he desired to kill the mother of Kāvya (cf. *abhidhyāya tataś cakram*). The *cakra* is also mentioned as an astra with which he cut her head off.[44] Tvaṣṭā is said to have fashioned the cakra of Viṣṇu.[45] Śiva is called *śāyaka-cakradhārin* (i.e. he wielded the *śāyaka-cakra*).[46] Vīrabhadra too is associated with its use.[47]

Carman (i.e. Shield?) — The sons of Nīlalohita are associated with its use.[48]

Daṇḍa — The use of Daṇḍa is mainly referred to in connection with Śiva who is called *daṇḍa, daṇḍadhṛk*,[49] *mahādaṇḍa, daṇḍa-dhara*,[50] *sadaṇḍin*.[51] The *daṇḍa* used by Vīrabhadra in his raid of Dakṣa-yajña is mentioned as being sharp and shining.[52]

Dhanus — The bow and the arrows:

There is a reference to *dhanurveda* as being one of the eighteen *vidyās* (or branches of knowledge). Jāmadagnya Rāma had learnt all these Vidyās including the Dhanurveda.[53] Satyadhṛti, son of the sage Śatānanda,

---

36. Cf. 97. 101. 37. Cf. 90. 32. 38. Cf. 23. 167. 39. Cf. 94. 49.
40. Cf. *Asurair api duḥsaham* : 88. 135. 41. Cf. 96, 74. 42. Cf. 96. 188.
43. Cf. 30. 237.
44. Cf. *kruddhas tad astram āvidhya śiraś ciccheda Mādhavaḥ* : 97. 138–9.
45. Cf. 84. 83. 46. Cf. 55. 44–5. 47. Cf. 30. 124.
48. Cf. 10. 47 Ka has *dharmiṇaḥ* for *carmiṇaḥ*. 49. Cf. 30. 251.
50. Cf. 30. 260. 51. Cf. 30. 266 etc.
52. Cf. *sita-tīkṣṇadaṇḍa* : 30. 130 Ka has *daṁṣṭra* for *daṇḍa*.
53. Cf. *sarva-vidyāntagaṁ śreṣṭhaṁ dhanur-vedasya pāragam* 91. 91.

was also skilled in the Dhanurveda[54] and the same was the case with Pracetasas, sons of Prācīnabarhis.[55]

Viśvakarman is said to have been the maker of the bows of gods.[56] Amongst the gods, Śiva is often described as wielding the bow. His bow—the *pināka*—is many times mentioned.[57] He is called *dṛḍhadhanvin* or *sudhanvā*.[58] He is addressed by Dakṣa in a prayer as "the bow amongst the *yantras*".[59] This would suggest that the bow was regarded as a kind of yantra.[60] The bow which Śiva used in the war caused by seduction of Tārā is mentioned as *ājagava*.[61]

The king Pṛthu was born out of the "churning" of Vena's arm "first" with a resounding bow named *ājagava* and (then ?) with arrows and a shining *kavaca* (armour) for the purposes of self-protection.[62] He pursued the earth in the form of a cow with a bow and arrows.[63] Tying the bow-string to his bow Kārtavīrya Arjuna shot five hundred (arrows ?) which bewildered the whole city of Laṅkā and Rāvaṇa became a captive.[64] The same king is said to have shot arrows which set fire to cities, towns and villages.[65] Epithets such as *dhanvin*,[66] *dhanurdhara*,[67] *uttama-dhanvin*,[68] etc., are frequently used in connection with kings. King Jyāmagha took up a bow and set out, in a chariot, to carve a kingdom for himself and was in the end successful.[69] The Devas and the Dānavas separately requested the king Raji to take up his *vara-kārmuka* (i.e. the best bow) and fight for them. Raji, however, acceded to the request of the Devas.[70] King Rukmakavaca had killed in former times many *dhanvins* (wielders of bow) and *kavacins* (wearers of armour) with his sharp arrows.[71] King Yayāti handed over his bow, arrows (*pṛṣatkān*) and his kingdom

54. Cf. 99. 203. 55. Cf. 30. 36.

56. Cf. *tridaśānāṁ ca dhanvakṛt* : 66. 29 Ka has a different reading

57. Cf. 25. 2 ; 24. 132 ; 54. 107–8 ; 54. 60 ; 55. 54 ; 97. 166–71 etc.

58. Cf. 97. 183–91. 59. Cf. *yantrāṇaṁdhanur evaca*.

60. Cf. 30. 235. 61. Cf. 90 31.

62. Cf. *ādyam ājagavaṁ nāma dhanur gṛhya mahāravaṁ śarāṁś ca bibhrad rakṣārthaṁ kavacaṁ ca mahāprabham* : 62. 127. 63. 62. 151.

64. Cf. *sa vai badhvā dhanur yāna utsiktaḥ pañcabhih śataiḥ Laṅkāyāṁ mohayitvā tu sabalaṁ Rāvaṇam balāt*......for *dhānur yāna* Gha and Ṅa have *dhanur-jyānām*. The word "*badhvā*" suggests that the bow-string was not fitted to the bow for all time : cf. 94–35.

65. Cf. 96. 184. 66. Cf. 95. 43. 67. Cf. 95, 40. 68. Cf. 92. 61.

69. Cf. 95. 30–3. 70. Cf. 92. 81–5.

71. Cf. *nihatya Rukmakavacaḥ purā kavacino raṇe dhanvino niśitair bāṇair* : 95. 25–6.

to his sons and retired to the peaceful life of the forest.[72] This shows the importance of the bow. The same king had received from the god Rudra two inexhaustible quivers.[73] It is said that in the Tretā age people were skilled in archery.[74]

We have already referred to the bow (*dhanus*) as a unit of measurement of distance and there is an interesting simile in which the bow is compared to *Oṁ*, the arrows to *ātman*, the *brahman* being the target.[75]

Gadā — Śiva is often addressed in prayers as the wielder of gadā.[76] Vīrabhadra in his raid of Dakṣa-yajña used gadā also.[77] It is also associated with Hari who reclines on the ocean-bed.[78] While Balabhadra was in Mithilā king Duryodhana went to him and learnt from him the divine art of wielding gadā.[79]

Hala — Balarāma, the elder brother of Kṛṣṇa, is called *halin* and *lāṅgalin*.[80] *Lāṅgalin* is also a name of the twenty-second incarnation of Śiva and he used *hala* as his weapon.[81]

Kavaca — Śiva is frequently called *Kavacin*.[82] The kavaca, which was meant for self-protection, is mentioned in connection with Akrūra or Babhrū.[83] There is a reference to *nārīkavaca* said to have been used by king Mūlaka who was afraid of Rāma. The exact significance of this *nārīkavaca* calls for an explanation.[84]

Khaḍga — When Kaṁsa heard the fatal voice foretelling his death he "drew out" his sword to kill Devakī. This suggests that the sword was sheathed.[85] Kārtavīrya Arjuna also used *khaḍga*.[86]

Khaṭvāṅga — King Dilīpa had a son named Khaṭvāṅgada.[87] Śiva is a *Khaṭvāṅgin* (i.e. wielder of Khaṭvāṅga).[88]

Kuliśa — Vīrabhadra used it.[89]

Kuśavajra (?) — The sages killed king Purūravas with Kuśavajras.[90]

Mudgara — Associated with Vīrabhadra[91] and with the Bhūtas.[92]

---

72. Cf. *dhanur nyasya pṛṣatkāṁś ca rājyaścaiva suteṣu ca* : 93. 93.
73. Cf. *akṣayau iṣudhī* : 93. 18. 74. Cf. *mahā-dhanur-dharāḥ* : 57. 66.
75. Cf. 20. 5. 76. Cf. 30. 237; 30. 247 etc. 77. Cf. 30. 124.
78. Cf. 24. 9 ff.; cf. also 55. 12 for Viṣṇu's association with *gadā*.
79. Cf. *gadā-śikṣāṁ tato divyām-Balabhadrād avāptavān* : 96. 83.
80. Cf. 96. 64; 96. 75. 81. Cf. 23. 199. 82. Cf. 24. 159; 97. 191 etc.
83. Cf. 96. 80. 84. Cf. 88. 179.
85. Cf. *niṣkramya* (*ṣkṛṣya*) *khaḍgaṁ tāṁ kanyāṁ hantukāmo' bhavat tadā* : 96. 222. Kha has *niṣkāsya* and Gha and Ga have *niḥkramya*.
86. Cf. 94. 21. 87. Cf. 88. 182. 88. Cf. 30. 237. 89. Cf. 30. 127.
90. Cf. 2. 22–3. 91. Cf. 30. 123. 92. Cf. 69. 253.

Nakha The nakhas with which Narasiṁha killed Hiraṇyakaśipu were neither moist nor dry.[93]

Paraśu Vīrabhadra wielded the *paraśu* in his raid of Dakṣa-yajña.[94] Śiva again is called *Khaṇḍa-paraśuh*.[95]

Pāśa Associated with Śiva.[96]

Paṭṭiśa Śiva is called *paṭṭiśin* (i.e. wielder of *paṭṭiśa*).[97] Elsewhere he is addressed as *paṭṭiśarūpadhārin*).[98]

Śakti Associated with Skanda.[99]

Śaṅkha It is associated with Viṣṇu. Śiva too used it[100] and Vīrabhadra also had it in his hand when he raided the Dakṣa-yajña.[101]

Śūla *Śūlin* (wielder of *śūla*) is a very common attribute of Śiva.[102] He is again called *śūlapāṇin*,[103] *śūlahasta*,[104] *śūladhṛk*,[105] *triśūlin*,[106] *triśūlapāṇin*,[107] *triśūlāṅga*,[108] *sahasrodyataśūla*[109] and *Jvalita-śūla*,[110] etc. *Śūlin* is also a name of Śiva's twenty-fourth incarnation.[111] Śiva's wife too wielded the *śūla*[112] and the Rudras are likewise called *śūlahastāḥ*.[113]

Tigma (?) Śiva is called *tigmāyudhadhara*.[114]

Vajra Indra, in different Manvantaras, wielded the *vajra*.[115] King Raji annihilated the Dānavas in the presence of Indra, the wielder of vajra.[116] Śiva is also called *vajra-hasta*.[117] In the prayer to the god Śiva, Dakṣa addresses the god as *vajra* amongst *praharaṇas* (i.e. weapons or striking weapons ?). That he is addressed also as *dhanus* amongst *yantras*, as previously noted, in the same context is rather interesting. Are we to suppose from this that there were two general classes of weapons, viz., the *yantras* and the *praharaṇas* ?[118]

Varman Associated with the sons of Śiva.[119]

Varūtha Śiva is often called *Varūthin* (i.e. wearer of *varūtha*).[120] His sons too are mentioned likewise.[121]

---

93. Cf. *anārdraśuṣkāḥ* : 67. 64-6. 94. Cf. 30. 124. 95. Cf. 25. 2.
96. Cf. 24. 159 ; 24. 117. 97. Cf. 24. 159.
98. Cf. 55. 45 Kha, Gha and Ṅa have a different reading altogether.
99. Cf. 41. 38-9 ; 54. 24. 100. Cf. 24. 159. 101. Cf. 24. 124.
102. Cf. 26. 2 ; 55. 30 ; 54. 3 ; 97. 166-71 ; etc.
103. Cf. 69. 289 ; 70. 8 ; 24. 36 etc. 104. Cf. 25. 17. 105. Cf. 55. 54.
106. Cf. 25. 70 ; 25. 89. 107. Cf. 54. 107-8. 108. Cf. 24. 55.
109. Cf. 30. 215. 110. Cf. 30. 92. 111. Cf. 23. 206.
112. Cf. *śūla-dharā* : 9. 91. 113. Cf. 23. 105.
114. Cf. 24. 135 ; cf. also 97. 183. 115. Cf. 64. 7.
116. Cf. *samakṣaṁ vajra-pāṇinaḥ* : 92. 85. 117. Cf. 54. 66. 118. Cf. 30. 235.
119. Cf. 10. 47. 120. Cf. 54. 77 ; 97. 191 etc. 121. Cf. 10. 47.

CHAPTER X

FLORA AND FAUNA

I. The Plant-World

Of Plants in General : The origin of the plant-world is connected with the birth of Soma. Elsewhere we find Soma mentioned as the consecrated lord of the vegetable kingdom.[1] In the Cākṣuṣa Manvantara it so came to pass that the Prachetasas were practising severe penance which brought a considerable calamity on the plant-world. The earth became bereft of trees and only a few branches of trees remained. Soma came to the rescue of the vegetable kingdom and on their behalf requested the Pracetasas to be merciful. On Soma's request the Pracetasas took Māriṣā (daughter of Soma ?) as their wife and procreated Prajāpati Dakṣa who created anew the whole world.[2]

Classification of Plants : In the Tretā age the lord Svayaṁbhū created the *grāmyāraṇya* and *yajñiya oṣadhis*.[3] It appears that here the plant-world is divided into three classes, viz., *grāmya*, *āraṇya* or *grāmyāraṇya* and *yajñiya.* We have also a list of grāmya and grāmyāraṇya oṣadhis but the text is so confusing that it is difficult to arrive at the point of difference between the two classes. Again we have no list of the yajñiya oṣadhis. The statement that grāmyāraṇya oṣadhis do not require cultivation[4] suggests that these plants are distinct from the grāmya ones on this point but the list given of them does not warrant such an inference. It should be noted that the word "oṣadhi" here signifies the plant-world in general.[5] In continuation of the same we find reference to *vṛkṣa*, *gulma*, *latā*, *vallī*, *vīrudh*, and *tṛṇajātis*, and these are probably the five classes under which the plant-world was known.[6]

In the chapter on the narration of the progeny of Kaśyapa we have it stated that Irā had three daughters, viz., Latā, Vallī and Vīrudhā. Of Latā were born the vanaspatis *without* flowers. She (again ?) gave birth to vṛkṣas *with* flowers and fruits. Vallī had her progeny in the gulmas and the tṛṇa-jātis and vīrudhas were the progeny of Vīrudhā.[7] This amounts to the system of classification which can be presented thus :

(1) Latās — Vanaspatis (without flowers); Vṛkṣas (with flowers and fruits)

(2) Vallīs — Gulmas; Tṛṇa-jātis (grassy plants)

(3) Vīrudhas

1. Cf. 70. 3 ; 31. 38. 2. Cf. 63. 27 ff.
3. Gha and Ṅa omit the reference to *yajñiya oṣadhis*.
4. Cf. *aphālakṛṣṭā oṣadhyo grāmyāraṇyās tu sarvaśaḥ* : 8. 156.
5. Cf. 8. 149–56. 6. Cf. 8. 157. 7. Cf. 69. 338–41.

Divyauṣadhis[8] and *Vanauṣadhis*[9] are also mentioned but they are of not much use in this connection and may be noted for the reason that the genera of the plant-world was expressed by the term "oṣadhi"

The following is the alphabetical list of plants :

Āḍhakya It is included in the list of *grāmya* plants.[10]

Aguru There is a forest of aguru plants in the Kuru land.[11] Mentioned in connection with śrāddha.[12]

Akṣoṭaka It grows on the region between the Nāga and Kapiñjala mountains.[13]

Ambuda (?) A tree named Ambuda (*Ambuda-vṛkṣa*) is mentioned with reference to the end of Yuga.[14]

Āmra Mentioned as a progeny of Kaśyapa.[15]

Aṇu Included in the list of grāmya plants.[16]

Aśoka Cf. *Nīlāśoka*.

Aśvattha It is called vanaspati.[17] On the summit of the Vipula mountain grows a great aśvattha tree which was once garlanded by Indra—a fact from which the name of Ketumāla-dvīpa is derived.[18] The Aśvattha trees grow at the source of the river Kāverī on the Auśīra mountain.[19] Its sticks are recommended for use in śraddha.[20] It symbolizes the spirit of kingship.[21] The fire which the Gandharvas presented to king Purūravas was to be prepared with the sticks of aśvattha tree ; and it is said that by kindling fire in this manner a king accomplishes his cherished goal in the world of Gandharvas.[22]

Atasī Cf. Badarī.

Badarī The forest of the following trees or plants are situated in the region between Nāga and Kapiñajala mountains :—*drākṣa, nāga, kharjūra, nīlāśoka, dāḍima, akṣoṭaka, atasī, tilaka, kadalī* and *badarī*.[23] The vanquished Indra—king Raji had deprived him of his status—requested Bṛhaspati, "Please arrange for me the *puroḍāśa*-offering, composed of *badarī* fruits only, so that I may regain the lustre I have lost."[24]

---

8. Cf. 47. 4 ; 49. 26-7 ; 34. 54. 9. Cf. 3. 14.
10. Cf. 8. 152 Kha and Ga : *Āṭhakya* ; Gha and Ṅa omit it.
11. Cf. No. 660 App. 12. Cf. 75. 32. 13. Cf. 38. 66 ff.
14. Cf. 94. 37. 15. Cf. 69. 307-8 ; cf. No. 31 App. for *Āmra-vana*.
16. Cf. 8. 150 omitted in Ṅa. 17. Cf. 35. 38. 18. Cf. No. 819 App.
19. Cf. 77. 29. 20. Cf. 75. 71. 21. Cf. *aśvatthe rājya-bhāvanā* : 75. 1.
22. Cf. 91. 42-8. 23. Cf. 38. 66-70.
24. Cf. *badarī-phala-mātraṁ vai puroḍāśaṁ vidhatsva me* : 92. 92.

Balvaja — It is taboo in śrāddha.[25]

Bhaṇḍī — Its flowers are taboo in śrāddha.[26]

Bilva — Mentioned as a progeny of Kaśyapa.[27] The following trees grow on the Auśira mountain : *pālāśa*,[28] *khādira*, *bilva*, *plakṣa*, *aśvattha* and *vikaṅkata*.[29] Again the following are the *yajñiya* trees : *samāna-plakṣa*, *nyagrodha*, *plakṣa*, *aśvattha*, *vikaṅkata*, *udumbara*, *bilva*,[30] *candana*,[31] *sarala* (?), *devadāru*, *śāla*[32] and *khādira*. Their sticks (*samidh*) are good for śraddha purposes. So should sticks of *kalkaleya* trees (?) be used.[33] For the description of *Bilva-vana* and *Bilva-sthalī* see No. 146–7 App. The use of a vessel (*pātra*) made of bilva wood is said to fetch wealth.[34]

Campaka — Cf. No. 168 App.

Caṇaka — Mentioned as grāmya oṣadhi.[35]

Candana — There is a forest of candana trees in the Kuru land.[36]

Dāḍima — See Badarī above.

Darbha — Darbha grass is used in śrāddha.[37] The Creator in his boar form was *dharbha-romā*.[38]

Devadāru — Cf. No. 226 App.; cf. also Bilva above.

Drākṣa — Cf. Badarī above.

Durvāra — Mentioned in connection with śrāddha.[39]

Falgu — A vessel made of falgu wood is recommended for use in śrāddha for the fulfilment of all the desires.[40]

Godhūma — It is a grāmya oṣadhi.[41]

Gṛñjana — *Laśuna*, *Gṛñjana*, *Palāṇḍu* and *Karambha* are taboo in śrāddha. Any food-preparation in which any of them is used should be avoided in śrāddha. Here is a reason why this is so enjoined.[42] Formerly, in the Deva-Asura war, Bali was wounded and the drops of blood that gushed forth from his wounds fell on the earth, and from that blood originated the above plants (?). They are again inferior on account of their smell and taste.[43]

---

25. Cf. 75. 61. 26. Cf. 75. 34. 27. Cf. 69. 307–8.
28. Kha, Gha and Ṅa : *Palāśa*. 29. Cf. 77. 29.
30. Ga, Gha and Ṅa have *viśva*. 31. Ga, Gha and Ṅa : *viśvacandana*.
32. Kha : *śālmali*. 33. Cf. 75. 70–4. 34. Cf. 75. 3–4.
35. Cf. 8. 152 omitted in Gha and Ṅa.
36. No. 660 App. cf. No. 332 App. for *candana* trees in the Gokarṇa forest. See also No. 437 for *candana* in Malayadvipa.
37. Cf. 75. 17–8 ; 83. 79. 38. Cf. 6. 16. 39. Cf. 75. 39. 40. Cf. 75. 3.
41. Cf. 8. 150 omitted in Ṅa. 42. Cf. *kāraṇaṁ cātra vakṣyate*.
43. Cf. *hīnāni rasa-gandhataḥ* : 78. 12–4 Ṅa omits all this information.

Ikṣu	The ikṣu (sugar-cane) plants grow in the Plakṣa dvīpa.[44] The Āgrayaṇa offerings to Pitṛs in the form of *śyāmākas* and *ikṣus* are particularly recommended in the śrāddha ceremony.[45]
Jambū	Cf. Nos. 436, 823 App. for the derivation of the name of Jambudvīpa.
Japā	Its flowers are a taboo in śrāddha.[46]
Kadalī	Cf. Badarī above.
Kālāmra	It grows in a forest in the Bhadrāśva (?) dvīpa.[47]
Kalkaleya	Cf. Bilva above.
Kalpavṛkṣa	It grows in the Kuru land.[48] There is also a reference to honey extracted from this tree.[49]
Kapittha	The following trees are tabooed in śrāddha : *śleṣmātaka*, *naktamāla*, *kapittha*, *śālmali*, *nīpa* and *vibhītaka*.[50]
Karambha	Cf. gṛñjana above.
Kārūṣa	One of the grāmya oṣadhis.[51]
Kāśa	It is good for śrāddha purposes.[52]
Kāśmarī	By using a vessel (pātra) made of kāśmarī tree one can bring about the destruction of demons.[53]
Khādira	Cf. Bilva above. Its sticks are used in śrāddha on the occasion of *pitṛ-tarpaṇa*.[54]
Kharjūra	Cf. Badarī above. Varūtrin was one of the four sons of Uśanas Śukra. Varūtrin again had four sons who were great Brahmins and offered oblations to Suras.[55] But they approached Manu to bring about the destruction of the Institution of Sacrifice.[56] Indra, however, seems to have scolded Manu who then migrated from that country (where the sons of Varūtrin lived ?).[57] The yatis (i.e. the sons of Varūtrin) now intended to annihilate Indra who hid himself in the southern side of the *vedī* (sacrificial altar). The yatis appeared on the scene of the altar with *śālāvṛkas* and probably proceeded to devour the eatables lying about it, but Indra cut their heads off and the heads that fell were turned into the *kharjūra* plants.[58]
Kiṁśuka	Cf. No. 584 App.

---

44. Cf. 49. 28-30. 45. Cf. 78. 7-8. 46. Cf. 75. 34. 47. Cf. 43. 6.
48. Cf. 45. 40. 49. Cf. 8. 128. 50. Cf. 75. 75-6.
51. Cf. 8. 152 omitted in Gha and Ṅa. 52. Cf. 75. 41.
53. Cf. 75. 2 omitted in Ṅa. 54. Cf. 74. 9.
55. Cf. *brahmiṣṭhāḥ Sura-yājakāḥ*. 56. Cf. *ijyā-dharmavināśārthaṁ Manum etya*.
57. Cf. *tasmād deśād apākramat*. 58. Cf. 65. 75-84.

Kūlatthaka	It is one of the grāmya oṣadhis.[59]
Kuraṇḍaka	Its flowers are tabooed in śrāddha.[60]
Kuśa	Cf. Nos. 673–6 App.
Lakuca	Its juice is a drink.
Laśuna	Cf. Gṛñjana above.
Lava	The lava grass is a taboo in śrāddha.[61]
Māṣa	One of the four grāmya oṣadhis.[62]
Masūra	One of the grāmya oṣadhis.[63]
Mātuluṅga	Cf. No. 804 App.
Mudga	One of the grāmya oṣadhis.[64]
Nāga	Cf. Badarī.
Naktamāla	Cf. Kapittha.
Nīlāśoka	Cf. Badarī.
Nīpa	Cf. Kapittha.
Niṣpāva	One of the grāmya oṣadhis.[65]
Nyagrodha	The Nyagrodha symbolizes prosperity.[66] We occasionally find similes such as "with arms as wide as the nyagrodha tree".[67] The fruits of this tree formed the food for Durgā when she practised austerities.[68] The people of the Ramaṇaka-varṣa live on the juice of these fruits.[69] We have also a description of a very big Nyagrodha tree on the peak of a mountain in the Ketumāla-varṣa.[70] The yakṣas worship the tree where Guhyaka, a yakṣa, lives.[71]
Padma, (*Ambuja*, *Kamala*, *Kumuda*, *Utpala*, etc.)	This is the plant mentioned either by way of similes or symbolically. Lakes beautiful with the lotus-plants are frequently described.[72] In the Padmavana there is a big lotus in which the goddess Śrī resides.[73] In the centre of a lake in Śabala forest is a great *sthala-padminī*, which is described in detail. In its centre grows a big Nyagrodha tree, about five yojanas in extent, where the god Hari dwells.[74] The *padma-pātra* (i.e. a vessel made of the lotus leaves) was

59. Cf. 8. 151 ; omitted in Gha and Ṅa. 60. Cf. 75. 34. 61. Cf. 75. 51.
62. Cf. 8. 151 omitted in Gha and Ṅa. 63. Cf. 8. 151 omitted in Gha and Ṅa.
64. Cf. 8. 151 omitted in Gha and Ṅa. 65. Cf. 8. 151 omitted in Gha and Ṅa.
66. Cf. *puṣṭikāmaṁ ca Nyagrodhaṁ* : 75. 2 omitted in Ṅa.
67. Cf. *nyagrodhapariṇāhāḥ* : 57. 66–7 ; 57. 78. etc. 68. Cf. 72. 8–9.
69. Cf. 45. 3–5. 70. Cf. 35. 40–2.
71. Cf. 69. 150 ; cf. also *Bilva* and *Padma*. 72. Cf. 41. 14–6 ; 37. 2–3 ; 45. 33.
73. Cf. 37. 6–8. 74. Cf. 38. 51 ff.

	used by the Gandharvas in the incident of the "milching" of the earth.[75] Brahmā's origin from the lotus whose stalk arose from the navel of Viṣṇu is very often mentioned.[76] The earth is said to have a shape like that of a lotus.[77] A lotus-mark on an arm of a king indicates that he will be a paramount sovereign (?).[78]
Palāṇḍu	Cf. Gṛñjana.
Palāśa	The Palāśa symbolises the lustre of a Brahmin.[79] A vessel made of palāśa wood was used by the plant-world in the incident of the "milching" of the earth.[80] It grows in the Campaka forest.[81]
Panasa	In the Bhadrāśva(?)-dvīpa grows a heavenly Panasa tree from which six kinds of *rasas* are obtained.[82]
Pārijāta	The Mahendra forest abounds in the Pārijāta plants the frangrance of whose flowers spreads over hundreds of yojanas.[83]
Parūṣaka	We have a description of Parūṣaka-sthali.[84]
Pāṭalā	Its fruits formed the food of Durgā in the course of her penance.[85]
Paṭola	Referred to in connection with śrāddha.[86]
Plakṣa	See Bilva and cf. also Plakṣa-dvīpa Nos. 988–990 in App. The Plakṣa-tree symbolizes the lordship of the world.[87]
Priyaṁgu	It is one of the grāmya oṣadhis.[88]
Puṣkara	See Puṣkara-dvīpa, Nos. 1027-30 App.
Śāka	See Śāka-dvīpa, Nos. 1099–1101 App.
Śāla	A Śāla-forest is mentioned as being situated in the Bhadrāśva(?)-dvīpa.[89]
Śālmala	See Śālmali-dvīpa, Nos. 1108–11 App.; cf. also Bilva and Kapittha.
Sarala	Cf. Bilva.
Sarjaka	Cf. Bilva. It is a taboo in śrāddha.[90]

75. Cf. 62. 187–8. 76. Cf. 24. 52; 23. 113; 54. 65; 24. 11–3; 5. 31 etc.
77. Cf. *Pṛthivī kīrtitā kṛtsnā padmākārāmayā dvijāḥ* : 41. 86.
78. Cf. 57. 79. 79. Cf. *pālāśaṁ brahmavarcasvaṁ* : 75. 1. 80. Cf. 62. 191.
81. Cf. 37. 18–9; cf. also *Bilva*. 82. Cf. 43. 4. 83. Cf. 39. 11 ff.
84. Cf. 38. 63 ff. 85. Cf. 72. 8-9. 86. Cf. 78. 9.
87. Cf. *sarva-bhūtādhipatyaṁ ca plakṣe nityam udāhṛtam* : 75. 1.
88. Cf. 8. 151 omitted in Gha and Ṅa. 89. Cf. 43. 6; cf. *Bilva*.
90. Cf. 78. 11 Kha, Ga, Gha and Ṅa read differently.

Savī(tī)naka	Kha has *sacīnaka*.[91] It is one of the grāmya oṣadhis.[92]
Śleśmātaka	Cf. Kapittha. The Brahma-Rākṣasas have their dwellings on this tree.[93]
Śyāmāka	Inspite of the opposition of Indra, Tvaṣṭā drank soma and was hurled down on the earth and the śyāmāka trees had their origin thence. In the Āgrayaṇa offerings to Pitṛs śyāmāka-sticks are recommended for use.[94]
Udāra	It is one of the grāmya oṣadhis.[95]
Udumbara	Cf. Bilva. The vessels, sticks and fruits of the udumbara are very good for śrāddha purposes.[96] We have also a description of an Udumbara-forest.[97]
Uśīra	Mentioned with *Tamāla* in connection with śrāddha.[98]
Tāla	We have a description of Tāla-forest.[99]
Tamāla	Cf. Uśīra.
Tila	It is a grāmya oṣadhi.[100] *Kṛṣṇa-tila* (i.e. black variety of tila) is also mentioned in connection with śrāddha.[101]
Tilaka	Cf. Badarī.
Vaṁśīkarīra.	It is a taboo in śrāddha.[102]
Vaṭa	Dakṣa, in his prayer to god Śiva, addresses him as *Vaṭa*.[103]
Veṇu	*Veṇu-pātra* is recommended for use in śrāddha.[104] We have also a Veṇumat mountain.[105]
Vibhītaka	Cf. Kapittha.
Vikaṅkata	Cf. Bilva.
Vrīhi	One of the grāmya oṣadhis.[106]
Yava	One of the grāmya oṣadhis.[107]

II. The Animal-World

Of the Animal-World in General : We have seen, in connection with the Kṛta age, that the animal-kingdom did not exist then and that the people enjoyed a life of bliss.[108] In the further account of creation, however, it is stated that after the creation of gods, the Creator proceeded to create the animals from the various parts of his

91. Kha has *sacīnaka*. 92. Cf. 8. 151 omitted in Gha and Ṅa.
93. Cf. 69. 135. 94. Cf. 78. 6–9. 95. Cf. 8. 151 omitted in Gha and Ṅa.
96. Cf. 75. 67, 97. Cf. 38. 3 ff. 98. Cf. 75. 32. 99. Cf. 37. 23 ff.
100. Cf. 8. 150. 101. Cf. 75. 31. 102. Cf. 78. 11. 103. Cf. 30. 250.
104. Cf. 75. 5. 105. Cf. No. 1427–8 App. 106. Cf. 8. 150. 107. Cf. 8. 150.
108. The text leaves the matter here and does not elucidate, as it does in the case of the vegetable kingdom, whether the animal world made its first appearance in the Tretā age ; cf. 8. 54.

body.[109] We have already noted above the birth of Prajāpati Dakṣa as a son of Pracetasas. Dakṣa is said to have created the animals, such as the bipeds and quadrupeds.[110] This was the history of animals in the Cākṣuṣa Manvantara and in this Vaivasvata Manvantara they are born as the progeny of Kaśyapa who is also the ancestor of the Devas, Asuras, Gandharvas, etc. and the plant-world.[111]

Classification of Animals : The four-fold classification, viz., *aṇḍaja*, *udbhija*, *svedaja* and *jarāyuja* is frequently alluded to in the Purāṇa. We are informed that at the sacrifice of Dakṣa all the creatures of the world such as jarāyujas, aṇḍajas, svedajas,[112] and udbhijjakas—were invited to attend the session.[113] We have also a list of svedaja creatures.[114]

The two-fold classification of bipeds and quadrupeds is mentioned above. Another system of classification is probably implied in the grāmya and āraṇya paśus. The grāmya (i.e. the domesticated) animals are : *go*, *aja*, *puruṣa* (man !), *meṣa*, *aśva*, *aśvatara* and *gardabha*. The *āraṇya* (i.e. wild) beasts are : *śvāpadas*, *dvi-khuras* (i.e. having two hoofs), *hastin*, *vānara*, *pakṣis*, *undakas*, and *sarī-sṛpas*.[115]

Domesticated Animals : The list of grāmya animals given above suggests that they were the domesticated animals. It should be noted that the elephant is included in the list of wild beasts and the list of domesticated animals does not mention the dog. We have, however, other references in the Purāṇas to suggest that the elephant was already domesticated. The horse and the cow are the most important of the domesticated animals. The buffalo is not to be found in the list of grāmya animals and we elsewhere find king Satyavrata hunting the Mahiṣas as if they were wild beasts but in the śrāddha chapters we find the milk of a she-buffalo as a taboo in śrāddha which suggests that the animal was domesticated.

The following is an alphabetical list of animals :

Aja It is born of the Creator's mouth.[116] It is included in the list of *grāmya-paśus*.[117] It is a useful animal in yajñas (as a victim)[118] along with cows, *mahiṣas*, *aśvas*, *hastins*, and birds.[119] It is said that at the end of the Kali age people will be keeping *aja*, *eḍaka*, *khara* and *uṣṭra* as their pet animals.[120] At the time of the birth of Skanda Kārtikeya, Vāyu gave him *mayūra* and *kukkuṭa* ; lord Svayaṁbhū gave him *aja* and Śiva gave him *meṣa* as presents.[121]

---

109. Cf. 9. 41 ff. 110. Cf. *dvi-pado' tha catuṣpadaḥ* : 63. 40.
111. Cf. 69. 290 ff. 112. Gha : *sadbhedajas*. 113. Cf. 23. 101.
114. Cf. 69. 298 ff. ; cf. also 30. 227. 115. Cf. 9. 44–8. 116. Cf. 9. 43.
117. Cf. 9. 46. 118. Cf. *upayuktā kriyāsv ete yajñiyāsu*. 119. Cf. 59. 16.
120. Cf. 99. 406. 121. Cf. 72. 46.

Aśva — The horse is said to have been born of the Creator's feet.[122] It is included in the list of domesticated animals.[123] We have noted references to stables for horses and to horse-riding. Horses are good gifts for Brahmins in śrāddha[124] and they are regarded useful in sacrifices. Horses were yoked to chariots. A horse was one of the select jewels (atiśaya-ratnāni) of a cakravartin in the Tretā age.[125] The horses of the Gāndhāra country are said to be the best amongst the species.[126] The *Aśvinī-nakṣatra* is said to be favourable to the acquisition of horses.[127]

Aśvatara — Included in the list of domesticated animals.[128]

Avi — Its milk is a taboo in śrāddha.[129]

Baka — Śyenī was a wife of Aruṇa.[130] She gave birth to the *Sārasas, Kuraras,* and *Bakas*.[131]

Bhramara — The Bhramaras are the progeny of Pulaha.[132] In the geographical chapters we are often reminded of the existence of the *ṣaṭ-padas* or *bhṛṅgas* on the mountain-tops and in the forests where their humming sound is alluded to.[133]

Biḍāla — The Bhūtas who worship Śiva on the Kailāsa mountain are said to have the faces of biḍālas.[134]

Cakora — The following are said to resound the forests such as Caitraratha, Nandana, etc. with their melodious sounds; *sārikās, mayūras, cakoras, śukas, bhṛṅgarājas, kokilas, sugrīvas* and *bhramaras* etc.[135]

Cakravāka — Dhṛtarāṣṭrī was a wife of Garuḍa. She gave birth to *haṁsas, kalahaṁsas, cakravākas,* and various other kinds of birds.[136] The attachment between the *cakravāka* and the *cakravākī* is alluded to in a simile.[137]

Chagala — Recommended for the offering of its flesh in śrāddha.

Eḍaka — Cf. Aja.

Gardabha — Regarded as a grāmya-paśu.

Garuḍa — Garutmat or Garuḍa had four wives, viz. Bhāsī, Krauñcī, Śukī and Dhṛtarāṣṭrī. Śukī gave birth to sons who are the enemies of snakes who occupy various regions

---

122. Cf. 9. 42–4. 123. Cf. 9. 46–7. 124. Cf. 80. 15. 125. Cf. 57. 68.
126. Cf. *Gāndhāra-deśajāś cāpi turagā vājināṁ varāḥ* : 99. 10.
127. Cf. 82. 14. 128. Cf. 9. 42–4. 129. Cf. ,8. 17. 130. Cf. 69. 326.
131. Cf. 69. 336. 132. Cf. 70. 64
133. Cf. 36. 1–5 ; 34. 18 ; 37. 7 ; 37. 20 ; 38. 53 ; 38. 9–10 ; 39. 20 ; 45. 32–3 ; 47. 70 etc, etc.
134. Cf. 54. 40. 135. Cf. 36. 1–5. 136. Cf. 69. 337–9. 137. Cf. 45. 19.

such as the Śālmali-dvīpa, and Devakūṭa and other mountains. Following are the progeny of Bhāsī: *ulūkas*, *kākas*, *kukkuṭas*, *mayūras*, *kalaviṅkas*, *kapotas* and *lāvatittiras*. Krauñcī gave birth to the *vārdhīṇasas* and the progeny of Dhṛtarāṣṭrī are already noted above.[138] Garuḍa as the vehicle of Viṣṇu is also mentioned.[139] Viṣṇu is called *garuḍa-dhvaja*[140] and Śiva too is mentioned as the lord of Garuḍas.[141] Garuḍa is the "consecrated lord" of the birds.[142]

Go: the cow, the bull, etc.

This species had its birth from the belly of the Creator[143] and is included in the list of domesticated animals.

The cow symbolizes the *gāyatrī* metre.[144] The cow that dropped from Maheśvara's mouth when Brahmā was engaged in meditation, was none else than the gāyatrī.[145] *Prakṛti* (or matter) too is called the cow.[146] Flying of the Earth in the form of a cow in the incident of the "milching of the earth" by Pṛthu is a good instance of symbolism.[147]

The cow figures considerably in ritual. Gift of cows in sacrifices is a highly commended act. The cow is included in the list of animals useful in sacrifices.

In the description of the end of the Kali age we find a reference indicating that the slaughter of cows is a sin. Again, in the same connection we are told that the number of cows "will be diminishing". But a different state of facts is reflected in the material that is available on non-vegetarian diet.

We have a solitary reference connecting Vāsudeva Kṛṣṇa with the cows. He is said to have been brought up amongst the cows[148] and in the chapter purporting to glorify the god Viṣṇu we find the sages asking Sūta, "How is it that the god who protects the whole world lived amongst the cows and protected them?"[149]

We find cows serving also as means of exchange and gavyūti is a unit of measurement of distance.

The bull figures in the Purāṇa mostly as a vehicle of Śiva[150] who is also mentioned as *vṛṣabha-dhvaja*

138. Cf. 69. 328–38. 139. Cf. 97. 22. 140. Cf. 24. 80. 141. Cf. 24. 108.
142. Cf. 70. 10. 143. Cf. 9. 42–4. 144. Cf. 23. 69. 145. Cf. 23. 5-12.
146. Cf. 23. 57. 147. Cf. 62. 136 ff.
148. Cf. *goṣu govindaḥ saṁvṛddhaḥ* : 96. 218.
149. Cf. *gopāyanaṁ yaḥ kurute jagatāṁ sārvalaukikaṁ sa kathaṁ gāṁ gato viṣṇur gopatvam akarot prabhuḥ* : 97. 12.
150. Cf. 30. 261; 54. 107–8; 55. 54 etc.

(i.e. having the Bull standard).[151] Śiva himself is addressed as Bull by Dakṣa in his prayer to the god.[152] The bull is the "consecrated lord" of the quadrupeds.[153]

Godhā — Already referred to as good for offering its flesh in śrāddha.

Golāṅgūlas — Cf. Vānaras.

Gṛdhra — The gṛdhras preyed upon the spoils of Dakṣa's sacrifice.[154] If a *kāka*, *kapota*, *gṛdhra* or any other bird that has fondness for the dead bodies touches the head of a person, he is sure to die within a period of six months.[155] The Bhūtas are said to have the faces of gṛdhras.[156]

Haṁsa — Cf. Cakravāka. On the Devakūṭa mountain there are many haṁsas.[157]

Hariṇa — Mṛgī was a wife of Pulaha. Her progeny are the *hariṇas*, *mṛgas*, *śaśas*, *nyaṅkus*, *śarabhas*, *rurus* and *pṛṣatas*. (Most of these are the different varieties of the species of deer.)[158]

Hastin — (*Nāga*, *Gaja*, *Dantin*, *Dvirada*, *Kuñjara*, *Karin*, *Dvipa*, *Mātaṅga*, etc.): Irāvatī was a wife of Pulaha. Her son was Airāvata, the vehicle of Indra. He was the first king of the elephants.[159] The various words for elephants are also explained in this account.[160] The word *sāmaja*, however, is interesting as it connects the animal with the Sāmaveda.[161] In the account of cosmology we find them described as being born of the Creator's feet.[162] It appears that "gaja" signified the class of the species born of domesticated parents.[163]

We have seen above that the elephant is included in the list of wild beasts (*āraṇyapaśus*). But there are numerous references to suggest that they were tamed. We have it in a simile that when a lion or an elephant is captured and made to serve he becomes *mṛdu* (i.e. tame).[164] A reference to stables for elephants had already been made and elephants are also

---

151. Cf. 30. 180; 24. 106; 24. 60 etc.
152. Cf. 30. 267–8.
153. Cf. 70. 10.
154. Cf. 30. 170.
155. Cf. 19. 6.
156. Cf. 40. 21–2.
157. Cf. 41. 70.
158. Cf. 69. 206.
159. Cf. *prathamaḥ sa mataṅgarāṭ* : 69. 211.
160. Cf. 69. 231–4.
161. Cf. *sāmajaḥ sāma-jātatvād* : 69. 244.
162. Cf. 9. 42–4.
163. Cf. *narair baddhāḥ kule teṣāṁ jāyante vikṛtā gajāḥ* : 69. 224.
164. Cf. 10. 83.

	recommended as good gifts to Brahmins in śrāddha.[165] The elephant is also a *yajñiya* animal (cf. *Aja*). Making of gifts under the shadow of an elephant is considered to be meritorious.[166] It is already seen that elephants were employed in war.
Kāka	Cf. Garuḍa and Gṛdhra.
Kalaviṅka	Cf. Garuḍa and Cakora.
Kapota	Cf. Gṛdhra and Garuḍa. Śiva is addressed as *Kapota* in a prayer by Dakṣa.[167]
Kāraṇḍa	On the Devakūṭa mountain there are many Kāraṇḍas.[168]
Khaḍga	Mṛgamandā was a wife of Pulaha. Her progeny are the *gavayas*, *mahiṣas*, *uṣṭras*, *varāhas*, *khaḍgas* and *gauramukhas*.[169]
Khadyota	Its flight in the night-time is a matter for simile.[170]
Khara	Cf. Aja.
Kīṭakas or *Pipīlakas*	There is a small passage in the account of the progeny of Kaśyapa on the insect-world. The insects are supposed to be *svedaja* creatures (i. e. those born of perspiration, heat or moisture). All the names of these insects are not enumerated here as the passage is confusing to some extent. Some of them may be mentioned, viz., *yūkas*,[171] *mīnakas*, *tittiras*, *siṁhalas*, *romalas*, *picchalas*, *nīlamakṣikas*, *sarpas*, *vṛścikas*, etc. Some of these are supposed to have their origin from foodgrains such as *mudga*, *taṇḍula*, *māṣa*, etc. and from fruits such as *panasa*, etc.[172]
Kokila	Cf. Cakora.
Krauñca	Cf. Garuḍa. Kārtikeya is called the destroyer of krauñcas.[173]
Kukkuṭa	Cf. Garuḍa and Aja. It is a taboo in śrāddha.[174]
Kumbhīra	He who recites the names of Devī (i. e. Śiva's wife) is assured protection from Kumbhīras and Vyāghras.[175]
Kuraras	They are the progeny of Śyenī, the wife of Aruṇa.[176]
Kūrma	Its utility for offering its flesh in śrāddha has already been referred to. Its contraction of limbs is mentioned as a simile.[177]
Lāvaṭittiras	Cf. Garuḍa.

165. Cf. 80. 15. 166. Cf. 80. 45. 167. Cf. 30. 241.
168. Cf. 41. 70. 169. Gha : *Gauramṛgas*. Cf. 69. 207.
170. Cf. 6. 7; 8. 4; 59. 207. 171. Omitted in Ka and Ga.
172. Cf. 69. 298 ff. 173. Cf. 54. 19-21. 174. Cf. 78. 38-40.
175. Cf. 9. 96. 176. Cf. 69. 336. 177. Cf. *kūrmo'ṅgānīva* : 11. 19; 93. 94.

Mahiṣa	Cf. Aja and Khaḍga.
Matsya	The utility of its flesh in śrāddha has been referred to already.
Mayūra	Cf. Aja, Cakora and Garuḍa. It is also a vehicle of Kārtikeya.[178]
Meṣa	It is included in the list of grāmya paśus. Meṣas as pets of Urvaśī have been mentioned before. See also Aja.
Mūṣika	The mūṣikas "will be" a menace to the people at the end of the Kali age.[179]
Nāgas and Sarpas	Brahmā was practising severe penance as a result of which sweat came forth from his body which gave rise to the serpent world. These *sarpas* had marks of *svastika* on them. Brahmā did not like this creation.[180] They are included in the insect-world which had its origin from perspiration, heat or moisture.[181] Vāsuki or Takṣaka is mentioned as their chief or consecrated lord.[182] Śiva too is their lord.[183] The lord of serpents who lives on the Devakūṭa mountain has a hundred hoods and is marked with the cakra of Viṣṇu.[184] It is said that at the end of the Kali age they "will be" a menace to the people.[185]
Nyaṅku	Cf. Hariṇa.
Pārṣata	The utility of its flesh in śrāddha has been noted.
Pṛṣata	Cf. Hariṇa.
Ruru	Cf. Hariṇa.
Śakuni	The utility of its flesh in śrāddha has already been mentioned. Śiva is addressed in a prayer as *Śakuni*.[186]
Śarabha	Cf. Hariṇa. Śiva is addressed in prayer as *Śarabha*.[187] They are supposed to be born of the Creator's feet.[188]
Sārikā	Cf. Cakora.
Sārasas	Cf. Baka.
Śaśa	Cf. Hariṇa. The utility of its flesh in śrāddha has been noted already. *Śaśāda* (hare-eater) was a nickname of Vikukṣi, son of king Ikṣvāku.
Siṁha, Śārdūla	The lion is often mentioned in the Purāṇa in the similes for expressing strength[189] and well-developed shoulders.[190] This beast is a terror to *mṛgas* (i. e.

178. Cf. 54. 19–21. 179. Cf. 58. 61. 180. Cf. 25. 64 ff.
181. Cf. *Kīṭakas*. 182. Cf. 70. 10–3. 183. Cf. 24. 108.
184. Cf. 41. 73 ; cf. also Garuḍa. 185. Cf. 58. 61. 186. Cf. 30. 260
187. Cf. 97. 180. 188. Cf. 9. 42–4. 189. Cf. 93. 68 ; 88. 165 ; 92. 74.
190. Cf. *siṁha-skandha* : 88. 192.

	other beasts).[191] Prasena was killed by a lion when he was on a hunting excursion in a forest but the lion in turn was killed by Jāmbavat (the lord of Ṛkṣa—i. e. Ṛkṣa mountain).[192] The lion is the "consecrated lord" of beasts.[193]
	There is a reference to the caging of lions. Vīrabhadra rushed towards the scene of Dakṣa-*yajña* as a lion let loose from a cage.[194] Cf. also Hastin regarding taming of lions. We have also an incarnation of Narasiṁha (Man-lion) of Viṣṇu who killed Hiraṇyakaśipu with *nakhas* (or nails).
Śuka	Cf. Cakra.
Śvā	It was a taboo in śrāddha.[195]
Tarakṣu	Cf. Vānara.
Ulūkas	Cf. Garuḍa.
Uṣṭra	Cf. Khaḍga. They are supposed to be born of the Creator's feet.[196] The milk of the uṣṭra is a taboo in śrāddha.[197]
Vānaras	Haribhadrā was a wife of Pulaha. Her progeny are the *Golāṅgūlas*, *tarakṣus*, *vānaras* and *vyāghras*.[198]
Varāha	Cf. Khaḍga. The utility of its flesh in śrāddha is already referred to. We also have a reference to the Varāha-incarnation of Viṣṇu.
Vārdhiṇasas	Cf. Baka.
Vyāghra	Cf. Vānara and Kumbhīra. Garments of tiger-skin were made.

---

191. Cf. 54. 55. 192. Cf. 96. 33–4. 193. Cf. 70. 10–3.
194. Cf. *bandhāt pramuktena siṁhena iva* : 30. 139. 195. Cf. 78. 38–40.
196. Cf. 9. 42–4. 197. Cf. 78. 17. 198. Cf. 69. 208.

PART II

CHAPTER I

SOCIAL ORGANIZATION

I. Social Theory

Cosmic Origin : The earliest evidence for the theory of society of four varṇas is found in the famous Hymn of Man occurring in the tenth Maṇḍala of the ṚV. It is here said that Puruṣa's mouth became the Brahmin, his arms the Rājanya (warrior), his thighs the Vaiśya and his feet the Śūdra.[1] But this hymn is generally regarded as "one of the very latest poems of the Ṛgvedic age ; for it presupposes a knowledge of the three oldest Vedas."[2] The Śatapatha Brāhmaṇa actually refers to the four varṇas and it has been conceded that it was a fact that the four varṇas existed in the days of the Brāhmaṇas which do not merely speak of "a theory which was to be striven for as an ideal". Conditions seem to have been considerably changed at the time of the Smṛti-writers who often seem to try to approximate the state of society existing in their times to the varṇas of the older literature which they held were of hoary antiquity.[3]

The contents of the Vāyu Purāṇa at once remind us of the Puruṣa Sūkta, the only difference being that it has Kṣatriya instead of the Rājanya of the latter. The stanza occurs in the Purāṇa at two places in the cosmological account which is greatly influenced by the Sāṁkhya ideas—a fact which, in addition to the mention of Kṣatriya for Rājanya referred to above, suggests that this Vāyu-material is considerably later than that of the Puruṣa Sūkta of the ṚV., if not coeval in point of time with the works of the Smṛti-writers.

Mythic Origin : The statement that Śiva is the originator of the varṇāśrama is merely an eulogy of the god by Dakṣa and may be dismissed altogether in connection with this enquiry. With regard to Manu, however, it may be stated here that even in the age of the ṚV. he was regarded as the "first sacrificer and the ancestor of the human race. The Śatapatha Brāhmaṇa makes Manu play the part of a Noah in the history of human descent."[4]

It is not clear whether our Purāṇa refers to this Manu. It does not even make an allusion to the story of the flood of the Śatapatha Brāhmaṇa. The reference to Smārta-dharma as being stated by Svāyaṁbhuva Manu and the association of Manu with the sages suggest that

1. Mac. *HSL*, 133. 2. *Ibid*. 3. Kane, II, 47. 4. Mac. *HSL*, 108.

we have here something to do with the author of the so-called Mānava Dharma-śāstra[5] though it is inopportune to guess more about that for the present.

Some observations may be made regarding the connection of Bali with the foundation of varṇāśrama. We know from the political history of the Purāṇas that this king Bali belonged to the Ānava branch of the Ailas and had five sons after whom the five kingdoms of the east, viz., Aṅga, Vaṅga, Kaliṅga, Puṇḍra and Suhma were so called.[6] If any historical significance is attached to the reference of the Vāyu under discussion we may be allowed to infer that this king Bali was regarded by the Purāṇa-tradition to be the propagator of Aryan culture in the eastern countries which we know did not come under the pale of Aryanism quite as late as the period of the early Dharma-sūtras and grammatical treatises.[7]

Varṇa, Āśrama and Dharma: "The word āśrama does not occur in the Saṁhitās or Brāhmaṇas"[8] but this does not mean that the stages of life indicated by this word were unknown in the Vedic period. Perhaps, the earliest reference to the four āśramas, though somewhat obscure, occurs in the Ait. Br. 33.[9] A much clearer reference to the three āśramas is found in the Ch. Up. II. 23. 1. But still one cannot say whether the four āśramas were certainly known in the time of the earliest Upaniṣads which, however, frequently allude to the three āśramas.[10] The Ch. Up. clearly relates the term āśrama to dharma though its connection with varṇa is not definitely indicated.[11] The Jātakas, however, are aware of the four āśramas, especially of a Brahmin, though the incidents found therein do not necessarily presuppose a schematic partition of the course of life of a Brahmin.[12] We are not, for the present, in a position to take it for granted that in these works the āśramas are so linked up with the varṇas and dharma as to suggest the evolution of a compact social theory. It is, however, in the Arthaśāstra of Kauṭilya that we get a definite and clear evidence of the blending together of these three concepts[13]—viz., those represented by the three terms varṇa, āśrama and dharma—so as to make a coherent whole. Even the earliest Dharma-sūtras refer to the four āśramas and in the whole range of the Dharma-śāstra literature these three concepts receive elaborate treatment and are closely interrelated.[14] Thus we can safely assign the highest antiquity of the social theory of varṇāśrama-dharma to the age of Kauṭilya.

---

5. *SBE*, 25, *Introduction*, p. xx ff. 6. *AIHT*, 109.
7. *History of Bengal*, Ed. by R. C. Mujumdar, 1. 36–7. 8. Kane, II. 418.
9. *Ibid.* 420. 10. *Ibid.* 422. 11. *Ibid.* 420. 12. Fick, 193 ff.
13. Cf. *Caturṇāṁ varṇānāṁ āśramāṇāṁ ca sva-dharma-sthāpana*...etc. p. 7.
14. Vide Kane, op. cit, 416 and 1 ff.

Out of the three concepts of varṇa, āśrama and dharma, the Vāyu appears to put more emphasis on dharma and certainly presupposes the existence of some works on the dharma-śāstra. The fact that it refers to the smārta-dharma as being primarily concerned with the varṇāśrama suggests a knowledge of some existing Smṛti-works of which the existence of one, namely the Manu Smṛti, may be accounted for by the statement that the Smārta-dharma, as based on tradition, is told by Svāyaṁbhuva Manu.

It should be noted that the term *śiṣṭācāra* is mentioned, in a technical sense, as an important source of law in many of the Dharma-śāstra works from the earliest times of Vasiṣtha and Baudhāyana.[15] As to the exact nature of the authority of śiṣṭācāra and its relation to the authority of the Śruti and Smṛti, there is some diversity of opinion amongst the ancient law-givers and their commentators[16] and our Purāṇa is apparently making here a reference to those of them who placed the authority of the śiṣṭācāra on the same footing as that of the Vedas and the Smṛtis.

Varṇa and Varṇa-saṁkara : So far as our knowledge goes the term *varṇa-saṁkara*, in its technical aspect, does not occur in the Vedic literature. The Sāmavidhāna Brāhmaṇa (3. 4. 2) and the Vaṁśa-Brāhmaṇa do mention the word ' saṁkara ' but not in connection with ' varṇa '. Though many instances of inter-caste marriages can be cited from the Vedic literature,[17] still we find there the rules regarding connubium appearing in a stage of development.[18] As regards the rules of commensality, however, there are no traces in the Vedas. It is in the Jātakas that we, for the first time, become aware of the ideas implicit in the varṇa-saṁkara though we are not certain for the present whether these works refer to the word ' varṇasaṁkara ' in this connection.[19] In them the rules both as regards connubium and commensality appear considerably developed[20] and the main force of their condemnation in this respect is laid against the Cāṇḍālas, the Pukkusas and similar despised classes existing in their time.[21] Kauṭilya mentions 'saṁkara' in connection with ' varṇa ' only once where he says that observance of one's own dharma leads one to heaven and that its transgression, due to saṁkara, amounts to the destruction of the world.[22] He further calls upon the sovereign not to swerve from the path of dharma. In the Dharma-śāstra works the term ' varṇa-saṁkara ' occurs frequently in connection with castes and sub-castes.[23] Baudhāyana mentions the Vrātyas as being the products of varṇa-saṁkara[24] and Manu (X, 1 ff.) enumerates the various saṁkara-jātis that have their

15. N. C. SENA GUPTA, *Sources of Law and Society in Ancient India*, 68 ff.
16. *Ibid*. 71. 17. KANE, II. 447 ff. 18. *Ved. Ind.*, 2. 257 ff.
19. Vide FICK, 31 ff. 20. RHYS DAVIDS, 52 ff. 21. FICK, 27 ff.
22. p. 8, cf. *sva-dharmas svargāyānantyāya ca tasyu utikrame lokas saṁkarād ucchidyeta.* 23. KANE, 2. 59. 24. *Ibid*. 60.

origin in the *anuloma* kind of marriage. The Dharma-śāstra works generally relate the term varṇa-saṁkara to the regulation of the relations of the four varṇas *inter se* particularly on the point of marriage. These works lay such a great emphasis on the prevention of varṇa-saṁkara that they consider it one of the principal duties of the king to see to the matter.[25] It is on account of this that so early as in the first centuries of the Christian era we see that the Sātavāhana king Vāsiṭhīputa Siri Puḷumāyi is extolled for having prevented the admixture of the four varṇas.[26]

The Vāyu also speaks in very strong terms against the prevalence of varṇa-saṁkara almost in the spirit of the Dharma-śāstra works. Its reference to the Ājīvas and Mlecchas as products of varṇa-saṁkara is more than interesting ; the same being the implications of its references to Pāṣaṇḍas, Yavanas, Śakas, etc. in connection with the society supposed to be existing at the end of the Kali age. In order to avoid repetition we may reserve a chronological discussion of these references for a later stage of our investigation.

Varṇāśrama and Vārtā : The term '*vārtā*', technically so called, does not occur in the Vedic literature. The earliest reference to 'vārtā' is found in the Arthaśāstra of Kauṭilya who calls it a branch of learning and quotes his predecessors on that point.[27] According to him vārtā deals with *artha* and *anartha* ; and the study of dharma, varṇa and āṣrama comes under that branch of learning called the *trayī* (i. e. the Vedas), while agriculture, cattle-breeding and trade, etc., come under the vārtā. The Manu-Smṛti also mentions vārtā as one of its four vidyās[28] and it elsewhere states that it is the function of a Vaiśya.[29] This would suggest that the vārtā of Kauṭilya or Manu signified, more or less, something like our science of economics. But its other sense as 'a means of subsistence' occurs in the Arthaśāstra which mentions "a saṁgha subsisting on the profession of arms."[30] Unfortunately the term vārtā denoting its technical sense is nowhere traceable in later literature though we find it occasionally mentioned in its literal sense of 'occupation'.[31]

There are many references to 'vārtā' in the Vāyu. At two places vārtā is directly connected with the origin of the varṇāśrama which in the sequence of creation takes place after the creation of the vārtās. Again the origin of vārtā in the Tretā age and its destruction at the end of Kali coincide with the similar history of the varṇāśrama. Of such views we are not aware either from Kauṭilya or from Manu. Was there any school or theory which regarded the varṇas purely from the occupa-

25. KANE, 2. 60. 26. *Ibid.* 61.
27. Vide p. 6 ff. 28. Cf. VII. 43. 29. Cf X. 80.
30. See p. 376, cf. *vārtā śastropajīvinaḥ*.
31. See D. R. BHANDARKAR, *Some Aspects of Ancient Hindu Polity*, 13.

tional point of view? If there was any, excepting the one probably reflected in our text, we have no knowledge of it so far.

We have at one place a reference to the trayī, vārtā, daṇḍa-nīti, etc. and we are here reminded of vārtā as a branch of learning mentioned by Kauṭilya and Manu. But the Purāṇa does not mention vidyā in this connection and adds *ijyā* and varṇāśrama which are not included as a vidyā by Kauṭilya and which come under the trayī in the four vidyās of Manu. D. R. BHANDARKAR informs us that after the fourth century A.D. we hear nothing of vārtā as a vidyā,[32] a conclusion which may be noted here as a chronological pointer to this material of the Purāṇa.

II. The Brahmins

The Brahmin's Claim for Superiority: The superiority of the Brahmin is recognized from the time of the ṚV. onwards. The claim to be a god, however, is not found in the ṚV.; but in later Vedic literature such claims are many times expressed.[33] The Vedic texts are full of references to civilities to be paid to the Brahmins. In the Jātakas too similar claims are found to have been made by the Brahmins,[34] though the Buddhist monks did not regard such claims with approval. The ideas of the sacredness and superiority of the Brahmins were carried forward and further emphasized by the Dharma-śāstra works some of which assign to them a status superior even to that of the gods. Manu tells us that a Brahmin, learned or not, is a deity.[35] The Mbh. also indulges in the expression of similar sentiments.[36]

Such theoretical claims that a Brahmin is a god or that he is superior even to gods are not found in the Vāyu. This is more to be noted when we are told that "most exaggerated and hyperbolical descriptions of the greatness of the Brāhmaṇas are sown broadcast over all the Smṛtis and the Purāṇas."[37] Certainly our Purāṇa is an exception to the above proposition; for nowhere does it refer *explicitly* to the sanctity or to the extravagant claim for superiority of a Brahmin. It no doubt shows us the Brahmins as a respectable class of people whom it often associates with gods but still it does not make such a straightforward claim for them as we find in the Smṛtis and the Mbh. The same can be said with regard to the incident which led to the origin of the avatāras of Viṣṇu, for in the narration of this incident we nowhere find a definite assertion that a Brahmin as such is a deity and can be superior even to the gods.

Kinds of Sages: We have no information for the present about the different theoretical gradations (and their characteristics) amongst

---

32. *Ibid.*

33. *Ved. Ind.*, 2. 80 ff., cf. also KEITH, *Religion and Philosophy of the Veda*, HOS. 32. 454 ff.

34. FICK, 30-1, and RHYS DAVIDS, 60-1. 35. KANE, 2. 135.

36. *Ibid.* 136. 37. *Ibid.* 135.

sages mentioned in the Vedas and in other ancient works. The mind-born sons of the Creator are not referred to in the ṚV. which however mentions the seven sages denoting the great Bear.[38] In the Śatapatha Brāhmaṇa we find a reference to the region between the sages and the setting of the Sun.[39] In the same work occurs the legend of the Kṛttikās and the seven sages.[40] Thus in the Vedic literature we find the saptarṣis associated with the astronomical sphere. The Gītā, however, mentions the seven mind-born sages[41] and the seven sages in heaven.[42] Again in the Mbh. we find the saptarṣis "sometimes confounded with the seven mind-born sons of Brahmā".[43] The Bṛhat-saṁhitā has a separate chapter on the saptarṣis (of astronomy) but it is silent on their "mind-born" characteristic. Varāhamihira gives their names thus: Marīci, Vasiṣṭha, Aṅgiras, Atri, Pulastya, Pulaha and Kratu.[44] The omission of Bhṛgu, whose name commonly occurs in the Vāyu lists of seven sages, is interesting.

In the Vāyu these seven sages are stripped of their astronomical attributes and they frequently figure as the mind-born sons of Brahmā, the Creator. But the fact that the *pralaya* does not affect them reminds us of their association with the *Ursa major*. They are, however, more than humanized when they, as maharṣis, hold anti-ritual ideas and think low of the sacrifice in which killing of animals invites their re-proof. Our Purāṇa here merely reflects the spirit of the great Epic.

Brahmarṣis, Devarṣis and Rājarṣis : Such a gradation amongst sages is not observable in the Vedic literature. The term *rājanyarṣi* appears in the Pañcaviṁśa-Brāhmaṇa[45] and the Gṛhya-sūtras mention the worship of the Brahmarṣis.[46] According to Manu the Madhya-deśa (middle-country) is the land of the Brahmarṣis.[47] The Mbh. is replete with references to Brahmarṣis, Devarṣis and Rajarṣis[48] and the Gītā mentions by way of analogy that Nārada is the chief of the Devarṣis.[49]

The Vāyu information suggests that these three were the commonly recognized gradations amongst the sages with the distinctive features of their own. For want of similar information from other sources we may leave the matter as it is for the present.

The Munis : The powers and practices of munis are found described in the ṚV. according to which they were probably a set of wandering ascetics devoted to a primitive cult of yoga.[50] At one place in that Veda we find Indra mentioned as a friend of munis.[51] "Transported by divine impulse, they pursued the course of the winds ; they could fly through the air and perceive all forms ; they were the friends

38. *Ved. Ind.*, 1. 117.
39. *SBE*, 44. 425.
40. *SBE*, 12. 282 ff.
41. *SBE*, 8. 86.
42. *SBE*, 8. 281.
43. Sörensen, 620.
44. Edited by Kern, 85 ff.
45. Cf. xii. 12. 6.
46. *SBE*, 29. 141.
47. Cf. II. 19.
48. Cf. Sörensen, 164, 237.
49. *SBE*, 8. 89.
50. *Rudra-Śiva*, 50.
51. *Ved. Ind.*, 2. 167–8.

of Gods and moved along the paths of the Apsaras, the Gandharvas and wild animals; and broke the unbending things by virtue of the cup of poison which they drank in the company of Rudra.''[52] But the muni of the ṚV. is more of the medicine-man than a sage. In the Upaniṣads he is described as a sage steeped in the problem of the Absolute. He was probably not approved by the priests who followed the ritual and whose views were essentially different from the ideals of a muni which are superior to earthly considerations such as desire for children and dakṣiṇā.[53] A quaint reference to Vaikhānasa-munis is found in the Tāṇḍya-Mahābrāhmaṇa (xiv, 4. 7) which mentions Munimaraṇa as a place where they were killed.[54] The muni also figures in the Buddhist canonical works which regarded him as a respectable personage.[55] Buddha himself gave a definition of a muni[56] and the Sutta-nipāta refers to a state of muni (cf. *mauneya*).[57] In the Jātakas the homeless ascetics are often termed as *samaṇas* and probably they are the same as the munis.[58]

The Vāyu also credits the munis with magic powers as we find them in the Ṛgveda. The munis of our Purāṇa do not appear to be mere ṛṣis and are sometimes distinguished from them. Their connection with yatis and bhikṣus and their adherence to non-violence probably reminds us of the doctrines of the Buddhist and Jain faiths. But of far more importance is their association with Śiva who himself is called muni many times. The fact that even Kṣatriyas are mentioned as munis suggests that they represent an order of ascetics which was open to other castes than that of the Brahmins.

Brahmins and the Ritual: The Brahmin as an officiating priest at sacrifices figures from the ṚV. onwards. It is doubtful whether this was an exclusive privilege of the Brahmins in the ancient Vedic days for the ṚV. mentions Devāpi as a purohita of Śantanu and according to the Nirukta at least we may admit that a Kṣatriya could officiate as a priest in the Vedic times.[59] It was in the days of the Brāhmaṇas that the Institution of Sacrifice had developed beyond all proportions and we find in those works the elaborate nature of the ritual functions of the Brahmins, who, it is averred, could even control the fortune of the gods, by virtue of their correct knowledge of the ritual.[60] In the Upaniṣads, however, there is a definite protest against the external sacerdotalism of the Brāhmaṇas. They re-interpret sacrifices and try to allegorise them and sometimes even go to the extreme of ridiculing their superficial character.[61] But the sacrificial religion was still the

52. Muir, *OST*, 4. 318. 53. *Ved. Ind.*, 2. 167–8. 54. Kane, 2. 418.
55. *SBE*, 10. 1. 65 ff. 56. *SBE*, 10. 2. 33–6, 91. 162–4, 179 etc.
57. *Ibid.* 128–31. 58. Fick, 60 ff. 59. Kane, 2. 109.
60. Keith, *Religion and Philosophy of the Veda*, *HOS*, 32. 451 ff.
61. Radhakrishnan, *Philosophy of the Upaniṣads*, 24–5.

dominating force in the days of the Upaniṣads.[62] With the rise of the new faiths of Jainism and Buddhism the Institution of Sacrifice suffered considerably in popular estimation. The Jātakas often contain polemics against the Brahmins profiteering in sacrificial ceremonies and quote a proverb current amongst the people regarding the priests at the ritual.[63] Soon after this period, which synchronizes with the age of the later Upaniṣads, we already find the germs of the Bhakti ideas taking root which finally revolted against the killing of animals at sacrifices.[64] But it will be incorrect to suppose that sacrifices ceased to be performed altogether from this period onwards. We have inscriptional evidence to suggest that a few centuries before the Christian era some kings had performed sacrifices. If we believe in the historicity of the statement contained in an inscription of Samudrgupta that he performed an aśvamedha after a long period of its abeyance,[65] we have to concede that sacrifices were rarely or not at all performed by kings who flourished in the centuries of the Christian era before the date of Samudragupta.

The Vāyu Purāṇa credits the instances of the performance of sacrifices with its kings of the 'past' and amongst its kings of the 'future', only Pravīra is said to have performed sacrifices. These instances appear to have some historical basis as they closely agree with the historical survey of the ritual given above. Again our text speaks of the institution of yajña as if it is a thing of the by-gone Tretā and Dvāpara ages. The Purāṇa is apparently unaware of the aśvamedha of Samudragupta and its political history does not take into account the far-flung and glorious empire of Samudragupta and his successors.[66] The fact that it gives credence to the views which went against the performance of rituals and the fact that the maharṣis—also called munis—themselves protest against the violence of killing animals at sacrifices may make us believe that here the influence of the Bhakti ideals had made itself felt. This is more than obvious from the speech of Śiva to Brahmā about the futility of sacrifice and its corollaries. Thus, chronologically speaking, the Purāṇa has left for us a state of facts about yajña which prevailed in the early centuries of the Christian era preceding the age of the Imperial Guptas.

Brahmins and Dāna : From the times of the ṚV. the right of the Brahmin to receive gifts has been recognised and it is equally obligatory on the other classes to make presents. The ṚV. also contains *dāna-stutis* ("in praise of giving") which immensely exaggerate these

---

62. *Ibid.* 141. 63. FICK, 197-8.

64. R. G. BHANDARKAR, *Vaiṣṇavism, Śaivism* etc., 106 ff.

65. FLEET, *Gupta Inscriptions*, 28.

66. The *Purāṇa* speaks only of the principalities of Anugaṅga, Sāketa, Prayāga and Magadha over which the Guptas ruled.

donations and the exaggeration grows in the Brāhmaṇas. The Śatapatha Brāhmaṇa states that "oblations go to the gods and the fee to the learned Brahmins who are the human gods".[67] It is important to notice that the enumeration of gifts in the Vedic literature, in the main, includes articles of personal property such as horses, kine, buffaloes, ornaments, etc., but not land. The Śatapatha Brāhmaṇa mentions gift of land but with disapproval. The Upaniṣads view dāna with the same estimation as they do in case of the sacrifice and the Ch. Up. contains an ironical statement describing a procession of dogs to march like a procession of the priests, each holding the tail of the other in front and saying, "Oṁ, let us eat. Oṁ, let us drink.........etc."[68] But the Upaniṣads never "influenced society as a whole".[69] The Jātakas are aware of gifts to priests but they often ridicule the swindling ways of the greedy Brahmins who filled their pockets from the sacrificial ceremonies.[70] Kauṭilya too recognises the right of the Brahmin to receive gifts and the corresponding duty of the other castes to make them.[71] The topic of dāna, however, receives a very elaborate treatment from the works on the Dharma-śāstra which contain many principles and regulations regarding the proper dāna, its kinds and religious efficacies. The early Dharma-śāstra works, in their definition of dāna, generally emphasize that the donees should be proper persons[72] and put a stress on their observance of śāstric rites.[73] They divide dāna into three kinds namely *nitya*, *naimittika* and *kāmya*. The three categories of best, intermediate and worst are also referred to but the basis for this classification is the value of the subject-matter of gift[74] and not the motive or purpose behind it for which they adopt the three-fold classification mentioned above. But the growth of the Brahmin population appears to have its repercussions on the principles and regulations of dāna and "it came to be said that a Brāhmaṇa, whether learned or ignorant, was to be a donee and may accept gifts without any scruples".[75] The first inroad on the old ideals of dāna was made in the great Epic which makes it a rule that "in rites meant for gods the character and learning of the Brāhmaṇas need not be deeply inquired into, but that such enquiry was proper only when they were to be invited for śrāddha and other rites for the dead".[76] Even these rules appear further relaxed in the later Smṛtis and Puraṇas which enjoin that in śrāddha gifts should be given to Brahmins without scrutinizing their conduct.[77]

There is another aspect of this topic of dāna. Verses regarding dāna are commonly cited in the inscriptions of land-grants of the

67. *Ved. Ind.*, 1. 336 ; cf. also KANE, 2. 837 ff.
68. RADHAKRISHNAN, *Philosophy of the Upaniṣads*, 25.
69. *Ibid.* p. 141.
70. FICK, 197 ; MEHTA, 247.
71. Cf. p. 7.
72. KANE, 2. 115-6.
73. *Ibid.* 842.
74. *Ibid.* 848.
75. *Ibid.* 117.
76. *Ibid.*
77. *Ibid.*

Gupta period and of later times. These verses have been traced in the Mbh. and in the Agni, Garuḍa, Kūrma, Liṅga, Matsya, Padma, Varāha and Bhaviṣya Purāṇas.[78] PARGITER says that these verses are peculiar to the Purāṇas though in the inscriptions they appear as quotations from the great Epic. The verses generally affirm the beneficial nature of the gifts and proclaim the merit accruing therefrom and condemn those who deprive the grantees of land to future evils.[79]

Though the Vāyu Purāṇa does not speak so strongly against dāna as do the Ch. Up. and the Jātakas still it contains a reference indicating its low estimation by the maharṣis (or munis) and by Śiva. Its classification of dāna is peculiar to it as it is not found in any of the early Dharma-śāstra works in the same sense as it does in our Purāṇa. Its idea of *dāna-lakṣana* indicates tendencies which appear to be earlier than those reflected in the definition of dāna found in the Anuśāsana Book of the Mbh.[80] This stanza is almost equivalent to the one in the Vāyu but the latter emphasizes the point that the subject-matter of a gift should be a lawfully acquired property (cf. *nyāyena upāgatam*) of the donor—a fact which is mentioned differently in the stanza quoted below. It is in its treatment of the śrāddha that the Purāṇa is more elaborate on the matter of dāna and here we find a statement that the conduct of a Brahmin should not be enquired into. This statement definitely shows traces of a later date and we are already informed that the śrāddha chapters of the Purāṇa cannot claim a very high antiquity.[81] But the absence in the Purāṇa of the imprecatory verses which occur in inscriptions and which are traced in most of the other Purāṇas and the Mbh. may be regarded as chronologically suggestive.

Brahmins at Tīrthas: Cf. App. B.

The Brahmins as Reciters of Kathās, Gāthās etc.: The term '*gāthā*' occurs in the ṚV. meaning usually a song or verse. The gāthās, though religious in content, are not mantras and hence are non-Vedic.[82] In the aśvamedha sacrifice, as described in the Brāhmaṇas,[83] we find mention of two lute-prayers, a Brahmin and a warrior, who in verses of their own composition (gāthās), glorified the generosity and war-like deeds of the sacrificer and his ancestors.[84] With the fate of the aṣvamedha, recitation of such gāthās also seems to have gone out of existence.

---

78. *JRAS* 1912, 248 ff. 79. *Ibid.*

80. Vide KANE, 2. 847. cf. *yad yad iṣṭatamaṁ loke yac cāpi dayitaṁ gṛhe tad tad guṇavate deyaṁ tad eva akṣayam icchatā.* cf. also Vā. 59. 49:—*yad yad iṣṭatamaṁ dravyaṁ nyāyenopāgataṁ ca yat tad tad guṇavate deyaṁ iti etad dāna-lakṣaṇaṁ.*

81. HAZRA, 167. 82. *Ved. Ind.*, 1. 224–5.

83. KEITH, *Religion and Philosophy of the Veda*, *HOS*, 32. 343–7.

84. WINTERNITZ, *History of Indian Literature*, 1. 311.

The word Kathā occurs in the Ch. Up. in the sense of "philosophical discussion".[85] Kauṭilya refers to a king interested in Kathā (i.e. conversation) with a courtier[86] but he does not enlighten us on the Brahmin reciter of Kathā. The early Dharma-śāstra works do not inform us anything about the Brahmin reciting or narrating Kathās though they refer to temple-priests with contempt. Manu says that a *devalaka* (i.e. a Brahmin who takes remuneration to perform service before the image in a temple) for three years continuously was unfit to be invited at a śrāddha or to officiate in a sacrifice to gods.[87] We have no information from these works whether these temple-priests, or any other class of Brahmins at such temples, maintained themselves by reciting Purāṇas and Kathās of old. About the beginning of the seventh century A. D. we find the Poet Bāṇa relating in his historical romance, the *Harṣa-carita*, how he attended a reading of the Vāyu Purāṇa "in his native village".[88] Thus it appears that some centuries before the date of Bāṇa the practice of reading Purāṇas—whether at village-temples or tīrthas, we do not know—had come into vogue.

The Gupta inscriptions mention Kathāvids by which they probably refer to Brahmins well-versed in Kathās, but the information of the inscriptions does not throw more light on this.[89]

The reference to recitation of gāthā by dvijas found in the Purāṇa may probably remind us of the lute-player Brahmins at aśvamedha performed in the period of the Brāhmaṇas. The references to Purāṇa and Kathā recitations, however, cannot claim such a high antiquity, though we may not take them to be later than the age of the Guptas.

Brahmins and Politics : The Purohita : In the ṚV. he appears as a domestic priest of the king or perhaps a great noble himself. Every king must have a Purohita according to the ṚV. But very often he appears to assure his lord's safety or victory by means of his spells or prayers.[90] In the Brāhmaṇa literature we find in the *rājasūya* sacrifice the Purohita as one of the eleven *ratnins*—also called king-makers (*rājakṛt*)—to whom *ratnahavis* were offered by the king who was about to be consecrated. He is here mentioned after the commander-in-chief.[91] He is studiously referred to as a Brahmin only in the majority of the Yajus schools and it would appear that he represented the Brahmin caste in the king's ministry and wielded much influence in matters of state policy. The Purohita, as can be made out from Ait. Br. VIII, 24-7, was the partner and co-adjutor of the *alter ego* of the king. More than that he was the active Providence ruling the kingdom as well as the king.[92] The Jātakas depict the person of the

---

85. *Ved. Ind.*, 1. 134.
86. p. 250.
87. KANE, 2. 109-10.
88. WINTERNITZ, op. cit., 526.
89. *BDCRI*, 2. 165.
90. *Ved. Ind*., 2. 5 ff.
91. JAYASWAL, 2. 16. ff.
92. GHOSHAL, 50-1.

Purohita in a wider perspective. There we find him as a domestic priest of his sovereign, as his teacher and guide, as his friend and companion in good or bad days and more than that an officer of purely temporal character. He is even described as a fortune-teller.[93] The Arthaśāstra, however, ruled him out from the list of proximate factors of government.[94] Kauṭilya no doubt advises the king to heed him "as a student his teacher, as a son his father, and as a servant his master,"[95] and places the Purohita in the first rank of state officials. But he is conspicuous by his absence in the list of "seven elements" nor is his skill in the use of charms and spells included in the list of the three powers of the king.[96] The early Dharma-śāstra works tend to show that kings often left the ecclesiastical matters to the Purohita and relied on their advice.[97] In the Rāmāyaṇa we find the Purohita Vasiṣtha wielding considerable influence in matters of state. He is mentioned sometimes as being prominent amongst the *mantrins* and sometimes acts as a *de facto* premier.[98]

The term *ratnin* is not traced in the literature later than that of the Brāhmaṇas. The Vāyu uses the term "*ratna*" in a different sense in which it has been used in the Brahmaṇas. It mentions seven jewels instead of eleven in addition to other seven heavenly (divya) ratnas. The words used by the Vāyu is *ratna* and not *ratnin*. Again the Purāṇa associates the term with a cakravartin of the Tretā age which according to it is a by-gone age. Significantly enough the Purāṇa mentions the term ratna elsewhere in connection with the consecration of king Pṛthu—a fact which leads one to believe that the Purāṇa has handed down for us, in this respect, a piece of very ancient information. It may be recalled here that the ratnins of the Brāhmaṇas are mentioned in connection with the rājasūya sacrifice.

In addition to what has been given above, the Purohita figures in the Vāyu as an important person in matters of state, as an adviser whose advice was heeded with respct and as one who could virtually become the ruler in the king's absence. As these incidents about the Purohita mainly refer to the kings of the pre-Mauryan period and agree in general with the Vedic information about him, we are right in assuming his historical rôle in ancient Hindu polity as being next in importance to the king himself.

BRAHMINS *versus* KṢATRIYAS :

(i) Vasiṣtha, Satyavrata Triśaṅku and Viśvāmitra : King Triśaṅku is not known to the Vedic literature and PARGITER takes him as the

93. FICK, 164 ff. 94. GHOSHAL, op. cit. 95. Trans. p. 1.

96. GHOSHAL, 88-9. DIKSHITAR, however, questions the correctness of these arguments, cf. his *Hindu Administrative Institutions*, 123.

97. KANE, 2. 363. 98. *Miss* DHARMA, *Rāmāyaṇa Polity*, 47 ff.

king of the Kṣatriya tradition.[99] He has discussed this episode in a separate article[100] where he has shown three stages in the narrative of the story, viz. (i) the exile of Satyavrata due to the intrigues of Vasiṣṭha, (ii) the great famine in which Satyavrata supported the family of Viśvāmitra, and (iii) Vasiṣṭha-Viśvāmitra struggle and restoration of Satyavrata. After considering all the bare facts of the story he comes to the conclusion that "it is really an ancient Kṣatriya ballad" which "may have been handed down by the court bards and then put into writing six or seven centuries before the Christian era,"[101] though it shows some traces of preliminary tampering by the Brahmins.[102] It should be noted that the Vāyu, (though elsewhere it merely alludes to the Vasiṣṭha-Viśvāmitra conflict,) does not narrate the details of the conflict between Vasiṣṭha and Viśvāmitra and the incident of the raising to heaven of Triśaṅku by Viśvāmitra occurs only in the version of the Ms. Kha. Thus our Purāṇa has handed down to us a reliable version of this "ancient ballad" the historicity of which may be judged accordingly.

We are here concerned primarily with the influence of the Brahmin Purohita vis-a-vis the king or his heir-designate. The ancient kernel of the story bears out the conclusion that the royal priest was a power to be reckoned with even by the heir-designate—the only son of his father (?). The intriguing Purohita was capable of effecting an heir's exile. Indeed he could become a *de facto* ruler of the kingdom and he "had all the religious and political power of the kingdom in his hands".[103] But this was politics and his position was such only by virtue of facts and could not be legalized by usage ; for Vasiṣṭha seems to have apprehended the nature of opposition to his regime as we can infer from his intention to anoint Satyavrata on the throne.[104] This according to PARGITER, indicates that the Kṣatriya order and the people disapproved of Satyavrata's enforced exile since we are not informed about any actual conflict about Satyavrata's restoration with the help of Viśvāmitra. Vasiṣṭha probably had to withdraw from the scene as "the whole kingdom was ill-affected towards him." Viśvāmitra now became the dominant influence and after Satyavrata's death, he[105] "probably did his king honour by raising him to the celestial dignity by naming a constellation *Triṣaṅku* after him." The whole story clearly indicates the true import of the term *rājakṛt* mentioned in the Brāhmaṇa literature. Indeed the significance of the position of Purohita becomes more apparent when we notice that Viśvāmitra, after undergoing the severity of penance should have aspired not for the throne of his ancestral kingdom but for the purohitaship of the king of Ayodhyā !

99. *AIHT*, 11. 100. *JRAS* 1913, 885 ff. 101. *Ibid*. 904.
102. *AIHT*, 74-5. 103. *JRAS* 1913, 899.
104. Other Purāṇas mention Satyavrata's son instead. Cf. *JRAS* 1913, 895, fn. 2.
105. *Ibid*. 900.

(ii) The Sages, Vena and Pṛthu : Pṛthu is the name of a semi-mythical personage who is mentioned in the ṚV. and later as a ṛṣi and more especially as the inventor of agriculture, and as the lord of both the worlds of men and animals. He bears in several passages the epithet Vainya "descendant of Vena".[106] In the ṚV. Vena is mentioned as a "generous patron".[107] The compilers of the Vedic Index consider Pṛthu as a "culture hero" rather than a real man[108] and PARGITER too thinks him to be mythical.[109] JAYASWAL, however, regards him a historical personage.[110] The incident of the "milching of the earth" is alluded to in the AV.[111] In the Śatapatha and Taittirīya Brāhmaṇas we have the rājasūya sacrifice described in details.[112] Here we are told of the six Pārtha Homas which are connected with Pṛthu Vainya who is expressly stated to be the "first anointed king" of the world. The Sūta is here mentioned as one of the Ratnins—reference to whom has already been made above—to whom the preliminary offerings called the *ratnahavis* are to be offered in the course of the ceremony. But before these offerings are made it is enjoined upon the king to seek a formal approval of the earth. We are also informed that waters of rivers and seas are to be brought for the sprinkling ceremony. The Mbh. account of the story of Pṛthu is more coloured and amplified and brings in altogether new elements. It does not associate him so much with the older ritual of the rājasūya as it connects him with its own theory of the origin of kingship.[113] The Rāmāyaṇa too narrates the tale in the same manner but gives more prominence to Brahmins.[114] The Manusmṛti appears more concerned about Vena than Pṛthu. Of Vena it tells us that in the reign of this king the levirate (*niyoga*) system—which it says is called the law of the jungle (*paśudharma*) by the learned Brahmins—had its origin.[115] The Smṛti further adds that this kind of varṇasaṁkara was promulgated by Vena who had no control over his passions[116] and that he met his ruin on account of his arrogance.[117] Of Pṛthu the same work informs us that Pṛthvī (earth) was his *bhāryā* (wife).[118]

This brief survey of the various versions of the story of Pṛthu at once enables us to fix the chronological position of the version of the same tale occurring in our Purāṇa. Chronologically the Vāyu version stands midway between those of the Brāhmaṇas and the Mbh. Even in the period of the ṚV. Pṛthu was regarded as a very ancient personage and the Śatapatha Brāhmaṇa merely testifies to the statement of that Veda by calling Pṛthu the "first anointed king". Our Purāṇa further

---

106. *Ved. Ind.*, 2. 16. 107. *Ibid.* 325. 108. *Ibid.* 16.
109. *AIHT*, 40. 110. *Hindu Polity*. 2, 48, fn. 3. 111. Cf. *ERE*, 4. 225.
112. KEITH, *Religion and Philosophy of the Veda*, *HOS.*, 32. 343 ff.; see also JAYASWAL, 2. 16-7 and KANE, 2. 1217 fn.
113. JAYASWAL, 2. 47 ff. 114. *Ibid.* for reference. 115. IX. 66.
116. IX. 67. 117. VII. 41. 118. IX. 44.

corroborates the same information by associating him with the period of the interregnum between the Cākṣuṣa and the Vaivasvata Manvantaras. The ṚV. calls Pṛthu the inventor of agriculture, the Śatapatha Brāhmaṇa makes a king in rājasūya seek formal approval of the earth and the Vāyu narrates the incident of the pṛthvī-dohana. For so much of the Vāyu account there is corroboration from the Vedic literature. The annihilation of Vena, however, finds no reference in Vedic literature; on the contrary, the ṚV. calls him a "generous patron". It is difficult to imagine the source from which Vāyu has obtained its information. With regard to the remaining details the Vāyu agrees fairly with the Brāhmaṇas, though it modifies the account to a certain extent. The Vāyu reference to the Sūta refusing at the outset to sing a panegyric of the king is also instructive; and we know from the rājasūya ritual of the Brāhmaṇas that the Sūta was one of the ratnins offerings to whom implied that their approval was necessary as a condition precedent to the coronation ceremony.[119] That the Vāyu version is earlier than that of the Mbh. will be apparent when we discuss the theory of the origin of kingship. It is unnecessary to comment on the comparatively later character of Manu's version.

A few words may be added here regarding the part of the Niṣādas and other tribes in the story. The Niṣādas are mentioned in the *viśvajit* sacrifice and the Vedic literature probably understands by them "a whole body of aborigines outside the pale of the Aryan organization".[120] The Niṣāda sub-tribes are not mentioned in the Vedas. If we believe that the story of Pṛthu has some historical basis, as JAYASWAL tells us,[121] we may venture the following explanation of the part played by the Niṣādas: There was a conflict between the tribal chief Vena and the sages who were supported by the common people. Vena seems to have sought the help of the aboriginal tribes—that is the Niṣādas—but still he could not maintain his position and finally met his ruin. That the people supported the sages is suggested by the fact that they seconded the speech of the sages at the consecration of Pṛthu. Whether we regard Pṛthu as a historical personage or not, it has to be admitted that the legend has something to inform us regarding the Aryan expansion in the eastern and central India; for it mentions the Māgadhas and Sūtas and the aboriginal tribes about the Vindhyas.

(iii) Brahmins and Janamejaya: In the Vedic literature, Janamejaya appears with his patronymic Pārikṣit who was famous at the end of the Brāhmaṇa period. He is known as the performer of aśvamedha. According to the Śatapatha and Aitareya Brāhmaṇas his capital was Āsandīvanta. The Ait. Br. states that at one sacrifice he did not employ

119. JAYASWAL, 2. 27. 120. *Ved. Ind.*, 1. 453-4.
121. *Hindu Polity*, 2. 48 fn. 3.

the Kāśyapas which eventually resulted in a tussle between them.[122] RAYCHAUDHARI has discussed the chronology of this Pārikṣit Janamejaya. From the evidence of the Brāhmaṇa-literature he states that this Janamejaya had performed two aśvamedhas and that it was at the performance of the second aśvamedha that he had quarrels with the Kāśyapas.[123] From the evidence of the collated Purāṇic tradition PARGITER concludes that the story of his ruin at the hands of Brahmins is a mixture of Kṣatriya and Brahmin traditions.[124]

So far as the performance of two aśvamedhas is concerned the Vāyu version of the story corroborates the information of the Brāhmaṇas. But our Purāṇa does not refer to the Kāśyapas and amplifies the Brāhmaṇa account of the quarrel by stating that he met his ruin at the hands of the Brahmins who consecrated his son Śatānīka as the king. RAYCHAUDHARI says that the Gārgyas had quarrels with Janamejaya, the son of Parikṣit I, while our Janamejaya according to him was the son of Parikṣit II.[125] If this be the case, the Vāyu may be taken to have confused the two Janamejayas. Again the Vāyu gives another account of his quarrel with the Gārgyas which is not found in the Vedic literature in connection with the same Janamejaya.

The Matsya Purāṇa gives a different version stating that the king made a successful stand in the beginning but later gave in and after making his son the king, went to the forest.[126] Thus the Matsya-account falls more in line with that of the Brāhmaṇas than that of the Vāyu and may be considered to be the earlier one of the two; and we may conclude with PARGITER that the Vāyu has here some mixture, if any, of the Kṣatriya and Brahmin traditions.

By the time of Kauṭilya the story of Janamejaya appears to have been regarded as one of the glaring examples of how a king can go to rack and ruin through his non-control of senses. He further tells us that "the wrath of the Brahmins brought him his ruin."[127]

(iv) Brahmins and Purūravas: Aila Purūravas is mentioned in the ṚV. which however does not definitely say whether he was a king.[128] The story of the antagonism of Purūravas against Brahmins is considered by PARGITER to be an ancient tradition. He further draws other conclusions with which we are not here concerned.[129]

Brahmins and Kārtavīrya Arjuna: Kārtavīrya Arjuna is not mentioned in the Vedic literature,[130] and PARGITER calls him a king of the Kṣatriya tradition. He considers the story of Kārtavīrya's death at

---

122. *Ved. Ind.*, 1. 273–4 and 2. 5 ff. 123. *PHAI*, 15 ff., 30. ff.

124. *AIHT*, 50. 125. *PHAI*, 15.

126. *PHAI*, 32. Cf. also PARGITER, *Purānic Texts of the Dynasties of the Kali Age*, pp. 86 ff.

127. P. 11. Cf. *Kopāj janamajeyo brāhmaṇeṣu vikrāntaḥ.*

128. *Ved. Ind.*, 2. 129. *AIHT*, 305–6. 130. *AIHT*, 7.

the hands of Jāmadagnya Rāma as historical,[131] though the account of Rāma's killing Kṣatriyas off the earth twenty-one times, as is found in the Mbh. and in the other Purāṇas, is according to him purely a tale of Brahmanical tradition without any historical basis behind it.[132] There is no doubt that "at the end of his long reign Arjuna came into collision with Jamadagni and his son Rāma." The genealogical accounts of the Purāṇas—the Vāyu included—do not explain how this happened except as a result of Āpava's curse.[133] The story of this curse is, according to PARGITER, largely Brahmanical and the contents of this story, as given in the Vāyu, also confirm his opinion. The introduction of the sun-god, the occurrence of marvels, exaggerations in the incident and also the curse of Āpava Vasiṣṭha for which the king was almost innocent, belie the historicity of the account. PARGITER tells us that there is no Kṣatriya version of this story, the nearest approach to which, he says, is found in the version of the Brahmāṇḍa Purāṇa which says nothing of the destruction of all the Kṣatriyas.[134] He has apparently missed our Vāyu version which too does not mention it. It should be noted that our Purāṇa does not narrate the exploits of Rāma especially his annihilation of the whole Kṣatriya order, which forms a very powerful theme for the redactors of the Mbh.,[135] nor does it mention the expression "thrice seven times" which appears to have been a favourite slogan with the bards of the great Epic[136] with regard to the tale of this extermination of the Kṣatriyas. Thus the Vāyu version is probably earlier than that of the Mbh.

Some observations may be made here with regard to the conclusion that can be deduced from these stories of the "Brahmin-Kṣatriya conflicts". The above discussion about them shows that only the first, third and the fifth can be taken to have some historical basis. About the second and the fourth it is doubtful whether we should treat them as historical. The fifth is largely tampered with, still the germ of the tale, viz., the conflict between Arjuna and Rāma, may be considered to be based on facts now lost to us. Do these incidents lead us to conclude that in those ancient times the Brahmins vied with the Kṣatriyas for supremacy? Or was there a class (or caste) struggle for ascendancy between the Brahmins and the Kṣatriyas? The answer, it appears, should be in the negative. For in the first instance of Vasiṣṭha we find it merely a personal rivalry and at no stage the conflict assumes a representative character, and again Vasiṣṭha appears there to be devoid of popular support. The third incident may be considered important in this connection but the mention of Paura-Jānapadas suggests that whenever the Brahmins came into conflict

131. *Ibid.* 265-7. 132. *Ibid.* 73. 133. *Ibid.* 266. 134. *Ibid.* 267, fn. 3.
135. SUKHTHANKAR, *Epic Studies*, VI. 6 (*ABORI*, 18). 136. *Ibid.* 65.

with the ruling sovereign they expected support from the people; and the last incident—on which the Vāyu does not throw much light—suggests that the Bhārgavas looked at the affair with the point of view of their own clan and probably were helped by other Kṣatriyas with whom they were related by matrimonial ties.[137]

Brahmins and Education: Study of the sacred texts formed the basis of the Brahmin's learning from the Vedic times. The expression '*svādhyāya*' occurs in the Śatapatha Brāhmaṇa which waxes eloquent on its advantages.[138] In the Jātakas we find a distinction made between the proper (i.e. learned) Brahmins and the other ones. The later Sūtra-literature contains many rules and regulations regarding his studies.[139]

The Vāyu does not contain any rules and regulations about the education of the Brahmins. It only gives us instances some of which can be traced to the Vedas and are probably ancient facts. The debate at Janaka's aśvamedha is described in the Br. Up.[140] But in that work we find the king himself putting questions to the sage Yājñavalkya and the questions are of a different nature.[141] In the Vāyu, however, we find Devamitra Śākalya contesting with Yājñavalkya the prize announced, the discussion centred on the topic of kāma, and its termination was the victory for Yājñavalkya and death for Devamitra Śākalya. This Yājñavalkya was a son of Brahmavāha who, according to PARGITER, was a contemporary of king Adhisīmakṛṣṇa of the Kuru-Paurava line. Śākalya was his contemporary teacher of a śākhā of the ṚV.[142] PARGITER is, however, silent on the historicity of the contest.

Suffice it to state here that debates at sacrifices were common which afforded good opportunity for the learned to display their knowledge. A disputation called *brahmaugha* had a regular place in the aśvamedha sacrifice and in the *daśa-rātra* (ten-night) festival. The reward for such learning was the gaining of the title of Kavi or Vipra.[143] The Vāyu Purāṇa, it is to be noted, calls Yājñavalkya a Kavi.[144]

The system of the teachings passing from father to son is found in the Vedas.[145] The sage Jaimini, however, is not mentioned in the Vedas though the Vedic works of the Sāmaveda on his name are extant.[146]

In the Vāyu we find Jaimini as a disciple of Vyāsa to whom the compilation of the Sāmaveda was entrusted. The Vedic silence on Jaimini, according to PARGITER, is due to the fact that the Vedas are regarded as existing from the primordial times and to admit that any one had compiled them struck at the very root of that belief.[147]

---

137. *AIHT*, 267. 138. *Ved. Ind.*, 2. 86 139. FICK, 190 ff.; MEHTA, 257.
140. *Ved. Ind.*, 2. 87. 141. Cf. Br. Up. VI. 1. 1-9, 20-9.
142. *AIHT*, 330-1. 143. *Ved. Ind.*, 2. 87. 144. Cf. Vā. 60. 41.
145. *Ved. Ind.*, 2. 88. 146. *Ibid.* 1. 290. 147. *AIHT*, 9. 320.

III. Kṣatriyas

Who were the Kṣatriyas?: The word *Kṣatriya* is used in the ṚV. frequently as an epithet of gods and in some verses it means 'a king or a nobleman'.[148] Its use in the sense of a caste, i. e., one of the four castes, is observable particularly in the later Vedic literature.[149] The term '*Kṣattra*' is also used in the ṚV. sometimes in a compound "*brahma-kṣattra*" but here the two words mean 'prayer' and 'valour' respectively.[150] In some Vedic works the term Kṣattra collectively stands for the Kṣatriyas.[151] The word *rājanya* is found in the ṚV. only once in the *Puruṣa-sūkta*,[152] but in the later Vedic literature it becomes a regular term for a man of the royal family.[153] It appears that by the time of the Jātakas the word *Khattiya* came more into general use and here it is applied not only to the descendants of the victorious classes under whose leadership the Aryan people acquired their new dwelling-places in the Gangetic lands but also to the rulers of the aboriginal peoples who, in their fight with the foreign invaders, maintained their independence.[154] Kauṭilya uses the term Kṣatriya more often than Kṣattra.[155] The epics probably take the word Kṣatriya in a wider sense but there is nothing in them to infer that every warrior was a Kṣatriya.[156]

Out of these terms the Vāyu uses only Kṣattra and Kṣatriya very frequently. It rarely mentions the term rājanya. The use of the term Kṣattra is found mostly in the genealogical lists where too we find the compound *brahma-kṣattra* also occasionally mentioned. This may lead us to speculate on the chronological aspect of these lists.

In the story of the king Sagara, our Purāṇa refers to the Śakas, Yavanas, etc., as Kṣatriya-gaṇas. Pargiter tells us that the ballad of Sagara's conflict with these Śakas, Yavanas and Kambojas, etc., is really ancient dating back to a period earlier than the Bhārata battle.[157] The Śakas, he says, "certainly were not Aryans by origin".[158] Then why are they here called Kṣatriyas? Pargiter suggests that they were originally Druhyus ruling in the Mleccha countries of the north who came back to India to help the Haihayas and were called Śakas.[159] He is probably labouring under a supposition that those who were not Aryans—i.e., who were foreigners or aborigines—could not be called Kṣatriyas. But the evidence of Jātakas shows us that in their time even princes of the aboriginal tribes could become Kṣatriyas and the epics too express the same view. The very fact that later tradition maintained

---

148. Kane, 2. 30. 149. *Ved. Ind.*, 2. 252. 150. Kane, 2. 30.
151. *Ibid.* 152. *Ved Ind.*, 1, 202. 153. Kane, 2. 30; and *Ved. Ind.*, 2. 216.
154. Fick, 78-9. For 'rājañña' in the Jātakas, cf. p. 153 fn. See also Rhys Davids, 56.
155. See *Index Verborum* by S. Sastry, 1. 371.
156. Hopkins, *JAOS*, 13. 73 ff. 157. *JRAS* 1919, 261.
158. *Ibid.* 159. *Ibid.*

that in the Kali age Kṣatriyas do not exist means that many foreign and aboriginal princes had been incorporated into the order which the later theorists viewed with disfavour.

Prominent Position of the Kṣatriyas : Jātakas almost always, in their enumeration of castes, mention the Khattiyas first.[160] The Mbh. equally shows, if cleared of the priestly gloss, that the military caste stood at the top, below whom were the priests and the people.[161]

In the cosmological account with regard to the origin of the varṇas or their functions, the Vāyu mentions the Kṣatriyas first and the other orders (varṇas)—including the Brahmins—are mentioned afterwards. No Brahmin compiler could have ever thought of so mentioning the Kṣatriyas first, for elsewhere, wherever the four varṇas are mentioned, the sense of gradation is never lost sight of. The Vāyu mentions the Kṣatriyas first and repeats the same again in the same account and this cannot be regarded merely as an oversight. Have we here anything to do with the Kṣatriya tradition[162] of PARGITER which regarded the Kṣatriyas as the foremost amongst the four castes ? But this would be speculating too much for the present for there is no general agreement[163] regarding an independent Kṣatriya tradition of PARGITER nor have we any information from PARGITER as to whether even cosmology was included as a topic in his Kṣatriya tradition.

INTELLECTUAL ACTIVITIES OF THE KṢATRIYAS

(i) Brahmavādin Kṣatriyas : (a) Purūravas :—Though Purūravas is mentioned in the ṚV.,[164] we have nothing from that Veda to infer that this king was so learned as to justify an epithet "brahmavādin". The Purāṇic tradition itself is not unanimous on this point. The Matsya[165] and Padma[166] Purāṇas do not know of this epithet of the king while the Brahma[167] Purāṇa has its information identical with that of the Vāyu.

(b) Malina : The Brahma Purāṇa credits the son—his name is not mentioned—of Taṁsu (i.e. Trasu of the Vāyu) with being a brahmavādin. His mother named Ilā (for which name Vāyu has Itinā) is also called a brahma-vādinī. She is referred to in the Matsya as Ilinā who bore four sons all of whom were brahma-vādins *par excellence*. It appears that Malina was the name of a king whose father was Taṁsu (or Trasu) and mother Ilinā. His name Malina sounds well with that of his mother. This king was known to have been a brahmavādin as the genealogies in the Purāṇas invariably mention the epithet though they confuse the names. PARGITER has completely missed this Malina

---

160. FICK, 84 ; RHYS DAVIDS, 54 ; MEHTA, 254.
161. HOPKINS, *JAOS*, 13. 73.
162. *Ved. Ind*. 2. 3.
163. 24. 10–25.
164. 5. 12, 62 ff.
165. See KIRFEL, *Das Purāṇa Pañcalakṣaṇa*.
166. 13. 50 ff.
167. 49. 8–10, cf. *Brahma-vāda-parikrānta*.

of the Vāyu as the name does not occur in any other Purāṇa. Indeed he has also missed this Trasu of the Purāṇa.[168]

(c) Sons of Mitrajyoti: The Brahmāṇḍa has its text identical with that of the Vāyu. The information about these sons of Mitrajyoti, however, is found in the other Purāṇas also.[169] PARGITER thinks that the passage is misplaced in the Purāṇas and is unable to find its true connection.[170] It appears that this is a piece of very ancient information which the redactors had to retain though they did not know where to place it. It would be unnatural to expect the Brahmin redactors to invent this information and insert it in the genealogies for which it appears there would be no reason for them to do so.

(ii) Kings who Retired to Forest-life and Practised Penance: (a) Bṛhadaśva: PARGITER remarks that though this story is in a fabulous form still it is worthy of note. He even suggests from the contents of the story that the southern part of the Rajputana desert was probably a sand-filled sea. The story is also found in the Mbh.[171] The Rākṣasī Dhuṇḍhā is referred to by Hemachandra and the anniversary of her death was observed as a ceremony in the 10th and 11th century Gujarat,[172] a fact which may have some historical significance.

(b) Trayyāruṇa: The Purāṇic tradition knows nothing more about him except that he left his kingdom and went to forest because of his son's behaviour.[173]

(c) Viśvāmitra: The story of Viśvāmitra has been discussed fully by PARGITER[174] and it is unnecessary to give the details here.

(d) Kapila: PARGITER has not discussed his political history. The Vāyu identifies his father Vasudeva to be the same Vasudeva as the father of Kṛṣṇa.[175]

(e) Bali: A boon was granted by Brahmā to this king who was the father of five sons to whom he gave five kingdoms of the east. He is also mentioned in the Matsya[176] and the Brahma Purāṇas.[177]

(f) Manu: Some Purāṇas omit his name in the genealogical list of Ikṣvāku kings of Ayodhyā. PARGITER, however, accepts the historicity of the Vāyu account.[178] The Matsya refers to Manu as a mahāyogin and as the promoter of the Kṣatriyas in "future yugas"; it also mentions him elsewhere with Devāpi while summing up the genealogical lists in which place, however, Vāyu does not mention his name.

---

168. KIRFEL, *Das Purāṇa Pañcalakṣaṇa*. 169. *AIHT*, 111.
170. *Ibid*. 86. cf. fn. 4 for references; cf. also KIRFEL, op. cit.
171. *AIHT*, 260 for references cf. fn. 5.
172. SANKALIA, *The Archaeology of Gujarat*, 242.
173. *AIHT*, cf. fn. for references; see also KIRFEL, op. cit.
174. *JRAS* 1913, 885 ff. and 1917, 37 ff. 175. See KIRFEL, op. cit.
176. 48. 26. 177. 13. 33 ff. 178. *AIHT*, 94.

(g) Saṁyāti : The other Purāṇas mention Yati for Saṁyāti of the Vāyu.[179] The Brahma says that Yati was the eldest brother of Yayāti and that he became a muni.[180] The Matsya states that Yati, while still young, became a yogin and embraced the life of a wanderer.[181] The Padma has the same śloka to describe Yati.[182] It appears that the Vāyu has mistaken Saṁyāti for Yati. It mentions both the names and its information should properly apply to Yati who, it mentions, was the eldest brother of Yayāti after whose "becoming a muni" Yayāti became the king.[183]

The Vedas refer to Yayāti but do not know anything about Yati, his elder brother.[184]

(h) Yayāti : He is mentioned twice in ṚV., once as an ancient sacrificer and once as Nāhuṣya, descendant of Nahuṣa, apparently a king.[185] The compilers of the Vedic Index further remark that " there is no trace whatever of his connection with Pūru as in the Epic, the tradition of which must be deemed to be inaccurate[186] and PARGITER has aptly refuted this argument to which it is unnecessary to add here anything more.[187] The Ṛgvedic king Yayāti is undoubtedly the Purāṇic king of the same name who too was a son of Nahuṣa.

The reference to his entering forest life is contained also in the other four Purāṇas including the Harivaṁśa.[188]

(i) Devāpi : The Ṛgvedic canon contains a hymn by Devāpi.[189] The Nirukta says that Devāpi and Śantanu were brother-princes in the line of the Kurus. Devāpi was the elder brother but Śantanu anyhow became the king. So there was draught which the Brahmins attributed to Devāpi being set aside by Śantanu who then was prepared to offer the kingdom to him. Devāpi refused the offer but acted as Purohita of Śantanu and rains came.[190] Other versions of the story also occur in the Bṛhaddevatā, the Mbh. and the other Purāṇas.[191] The compilers of the *Vedic Index* remark that there is nothing in the Vedic evidence to indicate that he was not a Brahmin. But this is ***argumentum ex silentio*** which cannot be treated as conclusive.[192] According to PARGITER his identity with Purāṇic Devāpi is quite obvious though his relation with Ṛṣṭiṣeṇa, mentioned as his father in the ṚV., is not found in the genealogical lists.[193]

(iii) LIST OF RĀJARṢI KINGS

Aṁbarīṣa : He is mentioned in the ṚV. as Vārṣāgīra[194] with Ṛjrāśva, Sahadeva, etc. Probably he was a king.[195] This becomes

179. *AIHT*, 86. 180. 12. 3. 181. 24. 51. 182. 5. 12. 104.
183. Cf. Vā. 93. 13–5. 184. *Ved. Ind.*, 2. 18. 185. *Ved. Ind.*, 2. 117.
186. *Ibid.* 187. *AIHT*, 12.
188. See KIRFEL, op. cit., p. 397 for references. 189. *AIHT*, 7.
190. *Ved. Ind.*, 1. 377–8. 191. *Ibid.* and also cf. *AIHT*, 252.
192. Cf. *AIHT*, 12. 193. *Ibid.* 165. 194. *Ved. Ind.*, 1. 31. 195. *AIHT*, 92.

more probable since he is mentioned with kings in the ṚV. The Purāṇic tradition knows two Aṁbarīṣas. The Mbh. refers to songs sung by king Aṁbarīṣa.[196]

Ajamīḍha : He appears in the ṚV. probably as a seer of a hymn.[197] In the Vāyu also he is called a mantrakṛt sage.

Divodāsa : He is mentioned in the ṚV. as a king, who was an energetic supporter of the fire ritual, for Agni is once called by his name in the ṚV. (VIII, 103, 2 cf. *Daivodāsa* i.e. worshipped by Divodāsa).[198] Hymn I, 130, 7, 10 of the ṚV. proves that some of the descendants of the *warrior* Divodāsa were sages and Brahmins. But in the ṚV. Divodāsa does not figure as a king of Kāśi.[199] The Purāṇic tradition shows him as a king of Kāśi[200] and tells a tale of his abandonment of his capital Vārāṇasī. The same incident is found in Brahmāṇḍa (iii. 67, 26–31).

PARGITER says there were two Divodāsas in the Kāśi dynasty of whom one was identical with the Ṛgvedic king Divodāsa.[201]

Kakṣīva : (The same as Kakṣīvat). He is frequently mentioned in the ṚV. as a seer. WEBER suggested that he was originally a Kṣatriya as he is mentioned with kings such as Vītahavya, Trasadasyu, etc.[202] To the purāṇic tradition two Kakṣīvats are known. The Kakṣīva in the rājarṣi-list was probably the son of Dīrghatamas through a *śūdra* maidservant of king Bali. This Kakṣīva practised severe austerities and became a Brahmin. Kakṣīvat was the earlier one of the two.[203] That he should be included in the list of royal sages is interesting. But let us here recall the Purāṇa information that king Bali claimed him as his son and Dīrghatamas set aside that claim. The opinion of WEBER quoted above deserves to be considered in this respect though the compilers of the *Vedic Index* take it to be "an unnecessary assumption".[204]

Māṁdhātā : The king Māndhātṛ of the first Maṇḍala of the ṚV. appears as a protégé of Aśvins.[205] The hymn X. 134 of the ṚV. is attributed to him.[206] LUDWIG and GRIFFITH equate this king Māndhātṛ with the rājarṣi Māndhātṛ of the epics and the Purāṇas but the compilers of the *Vedic Index* dismiss the suggestion as "unnecessary and improbable".[207] Māndhātṛ Yauvanāśva ('descendant of Yuvanāśva'), is in the Gopatha Brāhmaṇa, the name of an emperor who was instructed by Vicārin, son of Kabandha Ātharvaṇa.[208]

The Purāṇic tradition knows him by the patronymic.[209] The Vāyu quotes two stanzas current about him[210] and also calls him an incarnation

196. *Ibid.* 197. *Ved. Ind.*, 1. 13. 198. *Ved. Ind.*, 1. 363.
199. *Ibid.* 2. 30. 200. *AIHT*, 153. 201. *Ibid.* 153–5.
202. *Ved. Ind*, 1. 131–2 203. Cf. *AIHT*, 220–4. 204. *Ibid.*
205. *Ved. Ind.*, 2. 132. 206. *AIHT*, 7. 207. Op. cit.
208. *Ved. Ind.*, 2. 133. 209. *AIHT*, 42. cf. fn. 1 for references in Purāṇas.
210. 77. 67 ff.

of Viṣṇu. The Brahmāṇḍa also quotes the stanzas found in our Purāṇa. The specific information of the Gopatha Brāhmaṇa appears to corroborate the Purāṇic tradition that he was a learned rājarṣi.

Pṛthu Vainya : He is mentioned in the ṚV. as a seer.[211] PARGITER suggests that the Pṛthu Vainya in the list of the mantrakṛt sages was a descendant of Pṛthu, son of Vena, "for Vainya Pṛthu is included in a list of eighteen Bhārgava hymn-makers and appears as Venya Pṛthī in Ṛgveda X. 148, 8. Thus this Vainya Pṛthu is, according to him, a different person from the king Pṛthu of the hoary past.[212]

Purukutsa : "There are two Purukutsas with sons named Trasadasyu" known to the Purāṇic tradition[213] and PARGITER identifies the Ṛgvedic king Purukutsa,[214] not with the son Purukutsa of Māndhātṛ but with another and later Purukutsa who was a contemporary of Aśvamedha Bharata.[215] In the Vāyu the epithet rājarṣi does not occur in connection with either Purukutsa in the genealogical lists. But elsewhere in the list of rājarṣi kings it mentions Purukutsa after Saṁkṛti and Kapi who were descendants of Bharata, and this probably suggests that this rājarṣi Purukutsa is the same as the Ṛgvedic king of that name.

Janamejaya : About the rājarṣi Janamejaya, son of Purañjaya, we have no information from the Vedic literature. The Brahma and Matsya Purāṇas and the Harivaṁśa too mention him as a rājarṣi.[216] PARGITER has apparently missed his political history.[217]

Ṛṣabha : According to the Śatapatha Brāhmaṇa he was a king of Śviknas and had performed an aśvamedha. He is also mentioned there as having probably been the source of a saying of gauravītiśāktyas.[218] He is probably identical with the mantrakṛt Ṛṣabha of the Vāyu Purāṇa. But whether he can be identified with any of the Ṛṣabhas mentioned in the Purāṇic tradition is a moot point.[219]

(iv) Kṣatriyas and Vedic Learning : Of training and education of the Kṣatriyas we have no record from the ṚV. presumably because they were mainly instructed in the art of war. In the latest stratum of the Brāhmaṇa literature there are references to learned princes such as Pravāhaṇa Jaivāli, Janaka, Aśvapati Kekaya and Ajātaśatru.[220] Their eminence was due primarily to their knowledge of brahma-vidyā, though Janaka is mentioned by Yājñavalkya as one who had studied the Vedas as well as the Upaniṣads.[221] There occur various passages in the Jātakas which leave no room for doubt that sons of princes had to

211. *Ved. Ind.*, 2. 16. 212. *AIHT*, 202. 213. *Ibid.* 133.

214. *Ved. Ind.*, 1. 541. 215. *AIHT*, 133. 216. KIRFEL, op. cit., 523[15].

217. Cf. *AIHT*, 145. Here he mentions Purañjaya but omits Janamejaya, the rājarṣi who according to the Purāṇas and the Harivaṁśa was a son of this Purañjaya.

218. *Ved. Ind.*, 1. 115.

219. Cf. *AIHT*, 249 fn. 7 for PARGITER's remarks on the same.

220. *Ved. Ind.*, 1. 205-7. 221. KANE, 2. 106-7.

devote, like the Brāhmaṇa youths, a certain time of their life to religious studies.[222] Kauṭilya also expected a king to be well-educated in the Vedas and in various other sciences.[223] The Dharmaśāstra works enjoin that the Kṣatriyas should be well versed in the traditional lore of the Vedas; but these directions were probably meant to be an ideal.[224] It appears that by about the beginning of the Christian era the average prince and Kṣatriya "used to possess only a very limited knowledge of the Vedas and philosophy".[225]

The information of the Vāyu in this respect is not very instructive. It quotes only one instance of a king's education and of his learning the Vedas. But it has more to inform us about their connection with the compilation of the Vedas and about their interest in the life of the forest and the problem of the *brahman*.

It will not be out of place if we state here the conclusions that emerge out of this discussion on the intellectual activities of the Kṣatriyas. Most of the kings, mentioned above in this connection, have been found to be historical personages. Many of them were known to the Vedas which in some respects testify to the Purāṇa evidence that they were learned. What is striking about them is that the political history of the Purāṇic tradition shows them, excepting the doubtful instance of Manu, to belong to a very hoary antiquity and that is probably the reason why their names are traced in the Vedas. Some of them belong to a period anterior to that of the Ṛgveda and the ascription to them of the knowledge of brahman and of the practice of yoga and tapas—which were developments of an age posterior to their own—can hardly be considered as historical facts. Nevertheless the Purāṇic tradition, in common, knew that they had some connection with learning though not with what it tells us.

Some scholars have protested against the general assumption that the Brahmins alone were the custodians of the intellectual heritage of ancient India. Long ago DUESSEN pointed out that "numerous indications point to this that the proper guardians of this (i.e. Upaniṣadic) thought were not originally so much the priestly classes...as the Kṣatriyas."[226] R. G. BHANDARKAR also supported this view in his "*Vaiṣṇavism, Śaivism etc.*"[227] as did also GARBE and FICK.[228] GRIERSON says that the Kṣatriyas contributed a great deal to the development of the Bhakti school,[229] and WINTERNITZ has expounded the thesis that the Kṣatriyas were mainly responsible for the development of the ascetic literature of India.[230] The information of the Vāyu Purāṇa may be regarded

222. FICK, 92 cf. also MEHTA, 254. 223. See Trans. pp. 10–11.
224. KANE, 2. 363 ff. cf. also ALTEKAR, *Education in Ancient India*, 163 ff.
225. ALTEKAR, of. cit. 168. 226. *System des Vedanta*, 1883, p. 18. 227. p. 9.
228. Cf. FICK, p. 90 fn. 1, see also RHYS DAVIDS, p. 256 ff.
229. *ERE*, see *Bhakti*. 230. *Some Problems of Indian Literature*, 21 ff.

to support the view of WINTERNITZ. But we are warned that "to attribute wisdom to a king was a delicate and effective piece of flattery,"[231] and we have to judge the value of our evidence accordingly.

(v) Kṣatriya-Brahmin-Relations: There have been divergent views regarding the formulation of caste in the age of the Ṛgveda.[232] But the general opinion on this subject is that the caste system developed at the end of the Vedic period.[233] It has been suggested that the Kṣatriyas of the ṚV. were probably only a class—and not a caste—which was more or less fluid and the kings and Purohitas were not so known by virtue of their birth.[234]

The connection of the Kṣatriyas with Brahmins was very close in the Vedic times and the prosperity of the two is repeatedly mentioned.[235] The marriage of Brāhmaṇas with Rājanya women is illustrated by the cases of Sukanyā, the daughter of king Śaryāta, who married Cyavana and of Rathavīti's daughter, who married Śyāvāśva,[236] but such instances are few and it has been generally conceded that the system of caste with its rule regarding marriage within caste had taken a definite shape in the times of the later Saṁhitās,[237] though the rule about connubium was not so rigid as it was in later times. By the time of the Jātakas we find that marriage within the caste was a general rule, though we have certain examples of the transgression of this rule where the children of such mixed marriage were considered legitimate.[238] The early Dharma-śāstra works generally enjoin that one should marry within one's own varṇa though they do show a consciousness of a state of facts that this was not always so.[239] The epics, however, show occasionally that the Brahmins were matrimonially connected with the Kṣatriyas.[240]

The instances of Kṣatriya-Brahmins have been fully treated by PARGITER.[241] He says that the Purāṇic statements referring to them cannot have originated with the Brahmins because it was not in the interest of any Brahmin *gotra* to allege such a beginning. He further

231. *Ved. Ind.*, 1. 206.

232. For references cf. *Vedic Index*, 2. 247 ff. GHURYE, *Caste and Race in India*, 40 ff. and also *BDCRI*, 2. 34.

233. BHANDARKAR, *Collected Works*, 2. 511.

234. KANE, 2. 31. KANE here cites certein instances in support of his contention.

235. *Ved. Ind.*, 1. 204. 236. *Ibid.* 2, 260, cf. also KANE, 2. 447.

237. Cf. KANE, op. cit. GHURYE remarks, "while there are few traditional examples of Kṣatriya girls being married to Brahmins there is not a single example from among the personages of this age where a Brahmin girl has married a Kṣatriya," See his *Caste and Race in India*, 45.

238. FICK, 51 ff.

239. KANE, 2. 448 ff. We are not here concerned about the *anuloma* and *pratiloma* kinds of marriages.

240. HOPKINS, *JAOS*, 13. 241. *AIHT*, Chapt. 23.

adds that "these statements were too damaging to exclusive Brahmanic pretensions. The Brahmins then did not put them into the genealogies. The statements came from Kṣatriya sources and were notices which occurred naturally in the course of the royal genealogies......the statements, therefore, were genuine ancient tradition and were known to be true beyond gainsaying".[242]

The names of kings with whom the origin of these various Kṣatriya Brahmins are associated may be given below :

(a) Māṁdhātā—ancestor of the Hāritas and Viṣṇuvṛddhas and whose origins are separated from him not beyond three to five generations.

(b) Ajamīḍha—ancestor of the Kaṇṭhāyana Brahmins and the Maudgalyas who were not removed for more than five generations from him. This Ajamīḍha was the earliest king of the North Pañcāla dynasty.[243]

(c) Vitatha Bharadvāja,—adopted son (?) of Bharata (ancestor of Gāgras, Kapis and Sāṁkṛtis who were his immediate descendants).

(d) Divodāsa—ancestor of the Maitreyas who were his immediate descendants.

The origin of the Śāradvatas is, according to the Purāṇa, to be assigned to the period immediately after that in which king Śaṁtanu flourished.

It will be obvious from the discussion of the age of these kings, that they belonged to a period anterior to that of the ṚV. which mentions all of them.[244] Thus the origin of these Kṣatriya-Brahmins can be said to have taken place in the age anterior to that of the Veda except in the case of the Śāradvatas who appear to have sprung up in the time of the ṚV.[245] What is striking in this is that we do not find such instances in later genealogies probably because the caste system began to have its effect on the social structure of the post-Ṛgvedic period.

Chronologically the same conclusion is true of the instances of Kṣatriya-Brahmin marriages also (excepting the last two whose chronology it is difficult for us to make out). These cases are found in the Purāṇa without any vestige of an idea that they went against a settled custom prohibiting inter-caste marriages.

(iii) Brahmins appointed to raise issue for Kṣatriyas (for particulars see "*Niyoga*" in the chapter on Marriage).

(iv) A Kṣatriya adopting a Brahmin as his Heir: "In early societies, a son by levirate was always preferred to a son by adoption. An

---

242. *Ibid.* 124. 243. *Ibid.* 116, 251.
244. Bharata, father of Vitatha Bharadvāja is mentioned in the ṚV.; cf. *AIHT*, 7.
245. Cf. *AIHT*. 7.

adopted son presupposed a tremendous legal fiction for which society was not yet ripe." We have a statement in the ṚV. that an adoptive son born of another is no son at all.[246] This prejudice against an adopted son was due primarily to the fact that there existed other kinds of sonship known to the society of those days which were preferable to the sonship by adoption. The kinds of sons referred to in the early Dharma-śāstra works and the degree of preference in which the adopted son stood clearly testify to this. The Āpastamba Dharmasūtra, even though it condemns Niyoga, is equally opposed to giving away of a son in adoption.[247] But the more the other kinds of sonship fell into disuetude through the advance of morality and the increasing prevalence of child marriage, the more was the theory of adoption improved and was at last developed into one of the most important institutions of Indian Law.[248] In connection with adoption the Smṛti works generally cite the well-known legend of Śunaḥśepa in the Ait. Br. whom his father Ajīgarta sold to king Hariścandra under the pinch of poverty and who was afterwards adopted by Viśvāmitra.[249] That these texts do not note the case of adoption cited in our Purāṇa is really very significant. This omission may be due to the fact that the instance belongs to the Purāṇic tradition which had not the same authority as the source of law as the Vedic texts,[250] or it may also be due to the fact that the Smṛtikāras by referring to this instance would have involved themselves into a fallacy that a Brahmin could be adopted by a Kṣatriya which would have upset the principles which they held in general about caste in their law of adoption. The historicity of the instance of the Purāṇa is assured for us by PARGITER who remarks that "the statement that a distinguished Brahmin became a Kṣatriya's son could not have come from a Brahmin source". He regards the Vāyu version of the story as earlier which according to him is manifestly an ancient Kṣatriya tradition.[251] The Vāyu has an interesting information that Bharadvāja claimed ~~to~~ be both a Brahmin and a Kṣatriya and calls himself as one having "two fathers" which the Matsya tries to change.[252] Again the Purāṇa states that this Bharadvāja from being originally a Brahmin became a Kṣatriya. Such a state of facts could never have been viewed with favour by even the early Dharma-sūtra works according to whose theories of varṇāśrama such an occurrence should certainly have been stamped as a case of varṇasaṁkara.[253]

---

246. ALTEKAR, 169.
247. Cf. JOLLY, *Hindu Law and Custom*, (Eng. Trans. by GHOSH), 159.
248. *Ibid.* 249. *Vasiṣṭha Dharma Sūtra*, 17, 31 ff.
250. N. C. SEN GUPTA, *Sources of Law and Society in Ancient India.*
251. *AIHT*, 160. 252. *Ibid.*
253. It should be noted that according to the Smṛtis the adoptive son was required to be of the same caste and status as those of the adoptive father. Cf. JOLLY. op. cit. 162.

The Vaiśyas

"The Vaiśya plays singularly little part in the Vedic literature which has so much to say of the Kṣatriyas and the Brahmins." He was really an agriculturist and followed pastoral pursuits and commerce also. The Vaiśyas formed the bulk of the masses excluding, of course, the Śūdras.[254]

The name Vaiśya is first found in the Puruṣa-sūkta of the ṚV. and then frequently from the AV. onwards.[255] The ṚV. however uses the word "viś" quite a number of times though in a variety of senses. The expression is sometimes used to signify "a people" and is occasionally used as a synonym of *jana*.[256] It is certain that viś cannot in almost all the hymns of the ṚV. mean Vaiśya.[257] Fick says that the Jātakas do not show Vaiśyas as a caste. The *gahapatis* of these texts show some resemblance to the Vaiśyas of the Brahmanical theory.[258] In the great Epic, however, we find the Vaiśyas forming the caste of a people who were after money.[259]

We have an interesting instance of the expression 'viśāṁ patiḥ' used in the Purāṇa in connection with king Kārtavīrya Arjuna and his son Jayadhvaja. Here the word viś does not certainly mean the caste vaiśya but appears to signify "the peoples" or "countries" as we find the same expression used in the Vedic literature. That the expression 'viśāṁ patiḥ' should be found in the Purāṇa-genealogies only in connection with the king Kārtavīrya and his son is really significant though we are unable for the present to explain this connection.

The Vaiśyas mentioned in the story of Pṛthu probably indicate that they formed the bulk of the masses, for here the three varṇas—and not the śūdras—are mentioned and they are here recommended to pay homage to the king.

The other references to Vaiśyas in the Puraṇa can be easily assigned to a period subsequent to that of the Jātakas, for nowhere do we find them in the Purāṇa in such a respectable position as the *gahapati* in the Jātakas. On the contrary, they are occasionally condemned probably because many of them belonged to faiths which the Purāṇa-redactors held in contempt and whenever they are mentioned in a favourable light they are associated with Śūdras and women.

The Śūdras

The word *śudra* is unknown to the ṚV. except in the Puruṣa-sūkta. The ṚV. knows the Dasyus or Dāsas both as aborigines and as subjected slaves and the Śūdras of the later Vedic texts were certainly aborigines who were reduced to subjection by the Āryans. The term mostly

254. *Ved. Ind.*, 2. 333-5. 255. *Ibid.* 256. *Ibid.* 257. Kane, 2. 32-3.
258. P. 252 ff. cf. also Mehta, 255-7. 259. Hopkins, *JAOS*, 13. 73.

indicated those who were beyond the pale of the Āryan state. The Vedic references to his condition imply this. The Ait. Br. says that he is a "servant of another to be expelled at will" and "to be slain at will". The Pañcaviṁśa Brāhmaṇa says that even if he is prosperous he cannot but be servant of another and that his business is to wash the feet of his master.[260] Though the Jātakas mention the word *śudda* (i.e. śūdra) in their theoretical discussions of castes, there is nothing in them which points to the real existence of a fourth caste, the Śūdras. In their realistic picture of the society of their times in eastern India, however, there are frequent references to the low races such as those of Cāṇḍālas, Pukkusas, etc.[261] In the Dharma-śāstra-literature we find many disabilities imposed on Śūdras[262] and the Mbh. says that they cannot own property[263] and insists on their duty to serve.

In the Vāyu account of social origins we find them first described as a miserable, powerless and servile people. The occurrence of *delusion* and the consequent revision of the functions of the varṇas by the Creator may be regarded as significant. Does it indicate a reminiscence in the Purāṇa of a fact that the people who were loosely called Śūdras were originally aboriginal peoples rendered helpless by the invading Āryans who then later absorbed them into their society by assigning to them the lowest work of servitude? The reference to Śūdras in connection with king Yayāti, where they appear as distinct from the Dasyus must be considered inapplicable to the period of the king who is mentioned in the ṚV. It only shows that a large number of aboriginal inhabitants had been incorporated into the Āryan fold and the Dasyus signified probably the remaining aboriginal tribes. On the contrary, the absence of reference to Śūdras amongst the varṇas who were required to pay respects to the king Pṛthu indicates that the story has been preserved for us in an antiquarian form.

The Dasyus

The mention of the Dasyus in connection with Budha, father of Purūravas, clearly indicates the antiquity of the information, for here we find the Dasyus not as slaves but as enemies with whose annihilation Budha is credited as if it were his glorious achievement. In the Vedic tradition we find Indra credited with this achievement.[264] The Dasyu-dharma mentioned in connection with king Satyavrata Triśaṅku is equally suggestive of the antiquity of the reference because of the absence of the prohibition of eating cow-flesh in the story and because of the possibility of the Dasyus harassing the Brahmins in their possession of cows.

---

260. *Ved Ind.*, 2. 387–92. 261. Fick, 314. 262. Kane, 2. 154.
263. Hopkins, *JAOS*, 13, 13. 73. 264. *Ved. Ind.*, 1. 347.

Slavery and Slave-Trade

The word *dāsa* has the sense of 'slave' in several passages of the ṚV.[265] Slaves, both male and female, are found mentioned in the Vedic literature.[266] The Vaideha slaves are referred to as prize in connection with king Janaka of the Bṛ. Up.[267] The Jātakas too testify to the existence of slavery.[268] Slavery was probably not much in evidence in India of the 4th cent. B.C., for we find Megasthenes stating that none of the Indians employ slaves though it is admitted that slavery did exist then. The Dharma-śāstra also gives some consideration to slaves.[269]

There is one very striking instance of slavery found in our Purāṇa in connection with the sale of the child of Viśvāmitra by his wife. We have seen above how the story of Triśaṅku embodies an ancient tradition and in the reference to this tale we have a very ancient state of facts preserved for us. We find a similar account from the Ait. Br. regarding the purchase of Śunaḥśepa as a victim in a sacrifice.[270] The story of the prize of slaves, etc., told in our Purāṇas, is corroborated by the Bṛ. Up. in connection with the same king Janaka.

---

265. *Ved. Ind.*, 357. 266. Kane, 2. 180-1. 267. *Ibid.* 181.
268. Fick, 307-10. 269. See Kane, 2. 183 for details.
270. *Ved. Ind.*, 2. 385.

CHAPTER II

WOMAN AND MARRIAGE

I. Woman

Estimation of Women :—In the ṚV. we find that "the wife on her marriage was at once given an honoured position in the house ; she is emphatically a mistress in her husband's house."[1] But still uncomplimentary remarks about her, especially with regard to her unstable faith, are found in that Veda. Regard for her begins to diminish in the latter Saṁhitās and in the Brāhmaṇas to such an extent that the Maitrāyaṇī Saṁhitā generally classes her with dice and drink, as one of the three chief evils and she is even declared to be the very untruth and the embodiment of calamity.[2] Early Buddhism did not regard her with much respect and Buddha is shown very unwillingly admitting her to the uddhist Order which consequently led to the formation of a separate order of nuns.[3] Her wicked nature is frequently alluded to in the Jātakas.[4] In the early Dharma-śāstra works her position gradually becomes worse and worse and she is assigned a position of dependence[5] and is even charged with serious moral defects.[6]

The peculiarity of the information of our Purāṇa is such that condemnatory remaiks about her are rarely found in it. The only positive statement regarding her evil disposition is found in her association with the Kali age when women are said to outnumber men. ALTEKAR tells us that deliberate attempts were made to blacken her character from about the beginning of the Christian era[7] and the Vāyu statements may be supposed to reflect the social condition of the women of that age.

Women and Chattel : In some respects women were regarded as chattel even in the times of the ṚV., as is indicated in the famous hymn about gambling, which shows that confirmed gamblers would stake away their wives to their opponents. But the same hymn suggests that social conscience had begun to disapprove of such practices.[8] Women, captured in war, particularly, suffered in their status and were regarded as chattel and thus we find in the ṚV. Vimada described as having won his bride in battle[9] and similar incidents are found in the epics also.[10] It is clear that though the Kṣātra marriage—according to which the condition of woman as a chattel is implied—continued

---

1. *Ved. Ind.*, 1. 484 ; A. C. DAS, *Ṛgvedic Culture*, 238-9.
2. *Ved. Ind.*, 1. 485 ff. ; KANE, 2. 368, 575 ; ALTEKAR, 383 ff.
3. OLDENBERG, *Buddha*, 164 ff. ; 377 ff. ; cf. also LAW, *Women in Buddhist Literature*.
4. MEHTA, 286-9.
5. KANE, 2. 367.
6. *Ibid.*, 577-8 ; ALTEKAR, 383 ff.
7. P. 385.
8. A. C. DAS, *Ṛgvedic Culture*, 105 ; ALTEKAR, 408.
9. ALTEKAR, 45 ; cf. also DAS, op. cit.
10. HOPKINS, *JAOS*, 13. 361-2.

to be recognised by the Smṛtis and the epics, it had ceased to be approved, even by the enlightened Kṣatriyas in the 3rd century B.C.[11] In the Jātakas the wife is shown under the subjection of her husband and was his absolute property.[12]

The Vāyu has only one instance of this category and its antiquity may be judged accordingly. The first reference to women in connection with the king Yayāti is devoid of historical basis as Yayāti was a king of the pre-Ṛgvedic period. We are not sure whether we can say the same about the other statement about women in connection with the same king.

Women equal in Status to Śūdra: In Vedic times woman had equal status with men and initiation and other ceremonies were performed for her also.[13] The Vedas do not class her with Śūdras and the Jātakas are silent on this point.[14] In the Dharma-śāstra literature, however, we generally find that their position is similar to that of the Śūdras in many matters.[15] Manu positively states her to be equal in status to a Śūdra.[16]

The Vāyu has no explicit statement with regard to this and this silence may be regarded as suggestive though not as a conclusive evidence. The inference that her status was, according to the Purāṇa, equal to Śūdra becomes probable from the description of the Kali age. We have to note, however, that our Purāṇa classes even Vaiśyas with women.

Her Status as Wife: The sanctity of the marriage-tie is as old as the ṚV.[17] The perpetuity of the marriage-union is praised in the Vāyu and the reference presupposes the knowledge of the theory of rebirths and probably of the avatāras also. Thus this statement of the Purāṇa must be supposed to be coeval with or later than the antiquity of the theory of rebirth and avatāras. The ideal happiness which our Purāṇa wishes for a girl—to secure a good husband and be blessed with male progeny—is also as old as the Vedas and the sentiment was popular throughout the ages. Hence it is unnecessary to discuss its chronology.

Her Status as Mother: In the Vedic period the mother ranked after the father in the family. Details are given in the Sūtras about the respectful attention paid to a mother and about the ceremonies in which she is concerned.[18] The social conditions depicted in the Jātakas also imply her respectable position.[19] Whatever the condemnation of women in the whole of Dharma-śāstra literature, we find there her position as

---

11. ALTEKAR, op. cit. 12. MEHTA, 290.
13. *Ved. Ind.*, 1. 485; A. C. DAS, op. cit., 249. 14. See MEHTA, 276 ff.
15. KANE, 2. 594; cf. also ALTEKAR, 12. 19. 236 ff.
16. V. 139 cf. *strī śūdras tu sakṛt sakṛt*. 17. KANE, 2. 427; ALTEKAR, 34 ff. etc.
18. *Ved. Ind.*, 2. 151. 19. MEHTA, 291-2.

mother definitely exalted. Some of these works are even schematic on this point and work out the degrees in which she should be respected as compared with the preceptor, the father, etc.[20] Manu says that a mother is thousand times greater than the father.[21] The great epic also contains eulogies of this nature.[22]

The Vāyu does not discuss the niceties of the problem of the degrees of respect to be paid to the mother. We are not sure on the point whether this points to the antiquarian character of the Purāṇa. The incidents which indirectly show the high respect paid to her are purely mythical, but at any rate they reflect a state of society in which a mother was highly esteemed.

Immunity from Capital Punishment: "From very ancient times it appears that the idea was that women should not be killed on any account.[23] The Śatapatha Brāhmaṇa says that a woman ought not to be killed,[24] that only a king, (according to some Dharma-śāstra works, e.g. Gautama Dharma-sūtra and Manusmṛti) could punish a woman to death but even for this he had to undergo a slight penance and this punishment is allowed in the case of her adultery with a man of a lower caste.[25] The epics are equally emphatic on this point.[26]

The information of the Vāyu in this respect falls more in line with the Dharma-śāstra works and the epics than with the Śatapatha Brāhmaṇa. The incident stated in connection with king Pṛthu suggests that she did not enjoy an unconditional immunity and this reference accords well with the views expressed in the Gautama Dharma-sūtra and the Manusmṛti.

Women and Higher Studies: In the Vedic times women were capable of undertaking higher studies. They participated in the intellectual activities of the day.[27] Twenty women are recorded in the Sarvānukramaṇīkā as authoresses of the hymns of the ṚV.[28] The names of Maitreyī and Gārgī of the Upaniṣads are too well-known to need mention. The ancient grammarians were also familiar with women teachers.[29] The Jātakas, however, show that her education was on the decline. But still we find women admitted to the order of nuns.[30] At least, this was so at that time in eastern India. The Dharma-śāstra literature shows that "literary education amongst women was in a languishing state or almost nil."[31] The cause of women's education suffered a good deal after about 300 B.C., on account of the new fashion of child-marriage that began to come into vogue. Even the initiation ritual that was allowed her from the Vedic times was now reduced

20. KANE, 2. 580-81. 21. II. 145.
22. ALTEKAR, 118. 23. KANE, 2. 593. 24. ALTEKAR, 380.
25. KANE, op. cit. 26. ALTEKAR, op. cit. 27. *Ved. Ind.*, 1. 486.
28. ALTEKAR, 12; KANE, 2. 365. 29. KANE, 2. 366.
30. OLDENBERG, *Buddha*, 164 ff.; 377 ff.; MEHTA, 298. 31. KANE, 2. 368.

to a mere formality and then was dropped out altogether. This put an end to her education.[32]

The instances quoted from the Purāna are mostly mythical and thus of doubtful value. Of the instances from the genealogical portion of the Purāṇa the one about Dhūminī's penance is apparently fantastic. The only incident that deserves the credit of historicity is that of the wife of king Bāhu, though the penance practised by the wives of Sagara may also deserve some consideration. Whether we regard these references as historical or not, the Purāṇa has given us information about matters which rarely took place in the period after the 3rd cent. B.C.

Seclusion of Women : There is no evidence from the Vedas and the Jātakas[33] regarding the seclusion of women. "There can be no doubt whatsoever that the Purdah was quite unknown down to about the beginning of the Christian era".[34] But soon after this time it appears that a section of society began to advocate a greater seclusion of women.[35]

The Vāyu shows no instance of any seclusion of women. The case of Kumārīpura in a Kṛtrima fort does not appear to indicate seclusion of women. It only shows that women had separate residential arrangements for them in an ideal Kṛtrima fort, just as the harems of kings were known to us from very early times. Thus, according to the Vāyu, women could move freely in society. This may be taken as evidence for the antiquity of these references from the Purāṇa.

The Suttee : The custom of sacrificing the wife at her husband's death existed amongst the Indo-Europeans.[36] The Vedic age shows that self-immolation of the widow was then an ancient custom which began to fall out of practice.[37] We find the AV. mentioning suicide of the widow on the death of her husband as an "ancient duty" (XVIII. iii. 1). The custom, however, appears again to peep into existence at about 300 B.C. and afterwards grew in frequency till at about 400 A.D. It was common amongst the Kṣatriyas.[38]

The Vāyu has only one instance of the *suttee*. The text is not explicit whether she did actually ascend the funeral pyre. The Brahma Purāṇa and the Hari Vaṁśa fill up the blank. They say that king Bāhu's wife ascended the funeral pyre evidently to immolate herself and the sage Aurva dissuaded her from the act. The Viṣṇu and the Bṛhannāradīya say so explicitly.[39] The ground on which Aurva appears to have dissuaded the wife of Bāhu from her act of self-immolation suggests

32. ALTEKAR, 18-9.

33. There are certain indications in the Jātakas to the contrary but the evidence on the whole does not point to a rigid custom of seclusion of women. Cf. MEHTA, 290-1.

34. ALTEKAR, 19; KANE, 2. 596-8.

35. ALTEKAR, 200.

36. SCHRADER, *Prehistoric Antiquities of the Aryan Peoples*, 391.

37. ALTEKAR, 137 ff.

38. ALTEKAR, 140-3 ; *ERE*, 2. 207 ; KANE, 2. 624 ff.

39. *JRAS*, 1919, p. 355, fn. 4.

that the custom was not still regarded with disapproval. This instance thus falls in time and spirit with the period anterior to that of the ṚV. which reminds us of an ancient custom of the *suttee* but shows its discontinuance.[40] This leads us to conclude that the Purāṇa had preserved for us a fact which might be considered historical as it sinchronizes with the political history of king Sagara.

Matronymics and the Matriarchate : In the Vedic literature we find a person born of a maiden mentioned with his matronymic. In this custom may be found the origin of matronymics such as those which make up a greater part of the list of teachers (vaṁśa) of the Br. Up.[41] This practice of mention by matronymics might also be due to polygamy.[42] We find Dīrghatamas mentioned in the ṚV. by his matronymic Māmateya alone.[43]

We know that the Aryan society was essentially patriarchal from the Vedic times and such was the case also with the Indo-Europeans.[44] The occurrence of matronymics amongst them might be due to reasons stated above. Only one case of matronymic—i.e. of Aila Purūravas—is found in the Vāyu which, however, mentions many patronymics with the 'Aryan' names. But the reverse is the case when the Purāṇa mentions the names of Asuras, Rākṣasas, Yakṣas, etc. Preponderance of matronymics amongst them as against the preponderance of patronymics amongst the "Aryans" is a fact worthy of attention. It has been suggested that the Asura institutions were matriarchal on the ground that they are often mentioned with matronymics.[45] The evidence of our Purāṇa is really very suggestive in this connection. Again we find in the Purāṇa the speech of Kaśyapa to his wife Khaśā, who was a Rākṣasī which appears to confirm the above suggestion. The statement that a son is devoted to his maternal uncle may make us infer that the society of the so-called Rākṣasas or Asuras was probably matriarchal.

II. Marriage

Promiscuity : "The Vedic works contain no indications about a society in which the relations of the sexes were promiscuous or unregulated." The Mbh., however, shows Pāṇḍu stating to his queen Kuntī that women in former ages were under no control, that they indulged themselves as they liked, that they left one man and went after another and that this state of things continued to his day when Śvetaketu, son of Uddālaka, for the first time stopped all this licence and laid down certain rules regarding marriage. There is another passage in the Sabhāparvan referring to the unrestrained nature of

---

40. *Ved. Ind.*, 1. 488. 41. *Ved. Ind.*, 1. 481. 42. *Ibid.*, fn. 70.
43. *Ved. Ind.*, 1. 366. 44. Childe, *Aryans*, 81. 45. *JBORS*, 12. 533 ff.

Māhiṣmatī women.[46] KANE, however, puts little reliance on these passages, which PARGITER considers as "possibly true".[47] PARGITER also quotes another instance from the Mbh. which mentions Dīrghatamas as putting an end to promiscuity.[48]

If any historical significance is attached to these passages, they must be referred to the pre-Vedic times; for in the ṚV we already find marriage as a sacred institution.

The instances of the Vāyu should be considered in this light. In the first instance we find Tārā, the wife of Bṛhaspati, seduced by Soma. What is necessary to notice here is the procedure followed in deciding the vexed question of the paternity of the child born of that 'illicit union'. That procedure does not at all indicate that Soma's connection with Tārā was a case of 'illicit' union, offending the sanctity of the marriage tie.

Budha's relation with Ilā is equally significant. The text expressly says that she was 'invited' by him for cohabitation.

Equally interesting is the case of Budha's son Purūravas. That this Purūravas is mentioned by his matronymic Aila is equally significant. Was it that he was born of illicit union? Ilā was a maiden when Budha cohabited with her. It is doubtful if the relation between Purūravas and Urvaśī can at all be called 'marriage' as we understand it from the Ṛgveda onwards. A curious dialogue between him and a nymph Ūrvaśī occurs in the ṚV.[49] and the compilers of the Vedic Index conclude that Purūravas might be a mythical figure, pure and simple. We find, however, that the Śatapatha Brāhmaṇa (11-5-1), while narrating this story in details, mentions the 'condition' as stated in the Vāyu. This story of the Śatapatha Brhāhmaṇa offers closer resemblances to that of our text.[50] Though it is difficult to say whether this episode belonged to the ancient and original Purāṇic tradition, yet its character suggests that it might have been so. Fabricated stories stand on a different footing and PARGITER says that this is not one of them. "Purūravas and Ūrvaśī were the progenitors of the great Aila race; hence their legend must have existed in earliest times".[51] He, however, doubts the historicity of the story of Soma's abduction of Tārā on the ground that it belongs to mythological tradition. But still he immediately says that "myths that explain the origin of the chief races...may suggest clues for exploring earliest conditions".[52]

What interests us further is that all these instances are associated with the earliest ancestors of the so-called Aila race who were not much removed in time from each other; and it is tempting to assume

46. KANE, 2. 427-8. Cf. also ALTEKAR, 35 ff. 47. *AIHT*, 328, fn. 8.
48. *Ibid.* 49. *Ved. Ind.*, 2. 3.
50. MACDONELL, *Vedic Mythology*, 135. 51. *AIHT*, 38. 52. *AIHT*, 58.

that in the above three cases we have "explored the earliest conditions" of the institution of marriage as it prevailed amongst the "Ailas".

The fourth instance shows Bṛhaspati mating with his brother's wife Mamatā, and Bharadvāja, the issue of the union, is called Bārhaspatya and a Brahmin. What is important here to notice is the idea regarding sexual morality. Though there is a faint plea on the part of Mamatā that Bṛhaspati's behaviour amounts to violation of dharma, Bṛhaspati dismisses it on the ground that it is sheer modesty. The whole story assumes still more importance when we find Bharadvāja, (the issue of that union) adopted by Bharata.

This incident is found in the Matsya Purāṇa in a modified form. PARGITER considers the Vāyu version earlier and says that "neither version could have been composed by the Brahmans after the Purāṇa had passed into their hands". Thus this story must have belonged to the ancient Kṣatriya tradition.[53]

The instances, discussed above, do not exactly give us a picture of a society in which the relations of the sexes were promiscuous; still they show us that ideas regarding marriage-obligations were different. According to them, one is tempted to infer that sexual morality was not the *sine qua non* of the obligations that arose out of marriage.

It should be noted that many primitive tribes do not always regard marriage as an institution controlling sexual behaviour. Mating must not be confounded with marriage. A realistic analysis of the institution of marriage does not confound the theory and actuality in sex behaviour nor does it derive conjugal life from sexual drive. To merge the two concepts is to forego an insight into the distinctively human element of the phenomenon.[54] The above cases may then be supposed to offer glimpses of such primitive stage of the institution of marriage, a stage which, as seen above, must be assigned to times far anterior to those of the Vedas.

The Cult of Godharma: The text has confused king Bali with Vairocana Bali, the *asura*, probably because the *purāṇakāra* could not view such an incident connected with the progenitor of the five great families. The whole episode clearly indicates promiscuity. The story shows that Dīrghatamas *borrowed* the Cult from a Bull of Śiva and that he was persecuted. This implies that the practice was alien to the society to which Dīrghatamas belonged. PARGITER thinks that this incident finds support in the ṚV.[55] We have also to note that in the ṚV. Dīrghatamas is often mentioned by his matronymic. But the compilers of the VEDIC INDEX dismiss it by saying that it would be unwise to see any historical significance into this.[56]

53. *Ibid.*, 160.
54. LOWIE, *Encyclopædia of Social Sciences*, 10. 146.
55. *AIHT*, 158.
56. *Ved. Ind.*, 1. 366; cf. also Mbh. 1. 104. 4193–221.

Certain scholars hold that according to the ṚV., the aborigines practised the phallus cult.[57] The ṚV. mentions Śiśnadevas twice.[58] Perhaps a custom akin to this godharma might have existed amongst them which attracted the attention of Dīrghatamas to the extent of practising it himself. It must be stated that this is merely a speculation as, with the available evidence, it is difficult to suggest any historical explanation for this quaint practice of *Godharma*.

Levirate or Niyoga: There was a custom amongst the ancient Aryans to appoint a person to procreate male progeny for another under certain conditions. The ancient Dharma-sūtras like the Gautama allowed *niyoga*, still there were others, equally as old as the Gautama, who condemned the practice and forbade it. The Mbh. is replete with instances of niyoga. Satyavatī pressed Bhīṣma to procreate male progeny for his younger brother Vicitravīrya and though Bhīṣma refused to do so, Vyāsa acceded to her request. Pāṇḍu himself asked his wife Kuntī to procreate sons for him by *niyoga* from a Brahmin endowed with *tapas*.[59] This practice of niyoga was a relic of a very remote past and did not find favour with later writers.[60]

Now the law-books give certain rules as regards niyoga and it is necessary to state some of them here in order to examine the evidence of the instances from the Vāyu:

(1) The husband, living or dead, must have no son. This shows that the underlying motive was to continue the family line.

(2) The *gurus*, in a family council, should decide to allow the widow to raise the issue for her husband. The person appointed to raise the issue must be the *sapiṇḍa*, especially the brother, of the husband of the woman.[61]

(3) The person appointed must be annointed with ghee or oil. He must not be animated by lust.

(4) The issue belonged to the kṣetra (i.e. the husband of the woman who is allowed to practise niyoga). The text-books however differ on this point.[62]

In both the instances of the Vāyu we find the main motive to be the same as laid down in (1) above. (Cf. the expressions *santānārthaṁ* and *Ikṣvākukulavṛddhaye*). As regards point (2) it is noteworthy that the persons appointed (in the Vāyu) are not the *sapiṇḍas* of the husband, but are Brahmins. One is the preceptor himself. The other provision that in the case of the death of the husband, the *gurus* should decide in a council to appoint the person, deserves attention in this respect.

57. *Mohenjo-daro*, 1. 111.
58. *Ved. Ind.*, 2. 382.
59. KANE, 2. 602-4.
60. Cf. ALTEKAR, 170 ff.
61. KANE, 2. 599-601; ALTEKAR, 170 ff.
62. KANE, 2. 601.

Why are they to have any voice in the matter according to the law-texts? In the Mbh. we find Pāṇḍu advocating appointment of a Brahmin endowed with *tapas*. It seems that the primitive custom was that a Brahmin, especially the preceptor of the husband, was a fit person in this respect and the law-books give a later stage of the custom still showing a trace of the former practice in the form of the consultation with the gurus. This would mean that the Vāyu has (as also the Mbh.) preserved for us a very ancient stage of the custom. Of the third point we find a clear evidence in the narration of the appointment of Dīrghatamas in the case of Sudeṣṇā. This Vāyu passage, however, says that curd mixed with salt was applied to the naked frame of the sage. The Matsya adds honey also.[63] (The exact significance, medical or otherwise, of this practice, is difficult to be made out). As regards the fourth point, we find in both the instances from the Vāyu that the issues of niyoga belonged to the kṣetra.

The practice of niyoga was a relic of the remote past. It was theoretically a practice forbidden in the Kali age.[64] We do not find any instance of niyoga mentioned in the Vāyu in connection with the dynasties of the Kali age. Manu states that "in former ages men possessed tapas and knowledge and could strictly carry out the rules while in Dvāpara and Kali there is great deterioration of power and so men of these times cannot practise niyoga.[65] We have to judge the antiquity of the instances of Vāyu in the light of these observations.

---

63. 48.69. 64. KANE, 2.606. 65. KANE, 2.603.

CHAPTER III

POLITICAL INSTITUTIONS

I. Kingship

Origin of Kingship : In the R̥V., monarchy is the normal and the only form of government known.[1] The Vedic theory of the origin of kingship is found in the Ait. Br. "It asserts that the Devas......originally had no king. In their struggle against the Asuras, when the Devas found that they were repeatedly defeated, they came to the conclusion that it was because the Asuras had a king to lead them that they were successful. Therefore they decided to try the same experiment. And they agreed to elect a king." If this is taken to have a historical reference it would refer to the tribal stage of the Aryans in India and it would suggest that the institution of kingship was borrowed from the Dravidians.[2]

This theory is not found anywhere in later literature on political theories, nor is it found in the Vāyu.

The ancient Hindu political writers however held two theories regarding the origin of kingship which are found narrated in the Mbh. It is necessary to discuss them here as they have a bearing on the Vāyu passages.

First Theory : (a) A dreadful picture of the conditions of anarchy is described which precedes the origin of kingship. This is narrated to stress the evil consequences of king's non-existence.

(b) People tried to live by mutual contracts but being afflicted with sorrow they approached (collectively) Lord Brahmā and begged for a chief to protect them.

(c) The Lord appointed Manu as their ruler. Manu hesitated at first to accept this office but after the assurances from people regarding the payment of taxes, homages, etc., he accepted the office and made them do their duties.[3]

Here we find the notion of social contracts blended with the theory of divine creation of the king.

The Vāyu account differs considerably from this. It does not make much of the evil state of anarchy—technically known by the *Matsya-nyāya*. The Mbh. account introduces immediately at the close of the anarchical state of nature a stage which approximates closely to the notion of the social contract. The Vāyu, however, states that at first Brahmā had ordained the four varṇas and they lived in a state of bliss ;

---

1. *CHI*, 1. 94 ff. 2. Jayaswal, 2. 1-5.

3. Ghoshal, 174 ff. ef *Śāntiparvan*, 67. 17-32. Cf. also Dikshitar, *Hindu Administrative Institutions*, 16-7.

but somehow people were swayed away from the path of dharma by the spell of *moha*. And this gave rise to mutual conflicts which resemble the state of anarchy. Thus, as compared with the Mbh. account, the order of the two stages are inverted in the Vāyu. In the Vāyu the people approach Manu Prajāpati himself, who creates *two* kings. This mention of two kings is very queer. Has it any semblance to the theory of dual organization of PERRY ?[4] It should be noted that most of these references occur in the genealogical portion of the Purāṇa. The Vāyu passage suggests that kingship was a divinely ordained institution. Yet we are immediately told that "thenceforward are kings wielders of daṇḍa and entertainers of their subjects". This Vāyu passage knows nothing of the notion of social contract which smacks of the ideas prevalent in the old Buddhist canon.[5] Thus it appears that the Vāyu has handed down to us different ideas about the same theory and we may be allowed to state that they are probably the earlier ones than those of the Mbh. which introduces the technical term *matsya-nyāya* of which the Vāyu betrays complete ignorance.[6]

Second Theory :[7] Only the points of difference need here be noted.

(a) Here also the Mbh. gives a picture of the state of nature where there was no monarchy nor the monarch and that people protected each other according to the law. This mutual co-operation, however, failed to work and the law began to suffer. Lord Brahmā prepared a gigantic treatise on Daṇḍa-nīti and gods approached Viṣṇu who produced a son out of his own lustre. Vena was the fifth successor of this son of Viṣṇu.

This matter is absolutely new to the Vāyu which does not show any trace of it.

(b) The Mbh. is elaborate on the point of Vena's persecution of the Brahmins while the Vāyu only shows how he viewed ritual and the law (dharma) and says nothing of his persecution of the Brahmins.

(c) The Vāyu says nothing of the Pratijñā which the gods and sages proposed to the king Pṛthu.[8] On the other hand we find in the Vāyu account a ceremonial procedure which has a tinge of antiquity.

---

4. Children of the Sun. 5. Cf. GHOSHAL, 117–9.

6. Kauṭilya has another version though we are not sure whether of the same theory as found in the Mbh. and in the Vāyu. He mentions Vaivasvata Manu while our works mention Svāyaṁbhuva Manu. Again it is stated that Kauṭilya drives at the theory of the human origin of kingship in this passage referring to Manu; cf. DIKSHITAR, op. cit., 16–7.

7. We followed the account of this theory as it is given by GHOSHAL, 176 ff., cf. also JAYASWAL, 2-47 ff. ; and PANIKKAR, *Origin and Evolution of Kingship*, 25 ff.

8. This is important to note, for JAYASWAL lays much strees on the oath. Cf. his *Hindu Polity*, 2. 45.

In the procedure we find the sage—who made him king—occupying a subordinate position.

(d) The Mbh. says that "the divine Viṣṇu entered the person of the king and hence the whole universe worships the kings as if they were gods." This is not found in the Vāyu which, however, says that Pṛthu, being *Brahmayoni* and *sanātana*, must be respected by the three varṇas (i.e., Brāhmaṇas, Kṣatriyas and Vaiśyas. Note that the Śūdras are not mentioned), for their own sake.

(e) The Vāyu, however, adds the account of the "milching of the earth". The exact significance of this is difficult to make out. We have a suggestion from the compilers of the VEDIC INDEX that Pṛthu of the ṚV. was probably a vegetation deity.[9] The idea which appears prominent in the Vāyu is that the king must provide for his people means of sustenance especially through the vegetable world.

The Vāyu material is manifestly earlier than that of the Mbh. It does not, for certain, establish that kingship was the creation of the Divine will, nor does it show kingship associated with Viṣṇu.

The Matsya-nyāya: It would have been seen that *matsya-nyāya* forms an important element in both the theories of the Mbh. The ideas about the prevalence of anarchy which preceded the rise of kingship appear in their germs in the Ś. Br. and the Tait. Br. which were woven by the later canonical writers into elaborate theories of the state of nature crystallized into the celebrated popular maxim of the *matsya-nyāya*.[10] The Jātakas are aware of this matsya-nyāya and in them we find a description of the pre-stated condition of anarchy.[11] Kauṭilya knew it well (1.4) and we find its vivid description in the Rāmāyaṇa.[12] By the time of Manu[13] and the later Smṛti works it had already become popular.

It is significant that the second Vāyu passage does not even show a hint of the knowledge of the maxim. Nor is the first one colourful in its description of the state of things before the advent of monarchy. From its simple description that "the people did not observe the dharma and mutual conflicts arose" we cannot definitely make out whether this is exactly the state of anarchy implicit in the matsya-nyāya. Even if we think that it is so, still it seems that the ideas are not ripe enough to bloom into a celebrated maxim. It appears that our Purāṇa favours the term *moha* more than the term *matsya-nyāya* and probably is not aware of a commonly known maxim of the matsya-nyāya which otherwise would not have been missed by the Purāṇa.

The Conception of King's Divinity: The germs of the ideas of the king's divinity are found in the ṚV. where we find a king comparing

9. *Ved. Ind.*, 2. 16. 10. GHOSHAL, 42–2; DIKSHITAR, op. cit., 19 ff.
11. MEHTA, 79. 12. Miss DHARMA, *Rāmāyaṇa Polity*, 12–3. 13. 7. 20.

and identifying himself with the two leading deities of the Vedic pantheon. In the AV. the conception is inculcated in the form of a general doctrine while in the YV. and the Brahmaṇas his divinity is pre-eminently associated with his participation in the great political sacrifices. In all these cases we find mostly the deity Indra represented in the king's person. But these statements appear merely metaphorical for we find others also called divine. But the corner-stone of the theories of the king's divinity of the later canonical works, however, appears to be laid in a passage of the Ś. Br. where the king, "the rājanya is the visible representative of Prajāpati; hence while being one, he rules over many." Still it must be remembered that these texts do not declare the king to be a god by virtue of his hereditary descent. On the other hand they distinctly affirm the human origin of the king.[14] The Jātakas are not mindful of the theory of the king's divinity. Kauṭilya, however, appears to note it but Jayaswal comments that "no divine origin of the king is preached in the passage of the Artha-śāstra".[15] It was, however, the Manu-saṁhitā that lent its weight in support of this theory.[16] And we have already stated above the views expressed in the Mbh.

If we examine the Vāyu material in the light of this chronological sequence we are right in assuming the high antiquity for its contents. We are not led by it to expressly infer about the king's divinity except in its hints noted above. The creation of two kings by Prajāpati should be noted in connection with the statement in Ś. Br. that the king is the visible representative of the Prajāpati.

Other Fragmentary Statements regarding King's Divinity: These statements, especially those associated with Viṣṇu clearly remind us that they had been aware of a well-known theory of king being animated with the spirit of Viṣṇu, a view which had been well-established in the story of Pṛthu of the Mbh. Thus they should be viewed chronologically in the line of the Mbh. story.

The association of kings with gods (especially with Indra) may be pieces of panegyrics. It is, however, possible that associations with Indra might be remnants of the theory of Ś. Br. which saw in the king the essence of Indra. It should be noted that most of these references occur in the genealogical portion of the Purāṇa.

There are some Purāṇas which discuss the fine question as to how many deities are represented in the king's person. It must be said that the Vāyu is a stranger to such notions.

---

14. Ghoshal, 27–33; cf. also Banerjea, 70 ff.; Jayaswal, 2. 54–9; Dikshitar, op. cit., 57 ff. See also Ghoshal, *A History of Hindu Public Life*, pp. 33, 57–9, 162–3.

15. 2. 56; Ghoshal, 93–6; Dikshitar, op. cit., 64.

16. Jayaswal, 2. 54 ff.; Ghoshal, 173–4.

Protection of the People : The activity of the sovereign on which a great stress is laid in the ṚV., is his duty of protecting his subjects.[17] The Ś. Br. says that the king is the upholder of the law or dharma, by upholding the law he becomes rāṣṭrabhṛt (i.e. "sustainer of the realm").[18] It is on this striking dictum of the Ś. Br. that the early Dharma-sūtra works, such as those of Gautama and others, base their theory that the most important of the king's duty is to protect the dharma and the four-fold human race (i.e. the four varṇas). Thus the duty of the king to protect his subjects, as is found in the early Vedic literature, is now interpreted by the canonical works in the sense that the king as a part of his most important function must try to maintain the *status quo* of the varṇāśrama and that he must, at all costs, try to prevent the recurrence of the varṇasaṁkara during the course of his regime. It is this that the Dharma-śāstra works generally mean by their insistence on the king's duty to protect dharma and the people. Kauṭilya also expresses his views in the same manner.[19] According to GHOSHAL this was a necessary corollary to their theory of the divine origin of the king.[20] Ideas such as those of the king being the servant of his people and that the king's duty of protection is his service for the payment of taxes by the people are also expressed in the Dharma-sūtra of Baudhāyana,[21] in Manu[22] and occasionally in the Mbh[23] and later works,[24] but they do not seem to have secured general support.[25]

The Vāyu, similarly, emphasizes, by way of incidental reference, the duty of the king to protect his people. But there is nothing in the Vāyu references to confirm the contention of GHOSHAL that this duty of protection is a necessary corollary to the theory of the divine origin of the king. The story of Pṛthu, however, is interesting. We do not find there any allusion to king's duty to protect his people. On the other hand we find the people asking the newly consecrated king to offer them means of sustenance. The definition of the king (rājan) in the story makes him a "pleaser" without any idea of protection. But in the case of Vena, the predecessor of Pṛthu, we find the sages reminding him of his former promise to protect the people ; and here we do not find even a trace of an idea that Vena regarded himself as a creation of the Divine or as the Divinity itself.

The repeated occurrence of the expression dharma in connection with kings in the Purāṇa may make us infer tha ae Purāṇa has come greatly under the influence of the Dharma-śāstra eas.

---

17. *CHT*, 1. 95.18. GHOSHAL, 41, 63 ; DIKSHITAR, op. cit., 102.
20. GHOSHAL. 97. 19. GHOSHAL, 63.
21. *Ibid*. 65. BANERJEA, *Public Administration in Ancient India*, 72–3 ; DIKSHITAR, op. cit., 155. 22. *Ibid.*, 185 fn. 23. *Ibid.*
24. Such as Śukra-nīti etc. cf. JAYASWAL, 2, 163. 25. GHOSHAL, 65 fn.

Kings and Daṇḍa: We have no information on the technical sense of the word *daṇḍa* in the Vedic literature. The earliest reference to daṇḍa, technically so called, is found in the Artha-śāstra of Kauṭilya. Kauṭilya mentions a science (vidyā) *daṇḍa-nīti* about the exact connotation of which there has been a divergence of views amongst scholars. JAYASWAL takes it to mean "the Ethics of the Executive"[26] and GHOSHAL differs from him.[27] According to GHOSHAL, Kauṭilya himself gives its two senses, viz. (i) etymological—the art of punishment and (ii) broadly as the art of government. According to him Kauṭilya does not use *artha-śāstra* and *daṇḍa-nīti* as convertible terms as is found in the later literature on that subject.[28] D. R. BHANDARKAR, however, takes daṇḍa-nīti and artha-śāstra both as meaning the science of Polity which he says must have been known in at least the 7th cent. B.C., if not earlier.[29] We are again told that the expression daṇḍa-nīti of Kāuṭilya means the art and science of government which later on came to be known as artha-śāstra, rāja-dharma, rāja-nīti, nīti-śāstra, etc.[30]

The Manu-smṛti also mentions daṇḍanīti as a science (or vidyā)[31] and deifies it and says that this daṇḍa is the *summum bonum* of a state's existence.[32] The purpose of this deification, says JAYASWAL, was simply to bring the king under the rule of law, that is, in short, "the sovereignty of the law is preached with the greatest vigour."[33]

The term *daṇḍa*, technically socalled, figures considerably in the Mbh., especially in the Śāntiparvan. Here we find the concept of daṇḍa definitely assimilated to its idea of rāja-dharma.[34] The same work contains a tale of how the Daṇḍa-nīti came to be evolved. Here we are told that lord Brahmā originally created a gigantic treatise called the Daṇḍa-nīti which was handed down by him to Śiva who summarised it. From Śiva it came to Indra and then to Uśanas (i.e. Śukra) both of them having summarized it in turn.[35] The same work again works out, rather elaborately, the idea that daṇḍa itself is a deity, a conception, as we have seen above, which was familiar with the Mānava-dharma-śāstra.[36]

The Matsya Purāṇa elevates *daṇḍa* to the rank of different expedients such as *sāma*, *bheda*, *dāna*, etc., to which the king was advised to resort according to circumstances.[37]

---

26. *Calcutta Weekly Notes*, 15. 875. 27. p. 78.
28. *Ibid.* 29. *Some Aspects of Ancient Hindu Polity*, 5 ff.
30. DIKSHITAR, *Hindu Administrative Institutions*, 2. 31. VII. 43.
32. VII. 17-8; cf. JAYASWAL, 2. 58; DIKSHITAR, op. cit., 10.
33 *Manu and Yajñavalkya, Tagore Law Lectures*, 1917, 81. 34. GHOSHAL, 165.
35 *Ibid.*, 176-7; D. R. BHANDARKAR, op. cit., 21. 36. DIKSHITAR, op. cit., 10.
37. DIKSHITAR, *The Matsya Purāṇa, A Study*, 80.

The Vāyu takes the word daṇḍa in the sense of government and says that it is the most important function of a Kṣatriya. It does not deify daṇḍa nor does it make such a fetish of it as do Manu and the Mbh. It mentions nīti in association with Śiva and Śukra but its details are not so elaborate as we find them in the Mbh., nor does it narrate the tale of this nīti in connection with the origin of kingship. Again the Purāṇa does not expressly refer to daṇḍanīti and we are not sure whether we should treat the Vāyu account as having some connection with the one found in the Mbh. If it be taken to have such a connection, the Vāyu version of it must be deemed to be earlier. Our Purāṇa does not know the other expedients mentioned in the Matsya and thus the claim for a higher antiquity of this Vāyu material can be taken for granted. As far as Kauṭilya is concerned we are unable to find a basis for its relative chronology with our Purāṇa. It may be stated here that the Vāyu, in its enumeration of the eighteen vidyās (branches of knowledge), mentions *arthaśāstra* and not *daṇḍanīti*.

Devolution of Kingship : In the age of the ṚV. kingship was normally hereditary and even in the scanty notices of that Veda we can trace lines of succession.[38] The hereditary character of the monarchy is clearly apparent in the later Saṁhitās where in one case, that of the Sṛñjayas, we hear expressly of a monarchy which had lasted ten generations.[39] It has been maintained that there are instances in the Vedic literature that kings were sometimes elected to their office.[40] JAYASWAL says that the theory that Hindu kingship is elective was never forgotten, for the observance of the coronation ceremonies and rituals had kept it "ever green".[41] In the Jātakas election of the king by the people is nowhere mentioned.[42] According to them hereditary succession to the throne was the general rule.[43] The great epic, however, shows certain instances of the election of a king,[44] but here too we find many instances of hereditary succession.[45]

The Vāyu has no instance of the election of a king and it shows that kingship devolved according to the rules of hereditary succession. The only instance, if any, which may remind us of it is found in the incident of king Yayāti's nomination of his successor. The grounds of objection raised by the people and the manner in which His Majesty explained his position to justify his action are the points that deserve our attention. It appears that according to the original tradition contained in the

---

38. *CHI*, 1. 94. 39. *Ibid.* 130.

40. JAYASWAL, 2. 5 ff. ; BANERJEA, op. cit., 64 ; DIKSHITAR, of. cit. 68 ; KEITH quotes the opinions of ZIMMER, WEBER and BLOOMFIELD on this point that kings were sometimes elected, but he refutes their opinions though he states that "that sometimes election actually took place is quite probable". Cf. *CHI*, 1. 94 fn.

41. JAYASWAL, op. cit., 2. 51. 42. FICK, 125. 43. MEHTA, 99.

44. *JAOS*, 13. 143. 45. *Ibid.*, 317 ff.

Purāṇa the people formerly directed the course of devolution of kingship and that this people's right had been subsequently substituted by the conception of dharma though the formal approval of the people, implied in the Purāṇa reference, preserved itself. The tone of the king's speech and his repeated reference to the fact that the successor nominated by him was the people's favourite reflects the reality of the approval. The excuse of the boon of Śukra is certainly a later polish and appears to be a theoretical attempt by the Purānakāra even to do away with this formal approval of the people. It may be stated here that Yayāti was a tribal king of the pre-Vedic period and the tradition of this incident about him might be regarded to have some historical basis.

Primogeniture : In the Vedic age the kingdom generally devolved on the eldest son of the deceased king.[46] The same rule prevailed in the age of the Jātakas[47] and later,[48] the Vāyu also shows that generally this rule of primogeniture was followed in matters of succession to the throne. That this was almost the settled law or usage (dharma) in its days appears obvious from the incident which arose out of king Yayāti's nomination of Puru as his consecrated heir.

Oligarchies : It has been stated that side by side with the existence of monarchy there existed in the Vedic times other forms of government, such as the oligarchies or the republics.[49] ZIMMER sees traces in one passage of the ṚV. that in times of peace there was no king in some states, the members of the royal family holding equal rights.[50] In the Jātakas, however, we find many oligarchies existing in Eastern India.[51] The Kula-Saṁgha mentioned by Kauṭilya is taken by JAYASWAL to mean an aristocratic state in which the family—apparently the whole royal family—ruled.[52] The law-books, says JAYASWAL, always treat the Kulas as distinct from the Gaṇas, the latter being not based on the hereditary principle as the former was. The distinction however was ignored in later times[53] probably because such forms of government were not known then.

The instances of the first category collected from the Vāyu refer to the actual division of the kingdom, and we find their separate genealogies narrated in the Purāṇa. But the case of Yayāti's sons call for explanation. We have to note that Puru is said to have been consecrated to the heirship of *Svarājya* and that at the same time portions of the kingdom were assigned to his brothers. The exact significance of this term is not clear. It is found in the ṚV. and in the other Vedas. It is the

46. FICK, 123 ; HOPKINS, *JAOS*, 13. 137 ; *Ved. Ind.*, 2. 211.
47. FICK, op. cit., MEHTA, 99.
48. HOPKINS, op. cit., 139, 317 ff.
49. BANERJEA, op. cit., 42 ff.
50. Quoted in *Ved. Ind.*, 3. 216.
51. RHYS DAVIDS, 19 ; FICK, 135 ff.
52. II. 65 ; cf. also 1. 85.
53. 1. 85–6.

other technical term for the kings of the west according to the Ait. Br.[54] JAYASWAL says that the *Svarājya*-ruler was taken from amongst the equals and that he was made president.[55] It is difficult to suggest here whether this Svarājya of the Ait. Br. has anything to do with the Svarājya (another variant is Svarāṣṭra) of our Purāṇa. But this much can be said that the reference is peculiarly found in the Vāyu and occurs nowhere else in its text.

The instances of the third category appear to be mythical and even if their value is not discredited they do not add more than what is inferred from those of the first and second categories.

The instance of the second category stands on a different footing. The references to Pracetasas and Śibis suggest that probably here we have some information about the oligarchical form of government mentioned in the Jātakas and the Vedas. The fact that the Purāṇa does not trace their genealogies is full of significance. The other instances, however, use a word Janapada of which we shall see later on.

Kings and Ritual: Of the priest-king[56] we have no evidence in the whole range of the history of Ancient India. In the ṚV. we find the provinces of the priest and the king already separate.[57] Even the earlier traditions do not hint at the king who was a public magician or a *Shaman*. Nowhere do we find in him the magico-political tribal leader of primitive times. But kings were closely connected with the performance of sacrifices some of which were specially meant for them.

The Rājasūya: The *Rājasūya* is described in the Ś. Br. which mentioned king Pṛthu, as the "first annointed king".[58] The importance of the consecration ceremony is fully realized from the Jātakas according to which also investiture was a condition precedent to the validity of succession.[59] But they show that the ceremony had lost its ritualistic character in Eastern India.[60] This might be due to tbe anti-ritual policy of Buddhism. It is noteworthy that Kauṭilya mentions Rājasūya only once and that too in a simile.[61] The early Dharma-śāstra works too

54. *Ved. Ind.*, 2. 494.

55. 1. 91. BANERJEA, however, refutes the suggestion of JAYASWAL and interprets the term in the sense of "independent kingdom" or "extensive kingdom". Cf. his *Public Administration in Ancient India*, 42. fn. 1.

56. "Students of customs both ancient and modern have long been aware that the line which divides a king from a priest is a very faint one and often disappears altogether. They have therefore coined a term priest-king- or king-priest to indicate that doubtful personage of whom it is difficult to say whether he is a priest or a king. He is chiefly to be found in ancient times or in backward communities." Cf. A. M. HOCART, *Kingship*, 119.

57. *ERE*, 7. 720.

58. KEITH, *Religion and Philosophy of the Veda*, *HOS*, 32. 340-3. Cf. JAYASWAL, 2. 14 ff. where he explains fully the ceremony and its constitutional implications and also DIKSHITAR, op. cit., 82 ff.; *JAOS*, 13. 143 ff.

59. FICK, 128 ff.

60. MEHTA, 105.

61. Trans. p. 300. See also *Ind. Verb.*

describe the Rājasūya sacrifice. According to them only the Kṣatriyas are entitled to perform the sacrifice and Jaimini says that even Brahmins cannot perform it.[62] JAYASWAL tells us that the Purāṇas do not count the pre-coronation years of Aśoka's reign while they are included in the total for the dynasty; thus he suggests that Aśoka had performed the ceremony.[63] "The legalism about coronation was so strong that Kālidāsa in drafting Puṣyamitra's letter to Agnimitra takes care not to describe Puṣyamitra as king. The preparations for coronation by Rājasūya were still in progress and coronation had not yet taken place. He was not therefore king *de jure*.[64] JAYASWAL further states that the coronation ceremony was performed for the Emperor Khāravela in his 24th year and here he mentions the Rājasūya sacrifice,[65] but his reading of the word 'Rājasūya' in the Hāthigumphā inscription is not accepted by other scholars.[66] The earliest inscriptional reference to the performance of Aśvamedha is from the Ghasundi inscription of the Chhattisgarh Division of 1st cent. B.C.[67] and slightly later we find in the Deccan a Sātavāhana king to have performed the Rājasūya and Aśvamedha sacrifices.[68] These instances belie the boast of Samudragupta who claims to be "the restorer of the Aśvamedha that had long been in abeyance",[69] and consequently the contention that the Brahmanical revival began its vigorous career in the time of the Guptas has to be modified.[70]

Most of the instances of coronation ceremonies of the Vāyu are mentioned in connection with kings not belonging to the Dynasties of the Kali Age, and the Vāyu states that in the Kali Age these ceremonies 'will' cease to be performed. This Vāyu statement has to be explained in the light of inscriptional evidence. We have to note that Kauṭilya does not regard rājasūya and aśvamedha as important sacrifices. The Vāyu states it categorically that Mahāpadma Nanda was a Śūdra Emperor after whom all kings 'will be' Śūdras. After Mahāpadma no king is recorded by the Vāyu to have performed consecration. We have again statements in the Purāṇa equating the merits of the performance of the rājasūya and aśvamedha with gifts in śrāddha, thus probably making us infer that these sacrifices were no longer performed. The Vāyu estimation of its later kings that they 'will be' practically Yavanas in point of ideas of dharma, artha and kāma and that they will not be "sprinkled on their heads" is suggestive of an age—especially a period when foreigners were pouring in hoards into the plains of India and

---

62. KANE, 2. 153, 1214 ff. 63. 2. 53; cf. also *JBORS*, 1. 93.
64. JAYASWAL. 2. 53. 65. *JBORS*, 3. 438.
66. Cf. BARUA, *Old Brāhmī Inscriptions*, 15. 53. 67. *EI*, 22. 203.
68. *ASWI*, 5. 60; cf. D. R. BHANDARKAR, *Volume of Eastern and Iranian Studies presented in honour of F. W. Thomas*, 29–30., cf. also *JIH*, 22. 1–6.
69. FLEET, *Gupta Inscriptions*, 28. 70. *JIH*, 1941, 1–6.

establishing principalities. We know from the political history of ancient India that these conditions are best reflected in a few centuries after the fall of the great Mauryan Empire. But why should the Vāyu not mention the rājasūya and aśvamedha sacrifices which are said to have been performed according to the evidence of the inscriptions? The answer is found in the fact that the Vāyu—and also the Purāṇic tradition in general—was not prepared to regard the kings who ruled after the Nandas as being Kṣatriyas[71] and thus it could not entertain the possibility that these kings could rightfully perform the coronation ritual. It is clear that the Purāṇa is here relying on the authority of the law-texts according to which only the Kṣatriyas can perform such sacrifices.

The Aśvamedha: The Horse-sacrifice was performed by kings who were successful in their conquest of the quarters.[72] The Jātakas do not show instances of the performance of aśvamedha. Kauṭilya mentions it only once in a simile.[73] The Mbh., however, gives many instances of the performance of the ritual.[74] The inscriptional evidence has been pointed out above.

The same observations that are made in connection with the rājasūya apply here. The statement that a muttering of a mātrā of *oṁ* is more meritorious than monthly performance of aśvamedha for a hundred years is significant. It appears that aśvamedha was no longer performed and had fallen low in general estimation.

Vājapeya: The Vājapeya sacrifice was originally the proper ritual for an emperor but later on it became only a preliminary ceremony to the ritual of rājasūya.[75] It was probably not of a political nature in its origin and became later associated with the Brahmins only.[76] We hear nothing about it from the Jātakas and Kauṭilya does not mention it. This sacrifice was befitting a great emperor and the great imperialist Kauṭilya should not have mentioned it is a fact which is full of meaning.

The Vāyu gives one reference of the performance of these sacrifices by king Pravīra. But it is difficult to arrive at any conclusion from this single instance.

II. Popular institutions

Samiti, as an assembly of the people, is mentioned in the ṚV. and in the later Saṁhitās we still find its power felt by the sovereign though traces of the decline of its political influence are also observable.[77] "That the institution did not far outlive the later Vedic age...is borne

---

71. Cf. *AIHT*, 226-8.
72. Banerjea, 92. cf. Keith, op. cit., 343 ff. for the details of the ritual.
73. Trans. p. 294. 74. *JAOS*, 13. 75. Dikshitar, 82; Banerjea, 90 ff.
76. Jayaswal, 2. 14; Dikshitar, 86; Banerjea, 92.
77. *Ved. Ind.*, 2. 430; for detailed discussion on 'Samiti' cf. Jayaswal, 1. 11-6; Banerjea, op. cit., 94 ff.; R. C. Majumdar, *Corporate Life in Ancient India*, 113 ff.; Dikshitar, op. cit., 152 ff.

out by the Pāraskara Gṛhya Sūtra which treats the Samiti evidently as a reminiscence."[78]

In the Vāyu we have only one reference to the Samiti which most probably means "an assembly". But whether we should relate this Samiti with the Samiti of the Vedic age we are not sure as the Purāṇa gives no other elucidatory details about it.

Sabhā: The term 'Sabhā' is often mentioned in the ṚV. "but its exact character is not certain". It meant an 'assembly' of the Vedic Indians as well as the 'hall' where they met in assembly.[79] "The rise of the Sabhā," says JAYASWAL, "is to be dated like that of the Samiti in the latest period of the Ṛgveda. Its career is co-extensive with that of the Samiti."[80] Thus with the close of the Vedic period the *institution* Sabhā passed into oblivion though traces of its popular origin could still be found in the later times in the judicial Sabhā of the king.[81]

The Sabhā of the Vāyu suggests a later connotation of the term having its origin in the sense 'hall' of the word in the Vedic times. The significance of the "four Sabhās" cannot be for the present made out as we are not aware of such a use of the term in the other ancient sources on the topic of Sabhā. It should be noted that all these references to Sabhā are found in the portions other than the genealogical lists of the Purāṇa.

In the genealogical portion of the Purāṇa we find two references to the Sabhā. In the first reference we find *sabhā* and *saṁsad* as synonyms and here Sabhā apparently means an "assembly" in which Kṛṣṇa is reported to have made a speech addressed to Akrūra in connection with the Syamantaka jewel. It should be noted that JAYASWAL takes the Sātvatas,—amongst whom Kṛṣṇa was born, as a republican tribe known to the Ait. Br. and their character as a republican tribe is clearly indicated in descriptions about them in the Mbh.[82] "In the tradition quoted in the Mahābhārata, the party of Akrūra is bitterly complained against by Kṛṣṇa"[83] and we have also the epic stating that Kṛṣṇa's "heart was roasted by terrific speeches."[84] Our Purāṇa no doubt refers to the same matters as quoted from the Mbh. and thus corroborates the tradition known to the great epic. It is interesting to observe that according to the story told in our Purāṇa all the attempts of Kṛṣṇa to get possesstion of the jewel were of no avail and he could secure it only by addressing Akrūra straight in the assembly of the Sātvatas. That such a powerful

78. JAYASWAL, 1. 15.

79. *Ved. Ind.*, 2. 426. For detailed discussion on '*sabhā*' see JAYASWAL, 1. 17–21; BANERJEA, op. cit., 94 ff.; R. C. MAJUMDAR, op. cit., DIKSHITAR, op. cit., and cf. also references given in footnotes in *Ved. Ind.*, op. cit.

80. JAYASWAL, 1. 20. 81. *Ibid.* 82. 1. 39. 191 ff.

83. 1. 42. 84. 1. 176.

personality, as Kṛṣṇa was, should have resorted to an expedient of addressing him in the assembly for obtaining the possession of the jewel cannot be said to be without any significance about the constitution of the Sātvatas.[85] PARGITER says that "real difficulties occur with regard to Andhaka's and Vṛṣṇi's descendants" and their genealogical lists are very often confused in the Purāṇas, including, of course, the Vāyu. The Andhaka-Vṛṣṇis were one of the six republics known to Pāṇini and JAYASWAL claims that they were the same as the Sātvatas of the Purāṇas[86] and that they were a republican tribe. The confusion about their 'genealogies' in the Purāṇas might have been, partly at least, due to this fact which the Purāṇa redactors probably did not know.

We do not know from other sources whether the Nāgas were a republican people, having a representative institution such as the Sabhā. The Vāyu has no detailed information about them so as to enable us to discuss this reference to Sabhā further.

Gaṇa : As early as the later Vedic period, we find a reference to *gaṇa* as a corporate organization amongst the Vaiśyas.[87] In the early Buddhist works the term gaṇa occurs in a technical sense signifying a republic[88] and JAYASWAL says that Pāṇini too used the word in the same sense.[89] The term gaṇa, technically so called, is also mentioned in the Dharma-śāstra works[90] and JAYASWAL quotes a passage from the Mbh. regarding the exact significance of gaṇa known to the epic.[91] "By the time of the legal commentators, gaṇas, as political institutions, had long ceased to exist."[92]

The term gaṇa, in addition to its general collective sense, is mentioned in the Purāṇa also in a technical sense. We find gaṇa mentioned in connection with Daityas and Rākṣasas and what is interesting to notice here is the hereditary principle on which a gaṇa is named. The mention of Jāti in the same connection should also be noted. For want of similar evidence from other sources we are forced to defer this point to later investigation. To discuss the matter here is to involve ourselves in a controversy whether the Rākṣasas, Daityas, etc., of the tradition were non-Aryans or merely the demons of human imagination. The same observation may be, for the present, made with regard to the gaṇas of the Mlecchas existing in the various continents (*dvīpas*)

85. Kṛṣṇa is mentioned in the Purāṇa also as "Vāsudeva-purogama" (Vā 86. 28) [according to Kha, Gha and Ṅa only] and as being afraid of "division in the community" (jñāti-bheda) (Vā. 96. 85-7) etc., thus suggesting that he was a "leader" or "head" of his tribe, clan or party.

86. 1. 39. 87. R. C. MAJUMDAR, op. cit., 12.

88. JAYASWAL, 1. 26-8; cf. also RHYS DAVIDS. 89. Op. cit.

90. R. C. MAJUMDAR, op. cit., 142 ff.; DIKSHITAR, op. cit., 347; D. R. BHANDARKAR, op. cit., 105 ff.

91. 1. 30. 125 ff. 92. *Ibid.*

of the earth. But if any reliance is kept on these references we are led to infer that gaṇa was a sort of organisation known to the Purāṇic tradition to be existing amongst the "non-Aryans" also. The reference to gaṇa in connection with śrāddha definitely means some kind of organization, whether political or religious we cannot say. The nature of the reference suggests that gaṇas did exist then. The information on gaṇa, in connection with the story of Yājñavalkya, clearly shows gaṇa as a corporate organization in religious matters for the existence of which we have no definite evidence in the Vedic literature.[93] The power and functions of this gaṇa are evident from the story narrated in this connection. *Samayas*, meaning the laws of gaṇas, are mentioned in the Dharma-śāstra works[94] and the use of this term in the reference under discussion may be noted accordingly.

In the last category of references we find gaṇas of Kṣatriyas mentioned and here it appears we have something to do with the political 'gaṇa' (i. e. republic) of JAYASWAL. It should be noted that in section XIII of Rock Edicts of Aśoka we find a reference to Nābhā-paṅktis which according to JAYASWAL means "a league of Nābhas." Pāṇini mentions Nabhāka and JAYASWAL says that he is unable to identify this Nabhāka. The Ūrṇa-Nābhas are mentioned as a republican tribe by Pāṇini. JAYASWAL, however, concluded that "Nabhāka was probably a national title derived from the Nābha people".[95]

Our Purāṇa mentions Nābhāga as a name of a Kṣatriya-gaṇa with a strength of one thousand. The ṚV. mentions Nābhāka, i.e. "a descendant of Nabhāka" as a name of a sage[96] and PARGITER takes him to be the same as Nabhāga, son of Vaivasvata Manu, of the Purāṇic tradition.[97] The descendants of this Nābhāga are not mentioned in the Purāṇas[98] and the reason for this omission according to PARGITER is that probably "their line played no part in traditional history" [99] But it appears that the "omission" in the Purāṇas of the genealogy of the Nābhāgas is quite natural for they had formed a republican tribe whose genealogy the Purāṇic tradition could not have apparently handed down to posterity. This suggestion becomes more probable from the observations of JAYASWAL quoted above—the more so if we, with PARGITER, identify Nabhāka of the ṚV. with the Nabhāga of the Purāṇic tradition.

The same is probably the reason why the descendants of Dhṛṣṭa, brother of Nabhāga, are also not mentioned in the Purāṇa;[100] for the Vāyu also mentions "a Dhārṣṭaka gaṇa of three thousand Kṣatriyas," so named after Dhṛṣṭa, brother of Nabhāga. But about them we have

93. Cf. R. C. MAJUMDAR, op. cit., 13.
94. JAYASWAL, 1. 124.
95. 1. 145.
96. *Ved. Ind.*, 1. 442.
97. *AIHT*, 255.
98. *Ibid.*, 98.
99. *Ibid.*, 256.
100. *Ibid.*, 256.

no other corroborative information for the present. The republic of the Bhojas has been described by JAYASWAL from the evidence of other sources and the Vāyu may be said to be corroborating JAYASWAL's conclusions regarding their being a republican tribe.[101] About the other Kṣatriya gaṇas mentioned in the Purāṇa we have no corroborative evidence for the present.

Janapadas: The term '*jana*' is used in the ṚV. and later, in the sense of 'a tribe' or 'people'.[102] The term '*janapada*', however, occurs first in the Brāhmaṇas denoting both the 'people' as opposed to the king and the 'land' or 'realm'. The 'subjects' are also denoted there by the adjectival 'jānapada'.[103] JAYASWAL says that the term 'janapada' originally meant the seat of the nation "and was secondarily employed as denoting the nation itself". According to him this original sense of the term was lost in later literature where it generally came to signify "the province" or "the country".[104] The expression '*jānapada*', a derivative form of janapada, is mentioned in the Pāli Canon, in the epics and in inscriptions and JAYASWAL tells us that modern writers have wrongly taken the word as meaning "the people of the Janapada". "It really means", he continues, "the whole area of a kingdom minus the capital constitutionally". In support of this contention he further adds, "the technical significance of the jānapada as a collective institution has now been established by Khāravela's inscription of 165 B.C."[105] But this interpretation of the term has been objected to by N. N. LAW who says that in all the cases where JAYASWAL sees a technical jānapada he finds only "the people of the country meant".[106] It has been however contended that in some cases the term may signify what LAW means but "to totally deny the existence of such organized bodies of citizens is to miss the mark altogether".[107]

The Vāyu uses the term very frequently as a geographical term meaning a particular territory or region. But occasionally we find the expression used to signify a 'people' or 'tribe' also. Only at two places the Purāṇa uses the term Paura-Jānapada and these instances of the use of the term occur in the genealogical portion of the Purāṇa. There is reason to believe, that here we have the jānapada, technically so called, of JAYASWAL. The repeated reference by the king Yayāti to the fact that the successor nominated by him (contrary to the provisions laid down by ancient usage) was well-disposed to the Paura-Jānapadas suggests that His Majesty was trying to justify his position under

101. See 1. 39. 102. *Ved. Inā.*, 1. 269. 103. *Ibid.*, 273.

104. 2. 61–2. JAYASWAL, however, has not discussed the use of the terms 'jana' and 'jānapada' of the Vedic literature quoted above. He, on the contrary, attempts to show that the "jānapada" assembly of the post-Vedic times was an "incarnation" of the Vedic Samiti. Cf. *Ibid.*, 62.

105. *Ibid.* 106. *IHQ*, 2. 385 ff. 107. DIKSHITAR, op. cit., 157.

some pressure. It should be noted that here the Paura-Jānapadas are also referred to as "representatives (?) of the people with the Brahmins to lead them" and the passage concludes with the formal approval of the Paura-Jānapadas. The other reference to Paura-Jānapada in connection with king Janamejaya, too, suggests that they were the powerful organizations capable of making "the heads that wear the crown" feel uneasy. If this be not the case there is no other reason why the Purāṇa should at all refer to them in the course of narration.

Paura: JAYASWAL says that "the Paura was a communal association in which was vested the municipal administration of the capital" and that it also exercised great constitutional powers.[108] It was according to him "a twin-sister of the Jānapada in constitutional matters. The two are almost mentioned together, and sometimes one stands for both"

The two instances of Paura-Jānapadas mentioned in the Vāyu may be said to confirm the views of JAYASWAL. We have, however, one instance of the word "Paura" occurring alone. It is not clear whether here Paura stands for both the Paura and the Jānapada; nor are we sure whether we should take the Paura of this reference as signifying "a corporate association" of the capital.[109] Any way we have here a good case of the influence of public opinion on the sovereign who had to expel his son for the latter's activities prejudicial to the Pauras.

---

108. 2. 70. For LAW's objection to this interpretation also cf. op. cit.; cf. also DIKSHITAR, op. cit., regarding his comments on LAW's objection.

109. 2. 68.

CHAPTER IV

RELIGION

I. ŚAIVISM

Maheśvara, the Supreme God: Rudra is a minor god of the Ṛgvedic pantheon. He is celebrated in only three hymns of that Veda and his name is mentioned slightly less often than that of Viṣṇu.[1] In the later Saṁhitās Rudra has become, along with Viṣṇu, one of the two great gods of the Brahmins.[2] The Vājasaneyi Saṁhitā (Chapter 16) mentions many epithets of the god, such as, *Girīśa*, *Paśupati*, *Kapardin*, *Śarva*, *Bhava*, *Śiva and Śaṁbhu* and there he is also referred to as wearing hide-skin garments. The name Mahādeva of the god is also found elsewhere in the same Saṁhitā (Chapter 39).[3] In the AV. the conception of Rudra is further developed and he is elevated to a higher platform. We find here more names for the god which are also addressed as separate deities.[4] A reference to the cult of Rudra by the Vrātyas has been seen as the explanation of the curious Vrātya hymn of the AV.[5] but KEITH,[6] and HOPKINS[7] regard this view as untenable. In the Brāhmaṇas we find the power of Rudra at its height. The gods even are afraid of him lest they be killed by the god.[8] It is, however, in the Śvetāśvatara Up. that we find Śiva alone in the field as the supreme god and the germs of Bhakti or love which manifested themselves at that time were directed mostly towards him.[9] R. G. BHANDARKAR considers this work to be earlier than the Bhagavadgītā.[10] In this Upaniṣad the god is mentioned as the creator and destroyer of the world. Certain Yoga-processes are here prescribed for the purposes of proper meditation of the Supreme Soul and the treatise ends with an expression of self-surrender to the god.[11] But this Upaniṣad is not a sectarian work and there is no evidence in the work of the existence of a Śaivite sect which worshipped Śiva as its favourite god.[12] The Gṛhya-sūtras, too, do not testify to the existence of a Śaivite sect.[13] From the days of Patañjali onwards, the existence of some Śaiva sects can be taken for granted.[14] In the 'earlier' portions

---

1. MACDONELL, *Vedic Mythology*; cf. also KEITH, *Religion and Philosophy of the Veda, HOS*, 31. 142 ff.
2. KEITH, op. cit., 143.   3. R. G. BHANDARKAR, 103.   4. *Ibid.*
5. CHARPENTIER, *VOJ*, 23. 151 ff.; 25. 355 ff.   6. Op. cit., 149–50.
7. *Epic Mythology*, 231; fn. 2. Cf also C. V. N. AYYAR, *Origin and Early History of Śaivism in South India*, 17 ff., where a view similar to that of CHARPENTIER is advocated.
8. KEITH, op. cit., 144.   9. BHANDARKAR, 106 ff.   10. Pp. 110–111.
11. *Ibid.* 110.   12. Op. cit.
13. *Ibid.* 115; cf. also V. M. APTE, *Social and Religious Life in the Gṛhyasūtras*.
14. BHANDARKAR, 115 ff.

of the Mbh, we find both the sects, namely, the Śaivites and the Vaiṣṇavites existing without much antagonism between them, but in the later parts of the epic such antagonism is clearly traceable.[15]

Judging from the above discussion our Purāṇa shows traces of sectarian sentiments. We find attempts made, in some places, to humiliate the position of Viṣṇu. It should be noted, however, that these references occur mostly in connection with stories narrated about the god and the philosophical portion of the Purāṇa does not include any of them. Again these references do not suggest the violently sectarian character of the Purāṇa testifying to an actual antagonism between the two sects of the Vaiṣṇavas and the Śaivas and we may state here that the Vāyu in this respect falls more in line with the earlier portions of the Mbh. than with its later parts. This will be obvious when we discuss the important stories told about Śiva in our text.

Rudra, the Malevolent: The Rudra of the ṚV. is a fierce god destructive like a wild beast.[16] In the whole range of Vedic literature there are many instances indicating his malevolent character, though we find him here and there emerging as a great god capable of bestowing good on those that pray to him. Even up to the time of the Gṛhya-sūtras this darker side of the nature of this god was never forgotten and we find a sacrific called Śūlagava mentioned in these works which was meant to appease him.[17] With the growth of religious sentiments which exalted Śiva as a supreme god this darker side of his nature began to recede in the background though it was never wiped out altogether.

Of the demonaical qualities of the god Śiva the Vāyu is not so elaborate as it is on indicating his supremacy. The Purāṇa nowhere indicates that the wrath of the god should be appeased and it appears from the Purāṇa that in this respect tendencies exist posterior in time to that of the Gṛhya-sūtras.

Names of Śiva: Most of the names of Śiva are found mentioned in the later Saṁhitās and the Brāhmaṇas.[18] In the Mbh. many more names of the gods are mentioned.[19] The story of the eight names occurs in the Ś. Br. and in the Kauṣītaki-Brāhmaṇa where Rudra is mentioned as the son of Uṣas and the names are given to him by Prajāpati.[20] The eight names of these texts are Rudra, Śarva, Ugra, Aśani,

15. Hopkins, op. cit., 220.

16. For the malevolent qualities of Rudra cf. Macdonell, op. cit., Keith, op. cit., 142 ff.; Bhandarkar, 102 ff., *Rudra-Śiva*, 6-8.

17. Bhandarkar, 105; V. M. Apte, op. cit.

18. For names of Śiva cf. Bhandarkar, 102-5; *Rudra-Śiva*, 32 ff.; Macdonell, op. cit., Keith, op. cit.

19. Hopkins, op. cit., 173, 219, 223; cf. also *BDCRI*, 5. 151-2.

20. Bhandarkar, 105.

Bhava, Paśupati, Mahādeva and Īśāna. The first four af these names denote his destructive energy while the last four may be regarded as its benign counterpart.[21]

The Vāyu gives apparently a later version of the same tale as here we find Brahmā, instead of Prajāpati of the Brāhmaṇas, giving the eight names to the god. Again the eight names are here slightly changed probably with a view to show the benevolent character of the god. The names Śarva, Aśani of the Brāhmaṇas are dropped and the names Śiva and Ugra introduced. But still in these names we find three which indicate the malignant character of the god and except for the introduction of Śiva there is not much difference in the two lists of names. This probably should indicate that this portion of the Purāṇa is not very much removed in time from the accounts in the Brāhmaṇas.

Important Myths about Śiva

The Story of Dakṣa's Sacrifice : The main features of the Dakṣa story are found in the Vedic literature. Dakṣa is mentioned several times is the ṚV. The Brāhmaṇas also mention Dakṣa as a Prajāpati and a sacrificer. The account of the Dākṣāyaṇi sacrifice, so called because it was first performed by Prajāpati Dakṣa, is described in the Śatapatha and Kauśītaki Brāhmaṇas. Śiva's exclusion from Dakṣa's sacrifice is also supported by the Vedic evidence but here the cause of Rudra's attack on Dakśa's sacrifice is quite different. The reason here stated is that Prajāpati Dakṣa had intercourse with his daughter Uṣas and to remedy the evil effects of this the gods created a new being out of their fearful forms. This new being was the Bhūtavān (i. e. Rudra) who was commanded to pierce the Prajāpati and he accordingly carried out the behests of his creators. But in the Vedic evidence we nowhere find a reference to Śiva's marriage with Dakṣa's daughter.[22]

The Rāmāyaṇa has the story in a very simple form and it does not contain any reference to Vīrabhadra and to Umā, wife of Śiva. Śiva is only said to have wounded the gods.[23] The same story occurs thrice in the Mbh.[24] and Muir has shown that many of the verses in the narration of the Mbh. account of the story are found also in the Vāyu Purāṇa.[25] In one version of the story in the Mbh., Śiva himself puts an end to the sacrifice, while in another version we find Dadhīci as a staunch votary of Rudra, warning Dakṣa in a rather lengthy speech about the impudence of his decision in not inviting Śiva for the sacrifice. Both the Mbh. and the Rāmāyaṇa versions of the story, however, do not even remotely allude to Umā's parentage or Dakṣa's relation-

21. Op. cit. 22. Vide, *Rudra-Śiva*, 78-80.
23. Muir, *OST*, 4. 372-3 ; cf. also C. V. N. Ayyar, op. cit., 63 ff.
24. *Ibid.* 373 ff. 25. *Ibid.* 373 fn. 124, 374 fn. 126, 375 fns. 127-9.

ship to her. Thus it would be obvious that the Vāyu version of the story is later than those contained in those two epics, excepting perhaps the lengthy speech of Dadhīci in the Mbh. which appears, in brief, in the Vāyu. Had the Vāyu been a purely sectarian Purāṇa and had it been aware of such a verbose grandiloquence of Dadhīci[26] we would probably not have missed it in our text.

Kālidāsa, however, knew the story about Śiva's wife Satī, who was the daughter of Dakṣa and who put an end to her life owing to the insulting treatment of her father.[27] Thus the Vāyu version of the story can be assigned to the period between that of the Mbh. and Kālidāsa. This becomes more probable when we compare the Vāyu version with those contained in the other Purāṇas[28] which leads us to conclude with WILSON that the narration as found in our Purāṇa "from its inartificial, obscure and uncircumstantial construction is probably of an ancient date."[29]

The Story of how Śiva came to be called Nīlakaṇṭha: The ṚV. gives an account of the powers of a long-haired Muni who drank poison in the company of Rudra[30] and the YV. alludes to the latter's blue neck.[31] The AV. also knows his blue neck.[32] The two facts, namely, (i) the blue neck and (ii) the drinking of poison are, however, not connected in the Vedic literature and the story connecting them is certainly post-Vedic. The Vāyu account connects the two facts but is not very elaborate about the incident itself though it gives a far-fetched account of its transmission. It is not possible for the present to trace its relative chronology with the versions found in the epics and the other Purāṇas as our Purāṇa account appears in an abridged form and does not admit of such a discussion.

ŚIVA'S ASSOCIATES

The Bhūtas: The Bhūta of the Vedic literature does not bear the sense of 'demon' until possibly a very late period; but it denotes beings pure and simple.[33] Rudra as Bhūtapati is mentioned in the AV. but here *bhūta* means simply a "being". But the Buddhist literature knows the Yakṣas and Bhūtas as evil spirits who dwell in cemeteries. It would thus be seen that the Bhūtas, as associates of the god Śiva, is a post-Vedic development. The Mbh., however, knows Bhūtas as followers of Śiva who are also stated to have oppressed Indra.[34] Śiva

26. The existence of this speech in the Mbh. may be due to the "bhṛguisation" of the great epic. Cf V. S. SUKTHANKAR, *Epic Studies* VI. *ABORI*, 18.

27. See *Kumārasambhavam*, Canto I, verse 21.

28. See WILSON, *Translation of the Viṣṇu Purāṇa*, 61 ff. and notes. The Vāyu version of the tale is translated here and is compared with those occurring in the other Purāṇas which shows a definite sectarian influence.

29. *Ibid.* 61 fn. 1.

30. *Rudra-Śiva*, 18; cf. also KEITH, op. cit., 142.

31. KEITH, op. cit.

32. *Rudra-Śiva*, op. cit.

33. KEITH, op. cit., 153, 214-5.

34. HOPKINS, *Epic Mythology*, 131.

is there called "the Lord of the Bhūtas" which, however, may mean both "the lord of the creatures" or "the lord of the Bhūtas, the demons."[35] The Vāyu gives more information about them and may in this respect suggest the post-epic development.

The Rudras : The Rudras of the Vedic literature are not demons, though a view to this effect has also been advocated.[36] In the Vedic literature they figure as the children of Rudra and are identified with the Maruts.[37] In the Mbh. they figure as companions of Indra, servants of Śiva and of his son and also as the escort of Yama who appears as being surrounded by them.[38]

The Vāyu mentions Rudras not so often with Śiva as it does the Bhūtas.

The Asuras, the Rākṣasas and the Daityas : They are all of them mentioned in the Vedic literature mostly as demons and evil spirits,[39] but there we do not find a definite evidence about their close association with Rudra.[40] In the Mbh. also they do not figure closely along with Śiva.[41]

For the present we are unable to locate chronologically the information of the Vāyu with regard to this point.

Munis : The association of Munis with Rudra is found in the ṚV. But KEITH regards the passage in which the reference to Muni occurs, as curiously isolated in the ṚV. and even in the later Vedic texts, since the aspect of life which may be inferred from the reference does not fall within the outlook of the Vedas.[42] The AV. mentions Keśins (long-haired), who, it is asserted, were the Munis attending upon Rudra.[43] The Mbh. is silent on the special association of Munis with Śiva.

The Vāyu evidence on the matter shows them frequently as devotees of Śiva and it appears that they had something to do with the development of asceticism connected with that deity.

Śiva's Yoga and Tapas : Śiva in Mohenjodaro is pre-eminently the prince of Yogis, the typical ascetic and self-mortifier. Like Śaivism itself Yoga had its origin among the pre-Aryan population.[44] The existence of this proto-type of Śiva in the Indus civilization is now generally accepted though an objection is raised against the contention that Śiva was at all a non-Aryan god.[45] The term *yoga* in the sense

---

35. *Ibid.* 37. 142. 36. KEIEH, op. cit., 153. 37. Op. cit., 150-1.
38. HOPKINS, op. cit., 173. 39. KEITH, op. cit., 218, 231-4.
40. Rudra is, no doubt, addressed in the Taittirīya Saṁhita (I, iii, 14, 1), but this is not a clear evidence for an association of the god with the Asuras.
41. HOPKINS, op. cit., 38 ff., 47 ff. 42. Op. cit., 402.
43. C. V. N. AYYAR, op. cit., 11 ff. 44. *Mohenjodaro*, 1, 52-3.
45. *Rudra-Śiva.*

of "mystic union of the individual with the Absolute" does not occur in the ṚV. But some glimpses of the crude ideas about Yoga are available from that Veda. We have already noted above the connection of Munis with Rudra and it appears that they were devoted to some kind of primitive cult of Yoga. KEITH regards the passage describing them as somewhat isolated in the ṚV.[46] It has been also suggested that the forest-tribe of Niṣādas are brought into close connection with the Rudra of the ṚV. and that probaby they were his worshippers or their own peculiar gods were identified with the Aryan Rudra. The Munis might have belonged to such tribes as the Niṣādas and that is probably the reason why they are not approved of by the priest.[47] The Yatis also figure in the ṚV. as a tribe or people connected with the Bhṛgus and in the later Saṁhitās they are mentioned as enemies of Indra and were opposed to the ritual.[48] It appears that there existed a sect of ascetics who propounded an esoteric doctrine opposed to the cult of the ritual and they might have had some connection with Rudra who was a friend and a companion of the Munis.[49] With regard to the Vrātya hymn in the AV. it has been suggested that they were a class of Kṣatriya Yogins devoted to some form of worship of Śiva but this suggestion has been refuted by KEITH as being implausible.[50] If these Munis, Yatis or Vrātyas, as the case may be, signify a non-Aryan people, their predigree with the people of the Indus Valley becomes a tempting assumption. According to FRAZER, the practice of austerities was in great part at least adopted from the aboriginal tribes amongst whom the new-coming Aryans settled.[51] It is probable that Rudra had a parallel in some aboriginal god to whom *tapas* and similar occult powers, such as those of the primitive Yoga, were congenial and the cultural contacts with these tribes led the Aryan thinkers to absorb some of their beliefs and they found in Rudra the capacity to absorb such elements.

The Śvetāśvatara Upaniṣad, however, mentions Rudra-Śiva as the Supreme Soul for the perception of which it prescribes certain Yoga processes. Here Rudra is apparently a personal god ; but BHANDARKAR says that the Upaniṣad is not a sectarian treatise and the god Rudra is not here raised to the supreme godhead to the exclusion of another.[52] There is, however, another Upaniṣad, by name Atharvaśiras, which is purely sectarian in character and belonging to the sect of the Pāśupatas. This Upaniṣad is considered by BHANDARKAR as a much later work.[53] Rudra is here mentioned as the Gāyatrī. It expressly mentions the Pāśupata-vrata and the term *paśu-pāśa-vimokṣaṇa* also occurs in it.

46. Op. cit. 47. BHANDARKAR, 103.
48. *Ved. Ind.*, 2. 167-8. 49. KEITH, op. cit., 56.
50. HAUER, quoted by KEITH; op. cit., 148 fn. 1. 51. *ERE*, 2, 88.
52. Cp. pp. 110-111. 53. *Ibid.*

Besides, the muttering of the mātrā of *oṁ* is also enjoined to be practised by the Upaniṣad.

The theology of the Upaniṣad offers close resemblance to that of the Vāyu and the account of the avatāras of the latter are undoubtedly connected with the school of Pāśupatas according to which Lakulīśa was the last of the incarnations of Śiva.[54]

The Pāśupata School of Śaivism : The rise of the Pāśupata School is assigned by BHANDARKAR to the period of about 2nd century B.C. The school as such is mentioned in the Nārāyaṇīya section of the Mbh., as one of the five schools of religious doctrines known to it.[55] According to him there lived a certain person of the name of Lakulin (the holder of a *lakuṭa*, or *laguḍa* or *lakula* i.e. a club) who founded the Pāśupata system. "The fact that his rise has been represented by Purāṇas to be contemporaneous with Vāsudeva-Kṛṣṇa points to the inference that traditionally the system was intended to take the same place in the Rudra-Śiva cult that the Pāñcarātra did in the Vāsudeva-Kṛṣṇa cult.[56] The earliest inscriptional evidence regarding the existence of this sect is found in Mathura Pillar inscription of 380-1 A.D.[57] Here we find the teachers of the school mentioned who according to D. R. BHANDARKAR must have been "experts in the Pāśupata Yoga." We must, therefore, presume that they too must have passed away like the Yogins driving away their *prāṇa-vāyu* through the *brahmarandhra*. They must have thereby merged themselves into the godhead of Śiva. This explains why all those departed ascetics of the Lakulīśa sect have received the title of Bhagavat.[58] It should be noted that the inscription shows the Lakulīśa sect having connection with 'liṅga'. On the strength of the evidence of this inscription D. R. BHANDARKAR concludes that it might be considered as "well-nigh proved that Lakulīśa flourished in the first quarter of the first century A.D".[59] Formerly FLEET had also gone so far as to suggest from the evidence of the representation of Śiva with a club on the coins of Huvishka, the Kushan king, that the sect might have had its origin even earlier.[60] The wide diffusion of the sect in the later period is testified by the statements of Varāhamihira and the Chinese traveller Hiuen-Tsiang and the latter gives considerable information about them.[61]

The position of the Vāyu evidence *vis-a-vis* the above discussion is this : It certainly presupposes the contents of the Atharvaśiras Upaniṣad which though "a much later work" knows nothing of the incarnations of Śiva. The close connection of the Vāyu material with that of the Upaniṣad is, however, borne out by the former's elucida-

---

54. Cf. DIKSHITAR, *Some Aspects of the Vāyu Purāṇa.* 55. BHANDARKAR, 116.
56. *Ibid.* 57. *EI*, 21. 1 ff. 58. *Ibid.* 7. 59. *Ibid.*
60. Cf. *JRAS*, 1907, 424-5 ; cf. also *JBBRAS*, 22. 151-3 ; DIKSHITAR, op. cit., 24 ff.
61. BHANDARKAR, 117.

tion of the Pāśupata-vrata, the *mātrā* of *oṁ* and the *gāyatrī*,[62] all of which are intimately associated with Śiva by the Purāṇa. The importance of the Vāyu Purāṇa as containing the earliest reference to the Lakulīśa Pāśupatas has already been noted by D. R. BHANDARKAR who considers the Vāyu version on the incarnations of Śiva as being earlier than that of the Liṅga Purāṇa which too mentions them.[63] The material of the Vayu, again, appears to be earlier than the information found in the Mathurā inscription for the latter associates the cult of Lakulīśa with the Liṅga and the Vāyu does not establish such a connection though it narrates the story of liṅga in a different context.

It would be seen that the earliest reference, though somewhat vague, to the theology of the Pāśupatas is found in the Śvetāśvatara Upaniṣad which gives us some rudimentary ideas about the Yoga which seems to have been subsequently known as the Pāśupata Yoga. Our Purāṇa seems to have regarded this work as an authority and it contains two quotations from that Upaniśad.[64] The table of the incarnations of Śiva may be noted in this connection. It mentions Śveta as the first incarnation of Śiva and the four sons or disciples of god—who were really the teachers of the school—are : Śveta, Śikha [according to other MSS. Śveta], Śvetāśva and Śvetalohita. The emphasis on the word 'Śveta' is unnecessary. It appears that the tradition of the sect regarded Śveta or Śvetāśva as the original founder of the school and the same person might have had some connection with the Śvetāśvatara Upaniṣad which was probably named after him. Originally it might not have been a fully developed sect as it came to be in subsequent times especially through the efforts of Lakulin (or Nakulin). The names of the so-called disciples of the god Śiva seem, in some cases, to have a tinge of historicity. The names Kapila, Āsuri, Pañcaśikha and Vāgvali (cf. No. 8) are already noted by Dikshitar who, with regard to Sana, Sanandana (cf. No. 8) and Sanatkumāra, again, tells us that "they belonged to a common school of philosophy which became lost in obscure tradition at a very early period."[65] We may also recall the names of Akṣapāda, Kaṇāda, Ulūka and Vatsa (No. 27). We may further state that Praśastapāda characterises his predecessor Kaṇāda "as having composed the Vaiśeṣika-śāstra after propitiating Maheśvara by the greatness of his Yoga,"[66] and on the strength of this information R. G. BHANDARKAR had conjectured long ago that this "Kaṇāda, therefore, may have been a follower of the Pāśupata or Saiva system".[67] We may here venture a suggestion that the same Kaṇāda is referred to in this Vāyu list of teachers. The fact that the Kāṇāda of the Vāyu was the immediate predecessor of Lakulin may be

62. See Vāyu Chapter on *Oṁ Mātrā*.
63. *JBBRAS*, 1908, 151.
64. Cf. DIKSHITAR, op. cit., 13.
65. Op. cit., 27.
66. BHANDARKAR, 117.
67. *Ibid.*

chronologically suggestive though we need not be dragged into the matter for the present. It is further interesting to note that the hierarchy of teachers mentioned in the Vāyu shows some resemblance with those mentioned in the Mathurā inscription.[68]

Śiva and Liṅga: The phallus-worshippers are twice referred to with disapproval in the ṚV.[69] and it has been maintained that this phallus-worship was probably of prehistoric age in India. By the "phallus worshippers" of the ṚV. apparently the aborigines are meant and it has been generally asserted that the people of the Indus Civilization also were the followers of this cult.[70] The term "*liṅga*", however, appears first in the Śvetāśvatara Upaniṣad which says that Īśāna presides over every *yoni* and here the "liṅga" is directly affiliated to the god Śiva,[71] but BHANDARKAR is not sure whether this should be regarded as a characteristic of the worship of Śiva in the days of the Upaniṣads.[72] He further states that even in the days of Patañjali and Wema Kadphises such a worship was unknown.[73] By the time of the Mbh., however, it had already won its way into the orthodox Hindu Cult.[74] The Mathurā Pillar Inscription of 380–1 A.D. shows that liṅgas in honour of Upanīteśvara and Kapileśvara (i.e. with their portraits carved on the liṅgas) were installed in the Teacher's Shrine. These teachers belonged to the Lakulīśa sect. Thus the existence of the liṅga-worship appears to have existed in the 4th cent. A.D. connected particularly with the Lakulīśa Pāśupatas.[75]

In the Vāyu, however, there is no mention of liṅga in connection with Lakulīśa, the last of the incarnations of Śiva. There is, however, a separate chapter in the Purāṇa devoted to the story of liṅga. But the description of the liṅga given in this story does not allude to the physical fact of liṅga being connected with the yoni and we are not sure whether we should see here in the liṅga, "the phallus". There is no doubt a reference to the upper and lower extremities of the liṅga which Brahmā and Viṣṇu tried to reach but this does not establish that the liṅga here means the "phallus". The description of this liṅga as a shining object enveloped with flames is significant in so far as we are reminded of fire out of which the liṅga arose. There is a view[76] that the phallic emblem "grew naturally out of the sacrificial cult

---

68. *EI*, 21. 6 ff

69. *CHI*, 1. 85; cf. also KEITH, op. cit., 10; BHANDARKAR. 115; MUIR, *OST*, 4. 411, however does not think that the term "śiśnadevāḥ" of the ṚV. implies the existence of such a worship. Cf. also C. V. N. AYYAR, op. cit., 49 ff. and *Rudra-Śiva*, 36 ff.

70. *Mohenjodaro*, 1. 48–9. But this thesis has been opposed in *Rudra-Śiva*, 39 ff.

71. BHANDARKAR, 114 fn. 1. 72. *Ibid.* 114.

73. *Ibid.* 115, cf. *Rudra-Śiva*, 36 fn. 68 where a claim is made to have found an archaic liṅga of 2 cent. B.C. in South India.

74. *CHI*, 1. 85. 75. *EI*, 21. 9. 76. *Rudra-Śiva*, 54–5.

and fastened itself upon Rudra on account of his close association with Agni". The author of this thesis quotes with approval references from the Ś. Br. in support of his theory and the Vāyu evidence may be said to be equally confirming this view.

The other references of the Purāṇa to liṅga, however, suggest that liṅga meant a 'phallus' but still here there is no indication whatsoever that it was an object of worship and the interpretation of this liṅga can be the same as the one found mentioned in the Śvetāśvatara Upaniṣad. On the whole it can be stated that the Vāyu does not know the worship of liṅga as such and consequently its material in this respect may be said to ante-date the age of the Guptas.

Skanda-Kārttikeya: The name Kumāra occurs in the ṚV. and also in the Brāhmaṇas denoting the god Agni and not Skanda.[77] The earliest reference to Skanda is found in the Ch. Up. where he is identified with Sanatkumāra.[78] The Atharvaśiras Upaniṣad also mentions the god Skanda. But in these references to Skanda we do not find him connected with Śiva.[79] The Skanda of the great epic does not appear as a later addition but as a god rapidly increasing in importance. In the Pāraskara Gṛhya Sūtra we find the mention of a demon-cough in the form of a dog, named as Kumāra.[80] The same work again mentions Mahāsena as a disease-demon and here Mahāsena is an epithet of Skanda.[81] His sonship is debated in the epic but his connection is not lost sight of. The story of his birth is narrated in the epic at length[82] and it is considered to be an earlier version than those generally found in the Purāṇas as Śiva does not find a place in the story.[83] In the Mbh. we do not find his name Subrahmaṇya mentioned,[84] nor does he figure there as a demon, though his followers are often said to be imps and disease-demons.[85] Patañjali mentions the images of Śiva, Skanda and Viśākha as being worshipped in his time[86] and the existence of the worship of this god seems to have developed further in the days of the Guptas.[87] The names of the Gupta emperors such as Kumāragupta and Skandagupta are adduced as evidence indicating the flourishing state of the Śaivite sect in which Skanda had entered as a pet deity. It should be noted that even the seven mātṛkās, the female attendants of the god, had become objects of worship in these days.[88] It may also be noted that the name Brahmaṇya of the god is mentioned in the Gupta inscriptions.[89]

---

77. *Rudra-Śiva*, 71.
78. *Ibid.* 73.
79. *IHQ*, 7. 309 ff.
80. Keith, op. cit., 241.
81. Op. cit., 242.
82. Hopkins, op. cit., 229.
83. *Rudra-Śiva*, 73.
84. Hopkins, op. cit.
85. *Ibid.*
86. Bhandarkar, 150.
87. R. N. Saletore, *Life in Gupta Age*, 501.
88. *Ibid.*
89. *BDCRI*, 2. 162.

In the Vāyu, though Skanda figures as the generalissimo of the gods, there is nothing to indicate that he and the Seven Mothers had become objects of worship. This, in addition to the fact that the name Brahmaṇya is not mentioned in our Purāṇa, suggests that the Vāyu material is earlier than that of the Gupta inscriptions. The account of the birth of the god as given in our Purāṇa, however, shows that the Vāyu version of the story is later than that of the epic. But the Vāyu also connects the god with demons in a manner in which it is not found in the epics where more stress is laid on his being the military chief of the gods. It appears that this material reflects the condition of beliefs found in the Gṛhyasūtra of Pāraskara.

Gaṇeśa : In the Vedas we find Rudra with his hosts called the Gaṇas whose leader was Gaṇapati. The Taittirīya Brāhmaṇa mentions a god Dantin along with Kārttikeya and Nandi and it is probable that this Dantin was the same as the later elephant-faced god.[90] Besides the Gaṇas, Vināyakas are also associated with Rudra who himself is sometimes called Vināyaka. The Mānava-Gṛhya-Sūtra mentions four Vināyakas who were supposed to possess men and cause them evils and by the time of the Yājñavalkya-Smṛti these four Vināyakas had become one Gaṇapati-Vināyaka.[91] Gaṇeśa is mentioned only at a few places in the Mbh. and he is not here the god Gaṇeśa, for Viṣṇu himself is mentioned as Gaṇeśvara.[92] It should be noted that the invocatory verse with which the epic begins, according to some MSS., has been omitted in the critical edition of the text.[93]

There is no definite evidence of a Gaṇeśa-cult in India before the 5th cent. A.D. "There is a sculptural evidence of his popularity from the fifth century onwards, although no inscription has been found referring either to Gaṇeśa or to Gaṇapati as a god until after the Gupta period".[94] The first stage of Gaṇeśa's embryonic existence must have belonged to a far earlier period. The Mathurā school yields us a comparatively early likeness of the deity which FOUCHER is inclined to regard as an archaic image of Gaṇeśa.[95]

In the Vāyu Śiva often appears as attended upon by the Gaṇas, Bhūtas and also by the Vināyakas ; but the god Gaṇapati, Gaṇeśa or Gaṇapati-Vināyaka does not at all figure in the Purāṇa. The Purāṇa, however, narrates a story of one Gaṇeśa (also called Gaṇeśvara, Gaṇapati) who appears to have two other names Nikumbha and Kṣemaka (the literal meaning of Kṣemaka should be noted). This Gaṇeśa was a follower of Śiva who commanded him to bring about the expulsion

90. GETTY, *Gaṇeśa*, 1-2.

91. BHANDARKAR, 147-8.

92. Hopkins, op. cit., 106, 206.

93. *Prologomena*.

94. GETTY, op. cit., 10.

95. *Ibid.* introduction, xix. For the sculptural and inscriptional evidence on this matter cf. *BDCRI*, 1 ; 5, 150-1.

of king Divodāsa from the city of Vārāṇaśī. Here Gaṇeśa appears to be a vegetation deity particularly popular with the lower order of the populace as suggested by the fact that a barber installed his image outside (or at?) the city gates and it was worshipped particularly by women desiring male progeny. His popularity with the lower classes is further suggested by the fact that the king at first hesitated to offer worship to the deity and his desire being unfulfilled he calls the deity in anger *bhūtam* (note the neuter). The place of worship is called the *sthāna* of Gaṇapati. It is noteworthy that this Gaṇeśa (Kṣemaka) is also called Rākṣasa.

The context of this story suggests its antiquity as it involves the ancient king Divodāsa as a victim of Śiva's anger.[96] The features of Śiva here show him as a god of the wild (for he had no dwelling) and comments on his nature by his mother-in-law suggest that he was a lord of the lowly and the paupers. The god Gaṇeśa who was worshipped at the city-gates and whose image was installed by a *barber* and who is also mentioned as a Rākṣasa appears to have been a god originally of some aboriginal tribe. He was at first worshipped by the lower classes but later on, with the change of fortune in Rudra-Śiva, he also entered upon the stage as one of the first order of divinities among the higher classes also. It is held that Gaṇeśa was originally a kind of demon or "to put it more politely, a jungle genius".[97] Are we then to suppose that this Gaṇeśa, Gaṇeśvara or Gaṇapati who had a name Kṣemaka was a forerunner of the later Vighneśvara Gaṇeśa?

We have already seen how Gaṇeśa emerged as a divinity in about the 5th cent. A.D. and consequently the Vāyu material has to be considered as being considerably earlier.

II. Vaiṣṇavism and the other Sects

Vaiṣṇavism: Viṣṇu as a Sectarian God: There are but few hymns addressed to Viṣṇu is the ṚV. but his personality is by no means unimportant.[98] In the Brāhmaṇas we find clear traces of his rise as a great god.[99] The name Nārāyaṇa occurs in the Ś. Br. but there he is not in any way connected with Viṣṇu[100] and the conception of Nārāyaṇa as the Supreme Being had already been evolved by the end of the Brāhmaṇa period.[101] In the Taittirīya Āraṇyaka, however, we find the name Nārāyaṇa directly related to Viṣṇu.[102] By the time of Pāṇini

---

96. Pargiter appears to believe in its historicity though in a different connection. Cf. *AIHT*, 263. The Mbh., it should be noted, mentions Kumbha and Nikumbha as the two Rākṣasas. Nikumbha is there called the "Daitya-chief", father of Sunda and Upasunda and Gaṇeśa of Śiva's host, when he slaughtered Saudāsa's army at Benares. Cf. Hopkins, op. cit., 133.

97. Getty, *Gaṇeśa*, Introduction p. xx.

98. Bhandarkar, 33; Macdonell. *Vedic Mythology*; Keith, op. cit.

99. *Ibid.*

100. Raychaudhari, *Early History of the Vaiṣṇava Sect.* 7.

101. Bhandarkar, 32.

102. Raychaudhari, op. cit., 9.

the worship of Vāsudeva had become well-known[103] and it appears[104] that Vāsudeva came to be identified with Nārāyaṇa sometime afterwards, as in the Mbh. The evidence of the inscriptions found at Besnagar and Ghosuṇḍi in Rajputana suggest that the worship of the god Vāsudeva had already gathered a large following so that even the foreigners were attracted to it.[105] The Nārāyaṇīya section of the Mbh. sheds more light on the problem but it is not necessary to state its details here.[106] It is in the Mbh. that we get a definite evidence for the identification of Viṣṇu with Vāsudeva. But still in many parts of the great epic we find a state of things in which the divinity of Vāsudeva-Kṛṣṇa was not generally acknowledged.[107] The story of Kṛṣṇa's boyhood in Gokula was unknown till about the beginning of the Christian era[108] and the Harivaṁśa is probably the earliest authority on the matter.[109]

The Vāyu information no doubt testifies to the worship of Vāsudeva-Kṛṣṇa in whose connection the story of the incarnations of Viṣṇu is narrated in the Purāṇa. There is a reference in the Purāṇa to the five great men of the family of Kṛṣṇa, but here the term Vyūha is not used and we are not sure whether that is to be understood by implication, thus suggesting that our Purāṇa knew of the doctrine of Vyūhas of the Pāñcarātra school.[110] The Vāyu again alludes to the cowherd god, a fact which brings down the antiquity of the chapters containing it, at least to the beginning of the Christian era. But we have to note in this connection that the Vāyu does not further develop the idea probably because it thinks the matter to be within the purview of the Harivaṁśa with which it has much resemblance in certain respects.

Incarnations of the god Viṣṇu: The habit of thought which identifies one god with another is reflected in the Vedas though they had not arrived at the conception of the incarnation of a god.[111] The names Matsya, Kūrma, Varāha, Nṛsiṁha and the Dwarf (Vāmana) as manifestations of the divine are known to the Brāhmaṇas but here they are not—excepting the Dwarf—identified with Viṣṇu and are, on the other hand, identified with Prajāpati, the Creator.[112] The idea that a creator god appears in an animal form is certainly pre-epic.[113] Tortoise as a representation of Brahman is mentioned in the Ś. Br.[114] and the Fish and the Boar manifestations first belonged to Brahmā.

103. BHANDARKAR, 3; RAYCHAUDHARI, op. cit., 13. 104. BHANDARKAR, 32.

105. Cf. RAMAPRASAD CHANDA, *Archaeology and Vaiṣṇava Tradition*, *MASI*, 5. 151 ff.; cf. also BHANDARKAR, 3–4.

106. BHANDARKAR, 4 ff. 107. *Ibid*. 34–5. 108. *Ibid*. 36. 109. *Ibid*.

110. Cf. SCHRADER, *Introduction to the Pañcarātra System*.

111. BHANDARKAR, 41. 112. *IHQ*, 17. 370–1.

113. HOPKINS, *Epic Mythology*, 217. 114. *Ibid*. 29.

The Boar incarnation is not that of Viṣṇu but of Brahmā in the older Rāmāyaṇa and the gods do not at first recognise the Boar-form of Viṣṇu at all.[115] Th idea of incarnation is best expounded in the Gitā where it is stated : "Whenever there is a decline of the Law, O Bhārata, and an increase in inequity, then I put forth myself (in a new birth). For the rescue of the pious and the destruction of the evil-doers for the establishment of the Law I am born in every age." (iv, 7 f.). The Mbh. has no systematic account of the avatāras and even in the Harivaṁśa the list is not that of the later ten.[116] The Nārāyaṇīya section of the Mbh. gives first a list of six incarnations and after a short interval it refers to the ten avatāras of the god.[117] It is stated that the later epic alone has the ten avatāras but that they are not always the same. In short, the theory of avatāras is still developing in the epic which represents only a stage in brief where the factors were still not fixed.[118] Among the seven original avatāras the form of boar, man-lion, dwarf and tortoise were the foremost, the three remaining may have been fish, Rāma and Kṛṣṇa. It is only in the later epic that Jāmadagnya Rāma figures as an avatāra, and the Harivaṁśa mentions his function as an avatāra, viz., the annihilation of Kārtavīrya Arjuna. It should be noted that in the early portions of the Rāmāyaṇa, Rāma is only a great hero and not a god.[119]

The Vāyu gives the number of avatāras as ten but its list of these ten is peculiar. It does not include Varāha, Matsya and Kūrma in the list and these are the well-known incarnations of the god in the Purāṇas and also in the later epic.[120] The curse of Bhṛgu mentions *seven* "descents" of the god and not ten and it appears that the original text had seven incarnations. The fact that one Ms. omits the names of Maṃdhātā and Jāmadagnya Rāma is also significant, for the former is rarely known as an avatāra of Viṣṇu and the latter appears as an incarnation only in the later epic. Again there is an explanation in the Purāṇa which purports to classify the incarnation into two categories, viz., (i) heavenly (ii) earthly, and this tends to confirm the suggestion, already made, that the original Purāṇa knew only the seven incarnations which was probably the case also with the Mbh.[121]

The Conception of the Triad : "Though the ṚV. does not contain the conception of a supreme spirit manifested in three forms (trimūrti) which is the doctrine of Trinity, it contains elements which

---

115. *Ibid.* 197, 205, 210 fn. 116. *Ibid.* 217. 117. BHANDARKAR, 41.

118. HOPKINS, op. cit., 217.

119. *Ibid.* For the number of avatāras in other Purāṇas cf. *ERE*, 7. 193 ; cf. also DIKSHITAR, *Matsya Purāṇa, A Study*, 24 ff. where the author claims to have found the rudimentary notions regarding the theory of evolution ; cf. also *IHQ*, 17. 371.

120. Cf. also *IHQ*, 17. 370 ff. 121. Cf. HOPKINS, op. cit., 217.

have contributed to form that belief''. Agni, in the Vedic literature, is stated to have three forms and in connection with the ritual we find the three-fold character of the sacrificial fire sometimes referred to.[122] Thus the earliest triad is that of the fires.[123] In the Maitrāyaṇī Upaniṣad, Brahmā, Rudra and Viṣṇu appear as forms (*tanavaḥ*) of the Absolute which itself is incorporeal and again are declared to correspond respectively with the rajas, tamas and sattva aspects of the Absolute.[124] ''The union of the three highest gods into a trinity forms no part of the epic belief'' and the trinitarian doctrine is recognised only in one late epic passage ; others do not really imply it and the aim of the later epic poets is to equalise Kṛṣṇa-Viṣṇu and Śiva as two aspects of God rather than to establish a trinity or reconcile militant factors.[125] The Harivaṁśa, however, seems to have known the doctrine of trinity and by the time of Kālidāsa it had become quite well-known.[126]

The Vāyu shows traces of the doctrine of trinity and these portions may be supposed to fall in line with the Harivaṁśa. Our Purāṇa, however, does not indicate too much of sectarian preference as is often the case in later literature,[127] for in one case we find Brahmā as the Creator whose other forms are there mentioned to be Maheśvara and Nārāyaṇa.

The Cult of the Sun-god : Adoration of the Sun-god was a common practice with the Vedic Aryans ; and we find in the Brāhmaṇas that offerings were made to the Sun for the removal of sins.[128] The Chh. Up., however, refers to Devakī-putra Kṛṣṇa as a disciple of Ghora Āṅgirasa, a priest of the Sun.[129] But we have, however, no definite evidence from the Vedic literature on a special sect of Sun-god. Kauṭilya refers to the temples of other deities but not that of the Sun. In the Gupta age the prevalence of Sun-worship was known and practised and references to temples of the god are found from the inscriptions of the Gupta period.[130] There is evidence to testify to the existence of the Sun-cult in Gujarat before the 5th cent. A.D. and it continued in the subsequent period also.[131] Varāhamihira tells us that the installation and consecration of the images and temples of the Sun should be caused to be made by the Magas and it appears that in his days the Magas were the special priests of the Sun-god.[132] Thus it has been concluded that the cult of the sun-god was introduced into

---

122. KEITH, *ERE*, 12. 457. 123. HOPKINS, op. cit., 103. 124. KEITH, op. cit.
125. HOPKINS, op. cit., 231. 126. KEITH, op. cit. 127. *Ibid.*
128. BHANDARKAR, 151-2.
129. Cf. III. 17. 6 ; and also Kauśītaki Brāhmaṇa, 30. 6.
130. Cf. R. D. BANERJI, *Age of the Imperial Guptas*, 125 ff.; cf. also R. N. SALETORE, *Life in Gupta Age*, 509-14.
131. H. D. SANKALIA, *Archaeology of Gujrat*, 212. 132. BHANDARKAR, 153.

India from Persia and the construction of the temples of the god, alluded to above, was also due to foreign influence.[133] The Bhaviṣya Purāṇa contains a legend which too implies this.[134] There also existed a school for the exclusive worship of the Sun known by the name of Sauras, whose existence in South India in the days of Śaṁkarāchārya[135] can be inferred from the information of Ānandagiri who brings him into contact with the followers of that sect.[136] This sect appears to have evolved a theology of its own, but the system does not contain even the remotest allusion to a temple of the Sun and appears to have no connection with the cult of that god[137] as it prevailed in Northern India.

Most of the Vāyu information on the matter merely alludes to the adoration of the god and does not suggest an existence of a cult in honour of that deity. The story of Yājñavalkya appears to have some significance in this connection but the myths told about the origin of the Vājasaneya school of Yajurveda (whose founder Yājñavalkya was), occurring in various ancient Sanskrit works do not clearly imply that they were particularly devoted to a cult, as such, of the Sun-god, though that god figures prominently in these myths.[138] The Vāyu, however, appears to suggest their connection with the worship of the Sun but it is not clear on this point. The reference to the temple of the Sun-god at Vāyupura, also called Pavanapura, and the four tanks at that place, of which the tank of the Sun (Sūrya-kuṇḍa) was one, suggest that the prevalence of Sun-worship is here implied. It should be noted that the Purāṇa, in connection with the same Vāyupura, refers elsewhere to Vāḍavas as inhabiting the place whose customs are stated to be "many and varied". This reference to their customs appears somewhat unusual, and are we to infer from this that they were a foreign people akin probably to the Magas mentioned by Varāhamihira? The text of the Purāṇa is here confusing, a part of it having been omitted in some Mss., (Cf. No. 1422 App.), and it is not clear whether the above reference should be taken to be a genuine text of the Purāṇa or a later interpolation. This much, however,

133. *Ibid.* 155. 134. *Ibid.* 153.

135. That is about the 8th century A.D., the period generally assigned to him. Cf. RADHAKRISHNAN, *Indian Philosophy*, II.

136. BHANDARKAR, 152. 137. *Ibid.* 155.

138. See WILSON, *Translation of Viṣṇu Purāṇa*, 279 ff. The story occurs also in the other Purāṇas: cf. Brahmāṇḍa. II. 35. 14-26; Bhāgavata, 12. 6; Skanda, Nāgarakhaṇḍa, ch. 278 and Mbh. Śāntiparvan, 61. 5. No notice of this legend occurs in the Veda itself and according to WILSON it is nothing more than a Purāṇic invention. Cf. op. cit., 280, fn. 3. The name of Yājñavalkya himself does not appear in any other Vedic text than in the Ś. Br. and Sāṅkhyāyana Āraṇyaka. Cf. *Ved. Ind.*, 2. 189. The writer is indebted to Mr. H. M. APTE for supplying the necessary information with regard to this.

can be stated that the worship of the Sun-god in temples is known from the Vāyu and that this worship probably had nothing to do with the Saura system which prevailed in the south in the days of Śaṁkarācārya, i.e. in the eighth century A.D.

It is not clear whether the Vāyu information that the Rākṣasas named Yātudhānas were the followers of the Sun-god should make us infer that they were the worshippers of the god ; and we have no information of that kind available for the present from other ancient sources so as to confirm the same.

Ājīvas : The central figure in the history of the Ājīvikas is Maṅkhali Gosāla whose teaching served to supply a philosophic basis to the Ājīvika religion.[139] He was originally a disciple of Mahāvīra and lived with his teacher for six years practising the most austere asceticism. After that period, however, a dispute arose between them out of a very trifling matter and Gosāla separated himself from Mahāvīra and set up a religious system of his own.[140] These Ājīvikas, as is evidenced by the Jaina and Buddhist canonical works, were naked ascetics and had Śrāvasti as their headquarters.[141] The sect continued to flourish in later times and had gained considerable following in the days of the Mauryas. There are three cave inscriptions of Aśoka at Barābar in the Gayā Dist,[142] which record the dedication of cave-dwellings for the use of the Ājīvikas who "went about naked and were noted for ascetic practices of the most rigorous kind."[143] The Seventh Pillar Edict of Aśoka mentions them with Brahmins and Jainas.[144] The grandson of Aśoka, Daśaratha, had bestowed on the sect caves in Nāgārjunī hills.[145] KERN and BÜHLER had opined that the sect of the Ājīvikas was a subdivision of the Bhāgavatas but the view had been ably refuted by D. R. BHANDARKAR.[146] The further existence of the sect in the 5th and 7th centuries A.D. is testified by references to them by Varāhamihira and in the Harṣa-carita,[147] but the subsequent information about them becomes more scrappy and they are sometimes confused with the Buddhists and Jains. After about the 14th cent. A.D. we hear of them no more.[148]

The history of Buddhism and Jainism is well-known and their history need not be sketched here.

---

139. For a history of this sect cf. B. M. BARUA, *JDL*, 1920, 1–80 ; also *Calcutta Review*, 1927, 335 ff.

140. *CHI*, 1. 159. There is a deep mystery which hangs over the relations between these two personalities according to BARUA who differs from the view expressed above : cf. op. cit., 17.

141. BARUA, op. cit., 13, fn. 2. 142. Corpus Inscriptionum Indicarum, 1. 181–2.
143. SMITH, *Early History of India*, 177. 144. *Corp. Ins. Ind.*, 1.
145. *Ibid.* 1. 103–4, 134–6. 146. *IA*, 1912, 286 ff. 147. BARUA, op. cit., 73–6.
148. *Ibid.* 77 ff.

The Vāyu mentions the Ājīvas as a people who had Piśācas as their deities and the mention of Caityavṛkṣas in the same connection is significant. It is not certain whether by these Ājīvas the Purāṇa means the people who followed the Ājīvika sect or understands by the name all the heterodox sects who were oppposed to the orthodox religion. The reference to *nagnas* in a different context suggests that by that term the Purāṇa understands all these hostile non-Brahmanical sects known to it. This portion of the text (i.e. Śrāddha chapters) is assigned by HAZRA to 3rd century A.D. He states further : "The contempt shown to these religious sects could be possible only when their religions were in a decadent state".[149] It should be noted that the Vāyu speaks very highly of ascetics in general and uses the technical words peculiar to the religious doctrines of Buddhism. It is not clear, however, whether the use of these words suggests that the faith of the Buddhists was not quite unknown[150] or whether all these references should be taken to be complimentary to the religion of the Buddhists which would appear rather un-Purāṇic.

---

149. Cf. p. 16, 150. Cf. DIKSHITAR, *Some Aspects of the Vāyu Purāṇa*, 24.

CHAPTER V

YUGAS AND THE SYSTEM OF CHRONOLOGY

The Kalpa: So far as our knowledge goes we do not find Kalpa being mentioned in the Vedic literature. The belief in the periodical creation and destruction of the world is no doubt found in the AV. (X. 8, 39, 40). The early Buddhist canonical works often mention Kappa in the sense of aeons or cycles of time. They mention three principal aeons, viz., Mahākalpa, Asaṅkheyakalpa and Antarakalpa.[1] Here Kappa is also related to the cosmic life. An early Jaina canonical work, namely the Uttarādhyayana, refers to Kalpa but there the conception of Kalpa signifies only centuries of years and not a fabulously lengthy range of time.[2] The Gītā is well aware of a Kalpa which meant a length of time commencing from the period of creation to that of destruction. "At the expiration of a Kalpa, O son of Kuntī, all entities enter my nature and at the beginning of a Kalpa I again bring them forth." This is what Kṛṣṇa says to Arjuna.[3] The Mbh. connects 'Yuga' with Kalpa and at one place it mentions that 12,000 Yugas make a Kalpa. It also refers to "past Kalpa".[4] But the great epic does not much elaborate on the point. "Even the pseudo-epic does not have such calculations as are found in the Harivaṁśa and the Purāṇas...The earlier calculation is that of 12,000 years making a day of Brahman...An insert at 52, 51, 41 says that 3,600,000 years pass while Viṣṇu sleeps...Unless specially restricted, the years are to be calculated as human years, and probably till the period of later epic...as well as by the pseudo-epic the only period known was the Yuga-complex of twelve thousand years. Then a thousand such were made into a day of Brahman, and with the introduction of Manvantaras in the later epic speculation, this was replaced by astronomical calculations."[5]...The Manu-smṛti, however, says that 12,000 four-yuga periods make a Yuga of gods and one thousand of such Yugas of gods make a day or night of Brahmā. But in this connection it does not refer to the Manvantaras at all, though it refers later on to "innumerable Manvantaras."[6] It appears that the Manu-smṛti is not aware of a *standardized* system of "chronology" connecting the three concepts of Kalpas, Manvantaras and Yugas. Wilson shows that two systems of calculations regarding the duration of Kalpa are observable in the Purāṇas, the original and the simple one indicating that a Kalpa was equal to 1000 great ages and the later calculation had incorporated into it the conception of Manvantaras also.[7]

---

1. Davids and Williams, *Pali-English Dictionary*, see Kappa.
2. *SBE*, 45. 16.
3. *Ibid*. 8. 82.
4. Sörensen, 378.
5. Hopkins, *Epic Mythology*. 196–7.
6. 1. 71–81.
7. *Viṣṇu Purāṇa, Translation*, 24 fn. 6.

The Vāyu information on the Kalpas is definitely very elaborate, more elaborate than that obtaining in the early Buddhist and Jaina works as also in the Mbh. and the Manu-smṛti referred to above. But even here certain stages are observable. For at one place we find the duration of a Kalpa as one thousand four yuga-periods; and in the same context the number of Kalpas is ten. But at another place there is much of fanciful scheming for there we find the number of Kalpas as 33 and the names of some of these Kalpas are derived from terms in music. Again, here the duration of Kalpa is stretched to a fabulously lengthy period of time. Besides, the names of Kalpas in this narration do not include the Vārāha Kalpa which is narrated in the former case. Thus the Vāyu material shows two distinct stages in its information. The first stage is indicated in the purely cosmological setting of the Purāṇa while the second is found in connection with Śiva. It might be stated here that the first stage falls chronologically in a line with the later portion of the great epic, the latter belonging to a much later period.

The Manvantaras : The patronymics Vaivasvata, Sāvarṇi and Sāṁvaraṇa of Manu occur in the Vedic literature[8] but we do not find Manvantaras mentioned in the Vedas. The Buddhist canonical works, though they refer to Kalpas in their ideas of aeons or cycles of time, do not mention the Manvantaras. The same is the case with the early works of the Jaina faith. Though Kauṭilya mentions Yuga in his 'divisions of time' he is silent on the Manvantara and Kalpa. The Gītā mentions four ancient Manus, but another construction is also put on the passage containing the reference.[9] The Mbh. gives some information on the Manvantaras though its information is not certain on the number of Manvantaras which is occasionally mentioned as four, seven or fourteen.[10] The epic alludes to names of Manvantaras such as the Vaivasvata, Cākṣuṣa and the Svārociṣa. It should be noted that the Cākṣuṣa Manvantara is mentioned as being the sixth one.[11] The Manu-smṛti refers to Manvantaras being innumerable[12] and does not mention their number and here the commentator Kullūka puts it in his gloss that fourteen is the number known in the Purāṇas and the expression "innumerable" should be taken to signify the endless process of creation and destruction. The Smṛti, however, mentions seven to be the number of the Manvantaras[13] and whatever be the interpretation of Kullūka, the number fourteen of the Manvantaras had not become a matter of common knowledge at the time of the compilation of this Smṛti. Kullūka's gloss, however, suggests that in

8. *Ved. Ind.*, 2. 128.
9. *SBE*, 8. 86.
10. Hopkins, op. cit., 201, 202, 222.
11. *Ibid.* 36, 174, 202, 81, 85, 88, 201.
12. Cf. *manvatarāṇi asaṁkhyāni*, 1. 80
13. 1. 62-3.

his days the Purāṇas were regarded as authoritative works on the question of Manvantaras.

It should be noted that the description of Manvantaras is one of the five characteristics of a Purāṇa and it is on this ground that a particular Purāṇa is often considered by scholars to be 'ancient'. Whether the Purāṇic tradition in its floating stage conformed to these characteristics is a problem still to investigated. Judged from the contents of the Mbh., our Purāṇa definitely shows an advanced stage of information on the question of the Manvantaras. The Manvantaras are introduced in the scheme of chronology only in the later portion of the epic. Thus the Purāṇa scheme of chronology, namely that of the Yugas, Manvantaras and Kalpas must be supposed to be a post-epic development though its exact antiquity cannot be fixed at this stage of our researches.

The Units of Measurement of Time : In the Ś. Br. we have the following divisions of time : 15 *idānīs = etarhi* ; 15 *etarhis = kṣipra* ; 15 *kṣipras = muhūrta* ; 15 *muhūrtas* = day or night ; 15 days = half month... Here the year is the highest unit of the measurement of time. The Yuga, Manvantara and Kalpa are not mentioned in this connection at all.[14] The Arthaśāstra of Kauṭilya mentions the following divisions of time, in order : *truṭi*, *lava*, *nimeṣa*, *kāṣṭhā*, *kalā*, *nālikā*, *muhūrta*, forenoon, afternoon, day, night, *pakṣa*, month, *ṛtu*, *ayana*, year (*saṁvatsara*) and *yuga*.[15] Kauṭilya's 'Yuga' is equal to five years.[16] He, however, does not mention Manvantara or Kalpa. An early Jaina canonical work, namely, the Kalpasūtra, mentions *stoka*, *kṣaṇa*, *lava*, *muhūrta*, *nādikā*, *samaya*, etc., as divisions of time.[17] The Manu-smṛti, however, gives the following units of the measurement of time :—18 *nimeṣas* = *kāṣṭhā* ; 30 *kāṣṭhās = kalā* ; 30 *kalās = muhūrta* ; 30 *muhūrtas* = day and night. The context also makes references to Kalpas and Manvantaras and to 'days' of the manes and gods.[18]

It will be obvious that the Vāyu material of calculations regarding the divisions of time closely resembles that of the Manu-smṛti, the only difference being that in the Vāyu 15 *nimeṣas* make a *kāṣṭhā* while in Manu 18 *nimeṣas* are said to be equal to a *kāṣṭhā*.

The Yugas : The term 'Yuga' occurs in the ṚV. in the sense of generation. To the four ages there is no reference in the Vedic literature though the four names are mentioned as designations of the throws at dice. The four ages Puṣya, Dvāpara, Khārvā and Kṛta are mentioned in the Ṣaḍviṁśa Brāhmaṇa and Dvāpara in the Gopatha Brāhmaṇa. The name Kali occurs in the Vedic literature but it is not clear whether there it signifies the name of a Yuga.[19] Thus there is no definite evidence for the existence of the Yuga-system of chronology in the

14. *SBE*, 44. 168 ff. 15. *Trans.*, 133 ff. 16. *Ibid.* 135.
17. *SBE*, 22. 262. 18. *SBE*, 25. 20-4. 19. *Ved. Ind.*, 2. 192-3.

Vedic literature. We do not know if the Jātakas were aware of such a system. Kauṭilya, however, knew a Yuga of five years which he connects with a regular system of computation of time. The early Jaina canonical work, named Bhagavatīsūtra, the composition of which is assigned to a period of about 300 B.C.,[20] mentions the four Yugas and further evolves them into its own elaborate system of chronology. It should be noted that this work refers to two kinds of Yugas, viz., the great Yugas (*mahāyuga*) and the small Yugas (*kṣudra-yuga*).[21] The expression 'Yuga' occurs also in the Hathigumphā inscription of Khāravela but scholars have often taken it to signify 'a pair'.[22] The Manu-smṛti mentions Yuga in a familiar tone and its Yuga is different from that of Kauṭilya. It mentions all the four Yugas and shows awareness of the Manvantaras and Kalpas connected with its Yuga.[23] The Mbh. is familiar with the four Yugas though it is not so advanced on the whole scheme of chronology formed of Yugas, Manvantaras and Kalpas. In the epic, Kṛṣṇa is said to represent the four Yugas.[24] The durations of the four Yugas are the same as they appear in the Purāṇas.[25] As an entity, Time is subdivided into four ages—the Yugas and according to HOPKINS—"Of these only one is mythologically important. Kṛta, the perfect age, is no more personified than are the other time-divisions, nor is the succeeding Tretā age of more mythological worth while Dvāpara appears on the stage only with Kali, the last of the ages." Kali is here described to be the "bad present age."[26] Jāmadagnya Rāma is stated to have lived in the Tretā or in the period between Tretā and Dvāpara ages.[27] Viśvāmitra, the rival of Vasiṣṭha, too, is said to have lived in the same period.[28] There are two epic Kalis, however, one the musical demi-god, son of Muni, and the other the time-spirit of evil. The latter figures considerably in the great epic. It signifies the "wheel of time", the "fatal time", and sometimes is the same as "plain destruction" and even appears incorporated in all destructive kings. It appears as a human personage in the history of Nala. "As the fiend of the dice Kali is then playing only the part of his general character. In the great gambling scene of the epic he plays no part at all".[29] In the Gupta inscriptions we find that the Purāṇic view of the Yugas seems to have been known, for they mention the Kṛta as the perfect age, though the Kali is not expressly mentioned.[30]

---

20. CHARPENTIER, Introduction to his edition of *Uttarādhyayana*.

21. *Āgamodaya Samiti Edition*, 744, 958, 964. I am indebted to Mr. M. N. DESHPANDE for this information.

22. BARUA, *Old Brāhmī Inscriptions*, 1, 20, 41, 44. I am indebted to Dr. MEHENDALE for kindly supplying me this information.

23. I 61 ff. 24. HOPKINS, op. cit., 217. 25. *Ibid.* 75–6. 26. *Ibid.* 76.

27. *Ibid.* 211. 28. *Ibid.* 183. 29. *Ibid.* 76–7. 30. *BDCRI*, 2. 163.

PARGITER says that the Yuga reckoning, as is found in the Purāṇas, appears to have an historical basis though later speculations elaborate it into an amazing yet precise scheme of cosmogony. The repeated reference to the application of the theory of four ages only to Bhāratavarṣa (and not to the whole world) suggests that originally the 'Yuga' had nothing to do with cosmogony.[31] It should be noted in this connection that 'Yuga' in the ṚV. means "generation" and it is probable that some crude era was known in the Vedic times. The fact that Kauṭilya refers to a secular mode of reckoning a Yuga is significant. His 'Yuga' was of five years, a fact clearly attested in the Vāyu Purāṇa. The Vedic "generation" may have been subsequently treated as being equivalent to the period taken by the four Yugas of the secular scale. The Purāṇa further seems to emphasize that Yuga formed the central feature of its chronological system for Time, when personified, refers only to "Yuga" and not to "Manvantara" and "Kalpa" which means that the latter had been incorporated into the scheme only subsequently. But even this incorporation had taken place before the final edition of the Mbh., if not before the compilation of the Manu-smṛti, both of which testify to the system of chronology of Yugas, Manvantaras and Kalpas. We are told that the chapters of our Purāṇa which deal with these details were composed in the period about the 3rd century A.D.,[32] —a conclusion which corresponds closely to the observations made above. The fact that in this portion of the Purāṇa there should be no reference to the Yuga of five years is significant.

The Names of the Four Yugas : We have stated above that the four Yugas, as such, were not known in the Vedic period and later the Jātakas are silent on them. The earliest literary evidence on them is, however, found in the Jaina canonical work noted above it and is striking that Kauṭilya mentions a Yuga—(which we have called a secular Yuga) but not the four Yugas. It appears that in his time the four-yuga period was not a secular one and the four Yugas had been elaborated into a cosmogonic scheme which it was not his business to refer to. The Mbh., however, knows all the four Yugas with the same characteristics in which they appear in the Purāṇa and the Manu-smṛti shows the same.

The Descriptions of the Yugas : We are not in a position for the present to assume that the description of the Kṛta, Tretā and Dvāpara ages have any historical significance. These descriptions are given above in order that probably they may be found of some use for

31. *AIHT*, 175. G. BOSE has discussed the different eras found in the Purāṇas in his "Purāṇa-Praveśa" which unfortunately is written in the Bengali language. He has, no doubt, given a summary of his views on the matter in *JRASB*, 1939, 5. 74 ff. but his views are one-sided, so far as his summary goes, and it cannot be used for the present discussion. We have deliberately refrained from discussion which involves knowledge of astronomy. 32. HAZRA, 16.

subsequent investigation. The Kṛta age, as a perfect age, was known to the Mbh. and to the Dharma-śāstra works in general and the concept had its origin long before the age of the final edition of the Mbh. The notion was popular in the age of the Guptas—i.e. in the fourth and fifth centuries A.D.—for this is the only Yuga actually mentioned by name in the inscriptions of this period.[33] The Mbh. has not got such an elaborate description[34] as is found in the Vāyu and we are not sure whether on this ground we should assign that Vāyu portion to a later date. The same holds good as regards the description of the Dvāpara age for the Vāyu material, in this respect, is peculiar to it and is not found in the Mbh.[35]

The case of the description of the Kali age is, however, different. Some scholars have seen a historical significance into it, thinking that the Purāṇas are herein depicting an actual state of facts existing in the times when the chapters containing such description had been incorporated into the Purāṇas.[36] It should, however, be noted that such descriptions are common to many Purāṇas[37] and that they probably suggest a common source of the information. The Mbh. also indulges in similar description and its description of the incarnation of Kalki, on its own authority, is based on the Vāyu Purāṇa.[38] HAZRA has brought much evidence to bear upon these passages. He says that the evidence of the Buddhist literature also confirms what is described in the Purāṇas. "The similarity between the two accounts is very great. In numerous cases what the Purāṇas formulate, the Jātakas seem to illustrate. This striking agreement between the two accounts proves that they are not so imaginary as we may take them to be, but have some historical value."[39] According to him the state of society reflected in these descriptions belongs to the period before 200 A.D. "In spite of the obvious exaggeration, this description refers to the disintegration of the social fabric, on account of the vigour of Buddhism from the time of Aśoka Maurya, the position of the Śūdras as kings and perhaps also as high state officers, and the settlement of the immoral and casteless nomads, viz., the Śakas, Pahlavas and Ābhīras."[40] Though there is some justification in what HAZRA has argued, still, we have to bear in mind that there is much of wishful thinking in this description and so far as the *details* of this description are concerned, we are not prepared to attach any historical importance to them.

---

33. *BDCRI*, 2. 163. 34. SÖRENSEN, 679. 35. *Ibid.* 283–4.

36. G. BOSE refers to 'Social order in the Kali yuga' but does not develop the idea further. Cf. *JRASB*, 1939, 5. 75–6 ; cf. also HAZRA, 208 ff. where he has discussed the problem in details.

37. *Ibid.* 38. Cf. SÖRENSEN, 377 and HOPKINS, op. cit., 218.

39. P. 212. 40. P. 210.

CHAPTER VI

TOWNS, VILLAGES AND DWELLINGS

I. Towns and Villages

The Origin of the Communal Settlements: "We really know nothing whatever of the dwelling-places of men other than caves during Quarternary times; the first traces of huts built in the open appear with mesolithic industries."[1] Palaeolithic Man was primarily a cave-dweller, a nomad and a hunter. "The palaeolithic age was characterised by a purely hunting culture,...by a semi-nomadic way of life in which the only permanent forms of habitation were caves and rock-shelters. The men of the neolithic culture, on the other hand, followed a settled way of life in huts and villages, practising agriculture and the breeding of domestic animals..."[2] It should be noted that the neolithic age had followed a great change of climate which resulted from the passing of glacial conditions and the emergence of northern Europe from the great ice-sheets that had covered it. This is how the pre-historians tell us about the origin of the fixed habitation of man and the rise of the village organisation.

The description found in the Vāyu with regard to the same topic is really very striking.[3] The emphasis on climate which, according to our text, forced man to resort to fixed dwelling is certainly interesting. It should be noted, again, that the rise of civilization, according to the theory known to the Vāyu, had taken root in the Tretā age. The analogy, however, should not be stretched too far, for the preceding description in the context does not show an orderly and clear way of thinking over the matter. But still we have to admit that the description is striking as considered with the findings of pre-historians.

Different Terms used for Communal Settlement: "Upto the present no evidence has been found that the city of Mohenjo-daro was protected either by walling or by fortifications".[4] It is not certain, however, whether stone fortifications were known to the Aryans of the ṚV.[5] The village probably consisted of a certain number of houses built near each other for purposes of mutual defence, perhaps surrounded by a hedge or other protection against wild beasts or enemies.

1. Jacques De Morgan, *Prehistoric Man*, 154.

2. Dawson, *The Age of the Gods*, 45; cf. also Keith-Henderson, *Prehistoric Man*, 132 ff.

3. Cf. also Dikshitar, *The Matsya Purāṇa, A Study*, 101 ff. where he quotes the text of the Brahmāṇḍa Purāṇa which is almost the same as that of the Vāyu.

4. Mackay, *Mohenjo-daro*, 1. 282. Cf. also fn. 2 and also p. 9 where Marshall says that personally he "sees no sufficient reason at present for this supposition."

5. *CHI*, 1. 99.

Indra in the ṚV. is often described as destroying hundreds of strongholds of the Dasyus, called "Pur". But this "Pur" according to KEITH was no more than a mere earthwork fortification.[6] P. K. ACHARYA, however, says that the Vedic Indians "were not ignorant of stone forts, walled cities, stone houses and brick edifices."[7] The canonical books of the Buddhists more elaborately refer to the arrangement of villages, towns and forts.[8] Here we find *gāma*, *nigama*, *kula* and *nagaraka* often mentioned.[9] The early Jaina texts also refer to settlements such as *ghoṣa*, *kheṭa*, *kharvaṭa*, *grāma*, *pallī*, *pattana*, *saṁvāha*, *uagara* and *maṭamba*.[10] Kauṭilya refers to four kinds of forts, viz., water fortification, mountainous fortification, desert and forest fortifications.[11] The two epics also furnish us copious descriptions about towns and forts, though they do not give us structural details about the same. There are nine Purāṇas which have treated the subject more systematically (the Vāyu is not one of them). The Matsya Purāṇa has eight chapters entirely devoted to the subject of architecture and sculpture[12] and it mentions as many as eighteen teachers of Vāstu Śāstra.[13] The Bṛhatsaṁhitā of Varāhamihira has five chapters "wherein both architecture and sculpture are treated with a masterly hand".[14] Acharya says that Varāhamihira might have based his information on the Mānasāra which is the standard treatise on the subject handed down to us. But the date of this compilation is a moot point though it might probably be assigned to the period anterior to that of Varāhamihira.[15] This work refers to eight kinds of fortified cities, viz., the Nagara (royal and ordinary), Pura, Nagarī, Kheṭa, Kharvaṭa, Kubjaka and Pattana and also eight kinds of forts.[16]

It would thus be obvious that the material of the Vāyu is certainly earlier than that of the Matsya and antedates Varāhamihira. It does not know at all the eight kinds of durgas and nowhere shows any knowledge of a standard treatise on the subject such as the Mānasāra. Its material, however, shows closer resemblance with that of Kauṭilya, though the details of the four kinds of durgas given by the Vāyu do not agree with those mentioned by Kauṭilya. It should be noted that the Vāyu information is not so systematic, elaborate and clear as that of Kauṭilya, a fact which may make us infer that our Purāṇa has handed down to us a material which probably belongs to a

6. *Ibid.*; cf. also *Ved. Ind.*, 1. 538.

7. *History of Indian Architecture*; cf. also DAS, *Ṛgvedic Culture*; cf. also MEHTA, 317 ff.

8. P. K. ACHARYA, *Architecture of Mānasāra*, 4. Preface, xlviii; *Ibid.* xlix; cf. also RHYS DAVIDS, 96 and *CHI*, 1. 616.

9. Cf. *CHI*, 1. 200 ff.; RADHA KUMUDA MOOKERJI, *Hindu Civilization*, 299.

10. *Ibid.* 300–1. 11. Trans., 56 ff.

12. ACHARYA, op. cit., and cf. also DIKSHITAR, op. cit., 105. 13. *Ibid.*

14. ACHARYA, op. cit., 11. 15. *Ibid.* lvi. 16. *Ibid.* 95.

period anterior to that of Kauṭilya, though it cannot claim an antiquity as high as that of the Vedas.

Units of Measurement of Distance: *Aṅguli*, 'finger-breadth' is mentioned as the 'lowest measure' in the Ś. Br.[17] The term '*Prādeśa*' also frequently occurs in the Brahmaṇas as a measure of length equivalent to a 'span'.[18] Of '*Vitasti*', however, there is no mention in the Vedic literature. The word '*Aratni*' which primarily means 'elbow' is frequently met with from the ṚV. onwards as denoting a measure of length ('ell' or 'cubit'), showing the distance from the elbow to the tip of the hand.[19] The exact length is nowhere given in the early texts. The term '*Ratni*' is mentioned in the Ṣaḍviṁśa Brāhmaṇa and is a corruption of '*Aratni*'.[20] '*Dhanus*', '*Hasta*' and '*Kiṣku*' are not mentioned in the Vedic texts as units of measurement, though '*Yojana*' occurs very frequently in the ṚV. and in later works as a measure of distance but there is no reference defining its real length. Later, it is reckoned at four *Krośas* or about nine miles. It is also calculated at 8 *Krośas* or 18 miles and the estimate of 2 miles is also found.[21] The Pañcaviṁśa Brāhmaṇa mentions '*Gavyūti*' as a measure of distance.[22] The Taittirīya Saṁhitā mentions another measure of distance, namely, '*Bāhu*' which is often mentioned in the Sūtras.[23] This '*Bāhu*' may be the same as '*Hasta*'. The Ś. Br. mentions '*Pāda*' also as a measure of length.[24] The Jātakas seem to refer to other measures of distance as used in their time in Eastern India. Here we find references to '*sticks*' and '*ropes*' used for the purposes of surveying the land.[25] Kauṭilya, however, is more elaborate about his measurements of distance,[26] and it is unnecessary to repeat the whole thing here. FLEET, however, says that the Arthaśāstra "presents its table of measures of length in a somewhat disjoined form owing to the various parenthetical excursions into special subsidiary measures."[27]

The Vāyu has two tables regarding the measures of distance. It is clear that it shows the tables in a more systematic form than what can be made out from the Vedic literature. As compared with Kauṭilya, however, the first table of Vāyu is more antiquarian in its contents; for the Vāyu had not then advanced to such minute measures of distance as the atoms, *likṣā*, *yava*, etc., which are found in the Arthaśāstra.[28] It should be noted that these minute measures are not, so far as our knowledge goes, mentioned in the Vedic literature. Again the Vāyu does not mention the '*Rajju*' (rope) and '*Daṇḍa*' (stick) which are found as measures in the Jātakas and also in the Arthaśāstra.[29] It should be further noted that '*Gavyūti*', which occurs in the Vedic literature

17. *Ved. Ind.*, 2. 511. 18. *Ibid.* 50. 19. *Ibid.* 1. 34. 20. *Ibid.* 2. 199.
21. *Ibid.* 196. 22. *Ibid.* 1. 223. 23. *Ibid.* 2. 68. 24. *Ibid.* 1. 516.
25. FICK, 148–50; cf. also fn. 1 on p. 149; cf. also MEHTA, 143–4.
26. Trans., 131–3. 27. *JRAS*, 1912, 331. 28. Op. cit., 131. 29. *Ibid.* 133.

and in the Vāyu is not mentioned by Kauṭilya. The second table, however, shows closer resemblance with the information of Kauṭilya on the same subject. But this table is more elaborate in regard to minute measures of distance than Kauṭilya and probably shows traces of a later age. Here we find '*Daṇḍa*' also mentioned and the fact that this table mentions 1000 *Yojanas* as being equal to a *Krośa* of Indra suggests that it shows traces of a later speculation.

Town-planning: As regards town-planning the Vāyu does not show an advanced state of facts or knowledge. The Purāṇa information, especially in connection with the Tretā age, does not elucidate much, the probable antiquity of which we have already discussed above. The information occurring in the geographical chapters is more or less fanciful as is clear from the cities or the extent of the cities described therein.

Village-roads, etc.: The existence of path-ways and roads in the Ṛgvedic times appears to have been implied in references to Pūśan as a protector of paths and high-ways, chariots and carts;[30] and since carriages and chariots are frequently mentioned in the Vedic literature, it may be presumed that a system of communications might have been evolved in those days. In the Jātakas we already find trade and commerce in a flourishing state and these works clearly testify to an existence of a net-work of trade-routes known in those days.[31] Kauṭilya, however, gives better information on this subject. He describes names of the various kinds of roads and highways.[32] He mentions six principal roads in a city and he further enumerates several small roads and foot-paths and frames also rules and regulations regarding traffic.[33] According to him the royal road was to be 4 *Daṇḍas* wide.[34]

The Vāyu information, in this respect, does not agree with that of Kauṭilya nor is it so systematic as that of Kauṭilya and thus it is to be assigned to the stage of development as is indicated by the Purāṇa information on durga, pura, etc. which is described in the same context.

II. Houses and Dwellings

"The sort of houses inhabited by the Aryans would be of great interest could it be reconstructed. Equations exist for door, door-frame or porch and pillar as well as the whole structure. They certainly suggest something more substantial than a nomad's tent—even perhaps a porched house......From the series of *śāla*, *cella*, *höll*, SCHRADER infers some sort of pit-dwelling such as is common all over prehistoric Europe."[35] Such is the information on the dwelling of the

30. MACDONELL, *Vedic Mythology.* 31. *CHI*, 1. 213; FICK, 272 ff.

32. N. N. LAW, *Studies in Ancient Hindu Polity*, 66 ff.; cf. also DIKSHITAR, *Hindu Administrative Institutions*, 375.

33. Trans., 217. 34. LAW, op. cit., 71. 55. CHILDE, *The Aryans*, 86.

primitive Aryan. That the word '*śālā*' should have an Indo-European antiquity is interesting from the view-point of the information available from the Vāyu. "Of the construction of the Vedic house we learn little, but the bamboo seems to have been largely used for the beams which borrowed their name from it.[36] There is, however, a short hymn in the R̥V. wherein the deity of the house, Vāstoṣpati, is invoked to bless man and beast, to afford protection and to grant a favourable entry.[37] The Gr̥hya-sūtras lay down rules regarding building of houses and the ceremonies to be observed in that connection[38] and we need not probe into the later history of this subject as the Vāyu does not furnish such details as would justify such an attempt.

The origin of a fixed dwelling, as is explained by the Vāyu, is certainly very interesting as compared with the information noted above about the primitive Aryan house. It shows that a house was more or less a wooden structure and it does not refer to any other material in this connection. It is further interesting that one Ms. omits the etymological explanation of the word '*prāsāda*' which occurs immediately after '*śālā*', thus probably suggesting that the original tradition of the history of the dwellings of men did not know anything about a '*prāsāda*', meaning a palatial building.

The references to cave-dwellings in our Purāṇa occur in a purely mythological setting and we need not attach any historical importance to them. It is possible, however, that ascetics might have inhabited the caves, excavated by nature, for the references do not suggest any caves excavated by man.

The Vāyu has a very scanty information regarding the construction of buildings. It does not presuppose an existence of any treatise, well-known or otherwise, on the science of architecture. References to Tvaṣṭr̥ and Viśvakarman[39] occur in the Vedic literature and almost the same functions are assigned to them in the Vāyu. But the latter mentions Maya who is not referred to in the Vedas. The Mbh., however, gives us more information on this Maya but there he is recorded to be a brother of Namuci. The epic calls him Viśvakarman and his cleverness in building cities and palaces is often alluded to.[40] He is there the son of Diti[41] and was spared by Agni in the famous incident of the burning of the Khāṇḍava forest.[42] It will at once be obvious that the Vāyu information about him is comparatively earlier than that of the great epic.

---

36. *CHI*, 1. 99; cf. also Das, *R̥gvedic Culture*, 187 ff.
37. Keith, *Religion and Philosophy of the Veda*, *HOS*, 31. 188.
38. *CHI*. 1. 39. Keith, op. cit., 204–10. 40. Hopkins, *Epic Mythology*, 49.
41. *Ibid*. 9. 42. *Ibid*. 49.

CHAPTER VII

DRESS, ORNAMENTS, FOOD AND DRINK

I. Dress and Ornaments

Dress

Nudity: The information of the Vāyu, in this respect, is purely mythological and hence useless for the purposes of the present enquiry. Again we do not know of any stage in the history of the Indian people when they wandered naked.

The Vāyu information regarding the origin of clothing forms a necessary part of the description which tells us about the origin of fixed dwelling and is consequently very valuable. The latest contribution to the history of dress, as indicated by the Purāṇa, occurs in its śrāddha chapters. On the ground of other evidence, these chapters, according to HAZRA, were added to the Vāyu probably in the middle of the third century A.D.[1] There is no other criterion to judge the antiquity of this material.

Materials for Dress: The use of cotton and wool for the purposes of clothing is indicated by the finds of the Indus-Valley.[2]

The ṚV. shows that garments made of wool, skin and grass or leaves of trees (mostly for ceremonial purposes) were used in those days.[3]

About the use of cotton fabrics we have no information but silken garments are mentioned in the later Vedic literature.[4] Cotton clothes were, however, in common use in the period indicated by the Jātakas, at least in Eastern India.[5] It is unnecessary to deal with the period subsequent to that of the Jātakas wherein all the materials for clothing mentioned in the Vāyu were known and such a discussion is not useful for chronological purposes.

The Vāyu information on garments made of leaves and bark of trees occurs mostly in mythological setting and hence is of little historical value; and the same can be said with regard to skin-garments.

The reference to munis, however, suggests that the ascetics were accustomed to this material for their clothes. The Vāyu references to cotton, silk, wool and linen occur mostly in the śrāddha chapters, the antiquity of which has already been referred to above. The information on the clothing of the people at the end of the Kali age need not be taken seriously though the general description which embodies this information among other details, has been, on certain grounds, assigned to a period immediately preceding 200 A.D.

1. P. 16. 2. *Mohenjo-daro*, 1, 33. 3. *CHI*. 1. 101; DAS, op. cit., 210–5.
4. *CHI*. 1, 137. 5. *CHI*. 215; cf. also MEHTA, 194, 239.

Shape of Garments: Our evidence on the dress of the Indus-valley people is very scanty.[6] The Vedic Aryans used two garments to cover their nakedness – the upper and the lower garments. The Vedic evidence is not clear on the point whether males and females used different kinds of dress.[7] The style of clothing seems to have remained unchanged till the time of the later Brāhmaṇas.[8] "Suit of clothes was the ordinary dress" of the people depicted in the Jātakas.

"One Jātaka informs us that people wore under-garments in the pockets of which they put money or such valuable things. The richer class could afford to indulge in little luxuries in the matter of dress."[9] In the Mbh. we find women using only one garment covering both the upper and the lower parts of their bodies.[10] The warriors, however, are shown there using two garments.[11]

The Vāyu information on the shape of garments occurs only in the mythological and sacerdotal settings. The reference to upper and lower garments occurs in the śrāddha chapters. The only evidence of the dress of a female occurs in connection with the wife of god Śiva which may be supposed to represent the dress of women known at the time when the reference was incorporated into the text, but this information is chronologically of little value.

Hair-Dressing: "The Indus-Valley people had their hair taken back from the forehead and either cut short behind or coiled in a knot or chignon at the back of the head, with a fillet to support it." In the case of females it appears that the practice was to let the hair fall loosely behind.[12] In the time of the ṚV. women dressed their hair in braids,[13] so did men. The Vasiṣṭhas had long hair which was braided and coiled on the right. The term *kapardin* occurs in the ṚV. in connection with Rudra and Pūṣan. The Gṛhya-sūtras, however, contain two important Saṁskāras (the *cūdākarman* and *godāna*) which give numerous prescriptions regarding the arrangement of the hair.[14]

The Vāyu information on hair-dressing is mostly in connection with Śiva, the Bhūtas and the Piśācas. It is difficult to say whether the fashions of Śiva's hair-dressing had any historical reality. We find, however, the appearance of the Śikhī or Śikhaṇḍī which must presuppose the art of shaving. The expressions *muṇḍī*, *ardhamuṇḍa* also point to this.

Beards: The men of the Indus-valley wore short beards and whiskers with the upper lip sometimes shaven.[15] In the ṚV. Indra is

---

6. *Mohenjo-daro*, 1. 33.
7. DAS, op. cit., 210-5; ALTEKAR, 334-5; *Ved. Ind.*, 1. 292; *CHI*. 1. 101.
8. *CHI*. 1. 137.
9. MEHTA, 239. Cf. also DAVIDS, *Dialogues of Buddha*, 2. 180 fn.
10. ALTEKAR, 335; HOPKINS, *JAOS*. 13. 349 fn.
11. *Ibid*. 105-6.
12. *Mohenjo-daro*, 1. 33-4.
13. DAS, 217.
14. APTE, op. cit., 73.
15. *Mohenjo-daro*, 1. 33; cf. also *JIOSA*. 8. 66.

described as wearing beard and the information of the same Veda on the Tṛtsus and Vasiṣṭhas shows that men in those days sometimes wore beards and sometimes shaved them.[16] But it is difficult to state definitely whether it was a common practice to wear beards in the Vedic times for we also find shaving of beards often referred to.[17]

The practice, however, shows decline in later times for the sacraments of the Gṛhya-sūtra contain elaborate prescriptions regarding shaving which included shaving of the beard.[18] In the early Buddhist sculptures we find beards less common.[19]

It is intersting that Vāyu has its information connected with its genealogical lists. Though this information shows that shaving was known, still the details suggest that beards were generally worn by kings and the members of the nobility. The information may probably be considered to be true to its political setting.

Ornaments: The Vāyu information on the origin of ornaments is to be explained in the same manner as in the case of similar information on dress.

Armlets and Bracelets: *Keyūra* and *Aṅgada*: Bracelets were used by the Aryans of the Ṛgvedic period,[20] and no doubt continued to be used in later times. The Yakṣa statue from Patna of about the third century B.C. shows that both bracelets and armlets were used in that period.[21] Both aṅgadas and keyūras are frequently mentioned in the Mbh. and HOPKINS says that armlets are the most frequently mentioned ornaments in the great epic.[22] Their use is also indicated in the South India of the second century A.D.[23] The Vāyu associates their use with Śiva, the Rākṣasas and the people of the Kuru country. Its evidence does not admit of chronological verification.

Crowns and Turbans: *Kirīṭa*, *Mukuṭa* and *Uṣṇīṣa*: We have no evidence from the ṚV. whether the people used any head-dress such as a crown or a turban. The AV. mentions ***kumbha*** worn on the head but we have no information regarding its form or size.[24] The Ś. Br. describes Indrāṇī as wearing the uṣṇīṣa as her head-dress.[25] The Jātakas show that, in Eastern India of their times, use of turbans was very common.[26] Gods and men from the Bhārhut sculptures wear mostly the turbans and not the jewelled crowns,[27] and the same can be

16. DAS, op. cit., 219. 17. *Ibid.* 18. V. M. APTE, op. cit., 74-5.
19. BARUA, *Bharhut Sculptures*, 3. Plates.
20. *CHI.* 1. 101; MAC., *HSL.* 164; ALTEKAR, 360.
21. Cf. STELLA KRAMRISCH, *Indian Sculpture*, Plate I, No. 2.
22. *JAOS.* 13. 317 fn. 23. *BDCRI.* 2. 85. 24. VI. 138. 3.
25. XIV. 2. 1. 8. 26. MEHTA, 239.
27. BACCHOFER, *Early Indian Sculpture*, Plates 10 ff.; cf. also BARUA, *Bharhut*, 3, 52-4 and plates.

said from the evidence of the Sanchi sculptures.[28] The Nāgārjunikoṇḍā sculptures of about the second century A.D. show that in the South India of that period turbans formed the most common head-dress for men but here we find the wearing of crowns coming into practice especially by princes.[29] Both *Mukuṭa* (crown) and *uṣṇīṣa* (turban) are mentioned in the Mbh. and HOPKINS says that *mukuṭa* seems to be worn only by kings and princes while the *uṣṇīṣa* was worn by all. He attributes the former to a later usage when "the king, free from immediate personal danger, drove upon the scene (of war) to see, not to fight, permitting the use of the crown and not the older helmet."[30] That the wearing of crown was a "later usage" appears probable from the evidence of the sculptures noted above.

The Vāyu mentions uṣṇīṣa many more times than the mukuṭa. It is striking that it associates the use of mukuṭa not with the gods but with the Rākṣasas and with people of the Kuru country, a fact full of chronological significance, for we find in later sculptures the wearing of crowns associated with gods and princes. The epic kings wear the crown but no king is so described by the Vāyu ; it may be that the Purāṇa had no occasion for such a description. Nevertheless the evidence of the Purāṇa, in this respect, is striking and it shows the comparative antiquity of this information.

Necklaces : The use of necklaces as ornaments is as old as the ṚV. for we find in it such an expression as *maṇigrīva* (i. e. having a jewel on the neck).[31] They continued to be worn in later times. The early Buddhist sculptures testify to their common use both by males and females.[32] The Mbh. refers to jewelled necklaces.[33]

The Vāyu mentions '*dāman*', '*hāra*', and '*sūtra*', but we have no information to judge whether each of them had their distinctive characteristics. Again, this material of the Purāṇa does not suggest anything definitely chronological about them.

Use of Garlands : (cf. also *Akṣamālā*) : The fashion of wearing garlands of flowers appears to have been very popular with the Ṛgvedic Aryans. They wore also a golden lace. The very fact that the maker of *niṣka* and the maker of garland are mentioned in that Veda as having been troubled with evil dreams suggests the frequency of its use.[34]

Of the Vāyu evidence on the matter we may observe the same remarks as in the case of necklaces.

Waist-bands or Belts : *Mekhalā*, *Kāñcanapaṭṭa* and *Śroṇībandha* : The Ś. Br. shows that the waist-band was worn round the lower garment

---

28. BACCHOFER, op. cit. 29. *BDCRI*. 2. 66 ff. 30. *JAOS*. 13. 317 fn.
31. DAS, op. cit., 217 ; cf. also MAC., *HSL*. 164 and *CHI*. 1. 101.
32. Cf. BACCHOFER, op. cit., plates ; BARUA, op. cit. and *BDCRI*. 2. 81 ff.
33. *JAOS*. 13. 317 fn. 34. DAS, op. cit., 216.

and it appears that it was more a part of dress than an ornamental device.[35] The earliest sculptures, however, show it more as an ornamental device. The two Yakṣa statues from Patna of about the third century B. C. suggest that waist-bands were probably commonly worn.[36] The frequent use and the elaborate nature of this ornament are clearly seen from the Bhārhut sculptures.[37] Its use in South India of about the second century A. D. is clearly testified by the evidence of Nāgārjunikoṇḍā sculptures.[38]

The Vāyu mentions the use of waist-bands in mythological and sacerdotal settings only. The reference to *Kāñcanapaṭṭa* as a good gift in śrāddha may be assigned to the period to which the śrāddha chapters are assigned by HAZRA. The association of the use of *śroṇībandha* with the kings of the Aiḍa-vaṁśa does not occur in the genealogical portion of the Purāṇa and we do not know whether it can be considered to have any historical basis.

Ear-rings: *Kuṇḍala:* Ear-rings (*karṇa-śobhana*) are referred to in the ṚV.[39] and may have been used in later times. The Vāyu information on this matter does not admit of chronological discussion.

Anklets: *Valaya*: The ṚV. mentions anklets[40] and the Vāyu evidence has the same chronological implications as in the case of ear-rings.

Cosmetics: 'Kohl' vessels have been discovered in the Indus-Valley excavations suggesting the use of some sort of eye-paint.[41] A similar practice appears to have prevailed in the Vedic times. *Añjana* (eye-solve) is frequently mentioned in the AV.[42] The same work also makes frequent allusions to scents and perfumes the importance of which can be easily realized from the fact that they were presented to the bride in the beginning of the nuptial rights. It again refers to *guggula* and use of flowers for the purposes of decoration.[43] The Ś. Br. shows use of ointments for eyes and even gives a story of the origin of añjana.[44] In the Jātakas the art of cosmetics appears in a more developed form.[45] We find the ancient Pali texts giving a stock expression *mālāgandha-vilepana-dhāraṇamaṇḍana-vibhūṣaṇa-ṭhṭhāṇa* which apparently suggests that all these kinds of toilets had become a matter of common use.

Most of these are mentioned in the Vāyu but only in the mythological and sacerdotal settings. The genealogical account mentions none of them. The information contained in the śrāddha portion of the Purāṇa may be assigned to the period of about 200 A.D.

---

35. ALTEKAR, 334. 36. BACCHOFER, op. cit., Plate 10.
37. *Ibid.* Plates 17 ff. 38. *BDCRI*. 2. 87 ff.
39. DAS, op. cit., 216; ALTEKAR, 358; MAC. *HSL*. 164. 40. MAC. *HSL*. 164.
41. *JISOA*. 8. 62. 42. *Ibid.* 68–9. 43. *Ibid.* 70–72.
44. *Ibid.* 68–9. 45. *Ibid.* 73 ff. and cf. also MEHTA.

II. Food and Drink

Food-grains : *Yava* and *dhānya* are the only terms for food-grains mentioned in the Ṛgveda. The diet of a people of semi-pastoral habits must essentially be composed of milk and flesh of their cattle and thus we find few references to food-grains in the ṚV.[46] But a considerable change had taken place in the economic life of the people in the times of the Brāhmaṇas.[47] A good many food-crops—*Vṛīhi*, *Priyaṅgu*, *Tila*, *Godhūma*, *Māṣa*—are mentioned in these works. The censure of meat-eating, for the first time, in the Brahmaṇas is also suggestive of a possible change in the dietary of the people. The presence of a large number of cultivated food-grains, ready for use as food-stuffs, seems to have become an important psychological factor in the development of these ideas of animal *ahiṁsā*. These various food-grains had been introduced in the place of meat as important articles of food for the people. A further development in this state of things in the Jātakas is already noted above. In the Jātakas we find the following field-crops : *Sāli*, *Vīhi*, *Taṇḍula*, *Yava*, *Kaṅgu*, *Kalāye*, *Mugga*, *Māsa*, *Tila*, *Eraṇḍa*, *Marīca*, *Jīraka*, *Siddhaṭhakka*, *Lona*, *Aṁbila*, and *Addasugivera*.[48] The Arthaśāstra is even more elaborate.[49]

The Vāyu references to food-grains are merely illustrative and not exhaustive. Only those primarily associated with ceremonies such as śrāddha and yajña are mentioned. They show the use of *masura*, varieties of rice, *yava* and *tila* only. It is not clear whether the *dhānya* of Vāyu refers to barley or in general to any food-grain. The Vāyu material is clearly indicative of conditions of post-Ṛgveda times though we cannot set up the lowest limit thereof.

Food-preparations : In the Ṛgveda we find that the principal meals were prepared from barley and rice. The food preparations mentioned in the ṚV. are : *odana*, *kṣīraudana*, *mugdaudana*, *māṁsaudana*, *apūpa*, *pakti* and *karambha*.[50] Conditions must have fairly advanced in the times of the Brāhmaṇas, but we have no evidence to record here. Extraction of oil from tila was known in Brāhmaṇa times.[51] The field-crops of the Jātakas are noted above and they must have been used for the purposes of food-preparations. The Jātakas further show sugarcane as a common crop and its juice was used in plenty and sugar was obtained from sugarcane.[52] Salt-makers are also mentioned We even find food-stuffs, groceries and oil sold in bazaars.[53] Kauṭilya throws more light on this problem but his information is of an altogether different character which does not admit of comparison here.[54] The same conclusion as in the case of food-grains can be recorded here.

---

46. Cf. *CHI*. 1. 99-101.
47. *Ibid*. 136.
48. Mehta, 19.
49. Cf. pp. 142 ff. and 114 ff.
50. Das, 201-2.
51. Apte, op. cit., 117.
52. Mehta, 187.
53. *CHI*. 1. 214-5.
54. Cf. trans. 112 ff.

Milk and its Products : The chief articles of food in the Ṛgvedic times were milk and its products.[55] The word *dadhi* is mentioned in the ṚV. and the frequent occurrence of *ghṛta* was due to its use in sacrifices.[56] This predominance of milk and its preparations in the food of the people was due to the fact that the Ṛgvedic Aryans were, to a large extent, a pastoral people.[57] Things must have changed considerably when they settled to agricultural pursuits which means predominance of the food-grains and vegetables in the dietary of the people ; thus milk and its products would no longer remain as the chief articles of food. In later saṁhitās we find this clearly reflected ; for quite a large variety of grains came to be known in this period.[58] The Jātakas show a further advance in this state of things where we find even manufacturing industries connected with food-grains.[59]

The references to milk and its products in the Vāyu occur mostly in connection with the śrāddha ceremonies. It had also become a part of the mythological nomenclature, viz., *Kṣīroda*, the name of a sea ; and *Dadhivāhinī*, that of a river.

The Vāyu statement that Urvaśī's food consisted only of *ghṛta* when she lived with Purūravas is pregnant with chronological suggestions. It appears as if we are here reminded of Purūravas, a king of a pastoral people, a state of facts well suited to the Ṛgvedic or even pre-Ṛgvedic times. This only shows how facts of material culture strongly coincide with the facts of a corresponding greater antiquity indicated in political history. The story of the Pṛthvīdohana fits well in the folklore of a pastoral people, for it involves an idea showing milk as the main sustainer of the people.

Soma and Surā : These were the principal drinks of the Ṛgvedic Aryans.[60] Soma was probably a sacrificial drink and it must have originally been a popular drink also,[61] but with the Ṛgvedic people Surā was a more popular drink. Another drink named Pānta is also recorded in the ṚV.[62] A Distiller of Wine is mentioned in the Vāj. Saṁ.[63] and we find Ch. Up. 6.10 mentioning drinking liquor as a *madāyātaka*. Liquor was manufactured and consumed on a large scale in the times of the Jātakas in eastern India and there were a good many liquor-shops open day and night.[64] Kauṭilya has an independent officer as a Superintendent of Liquor and he mentions the manufacture of different kinds of liquor.[65]

The Vāyu has also a general tendency to regard Surā as an evil and calls one who drinks it as a *mahāpātakin*. But it refers to Śiva as Surāpa and derives the origin of the name Kaśyapa from his habit of drinking

---

55. *CHI*. 1. 101 ; Mac. *HSL*. 164 ; Das, 202.
56. Das, 202.
57. *CHI*. 1. 101.
58. Apte, op. cit., 117.
59. Mehta, 196–7.
60. Das, 208 ff.
61. *CHI*. 1. 102,
62. Das, 210.
63. Cf. Apte, op. cit., 118.
64. Mehta, 197.
65. Trans. p. 147 ff.

Kaśya—a kind of spirituous liquor. It is difficult to say whether these references indicate an age when the drinking of Surā was not regarded as a sin, i.e. to an age earlier than that of the Ups. when it was not so much regarded with disapproval.[66]

The Vāyu refers to Soma many times and associates it with gods only, thus suggesting that it was not a drink of human beings at all; but we have at one place a reference to a Dealer in Soma who was not invited for śrāddha. This reference suggests that traffic in Soma was regarded with disapproval though such traffic was taking place. The prohibition is equally suggestive of the fact that Soma was primarily used in sacrifices and hence was considered too sacred to be an article for sale.

It is fruitless to make chronological suggestions on this evidence.

Amṛta: In the ṚV. *amṛta* is not found as a name of a divine drink. The term, however, occurs as an attribute of Soma which was regarded as a divine drink.[67] Soma was a stimulant and conferred immortality upon the gods.[68] The term Amṛta itself, signifying a celestial drink, occurs very often in the Ś. Br.[69] Still it has close connection with Soma. We find Soma called the nectar (*amṛta*) of immortality.[70] There is also a reference to Amṛta being recovered by gods.[71] Amṛta, as purely a drink of immortality, is many times mentioned by the Gītā.[72] Here we do not find it connected with Soma at all.

In the Vāyu Amṛta occurs as a drink of the gods; but there are some instances connecting it with Soma, the moon, and not with Soma the plant. This information of the Vāyu is thus assignable to a period subsequent to that of the Ś. Br. though it is difficult to say about the lowest limit of time. There is one reference stating that Amṛta was stored by the gods on the Somaka mountain but it is not clear whether this name Somaka should be connected with Soma, the drink or Soma, the moon.

Honey: Honey was used with food by the Ṛgvedic Indians.[73] The Ś. Br. mentions honey as the life-sap of the sky.[74] It even calls it a form of Soma,[75] and shows its use in the ritual.[76] The *madhuparka* offered to guests is mentioned in the AV.[77] Kauṭilya mentions it many times even in similes.[78] It includes also the juice of grapes in 'honey' (*madhu*).[79]

With the Vāyu honey is amongst its favourites, and we find even a river of honey mentioned.

---

66. *CHI*. 1. 102. 67. Mac. *HSL*. 98. 68. *Ibid*.
69. *SBE*. 26. 374; *SBE*. 44, 87; *SBE*. 41. 164 etc.
70. *SBE*. 26. 385(n). *Ibid*. 43. 251 ff. 71. *Ibid*. 43. 355 ff.
72. *Ibid*. 8. 62, 88 ff., 126, 391. 73. Das, 206. 74. *SBE*. 41. 390.
75. *Ibid*. 44. 243. 76. *Ibid*. 43. 182 ff. 77. *Ibid*. 42. 84.
78. Text. p. 70. 79. Trans. p. 114.

Juices : Fruits of Jaṁbu, Panasa and Paruṣaka are mentioned in Kauṭilya[80] but it is not clear whether juice was extracted from them.

For want of evidence from other sources it is not possible to discuss the implications of this Vāyu material

Non-Vegetarian Diet : 'The Vedic Indians were a nation of meat-eaters'.[81] This might have been due to the fact that they were a pastoral people.[82] Beef was probably the kind of meat most frequently eaten by them.[83] Cow is no doubt called *aghnyā* sixteen times in the ṚV. thus probably indicating a new school of thinkers who were opposed to the killing of cows.[84] Ideas of general prohibition against meat-eating appear in the Brāhmaṇa literature, but it was in the time of the Ups. that we find these ideas gaining ground and becoming widely accepted. Meat-eating was regarded by Upaniṣadic teachers as one of the heinous sins.[85]

The Gṛhya-Sūtras also have a considerable evidence for flesh as one of the common articles of food of the people. Cows and bulls were sacrificed and the deification of the cow was still to become a settled belief. The general rule in a śrāddha is that flesh is compulsory ; in its absence only vegetable food is allowed (*śrāddhe maṁsaṁ nityaṁ, maṁsābhāve śākam*).[86] "Not only animals but even the cow was, on certain occasions, killed according to Gṛhya or Dharma Sūtras[87] and the Dharma-śāstra works contain numerous rules regarding flesh-eating. Gradually, however, a change came over the sentiments of the people. Megasthenes and Strabo state that the caste of philosophers abstained from animal food. We find in the Jātakas that fish and meat had a flourishing market and slaughter-houses were common. Such was the state of things then in eastern India.[88] Kauṭilya has a separate officer of state known as Superintendent of Slaughter-houses. Such Arthaśāstra, however, contains a provision prohibiting slaughter of cows and bulls.[89] We have the edicts of Aśoka testifying to a fact how originally thousands of animals were killed in royal kitchens and how the great emperor was determined to prevent this state of things. The Smṛti works, most of which were post-Aśokan in date, put a general ban on flesh-eating. Manu particularly appears to be a staunch opponent of flesh-eating, though he had on certain points tried to square with the views of the ancient śāstra which permitted animal food in sacrifices. He allows the use of flesh in śrāddha. But conditions seem to have been different even in Manu's days and flesh-eating was common. Gradually, however, flesh-eating was abandoned by the people of India when Vaiṣṇavism began to sway their minds.[90]

---

80. Text. p. 94. 81. *CHI*. 1. 101. 82. Cf. DAS, 203.
83. MAC. *HSL*. 164. 84. *Ved. Ind.*, 2. 146 ; DAS, 205.
85. APTE, op, cit., 117-8. 86. *Ibid*. 122. 87. KANE, 2. 776.
88. Cf. MEHTA, 196. 89. Trans. 151-2. 90. KANE, 2. 776-80.

There is a good deal of material on flesh-eating in our Purāṇa. Use of flesh in śrāddha was considered very meritorious and details regarding the nature of its merit are given. There is not even a trace in these details about the prohibition of eating flesh. The occasion in the story of Vikukṣi, who was nick-named Śaśāda (hare-eater) was due to a śrāddha to be performed by Ikṣvāku. We find also the use of flesh, of various qualities, in Dakṣa-yajña. This state of things must be considered more ancient as compared with the Smṛti works, though it must remain a tentative inference. There are three incidents which occur in the genealogical accounts connected with flesh-eating. (i) The reference to the hunting of buffaloes indicating that they were wild beasts still undomesticated. It means that this fact of material culture squares well with the antiquity of the king Ikśvāku as indicated in political history. The statement that his son Vikukṣi ate the flesh on his way might be suggestive of crude methods of cooking, thus strengthening the above chronological point. But we find an explanation of the term *māṁsa* which occurs *verbatim* in the Manu-smṛti (V. 55). This stanza appears quite unnecessary in the context and must be considered as a later interpolation probably by a redactor who sided with the views of Manu. It is necessary to mention here that the Mbh. does not include this stanza in connection with Vikukṣi.

The incident of Pṛṣadhra does not essentially indicate that cow-slaughter was regarded as a sin. It seems more probable that Cyavana cursed him because *his* cow was slaughtered, that being an offence against his ownership of the cow. Thus this incident is not a definite instance of the prohibition of eating beef, less so of flesh-eating in general. On the other hand, it proves that beef was eaten by the Kṣatriyas while among the Śūdras it was a common practice.

The story of Triśaṅku also leads us to the same conclusion. Pargiter considers the incident of Satyavrata killing Vasiṣṭa's cow as "not improbable." It is important to note that Vasiṣṭha did almost nothing against Satyavrata except that he stigmatised Satyavrata as Triśaṅku (i.e. a man of three stains of sins). He did not even curse him. The whole incident does not indicate anything about the sanctity of the cow and prohibition of cow-slaughter for ordinary purposes (i.e. other than sacrificial). Had such a state of things existed, as it apparently was, at the time of Kauṭilya, we would have found traces of it in that work. This leads us to conclude that the story fits well in the matter of flesh-eating with its antiquity indicated by the political history.

CHAPTER VIII

MUSIC AND DANCING

Music in General: In the age of the ṚV. music had already advanced beyond the primitive stage and some musical instruments were used. The hymns themselves prove that singing was highly esteemed.[1] The best evidence for the antiquity of music is, of course, the Sāmaveda. It is even suggested that it was practically a musical rendering of the ṚV.[2] The Sāmaveda was sung according to very strict rules.[3] The Jātakas show music and dancing as despised callings.[4] But the earliest reference to musical theory as such is found in the Ṛkprātiśākhya.[5]

Association of the Gandharvas, etc., and of the Ritual with Music: The ṚV. shows music as connected with ritual. The singing of the Brahmins at the time of pressing the Soma is alluded to in the Frog-hymn (VII. 103, 7-8). But the Gandharvas of the Vedic mythology nowhere appear as celestial singers.[6] The germs of this idea, however, can be traced in the Vedas. For instance, we find in the Ś. Br. (II. 5. 1) the Gandharvas connected with the ritual where Purūravas is said to have obtained the sacrificial fire from the Gandharvas. They are also often associated with Soma in the ṚV.[7] But the idea becomes more prominent when we find in the Ś. Br. (11, 6, 1) the Apsarasas—the female associates of Gandharvas from the ṚV. onwards—[8] described as engaged in dance, song and play. By the time of the Jātakas, however, the close association of Gandharvas with music had become an established fact; for we find there the art of music called by the name Gāndharva Veda as being one of the 18 *śippas* or subjects of study.[9] In the Jātakas they often appear as heavenly musicians.[10] It is unnecessary to dilate on the subsequent history of this association.

It should be noted that there is no evidence of the connection of Gandharvas of the Sāmaveda either in the Vedas or in the Jātakas and it is difficult to say at this state of our knowledge whether such an evidence can be traced in the epics and later literature.

In the light of this history of associations, the Vāyu references to Gandharvas as celestial musicians might be either contemporaneous with or later than the period of the Jātakas. It is interesting in this connection to note that the Vāyu also says that the Gāndharva-vidyā is

---

1. *CHI*. 1. 103; Das, 234 ff.; Dikshitar, *Aspects of the Vā. Pur.*, 34.
2. Dikshitar, *ibid.*
3. Popley, 8-9.
4. *CHI*. 1. 207; cf. also Fick, 291; Mehta, 312 ff.
5. Popley, 9.
6. Macdonell, *Vedic Mythology*, 137.
7. *Ibid*. 136.
8. *Ibid*. 134 ff.
9. Law, *India as Reflected in the Early Texts of Jainism and Buddhism*, 249; Mehta, 342 ff.
10. Davids, 220.

one of the 18 vidyās—a fact worthy of comparison with the 18 śippas of the Jātakas mentioned above.

The Gandharvas of the Vāyu are connected with the ritual especially in connection with the chanting of the Sāmaveda. In the Vedas they are no doubt associated with the ritual and especially with Soma and not with the Sāmaveda. The Udgātā was a special priest who chanted the Sāmans. As already stated above, it is not possible to comment on this at this stage.

Association of Śiva with Music : Nowhere in the Vedic mythology do we find Śiva connected with music and dancing.[11] In the Rāmāyaṇa, however, there is an indirect connection between Śiva and music where Rāvaṇa is described in that epic (VII. 16. 35) as praising the god Śaṅkara with Sāma hymns.[12] But this is found in the 7th Kāṇḍa of that work which is considered by scholars to be a later interpolation.[13]

The Vāyu evidence shows Śiva very often associated with music and the antiquity of this evidence cannot be discussed here for want of relevant information from other sources.

MUSICAL INSTRUMENTS :

Bherī : It is not mentioned in the ṚV. But the Jātakas mention it.[14] In the Rāmāyaṇa its use is found in the military band, i.e., as a trumpet.[15] In the Mbh., too, it is frequently mentioned.[16]

The Vāyu sets it in connection with Śiva-worship and does not show its use in war.

Diṇḍima: It is not mentioned in the Vedic literature, but the Jātakas have it.[17] The Rāmāyaṇa[18] testifies to its existence as also the Mbh.[19] The Rāmāyaṇa says that it had a leather facing.

The Vāyu information is the same as in the case of Bherī.

Dundubhi : In the early Vedic times it was used both in war and peace.[20] The Jātakas are silent about it, but in the epics we find it very commonly used on the battle-field.[21] In Kauṭilya it is the same.[22]

The Vāyu also seems to hint that it was used in war, for the noise of the drums of Suras is described as being as terrible as death.

Gomukha : It is said to be "a wind instrument" of shell species, a kind of conch somewhat resembling the mouth of the cow, whence it derives its name.[23] The Vedas do not know it though it appears that the flute (another kind of wind instrument) has a Vedic antiquity

11. Macdonell, op. cit. 12. *IC*. 4. 445.
13. See Jacobi, *Das Rāmāyaṇa* ; cf. also Mac. *HSL*. 304. 14. Mehta, 315.
15. *IC*. 4. 451. 16. *JAOS*. 13. 17. See *paṇava-deṇḍima*, cf. Mehta, 315.
18. *IC*. 4. 451. 19. *JAOS*. 13. 20. Das, 234. 21. *IC*. 4. 451 and *JAOS*. 13.
22. P. 401. 23. Tagore, *Hindu Musical Instruments*, 4.

(see Veṇu). The Jātakas are silent about it and Kauṭilya also does not mention it. But there are many references to it in the epics.[24]

About the Gomukhas in the Vāyu we can say the same as in the case of Bherī.

Jharjhara: It was a kind of drum.[25] Though the ṚV. mentions Dundubhi (i.e. a drum) we do not find Jharjhara there. The Jātakas too are silent and so is the Rāmāyaṇa.[26] The Mbh. has it.[27] About its use in later times it is difficult to be definite at the present state of our knowledge.

The Vāyu mentions it in the same manner as in the case of Bherī.

Mukhavāditra: Probably this term signified a general class of musical instruments to be played upon with the mouth. The same might be said of Mukhamardalavāditra. The Bherī, Diṇḍima, Dundubhi, Jharjhara, Mṛdaṅga, etc., might have belonged to another class.

We do not find the term in the ṚV. which knows only the Dundubhi, belonging to this class. Though the Jātakas refer to various kinds of drums we do not know whether this was then known. We are right in assuming from the number of such instruments and from the then general condition of the science of music that the term might have been known.[28]

The Vāyu shows that they were "beaten" (*sphoṭitaiḥ*) with force and connects them exclusively with Śiva.

Mṛdaṅga: It is not mentioned in the ṚV. The Jātakas[29] mention *Mūtiṅgā* probably the same as Mṛdaṅga. But Kauṭilya knows it well.[30] The Rāmāyaṇa[31] mentions Mṛdaṅga as also the Mbh.[32] In later literature we find the origin of this instrument attributed to Brahmā made to serve as an accompaniment to the dance of Śiva in honour of his victory over the three cities and that Gaṇeśa first played upon it.[33]

The Vāyu associates this instrument with the Kurus who used it in their sports for entertainment. The information occurs not in the genealogical accounts but in the chapters on geography. Of the later story of its origin the Vāyu knows nothing. The Rāmāyaṇa tells us that it was also used in war but there is no such reference in the Vāyu.

Paṇava: It is not found mentioned in the ṚV. and the *paṇavadeṇḍima* is mentioned in the Jātakas ; and this Paṇava is probably the same as our Paṇava.[34] The Rāmāyaṇa mentions its use in military bands,[35] and the Mbh. confirms this.[36]

---

24. *JAOS.* 13. Miss DHARMA does not mention it as being found in the Rāmāyaṇa. But TAGORE says so without quoting the exact source of his information.
25. MONIER WILLIAMS, *Sanskrit English Dictionary.*
26. *IC.* 4. 451.
27. *JAOS.* 13.
28. Cf. MEHTA, 312-5.
29. *Ibid.*
30. P. 125.
31. *IC.* 4. 451.
32. *JAOS.* 13.
33. POPLEY, 120. No reference is given by the author.
34. Cf. MEHTA, 315.
35. *IC.* 4. 451.
36. *JAOS.* 13.

The Vāyu associates its use with the Kurus as above.

Paṭaha. It is not mentioned in the Vedas nor in the Jātakas. It is, however, mentioned in the epics.[37]

The Vāyu mentions it in the same manner as the Bherī.

Raṇitālasita: Was it a musical instrument at all? There is no reference to it in works on music.

The Vāyu mentions it with Bherī and others mentioned above.

Śaṅkha: The ṚV. does not refer to it; but the Jātakas mention it. In the epic war-scenes use of the śaṅkhas is very common,[38] and we find in the Gītā the śaṅkhas of various warriors mentioned by name.[39] Kauṭilya testifies to the use of śaṅkhas in war.[40]

The Vāyu, however, shows its use only in connection with the worship of Śiva by the Bhūtas.

Tumba: We have no information on it from the other ancient sources.

The Vāyu mentions it to be the pet instrument of Śiva.

Vīṇā: The ṚV. mentions that Kṣoṇī or Viṇā was the musical instrument of the Maruts.[41] The Jātakas shed more light on the construction, size and use of this instrument. It was very popular in the period of the Jātakas.[42] In the Rāmāyaṇa it is a favourite instrument of the songsters,[43] and similar is the case with the Mbh.[44] Kauṭilya also mentions it.[45]

The Vāyu refers to Vīṇā at four places mostly associating it with Śiva and the Kurus. Of Śiva it was a pet instrument.

Veṇu: The ṚV. mentions Vāṇa and DAS suggests the Veṇu might have been a later corruption of Vāṇa. But there is no definite opinion on this point.[46] In the Jātakas, however, the Veṇu or flute is found to be a popular wind instrument.[47] The epics also mention Veṇu.[48]

The Vāyu associates it with the Kurus already mentioned above.

Dancing: In the ṚV. we find that "dancing was practised and dancing of maidens is several times mentioned; it seems that men also danced occasionally in the open air, as a metaphor alludes to the dust of the dancing feet of men.[49] In the Ś. Br. the Apsarasas are described as engaged in dance, song and play.[50] But the Kinnaras are not mentioned in the Vedas. In the Jātakas we find dancing as a despised

---

37. Cf. *IC*. 4. 451 and *JAOS*. 13.
38. *IC*. 4, 451 and *JAOS*. 13.
39. *SBE*. 8. 38.
40. P. 401.
41. DAS, 234.
42. MEHTA, 313-34.
43. *IC*. 4. 450 ff.
44. *JAOS*. 13.
45. P. 125. For the history of Viṇā in later period, cf. *ABORI*. 12. 362 ff.
46. Cf. DAS, 233.
47. MEHTA, 315.
48. *IC*. 4. 451 and *JAOS*. 13.
49. *CHI*. 1. 102-3 and DAS, 236.
50. MACDONELL, op. cit., 134.

calling.[51] In them we find Apsarasas and Kinnaras associated with dancing.[52] Pāṇini, in his comments upon the root nṛt—to dance—mentions two persons named Śilālin and Kṛśāśvin as the authors of two sets of sūtras on dancing.[53] The Arthaśāstra deals with the life and duties of dancing girls.[54]

It appears that the art of dancing was cultivated by the ladies of the royal family and the families of the rich from very early times.[55] But by the period of the Jātakas it seems to have declined in the estimation of the members of the higher strata of society. It subsequently tended to become a profession of a hereditary caste.

The custom of association of dancing girls is nowhere evident till the time of Kauṭilya at the latest; and its origin might be assigned to a period of about 300 A.D. as Kālidāsa some time later shows awareness of it and several Purāṇas devote their attention to it.[56]

In the Vāyu we find dancing connected mostly with Śiva and with Kinnaras, Apsarasas and Gandharvas. Our text is silent on the point whether dancing was a despised calling but the fact that god Śiva himself danced and the munis worshipped that deity with dance and song would lead us to infer otherwise. Except in one instance, all references to dancing in the Vāyu occur in mythological setting and their value may be judged accordingly. The one instance, referred to above, which occurs in genealogical accounts is also doubtful as the reading is confusing, and thus there is nothing to suggest as to whether dancing was a favourite pastime with the royal ladies or not. There is, however, one certain chronological pointer to the Vāyu material on dancing, i.e., regarding the custom of dancing girls, attached to temple-establishments. The Vāyu is absolutely ignorant of it. Since this custom had attracted the attention of several Purāṇas we might naturally have expected reference to it in the Vāyu if it had known it. Thus tentatively it becomes a good proposition to make that the Vāyu-material on dancing can be relegated to a time prior to the third century A.D.

On the art of dancing itself the Vāyu has some technical details to give us and they are already dealt with by Mr. DIKSHITAR in his work quoted above. In the absence of any studied information on the ancient history of this aspect of dancing we are unable to comment on the same. It must be stated, however, that this material also is included in the probably interpolated portion referred to above.

RE'SUME'

Some observations may here be made as they are indicated in our discussion of the musical instruments. The number of these instruments found in the Vāyu is not very large. Few of them are mentioned

51. *CHI*. 1. 207; LAW, op. cit., 179; MEHTA, 312-3. 52. MEHTA, 313.
53. POPLEY, 9. 54. ALTEKAR, 214. 55. *Ibid*. 213. 56. *Ibid*. 214-5.

in the RV., many in the Jātakas and a few in the epics and later literature. Our text shows no reminiscences of the various theories of the origin of music current in later mythology. We, no doubt, find Śiva closely associated with music but the information does not amount to a set theory that Śiva was the founder-deity of Hindu music. The association of music with the ritual is as old as the Vedas but its connection with the Gandharvas is certainly not Vedic though anterior to the period of the Jātakas. It must also be noted in passing that the whole of our information from the Vāyu on music is unconnected with the historical setting and is wrapped up with mythological lining. It is in this perspective that we have to judge the antiquity of this material.

There is a *lacuna* in the Vāyu statements regarding the chanting of the Sāmaveda by the Gandharvas. With the present condition of our researches it is impossible to fix its location chronologically.

The Vāyu has two chapters (86. 3 ff. to 87 end) which deal exclusively with music—especially on the theoretical side of it. It should be noted that some Mss. omit this portion of our text. As DIKSHITAR has dealt with this material in his "*Some Aspects of the Vāyu Purāṇa*",[57] it would be an unnecessary repetition to discuss the same here. It will suffice to refer to his chronological findings in this connection. "Taking the first chapter we find that the rules which are laid down are a mingling of both the schools, orthodox and secular. The Purāṇa does not mention either the famous author Bharata or his treatise. We have, therefore, to credit these portions of the Purāṇa as materials of an earlier epoch, earlier than the Bharatanāṭya Śāstra. It may be noted in passing that in some respects the injunctions agree with those of the Nāradīya Śikṣā.[58]

Again the names of *tānas* which are found in the text are different from those found in extant works on music. Thus we are forced to assume that the Vāyu contents of music are certainly old, older than any regular treatise on the science of music.[59]

It has already been observed that some Mss. omit this portion of the text and it is likely that it did not form part of the original text and was probably incorporated into the text afterwards. But even this interpolated matter is old as will be obvious from the findings of DIKSHITAR.

57. Pp. 34-7. 58. *Ibid.* 34. 59. *Ibid.* 35.

CHAPTER IX

WAR AND WEAPONS

Of War in General : Unfortunately the Vāyu sheds little light on the art of war in ancient India. The wars alluded to in the text belong mostly to the domain of mythology and hence of little historical value.

Composition of the Army : The technical term *caturaṅga-senā* which first occurs in the Jātakas[1] and which became a common feature in the description of an army in the epics and the later literature is not mentioned by our text,[2] nor does the text show us anything of the sixfold division of the army, the earliest references to which are found in Kauṭilya and the Mbh.[3] An army composed of elephants, horses and chariots (infantry is omitted probably for the sake of convenience) is no doubt mentioned in the description of war at the end of Kali. This reference might indicate the knowledge of a four-fold army. Here we might have a recognition of an existing fact of the time when the reference was incorporated into the text—i.e. perhaps at a time when such an army was known but still not so standardized as to be expressed by such a technical term as the caturaṅga-senā. Had this term become very common we would probably have not missed it in the text.

(i) *Infantry* : About this we have no gleaning from the texts.

(ii) *Cavalry* : In the later Saṁhitās we find references suggesting the use of horses, for riding had certainly become more common ; but no clear reference is made to the employment of cavalry in war.[4] Upto the period indicated by the Jātakas we do not find cavalry in the armies of ancient India. But by the time of Alexander cavalry had secured a place in the army of king Porus, though it did not prove effective against the disciplined Greek cavalry. We find also Kauṭilya emphasizing the use of cavalry in war.[5] In the Mbh. cavalry is recognized as a part of the armed forces.[6]

The Vāyu in its accounts of the genealogies is silent on cavalry. We have one instance in which Śatadhanvan is shown riding on a mare and Kṛṣṇa pursuing him in a chariot. But this had nothing to do with cavalry. The only instances referring to cavalry occur in connection

1. Dikshitar, *Hindu Administrative Institutions*, 293. Dikshitar says that the organisation of the Indian army which came to be known as *Caturaṅga*, both in epic Sanskrit and Pāli literature, was based on the ancient game of Chess. See his *War in Ancient India* pp. 153–156, for details of the discussion on this topic.

2. Cf. Chakravarty, 1–2. 3. *Ibid*. 3.

4. *CHI*. 1. 137 ; Dikshitar, op. cit., 174 ; cf. also Das, op. cit., 347 who says that employment of cavalry was known in the Ṛgvedic period.

5. Chakravarty, 35-6 ; see also Dikshitar, op. cit., 175–9. 6. *JAOS*. 13. 265.

with the accounts of the end of the Kali age and they point to an age indicated in the above discussion on the composition of the army.

(iii) *Elephants:* Elephants were not used in war in Vedic times. The YV. first mentions "an elephant trainer" (*hastipa*) and we find references in the AV. to domesticated elephants.[7] It is, however, in the Jātakas that we, for the first time, find elephants used in military operations[8] and the Great Epic has many instances of this kind.[9] Their use in the Indian armies of later times is too well-known to need mention here.[10]

The Vāyu genealogical accounts are silent on this except in its description of the end of the Kali age.

(iv) *Chariots:* In most of the ancient countries of the world we find that chariots were used in war. The war-chariot was known to ancient Egypt, Assyria and Babylonia.[11] The Aryans were experts in the use of war-chariots long before their entry into India and it is said that the introduction of the use of horse-drawn war-chariots into Babylonia in about 2000 B.C. was primarily due to them.[12] Two model chariots have been found at Harappa and cart-frames are common in the finds of Mohenjo-daro.[13] There are numerous references to war-chariots in the ṚV.[14] The AV. (IV. 125) contains a hymn addressed to war-chariot. But it appears that by the time of Alexander chariots had ceased to be the important arm of the armies of ancient India.[15] King Porus did make use of his chariotry against Alexander but with no useful result. The evidence from the Arthaśāstra shows that the Mauryas kept a chariot arm.[16] But we find a gradual decline of war-chariots from the scenes of war after the Mauryan period so that at the end of the 8th century A.D. we hear of them no more in the battles fought on the soil of India.[17]

In the Vāyu a halo of sanctity is attached to the chariot of Yayāti so much so that its history had been a topic of narration. The same was the case with the chariot of Kārtavīrya Arjuna and the epithet *rathin* has been used in the case of many kings too numerous to mention. This preponderance of the war-chariot tends to suggest that it was the only vehicle of war that could find a place in the summary narration of the dynasties of the kings of yore. The absence of references to cavalry

7. *CHI*. 1. 137. 8. CHAKRAVARTY, 47 ff. 9. *JAOS*. 13. 265.

10. See CHAKRAVARTY, 47 ff. and also DIKSHITAR, op. cit., p. 166 ff.

11. H. R. HALL, *The Ancient History of the Near East*, 181, 213, 446; SYDNEY SMITH. *Early History of Assyriya*, 11, 58, 213–4, 254.

12. HALL, op. cit., 213 and cf. also CHILDE, *Aryans*, 18, 27.

13. *Mohenjo-daro*, 2, 554 ff., 1. 273 fn. 2. *Further Excavations at Mohenjo-daro*, 1. 568–70.

14. Cf. DIKSHITAR, op. cit., 157 ff., DAS, op. cit., 226–7.

15. CHAKRAVARTY, 23. 16. DIKSHITAR, *War in Ancient India*, 161–3.

and elephants is instructive. The genealogical accounts are faithful to the facts of antiquity which testify that chariots alone have a hoary antiquity to their credit in the history of the art of war. The reference to war-chariots in the turmoil at the end of Kali need not be taken seriously in this connection.

Of the equipment and size of chariots we have little information from the Vāyu. The reference to 1000 horses drawing the chariot of Brahmā is historically valueless as it occurs in a mythological setting. It is likely that the chariot in which Kṛṣṇa pursued Śatadhanvan was a small-sized vehicle drawn by at least four horses (cf. *hayāḥ*, plural, not dual) for only Kṛṣṇa and Rāma appear to have been in that chariot. This is merely an inference though it is supported by the Mbh. which often mentions Kṛṣṇa in that manner.[18] The most common embellishment of the war-chariot which the Vāyu often mentions is its *dhvaja*. The standard or flag might have served as a distinctive device of the warrior as is often the case in the Mbh.[19] The Mbh., however, often mentions *chhattra* also in this connection and HOPKINS says that references to it in the Great Epic must have belonged to a later age and that it is to be "associated with the mass of effeminate luxuries depicted long after the original".[20] It is significant that the Vāyu does not mention this chhattra, a fact which is chronologically so suggestive that it can be incorporated in the floating tradition "long after the original."

It appears that only horses were yoked to the chariots. The references to asses, monkeys, etc., yoked to chariots as seen in a dream occur in a different context not concerned materially with our topic.

THE ANCIENT INDIAN ARMS AND WEAPONS

The Bow and the Arrows : The origin of the bow is still a mystery. It was used in ancient Egypt, Babylonia and Assyria. We find evidence of its use in about the 3rd or 4th millenium B.C. by the people of the Indus Valley.[21] The evidence of comparative philology takes its use right upto the time of the primitive Indo-Europeans.[22] In the ṚV. it is most frequently mentioned and practically no other weapon played any substantial part in the Vedic warfare.[23] "Throughout the ancient period it was the weapon *par excellence* of the Hindus." It gave its name to the military science and proficiency in its use was

---

17. For Bāṇa, the author of *Harṣa-Carita* (7th century A.D.) in his description of Emperor Harṣa's army does not make any reference to the use of chariots in war. See DIKSHITAR, op. cit., 165-6.

18. CHAKRAVARTY. 29. 19. *JAOS*. 13. 243-4. 20. *JAOS*. 13. 246.

21. *Mohenjo-daro*, 2. 392-3.

22. Cf. SCHRADER, *Prehistoric Antiquities of the Aryan Peoples*, and cf. also CHILDE, op. cit., 85, 92, 185.

23. *Ved. Ind.*, 1. 388.

the measure of one's reputation as a warrior.[24] In the Jātakas we find the science of archery having attained a high state of efficiency.[25] In the Mbh. we find that the bow, the arrow and the quiver are inevitably the most important.[26]

In the Vāyu also the bow is the most frequently mentioned weapon of war. There are some references which smack of its antiquity. The primitive king Pṛthu is said to have been born with a bow, arrows and an armour. It is difficult to decide whether '*ādyaṁ*' in the text is to be construed with the bow. If this is the interpretation, it would mean that Pṛthu was the inventor of the bow. But there is no other evidence to maintain this. The fact that king Yayāti, on the eve of his retirement to forest-life, relinquished his kingdom, bow and arrows to his son is highly suggestive of antiquity. It is interesting in this connection to note that in the funeral hymn of the ṚV. the last act of the funeral rite included removal of the bow from the right hand of the dead man (ṚV. X. 18. 9); and entry into the life of retirement almost amounted to civil death. The bow was also a unit of measurement and the science of archery passed into the list of the eighteen vidyās. The bow and arrows are also the objects of boons to warriors and of magical devices. Bows are also given pet-names and prominent personages of the tradition are often mentioned as having been the masters of the art of archery. All these facts about the bow and the arrow show their importance in the estimation of the Vāyu Purāṇa tradition.

About the size of the bow and the material of which it was made our text indicates nothing except that the bow-string was not tied to both ends always.

The Arrows and the Quiver: The arrows are often the subjects of magical devices in the Vāyu; e.g. we find arrows 'burning' cities and 'stunning' a whole city. It is equally interesting to hear of 'ever-full' quivers. Except from the word *śara* implying that arrows were made of reed there is no information from the Vāyu about the size and materials of arrows.

The Sword : *Asi and Khaḍga* : The use of the sword was known in ancient Near East[27] and to the ancient Greeks of Homer.[28] The kind of sword used by the Indo-Europeans was not originally a slashing but a thrusting weapon.[29] No sword or sword-blade was found in the Mohenjo-daro and Harappa excavations.[30] The Vedic Aryans used it rarely. In the Mbh., however, we find Bhīṣma favouring it even more

24. CHAKRAVARTY, 152, cf. also DIKSHITAR, op. cit., pp. 93-101.
25. MEHTA, 311. 26. *JAOS*. 13. 269 ff.
27. *Babylonia and Assyria*; cf. PETRIE, *Tools and Weapons*.
28. HALL, op. cit., 38; CHILDE, op. cit., 29, 51. 29. CHILDE, op. cit., 85.
30. *Mohenjo-daro*, 2. 35, cf. *JISOA*. 4. 101.

than the bow. The same book of the Mbh. also contains a legend regarding the mystic and divine origin of the sword.[31] "The epic age seemed to represent an epoch where the bow is yielding to the sword. In the final epic it reigns supreme."[32]

The Vāyu mentions *asi* only in connection with Śiva and the Bhūtas, i.e., in a mythological setting. Khaḍga is mentioned twice. The sword of Kaṁsa was sheathed and he had 'drawn' the weapon out of its sheath to kill his sister. The other reference is in connection with Kārtavīrya who is called a Khaḍgin. About the kinds of sword, its size and manner of use, the text tells us nothing. It is not clear whether Khaṭvāṅga was more of a kind of khaḍga than a separate weapon. Thus with our text the sword is not a popular and important weapon of war; and it is interesting to compare this with the information of the Mbh. The historical stages in the evolution of the use of the sword are pointers to the antiquity of the Vāyu material.

The Battle-axe: *Khaṇḍaparaśu*, *Kuliśa*, *Paraśu*, *Paraśva*, *Paṭṭiśa*: Copper axes have been discovered at Mohenjo-daro.[33] The use of the axe was known to the primitive Aryans.[34] It is mentinned in the ṚV. where it is more of a tool than a weapon.[35] Kauṭilya refers to *paraśu* and *kuṭhāra* as being two kinds of axes and the commentator explains the latter as the "kind of axe well-known".[36] The axe (*paraśu*, *paraśvadha*, *kuliśa*, and *kuṭhāra*) of the Mbh. might be termed as a royal weapon being chiefly used by the nobles and is often mentioned as a missile.[37]

The Vāyu does not mention the *kuṭhāra* known to Kauṭilya. Our Purāṇa associates the axe only with Śiva and not with any historical personage. It would be natural to expect *paraśu* mentioned in connection with Jāmadagnya Rāma as in the Mbh.,[38] but the Vāyu is silent on this. This is a fact which may reflect on the relative chronology of the respective references of the two works. Our Purāṇa, however, mentions two more varieties of the weapon noted neither by HOPKINS nor by CHAKRAVARTY. They are the *paraśva* and the *khaṇḍa-paraśu*. For want of corroborative evidence from other sources it is difficult to say as to what they exactly signify.

Kauṭilya classified *paṭṭiśa* with paraśu and kuṭhāra and it is stated that this paṭṭiśa was "a kind of bill or halbred".[39] But HOPKINS

31. HOPKINS, *Epic Mythology*, 176.
32. *JAOS*. 13. 284.
33. *Mohenjo-daro*, 1. 35 ff.; 2. 495.
34. CHILDE, op. cit., 85.
35. DAS, op. cit., 335; CHILDE, op. cit., 30.
36. CHAKRAVARTY, 171 fn. 1.
37. *JAOS*. 13. 291.
38. So far as the critical edition of the Ādiparvan goes he is simply called as "wielder of weapons" and is not associated with the *paraśu* distinctively; cf. *BDCRI*. 5. 157; but on the whole he does figure in the epic in this character. Cf. HOPKINS, *Epic Mythology*.
39. CHAKRAVARTY, 171 fn. 1.

takes the Mbh. paṭṭiśa to be a kind of spear.[40] It is difficult to say which of these two is signified by the Vāyu paṭṭiśa.

Discus : *Cakra* : It is suggested that a kind of boomerang which is supposed to return after striking the enemy, was used by the Sumerians in Assyria.[41] Even today the aborigines of Australia use this kind of weapon.[42] But it is not certain whether the discus is the same kind of weapon. The ṚV. mentions discus as a weapon of Indra but it does not appear to have ever become a national favourite.[43] Kauṭilya defines it as a movable machine (*cala-yantra*)[44] and the Mbh. describes it as a revolving weapon made of iron or steel and sharp-edged.[45]

The Vāyu associates its use mostly with Viṣṇu. The *cakra* of Viṣṇu appears to have been a missile and is called *astra*. It was probably a magical device for we are told that Viṣṇu "meditated" upon it before he made use of it. The reference to Śiva's *śāyaka-cakra* needs an explanation which it is difficult to suggest at this juncture.

The Club or the Mace : *Gadā* and *Mudgara* : It was known also to the people of the Indus Valley, as maces of stone and copper have been discovered at Mohenjo-daro and Harappa.[46] The use of a club or a mace was known to the Indo-Europeans.[47] The Ṛgvedic Aryans continued to use it.[48] The Śibis who opposed Alexander used mostly clubs and we have a statement from Plutarch that in the capital of Malloi Alexander received a blow on his neck from a club which forced him to lean for support against the wall with his face towards the enemy.[49] In the Mbh. it stands second to the bow in general esteem and appears to have been used more often than the sword. There we find a favourite club of a warrior having its own name and set-duels of club-men are often described in the epic.[50]

Except for the instance of Duryodhana acquiring the divine knowledge of wielding the *gadā* from Balabhadra all the Purāṇa references to *gadā* occur in the mythological setting connecting its use mainly with Śiva and Viṣṇu. We find *mudgara* also mentioned in connection with Śiva and the Bhūtas. But was it a mace? HOPKINS takes the epic *mudgara* to be a hammer made of iron which, according to him, was distinctly a missile.[51]

---

40. *JAOS*. 13. 289. 41. SYDNEY SMITH, op. cit., 63.

42. SOLLAS, *Ancient Hunters and their Modern Representatives*.

43. CHAKRAVARTY, 171. 44. *Ibid.*

45. *Ibid.* cf. also *BDCRI*. 5. 154 for Viṣṇu's cakra. According to DIKSHITAR it was a circular disc with a small opening in the middle. It was of three kinds of eight, six and four spokes. It was used in five or six ways. It resembled the quoit of the Sikhs today. The various uses of the disc were felling, whirling, rending, breaking, severing and cutting. See op. cit., p. 109.

46. CHILDE, op. cit., 85. 47. *Mohenjo-daro*, 1. 36. 48. DAS, op. cit.

49. CHAKRAVARTY, 168-9. 50. *JAOS*. 13. 281. 51. *Ibid.* 291.

Spear : *Śakti*, *Śūla* : Spear-heads have been discovered in Mohenjo-daro and Harappa.[52] The primitive Aryans knew the use of spear as a weapon of war[53] and the Vedic Aryans continued to use it.[54] The word *śakti* meaning 'spear' is found in the ṚV.[55] Kauṭilya defines it as a weapon provided with edges like a ploughshare.[56] In the Mbh. '*śakti*' means a spear or a javelin particularly used as an adjunct to the bow by the warrior in the chariot. There it does not essentially belong to the knight's furnishings.[57] The *śūla* is almost always associated with Śiva in early Indian coins. The *triśūla* is found on the coins of the Pāñcāla king Rudragupta, on other early coins and on the coins of Vema Kadphises.[58]

The Vāyu associates *śakti* only with Kārtikeya and *śūla* and *triśūla* with Śiva.

Ploughshare : *Hala* : The Vāyu mentions this as a weapon of Kṛṣṇa's brother Balarāma who is called Halin ; the only other wielder of this weapon is Śiva according to the Vāyu.[59]

Vajra : It is mentioned in the ṚV. mostly as a weapon of Indra.[60] It is suggested that it was originally made of stone and later of bone.[61] In later literature its use as a weapon becomes rare.

The Vāyu uses it mostly in connection with Indra and Śiva. It, however, shows a stage when vajra as a weapon was probably no longer in use and the term was often metaphorically used.

Śṛṅga : From the solitary reference to Indra as a bearer of *śṛṅga* in our Purāṇa it is difficult to arrive at any conclusion.

Tigma : Only Śiva is mentioned by the Vāyu to have used it. We have no information from other sources to discuss anything about it here.

Astra : They are mostly magical weapons supposed to have been used.[62]

Aṅkuśa : It was probably not a weapon of war, and was probably used only to control elephants.

Conch : *Śaṅkha :* Already referred to as a musical instrument.

Noose or Lasso : *Pāśa :* "The pāśa was a sort of lariat or lasso. It is mentioned in the ṚV. as one of the weapons of Varuṇa and Soma.[63] The Mbh. also makes allusions to it.[64]

The Vāyu mentions it only in connection with Śiva.

Defensive Armour : No defensive armour has been discovered from the Indus Valley. The ṚV. mentions *drāpi* and *varman* in the

52. *Mohenjo-daro*, 1. 53. Childe, op. cit., 85. 1. 54. Chakravarty, 166.
55. Das, op. cit., 334. 56. Chakravarty, 166. 57. *JAOS*. 13. 287-8.
58. Sankalia, *BDCRI*. 5. 153.
59. The Mbh. also associates Balarāma with this weapon ; cf. *BDCRI*. 5.
60. Das, 51. 61. *Ibid.*
62. Cf. *JAOS*. 13. 296 ff. for the views of Hopkins on the matter.
63. Chakravarty. 64. *Ibid.*

sense of coat-of-mail or body-armour.[65] The *varūtha* also finds mention in the ṚV. but it does not seem to have been much used by the warrior in those days.[66] The AV. uses the term *kavaca* in the sense of corselet or breast-plate.[67] In the 4th century B.C. we find that coats-of-mail were used by Indian kings in their wars against Alexander; for king Porus, according to the Greek writers, used metal armour.[68] Kauṭilya refers to different kinds of body-armour and he also furnishes us details about the construction of shields in his days. '*Kavaca*' according to him was an iron armour and he says that *varman* is a kind of protective clothing made of skin-hides of elephants, cattle, etc.[69] The Mbh. also makes frequent references to them.[70] Most of them are associated by our Purāṇa with Śiva and his associates. '*Kavaca*' however is mentioned by the Vāyu with reference to kings Pṛthu and Rukmakavaca. The fact that king Rukmakavaca killed "many who wore *kavaca*" with sharp arrows shows that these *kavacas* were probably not made of iron. If this can be assumed to have been the case, we have to remark that the genealogical portion in which this reference to *kavaca* occurs is faithful to the antiquity which it depicts; for we have no definite evidence up-to-date whether metal-armours were used by the warriors of Ṛgvedic Aryans; it is mentioned probably for the first time, in the AV.

Résumé :

It would be seen from the recorded information above that most of these weapons are associated either with Śiva, his followers and sons or occasionally with Viṣṇu and Indra. The only weapons associated with historical personages are: the bow, the club, the sword and the ploughshare. Of the defensive armour only the *kavaca* occurs in historical setting. Of all these weapons only the bow has the widest range of references to its credit. These facts corroborate the antiquity of the historical personages gleaned from works on political history. The genealogical lists of the Vāyu, as far as our information on weapons goes, do not show a type of tampering common in the Mbh. where we find cultural traits of later times mixed with the facts of antiquity. The Vāyu shows us the kings of yore only in their ancient military equipment and does not generally try to 'revise' the tradition in the light of its own material culture. This becomes more obvious when we take into account the observations already made regarding composition of the army, cavalry and war elephants. This is, of course, ***argumentum ex silentio***, still the chronological implications presented by them cannot be easily set aside unless shown otherwise.

---

65. DAS, op. cit. 336.
66. *Ibid.*
67. CHAKRAVARTY, 178.
68. *Ibid.*
69. *Ibid.*
70. *Ibid.* and also *JAOS*. 13. 305 ff.

CHAPTER X

FLORA AND FAUNA

I. PLANT-WORLD

Of Plants in General: In the ṚV. plants (*oṣadhi*) are personified as divine and a whole and a long hymn is devoted to their praise mainly with reference to their healing powers.[1] The same Veda often refers to Soma as the king of the plant-world.[2] By the time of the Br. Up. (IV. 5. 1) we find people holding a view that essence of water is embodied in the plants. If any other views were held regarding the origin of the plant-world we have no information on them so far.

In the Vāyu also the plant-world is closely associated with Soma who is called the "consecrated lord" of the vegetable kingdom.

Classification of Plants: Rudimentary ideas about classification of plants can be found in the ṚV. and the AV.[3] Roughly speaking the vegetable world is divided, in the Vedic literature, between *oṣadhi* or *vīrudh* (plants) and *vana* or *vṛkṣa* (trees).[4] The Manu-smṛti, however, divides the plant-world into four classes[5] which are also found in the works of Caraka and Suśruta.[6] This fourfold classification is:

(i) *Vanaspati*: Trees not bearing flowers.

(ii) *Vānaspatya*: Trees bearing flowers and fruits.

(iii) *Auṣadhis*: Plants. Commentators further subdivide it into two classes, such as (a) annuals or perennials and (b) grass or *tṛṇa*.

(iv) *Vīrudh*: Creeper. They are further subdivided into (a) *latā* and (b) *vallī* and *gulma*.

The Vāyu classification of plants into *grāmyāraṇya* (or *grāmya* and *āraṇya*) and *yajñiya* is not found in any of these works. This classification, however, reminds us of an age when sacrifices were very often performed so that popular nomenclature regarded plants used in sacrifices as forming a separate class altogether. Such a system of classification would obviously be in harmony with the spirit of the Brāhmaṇas but we have no information so far whether there were any works which adopted such a classification.

The other system of classification is certainly cruder than that of the Manu and Caraka, though it comes closer to them than to the one found in the ṚV. For we find Vanaspati and Vṛkṣa (i. e. Vānaspatya

---

1. MACDONELL, *Vedic Mythology*, 154. 2. *Ibid.*
3. *Cultural Heritage of India* (Rāmakrishna Centenary Volume), 3. 42.
4. *Ved. Ind.*, 1. 125. 5. *Cultural Heritage of India*, 3, 429.
6. G. F. MUJUMDAR, *Vanaspati*, and cf. also B. N. SEAL, *Positive Sciences of the Ancient Hindus*, 169.

in Caraka)—both the terms of the Vāyu have the same sense as in Caraka—as sub-species of Latā. But in Caraka and Suśruta Latā itself appears as a sub-species of Vīrudh, Vṛkṣa and Vānaspatya being there regarded as main classes. Again, in the Vāyu we find Vallī as a main class of which Gulmas and various kinds of grasses form the sub-species and Vīrudh is here regarded as a separate main class. The case is apparently different with Caraka where Virudh alone is the main class, the other being its sub-species. There is another difference to be noted. In the Vāyu Auṣadhi signifies the genera of the whole plant-world while in Caraka Auṣadhi signifies one of the four main species of the plant-world. It has already been noted that the Manu has the same system of classification as in Caraka and the antiquity of the Vāyu classification has to be estimated accordingly.

About the other modes of classification—medicinal, dietetic, etc.—we hear nothing from the Vāyu. This is another evidence of the comparatively archaic character of the system of classification employed in our Purāṇa. The plants referred to in the Purāṇa have been given below in alphabetical order :

Aguru : Kauṭilya knew it and gives its characteristics.[7] Caraka mentions it[8] and so does Suśruta who alludes to the oil being extracted from it and includes it in *tailavarga*.[9]

Akṣoṭa : Caraka mentions it in his *phalavarga* class of plants.[10]

Āmra : It is mentioned by Kauṭilya[11] and by Caraka and Suśruta in their system of classification.[12]

Aśvattha : It is the most important tree of the ṚV. and its fruit is described as sweet. Its wood was used for Soma vessels.[13] It is called *vanaspati* in the ṚV.

The Vāyu connects this tree with the grandeur of royalty, quite in fitting with its sanctity and its association with Soma as in the ṚV. Our Purāṇa, however, relates its use mostly in connection with the śrāddha.

Atasī : Kauṭilya mentions it[14] and according to Caraka it belongs to his 'oil group'.[15] It is called lin-seed and is included in *tailavarga* by Suśruta.[16]

Badarī : It is mentioned by Kauṭilya as an acid fruit.[17]

Campaka : It is referred to by Suśruta and also in the Bṛhat-Saṁhitā.[18]

---

7. *Trans.* 90. 8. *Vsp.* 96. 9. *Ibid.* 100, 121.
10. *Ibid.* 112. 11. See *Ind. Verb* 12. *Vsp.* 92–111.
13. Apte, op. cit., 143, and cf. also Mac. *HSL.* 146. 14. P. 202.
15. *Vsp.* 113. 16. *Ibid.* 115–20. 17. *Trans.* 114. 18. *Vsp.* 119, 132.

Caṇaka : Caraka mentions Caṇaka[19] and Suśruta takes it amongst pulses.[20]

Candana : Kauṭilya,[21] Caraka and Suśruta mention it.[22]

Dāḍima : Caraka and Suśruta mention it.[23] Varāhamihira states how it should be planted and associates its growth with Anūpa region.[24]

Darbha : Kauṭilya mentions it.[25]

Devadāru : It is mentioned by Kauṭilya.[26] According to Suśruta oil can be extracted from it.[27]

Drākṣa : Caraka and Suśruta mention it.[28] Varāhamihira describes how it should be planted and states that it grows in Anūpa region.[29]

Durvāra : It is mentioned in the AV.[30] and in the Bṛhat-Saṁhitā.[31]

Godhūma : In the ṚV. we find only the Yava referred to which in later Saṁhitas means barley. We do not know whether cultivation of wheat was known to the Ṛgvedic Aryans.[32] In the later Saṁhitas we find that wheat was cultivated.[33] By the time of Kauṭilya it had become quite familiar.[34] Caraka says that it unites fractures, prolongs life and promotes nutrition.[35] Suśruta also describes its nutritive value.[36]

Gṛñjana : Caraka includes it in his classification under the group of greens (*haritavarga*). He mentions it as *gṛñjanaka*.[37]

Ikṣu : The AV. mentions *ikṣu* (I. 34. 5). Kauṭilya terms it under *kṣāra*.[38] He states that sugar-cane crops are worst (i. e. very difficult to grow as they are subject to various evils and require much care and expenditure).[39] He also refers to sugar.[40] Caraka mentions its medicinal properties[41] and the Bṛhat-Saṁhita also refers to it.[42]

Jambū : Kauṭilya mentions *jambūphala*.[43] The Jaina Sūtras refer to *jambū* tree as an abode of a deity.[44] Caraka mentions its medicinal property and says that it relieves one of vomitting.[45] The Bṛhat-Saṁhitā lays down certain rules regarding its planting.[46] According to him it grows in the Anūpa region.[47]

Kadalī : Kauṭilya mentions *kadaḷī*. He says that it is procured from Aroha which according to a commentator is a place in the Himalayas.[48] He even mentions a process of making metals soft by treating them with the powder of *kadalī*.[49] It is known to Suśruta and Varāhamihira.[50]

Kālāmra : It is alluded to in the AV.[51]

---

19. *Ibid.* 107. 20. *Ibid.* 115. 21. *Ind. Verb.*
22. *Vsp.* 97–103, etc. 23. *Ibid.* 102–14. 24. *Ibid.* 40, 63, 68.
25. *Ind. Verb.* 26. *Ibid.* 27. *Vsp.* 121. 28. *Ibid.* 91–116.
29. *Ibid.* 40, 63, 68. 30. *Ibid.* 163. 31. *Ibid.* 134.
32. *CHI.* 1. 99–100. 33. *Ibid.* 135. 34. *Trans.* 144. 35. *Vsp.* 106.
36. *Ibid.* 115. 37. *Ibid.* 113. 38. *Trans.* 114. 39. *Ibid.* 145.
40. *Ibid.* 113. 41. *Vsp.* 91. 42. *Ibid.* 134. 43. *Trans.* 95.
44. *SBE.* 45, 48. 45. *Vsp.* 95. 46. *Ibid.* 38–40. 47. *Ibid.* 68.
48. *Trans.* 92. 49. P. 82. 50. *Vsp.* 63, 68, 99, 123.
51. *Vsp.* 174.

Kapittha : Kauṭilya shows that oil was extracted from this plant.[52] It is also mentioned by Buddhaghoṣa in his commentary on the Dīgha Nikāya.[53] Caraka and Suśruta knew it.[54] The Bṛhat-Saṁhitā mentions the mode of its planting.[55]

Kāśa : It is suggested that the *darbha* of the hymns of the AV. might be the same as *Kāśa*. It is still used for sacrificial purposes.[56] The Bṛhat-Saṁhitā refers to it.[57]

Kāśmarya : Caraka mentions its medicinal properties and also its dietetic value.[58] Suśruta does the same.[59]

Khādira : It is mentioned in the AV.[60] Caraka says that these trees grow in the Jāṅgala (forest) region.[61] Suśruta takes these plants as beneficial in the Pāṇḍu disease.[62] According to Varāhamihira its overgrowth indicates impending famine.[63]

Kharjūra : The Taittirīya Saṁhitā (II. 4. 9. 2) contains a myth about the origin of this plant. Formerly *yatis* did not offer sacrifice to Indra. Indra was incensed and cut off their heads into pieces and threw them to wild dogs. The hungry dogs tore open the skulls of these yatis and as these were scattered about on the ground they took root and grew into *Kharjjūras*.[64] Caraka and Suśruta give its medicinal and dietetic properties.[65]

The Vāyu apparently contains a version of the same story as it is found in the Taittirīya Saṁhitā. But we do not know as to why Manu should come into the story of the Vāyu at all. Again the *yatis* here are Varūtrins who were the descendants of Bhṛgu and that they should be opposed to sacrifices to Indra is really interesting to note. Instead of dogs the Vāyu mentions Vṛkas (wolves). The description of the Varūtrins appears to be strange in the true Purāṇic setting. They appear as sacrificers to gods (*Surayājakāḥ*) and in the same breath we are told how they contrived to destroy the institution of sacrifice. Their connection with the origin of the date-palms is pregnant with some ethnological suggestions, probably locating the Bhṛgus in Persia—the home of date-palms—who were opposed to the set of Indo-Aryans migrating into India.

Considering the contents of this story of the Vāyu which offer contradictory details, one is tempted to infer that its material is really very ancient which the final redactors of the Purāṇas retained though they did not seem to have understood it.

Kiṁśuka : Suśruta mentions it.[66]

Kuraṇḍaka : Suśruta mentions *Kurantaka*.[67]

---

52. *Trans*. 116. 53. *Vsp*. 65. 54. *Ibid*. 11-7.
55. *Ibid*. 44. 56. *Ibid*. 178. 57. *Ibid*. 138. 58. *Ibid*. 111.
59. *Ibid*. 116-9. 60. *Ibid*. 168-72. 61. *Ibid*. 67.
62. *Ibid*. 99. 63. *Ibid*. 133. 64. *QJMS*. 21. 177.
65. *Vsp*. 66. *Vsp*. 117-9. 67. *Ibid*. 119.

Kuśa: In the Jātakas we find people accustomed to the art of ascertaining the presence of water through its vegetable accessories amongst which Kuśa is mentioned as one.[68] It might be the same as *darbha* of the Vedas.[69] Kauṭilya mentions the oil extracted from its fruit and states that its oil, if it is poured over the fire, burns even in the storm.[70]

Lakuca: Caraka and Suśruta mention it.[71] Varāhamihira says that it should be planted by means of cuttings[72] and that they grow it in Anūpa region.[73]

Laśuna: It is mentioned by Caraka and Suśruta.[74]

Māṣa: Kauṭilya mentions the proper time for its cultivation.[75] It is referred to by Caraka, Suśruta and Varāhamihira.[76]

Masūra: Kauṭilya refers to the proper season of its cultivation.[77] It is known to Caraka and Suśruta.[78]

Mudga: Kauṭilya mentions the proper season of its cultivation.[79] It is also mentioned by Caraka and Suśruta.[80]

Mātuluṅga: According to Kauṭilya it bears acid fruits.[81] Caraka states its medical properties namely that it promotes cheerfulness and relieves one of vomitting effect.[82]

Nāga: It is mentioned in the book of "Milindā".[83]

Naktamāla: Kauṭilya mentions the sticks of *naktamāla* used for caning offenders.[84] Caraka says that it cures *Pruritius*[85] and according to Varāhamihira it grows in Anūpa region.[86]

Nīpa: Mentioned by Caraka and Suśruta. Varāhamihira[87] says that it grows in Anūpa region.[88]

Nyagrodha: The ṚV. does not mention it but it is referred to in the AV. though only twice.[89] The Ś. Br. mentions its sweet drink.[90] In the Ups. we find seeds of this tree mentioned in similes.[91] But there it does not seem to indicate the symbolism of strength. Kauṭilya does not mention it and Caraka and Suśruta allude to its various properties.[92]

In the Vāyu we find it regarded sacred, symbolising strength and is mentioned accordingly in similes thus pointing to the post-Vedic character of the references.

Padma (*Ambuja*, *Kamala*, *Kumuda*, *Utpala*, etc.): The lotus had not become an object of similes or metaphor in the ṚV.[93] but by

68. *Ibid.* 138-9. 69. *Ibid.* 178. 70. *Trans.* 502-4. 71. *Vsp.* 111-6.
72. *Ibid.* 63. 73. *Ibid.* 68. 74. *Ibid.* 113-8. 75. *Ibid.* 202.
76. *Ibid.* 44-8, 107-16. 77. *Ibid.* 202. 78. *Ibid.* 107-15. 79. *Ibid.* 302.
80. *Ibid.* 107-15. 81. *Trans.* 114. 82. *Vsp.* 92-4. 83. *SBE.* 36. 130.
84. *Trans.* 278. 85. *Vsp.* 92. 86. *Ibid.* 68. 87. *Ibid.* 93, 112, 16, 138.
88. *Ibid.* 138. 89. MAC. *HSL.* 146-7. 90. *SBE.* 44. 317.
91. *Ibid.* 1. 104. 92. *Vsp.* 102, 112. 93. APTE, op. cit.

the time of the Ś. Br. we find it achieving a symbolic character; for we find there[94] the lotus-leaf as a symbol of the womb of speech and water. It is even called immortal light.[95] The symbolism of the lotus is closely woven into the theories of cosmology in the Ups. where the concept of the lotus-birth of the manifested creative deity often occurs.[96] The idea of the lotus symbolising the earth is found in the Taittirīya Saṁhitā and the Ś. Br.[97] But the conception of Brahmā, the Creator, himself born of a lotus which arose out of the navel of Nārāyaṇa, is not found in the Vedic texts; and corresponding representations in art do not appear before the fifth or sixth centuries A.D.[98] The idea is no doubt found in the Vāyu but not in its cosmological chapters.

Śrī in the ṚV. is an attribute of Agni and in the Brāhmaṇas and the Ups. we find Śrī-Lakṣmī often as an angel. There is, however, a Śrīsūkta, said to be of the period of Bṛ. Up.[99] which corresponds in all respects with the iconographic formula of the early Indian art. Here we find her closely associated with the lotus symbol The early Buddhist sculptures of about the 2nd century B.C. already show her connection with lotus.[100]

Palāśa: It is mentioned in the ṚV.[101] The Ś. Br. refers to *palāśa* and compares it with Brahman and Soma.[102] It was often used in the ritual.[103] The Ait. and Ś. Br. contain myths about its origin.[104] In later works we naturally find it mentioned.[105]

Panasa: Kauṭilya, Caraka, Suśruta and Varāhamihira[106] mention it, the last one saying that it grows in Anūpa region.[107]

Pārijāta: Kauṭilya mentions its pleasant colour in his description of Saugandhika gem.[108]

Parūṣaka: Kauṭilya, Caraka, Suśruta and Varāhamihira[109] mention it.

Pāṭalā: Pātalā is mentioned by Caraka and Suśruta.[110] Varāhamihira also mentions it as a commodity.[111]

Paṭolā: It is mentioned by Caraka and Suśruta.[112]

Plakṣa: The AV. refers to it.[113] Kauṭilya mentions the seed of *plakṣa*.[114] It is mentioned in the Gītā as the first of immovable entities.[115]

Priyaṅgu: Kauṭilya,[116] Caraka and Suśruta mention it.[117]

---

94. *SBE*. 41. 215 ff. 95. *Ibid*. 43. 365 ff.
96. A. K. Coomarswamy, *Elements of Buddhist Iconography*, 18 ff.
97. *Ibid*. 18. 98. *Ibid*. 99. *Ibid*. 100. *Ibid*. 22. 101. *Vsp*. 155.
102. *SBE*. 12. 90; 41. 53; 44. 221. 103. *Ibid*. 41. 298; 44. 373–5.
104. *QJMS*. 22. 214 ff. 105. *Ind. Verb*. 106. *Vsp*. 68, 106–12.
107. *Ibid*. 68. 108. *Trans*. 88. 109. *Vsp*. 102–37. 110. *Ibid*. 96, 120.
111. *Ibid*. 132. 112. *Ibid*. 92, 120. 113. *Ibid*. 168. 114. *Trans*. 348.
115. *SBE*. 8. 354. 116. *Ind. Verb*. 117. *Vsp*. 91–100.

Śāka: Kauṭilya mentions it many times[118] and Varāhamihira also refers to it.[119]

Śālmala: It is mentioned in the ṚV.[120] According to Kauṭilya *śālmali* trees are good for denoting boundaries of villages.[121]

Sarala: It is mentioned by Kauṭilya[122] and Suśruta.[123]

Śleṣmātaka: It is mentioned by Kauṭilya,[124] and by Caraka and Suśruta.[125]

Udāra: Udāraka is mentioned by Kauṭilya as food.[126]

Udumbara: It is very frequently mentioned in the Brāhmaṇas.[127] A throne-seat made of Udumbara was used in the coronation ritual.[128] It was also considerably used in other sacrifices. Kauṭilya mentions it twice.[129]

Uśīra: Kauṭilya mentions its plantation.[130] Suśruta and Varāhamihira also refer to it.[131]

Tāla: Kauṭilya,[132] Caraka and Suśruta mention it.[133]

Tamāla: Caraka mentions it.[134]

Tila: Kauṭilya,[135] Caraka, Suśruta and Varāhamihira mention it.[136]

Vaṭa: Kauṭilya mentions it.[137]

Veṇu: It is often mentioned by Kauṭilya.[138] Suśruta also refers to it.[139]

Vibhītaka: It is mentioned by Caraka, Suśruta and Varāhamihira.[140]

Vrīhi: It is known to Kauṭilya,[141] Caraka and Suśruta.[142]

Yava: The exact significance of Yava in the ṚV. is uncertain[143] but in later Saṁhitās it indicates 'barley'.[144] Kauṭilya mentions it many times.[145]

It would have been noted so far that most of these plants mentioned by the Vāyu are found in the Arthaśāstra and the standard works of Caraka and Suśruta. These latter, however, mention other numerous plant-names which are not found in the Vāyu. It is difficult to make any chronological findings from this but certain indications have been already noted above. The names of *dvīpas* after plant-names deserve some treatment here. They are Kuśadvīpa, Śākadvīpa, Śālmalidvīpa, Plakṣadvīpa, Jambudvīpa, Puṣkaradvīpa. It has been suggested that

118. *Ind. Verb.* 119. *Vsp.* 138. 120. *Ibid.* 155. 121. *Trans.* 51.
122. *Ibid.* 121. 123. *Vsp.* 121. 124. *Trans.* 512. 125. *Vsp.* 112–9.
126. *Trans.* 115. 127. *SBE.* 41. 35 ff.; 43. 189; 203 etc.
128. *Ibid.* 41. 35 ff, 73, 83. 129. *Ind. Verb.* 130. P. 117.
131. *Vsp.* 100–2, 138. 132. *Ind. Verb.* 133. *Vsp.* 116–20. 134. *Vsp.* 68.
135. *Ind. Verb.* 136. *Vsp.* 68, 108, 115, 132. 137. *Ind. Verb.*
138. *Ibid.* 139. *Vsp.* 115–9. 140. *Ibid.* 96–120. 141. *Ind. Verb.*
142. *Vsp.* 106–26. 143. *CHI.* 1. 100. 144. *Ibid.* 145. *Ind. Verb.*

these names might be indicative of regions where these trees predominated.[146] The Purāṇa explicitly mentions their derivation from a big tree of that name in the particular dvīpa. All these trees have no history so old as the ṚV. Only the *Śālmali* was known to the Ṛgvedic Aryans. The *Aśvattha*, the most important of the ṚV. plants, has no dvīpa after it. Again *Udumbara* is very frequent in the ritual of the Brāhmaṇas and still it has no dvīpa to its credit. The *Nyagrodha* comes to be used in later Vedic literature and it too has no dvīpa. The same can be said of the *Palāśa*. Of these dvīpas only the Jambudvīpa is mentioned by the Jātakas[147] which, though they mention *plakṣa*, do not refer to Plakṣadvīpa. We have seen above that the names after whom dvīpas were so called were all of them known to Kauṭilya and to later writers. Kauṭilya, however, does not mention the dvīpas of those names. It would thus lead us to infer that the practice of naming dvīpas after particular names of trees has come into vogue in the period of the Jātakas and the idea might have been developed further in later times.

None of these plants are associated with the genealogical lists except the Ṛgvedic *aśvattha* tree. This reflects something on the antiquity of that portion of the Purāṇa.

II. Animal-world

Of the Animal-World in General : The twofold classification of animals (viz., domestic and wild) is found in the Ś. Br. which mentions seven domestic and seven wild animals.[148] The number seven should be noted. This classification was based on practical experience and had no scientific precision. The fourfold classification into *aṇḍaja*, *udbhijja*, *svedaja* and *jarāyuja* may be traced to the period of the Chh. Up. which mentions the terms *aṇḍaja*, *jīvaja* and *udbhijja*.[149] The Jain Sūtras also mention this fourfold classification[150] and the same is found in the Gītā,[151] the Manu-smṛti[152] and in the 'Questions of Milindā'.[153] Thus before the rise of the Christian era this method of classification of animals had become a matter of common knowledge and later on we find Caraka and Suśruta very much familiar with it.[154] Suśruta, however, is more elaborate in his system of classification and mentions *vyāla*, *paśu*, *kṛmi*, *kīṭa*, *pipīlaka*, *sarīsṛpa*, etc.[155]

There is also another classification which divides the animal-world into two broad categories, viz., (i) *yonija* (sexually generated), (ii) *a-yonija* (not sexually generated). The *jarāyuja* and *aṇḍaja*, according to this classification, come under *yonija*. This is the system of classification adopted by Patañjali and he gives several alternative

146. *Vsp*. 70. 147. Mehta. 148. *SBE*. 26. 213 ; 41. 40 fn. ; 43. 211, 277.
149. Seal, 181. 150. *SBE*. 22. 11. 151. *Ibid*. 8. 339. 152. *Ibid*. 25. 15 ff.
153. *Ibid*. 36. 101. 154. Seal, 181. 155. *Ibid*. 178–80.

definitions of the animals of the *a-yonija* class. He calls them *kṣudra-jantavaḥ* (small animals).[156]

It is interesting to note here that the Vāyu agrees closely with the classification of the Ś. Br. which is not observed by later writers. The mention of seven domestic animals in Ś. Br. confirms the above finding. Unfortunately, the Ś. Br. does not mention their names while the Vāyu does. The antiquity of this Vāyu material can be further judged from the fact that the elephant is included in wild animals by the Vāyu.

The fourfold classification of the Vāyu can be reasonably assigned to a period later than that of the Chh. Up. and earlier than that of Suśruta ; for we have found Suśruta more elaborate and systematic than the Vāyu in this connection. The Vāyu gives (without order) a list of *svedaja* creatures while Suśruta's knowledge of the subject decidedly appears to be more advanced. He mentions 18 classes of *kīṭas*, and 3 varieties of scorpions and he describes *pipīlakas*, *makṣikas*, *maśakas*, etc., in a more systematic manner.[157]

The last mode of classification of which Patañjali had some knowledge, also has no corroboration in the Vāyu. The Purāṇa, no doubt, uses the words *yonija* and *a-yonija* but in a quite different context, viz., in regard to the origin of sages. Even if this is regarded as being a fore-knowledge of such classification still it can be maintained that the Vāyu material is more archaic in character.

For want of detailed information on various animals, referred to in the First Part from other sources, we have dealt here only with the most important of them about whom we get at least some information from elsewhere.

Aśva : The horse figures considerably in the Vedic ritual. The aśvamedha sacrifice is well-known. The story of its domestication goes over to the Indo-European age[158] and the Vedic Aryans had their chariots drawn by horses though riding does not appear to have been known.[159] The Ś. Br. says that a horse draws nothing else than a chariot.[160] We have seen above how cavalry came to be employed in ancient India.

The conclusions arrived at in our discussion of the cavalry can be confirmed here and nothing more need be added.

Cow : The belief in the sanctity of the cow seems to have been inherited by the Indo-Aryans from prehistoric times before they had separated from the Iranians.[161] The cow is sacred to the Ṛgvedic

---

156. *Ibid.* 177–8.

157. *Suśrute Kalpasthāna*, Chapter VIII (Calcutta ed. 2. 287–301).

158. SCHRADER, op. cit., 261 ff. ; CHILDE, op. cit.

159. MAC., *HSL*. 150. 160. *SBE*. 44. 317. 161. *ERE*. 4. 224.

Aryans for we find cow addressed as Aditi. The earth itself is often spoken of as the cow.[162] In the AV. we find the earth conceived under the figure of a cow and a clear reference to the story of her being 'milched' by divine beings and men.[163] The history of this belief continues to our own times. In the Ups. we find speech meditated upon as cow.[164]

The practice of making gifts of cows to priests as fees for their services in rituals was very common in Vedic times. This might be due to the fact that the cow often served as a standard of value right from the times of the ṚV.[165]

"Though the cow-killer is in the White Yajurveda already said to be punishable with death, the ṚV. does not express an absolute prohibition, for the wedding hymn shows that even the cow was slaughtered on solemn occasions while bulls are several times described as having been sacrificed to Indra in large numbers."[166] The Ś. Br. prohibits eating of cow-flesh but still we find there Yājñavalkya saying, "I, for one, eat it, provided it is tender". The Gṛhya Sūtras permit the slaughter of cow on the arrival of a guest especially at a wedding or a sacrifice.[167] Not only the cow but its five products (*pañcagavya*) also appear to be sacred in the Mbh. as purifying agents[168] and similar is the case with the Dharma-śāstra works.[169] The Vedas appear to be silent on this aspect of her sanctity.

The Vāyu too shows the sanctity of the cow but regarding the *pañcagavya* it is silent. Regarding the relation of cow to speech it appears we can point to the story of Gāyatrī in the Vāyu as its equivalent. The Vāyu also shows us that cow served as a means of exchange and except *niṣkas*, *suvarṇas*, etc., we have no other evidence for use of coinage as currency. We have in the Vāyu an instance of how the cow served as a means of exchange, e.g. Viśvāmitra's wife sold her middle son for 100 cows. This culture-complex which is found in the genealogical lists must then be considered as antic, thus indicating the authenticity of the contents of the lists.

Elephants: The Ṛgvedic sages seem to have regarded it a strange creature and it is mentioned only in two passages of the ṚV. It appears, however, that by the end of the Ṛgvedic period attempts were made to catch the animal. In the YV. and the AV. the elephant is quite familiar[170] though its domestication must have taken some time.

---

162. MAC., *HSL.* 110. 163. *ERE.* 4. 225. 164. *SBE* 15. 193.
165. *CHI.* 1. 97; MAC., *HSL.* 167; cf. also *SBE.* 41. 46–51; *SBE.* 44. 46, 113, 115, 503 etc.
166. MAC., *HSL.* 149. 167. *ERE.* 4. 225. 168. *Ibid.* 4. 225.
169. *SBE.* 2. 276 fn.; 7. 89; 14. 168–72; 25. 187–90 etc. 170. MAC., *HSL.* 148.

The elephant figures considerably in the Jātakas.[171] By 300 B.C. it was quite familiar as a domesticated animal.[172]

It should be noted that the Ś. Br. enjoins that elephants should not be accepted as gifts[173] and elephants do not at all figure in the ritual as do the cows, goats and horses.

The Vāyu evidence indicates two different chronological stages in in its contents about this animal. In the first, the elephant was purely a wild animal and was not domesticated. In the second, it shows elephants as objects of gifts to Brahmins in śrāddha and mentions it as a yajñīya animal. It refers to elephant-stables and to their use in war at the end of the Kali age. Accordingly this material of the text belongs to a later chronological stratum (i.e. from about the time of Buddha) though we are unable to fix the lower limit of time. The geographical implications of this evidence is obvious from the fact that elephants abound in the north-east end of India and at the foot of the Himalayas. It is regarded as one of the 'jewels' of the paramount sovereign. The redactors of the Purāṇa were very familiar with the animal as they mention the use of Aṅkuśa for controlling it.

Lion : The lion was very familiar to the Ṛgvedic Aryans and they often allude to his roaring and they were even aware of catching lions in snares.[174] The lion typifying vigour is mentioned in the Ś. Br.[175] In the days of Kauṭilya we find that a Superintendent of Forest had to look after certain forest products which included lion-skin.[176]

The information of the Vāyu is of a very general nature and does not make us infer anything about its chronology. The statement that lions are made to serve when domesticated and the reference to caging of lions appear to show some advance after the Vedic period. It is difficult to say whether the yoking of lions to Skanda's chariots had any semblance of reality.

Tiger : It is unknown to the ṚV. but in the other Vedas it often figures as a beast of prey and the AV. describes the animal as man-eater (*puruṣāda*).[177] In the Ś. Br. we find the tiger as typifying vigour.[178] Kauṭilya mentions its skin as a forest product.

As compared with the lion the tiger figures less in the Vāyu. It does not appear as a vehicle of Durgā as in later mythology ; but a stage for this seems to have been prepared in the Vāyu statement that recitation of the Devī's name protects one from a tiger.

---

171. Mehta, Fick. 172. Mac., *HSL.* 148. 173. *SBE.* 26. 13.
174. *CHI.* 1. 100 ; Mac., *HSL.* 147. 175. *SBE.* 43. 38. 176. *Trans.* 123.
177. Mac., *HSL.* 147-8. 178. *SBE.* 43. 38. 179. *Trans.* 123.

APPENDICES

APPENDIX A

I

IDENTIFICATION OF PLACE-NAMES AND TRIBES

There exists considerable literature on the geography of ancient India[1] which occasionally takes notice of the material of the Purāṇas. There are, again, different views regarding the accuracy of the geographical information contained in the Purāṇas.[2] There are some who attempt to identify the *dvīpas* or island-continents of the Purāṇas and others who regard them merely as the product of geographical fancy.[3] About the exact geographical definition of the *Jambudvīpa* also there are different views and scholars are further divided on the point whether the nine divisions of Bhāratavarṣa of the Purāṇas means our modern India or only its ninth division is what we call India today. By entering into the arena of these controversies we would be involving ourselves into a separate investigation altogether. We have, therefore, avoided any discussion on the point. Again the names of tribes and places in the Appendix A are too numerous to discuss the identification of all of them in this work, which is not a treatise mainly on geography. It is clear that such a discussion should form an independent enquiry altogether and we hope to undertake it in future. The identifications of some names, however, are attempted here only to show how far the Vāyu information admits of verification in the light of a similar information from the other sources.

Ābhīras: We learn from the Greek sources that the Ābhīras " were on the Indus, north of the Sauvīras, where they gave their name to the Greek Satrapy of Abiria ".[4] Patañjali locates them in Sindhudeśa with their settlements near the Sarasvati,[5] and connects them with Śūdras.[6] According to the information of the Mbh. we learn more of their movements from the region about the Punjab and Mathura to the region now known as the Konkan[7] and here too they are at places associated with the Śūdras.[8] The Mbh., however, shows them in another light, that is, as a nomadic tribe of cowherds "amongst whom the boy-god Kṛṣṇa lived."[9] In the Nasik cave inscription we find mention of an Ābhīra king Iśvarasena who flourished about the end of the

---

1. CUNNINGHAM, *Ancient Geography of India,* xvii. ff.; cf. also RAYCHAUDHARI, *Studies in Indian Antiquities,* 46.
2. See *JRAS.* 1894, 231. 3. See *Ibid.* and cf. also RAYCHAUDHARI, op. cit., 62 ff.
4. TARN, *Greeks in Bactria and India,* 172. 5. *Ibid.* 235; *PHAI.* 204.
6. *PHAI.* 418. 7. BHANDARKAR, 37. 8. *PHAI.* 418. 9. BHANDARKAR, 37.

2nd cent. A.D.[10] This is probably the earliest reference to their southward march. Their location in the region about the Aparānta (Konkan) and Surāṣṭra is also attested by the Viṣṇu Purāṇa and by Varāhamihira,[11] and the latter also refers to them as a southern people.[12] They are again connected with the Paṇḍu migration to the south.[13] Even today the Ahirs (probably the same as the Ābhīras) are found in the Punjab,[14] Kathiawad[15] and parts of the Nasik and the Khandesh districts.[16]

The Vāyu places them both in the north and in the Dakṣiṇāpatha but not in the extreme south.

Acchoda: The Acchoda lake is mentioned by Bāṇa in his 'Kādambarī' and it is located, on the ground of this reference, in Kashmir.[17]

The Vāyu calls it, at one place, a heavenly lake and at another locates it on the Kailāsa. It is difficult to say whether the above Acchoda is the same as our lake Acchoda.

Āhukas: The Āhuka tribe is mentioned in the Mbh. and Rukmī is mentioned as being their leader or chief.[18]

The Vāyu calls them a northern '*deśa*'. The other reading '*Bāhuka*' appears to be dubious for we have no information of a tribe of this name from any source so far.

Alakā: Alakā as a city of Kubera figures very often in the 'Meghadūta' of Kālidāsa who also gives its picturesque description.

The Vāyu also associated it with Kubera but at one place we find a mention of king Purūravas having resided there, thus suggesting its location somewhere near Pratiṣṭhāna in the Himālaya.

Alakanandā: It is mentioned as a tributary of the Ganges[19] and the Vāyu appears to support the inference.

Alimadras: The Mārkaṇḍeya Purāṇa has 'Animadras in the same connection as in the Vāyu'.[20] No information is available from any other source so as to locate the region where they flourished.[21]

Amāladas (or *Māladas*): The Mārkaṇḍeya has Mānadas instead.[22] The Mbh. mentions Maladas as a people of the east who were vanquished by Bhīmasena in his *digvijaya* (conquest of quarters).[23] This may probably refer to their location in the region now known as the Maldah District of Bengal.[24]

---

10. *OHAI*. 418. 11. BHANDARKAR, 3.
12. *IA*. 22, 272. 13. K. PILLAI, *Tamils 1800 Years Ago*, 57.
14. CROOKE, *Castes and Tribes of North-west Province and Audh.*
15. ENTHOVEN, *Castes and Tribes of the Bombay Presidency.* 16. *Ibid.*
17. DEY, 1. 18. SÖRENSEN, 25. 19. DEY, 3. 20. *ABORI*. 17. 238.
21. *Ibid.*; B. C. LAW has wrongly taken the Vāyu readings as *Cānimadras* or *Cālimadras*. 22. *Ibid.* 23. SÖRENSEN.
24. LAW here refers to a "shrewd guess" of PARGITER who locates them in the east. Cf. *ABORI*. 17.

It would thus be seen that the Vāyu reference to these people as an eastern janapada or deśa testified by the above evidence and the readings of the Ānandāśrama edition, which do not include the name Māladas, may be modified to this extent.

Ambaṣṭhā : The Ait. Br. mentions an Ambaṣṭha king.[25] The Greek historians of Alexander mention Abastanoi as an Indian people who had come into conflict with Alexander. They had settled on the lower Chinab.[26] They are identified with the Ambaṣṭhas of Sanskrit and Pāli works.[27] The Mbh. refers to the Ambaṣṭhas with Śivis, Kṣudrakas and Mālavas and other north-western tribes.[28] The Bārhaspatya Arthaśāstra mentions an Ambaṣṭha country in connection with Sind. Patañjali mentions Ambaṣṭha as a name of a country or state and its inhabitants he calls as Āmbaṣṭheyas.[29] According to the Smṛti writers Ambaṣṭha denotes a man of mixed Brahmin and Vaiśya parentage.[30] Varāhamihira locates them in the east and south-west.[31]

The Vāyu seems to refer to Ambaṣṭhā as a name of a city and not of a people or tribe. But from the evidence of Purāṇic tradition in general, as collated by PARGITER, we can take it to mean a people of that name rather than a city Ambaṣṭhā. It has been surmised that the Purāṇic references to these people are to be considered earlier than those of the Greek writers;[32] and the fact that the Vāyu does not speak of them so contemptuously as the Smṛtis do and as the Purāṇa itself does in the case of other peoples, may be said to support the inference. It should be noted that the Vāyu also associates them with Śivis and the Yaudheyas as in the Mbh.

Amarakaṇṭaka : In his "Megha-dūta" Kālidāsa mentions the mountain named Amarakūṭa. In the Skanda Purāṇa we have its sanctity described and there it is mentioned as holy, it being the source of the river Narmadā.[33] Its sanctity, especially for the purposes of śrāddha, is mentioned in the Viṣṇu-saṁhitā.[34]

The Vāyu also probably means the same mountain by its reference to Amarakaṇṭaka, which it mentions as holy for śrāddha purposes (cf. also Kaliṅga).

Ānartta : In the Mbh. we find the country of Ānartta mentioned in connection with Kṛṣṇa who himself refers to his absence from that country but for which absence he would have prevented the fatal gambling scene of the epic.[35] In the Sabhāparvan, the people, Ānarttas, are mentioned as having been conquered by Arjuna.[36] The territory of Ānartta, as being ruled by Rudradāman, is alluded to in the Junāgadh

25. Cf. *PHAI*. 206. 26. *PHAI*. 206 ff. 27. *Ibid*. 28. SÖRENSEN.
29. *PHAI*. 206 ff.
30. Cf. LAW, *Ancient Indian Tribes*, 2. 34 ff. for details cf. also *PHAI*. 207.
31. *IA*. 22. 272-3. 32. JAYASWAL, 1. 74. 33. DR, 4. 34. *Ibid*.
35. III. 14. 14 (Critical Edition). 36. SÖRENSEN.

Rock Inscription of the year 72.[37] It is suggested that this Ānartta might signify the territory around Dvārakā.[38] But the exact definition and boundaries of Ānartta have always been vague both in the literary and epigraphic references to that name.[39] In the Mbh., again, we find Kuśasthalī as being another name for Dvārakā,[40] which was situated in Ānartta.

The evidence of the Mbh. and the inscription of Rudradāman suggest that Ānartta may mean the region about Dvārakā for here we find Kuśasthalī as the capital of Ānartta. One of the Vāyu references to that name (No. 38) would probably take it to be the same region. But the other reference (No. 39) suggests (—Surāṣṭra, Kacciya and Arbuda are also mentioned in its context)—that it means a different region, probably the same as the Northern Gujarat of to-day.[41] It should be noted that the name Lāṭa is not mentioned in the Vāyu. This may make us infer that Ānartta included Southern Gujarat also.

Āndhras: The Āndhras as a people are mentioned in the Brāhmaṇas. The Ait. Br. speaks of them as the exiled sons of Viśvāmitra, that is, as non-Aryans.[42] In the Jātakas a city named Andhapura and the Āndhra country are referred to[43] and in the inscriptions of Aśoka,[44] they are mentioned as inhabiting the borderland of his empire. Megasthenes calls the Āndhras as a separate race altogether and according to the Manusmṛti,[45] they were a barbarian people. In the Mbh. they are often found mentioned with Śabaras, Pulindas, etc.[46] In all these references to them there is no direct indication of an express mention of a country known particularly after their name.

The Vāyu mentions the Āndhras as inhabiting the Dakṣiṇāpatha and its reference to them as people who are a taboo in śrāddha suggests that according to it also they were a non-Aryan people.

Āndhrakas: They are probably the same as the Āndhras mentioned above. The Mbh. refers to them with Śakas, Yavanas, Daradas, Mlecchas, etc.[47] The Vāyu also mentions them in the same manner. The absence of the name "Āndhras" in the list of tribes wherein Āndhrakas are mentioned lends support to the above inference that both these names signify the same tribe.

Āndhravākas: The Mārkaṇḍeya Purāṇa reads Āndhrārakas in the same connection as in the Vāyu.[48] There is no other information about

---

37. Cf. *PHAI*. 424. 38. *Ibid*.

39. Cf. ALTEKAR, *Ancient Towns and Cities in Gujarat and Kathiawar*, 4; and also SANKALIA, *Archaeology of Gujarat*, 4–5.

40. SÖRENSEN, 433. 41. Cf. *Bombay Gazetteer*, 1. 6; cf. also fn. 5 above.

42. GOPALACHARI, *Early History of the Andhra Country*, 1.

43. MEHTA, 370. 44. *Corpus Inscriptionum Indicarum*, 1.

45. See SALETORE, *Wild Tribes in Indian History*, 9. 46. Cf, *ABORI*. 17. 324.

47. SALETORE, op. cit., 32. 48. GOPALACHARI, op. cit., 1.

them for the present so as to fix their location. It should be noted that our Purāṇa places them in the east and thus they may not be the same as the Āndhras noted above.

Aṅga : The AV. mentions a people of this name with the Mūjavats, Magadhas, etc.[49] In the Jātakas the Aṅgas and Magadhas are often associated together[50] and their janapada is mentioned first amongst the sixteen great janapadas known to these works.[51] It appears that the Aṅga dominions at one time included Magadha also[52] and that the important city in this territory was Campā which is famous in the Jātakas.[53] The Rāmāyaṇa gives a story about the origin of the name 'Aṅga' from Madana,[54] which is apparently an attempt at etymology probably confusing the name Aṅga with *anaṅga* (i.e. Madana). The Mbh. and the other Purāṇas (Vāyu included), however, derive the name from Aṅga, son of king Bali. There appears to have been some truth in this tradition.[55]

The Vāyu mentions the same Aṅga as that of the Mbh. and mentions the city of Campāvatī in connection with the region.

Aṅgadīyā : The mention of Kārāpatha occurs in the Raghuvaṁśa[56] in connection with the two sons of Lakṣmaṇa who were placed there by the order of Rāma. There is, however, no reference to its capital cities. The Rāmāyaṇa calls it Kārupatha.[57] It is identified with Kārābāgh or Kālābāgh on the banks of the Indus at the foot of the salt range in the Bannu District. Most of the Purāṇas read it as the Kārapatha-deśa[58] and not Kārāpatha as in the Raghuvaṁśa. The identification proposed above appears improbable from the evidence of the Purāṇas including the Vāyu which locates it near the Himavat mountain ; and in the region with which Kārāpatha is identified we find the sons of Bharata ruling. It is, however, not possible at this state of our knowledge to suggest anything about the location of the city called Angadīyā.

Añjana : The Jātakas mention the Añjana mountain as situated in the Great forest.[59] It is identified with the Suleiman Range in the Punjab on the strength of the evidence of the Rāmāyaṇa and the Mārkaṇḍeya and the Vārāha Purāṇas.[60] The Jātakas also mention Añjana forest near Sāketa which is identified with the Kālakāvana of the Dharmasūtras and the Kālakāśrama of the Buddhists.[61]

The evidence of the Vāyu does not throw any light on this information.

---

49. *JASB.* 1918, 317.
50. *Ibid.* 320 fn. 7 ; cf. also DAVIDS, 23.
51. DAVIDS, 23.
52. *PHAI.* 91.
53. *Ibid.*, cf. also MEHTA.
54. Cf. *JASB.* 1918. 317.
55. Cf. *PHAI.* 93.
56. XV. 90.
57. DE, 92.
58. *AIHT.* 279 fn. 1.
59. MEHTA, 369.
60. *Ibid.*, cf. DE, 8.
61. *IHQ.* 4. 93–4.

Anūpas: The Jātakas mention a town named Anūpiya which was probably situated in the Madhy-deśa (Middle country)[62] but here it is not clear whether it has anything to do with the Anūpa country. In the Mbh. we find kings Kārtavīrya Arjuna and Nala associated with the Anūpa country and references to it in the Harivaṁśa suggest its proximity with Surāṣṭra and Ānartta.[63] The country of Anūpa is mentioned in the Nasik inscription of Gautamīputra Balaśrī with Aparānta, Vidarbha and Avanti and it is suggested that there it signifies the district around Māhiṣmatī on the river Narmadā.[64] The same location is probably indicated also by the Junāgadh Rock Inscription of Rudradāman.[65] The Mārkaṇḍeya and the Matsya Purāṇas have Annajas and Arūpas instead of Anūpas of the Vāyu, in the same connection and these readings have been considered to be erroneous.[66]

The Vāyu mentions a janapada of Anūpas as situated on the Vindhya plateau (Vindhya-pṛṣṭha) and associates this name with the *Vītihotras* and *Tuṇḍikeras* who are elsewhere mentioned in the Purāṇa[67] as the branches of the Haihayas, thus suggesting the proximity of the region over which Kārtavīrya Arjuna probably ruled. At another place the Vāyu refers to Narmadānūpa. Thus this information of our Purāṇa appears to support the evidence of the Mbh. and the inscriptions. There is, however, another reference to the Anūpa-deśa in connection with the story of Pṛthu and here it appears that the region has some connection with the territory of Magadha. It has been suggested that this Anūpa might mean a part of Bengal, east of Magadha.[68] It should be noted that "*anūpa*" means "watery tract or region".

Aparāntikas: The Edicts of Aśoka mention Aparāntas as including Surāṣṭra, thus suggesting that Aparānta meant all the countries in Western India.[69] It appears that according to the Mbh. Aparānta included the whole of the Western Coast.[70] The Nasik inscription of Gautamīputra Balaśrī takes the same term as meaning a narrow region of the present Northern Konkan and the same inference appears to be evident from the other inscriptions of the Sātavāhana kings and of Rudradāman.[71] According to R. G. BHANDARKAR the Aparānta of the Purāṇas means the modern region of the North Konkan.[72] From the reference to Ariake in the Periplus, BHAGAVANLAL INDRAJI suggested that Aparāntaka signifies the Western sea-board of India[73] and the same appears to be the inference from the information of Ptolemy on that point.[74] The Mārkaṇḍeya seems to take Aparānta in a general sense

62. Cf. MALALASEKHARA, *Dictionary of Pāli Proper Names*, 91 for references; cf. also LAW, *Geography of Early Buddhism*, 24.
63. Cf. *ABORI*. 17. 330. 64. *PHAI*. 411. 65. *Ibid*. 424.
66. Cf. *ABORI*. 17. 330. 67. *Vā*. 94. 50 ff. 68. *AIHT*. 16.
69. *PHAI*. 259. 70. ALTEKAR, op. cit., 2. 71. *PHAI*. 411, 420, 425.
72. *Early History of the Dekhan*. 73. *IA*. 8. 140. 74. Cf. ALTEKAR, op. cit., 2.

meaning all the countries of Western India,[75] and that was also the information known to Yuan Chwang, the celebrated Chinese-Buddhist traveller.[76]

The reading of the Mārkaṇḍeya is changed in the Vāyu to "other countries" (cf. *aparāṁs tān*) and elsewhere we find mention of Vindhyāparāntikas; and the people Aparāntas are shown as inhabiting the region of the Vindhyas, probably its westernmost extremity. Thus Vāyu shows that Aparānta region is a restricted area, that being probably the geographical knowledge of the redactor of the Purāṇa. The Gha reading of the Purāṇa, however, mentions Aparānta in the sense in which Mārkaṇḍeya uses it which appears to be the original reading changed by the other versions to '*saṁparītāḥ*' from '*hyaparantāḥ*'.

Āpagās: The ṚV. mentions the river Āpayā with the Sarasvatī and Dṛṣadvatī.[77] The river Āpagā is mentioned in the Mbh. as flowing through the country of the Madras.[78] The Mārkaṇḍeya has Aupagās in the same connection as in the Vāyu,[79] and from the reference to the region of Āpagā in the Brahmāṇḍa Purāṇa its identification with Afganistan has also been surmised.[80]

The fact that the Vāyu places the Āpagās in the north may perhaps corroborate the information of the ṚV. and the Mbh. but it is difficult to say whether we are justified to see here the modern region of Afganistan.

Aparītas: The Mārkaṇḍeya has Aparāntas and the Matsya Purandharas in the same connection as in the Vāyu. The Mbh. mentions a tribe Aparānta and Mārkaṇḍeya's astronomical list locates it in Sindhu-Sauvīra country, and the Vāyu reading 'Aparīta' is supposed to be wrong.[81] It must be stated that the Aparītas in the Vāyu are the *deśa* in the north and might mean an independent tribe of that name inhabiting the northern region of India. The Mārkaṇḍeya Purāṇa gives a separate list of Aparānta countries taking it in a broad sense and there the mention of the name Aparānta as a northern country is improbable.

Arbudas: The mountain Arbuda is mentioned in the Mbh.[82] The people Arbudas of the Mārkaṇḍeya[83] and the Vāyu may be supposed to be inhabiting the region about that mountain.

Asmakas: The Asmakas are one of the sixteen great janapadas in the Jātakas.[84] They had, in Buddha's time, a settlement on the banks of the Godāvarī and in the Jātakas they are associated with the Avantis.[85] "The name, however, is ambiguous; for in Sanskrit we have names of two tribes, viz., the Aśmakas and Aśvakas as they are mentioned in

---

75. *ABORI*. 17. 325. 76. CUNNINGHAM, *Ancient Geography of India*, 690.
77. DAS, op. cit., 161, 178, 353. 78. SÖRENSEN. 79. *ABORI*. 17. 238.
80. DE, 10. 81. *ABORI*. 17. 231-2. 82. See DE, 10.
83. See *ABORI*. 17. 327. 84. DAVIDS, 23. 85. *Ibid*. 27.

the Mbh." and "either there were two distinct tribes so called or the Sanskrit form 'Aśvakā' is a wrong reading or a blunder in the sanskritisation of Assakā".[86] Pāṇini also mentions Aśmaka in one of his Sūtras.[87] A legend regarding the origin of the Aśmakas is found in the Bṛhannāradīya and Viṣṇu Purāṇas,[88] and it is suggested that the Aśmakas were an offshoot of the Ikṣvākus of Ayodhya.[89] The mention of Assakenoi by the Greek writers and the evidence of Bṛhatsaṁhitā and the Kūrma Purāṇa[90] suggest that their country was in the north-west.[91] But it has been suggested that the Assakenoi of the Greeks means the Aśvakas and not the Aśmakas.[92] Pāṇini, however, mentions, the Aśmakas in the Deccan.[93] The Hathigumphā Inscription of Khāravela mentions Asikanagara.[94]

The Vāyu has the Asmakas (not Aśmakas) as a janapada of the Dakṣināpatha and thus its information sides with the Jātakas and Pāṇini. They are mentioned with Maunikas, Paunikas and Bhogavardhanas. There is a suggestion that Aśmaka and Mūlaka of the Ikṣvākus founded the two kingdoms of Aśmaka and Mūlaka regions[95] and D. R. BHANDARKAR suggests that they were independent kingdoms.[96] The Vāyu no doubt mentions the king Aśmaka and his successor Mūlaka but from the Vāyu evidence it is improbable that this line can be brought to the Deccan; for we find in the Purāṇa Raghu and Rāma as descendants of this Aśmaka who certainly ruled in the region of Ayodhyā. There is no indication in the Purāṇa that this king ruled in the Deccan also. It appears that sameness of names—which according to PARGITER has brought many errors in the Purāṇic dynastic lists[97]—has confused the redactors of the Bṛhannāradīya and Viṣṇu Purāṇas and thus they try to relate the king Aśmaka with the region Aśmaka. It should be noted that the Jātakas do not throw any light on this assumption.

Aśvamukhas or Aśvakamukhyas: (See Aśmakas above.) They are mentioned in the Bṛhatsaṁhitā[98] and were probably a north-western people. Its literal meaning "horse-faced" is interesting and there appears to have been a similar inference about them from the Greek sources also.[99] They are probably the same as the Assakenoi of the Greeks or the Aśvakas referred to above.

Āṭavyas: The Mārkaṇḍeya has Aḍhakyas and the Matsya agrees with the Vāyu reading in the same connection and it is supposed that the Vāyu reading is correct.[100] Āṭavī as a city in the Deccan is mentioned in the Mbh.[101] and the Āṭavyas of the Allahabad Pillar Inscrip-

---

86. *Ibid*. 28. 87. LAW, op. cit., 87. 88. WILSON, *Trans*.
89. LAW, op. cit., 88 ff. 90. See DE, 12. 91. *PHAI*. 121 ff.
92. *Ibid*. fn. 5. 93. *Ibid*. 94. See MEHTA, 372 for reference.
95. *PHAI*. 122. 96. *Ibid*. 121. 97. Cf. *AIHT*. 131.
98. *IA*. 22. 174. 99. *CHI*. I. 159 fn. 100. *ABORI*. 17. 322.
101. SÖRENSEN.

tion of Samudragupta[102] probably signify the Āṭavyas of the Purāṇa who were probably the aboriginal tribes of Central India.[103] The Vāyu appears to confirm this view by locating them in the Dakṣiṇāpatha.

Ātreyas: The Vāyu has the same information as in the Mārkaṇḍeya Purāṇa.[104]

Aṭṭahāsa: The region Aṭṭahāsa is mentioned in the Padma Purāṇa and in the Kubjikā Tantra and an attempt is made to identify it with the eastern part of Lābhalpur in Bengal. The Vāyu information makes it a mountain chain of the Himalayas thus coming into conflict with the above assumption.[105]

Avantis: The Avantis are one of the sixteen janapadas of the Jātakas with its capital Ujjeni.[106] The janapada of Avantis, according to D. R. BHANDARKAR, was divided into two parts: Northern part with its capital Ujjeni and the southern one in Dakṣiṇāpatha with its capital Māhiṣmatī; but RAYCHAUDHARI hesitates to accept this conclusion.[107] The Mahāgovinda Suttanta mentions Māhissatī as the capital of the Avantis but the Mbh. distinguishes between the kingdoms of Avanti and Māhiṣmatī.[108]

The Vāyu mentions the janapada of the Avantis on the *Vindhyapṛṣṭha*. In the account of Kārtavīrya Arjuna we find Māhiṣmatī as "conquered" by him from the Nāgas and his sons in "Avantis" are afterwards mentioned. This probably suggests that Māhismatī was the capital of Avanti. The five gaṇas of Haihayas, as enumerated in the Purāṇa, do not mention the Avantis but mention Āvartis. The Matsya Purāṇa has the former reading. But in the list of the janapadas Avantis are mentioned with Tuṇḍikeras and Vītihotras (two of these gaṇas). This would make us infer that Avanti as a separate janapada came into existence in later times while formerly it comprised the territory of all the five gaṇas. The Bṛhatsaṁhitā takes Avanti and Ujjayinī as meaning the same city.[109] But the Vāyu does not mention Ujjayinī at all. It should be noted that 'Avantī' definitely meaning "a city" is not mentioned in our Purāṇa.

Avantī (river): Avantī and Śiprā are understood as being the two names of the same river.[110] But the Vāyu mentions Śiprā and Avantī separately, thus suggesting names of two rivers both of which had their source in the Pāriyātra mountain.

Ayodhyā and Sāketa: Both the cities of Ayodhyā and Sāketa are mentioned in the Jātakas.[111] Sāketa is supposed often to be the same as Ayodhyā but it is pointed out that they were possibly adjoining

---

102. FLEET, *Gupta Inscriptions*. 103. *ABORI*. 17. 322.
104. Cf. LAW, *ABORI*. 17. 237. 105. DE, p. 13.
106. MEHTA, 372; DAVIDS, 23–8. 107. *PHAI*. 122 fn. 4. 108. *Ibid*. 123.
109. *IA*. 22. 174. 110. P. 14. 111. MEHTA, 3?0–1.

cities like London and Westminster.[112] It was a town on the river Śarayū.[113] The Bṛhatsaṁhitā mentions the inhabitants of Ayodhyā.[114]

The Vāyu mentions both 'the city' and 'the kingdom' of Ayodhyā. According to the Jātakas the city of Ayodhyā was included in the territory of Kosala being one of its three great cities.[115] Ayodhyā seems to have been the earliest and Sāketa the next capital of the Kosalas of the Buddhist works.[116] After the Ikṣvāku dynasty, it appears that this city had never had the privilege of being a capital; but it is suggested that the successors of Skanda-Gupta had a capital in Ayodhyā till the rise of the Maukharis.[117] It should be noted that in connection with the region of the Guptavaṁśajas we find the Vāyu Purāṇa mentioning Sāketas (and not Ayodhyā) as being one of their four important janapadas. The absence of Ayodhyā in the later Kali age accounts of the Purāṇa is significant.

Bāhudā: The river Bāhudā is mentioned in the Mbh.[118] as one of Eastern India. PARGITER identifies this river with that of the Rāmāyaṇa which joins the Ganges near Kanauj but DE' rejects this identification and identifies it with the Dhalabha, a feeder of the Rāpti in Oudh.[119]

The Vāyu mentions it with Gomatī and Dṛṣadvatī, thus confirming PARGITER'S view.

Barbaras: The Mbh. locates them in the north-west region with Śakas, Yavanas, etc. It has been contended that the "Barbaricum" of Periplus is the same as Barbarika of the Dhanvantarīya Nighaṇṭu, an Āyurvedic work and that it was the city of the Barbaras.[120] It was the same as the Barbarii of Ptolemy which along with Patala formed the two towns of the islands formed by the river Sindhu.[121] The Bṛhatsaṁhitā mentions the Barbara people in the region of south-west which appears strange from the evidence sketched above.[122] It is held that they were a north-western tribe according to the Bṛhatsaṁhitā but no reference is quoted to support his statement. The Bṛhatsaṁhitā also mentions the Sindhu-Sauvīras, the Kambojas, the Ambaṣṭhas and the Kirātas in the south-west (*Nairṛti diśi*).[123]

The Vāyu too calls it a northern *deśa* and elsewhere the river Cakṣu is shown watering this land and passing through the Sindhu-maru country as in the Matsya Purāṇa.[124]

Bhadrakāras: The Mbh. mentions a people Bhadrakāras and also Bhadras. It is stated that both these people might mean the same. It is also suggested that they might have had their habitat near about

112. DAVIDS, 39. 113. *PHAI*. 85; cf. DE, 14 for details.
114. *IA*. 22. 174. 115. *PHAI*. 85. 116. *PHAI*. 90.
117. *Ibid*. 496. 118. SÖRENSEN. 119. DE, 16.
120. *IC*. 1. 389; CUNNINGHAM, op. cit., 694–5. 121. *IC*. 1. 389.
122. *IA*. 22. 174; LAW, *ICI*. 389. 123. XIV. 18. 124. *IC*. 1. 389.

the Kurus, the Matsyas and that the Uttamabhadras, known in historical times as a republican tribe, might have been a section of the Paurāṇic Bhadrakāras. The Mārkaṇḍeya has Bhadrakaras[125] in the same connection as in the Vāyu.

The Vāyu places them in the Madhya-deśa and thus confirms the evidence of the Mārkaṇḍeya.

Bhadrāśvas: The people of the name Bhadrāśvas are referred to in the Bṛhatsaṁhitā which mentions the king of Bhadrāsvas and KERN, in his note to his translation of the same work, remarks: "The Bhadrāśvas are a mythical people fabled to have lived in the remote East...The origin of the Bhadrāśvas living near the Udayagiri may be traced to the ṚV. (1. 115. 2 ff.)".[126] KERN further adds that they were probably the same as the Bhadras of the Madhya-deśa.

In the Vāyu also they appear to be a mythical people of the East and there is no indication as to where we should place them.

Bhānukacchas: The Mārkaṇḍeya has Bhīrukacchas in the same connection as in the Vāyu. They are stated to be the same as the Bhṛgukacchas of Sanskrit literature. The region about modern Broach represents their country which is the same as the Baryagaza of early Greek Geographers.[127] Bharukaccha as "a seaport town of the Bharu kingdom" is also mentioned in the Jātakas.[128]

The Vāyu also has the reading Bharukacchas and it locates them in the same region as above.

Bhāradvājas: The Bhīṣma Parvan of the Mbh. mentions them with the Ātreyas. The evidence of the Epic seems to locate them "not far from the upper regions of the Ganges near the hills".[129]

The Vāyu agrees to a certain extent with the above assumption by referring to the Bhāradvājas as a northern deśa and by mentioning them with the Ātreyas.

Bhārgavas: The Mbh. mentions Bhargas who are taken to be the same as the Bhārgavas. It is further stated that they were perhaps the eastern branch of the Bhaggas of Suṁsumāragiri.[130] The Vāyu has the same information as in the Mārkaṇḍeya in which connection the above inferences are made.

Bhīmarathī: This river is mentioned in the Purāṇa with Godāvarī and Kṛṣṇā as flowing from the Sahya mountain and thus is the same as the modern Bhīmā river. Varāhamihira mentions the same river by the name Bhīmarathā.[131]

125. *ABORI*. 17. 228–9. 126. *IA*. 22. 175.

127. *ABORI*. 17. 326; DE, 32; CUNNINGHAM, op. cit. For details about Bharukaccha see also ALTEKAR, op. cit., 33–5.

128. MEHTA, 412. 129. *ABORI*. 17. 238. 130. *Ibid*. 17. 241.

131. *IA*. 22. 175.

Bhogavardhanas : The Bharhut Inscription mentions Bhogavaḍham[132] but the identification of the tribe, Bhogavardhanas, is difficult to suggest. Varāhamihira mentions the Bhogavardhana country (or a city of that name?) summarily and the mention is 'perhaps' an interpolation.[133] Their association with the Asmakas in the Purāṇa suggests that they inhabited a region close to the Asmakas, i.e., in the Dakṣiṇāpatha.

Bhojas : They are mentioned in the Brāhmaṇa literature and had spread over Central and Southern India from the period represented by the Brāhmaṇas[134] onwards. There is also an evidence about their association with Vidarbha[135] and the Bhojas are mentioned in the edicts of Aśoka.[136] Kauṭilya's information suggests that the Bhojas were ruling in his time in the Daṇḍaka.[137] The Vāyu mentions them with Utkalas, Uttamārṇas, Daśārṇas and Kiṣkindhakas thus probably locating them somewhere about Vidarbha and not in Daṇḍaka which occurs separately in the list. It should be noted that the Vāyu mentions them as occupying the Vindhyapṛṣṭha (Vindhya plateau).

Bhṛgutuṅga : On the evidence of Varāha-Purāṇa it is located as a mountain in Nepal to the eastern bank of Gaṇḍakī.[138] This appears improbable from the statement in the Vāyu that after ascending the Bhṛgutuṅga one goes to the holy river Sarasvatī.

Bindusaras : On the evidence of the epics and the Matsya Purāṇa it is located as a place 2 miles south of Gangotrī.[139] The Vāyu agrees with the Brahmāṇḍa Purāṇa in showing its situation at the foot of the Gauḍa (Gaura in Vāyu) mountain.[140] Our Purāṇa further says that in the vicinity of this lake king Bhagīratha dwelt for many years, an information confirmed by the Rāmāyaṇa and the Matsya Purāṇa.[141]

Bodhas : They are mentioned also in the Mbh. and the Rāmāyaṇa. Their location somewhere in the eastern districts of the Punjab is suggested by LAW.[142] The Matsya Purāṇa has Bāhyas in the same connection as in the Vāyu.[143] The Vāyu calls them a janapada of the Madhyadeśa.

Brahmottaras : It is suggested that Suhmottara is the original reading implying thereby their location to the north of the Suhma country.[144] This is probable because Sumha, son of king Bali, after whom the janapada Suhma was known, is also mentioned as Brahma in our Purāṇa.[145] Their location in the east by our Purāṇa confirms the

132. BARUA and SAMHA, *Bharhut Inscriptions*, 15. 133. *IA*. 22, 175.
134. For detailed information from other sources on the Bhojas, cf. LAW, op. cit., 176 ff.
135. *PHAI*. 77. 136. See *Ibid*. for reference 137. *Ibid*.
138. DE, 34. 139. *Ibid*. 38. 140. *Ibid*. 141. *Ibid*. for references.
142. Cf. *ABORI*. 17, 229. 143. *Ibid*. 144. *Ibid*. 17, 241.
145. Cf. Vāyu, 99. 85.

same. It should also be noted that the Vāyu Purāṇa mentions the region of Brahmottaras with Aṅgas, Vaṅgas and Magadhas as being watered by the river Gaṅgā. Aṅga and Vaṅga were the two other sons of king Bali. The interpretation that the Brahmottaras were a people who inhabited the region north of the Brahma or Sumha country may probably be not correct and it appears that the Brahmottaras are the same as the Brahmas who, however, are not mentioned as such.

Charmakhaṇḍikas: The Mārkaṇḍeya has the same reading as in the Vāyu in this connection but the Matsya has Ātta-Khaṇḍikas (or Cātta-Khaṇḍikas) while the Mbh. has Carmamaṇḍalas. It is suggested that the region occupied by them might be identified with the one about Samarkand.[146] We have a reference in the Bṛhat-Saṁhitā to 'Charmaraṅga' as people in the north-west division, and the same source refers to an island named a Carmadvīpa (lit. island of bark) in the south-west division.[147] But it is difficult to suggest anything about their identification on this very account. The reference to a river named Carmaṇvatī in our Purāṇa flowing from the Pāriyātra mountain may be a pointer towards location of the people who, it is tempting to suggest, might be the same as the Charmaraṅgas of Varāhamihira.

Caulyas or Colas (?): The Colas are mentioned in the inscriptions of Aśoka. Their country is roughly the modern region of the Districts of Trichinopoly and Tanjore drained by the river Kāverī.[148] It is interesting here to note that in the Tamil tradition the Colas have also Śembiyan as their name which is "generally taken to mean a descendant of Śibi".[149] In the Mbh. they are seen fighting on the side of the Pāṇḍavas and are mentioned with Drāvidas, Āndhrakas and Pāṇḍyas.[150]

The Vāyu locates them with Pāṇḍyas, Keralas, etc., in the Dakṣiṇāpatha. They are again shown vanquished by king Sagara along with the Khasas, etc., as Kṣatriya-gaṇas and the Cola-janapada is derived from a son of Janāpīda, a descendent of Turvasu. Thus if we believe in the Vāyu tradition they were once in the north as Kṣatriyas having some connection with the Turvasu branch of Yayāti. PARGITER, however, thinks that their connection with Sagara's story is erroneous.[151] But in this account of the Vāyu Purāṇa they are not associated with either the Pāṇḍyas or the Keralas or such other admittedly southern people. It is on this ground that PARGITER suggests that "the Colas it seems were not the Colas of South India but rather another frontier tribe whose name appears as Culikas in later times".[152] He also asserts that the kingdoms of Cola, Pāṇḍya and Kerala were offshoots of the Turvasu branch of the Ailas.[153]

---

146. B. C. LAW quotes a suggestion of PARGITER on which he bases his statement but does not quote a reference in that connection. Cf. *ABORI*. 17. 233.

147. *IA*. 22. 176. 148. *PHAI*. 271.

149. K. A. NILAKANTHA SASTRI, *Colas*, 25. 150. SÖRENSEN.

151. *AIHT*. 278. fn. 5. 152. *JRAS*. 1919, 358. 153. *AIHT*. 382.

It is interesting to note here that the Vāyu does not mention the Colas in its list of tribes in India. It mentions the Cūlikas in the north and the Caulyas in the Dakṣiṇāpatha. The Colas are mentioned in reference to genealogies. The question remains whether the Colas in Sagara account should be identified with the Cūlikas or the Caulyas or whether all the names mean distinct tribes. The Colas, descendents of Janāpīḍa are mentioned with Keralas, etc., and they appear to be an offshoot of the Turvasu line and thus mean a Southern people.[154] Śibi, we know, belonged to the line of Druhyas. But at any rate, Śibi and Janāpīḍa were descendents of Yayāti. Still the connection of Śibi with Colas, so far as the Vāyu is concerned, is far-fetched though certainly suggestive. If we regard the Colas in Sagara account as the same as Cūlikas suggested by PARGITER their location in the north becomes probable.

Cūlikas: PARGITER places them, tentatively, in about the north-west region and connects them with the Piśācas.[155] He quotes the Matsya, Mārkaṇḍeya, Vāyu, etc., in support.

Cīnas: The Mbh. locates them both in the extreme north-west and in the east and also at the source of the Ganges.[156] The Rāmāyaṇa mentions the Western Cīnas (in the west).[157] For the Cīnas in the Mārkaṇḍeya list, Vāyu has a corresponding reading Pīna (except in Ṅa which has Pina). Thus Vāyu does not show them in the north but probably locates them in the extreme east. We find also here a mention of Cīnamaru country but it is difficult to identify it.

Daśārṇas: A town named Erakaccha in the Dasaṇṇa (Daśārṇa) country is referred to in the Pāli literature but this reference does not help much in locating the country of the people.[158] Kauṭilya also mentions the Daśārṇas, the elephants from whose region are, according to him, of a secondary category as compared with those from Aṅga and Kaliṅga.[159] The Mbh. refers to the Daśārṇas and during the period represented by the epics, it is suggested, that these people seem to have more than one settlement and the Mbh. thus refers to two Daśārṇas, one in the west conquered by Nakula and another in the east (or south-east) subjugated by Bhīmasena.[160] According to the Rāmāyaṇa and the other Purāṇas, the Daśārṇas are often shown as grouped with the Mālavas, Karūṣas, Utkalas, Mekalas, etc. In the Periplus there is a reference to Dosarena which might indicate a knowledge of these people. Kālidāsa, however, gives a better information about them and in his 'Meghadūtaṁ' he refers to their country with its

154. *Ibid*. 292.
155. *JRAS*. 1912, 713.
156. For details cf. *ABORI*. 17, 236-7.
157. *Ibid*.
158. LAW, op. cit., 2. 30.
159. Book II, Ch. II.
160. LAW, op. cit., 29; cf. also B. A. SALETORE, *Wild Tribes in Indian History*, 103 ff.

capital Vidiśā (i. e. modern Bhilsa), situated on the river Vetravatī. They seem to have occupied the region about the river Daśārṇā (i. e. the modern river of the name Daśān) which is a tributary of the Vetravatī.[161]

The Vāyu mentions them with the Mālavas, Karūṣas and Utkalas and thus places them somewhere in Central India (cf. also the river Daśārṇā).

Daśārṇā: The name of a river Dosaron mentioned by Ptolemy[162] sounds very much like the Daśārṇā, which actually occurs in the list of rivers issuing from the Ṛkṣa mountain as given in many other Purāṇas including the Vāyu-copy used by Alberuni.[163] This Daśārṇā, it is suggested, is the modern river named Dhasan near Saugor in the C. P.[164] In the Periplus also the name Dosarena occurs thus suggesting a knowledge of the same river.

The Vāyu, in addition to the reference quoted above, also associates the river with Kālañjara suggesting that this holy place (of Kālañjara) was situated on its banks. The Mbh., however, associates Kālañjara with the mountain Citrakūṭa. Thus the identity of the river Dāśārṇa becomes more difficult in view of its association with Kālañjara.

Dṛṣadvatī: According to the Mbh. Kurukṣetra was situated on the banks of the river[165] and in its Vana-parvan it is mentioned as forming the southern boundary-line of the holy land.[166] CUNNINGHAM identifies it with the river Rakshi which flows by the south-east of Thaneshwar.[167] It should be noted that Varāhamihira knew of a tank at Thaneshwar which was famed holy in his days.

The Vāyu too appears to support this suggestion of CUNNINGHAM as it expressly states, as does the Mbh., that Kurukṣetra was situated on the banks of this river (see Kurukṣetra).

Dvārakā, Dvārāvatī or Kuśasthalī: The first and perhaps the only early epigraphical reference to Kṛṣṇa's Dvārakā is found in the Pālitānā Plates of Sāmanta Siṁhāditya of about 600 A.D.[168] The location of the city of Dvārakā in which Kṛṣṇa lived and its identity with the modern city of the same name is still a moot point.[169] The name of a city of Dvārakā occurs in the Pāli literature in connection with the Kāmbojas but it is not here expressly stated that it was a capital city of the Kāmboja people.[170] The Mbh. abounds in references to this city in connection with Kṛṣṇa and it contains a legend to the effect that the

161. *Ibid.* 162. VII. i 39–41.
163. RAYCHAUDHARI, *Studies in Indian Antiquities*, 124. 164. *Ibid.*
165. SÖRENSEN. 166. For details cf. CUNNINGHAM, op. cit., 382 ff.
167. *Archaeological Survey Reports*, 14.
168. Cf. SANKALIA, op. cit., 227, App. 21.
169. Cf. ALTEKAR, op. cit., 25; cf. also *IHQ*.
170. LAW, *Geography of Early Buddhism*, 50.

city was washed off by the encroachment of the ocean upon the mainland where the city was situated.[171] Many other Purāṇas refer to this event.[172]

The Vāyu evidence does not throw much light on the problem. But the fact that Prasena, when he went for hunting, lost his life in the region where the Ṛkṣa-rāja, probably a chief of a people inhabiting the Ṛkṣa mountain, ruled, suggests that the Vāyu Dvāravatī is not the same as the modern one. The story of the flooding away of this city is nowhere hinted at in the Purāṇa.

In the Mbh. the cities Kuśasthalī and Dvārakā are mentioned as identical. But the Vāyu however appears to suggest that they were two cities (cf. No. 681) but the fact that two Mss. omit the reference to Dvāravatī is significant.

Gāndhāras: The people of this name are known from the very early times.[173] The Jātakas include the Gandhāra country in their list of the sixteen great janapadas. The Behistun inscription of Darius (of about 516 B.C.) purports to record that Gadara or Gandhāra was one of the kingdoms subject to the Persian Empire.[174] In the time of Aśoka, however, Gandhāra formed part of the Empire of the great Buddhist emperor ; and the Gāndhāras with their capital Takkasīlā are mentioned in the Fifth Rock Edict of Aśoka.[175] The Mbh. also refers to Takṣaśilā as their capital city.[176] According to the Matsya and the other Purāṇas the Gāndhāra kings were the descendents of Druhya, a son of Yayāti. The king Druhya and his people are mentioned several times in the ṚV. and it is stated that it is probable that the Druhyas were probably a north-western people.[177] Thus the Purāṇic tradition about the connection of the Gāndhāras with Druhya accords with the Vedic evidence.[178]

The Vāyu has the same tradition as in the Matsya about the origin of the name of the people. Its information about the two important cities of Takṣaśilā and Puṣkarāvatī accords well with that of the great epic. The particular reference in our Purāṇa to the best breed of horses in this region is significant.

Gokarṇa: There are in India more than one sacred place bearing the name Gokarṇa.[179] The Tīrtha of Gokarṇa is in the N. Kanara district of the Bombay Province and is still a celebrated place of

---

171. Mbh. XVII. 7.
172. See ALTEKAR ; no references are, however, quoted here.
173. See LAW, *Some Kṣatriya Tribes in Ancient India*, Chapter IX.
174. Cf. LAW, *Geography of Early Buddhism*, 50 ; RAYCHAUDHARI, *Studies in Indian Antiquities*, 22.
175. See *PHAI*. 93. 176. Cf. LAW, op. cit., 49. 177. See *Ved. Ind.*, 1. 385.
178. Cf. *PHAI*. 93. 179. *IC*. 4. 265.

pilgrimage.[180] Another holy place of the same name is located in Nepal[181] which is probably the same Gokarṇa that is mentioned in the Monghyr Copper-plate inscription of king Devapāla of the Pāla dynasty of Bengal. There is much of literary tradition about the former Gokarṇa.[182]

It is not clear whether the Vāyu Gokarṇa is the same as the Gokarṇa in the North Canara District. The Purāṇa, however, locates it in the southern region. The mention of the river Tāmraparṇi[183] as having its source in the mountainous region near Gokarṇa suggests that the Vāyu Gokarṇa is not the same as the present Gokarṇa in the North Canara District.

Hairaṇvatī: The river Hiraññavatī is mentioned in the Dīgha-Nikāya. It is the Little Gandak and the same as Ajitavatī near Kuśinārā or Kusinagara. It flows through the Gorakhpur District and joins the Ghogra (i.e. Śarayu).[184]

Hastināpura: The city of this name is mentioned in the Jātakas and the Pāli Canonical literature.[185] The Hatthipura of the Jātakas may be the same as the Hastināpura of the epic and Purāṇic tradition and it has been identified with an old town in the Mawana Tehsil in Meerut division.[186]

The Vāyu informs that the city was founded by king Hastin of the Paurava line and it was in later times flooded by the Ganges. The exact location of the city, however, is not indicated in our Purāṇa.

Hūṇas: The Mbh. knows the Hūṇas and generally associates them with the Pārasīkas.[187] The Rāmāyaṇa, however, does not allude to them.[188] It has been found that no literary work, the date of which can be definitely assigned to a period earlier than the 5th century A.D., speaks anything about them.[189] They are, however, referred to in the Raghuvaṁśa of Kālidāsa.[190] They probably appeared for the first time on the Indian soil in the time of Skandagupta (455–67 A.D.) under the distinctive name Hūṇa.[191]

The Vāyu mentions them summarily as one of the peoples who inhabited the mountainous regions with Dārvas, Khasas, etc. It should be noted that the Mārkaṇḍeya mentions Ūrṇas, instead of the Hūṇas of the Vāyu in the same connection.[192]

---

180. See *Bombay Gazetteer*, 15. 2. 288 ff. 181. *IC*. 4. 265–7.
182. For details cf. *Bombay Gazetteer*, op. cit., and see also De, 70.
183. Cf. Raychaudhari, *Studies in Indian Antiquities*. 60. 111.
184. Law, *Geography of Early Buddhism*, 37. 185. Law, op. cit., 19, 39.
186. Cunningham, op. cit., 702; cf. also *PHAI*.
187. Bagchi, *Presidential Address to Indian History Congress*, 1943, 24.
188. *Ibid*. 25. 189. *Ibid*. 190. *Ibid*.
191. *Ibid*. and also cf. R. D. Banerji, *Age of the Imperial Guptas*, 46 ff.
192. Cf. 57. 56–7.

Kaliṅga : The country of the Kaliṅgas is mentioned by Pāṇini and Baudhāyana brands their land as impure including it in his list of *saṃkīrṇa-yonayaḥ*. According to Kauṭilya Kaliṅga elephants are amongst the best of the species. All these authorities, including also those of the classical Greek writers, such as Pliny and others, mean by Kaliṅga the region of or about the modern Orissa bordering along the sea-coast.[193] In the Hathigumphā Cave Inscriptions we find the capital of Khāravela mentioned as Kaliṅga-nagara. The Mbh. and the other Purāṇas tell a story of the five sons of king Bali amongst whom Kaliṅga was one whose name the region under him bore.

The Vāyu also tells the same story and, as in Baudhāyana, our Purāṇa also mentions the region as impure and taboo for śrāddha where the Āśramadharma does not prevail. It is a southern land probably near the region of the Māhiṣikas. Our Purāṇa gives its location as being to the south-east of the Amarakaṇṭaka mountain.

Kāmbojas : The reference to the people Kāmbojas by Yāska may probably be the earliest literary information about them.[194] In the Indian tradition they are often associated with the Gāndhāras. They are mentioned accordingly in the early Pāli Canonical literature of the Buddhists.[195] The Mbh. also refers to them often with the Gāndhāras.[196] Although the name of Gandhāra survived for long centuries that of the Kāmbojas was later forgotten. "This makes it probable that they belonged to the nomad hordes of Central Asia which were moving from place to place".[197] The numerous references to Kāmboja horses as being of the best breed in both the epics may be considered as significant in this connection.[198]

The Vāyu refers to them as a northern people and mentions them in the story of Sagara who is said to have vanquished them with the Śakas, Haihayas, etc., who according to PARGITER, were the foreign tribes of the north. The Vāyu, however, refers to "the best breed of horses" not in connection with the Kāmbojas but with the Gāndhāras.

Kauśāmbī : The expression Kauśāmbeya as a local epithet of a person occurs in Śatapatha and Gopatha Brāhmaṇas[199] and "it may be safely inferred that the name Kauśāmbī was prevalent as early as the age of the Brāhmaṇa literature.[200] The high antiquity of the city of Kauśāmbī, as the capital of the Vatsa country, is further testified by frequent references to it in the text of the Pāli Canon and in the epics

---

193. For details cf. *ABORI*. 21. 203-9.

194. See BAGCHI, op. cit., 2, cf. B. C. LAW, *Some Kṣatriya Tribes of Ancient India*, Ch. VIII, for details about them.

195. LAW, *Geography of Early Buddhism*, 26.

196. Cf. *ABORI*. 17. 236.

197. BAGCHI, op. cit., 3.

198. *ABORI*. 17. 236.

199. LAW, *Kauśāmbī in Ancient Literature*, (*MASI*, 60), 1.

200. *Ibid*.

and the other Purāṇas.[201] As to the exact identification of the place where this ancient city stood, there is some difference of opinion amongst scholars. According to CUNNINGHAM the present village Kosam stands on the actual site of Kauśāmbī.[202] But VINCENT SMITH says that the site is still to be looked for and when looked for it will be found in a native state in Baghelkhand Agency probably on the Tons river, not very far from the East Indian Railway which connects Allahabad with Jubbulpore.[203] CUNNINGHAM's identification is now generally accepted.[204]

The Vāyu does not help in fixing the location of the site of this city. It only says that the city of Hastināpura was washed off by the Ganges and that the king Nirvaktra, son of Adhisāmakṛṣṇa, who was ruling at that time, shifted his capital to Kauśāmbī. The explanation that the city of Hastināpura was flooded by the Ganges is considered as inadequate by PARGITER[205] and the Purāṇic tradition only means that he was forced to abandon the city. The Purāṇa does not appear to indicate that Kauśāmbī, his new capital, was founded by the king.

Kulyas : There is, for the present, no information about them from any other source. LAW takes them to be the same as the Kulutas who, according to him, dwelt in the Punjab and are mentioned in the inscriptions of about the 1st century A.D.[206]

But it should be noted that the Vāyu places them both in the north and south and it is doubtful whether their identification with the Kulutas should be regarded as correct.

Kuntalas : The Mbh. locates them in the region about Kāśī and Kośala and also in the western and southern India.[207]

The Vāyu, however, shows them in the north and in the south and does not show their association with either the Kāśis or the Kośalas.

Kurus : The Kuru country is mentioned in the ṚV.[208] and the Pāli literature alludes to the Kuru country (i. e. Uttarakuru) as a mythical region. The case of South Kurus is, however, different and is as such one of the sixteen *mahājanapadas* of *Jambudvīpa* in the Buddhist literature.[209] The region about Thaneśvar, Panipat and Sonapat may indicate the ancient Kuru land.

The Vāyu gives a picturesque description of the Uttarakuru country and it must be deemed to be a fabulous region. Elsewhere the Vāyu associates the people Kurus with Pañcālas probably suggesting the geographical contiguity of the regions occupied by them.

---

201. *Ibid.*, cf. also MEHTA, 387 ; for details see LAW, op. cit.
202. Op. cit., 454 and 709. 203. See *JRAS*. 1898, 503.
204. See GHOSH, *Early History of Kauśāmbī*, 93-4. 205. *AIHT*. 285.
206. *ABORI*. 17. 224. 207. *Ibid.* 208. *Ved. Ind.*, 8.
209. LAW, *Geography of Early Buddhism*, 17.

The Ait. Br. mentions the Uttarakurus as distinguished from the Kurus in the Punjab.[210] The existence of the Uttarakurus in the region of Central Asia beyond the Himalayas is noted by Greek writers of the 5th cent. A.D. Ptolemy mentions, for the first time, a town named Ottarakorrha and of a river and a mountain bearing the same name in the Serique (Chinese Turkestan) near the mountain Emodos (Himavat). Uttarakuru thus signified Chinese Turkestan.†

Mālavas : According to D. R. BHANDARKAR[211] there are three stages in their history. Their earliest location is found in the Punjab where they opposed the invading Alexander. The Greek writers knew them as Malloi.[212] Later on they migrated to the South in Rajputana near about the Jaipur State, for their coins have been found just over here.[213] The Mbh. also locates them there.[214] Their occupation of this region is testified by the Nasik cave inscriptions of Śaka Uṣavadāta.[215] In the Gupta period, however, they seem to have migrated still to the south and settled somewhere in the north-western part of Central India.[216]

The Vāyu calls them the inhabitants of the Vindhya and of the mountainous territories and thus shows us their location in the area indicated by the inscription of Samudragupta.

Pāradas : On the strength of an almost unanimous Purāṇic and Epic tradition which associates them with the barbarous foreign tribes of the north, PARGITER locates them in the North-west.[217] The Manu-smṛti says that they were originally Kṣatriyas and lost this status through their avoidance of the sacred rites.[218] The Mbh. at one place associates them with the Ābhīras.

A tribe named Palidas is mentioned in the Edicts of Aśoka with Āndhras, Bhojas, etc., and a variant of this name in another version of the same edict at Girnar and Kalsi is Pālada. Due to this fact a controversy has arisen whether this tribe is to be known as the Pāradas or Pulindas in Sanskrit. If they be taken as Pāradas they are to be located in the south. It is doubtful whether such interpretation should be considered as correct.[219]

The Vāyu mentions them with the foreigners from the north and nowhere locates them in the south.

---

210. BAGCHI, op. cit., 2. † BAGCHI, op. cit.
211. *Charmichael Lectures*, 1918, 12–3. For details about them cf. also LAW, *Ancient Indian Tribes*, 2. 37 ff.
212. JAYASWAL, 1. 68 ff., cf. also *PHAI*.
213. *Ibid*. 154–5 ; cf. also *ABORI*. 13. 223 ff. 214. JAYASWAL, 1. 155.
215. *ABORI*. 13. 225. 216. *Ibid*. 227.
217. Cf. *JRAS*. 1917, 40–47 ; 1910, 9–10 ; 1919, 354–61. 218. X, 43–4.
219. *PHAI*. 259 ; cf. also *ABORI*. 21, 211–2,

Ramaṭas: The Mbh. calls them a western people and Varāhamihira gives a similar information.[220] According to some Purāṇas (Matsya and Kūrma), however, they are to be located in the north.[221]

The Vāyu too mentions them as a northern deśa.

Tuṣāras: The Greek writers, Ptolemy and the Periplus, appear to locate them in the province round Bactria and the Mbh. and the Harivaṁśa refer to them as an outside northern race along with the Mlecchas and Dasyus. According to LASSEN they inhabited the region north of Hindukush.[222] It has been only recently pointed out that the Tokharians of the Greek geographers were a Central Asian people living to the north of Kashmir.[223] There is considerable information from the Chinese sources in this connection but we need not dilate upon it here.[224] Some Purāṇas confuse the Tuṣāras with Turuṣkas (i.e. the Turks)[225] but the Vāyu does not do so.

The Vāyu mentions Tuṣāras with Yavanas, Śakas and Barbaras and with Āndhras also. Elsewhere it calls them a Northern deśa which probably means the same as the one inferred from the above evidence.

Vaitaraṇī: The Buddhist tradition supports that of the Brahmaṇa that the Vetaraṇī is Yama's river. It is the river Vaitaraṇī in Orissa and is referred to in the Mbh. as flowing in Kaliṅga. According to the Padma and Matsya Purāṇas, however, it is the river that flows north of Bassein which was brought down on earth by Paraśurāma and the Epic elsewhere takes it to Kurukṣetra. Thus its identification is difficult to ascertain.[226]

The Vāyu refers to it as a sacred river and taking into consideration the unholy character of Kaliṅga land the Vāyu probably does not show it flowing through that country. But it says that the river has its source in the Vindhya and it may be we have here something to do with the tradition in the Matsya Purāṇa.

Vatsas: The Mārkaṇḍeya has Matsya for the Vatsa of the Vāyu.[227]

Vetravatī: The river Vetravatī and a city of that name is mentioned in the Jātakas. Kālidāsa mentions the river of this name in his Meghadūta. It is undoubtedly the modern Betva, a small tributary of the Ganges.[228]

That the Vāyu means the same Vetravatī as that of Kālidāsa is clear from its mention of Śiprā and Avantī along with the river Vetravatī.

---

220. *IA.* 22.
221. Cf. *ABORI.* 21, 210.
222. For details see *ABORI.* 22, 95-6.
223. BAGCHI, op. cit., 14 ff.
224. See *Ibid.* for details.
225. *Ibid.* 20.
226. LAW, *Geography of Early Buddhism*, 40.
227. See *ABORI.* 17. 224; also LAW, op. cit., 16-17.
228. LAW, op. cit., 35.

Yaudheyas : Pāṇini refers to the Yaudheyas as "*āyudhajīvi saṁgha*" i.e., probably as a republican tribe subsisting on the profession of arms. Here they are mentioned with the Trigarttas[229] and the Mbh. says that they were defeated by Arjuna along with the Mālavas and the Trigarttas. The epic references to them suggest that they were also associated with the Śivis and Ambaṣṭhas.[230] According to the epic evidence they were probably settled somewhere in the Punjab and their migration to southern regions is suggested by the inscriptional and numismatic evidence about them.[231] According to the Purāṇic tradition in general, including the Vāyu, they were the descendents of king Uśīnara and were related to the Śivis and Ambaṣṭhas as their kinsmen.[232] CUNNINGHAM identifies them with the Johiya Rajputs of today who inhabit the region round Multan.[233]

It should be noted that the Vāyu does not refer to them in its lists of tribes. It is only in the genealogical portion that the name Yaudheya occurs and a reference to them is found commonly in the Purāṇic tradition, a fact which is already noted above.

II

This part of the Appendix has been prepared with a view to make available the geographical and tribal material of the Purāṇa in the form of a ready reference work. All geographical names have been included in this section. The tribal names, such as, Pāraśavas, Śudras, Āndhras, Śakas, Pulindas, Tūlikas, Yavanas, Kaivartas, Ābhiras, Śabaras, and the various *jātis* of the Mlecchas (Vā. 99. 268-9) and also Gardabhins, Tuṣāras, Manaṇṭas [Kha, Gh, Gha and Ṅa : Maruṇḍas ; Ga : Muruṇḍas elsewhere in the same context], Maunas, Vṛṣalas, Kolikilas, Nāgas (Vā. 99. 358-66), Vindhyakas, Vāhlīkas, Meghas [Ṅa has Medhātithi which dispenses with a tribal name], Pañcakas, and Brāhmaṇas (Vā. 99. 373-8) have not been included in the appendix as they are merely referred to in the Purāṇa as dynastic names said to be ruling in the 'future'. (For the relevant details about them see PARGITER : *Purāṇic Text of the Dynasties of the Kali Age* pp. 2-3, 44-8 and 50-1). All other tribal names are included in the list.

It will be obvious to one acquainted with the Purāṇas that it is sometimes difficult to understand the distinction between an adjective and a proper name. Wherever a doubt as to this had arisen it is indicated by a question mark. Again, sometimes a compound word

---

229. See LAW, *Ancient Indian Tribes*, 2: 43 ff. for details cf. also JAYASWAL, 1.
230. Cf. LAW, op. cit., for reference.
231. See *PHAI*. and cf. also JAYASWAL, op. cit.
232. Cf. *AIHT*. 264.
233. *Ancient Geography of India*, 281-2.

occurs which appears to signify a name and it is difficult to decide whether we should split up the compound and understand different names or simply take up the whole word as signifying one name. Such doubts are also expressed by a question mark.

There are certain geographical names which, according to general assumption, belong purely to the domain of mythology but some scholars have attempted to identify even such names. It would be prejudging an issue for us to exclude these names for the present and hence these names are included in the list.

This Section has been arranged as follows: (1) Serial Number, (2) The name proper, (3) Its distinctive geographical or tribal feature, (4) Relevant details about it, and (5) Reference figures in brackets.

The abbreviations used for (3) are as follows:

Cy.	—	City	P.	—	People or tribe
D.	—	Deśa	Rg.	—	Region
Dv.	—	Dvīpa	Rv.	—	River
F.	—	Forest	S.	—	Sea
H.	—	Hill	St.	—	Sthalī or marshy tract
Ja.	—	Janapada	T.	—	Tank
Kṣ.	—	Kṣettra	Tī.	—	Tīrtha
L.	—	Lake	Vr.	—	Varṣa
Mt.	—	Mountain	Vṣ.	—	Viṣaya

---

1. Ābhīras—(D.)—No. 130
2. A(Ā)bhīrras—Ja.—No. 130.
3. Ābhīras—Ja.—No. 470.
4. Acalakūṭakas or (Māheyācalakuṭakas ?)—Ja.—No. 569.
5. Acchoda—L.—Acchodā was a *mānasī* daughter of the Agniṣvātta pitṛs. She is called a river (*nimnagā*). From her is the heavenly lake Acchoda so called. Acchodā was originally a heavenly river but had fallen down on the earth due to her sinful behaviour. [Ka, Ga, Gha and Ṅa omit this portion of the text.] (73. 1-5)
6. Acchodā—L.—No. 470.
7. Acchodā—Rv.—No. 5.
8. ,, —Rv.—Its source is the Acchodaka lake. (77. 76)
9. ,, —Rv.—No. 470.
10. Acchodaka—L.—No. 8.
11. Acchodikā– Rv.—No. 470.
12. Agastyas—P.—A class of learned Brahmarākṣasas who were followers of Kubera in Hariśṛṅga. (47. 60-1)
13. Āhukas—D.—No. 130 [Ṅa reading is Bāhukas].

14. Ajatuṅga—Tī.—Where *tarpaṇa* to pitṛs should always be performed. (77. 48)

15. Ājīvas—P.—They were so called by Suras. They were irreligious, having been the issues of the contamination of castes (*varṇāśramasaṅkarikāḥ*). Of such people—belonging to the class of artisans (*kāruśilpijanāḥ*)—who were likewise thieves, who could not be trusted—the Piśācas were their deities. (69. 281-8)

16. Alakā—Cy. (?)—An extensive city (?) where Purūravas lived with Urvaśī. (91. 5-8)

17. Alakā—Cy. (?)—No. 470, 779.

18. Alakanandā—Rv.—No. 469 [Ga, Gha, Ṅa : Kanakanandā].

19. ,, —Rv.—No. 1022.

20. Alimadras—D.—No. 130.

21. Amaladas or Āmaladas?—D.—No. 130 [Gha reads Maladas and Ga, Amalavas or Āmalavas].

22. Amarakaṇṭaka—Mt.—This holy mountain is inhabited by Siddhas and Cāraṇas. There lord Aṅgiras practised penance for a thousand years. It is beyond the reach of death and demons (*asura-rakṣasām*). (It is located probably to the southern side of the river Narmadā). Here should *piṇḍas* be offered. To its south-east, situated in a mountain which forms half the boundary-line of Kaliṅgadeśa, is the *vāpī* (pond?) called Sāvartā. The great sages call it (?) a Siddhakṣetra. A verse by Uśanas says: "Blessed are they who having gone to Amarakaṇṭaka perform śrāddha there." A little penance is sufficient here to achieve emancipation. Merely worshipping leads one to svarga. (77. 4-16)

23. Amarapurī—Cy.—No. 366.

24. Amarāvatī—Cy.—By bathing in the river Tāmraparṇī one goes to Amarāvatī, free from all mental and physical maladies. (77. 26)

25. Amarāvatī—Cy.—By bathing (?) in the tīrthas of Śrīparvata and of the Vaikṛta mountain one goes to Amarāvatī. (77. 30)

26. Amarāvatī—Cy.—Nos. 184, 826.

27. Ambara-nadī—Rv.—Falling from the peak of Meru and circumambulating it, it waters the Devabhrāja forest and enters the Sitoda lake. Then it passes along the Supakṣa, Śikhi, Kaṅka (Kāka), Vaidūrya, Kapila, Gandhamādana, Piñjara, Sarasa, Kumuda, Madhumat, Mukuṭa, Kṛṣṇa, Śveta, and Sahasraśikhara mountains and falls on the mount Pārijāta. Then watering through the Ketumāladvīpa of various Mleccha gaṇas it joins the western sea. (Cp. also No. 1022). (42. 43-57)

28. Ambaranadī—Rv.—No. 1022.

29. Ambaṣṭhā—Cy.—Belonging to Suvrata, son of Uśīnara of the Yayāti line [Ka : Vṛṣṭā]. (99. 22)

30. Āmbikeya—Mt.—No. 1100.

31. Āmravana—F.—Situated between the Viśākha and Pataṅga mountains, and to the east of Tāmravarṇa lake. There Gandharvas, Kinnaras, Yakṣas, Nāgas and Vidyādharas enjoy the drinks of mango-juice in such a way that their frolic is resounded in the forest. [Ga has "Āmravaṇa".] (36. 18–22)

32. Amṛtā—Rv.—No. 989 [Ka omits this].

33. Anala—Mt.—There Rākṣasas dwell. (39. 53)

34. Ānandas—Ja.—No. 989.

35. Ānanda—Rg.—No. 988 [Kha, Gha : Ānalda].

36. ,, Vr.—Nos. 988, 989.

37. Ānandajala—L.—No. 456 [Gha, Ṅa : Nandajala].

38. Ānārta—Vr.—Śaryāti had a son Ānārta or Anarta. His successor was Reva.

,, Rg.—To Reva the *viṣaya* Ānarta and its capital Kuśasthalī belonged.

39. Ānartas—Ja.—No. 130 [Ka reading is Anartas].

40. Andhakāraka—D.—A deśa in Krauñcadvīpa called after Andhakāraka, son of Dyutimat, lord of that dvīpa [Kha, Gha omit this].

41. Andhakāraka—Vr.—No. 606.

42. ,, Mt.—No. 606.

43. Āndhras—Ja.—Will be ruled by Guha (after the Guptas ?) [Andhras may well be the reading.] (99. 385–6)

44. Andhras—Ja.—No. 130.

45. Āndhras—D.—A country inflicted with sin (*pāpa-deśa*). *Śiṣṭhas* and learned Brahmins do not go there. (78. 69–70)

46. Andhrakas—P.—They will be annihilated by Kalki, when this yuga will begin to close. [Ka, Ga : Andhaka]. (98. 103–8)

47. Andhravākas—Ja.—No. 470.

47a. Aṅga—D. ?—Janamejaya was Kharva (?) of the inhabitants of Aṅga. (99. 255)

48. Aṅgas—Rg.—Where people will take shelter at the end of the Kali age. (99. 402)

49. Aṅgas—Ja.—No. 470.

50. ,, —Ja.—A janapada called after Aṅga, son of King Bali. (99. 33)

51. Aṅgadīyā—Cy.—Situated in Kārapatha deśa near the Himālayas. Probably named after Aṅgada, son of Dāśarathi Lakṣmaṇa. (88. 188)

51a. Aṅgadīyā—Cy.—No. 524.

52. Aṅgadvīpa—Rg.—No. 437.

53. Aṅgalokavaras ?—D.—No. 470.

54. Añjana—Mt.—Situated to the west of Sitoda lake. (36. 26–29)

55. ,, —Mt.—No. 867, 1179.

56. ,, —Mt.—Inhabited by Mahoragas. (39. 59)

57. Antaśilā—Rv.—No. 130.
57a. Anugaṅga—Ja.—Where descendants of Guptas will rule. [Ga, Kha, Gha and Ṅa : Anugaṅgā]. (99. 383)
58. Anūpa—D.—King Pṛthu made a gift of Anūpadeśa to Sūta for his panegyric. (62. 147)
59. Anūpa—Ja.—No. 130. [Aṇupa in another reading.]
60. ,, —Rg.—No. 888.
61. Anutaptā—Rv.—No. 989 [Omitted in Ka.]
61a. ,, —Rv.—No. 1100.
62. Apagas—D.—No. 130.
63. Aparāntikas—P.—The Vindhyāparāntikas will be annihilated by Kalki at the end of this yuga. (98. 106-8)
64. Aparāntikas—P.—The Aparāntikas on the Vindhya plateau were annihilated by Pramiti at the end of Kali. (58. 75-81)
65. Aparītas—D.—No. 130.
66. Arbudas—Ja.—No. 130.
67. Arthapas—Ja.—No. 130. [Ka reading dispenses with the name.]
68. Aruṇa—Mt.—No. 470.
69. Aruṇāvatī—Rv.—No. 108.
70. Aruṇoda—L.—No. 1022.
71. ,, —L.—No. 1178.
72. Ārya—Ja.—No. 130.
73. Āryas—P.—No. 844.
73a. Asitā—Rv. ?—Holy for śrāddha. (77. 39)
74. Asmakas—D.—No. 130.
75. Aśoka—Mt.—No. 569 [Ga omits this name.]
76. Asta—Mt.—No. 1100.
77. Aśvamukhas—D. ?—No. 470.
78. Aśvakamukhyas—D. ?—Janamejaya was Kharva (?) of the Aśvakamukhyas. (99. 255)
79. Atala—Rg.—No. 1048.
80. Āṭavyas—Ja.—No. 130.
81. Ātreyas—D.—No. 130.
82. Aṭṭahāsagiri—Mt.—Śiva in his Aṭṭahāsa incarnation will live on the Aṭṭhāsagiri of the Himalayas in 20th dvāpara (?). (23. 189-91)
83. Atyākarālagojvālas—Ja.—No. 569.
84. Avantis—Ja.—No. 130.
85. Avantī—Rv.—No. 130.
86. Avanti—Cy.—Vatsa is called Āvantaka King. (99. 173)
87. Āvanti— ? ? (96. 157)
88. Ayodhyā—Cy.—Vaśiṣṭha protected the kingdom of Ayodhyā when the king had retired to forest. (88. 94)
89. Ayodhyā—Cy.—King (name ?) of Ayodhyā alluded to. (88. 20)

90. Ayodhyā—King Divākara of Ikṣvaku line is 'now' ruling Ayodhyā city. (99. 282)
90a. Ayodhyā—Cy.—No. 345.
91. Bāhudā—Rv.—No. 130 [Ṅa reading is Bahudā.]
92. Bakulā—Rv.—No. 569 [Ga, Ṅa : Bahulā].
93. Balāhaka—Mt.—Sub-merged in the southern sea. (47. 75)
94. ,, —Mt.—No. 1108.
95. Balārakas—P. ?—One of the four Pakṣas of men. Born in Atri gotra. [Kha reading is Valgūraga.] (70. 78)
96. Barbaras—P.—They will be annihilated by Kalki at the end of the Kali age. (98. 108)
97. Barbaras—P.—Pramiti annihilated them at the end of the Kali age. (58. 83)
98. Barbaras—P.—No. 842.
99. ,, —D.—Nos. 130, 470.
100. Bhadra—F.—No. 765.
101. Bhadrā—Rv.—No. 569.
102. Bhadras—Dv.—One of the four mahādvīpas of the earth. (41. 85)
103. Bhadrākara—Dv.—To the west of Candradvīpa. It covers 10,000 yojanas in a round ; and Vāyu is worshipped there. (45. 61-5)
104. Bhadrakāras—Ja.—No. 130.
105. Bhadrasīmā—Rv.—Nos. 180, 660.
106. Bhadrasomā—Rv.—(This river forms the northern course of the river Puṇyodā—see Puṇyodā). It originates from the Supārśva mountain—i. e. a mahāpāda of Meru—and joins the Mahābhadra lake whence its name Bhadrasomā. Then it crosses the Śaṅkhakūṭa, Vṛṣa, Vatsa, Nāgaśaila, Nīla, Kapiñjala, Indranīla, Mahānīla, Hemaśṛṅga, Śveta, Sunaga, Śataśṛṅga, Puṣkara, Varāha, Mayūra, Jatudhī, Triśṛṅga and Vīrudha Mountains. Then it waters (the land of) Uttara Kurus and crossing the Mahadī(dvi)pa joins the northern sea. (42. 58.77)
106a. Bhadrasomā—Rv.—No. 660.
107. Bhadraśvas—P.—No. 765.
108. Bhadrāśva—Dv.—There are five Kula-mountains in this dvīpa. They are:: Saivāla, Varṇamālāgra, Korañja, Śvetavarṇa and Nīla. These mountains have their own innumerable branches. The janapadas of this dvīpa are : Sumaṅgalas, Śuddhas, Candrakāntas, Sunandanas, Vrajakas, Nīlamauleyas, Sauvīras, Vijayasthalas, Mahāsthalas, Sukāmas, Mahākeśas, Sumūrdhajas, Vātaraṁhas, Sopasaṅgas, Parivāyas, Parācakas, Saṁbhavaktras, Mahānetras, Saivālas, Tanapas, Kumudas, Śākamuṇḍas, Uraḥsaṁkīrṇabhaumakas, Sodakas, Vatsakas, Caikas (?), Vārāhas, Hāravāmakas, Śaṅkhākhyas, Bhāvimandras, Uttaras (?), Haimabhaumakas, Kṛṣṇabhaumas, Subhaumas, and Mahābhaumas.

The rivers in this dvīpa are ; Śītā, Cakrā, Vaktrā, Kāñcī, Surasā, Śākhāvatī (?), Indranadī, Meghā, Maṅgāravāhinī, Kāveri, Haritoyā, Somāvarttā, Vanamālā, Vasumatī, Pampā, Pampāvatī, Suvarṇā, Pañcavarṇā, Vapuṣmatī, Maṇivaprā, Suvaprā, Brahmabhāgā, Śilaśinī, Kṛṣṇatoyā, Puṇyodā, Nāgapadī, Śaivālinī, Maṇitaṭā, Kṣārodā, Aruṇāvatī, Viṣṇupadī, Hiraṇyavāhinīlā, Skandamālā, Surāvatī, Vamodā, Patākā and Vetālī.

109. Bhandrāśva—Dv.—Nos. 232, 819, 1022.
110. ,, —Rg.—No. 818.
111. Bhāgīrathī—Rv.—Holy for śrāddha. (77. 92-3)
112. ,, —Rv.—King Bhagīratha with his own afforts 'brought' her and that is why the knowers of vaṁśa call the river Bhāgīrathī. (88. 169)
113. Bhāgīrathī—Rv.—Nos. 306, 470.
114. Bhakṣas—P.—One of the 15 pakṣas of Aṅgirasas. (65. 107)
115. Bhakṣyakas—P.—They will be ruled over by one named Kanaka. [Kha, Ga, Ṅa : Bhokṣyakas]. (99. 387)
116. Bhānukacchas—Ja.—No. 130. [Gha, Ṅa reading is Bhārukaccha].
117. Bharadvājas—D.—No. 130.
118. Bhāradvājas—P.—One of the 15 pakṣas of Aṅgirasas. (65. 106)
119. ,, —P.—Belong to the same stock as the Aṅgirasas. (65. 97)
120. Bharata—D.—No. 818.
121. Bharatas—Dv.—One of the four mahādvīpas of the earth. (41. 85)
122. ,, —Ja.—No. 470.
123. Bhārata—Vr.—Bhārata and other varṣas are described (in the Vāyu Purāṇa) with their rivers and mountains. (1. 87)
124. Bhārata—Vr.—There are four yugas in Bhārata varṣa. (24. 1)
125. ,, —Vr.—The southern varṣa called Himāhva was assigned to Bharata by his father Ṛṣabha ; and that is why this varṣa is known by the learned as Bhāratavarṣa. (33. 51-2)
126. Bhārata—Vr.—Śatajit had hundred sons who were all of them rājānaḥ. They divided this Bhārata varṣa into seven Khaṇḍas. [The expression 'into seven Khaṇḍas' is not found in Ṅa.] (33. 60-1).
127. Bhārata—Vr.—This Haimavata varṣa (i. e. varṣa with the Himavat mountain at its north ?) is known by the name Bhārata. (34. 28)
128. Bhārata—Vr.—Of the Bhārata varṣa there are nine divisions. (47. 78)
129. Bhārata—Vr.—There are four yugas in Bhārata-varṣa. (57. 22)
130. Bhārata—Vr.—There are fourteen Manus (Svāyambhuva and others) in this Bhārata varṣa. The Paurāṇika sūta Lomaharṣaṇa narrates its *nisarga* (physical features) thus :—I will enumerate the janapadas scattered about in this holy land (puṇyatīrtha)

which is to the south of Himavat mountain. It is in the centre, to the north of the sea and to the south of the Himavat mountain. Manu is called Bharata as he supported the people; hence etymologically (*niruktavacanāt*) this varṣa is called Bhārata. There *svarga*, *mokṣa*, the middle and the end are known; indeed nowhere else do mortals know *karman*.

This varṣa is divided into nine subdivisions, separated by seas and inaccessible to each other. These subdivisions are: Indradvīpa, Kaseru, Tāmravarṇī, Gabhastimān (?), Nāgadvīpa, Saumya (?), Gandharva, Vāruṇa and (?). This ninth dvīpa (?), amongst them, is surrounded by sea. It is 1000 yojanas north-south, extending from Kumarikya to the source of the river Gaṅgā. It is 9000 yojanas (? cf. *tiryaguttara*). Its frontiers are always inhabited by Mlecchas—to the east are the Kirātas and to the western extremity the Yavanas. The Brāhmaṇas, Kṣatriyas and Vaiśyas live in the centre with Śūdras scattered about. They follow their particular avocations, namely sacrifice, war and trade. He who conquers the whole of this ninth dvīpa is called the *Samrāṭ* (paramount lord or emperor). This *loka* is *Samrāṭ*, the *antarikṣa* is called *Virāṭ*, while another loka is called *Svarāṭ*.

There are seven Kula mountains in this varṣa, e.g., Mahendra, Malaya, Sahya, Śuktimat, Ṛkṣa, Vindhya, and Pāriyātra which have their own innumerable branches, e.g., Mandara, Vaihāra, Dardura, Kolāhala, Sasurasa, Maināka, Vaidyuta, Pātaṁdhama, Pāṇḍura, Kṛṣṇa, Gantuprastha, Godhana, Puṣpagi, Yuj, Jayanta, Raivataka, Śrī, Kāru, and Kūṭaśaila. 'Mixed' (vimiśrāḥ) with them are the various Arya and Mleccha janapadas drinking the waters of the rivers: Gaṅgā, Sindhu, Sarasvatī, Śatadru, Candrabhāgā, Yamunā, Sarayū, Irāvatī, Vitastā, Vipāśā, Devikā, Kuhū, Gomatī, Bāhudā, Dṛṣadvatī, Kauśikī, Niścīrā, Gaṇḍakī, Ikṣu, and Lohritā which flow from the Himavat mountain. Those flowing from Pāriyātra mountain are: Vedasmṛti, Vedavatī, Vṛtraghnī, Sindhu, Varṇāśā, Candanā, Satīrā, Mahatī (?), Parā (?), Carmaṇvatī, Vidiśā, Vetravatī, Śiprā, and Avantī. From the Ṛkṣa mountain flow the following rivers: Śoṇa, Narmadā, Mandākinī, Daśārṇā, Citrakūṭā, Tamasā, Pippalā, Śroṇī, Karatoyā, Piśācikā, Nīlotpalā, Vipāśā, Jambulā, Siterajā, Śuktimatī, Makruṇā, and Tridivā. Those that flow from the Vindhyas are: Tāpī, Payoṣṇī, Nirbandhyā, Madrā, Niṣadhā, Venvā, Vaitaraṇī, Śitibāhu, Kumudvatī, Toyā, Mahāgaurī, Durgā, and Antaśilā. These rivers of the Dakṣiṇāpatha flow from the Sahya mountain: Godāvarī, Bhīmarathī, Kṛṣṇā, Vaiṇī, Vañjulā, Tuṅgabhadrā,

Suprayogā, and Kāverī. Those flowing from the Malaya mountain are: Kṛtamālā, Tāmravarṇī, Puṣpajātī, and Utpalāvatī. The rivers Trisāmā, Ṛtukūlyā, Ikṣulā, Tridivā, Laṅgūlinī, and Vaṁśadharā are the 'daughters' of the Mahendra mountain. The rivers Ṛṣīkā, Sukumārī, Maṇdagā, Kūpā and Palāśinī flow from the Śuktimat mountain. All of them are holy and join the sea; and they have their own innumerable tributaries.

The janapadas of the madhyadeśa, to wit, are: Kurus, Pāñcālas, Śālvas, Sajāṅgalas, Śūrasenas, Bhadrakāras, Bodhas, Śatapatheśvaras, Vatsas, Kisaṣṇas, Kulyas, Kuntalas, Kāśikośalas, Arthapas, Tilaṅgas, Magadhas, and Vṛkas. The place in the northern half of the Sahya mountain whence the Godāvarī flows is a charming site on this earth; here did the king of gods create the Govardhana for the good of Rāma (?).

The northern deśas are: Vāhlīkas, Vāṭadhānas, Ābhīras, Kālatoyakas, Aparītas, Śūdras, Pahnavas, Carmakhaṇḍikas, Gāndhāras, Yavanas, Sindhu-sauvīra-Bhadrakas, Śakas, Hradas, Kulindas, Paritas, Hārapūrikas, Ramaṭas, Raddhakaṭakas Kekayas, Daśamānikas, Kāmbojas, Daradas, Barbaras, Pīnas, Tuṣāras, Pahlavas, Ātreyas, Bharadvājas, Prasthalas, Kaserukas, Lampākas, Stanapas, Pīḍikas, Juhuḍas, Apagas, Alimadras, the various classes (*jātayaḥ*) or Kirātas, Tomaras, Haṁsamārgas, Kāśmīras, Taṅgaṇas, Cūlikas, Āhukas and Pūrṇadarvas.

The eastern countries (*deśāḥ*) are: Andhravākas, Sujarakas, Pravaṅgas, Vaṅgeyas, Amaladas, Mālavartins, Brahmottaras, Pravijayas, Bhārgavas, Prāgjyotiṣas, Muṇḍas, Videhas, Tāmraliptakas, Mālas and Magadha-Govindas.

The janapadas of the Dakṣiṇāpatha are: Pāṇḍyas, Keralas, Caulyas, Kulyas, Setukas, Mūṣikas, Kumanas, Mahārāṣṭras, Māhiṣakas, Kaliṅgas, Abhīras, Sahacaiṣīkas (?), Āṭavyas, Varas, Pulindas, Vindhyamūlikas, Vaidarbhas, Daṇḍakas, Paunikas, Maunikas, Asmakas, Bhogavardhanas, Nairṇikas, Kuntalas, Andhras, Udbhidas, and Nalakālikas.

The other countries (*dākṣiṇātyāḥ deśāḥ*) are: Śūrpārakas, Kolavanas, Durgas, Kālītakas, Puleyas, Surālas, Rūpasas, Tāpasas, and Turasitas. All these are Parakṣaras (?). The Nāsikyādyas (i.e. Nasikyas and others), Antara-Narmadas (i.e. about the river Narmadā), Bhānukacchas, Samāheyas (?), Kacchiyas, Surāṣṭras, Ānartas and Arbudas—all these are *saṁparītāḥ* (?).

The inhabitants of the Vindhya are: Mālavas, Karūṣas, Rokalas, Utkalas, Uttamārṇas, Daṣārṇas, Bhojas, Kiṣkindhakas, Tosalas, Kosalas, Traipuras, Vaidikas, Tumuras, Tumburas, Ṣaṭsuras, Niṣadhas, Anūpas, Tuṇḍikeras, Vītihotras, and

Avantis—All these janapadas occupy the plateau of the Vindhyas.

The other deśas sheltered by the mountains are: Nigarharas, Haṁsamārgas, Kṣupaṇas, Taṅgaṇas, Khasas, Kuśaprāvaraṇas, Hūṇas, Darvas, Sahūdakas, Trigartas, Mālavas, Kirātas and Tāmasas.

131. Bhāratī—Rv.—No. 569 [Omitted in Gha].
132. Bhārgavas—D.—No. 130.
133. Bhāvimandras—Ja.—No. 108.
134. Bhīmā—Rv.—No. 569.
135. Bhīmarathī—Rv.—No. 130.
136. Bhogavardhanas—Ja.—No. 130.
137. Bhojas—Ja.—No. 130.
138. Bhramaras—Ja.—No. 569. [Ṅa reading is Bhrāmaras.]
139. Bhramaras—Ja.—No. 470. [Another reading is Bhramaṭas.]
140. Bhṛgus—P.—With Ādityas, Maruts, etc. (10. 71)
141. ,, —P.—Their expansion is narrated in the Purāṇa. (1. 137)
142. Bhṛgutuṅga—H.—A peak of the Himavat mountain, named after Bhṛgu. Four sons of Śiva will reside there in the tenth Dvāpara. (23. 148)
143. Bhṛgutuṅga—H.—After ascending the Bhṛgutuṅga one goes to the holy river Sarasvatī. (79. 20)
144. Bhṛgutuṅga—H.—In Bhṛgutuṅga king Yayāti practised penance after his retirement from kingship. (93. 102)
145. Bhṛgutuṅga—H.—Holy for śrāddha. (77. 82)
146. Bilva—F.—It is to the east of the Śrī lake. This Bilva-vana is also known by the name of Śrī-vana. It is situated in the valleys between the Śītānta and Kumuñja mountains. It is 100 × 300 yojanas in extent. (37. 1–15)
147. Bilva—St.—It is situated between Samūla and Vasudhāra mountains. There Yakṣas, Gandharvas, Kinnaras, Siddhas, Nāgas, etc. live on bilva fruits. It is 100 × 800 yojanas in extent. (38. 23-6)
148. Bindusaras—L.—No. 470.
149. Bodhas—Ja.—No. 130.
150. Brahmabhāgā—Rv.—No. 108.
151. Brahmakṣetra—Kṣ.—Viṣṇu is born as man at Brahmakṣetra in the end of yuga. (97. 4–5)
152. Brahmakṣetra—Kṣ.— This great tīrtha was founded by Brahmā in former times. It is the same as Kurukṣetra (?). There gods, sages and munis dwell. (59. 106–7)
153. Brahmakuṇḍa—T.—Holy for śrāddha. (82. 20)
154. Brahmarakṣasas—P.—A class of Rakṣasas, known after their maternal uncle Brahmarākṣa (?). (69. 133–4)

155. Bhahmatīrtha—T.—Holy for śrāddha. (77. 55)
156. Brahmatuṅga—H.—Holy for śrāddha. (77. 82)
157. Brahmatuṅgahrada—T. ,, (77. 71)
158. Brahmavedī—?— ,, (82. 20)
159. Brāhmī—Rv.—No. 569 [Omitted in Gha].
160. Brahmottaras—D.—No. 130.
161. ,, —Ja.—No. 470.
162. Caitraratha—F.—It is in the east of (?) where gods have their play-houses (*krīḍanakāni*). (36. 10–1)
163. Citraratha—F.—Here Purūravas enjoyed with Urvaśī. (91. 6–8)
163a. ,, —Nos. 470, 779.
164. Cakrā—Rv.—No. 108.
165. Cakragiri—Mt.—No. 437.
166. Cakṣu—Rv.—No. 470.
167. Campā—Cy.—The descendants of the Guptas will rule over the lovely city of Campā, protected by gods. (99. 385)
168. Campaka—F.—It is situated between Vikaṅka and Maṇiśaila mountains. It is 100 × 200 yojanas in area. There Devas, Dānavas, Gandharvas, Kinnaras, etc. dwell. The hermitage of Kaśyapa is also to be found there. (37. 16–22)
169. Campāvatī—Rv.—No. 569 [Omitted in Gha].
170. ,, —Campa was the son of king Pṛthulāśva. The city (founded by him ?) was Campāvatī (or Campā). It was inhabited by the four varṇas [Gha, Ṅa omit this]. (99. 105–6)
171. Campāvatī—Cy.—This city will be ruled by the Navanākas. (99. 382)
172. Candanā—Rv.—No. 130.
173. Candra—Mt.—No. 989.
174. Chandrā—Rv.—No. 1108.
175. Candrabhāgā—Rv.—The river loved by Fire (*Havyavāhana*) [Omitted in Ṅa]. (29. 13)
176. Candrabhāga—Rv.—No. 770.
177. ,, ,, No. 130.
178. Candradvīpa—Dv.—Nos. 103, 660.
179. Candrakaṅka—Mt.—It is sub-merged in the northern sea. (47. 73)
180. Candrakānta—Mt.—In between the Candrakānta and Sūryakānta mountain ranges. In the Uttarakuruvarṣa passes the river Bhadrasīmā. (45. 25)
180A. Candrakānta—Mt.—No. 660.
181. Candrakāntas—Ja.—No. 108.
182. Candraprabha—H.—No. 470.
183. Candraśaila—Mt.—
184. Candratīrtha—T.—A holy tīrtha at the source of the river Kāverī, where those who die go immediately to Amarāvatī. [Ka, Ga, Gha and Ṅa omit this.] (77. 28)

185. Candravaktrā—Cy.—The capital (?) city of Candraketu, son of Dāśarathi Lakṣmaṇa. It was situated in a deśa (named Kārapatha ?) at the foot of the Himavat mountain. (88. 187-8)

186. Candrāvartā—Rv.—No. 660.

186a. Candrāvatī—Rv.—No. 569. [Omitted in Gha.]

187. Carakas—P. ?—A branch of the followers of Yajurveda. (61. 24)

188. Carmakhaṇḍikas—D.—No. 130.

189. Carmaṇvatī—Rv.—No. 130.

190. Caulyas—Ja.—No. 130.

191. Cedi—Rg.—Vasu mentioned as Cedipati. (93. 26)

192. (Cedi)—Rg. (?)—Cidi was son of Kauśika of the Kroṣṭu line. After him his descendants were known as Caidyas. (95. 37-8)

193. (Cedi)—Rg.—Śiśupāla is mentioned as Caidya. (96. 157)

194. Chāgala—Mt.—It is on the peak of the Himavat (?) where the four disciples of Śiva will reside. (23. 116)

195. Cīnas—P.—They were annihilated by Pramiti at the end of the Kali age. [Gha reads Cānyān instead of Cīnān, thus dispensing with the name of a tribe or people.] (58. 78-83)

196. Cīnas—D.—No. 470.

197. Cīnamarus—D.—No. 470.

198. Citrakūṭa—Rv.—No. 130.

199. Cola—Ja.—Cola was the son of Janāpīḍa of Turvasu line. After him the Janapada was known as Cola. (99. 5-6)

199a. Colas—P.—No. 345.

200. Cūlikas—D.—No. 130.

201. Dadhimaṇḍodaka—S.—No. 1100.

202. ,, —S.—

203. Dakṣā—Rv.—No. 569.

204. Dakṣiṇa—Rg.—Śankhapada was descendant the of the Prajāpati Pulaha. He loved the south. (It is doubtful whether by the 'south' here we should understand a particular geographical area.) (28. 28)

205. Dakṣiṇāpara—Rg.—This was the region assigned to Yadu by his father Yayāti. (93. 89)

206. Dakṣiṇāpatha—Rg.—Nos. 130, 886.

207. Dakṣiṇapūrva—Rg.—This region was assigned to Turvasu by his father Yayāti. (93. 89)

208. Dākṣiṇātyas—D.—No. 130.

209. Dākṣiṇātyas—P.—They were annihilated by Pramiti at the end of the Kali age. (58. 82)

210. Dākṣiṇātyas—P.—They will be annihilated by Kalki at the end of this Kali age. (98. 107)

211. Daṇḍā—Rv.—No. 569.

212. Daṇḍakas—Ja.—No. 130.

213. Daradas—D.—No. 130.
214. ,, —Ja.—No. 470².
215. Daradas—Ja.—No. 842.
216. ,, —P. ?—They were annihilated by Pramiti at the end of the Kali age. (58. 83)
217. Daradas—P. They will be annihilated by Kalki at the end of this Kali age. (98. 108)
218. Darbhāvatī—Rv.—No. 569.
219. Dardura—Mt.—No. 130.
220. Darvas—D.—No. 130.
220a. Dārvas—P.—No. 345.
221. Daṣamānikas—D.—No. 130.
222. Daśārṇā—Rv.—Nos. 130, 477.
223. Daśārṇā—Rv.—Kalañjara, on the river Daśārṇā is holy for śrāddha purposes. (77. 9)
224. Daśārṇas—Ja.—No. 130.
225. Devabhrāja—F.—No. 27.
226. Devadāru—F.—The place where Śiva will reside in his incarnation of Dāruka in 21st dvāpara will be known as Devadāruvana. (23. 195)
227. Devadāru—F.—Holy for śrāddha. (77. 91)
228. Devakūṭa—Mt.—Inhabited by Garuḍas. (69. 332)
229. Devakūṭa—Mt.—Here is a place of the birth of Vainateya Suparṇa. This place covers an area of 100 (square ?) yojanas. Many kinds of birds and Garuḍas live here. There is also a mansion of the king of birds, the inhabitant of Śālmalidvīpa.

Again there are seven cities of the Āgneya Gandharvas, who are the followers of Kubera, on this mountain. [This portion re : the cities of Gandharvas is omitted in Ga.]

On its northern summit is the city of Saiṁhikeyas, the enemies of Devas. There is also a city of Kālakeya Asuras. This city is known as Sunāsa. It covers 60 × 100 yojanas and is difficult of access.

On its southern peak is the city of Autkaca Rākṣasas covering an area of 20 × 62 yojanas. On the central summit is the mansion (or temple, cf. *āyatana*) called Bhūtavaṭa of lord Mahādeva. There Bhūtas, gods, sages, Gandharvas etc. are forever worshipping the lord Bhūtapati.

230. Devakūṭa—Mt.—No. 819.
231. ,, Mt.—No. 1022.
232. ,, Mt.—To the east of this mountain is the Bhadrāśva dvīpa. (43. 12)
233. Devapura—Cy.— ? (89. 1)
234. Devaśṛṅga—H.—No. 1022.

235. Devikā—Rv.—Holy for śrāddha. (77. 41)
235a. ,, Rv.—No. 130.
236. Dhārā—Cy.(?)—In the holy Vindhya mountain the virtuous see not the stream of sin but Dhārā. (77. 34)
237. Dhātakī—Rg.—It is a name of a Khaṇḍa after Dhātaki, son of Savana, lord of Puṣkaradvīpa. [Kha, Gha and Ṅa : Dhātuki.] (33. 15)
238. Dhātakī—Rg.—No. 1027.
239. Dhenukā—Rv.—No. 1100.
240. Dhīvaras— Ja.—No. 470.
241. ,, P.—No. 576.
242. Dhṛtimat—Vr.—No. 673.
243. ,, Vr.—No. 674.
244. Dhruva— Vr.—No. 989.
245. ,, Vr.—No. 988.
246. Dhruvas— Ja.—No. 989.
247. Dhūmajas—Ja.—No. 569.
248. Dhūmra—Mt.—It is sub-merged in the eastern sea. (47. 71-2)
249. Dhūtapāpā—Rv.—No. 674.
250. Divāvṛta—Mt.—No. 605.
251. Divinda—Mt.—No. 606.
252. Draviḍas—P.—They were annihilated by Pramiti at the end of the Kali age. (58. 82)
253. Draviḍas—P.—They will be annihilated by Kalki at the end of the Kali age. (98. 107)
254. Droṇa—Mt.—No. 1108.
255. Dṛṣadvatī—Rv.—The sages performed sacrificial session at the holy place of Kurukṣetra on the banks of the holy river Dṛṣadvatī. (1. 14)
256. Dṛṣadvatī—Rv.—Its original name was Ratnāvatī but in the Kali age it is known by the name Dṛṣadvatī. The Vāyupura is on its bank. (59. 127-8)
257. Dṛṣadvatī—RV.—No. 669.
258. ,, —RV.—No. 130.
259. Druhas—Ja.—No. 470.
260. Dundubhi—D.—No. 608.
261. ,, —Mt.—It is sub-merged in the eastern sea. (47. 71-2)
262. ,, —Mt.—No. 989.
263. Dundubhisvana—Mt.—No. 606.
264. ,, —Vr.—No. 606.
265. Durgā—Rv.—No. 130.
266. Durgas—Ja.—No. 130.
267. Dvārakā—Cy.—Kṛṣṇa was absent from Dvārakā as he had been to the city of Vāraṇāvata to perform the obsequial ceremonies

for the Paṇḍavas (who were supposed to have been burnt to death in the *lākṣāgṛha*). In the meanwhile Bhoja Śatadhanvan killed Bhadrakāra (or Bhaṅgakāra) and besieged the city of Dvārakā. The *syamantaka* jewel was with Akrūra who had fled away. Kṛṣṇa received the news of what had happened in his absence and he pursued Bhoja Śatadhanvan to his capital Mithilā and killed him. But the jewel could not be secured at which Rāma grew angry and refused to leave the city of Mithilā. It was at this time that king Duryodhana came to Mithilā and learned the art of wielding the gadā from Rāma. After many entreaties Rāma came back to Dvārakā. (96. 60-84)

268. Dvāravatī—Cy.—In the episode of the jewel Syamantaka those who were with Kṛṣṇa in their search for Prasena went back to Dvāravatī thinking that Kṛṣṇa was killed in the cave into which he had gone and had not returned for a long time. (96. 46)

269. Dvāravatī Cy.—When Akrūra came back to the famine-stricken city of Dvāravatī there was again rainfall and plenty. (96. 89-90)

270. Dvāravatī—Cy.—It was inhabited by the Yādavas. It had many gates and was protected by Bhojas, Vṛṣṇis and Andhakas with Vasudeva (or Vāsudeva) as their leader. (86. 27-8)

270A. Dyutimat—Mt.—Nos. 437, 674.

271. Ekākṣā—Rv.—No. 569. [Omitted in Gha.]

272. Ekaśṛṅga—Mt.—No. 820.

273. Gabhastala—Rg. (?)—No. 1048.

274. Gabhastimat—Rg.—No. 130.

275. Gajaśaila—Mt.—No. 820.

276. ,, —Mt.—There the Rudras reside. (39. 47)

277. Gaṇḍakī—Rv.—No. 130.

278. Gandhamādana—Mt.—The four sons of Śiva will reside in the Vāli(la)khilyāśrama on the Gandhamādana mountain in the 13th dvāpara. (23. 159)

279. Gandhamādana—Mt.—Nos. 779, 823.

280. ,, —Mt.—No. 818.

281. ,, —Mt.—No. 819.

282. ,, —Mt.—No. 27.

283. Gandhamādana—Mt. (?) —On one side of the Gandhamādana (mountain ?) is a vast gaṇḍikā (plain ?) 32000 × 34000 yojanas in area. There the people are called Ketumālas (?). There is also a heavenly tree of Panasa of six *rasas*. (43. 1-4)

284. Gandhamādana—Mt.—No. 1022.

285. ,, —Mt.—There Purūravas enjoyed with Urvaśī. (91. 6-8)

286. ,, —F.—No. 1022.

287. ,, —Vr.--No. 434.

288. Gāndhāras—P.—They will be annihilated by Kalki at the end of the Kali age. (98. 106–9)
289. Gāndhāras—P.—They were annihilated by Pramiti at the end of the Kali age. (58. 78–83)
290. Gāndhāra—Vṣ.—Bharata, son of Daśaratha, had two sons, Takṣa and Puṣkara. Their respective capital cities were Takṣaśilā and Puṣkarāvatī which were situated in the Gāndhāraviṣaya. (88. 188–90)
291. Gāndhāra—Vṣ.—Gandhāra was a son of Aruddha, a descendant of Yayāti. After him is the Gāndhāra-viṣaya so called. (99. 9–10)
292. Gāndhāra—D.—The horses of the Gāndhāradeśa are the best of their species. (99. 10)
293. Gāndhāras—Ja.—No. 130.
294. ,, —Ja.—No. 470.
295. Gandharva—Rg.—No. 130.
295a. Gandharva—Ja.—No. 470.
296. Gaṅgā—Rv.—No. 606.
297. ,, Rv.—It is the best of rivers and is the source of waters of all the tīrthas. In the holy region at the source of this river on the Himavat mountain Dakṣa started performing a sacrifice which led to the incident of the Dakṣa-Śiva conflict. (30. 92 ff.)
298. Gaṅgā—Rv.—This river once flooded the place (*deśa*) where king Jahnu was performing a sacrifice. The enraged king drank the whole stream. (The gods and sages appear to have appealed to the king to let the stream flow again.) Thence is the river called Jahnavī, i.e., daughter of Jahnu. The water of the river is said to be yellow (*pīta*) ; [but this sense is dispensed with by the readings of Kha and Ga]. (91. 54-60)
299. Gaṅgā— ? —Gaṅgā bore the garbha (of Urvaśī ?). (2. 17)
300. ,, Rv.—It is the best of rivers, being also the wife of Lavaṇōdadhi (i.e. sea) [Omitted in Ṅa]. (30. 32)
301. Gaṅgā—Rv.—Śiva is praised as being Gaṅgātoyārdra (wet with the water of Gaṅgā). (30. 225)
302. Gaṅgā—Rv.—Śiva's hair [body according to Gha] were dishavelled by the water of (the river) Gaṅgā. (54. 97)
303. Gaṅgā—Rv.—Holy for śrāddha. (77. 68)
304. ,, Rv.—Holy for śrāddha [Gayā according to Ka, Ga and Ṅa]. (77. 96)
305. Gaṅgā—Rv.—Holy for śrāddha. (77. 117)
306. ,, Rv.—The Paurāṇika quotes a stanza which says that those versed in genealogies tell that Gaṅgā is called Bhāgīrathī because King Bhagīratha made successful efforts to make it flow down on the earth. (88. 168–9)

307. Gaṅgā—Rv.—Pramiti perished (*niṣṭhāṁ prāptaḥ*) in the region between Gaṅgā and Yamunā. (58. 88)
308. Gaṅgā—Rv.—Kali will perish (*niṣṭhāṁ prāpsyati*) in the region between the rivers Gaṅgā and Yamunā. (98. 117)
309. Gaṅgā—Rv.—Nos. 130, 839, 867, 989, 1022.
310. ,, Rv.—Nos. 470, 1256.
311. ,, Rv.—No. 607.
312. ,, Rv.—No. 708.
313. ,, Rv.—No. 770.
314. ,, Rv.—No. 817.
315. Gantuprastha—Mt.—130.
316. Gaura—Mt.—No. 470.
317. Gaurī—Rv.—No. 606.
318. Gautama—F.—Sons of Śiva will reside in the Gautama forest in the Kali age (i.e. in the 14th dvāpara age?). (23. 163)
319. Gautamas—P.—They belonged to the stock of Aṅgirasas. (65. 97)
319a. Gayā—(See Introduction.)
320. ,, Tī. ?—Holy for śrāddha. (77. 97)
321. ,, Tī.—Very meritorious for śrāddha. One who offers śrāddha in Gayā in the middle of the year gets everything he desires, and is respected in the heaven, etc. [This portion is omitted in Kha.] (82. 14–42)
322. Gayā—Tī.—Holy for śrāddha [Omitted in Kha]. (82. 43)
323. Ghṛtoda—S.—No. 674.
324. Ghṛtodaka—S.—No. 606.
325. Girivraja—Cy.—The son of Śiśunāka will occupy Girivraja on (the river) Vārāṇasī. (99. 315)
326. Girivraja—Cy.—Sahadeva of Magadha was killed in the Bhārata war. His son Somādhi ruled in Girivraja for 58 years. (99.296)
327. Godāvara—Tī.?—Bathing at Saptagodāvara is equal in merits to performance of aśvamedha. (77. 19)
328. Godāvarī—Rv.—Agni (Havyavāhana) loved her. [Omitted in Ṅa.] (29. 12–4)
329. Godāvarī—Rv.—No. 130.
330. Godāvas—Ja.—No. 559.
331. Godhana—Mt.—No. 130.
332. Gokarṇa—F.—By bathing here a sinner gets rid of all his sins and attains merits of aśvamedha. Here did Maheśvara practise penance. Here do *vipras* preach the tenets of the atheists (*nāstikānām*). If a non-Brahmin recites Sāvitrī here he is bound to face destruction. The place is beautiful with sandalwood trees and the river Tāmraparṇī has its source here. (77. 19–24)

333. Gokarṇa—F.—The sons of Śiva will reside in the Gokarṇa forest in the 16th dvāpara. [Omitted in Gha.] (23. 172)
334. Gokarṇa—F. ?—No. 437.
335. Gomanuṣyas—Ja.—No. 569. [Omitted in Gha.]
336. Gomatī—Rv. ?—Nos. 130, 1403.
337. Gomeda—Vr.—No. 989.
338. Gomedaka—Mt.—No. 989.
339. Govardhana—Mt. ?—No. 130. [Omitted in Ga and Gha.]
340. Gṛdhrakūṭa—H.—Holy for śrāddha. In an area covering five yojanas around this place there is (always ?) snowfall. (77. 97)
341. Guhyakas—P.—Nos. 470, 817.
342. ,, —P.—The Yakṣa Rajatanābha was their pitāmaha. He had married a daughter of the Daitya Anuhrāda and had a son named Maṇivara. (69. 151)
343. Guhyakas—P.—They were the descendants of Maṇivara. They are described both as handsome and crooked ; and are also mentioned as Yakṣas. (69. 162)
344. Guhyakas—P.—They are called Rākṣasas as are called also the Yakṣas. They were inferior to Gandharvas by three degrees (pādaiḥ) but are equal to Yakṣas. (69. 194–201)
345. Haihayas—P.—King Bāhu of Ayodhyā was deprived of his kingdom by the Haihayas, Tālajaṅghas, Śakas, Yavanas, Kāmbojas, Pāradas and Pahlavas. But his son Sagara vanquished them and made them captives. But, on his preceptor's advice, he set them free under pain of certain indignities. He also vanquished Kalisparśas, Māhiśikas, Dārvas, Colas and Khasas. (88. 121–42)
346. Haimabhaumakas—Ja.—No. 108.
346a. Haimavata—Vr.—No. 127.
347. Hairaṇvatī ?—Rv.—No. 406.
348. Haṁsa—Mt.—No. 713.
349. Haṁsamārgas—D.—No. 130.
350. ,, —D.—No. 470.
351. Hārapūrikas—D.—No. 130.
352. Hāravāmakas—Ja.—No. 108. [Ga and Gha and Ṅa : Harivāmakas.]
353. Hari—Mt.—No. 569.
354. Hari—Vr.—All the people here are refugees from the Devaloka. Their appearance is as those of Devas. They relish the sugarcane juice. Each of them enjoys a life of 11,000 years. They are all happy without any fear of old age. (46. 8–10)
355. Harigiri—Mt.—No. 674.
356. Harivarṣa—Vr.—Nos. 434, 818.
357. Harikūṭa—H.—God Hari resides here. (39. 58)
358. Harita—Vr.—No. 1108.

359. Harita—Vr.—No.:1107-
360. Haritas—P.—One of the fifteen *pakṣas* of Aṅgirasas. (65. 107)
361. Haritoyā—Rv.—No. 108.
362. Haryaśvas—P.—They were the sons of Dakṣa. They were brought to ruin by Nārada. (65. 139-50)
363. Hastināpura—Cy.—Hastin was a son of Suhotra, a descendant of Dauṣyanti Bharata. He founded the city of Hastināpura. (99. 165)
364. Hayaśiras—T.—Holy for śrāddha. (77. 46)
365. Hema—Mt.—No. 674.
366. Hemakakṣa—Mt.—On this mountain is a city of the Gandharvas like the eighty cities of gods with big ramparts and gates. There the war-like Gandharvas, by name Apattana, with their chief Kapiñjala dwell. (39. 51-2)
367. Hemakūṭa—Mt.—This *varṣaparvata* is described in Vāyu. (1. 85).
368. Hemakūṭa—Mt.—There the Garuḍas reside.
369. ,, —Mt.—This mountain is to the south of...(?). To the north or south (?) of the Himavat is the well-known city of Puṇḍra. (51. 48).
370. Hemakūṭa—Mt.—The Sāyana lake is situated on the Hemakūṭa. (47. 63)
371. Hemakūṭa—Mt.—Gandharvas and Apsarasas live here. (46. 33)
372. ,, —Mt.—Nos. 812, 818, 1022.
373. ,, —Mt.—No. 435.
374. ,, —Vr.—No. 434.
375. Hemaśṛṅga—Vr.—On it is the abode of the great Prajāpati, the four-faced Brahmā. (39. 46)
376. Hemaśṛṅga—Mt.—No. 106.
377. Himāhva—Vr.—No. 434. [Kha : Himāda.]
378. ,, —Vr.—No. 125.
379. ,, —Vr.—No. 470.
380. Himavat—Mt.—The Śaravaṇa is in the corner (kukṣi) of the Himavat mountain. (72. 32).
381. Himavat—Mt.—On its peak the Viśvedevas practised penance. Here do Gandharvas and gods dwell with Apsarasas. The Pitṛs were pleased with the penance of the Viśvedevas and asked them to demand any boons. (76. 1-7)
382. Himavat—Mt.—At the end of the Kali age people will fly to the Himavat mountain for shelter. (99. 403)
383. Himavat—Mt.—1080 (?) yojanas in extent. It is also rich in various minerals. (77. 114)
384. Himavat—Mt.—On the Chāgala hill (?) in its peak will reside the four disciples devoted to Śiva. (23. 116)

385. Himavat—Mt.—In the 15th dvāpara, there will be a mountain called Vedaśirṣa on the Himavat. On the Sarasvatī hill (a branch of this mountain ?) will dwell the sons of Śiva. (The sense is very confusing here.) (23. 168–9)

386. Himavat—Mt.—On the peak of the Himavat is the Jaṭāyu mountain where the sons of Śiva will reside in the 19th dvāpara. (23. 186–7)

387. Himavat—Mt.—On the Aṭṭahāsa range (?) of the Himavat the sons of Śiva will reside in the 20th (dvāpara ?). (23. 191–2)

388. Himavat—Mt.—The Mahāpuruṣa created by Śiva was like the Himādri. (30. 130)

389. Himavat—Mt.—It is called a varṣaparvata. (1. 85)

390. Himavat—Mt.—The Agniṣvātta Pitṛs gave their daughter Menā to Himavat. (30. 31)

391. Himavat—Mt.—It extends north-south and east-west right upto the sea (?). (35. 9)

392. Himavat—Mt.—Śiva in his incarnation of Guhāvāsī resided on the summit of the Himavat in the holy Siddhakṣetra in th 17th dvāpara age. (23. 174–5)

393. Himavat—Mt.—It was consecrated as the lord of mountains. (70. 9)

394. Himavat—Mt.—On the occasion of the milking of the earth Meru was one who milked, Himavat was the calf and Śaila (mountain) was the pot. (62. 190)

395. Himavat—Mt.—Nos. 369, 524, 607, 812, 818, 819.

396. ,, —Mt.—Nos. 185, 820, 831, 1022, 1155.

397. ,, —Mt.—No. 130.

398. ,, —Mt.—No. 194.

399. ,, —Mt.—No. 435.

400. ,, —Mt.—No. 469.

401. ,, —Mt.—No. 470.

402. ,, —Mt.—No. 142.

403. ,, —Mt.—No. 297.

404. Hīnānas—Ja.—No. 569.

405. Hiraṇmaya—Mt.—No. 818.

406. Hiraṇvat—Vr.—This varṣa is to the north of Śveta and to the south of Śṛṅgasāhva mountains. There the Mānavas live 12500 (?) years. They are happy and lovely in appearance with their desires fulfilled in all seasons. They drink the juice of the fruits of a big Lakuca tree which grows in that varṣa. The river Hiraṇvatī also flows there. (45. 6–10)

407. Hiraṇyapura—Cy.—In this city the Dānavas named Paulomas and Kālakeyas lived. (68. 25–7)

408. Hiraṇyavāhinīlā—Rv.—No. 108.

409. Hradas—D.—No. 130.

410. Hradas—Ja.—No. 470.
411. Hrādinī—Rv.—Agni (i.e. Havyavāhana) loved her. [Ṅa omits this.] (29. 13-4)
412. Hrādinī—Rv.—No. 470.
413. Hūṇas—D.—No. 130.
414. Ikṣu—Rv.—No. 130.
415. „ —Rv.—No. 1100.
416. Ikṣulā—Rv.—No. 130.
417. Ikṣurasodaka—S.—No. 1108.
418. Ilāvṛta—Vr.—It is in the centre of Jambudvīpa (?). There the sun, the moon and the *nakṣatras* do not shine. The people, who are really refugees from the Devaloka, live on the fruits and juice of Jambu tree, having a life of 13000 years each. This varṣa is to the opposite side (pratidiśaṁ) of the Mount Meru covering 9000 (or 1026 ?) yojanas. Its shape is like that of a *śarāva* (earthenware ?) (46. 11-6)
419. Ilāvṛta—Vr.—No. 818.
420. Indradvīpa.—Rg.—No. 130.
421. „ —Rg.—No. 470.
422. Indradyumna.—L.—No. 470.
423. Indrakāsas.—Ja.—No. 470.
424. Indranadī—Rv.—No. 108.
425. Indranīla—Mt.—No. 106.
426. Indraśaila—Mt.—No. 713.
427. Irāvatī—Rv.—Agni (Havyavāhana) loved her. [Omitted in Ṅa.] (29. 12-4)
428. Irāvatī—Rv.—No. 130.
429. Jalada—Vr.—No. 1099.
430. „ —Vr.—No. 1100.
431. Jaladhāra—Mt.—No. 1100.
432. Jambūdvīpa—Dv.—The Jambudvīpa and other dvīpas are described in the Vāyu Purāna. [Kha, Gha and Ṅa : Jambudvīpa.] 1. 88.
433. Jambudvīpa—Dv.—Priyavrata was the son of Svāyaṁbhuva Manu. He had ten sons and two daughters. He divided the whole earth of seven dvīpas amongst his sons thus :—Jambudvīpa he assigned to Agnīdhra, Plakṣadvīpa to Medhātithi, Śālmalidvīpa to Vapuṣmat, Kuśadvīpa to Jyotiṣmat, Krauñcadvīpa to Dyutimat, Śākadvīpa to Havya and Puṣkaradvīpa to Savana. 33. 1-14.
434. Jambudvīpa—Dv.—Priyavrata consecrated Agnīdhra (i.e. Priyavrata's daughter's son) [Ga and Ṅa read differently] as the lord of Jambudvīpa. This Agnīdhra has the following sons, viz., Nābhi, Kiṁpuruṣa, Harivarṣa, Ilāvṛta, Ramya, Hariṇmat

(Gha : Hiranmat), Kuru, Bhadrāśva, and Ketumāla. The deśas assigned to them are as follows: The southern varṣa named Himāhva was assigned to Nābhi, the Hemakuṭa varṣa to Kimpuruṣa (?), Naiṣadha varṣa to Harivarṣa, the central portion of Sumeru to Ilāvṛta, Nīlavarṣa to Ramya, the northern Śveta (varṣa) to Hariṇmat, the northern Śṛṅgavat varṣa to Kuru, Mālyavat varṣa to Bhadrāśva and Gandhamādanavarṣa to Ketumāla. 33. 37-45

435. Jambudvīpa—Dv.—The Jambūdvīpa of the nine varṣas is described thus :—It is 100 thousand yojanas in expanse, and it teems with various janapadas and puras. It is encompassed by nine bhuvanas and is adorned with mountains inhabited by Siddhas, Cāraṇas and Gandharvas. The Lāvaṇa sea surrounds it [Kha and Gha omit this sentence]. Extending east-west to the seas (thus equal in extent to the dvīpa) are the following six varṣa mountains : Himavat, Hemakūṭa, Niṣadha, Sauvarṇa, Meru, and Caturasra (?). (34. 9-16)

436. Jambudvīpa—Dv.—On the peak of the southern mountain (i.e. Gandhamādana—cf., Meru No. 819) do jambū trees grow ever decked with fruits and flowers. The river Jambūnadī flows thence, and the Jambūnada is also there. There the Devas, Gandharvas, Dānavas, Yakṣas, Rākṣasas, and Paunagas relish the sweet jambū juice and hence (?) is the sanātana Jambudvīpa so called. (35. 26-32)

437. Jambudvīpa—Dv.—There are six sub-divisions of Jambudvīpa, which are : Aṇgadvīpa, Yamadvīpa, Malayadvīpa, Śaṅkhadvīpa, Kuśadvīpa and Varāhadvīpa. [The last three are omitted in Kha.]

The Aṅgadvīpa is occupied by the various *gaṇas* of the Mlechhas. In it is the Cakragiri in the centre of Nāgadeśa. In Yamadvīpa there is a mountain called Dyutimat which is a source of gold and pearls (samudragānāṁ prabhavaḥ). [This information about Dyutimat is not found in Ṅa.] The Malayadvīpa is inhabited by the Mlecchas and there sandalwood trees grow in abundance. It is equally a store-house of gold and pearls. In this dvīpa are the Malaya and Mandara mountains. On the Mandara is the abode of Agastya revered by gods and asuras alike. The Malaya excels even the svarga in its foliage. On the Trikūṭa mountain (of this dvīpa) is the spacious city of Laṅkā, 100 × 30 yojanas in extent. It belongs to Kāmarūpin Rākṣasas, who pride in their power and hate the Devas. It is a *terra incognita* to men and is difficult of access. In the eastern tīra (?) of this dvīpa (i.e. Malayadvīpa) is Gokarna, an abode of Śaṅkara [according to Kha and Gha, of Deva.]

The Śaṅkhadvīpa, which is a home of the various gaṇas of the Mlechas, is 100 yojanas in extent. It has only one king, viz. Śaṅkhamukha, the lord of the Nāgas (*nāgarāja*). In it are the mountain Śaṅkhagiri and the river Śaṅkhanāgā. In the Kumudadvīpa (i.e. Kuśadvīpa ?) Kumudā, a sister of Mahādeva, is worshipped. The Varāhadvīpa is occupied by the various gaṇas of the Mlecchas. This prosperous dvīpa has a mountain named Varāha whence the river Vārāha flows. Here the lord (Viṣṇu) in his Vārāha form is worshipped by gods. Such is the description of the six anudvīpas of (Jambudvīpa) and in the south (of this Jambudvīpa ?) is the Bharatadvīpa-deśa. (48. 13-43)

438. Jambudvīpa—Dv.—No. 469.

439. ,, —Dv.—Nos. 818, 823, 989.

440. Jambūlā—Rv.—No. 130.

441. Jambūmārga—?—Holy for śrāddha. (77. 38)

442. Jāmbunada—Rv. ?—No. 818.

443. ,, —Rv. ?—No. 819.

444. ,, —Rv. ?—No. 436.

445. Jambunadī—Rv.—No. 436.

446. ,, —Rv.—No. 824.

447. Janasthāna—Rg —At Janasthāna, Rāma, the son of Daśaratha, lived and fulfilled the desire of gods by killing the son of Pulastya (i.e. Rāvaṇa). (88. 194-5)

448. Jaṅgas—Ja.—No. 569. [Gha : Jaṅghas.]

449. Jāhnavī—Rv.—Viśvasphāni of Magadha will offer his body (i.e. die) in the stream of the river Jāhnavī after paying respects to gods, manes and Brahmins. (99. 381)

450. Jāhnavī—Rv.—Nos. 298, 709.

451. Jārudhi—Mt.—No. 660.

452. ,, —Mt.—No. 713.

453. Jaṭāyu—Mt.—No. 386.

454. Jaṭhara—Mt.—No. 819.

455. ,, —Mt.—No. 1022.

456. Jātudhi—Mt.—In the northern deśa is the devaparvata Jātudhi [Gha and Ṅa : Jārudhi]. There Yakṣas, Kinnaras, Gandharvas, Nāgas, Rākṣasas and Daityas dwell. In its central kūṭa (hill) is a beautiful lake named Ānandajala [Gha, Ṅa : Nanadajala] which covers an area of 30 yojanas. There the lord of the Nāgas named Caṇḍa of hundred faces dwells. He has, as his emblem, the discus (cakra) of Viṣṇu. (41. 66-73)

457. Jātudhi—Mt.—No. 106. [Gha and Ṅa : Jārudhi.]

458. Jayanta—Mt.—Nos. 130, 569.

459. Jīmūta—D.—No.

460. ,, —Vr.—Nos. 1107, 1108.

461. Juhuḍas—D.—No. 130.
461a. Jyotsnā—Rv.—No. 1278.
462. Kācalas—Ja.—No. 569.
463. Kacchīyas—Ja.—No. 130.
464. Kaikaṭa— ?—No. 1316. [Kha, Ga and Ṅa : Vaikaṭa.]
465. Kailāsa—Mt.—The Mahāpuruṣa created by Śiva was like Kailāsa. (30. 130)
466. Kailāsa—Mt.—Bali, the Dānava, is compared to Kailāsa. (50. 48)
467. ,, —Mt.—The summit of the Kailāsa is frequented by the Cakravākas, Mayūras, Krauñcas, Kokilas and also by Siddhas, Cāraṇas, Apsarasas, Kinnaras and the Bhūtas and Vināyakas. Here did the wife of Śiva ask him a question as to why he is called Nīlakaṇṭha. (54. 30-45)
468. Kailāsa—Mt.—The lord of the Yakṣas has his place of residence on the Kailāsa. (30. 85)
469. Kailāsa—Mt.—The Kailāsa is an abode of the devotees of god. On its central hill (kūṭa) is situated the city of Dhanādhyakṣa Kubera. This city occupies an area of 100 × 50 yojanas. At the centre of this city is a spacious *sabhā* called Vipulā. The great *vimāna* which is a vehicle of Kubera, the king of the Yakṣas, is kept here. Here does Kubera, the friend of Mahādeva, dwell with Apsarasas, Gandharvas, Yakṣas, Siddhas and Cāraṇas. The eight *mahānidhānas* of Kubera are also kept in this sabhā. In this city Indra, Agni and Yama also reside. A beautiful pond (vāpī) named Mandākinī adds to the beauty of the city. The rivers Alakanandā and Nandā flow here. On the eastern hill of this mountain are situated the ten cities of the Gandharvas. These cities occupy 1000 × 30 yojanas of area. On the western hill (kūṭa), which is 80 × 40 yojanas in area, are the thirty mansions of thirty Yakṣa-chiefs whose paramount lord is Vaiśravaṇa. On the snow-clad peak in the south are the 100 cities of Kinnaras. There Rudra married Umā ; there did she practise penance ; there Śiva played in his Kirāta form ; and Śiva and Umā had a view of Jambudvīpa from this very place. Here is also the Umāvana where Śiva assumed the *ardhanaranārī* form, as also the Śaravaṇa where the six-faced (Skanda) was born. On the Krauñcaśaila of this mountain were lions yoked to the chariot of Kārtikeya. It was here that Guha (i.e. Skanda ?) was consecrated to the generalship of the gods. On the eastern *taṭa* of Kailāsa is the Kalāpagrāma where the sages, viz., Mṛkaṇḍa, Vasiṣṭha, Bharata, Nala, Viśvāmitra, Uddālaka and others have their hermitages in hundreds and thousands in this Himavat (mountain). (41. 1-47)

470. Kailāsa—Mt.—It is to the left side of the Himavat. Kubera, the lord of the city of Alakā lives here with Rākṣasas and Apsarasas. Here is a lake named Kumudvat at the foot of the mountain whence the river Mandākinī flows. On its bank is a great forest. A little north of the Kailāsa is the hill called Candraprabha at the foot of which is the Acchoda lake which is the source of the river Acchodā whose banks are lined with a forest named Caitraratha. On the Candraprabha hill the commander of the Yakṣas, by name Maṇibhadra, dwells surrounded by the cruel Guhyakas The rivers Mandākinī and Acchododikā flow south-east and passing along the Piśaṅga mountain join the great sea. At the foot of the Lohita hill is the Lohita lake which is a source of the river (?) Lauhityā on whose banks is a forest named Viśoka. On the Lohitā the Yakṣa Maṇivara resides with the pious Guhyakas. To the south of the Kailāsa are the Trikaku(?) [Ṅa-Trikaṭu] and Vaidyuta hills. At the foot of the Vaidyuta hills is the Mānasa lake, the source of the river Sarayū with the Vaibrāja forest on its banks. Here dwells the powerful Rākṣasa, named Brahmapāta [Ga and Gha : Brahmāpeta] who is a follower of Kubera and is followed by hundreds of Yātudhānas. The Aruṇa mount, the abode of Girīśa, at the foot of which is the Śailoda lake whence the river Śailodā flows, is also to the south of the Kailāsa. This river joins the Lavaṇodadhi. The forest Surabhi is on its banks. To the north of Kailāsa is the hill named Gaura with the beautiful lake Bindusara at its foot. It was near this lake that the royal sage Bhagīratha dwelt for many years for the river Gaṅgā. It was here that the heavenly river of the three courses descended on the earth and started its sevenfold course. While falling from the heavens the drops of water so collected formed the lake Bindusara (hence its name) whence this river flows in seven channels—three to the east and three to the west, the one to the south which followed Bhagīratha, after whom it was called Bhāgīrathī. All these seven courses of the river grace the Himāhva varṣa. The names of the eastern courses of this river are : Nalinī, Hrādinī, and Pāvanī ; those of the western are : Sītā, Cakṣu and Sindhu. All these courses water the following deśas :—Sirindhras, Kuntalas, Cīnas, Barbaras, Yavasas, Druhas, Ruṣāṇas, Kuṇindas, Aṅgas and Lokavaras (or Aṅgalokavaras ?). The river Sītā thus divides the Sindhumaru land and joins the western sea. The river Cakṣu waters the following janapadas :—Cīnamarus, Taṅgaṇas, Sarvamūlikas [Kha, Ga, Gha and Ṅa : Sarvaśūlikas], Āndhras, Tuṣāras, Tampākas, Pahnavas, Daradas and Śakas. The river Gaṅgā blesses the following ārya jana-

padas :—Daradas, Kāśmīras, Gāndhāras, Varapas, Hradas, Śivapauras, Indrahāsas, Vadātis, (Visarjayas ?), Saindhavas, Randhrakarakas (or Randhras and Karakas ?) [Gha : Randhravarakas], Bhramaras, [Kha, Gha and Ṅa : Bhramaṭas], Ābhīras, Rohakas, Śunāmukhas, Ūrdhvamanus [Kha, Gha and Ṅa : Ūrdhvamarus. The same Mss. read that these janapadas were watered by the river Sindhu], Gandharvas, Kinnaras, Yakṣas, Rākṣasas, Vidyādharas, Uragas, Kalāpagrāmakas, Pāradas, Sīgaṇas [Kha and Ṅa : Tāṅgaṇas], Khasas, Kirātas, Pulindas, Kurus, Bharatas, Pāñcālas, Kāśis, Mātsyas, Magadhas, Aṅgas, Brahmottaras, Vaṅgas and Tāmraliptas and being obstructed by the Vindhya (mountain) it joined the southern sea. The river Āhlādinī, (in the above list of seven courses of the river the name is Hrādini), runs to the east through the Upabhogas (or territories) of the various *jātis* of the Niṣādas, and of the Dhīvaras, Ṛṣīkas, Nīlamukhas, Keralas, Uṣṭrakarṇas [Kha, Ga and Gha : Naṣṭakarṇas] Kirātas, Kālodaras, Vivarṇas, Kumāras [Kha, Ga, Gha and Ṅa : Kumārīs], and Svarṇabhūṣitas (?). The course Pāvanī, wading through the Indradyumna lake and watering (the land of ?) Kharāpathas, Indraśaṅkupathas and Kuthaprāvaraṇas (?) enters the Lavaṇodadhi (?) near the sea of Indradvīpa. The course Nalinī also rushes up to the east watering (the land of ?) Tomaras, Haṁsamārgas, Saddūhukas (?), Karṇaprāvaraṇas, Aśvamukhas and Vidyādharas and thus joins the great sea. These courses, in their turn, have their own numerous tributaries. (47. 1-60)

471. Kailāsa—Mt.—Nos. 694, 845.

472. ,, —Mt.—No. 817.

473. ,, —Mt.—No. 819.

473a. ,, —Mt.—No. 820.

474. Kāla—Mt.—Nos. 1022, 1179.

475. Kalas—Ja.—No. 567.

476. Kālaṁjara—Mt.—On this mountain Śiva will pass away his time in the 23rd dvāpāra; that is why this mountain is called Kālaṁjara. (23. 204)

477. Kālañjara—Cy. ?—Situated on the banks of the (river) Daśārṇā. It is holy for śrāddha. (77. 93)

478. Kalāpagrāma—Cy.—The king Aiḍa (Purūravas) is called the inhabitant of Kalāpagrāma. (1. 189)

479. Kalāpagrāma—Cy.—Purūravas enjoyed with Urvaśī in Kalāpagrāma. (91. 7)

480. Kalāpagrāma—Cy.—Manu, a descendant in the Ikṣvāku line, resorted to yoga and resided in Kalāpagrāma in the 19th *prayuga*. He is also called Kṣatraprāvartaka. (88. 210)

481. Kalāpagrāma—Cy.—Devāpi, a Paurava king, was a great yogin. He resided in Kalāpagrāma.
482. Kalāpagrāma—Cy.—Nos. 469, 779.
483. Kalāpagrāmakas—Ja.—No. 470.
484. Kālasarpi—Tī.—The tīrtha of Kaśyapa [Kāśyapa in Gha] is known as Kālasarpi. It is holy for śraddha. (77. 87)
485. Kālatopakas—Ja.—This janapada will be ruled over by the Maṇidhānyajas. (99. 384)
486. Kālatoyakas—D.—(No. 130).
487. Kālindī—Rv.—(No. 569). [Omitted in Gha.]
488. Kaliṅgas—D.—Here the āśramadharma does not prevail and it is taboo for śrāddha purposes. (78. 23)
489. Kaliṅgas—Ja.—It was the janapada of Kaliṅga, son of king Bali (of Yayāti's line) who reigned in the east. (99. 33-4)
490. Kaliṅgas—Ja.—This janapada will be protected by Guha. (99. 386)
491. Kaliṅgas—Rg.—There people will fly in the end of the Kali age. (99. 402)
492. Kaliṅgas—D.—No. 22.
493. Kaliṅga—Mt.—No. 820.
494. ,, —Mt.—No. 1022.
495. Kaliṅgas—Ja.—No. 130.
496. ,, —? —No. 470.
497. Kalisparśas—Ja.—No. 345.
498. Kālodaras—Ja. ?—No. 470.
498a. Kambalas—Ja.—No. 567.
499. Kambala—Mt.—No. 569.
500. Kambalā—Rv.—No. 569.
501. Kāmbojas—D.—130.
502. ,, —Ja.—No. 345.
502a. Kāmodakas—Ja.—569.
503. Kāmpilya—Cy. ?—Samara, one of the Nīpas and a descendant of Yayāti, ruled in Kāmpilya. (99. 106-8)
504. Kanakanandi—Tī.—By having a bath here one goes to heaven. (Cf. No. 856). (77. 105)
505. Kanakhola—Tī. ?—Holy for śrāddha. (82. 21)
506. Kanakaśrṅga.—Mt.—No. 713.
507. Kaṅka—Mt.—(No. 27). [Gha and Ṅa : Kāka.]
508. ,, —Mt.—No. 1108.
509. Kānanasthalī— ?—It is situated between the Puṣpaka and Mahāmegha mountains. It is 100 × 60 yojanas in extent. (38. 71-3)
510. Kāñcanakā—Cy.—The descendants of Vindhyaśakti (?) will rule in this city for sixty years. (99. 371-2)
511. Kāñcī—Rv.—(No. 103). [Ka : Kañcī].

512. Kañcī—Rv.—No. 569.
513. Kāṇva—P.—One of the fifteen Pakṣas of Aṅgirasas. (65. 106-8)
514. Kapila—Vr.—Nos. 673, 674.
515. ,, —Mt.—No. 713.
516. ,, —Mt.—No. 1179.
517. ,, —Mt.—No. 27.
518. Kapilakarṇikas—Ja.—No. 569.
519. Kapiñjala—Mt.—Between Kapiñjala and Nāgaśaila there is a big *sthalī* which is 100 × 200 (or 102 ?) yojanas in extent. It is overgrown with trees of Kharjjūra, Nīlāśoka, Dāḍima, Atasī, Kadalī, Akṣoṭaka, Badarī, Nāga and Drākṣa. (38. 66-70)
520. Kapiñjala—Mt.—No. 106.
521. Kapotakas—Ja.—No. 569.
521a. Karambhavas—Ja.—No. 567.
522. Karañja—Mt.—On this mountain there is an abode of Śaṅkara, the lord of the Bhūtas. Here the Bhūtas dwell in their different forms. (39. 42-3)
523. Karañjas—Ja.—No. 569.
524. Kārapatha—D.—Aṅgada, son of Dāśarathi Lakṣmaṇa, had his janapada at the foot of the Himavat mountain. This janapada is the same as the Kārapatha deśa in which the capital city known as Aṅgadīyā was situated. (88. 187-8)
524a. Kārapatha—D.—No. 51.
525. Kāraskaras—D.—Here the āśramadharma does not prevail and this deśa is taboo for śrāddha performances. [Ka : Kāraṅkaras.] (78. 23)
526. Kāraskaras—P.—They live in a country (deśa) of sin. The virtuous evade contact with them. By visiting this unholy land one is inflicted with sin. (78. 69-72)
527. Karatoyā—Rv.—No. 130.
528. Karavāṭas—Ja.—No. 569.
529. Karkoṭaka— ? —Kārtavīrya Arjuna conquered Karkotakasabhā (i.e. the sabhā of Karkoṭaka Nāgas ?) with the thousand Nāgas and entered the city of Māhiṣmatī. (94. 26)
530. Kāru—Mt.—No. 130.
530a. Karūṣa—Rg.—Dantavaktra was lord of Karūṣa. (96. 155)
530b. Karūṣas—P.—No. 130.
531. Kaseru—Rg.—No. 130.
532. Kaserukas—D.—No. 130.
533. Kāśi—Cy. ?—Kuśadhvaja was the lord of Kāśi. He was a son of Sīradhvaja Janaka. [Gha : Sāṁkāśi.] (89. 18)
534. Kāśi—Cy. ?—Vibhu [Kha and Gha : Babhru] was the king of Kāśi. In his *viṣaya* rain did not fall for three years. Then he invited Śvafalka (or Svafalka) to stay with him and the rains came. 96. 103-4)

535. Kāśi—Cy. ?—Satyaka's wife was Kāśiduhitā (i.e. a daughter of the king of Kāśi). (This Satyaka was one of the Vṛṣṇis or Andhakas.) (96. 115)
536. Kāśi—Cy. ?—People will fly to Kāśikośalas (i.e. Kāśis and Kosalas ?) at the end of the Kali age. (99. 402)
537. Kāśi— ? —Kāśa was one of the three sons of Suta-hotra. His rāṣṭa (rāṣṭra ?) was called Kāśis (or Kāśaya ?). (92. 1-6)
538. Kāśi— ? —Dīrghatapas was a son of Kāśa. He had no son and hence he practised penance. Dhanvantari was pleased and as a consequence of the boon demanded by the king he was born as the king's son in the second dvāpara age. This Dhanvantari (i.e. son of Dīrghatapas) is described as Kāśi-rāja. (92. 18-21)
539. Kāśi— ? —King Alarka, called Kāśisattama, achieved a long life due to the favour of Lopāmudrā. (92. 67)
539a. Kāśi— ? —No. 1403.
540. ,, —Ja.—No. 470.
541. ,, — ? —No.
542. ,, —Ja.—No. 130.
543. **Kāśmīras**—D.—No. 130.
544. ,, —Ja.—No. 470.
545. ,, —Rg.—People will fly to (the land of ?) Kāśmīras at the end of the Kali age. (99. 402)
546. Kaumāra—Vr.—No. 1100.
547. ,, —Vr.—No. 1099.
548. Kauraja—Mt.—It is inhabited by the Garuḍas. (69. 330-4)
549. Kauśāmbī—Cy.—No. 361.
550. Kauśika—Rg.—No. ?
551. Kauśikas—P.—At the end of the Kali age the Kauśikas will inhabit countries afflicted with hunger and fear. (58. 62)
552. Kauśikī—Rv.—Agni (i.e. Havyavāhana) loved her [Ṅa : omits this]. (29. 14)
553. Kauśikī—Rv.—It is the best of rivers, named after (?) Kauśikī or Satyavatī, wife of the sage Ṛcīka. (91. 88-9)
554. Kauśikī—Rv. ?—Holy for śrāddha (cf. Nos. 184 & 1197). (77.101
555. ,, —Rv.—No. 130.
556. Kāverī—Rv.—It is the best of rivers. King Jahnu's wife was Kāverī. (91. 59)
557. Kāverī—Rv.—Holy for śrāddha. (77. 28)
558. ,, —Rv.—Agni (i.e. Havyavāhana) loved her. (29)
559. ,, —Rv.—Nos. 130, 184.
560. ,, —Rv.—No. 108.
560a. Kāyārohaṇa—T.—No. 814.
561. Kekayas—Ja.—Kekaya was one of the four sons of Śibi. His janapada was Kekaya. (99. 24)

562. Kekayas—Ja.—No. 130.

563. Keralas—Ja.—Kerala was one of the four sons of king Janāpīḍa of Turvasu line. His janapada was known as Kerala. (99. 5-6)

564. Keralas—Ja.—No. 130.

565. „ —Ja.—No. 470.

566. Kesara—V.—This Kesara-droṇi is situated between the Kumuda and Añjana mountains. Here is also the Śabala forest in which is a mansion of Viṣṇu, the guru of the Suras. (38. 45-8)

567. Keśari—Mt.—No. 1100.

568. Ketas—P.—They were annihilated by Pramiti at the end of the Kali age. (58. 78-83)

569. Ketumāla—Dv.—This dvīpa is to the west of the Niṣadha mountain. The seven Kula mountains in this dvīpa are : Viśāla, Kambala, Kṛṣṇa, Jayanta, Hari, Aśoka and Vardhamāna. [Ga omits the last two names.] These mountains have their own numerous ranges. The janapadas which are 'mixed' (*vimisrāḥ*) with these mountains and which are protected by many kings are as follows :—Pauras (is Paura here a generic term as the janapada ?) [Gha and Ṅa, however, read Sauras instead], Gomanuṣyas, Kapotakas [Gha omits these three names], Tatsukhas (?), Bhramaras [Ṅa : Bhrāmaras], Yūthas, Māheyas, Acalakūṭakas, Sumaulas, Stāvakas, Krauñcas, Kṛṣṇāṅgas, Maṇipunjakas (Ṅa : Maṇiyuñjakas), Kuṭas, Kambalas, Mauṣīyas, Karambhavas, Kucas, Śvetas [Gha and Ṅa : Śyenas], Suvarṇakaṭakas (?) [Ga, Gha and Ṅa : Suvarṇataṭakas], Śvetāṅgas, Kṛṣṇāpādas, Vihas [Ga : Vidas ; Gha : Vindas], Kapilakarṇikas, Atyākarālagojvālas, Hīnānas, Vanapātakas [Ga, Gha and Ṅa : Vānapātakas], Mahivas, Kumudābhas, Karavātas, Utkacas, Śunakāsas [Gha : Śukanāsas], Mahānāsas (?), Vanāsagajabhūmikas (?) Karañjas, Mañjamas, Vāhas, Kiṣkiṇḍīs (?), Pāṇḍubhūmikas, Kuberas, Dhūmajas, Jaṅgas [Gha · Janghas], Vaṅgas, Rājīvakokilas (or Rājīvas and Kokilas ?), Vācāṅgas, Mahāṅgas, Madhaureyas, Surecakas, Pittalas [Gha and Ṅa : Pittatas], Kācalas, Śravaṇas, Mattakāsikas [Gha : Mattavāsikas], Godāvas, Vakulas, Vāṅgas, Vaṅgas, Kāmodakas and Kalas. They drink the waters of the following rivers : Suvaprā [Ga and Ṅa : Suvakṣā], Kambalā, Tāmasī, Śyāmā, Sumedhā, Bakulā [Ga and Ṅa : Bahulā], Vikīrṇā, Śikhimālā, Darbhāvati, Bhadrā, Śukanadī, Palāśā, Bhīmā, Prabhañjanā, Kāñcī, Cuśāvatī, Dakṣā, Śākavatī, Puṇyodā, Candrāvatī, Sumūlā, Ṛṣabhā, Samudramālā, Campāvatī, Ekākṣā, Puṣkalā, Vāhā, Suvarṇā, Nandinī, Kālindī, Puṇyodā, Bhāratī, Brāhmī and Viśālā [Names from Candrāvatī to Viśālā are omitted in Gha], Pīvarī, Kumbhakārī, Ruṣā, Mahiṣī, Mānuṣī and Daṇḍā. Such is this western mahādvīpa. (44)

570. Ketumāla—Dv.—Nos. 27, 819.
570a. ,, —Dv.—No. 818.
571. Khasas—P.—They were annihilated by Pramiti at the end of the Kali age. (58. 83)
572. Khasas—P.—They will be annihilated by Kalki at the end of the Kali age. (98. 106-9)
573. Khasas—D.—No. 130 [Ga : S[illegible]asas].
574. ,, —P.—No. 345.
575. ,, —Ja.—No. 470.
576. Khasas—P.—The angry sages 'churned' the left arm of Vena and thence arose a pigmy-like (*hrasva*) black figure ; he was frightened and stood aghast with his hands folded begging for mercy. The sages ordered him to sit (*niṣīda*). Thus did he become the founder of the race (*vāṁśa*) of the Niṣādas. He also procreated the Dhīvaras who inherited the vices of Vena ; and those who were the inhabitants of the Vindhya, viz., Tumburas, Stuvaras, (or Tuvaras ?) [Ga : Varbaras], and Khasas, were irreligious and they too inherited the vices of Vena. (62. 119-25)
577. Khyāti 7—Rv.—No. 606.
578. Kiṁbhayas—P.—One of the fifteen pakṣas of Aṅgirasas. (65. 106-8)
579. Kiṁpuruṣa—Vr.—The people in Kiṁpuruṣa varṣa enjoy a life of 10,000 years : Their complexion is like gold in colour. With their minds pure they are always happy. In this varṣa there is a plakṣa tree the juice of which the people drink. (46. 2-7)
580. Kiṁpuruṣa—Vr.—No. 434.
581. ,, Vr.—No. 818.
582. Kiṁpuruṣas—P.—They were the descendants of Hari (-bhadrā ?), a daughter of Krodhā, who was a Rākṣasī. (69. 208)
583. Kiṁpuruṣas—P.—The Mayā-kiṁpuruṣas were descendants of Pulaha. (70. 65)
584. Kiṁśuka—F.—It is situated between Vasudhāra and Ratnadhāra mountains covering an area of 100 × 30 yojanas. Here Siddhas, Cāraṇas and Apsarasas reside. In this forest is a mansion (*āyatana*) of Āditya (i.e. sun-god) where he descends every month. (38. 27-32)
585. Kirātas—P.—They were annihilated by Pramiti at the end of the Kali age. They had various jātis. (58. 78-83)
586. Kirātas—P.—They will be annihilated by Kalki at the end of the Kali age. (98. 106-9)
587. Kirātas—P.— No. 130.
588. ,, Ja.—No. 130.
589. ,, Ja.—No. 470.

590. Kirātas—P.—No. 470.

591. Kisaṣṇas—Ja.—No. 130 [Ga : Kisaṣṭas].

592. Kiṣkindha—C.—The god Śiva, after narrating to his wife the story of how he came to be called as Nīlakaṇṭha, retired to the Kiṣkindha cave with his wife Umā. (54. 116)

593. Kiṣkindhakas—P.—No. 130.

594. Kiṣkiṇḍīs (?)—Ja.—No. 569.

595. Kolāhala—Mt.—No. 130.

596. Kolavanas—D.—No. 130.

597. Komalā—Cy. or Rg.—In Komalā there will be powerful kings who will be known as Meghas of whom there will be nine kings [Ṅa reads Medhātithi instead of Meghas]. They will (also) be known as Niṣadha kings, as they were (cf. *prasūtāḥ*) descendants of Nala. (99. 375-7)

597a. Korañja—(No. 108)—[Ṅa : Kaurañja].

598. Kośalas—Ja.—This janapada will be protected (i.e. ruled) by Guha. (99. 385)

599. Kośalā—Rg.—The kingdom of Kuśa, son of Dāśarathī Rāma was known as Kośalā. Its capital was Kuśasthalī situated amidst the hills of the Vindhya mountain. In the Uttarākośala was the kingdom of Lava (brother of Kuśa), with its capital city Śrāvastī. [Gha reads Kośalā only for Uttarākośala and does not connect it with Śrāvastī]. (80. 199-200)

600. Kosalas—Ja.—No. 130.

601. Kośalā—T.—In Kośalā there is a pond or well (vāpī). By merely bathing there one goes to heaven. (77. 36)

602. Kośalas—Ja.—Nos. 536, 542.

602a. Kratu—Rv.—No. 989.

603. Krauñca—Mt.—Skanda killed Tārakāsura on the Krauñca mountain. (72. 47)

604. Krauñca—Mt.—Nos. 469, 606.

605. Krauñcas—Ja.—No. 569.

606. Krauñcadvīpa—Dv.—This dvīpa is twice in area as that of Kuśadvīpa ; it surrounds the Ghṛtodaka sea. The following are the mountains in this dvīpa : Krauñca, Vāmanaka, Andhakāraka, Divāvṛt, Divinda, Puṇḍarīka, and Dundubhisvana ; and the corresponding varṣas are : Kuśala, Manonuga, Uṣṇa, Prāvaraka, Andhakāraka. Muni and Dundubhisvana. The seven great rivers corresponding to these varṣas are : Gaurī, Kumudvatī, Saṁdhyā, Rātri, Manojavā, Khyāti and Puṇḍarīkā. Thus is Gaṅgā sevenfold (i.e. having seven courses; cf. *saptavidhā*). (49. 61-71)

607. Krauñcadvīpa—Dv.—Menā was the wife of Himavat. She gave birth to Maināka and Gaṅgā. Maināka's younger brother (*anuja*) was Krauñca after whom Krauñcadvīpa is so called [Ṅa omits this]. (30. 32)

608. Krauñcadvīpa—Dv.—Dyutimat, lord of Krauñcadvīpa, had the following sons : Kuśala, Manuga, Uṣṇa, Pīvara, Andhakāraka, Muni and Dundubhi [these names are omitted in Kha and Gha]. Uṣṇa-deśa belonged to Uṣṇa ; Pīvara-deśa to Pīvara ; Andhakāradeśa to Andhakāra ; Munideśa to Muni and Dundubhi-deśa to Dundubhi (here two names are omitted). These are the seven janapadas in the Krauñcadvīpa. (33. 21–3)

609. Krauñcadvīpa—Dv.—No. 433.

610. Kṛmilā—Cy.—No. 891.

611. Kṛṣṇa—Mt.—Between Kṛṣṇa and Pāṇḍura mountains is a plateau 30 × 90 yojanas in area. There in the centre of a lake is a *sthalapadminī* [Gha : *jalapadminī*] haunted by Yakṣas, Gandharvas, Siddhas and Cāraṇas. In the centre of this sthalapadminī is a great Nyagrodha tree covering a space of five yojanas. It is here that the thousand-faced god Hari dwells and is worshipped by Yakṣas, Gandharvas, Vidyādharas, Siddhas and Cāraṇas with lotus offerings. (38. 49-50)

612. Kṛṣṇa—Mt.—On the Kṛṣṇa (mountain) are situated the cities of Gandharvas. (39. 59)

613. Kṛṣṇa—Mt.—No. 130.

614. ,, —Mt.—No. 27.

615. ,, —Mt.—No. 569.

616. Kṛṣṇabhaumas—Ja.—(No. 108). [Ga and Na : Kṛṣṇas and Bhaumas.]

617. Kṛṣṇagiri—Mt.—No. 130.

618. Kṛṣṇāpādas—Ja.—No. 569.

619. Kṛṣṇatoyā—Rv.—No. 108.

620. Kṛṣṇaveṇī ?—Rv.—Agni (i.e. Havyavāhana) loved her. (29. 13–4)

621. Kṛtamālā—Rv.—No. 130.

621a. Kṣārodā—Rv.—(No. 108). [Gha : Kṣīrodā].

622. Kṣemaka—Vr.—No. 988.

623. ,, —Vr.—No. 989.

624. Kṣīroda—S.—In the northern portion of the Kṣīroda (or Amṛta) sea Viṣṇu sleeps having resorted to an eternal yoga. (97. 22)

625. Kṣīroda—S.—Viṣṇu is near Kṣīroda. (55. 5)

626. ,, —S.—While returning from the south, the sun is at Viṣuva ; (then ?) he passes in the direction north of the Kṣīroda sea. (50. 125)

627. Kṣīroda—S.—No. 1027.

628. ,, —S.—No. 1100.

629. Kṣīroda—No. ?.
630. Kṣupaṇas—D.—(No. 130). [Gha ; Kulapas ; Ṅa : Kuṇapas.] (77. 78)
630a. Kuberatuṅga—H.—Holy for śrāddha.
631. Kuberas—Ja.—No. 569.
632. Kulindas—D.—No. 130. [Ga : Kunindas].
633. Kulyas—Ja.—Janāpīḍa was a descendant of Turvasu. Kulya was one of his four sons. His janapada was Kulya. (99. 5-6)
634. Kulyas—Ja.—No. 130.
635. Kumanas—Ja.—No. 130.
636. Kumārakośalā—Ti.—Holy for śrāddha [G : Kumārakuśilā].
637. Kumāras—P.—No. 470.
638. Kumārī—Rv.—Nos. 1100, 1197.
639. Kumārikya—?—No. 130.
640. Kumbha—T.—Holy for śrāddha. (77. 47)
641. Kumbhakārī—Rv.—No. 569.
642. Kumuda—Mt.—No. 1174.
643. ,, Mt.—No. 566.
644. ,, Mt.—Between the Sahasra-śikhara (?) and Kumuda mountains is the hermitage of Śukra. It is 50 × 30 yojanas in area. (38. 60-62)
645. Kumuda—Mt.—No. 1179.
646. ,, Mt.—No. 27.
647. ,, Mt.—No. 1108.
648. ,, Mt.—Kinnaras dwell on Kumuda mountain. (39. 59)
649. Kumudas—Ja.—No. 108.
650. Kumudābhas—Ja.—No. 569.
651. Kumudadvīpa—Dv.—No. 437.
652. Kumudvatī ?—Rv.—No. 130.
653. ,, —Rv.—No. 606.
654. Kumuñja—Mt.—No. 146.
655 ,, Mt.—Between Kuñja [Ga : Mumuñjaka] and Śītānta mountains. There are big valleys (*droṇyaḥ*) and is 300 × 100 yojanas in area [this portion about the area is omitted in Ṅa and Ka omits the following :] Here is also a lake named Śrī where Mahoragas, Gandharvas, Devas and Dānavas dwell. There is a big lotus in this lake where the goddess Śrī herself resides. (37. 1-8)
655A. Kumuñja—Mt.—Nos. 1174, 782, 1290.
656. Kuṇindas—Ja.—No. 470.
657. Kuntalas—Ja.—No. 130[2]
658. ,, D.—No. 470.
659. Kūpā—Rv.—No. 130. [Gha and Na : Kṛpā].

660. Kuru—Vr.—To the extreme borderline of the northern sea and to the south (?) is the holy Kuru inhabited by Siddhas. Here trees, called *kṣīrin*, grow. From them Kṣīra, composed of six rasas gently oozes out. It is sweet like amṛta. Here and there in this varṣa can be found trees which fulfil all desires of men and from which sweet honey flows. The people of this varṣa are refugees from Devaloka. The men are ever young and enjoy the kṣīra with their beautiful wives. They are equal in all respects, even in respect of the time of their death. Like Cakravākas they love their wives. Adultery is unknown. They enjoy a life of 13500 years : This varṣa is to the north of the Jārudhi. There are two mountains in this varṣa, viz., Candrakānta and Sūryakānta. They are inhabited by Siddhas and Cāraṇas. Between them flows the great river Bhadrasīmā. There are numerous other rivers which are flooded by ghee, honey, curds and maireya (?), etc. There are also forests of sandle-wood, tamāla and aguru trees in this varṣa. Here can one listen to the sweet melodies of Mṛdaṅga, Veṇu, Paṇava, Vīṇā, etc. Everywhere do we see here gardens and cities. The svarga by name Bhoma is situated in this varṣa. The people are great and bear the lustre of gods. They use the following ornaments for decoration : valaya, aṅgada, keyūra, hāra, kuṇḍala and mukuṭa. Their dress is picturesque. They are not tainted by egoism (*mamatva*), and dharma and adharma have no meaning for them. Similarly old age, disease and fatigue do not distress them and at the scheduled time of their death they vanish away like bubbles of water. To the southern side of this varṣa, after crossing a distance of 5000 yojanas, we come to the home of Suras, known by the name of Candradvīpa. In its centre is a mountain attended by Siddhas and Cāraṇas. From this mountain flows the river Candrāvartā. On the same mountain is a place (i.e. residence) of Candramas, the lord of the Nakṣatras. (This very mountain) is known by the name Candramas. (45. 11–60)

661. Kuru—Vr.—No. 818.

662. ,, —D.—No. 819.

663. ,, —D.—No. 130.

664. Kurus—Ja.—No. 470.

665. Kurujāṅgala— ? —Holy for śrāddha. (77. 93)

666. Kurukṣetra—Ti.—After a long and weary search, king Purūravas saw his beloved Urvaśī at Kurukṣetra in Plakṣatīrtha sporting with five aparasas in a puṣkariṇī. (91. 31–2)

667. Kurukṣetra—Cy.—Kuru was the son of king Saṁvaraṇa, a descendant of Puru. He crossed over to (?) Prayāga and founded the Kurukṣetra. (Cf. *Yaḥ Prayāgaṁ padākramya kurukṣitraṁ cakāra ha.*) (99. 214–5)

668. Kurukṣetra—Ti.—It is a holy tīrtha of Sanatkumāra, the lord of yoga. It is holy for śrāddha.

669. Kurukṣetra—Ti.—The pious king Adhisāmakṛṣṇa is now ruling. It is in his reign that this (Vāyu Purāṇa) is being narrated to you on the occasion of this difficult and long-drawn sacrificial session of three years at Kurukṣetra on the banks of the river Dṛṣadvatī and two years have already passed (since the time of its commencement ?). (This is what the Sūta says to the sages of the Naimiṣa forest who had started the session which had been the occasion for the narration of the Vāyu Purāṇa.) [Kha mentions the name of the king as Adhimāsakṛṣṇa.]

670. Kurukṣetra—Ti.—No. 152. [Omitted in Gha.]

671. Kurukṣetra—Ti.—No. 215.

672. Kurupāñcālas—Ja.—No. 130.

673. Kuśadvīpa—Dv.—Jyotiṣmat, lord of Kuśadvīpa had the following seven sons :—Udbhida, Veṇumat, Svairatha, Lavaṇa, Dhṛti, Prabhākara and Kapila. Their respective varṣas are : Udbhida, Veṇumaṇḍala, Svairathākāra [Kha : Svarathākāra], Lavaṇa, Dhṛtimat, Prabhākara and Kapila. The people of these varṣas follow the āśrama system. (33. 24–7)

674. Kuśadvīpa—Dv.—This fourth dvīpa surrounds the Surodaka sea. The seven mountains in this dvīpa are : Vidrumoccaya, Hema, Dyutimat, Puṣpavat, Kuśeśaya, Harigiri, and Mandara. Mandara is so called because the streams that flow from it have very still and gentle courses (?). This dvīpa is twice in area to Śālmaladvīpa. The seven varṣas in this dvīpa are : Udbhida, Veṇumandala, Svairathākāra [Kha : Vairathākara], Lavana, Dhṛtimat, Prabhākara and Kapila. Devas and Gandharvas rejoice in these varṣas, where there are no Dasyus nor any jātis of Mlecchas. The people are of fair complexion. The seven rivers in this dvīpa are : Dhutapāpā, Śivā, (the plural for these two names should be noted), Pavitrā, Saṁtati, Dyutigarbhā [Ga and Ṅa : Dyutidarbhā ; Gha : Dyutirdarmbhā] and Mahī. There are numerous other rivers and all of them flow to the region where rain falls. The Ghṛtoda sea, equal in area to Kuśadvīpa, encircles this Kuśadvīpa. The Krauñcadvīpa is twice in area as that of the Kuśadvīpa.

675. Kuśadvīpa—Dv.—Nos. 437, 606.

676. ,, —Dv.—No. 433.

677. Kuśala ?—Ja.—No. 608.
678. ,, —Vr.—No. 606.
679. Kuśala ?—F.—Diti, wife of Mārīca Kaśya, practised severe penance in Kuśala [Ga, Gha and Ṅa : Kuśapla] forest to enable her to beget a son capable of killing Śakra who had slain her sons. (67. 84)
680. Kuśaprāvarṇas—D.—No. 130.
681. Kuśasthalī—Cy.—Śaryāti was a son of Vaivasvata Manu. His son (? mithuna or putra) was Ānārta [Kha : Anarta]. He had also a daughter who was married to Cyavana. Ānārta's successor was Reva whose viṣaya was Ānārta and whose city was Kuśasthalī. Reva's eldest son was Kakudmin who ruled over Kuśasthalī. (It appears that Kakudmin's daughter, by name Revatī, was married to Baladeva or Rāma in Dvāravatī. But this is omitted in Kha and Gha.) (Cf. also No. 270.) (86. 23)
681a. Kuśasthalī—Cy.—After Kakudmin, son of Reva, had gone to that loka (i.e. died ?), the Rākṣasas raided (the city of) Kuśasthalī. The hundred brothers of Kakudmin fled away. (88. 1-3)
681b. Kuśasthalī—Cy.—No. 599.
681c. Kuśāvatī—Rv.—No. 569.
681d. Kuśeśaya—Mt.—No. 674.
681e. Kusuma—Cy.—There will be a great (Śaiśunāka ?) king named Udāyin [Kha and Gha : Udayin]. By him will be founded the city of Kusuma on the southern bank of the Ganges, [or according to Gha, Koṇa instead of *Kūla*] in the fourth year of his reign. [Ṅa omits the name of Udāyin and refers the foundation of the city to Ajātaśatru who was a predecessor of Udāyin.] (99. 316-9)
681f. Kusumottara—Vr.—No. 1100.
681g. Kūṭaśaila—Mt.—No. 130.
682. Lampākas—P.—They were annihilated by Pramiti at the end of the Káli age. (58. 83)
683. Lampakas—P.—They will be annihilated by Kalki at the end of the Kali age [Kha, Ga and Gha : Lampākas]. (88. 108)
684. Lampākas—D.—No. 130.
685. Laṅkā—Cy.—Kārtavīrya overcame Rāvaṇa in his Laṅkā and brought him as a captive to Māhiṣmatī. (94. 35)
685a. Laṅkā—Cy.—No. 437.
686. Lauhitya—Ti.—Holy for śrāddha. It was situated on the banks of the river Vaitaraṇī ? (77. 95)
687. Lavana—Vr.—Nos. 673, 674.
687a. Lāvaṇa—S.—No. 435.
688. Lavaṇodadhi—S ?—Nos. 300, 470.
689. Lavaṇodaka—S.—No. 989.

690. Lohita—Vr.—No. 1108.
691. ,, —L.—No. 470.
692. ,, —F.—No. 470.
693. Lohrita—Rv.—No. 130.
694. Lomaharṣaṇa—F.—It is situated between the Kailāsa and Pañcakūṭa mountains. It is 36 × 100 yojanas in area. The forest is impenetrable even to tiny creatures. (38. 33-4)
695. Madhaureyas—Ja.—No. 569.
696. Madhu—F.—Śatrughna, son of Daśaratha, went to the forest named Madhu and killed Mādhava Lavaṇa. There he founded the city of Mathurā. Śatrughna had two sons, viz., Subāhu and Śūrasena. With them he protected the city of Mathurā in Vaidehī. (88. 184-6)
697. Madhumat—Mt.—No. 1179.
698. ,, —Mt.—No. 27.
699. Mādhvī—Rv.—No. 1278a.
700. Madhyadeśa—D.—In connection with the distribution of the śākhās of Yajurveda, Āruṇi was the foremost in Madhyadeśa. (61. 8-9)
701. Madhyadeśas—P.—They were annihilated by Pramiti at the end of the Kali age. (58. 81)
702. Madhyadeśa—Rg.—No. 130.
703. Madhyadeśas—P.—They will be annihilated by Kalki at the end of the Kali age. (98. 106-9)
704. Madrā—Rv.—No. 130.
705. Mādrakas—Ja—King Śibi had four sons viz. Vṛṣadarbha, Suvīra, Kekaya and Madraka [Ṅa : Bhadraka]. Their janapadas were : Kekayas, Mādrakas, Vṛṣadarbhas and Sūcidarbhas [Ga, Gha and Ṅa : Śucidarbha]. (99. 23-4)
706. Magadha—Rg.—Bṛhadratha [Gha and Ṅa : Mahadratha], a descendant of Puru, was king of Magadha [Ka reads Bhagadharo, i.e. probably a personal name]. (99. 221)
707. Māgadhas—Rg. ?—The Bṛhadrathas are mentioned as Māgadheyas [Ga, Gha and Ṅa : Māgadhas]. One of these, Sahadeva, was killed in the Bhārata war (bhārate saṅgrāme). Jarāsaṁdha also was one of them. (99. 294-6)
708. Magadhas—Ja.—The Guptas will rule the following janapadas : Anugaṅga, Prayaga [Kha, Ga, Gha and Ṅa : Anugaṅga-Prayāga i.e. Prayāga situated on the banks of the river Gaṅgā ?] Sātektu [Gha : Sāketaṁ] and Magadhas. (99. 383)
709. Māgadhas—Rg. or P ?—Viśvasphāni [Ga and Gha : Viśvasphāṇi] will be the king of Māgadhas. He will annihilate all kings and will create other varṇas, viz., Kaivartas, Pañcakas, Pulindas and Brāhmaṇas. He will set up principalities in various deśas.

This Viśvasphāni will be as powerful as Viṣṇu. He will destroy the Kṣatra (i.e. the whole Kṣatriya order) and create another Kṣatra. After offering oblations to gods, manes and vipras he will breathe his last on the banks of the river Jāhnavī. [This last sentence is omitted in Ga.] (99. 377-81)

710. Magadhas—D. ?—King Pṛthu made a gift of Magadhas (i.e. land of Magadhas?) to Māgadha for his panegyric. Māgadha and Sūta were born in a yajña performed on the occasion of Pṛthu's consecration. (62. 137-47)

710a. Magadhas—D. ?—Nos. 325, 449.

711. ,, —Ja.—No. 130².

712. ,, —Ja.—No. 470.

713. Mahābhadra—L.—To the north of Mahābhadra lake are the following mountains : Śaṅkukūṭa, Vṛṣabha, Haṁsa, Nāga, Kapila, Indraśaila, Nīla, Kanakaśṛṅga, Śataśṛṅga, Puṣpaka, Meghaśaila, Virāja and Jārudhi. (36. 30-33)

714. Mahābhadra—L.—No. 106.

714a. ,, —L.—No. 1178.

715. Mahābhaumas—Ja.—No. 108.

716. Mahādruma—Vr.—No. 1099.

717 ,, —Vr.—No. 1100.

718. Mahāgaurī ?—Rv.—No. 130.

719. Mahākeśas—Ja.—No. 108.

720. Mahākūṭa—Mt.—Holy for śrāddha. (77. 57)

721. Mahāmegha—Mt.—No. 509.

722. Mahāmūla—Mt.—No. 820.

723. Mahānada—Rv.—No. 130.

724. Mahānāsas—Ja.—No. 569.

725. Mahānetras—Ja.—No 108.

726. Mahānīla—Mt.—No. 782.

727. ,, —Mt.—There are fifteen cities of Kinnaras known as Hayānanas (horse-faced?) on this mountain. The fifteen kings of Kinnaras, viz., Devasena, Mahābāhu, etc., rule here. These cities have bila entrances or gates (cf. *bila-praveśaiḥ nagaraiḥ*). (39. 32-5)

728. Mahānīla—Mt.—No. 106.

729. Mahāṅgas—Ja.—No. 569.

730. Mahārāṣṭras—Ja.—No. 130.

731. Mahāśaila—Mt.—No.

732. Mahāsthalas—Ja.—No. 108

733. Mahātala—Rg.—No. 1048.

734. Mahatī—Rv.—No. 130.

735. Mahāvīta—Vr.—No. 1027.

736. ,, —Vr.—No.

737. Mahendra—Mt.—On the Mahendra mountain is the holy abode of Śakra. Bilva trees grow here in abundance. The mountain is holy for śrāddha purposes. (77. 17-8)
738. Mahendra—Mt.—No. 130..
739. ,, —The janapadas inhabiting the Mahendra (mountain) will be ruled over by Guha. (99. 386)
740. Māhendrī—Cy.—No. 826.
741. Māheyaṣ—Ja.—No. 569.
742. Mahī—Rv.—No. 674.
743. Mahiṣas—Ja.—This janapada will be ruled over by Guha. (99. 386)
744. Mahiṣa—Mt.—No. 1108.
745. Māhiṣakas—Ja.—No. 130.
746. Māhiṣīs—P. ?—Śakyamā will be the king of Māhiṣīs (or Māhiṣis ?) [Ga, Gha and Ṅa : Mahiṣīs].
747. Mahiṣī—Rv.—No. 569.
748. Māhiṣikas—P.—No. 345.
749. Māhiṣmatī—Cy.—No. 529.
750. Māhiṣmatī—Cy.—No. 685.
751. Mahivas—Ja.—No. 569.
752. Maināka—Mt. ?—In the northern Mānasa where those (?) of the name Maināka are holy for śrāddha purposes. The same is the case with the southern Mānasa and with Kanakhala in the north (or with Khanakhala and Udīcī ?). (82. 21)
753. Maināka—Mt.—Holy for śraddha purposes. (77. 68)
754. ,, —Mt.—Sub-merged in the southern sea. (47. 75)
755. ,, —Mt.—No. 607.
756. ,, —Mt.—No. 130.
757. Makruṇā—Rv.—No. 130.
758. Mālas—Ja.—No. 130.
759. Māladas—Ja.—No. 130. [Ga : Mālavas.]
760. Mālavas—Ja.—No. 130[2].
761. Mālavartins—Ja.—No. 130. [Ga : Malavartins.]
762. Malaya—Mt.—No. 130.
763. ,, —Mt.—No. 437.
764. Malayadvīpa—Dv.—No. 437.
764a. Mālinī—Cy.—No. 170.
765. Mālyavat—Mt.—To the east of the Mālyavat (mountain) is a plain (*gaṇḍikā*). The people here are called Bhadrāśvas who enjoy a life of 10,000 years : The people are white (in complexion) and the women-folk are very beautiful. They enjoy the juice of Kālāmra fruits and are thus ever young. There is also here a forest of sāla trees called by the name of Bhadra. (43. 5-9)
766. Mālyavat—Mt.—No. 818.
767. ,, —Mt.—No. 1022.

768. Mālyavat—Mt.—No. 823.
769. ,, —Vr.—No. 434.
770. Mānasa—L.—By going to the north of Mānasa one achieves emancipation (siddhi). There a great wonder is seen and it is a good placc for performing śrāddha. There the river Gaṅgā, of the three courses (*tripathagā*) is seen in the sky. From here flow the holy rivers, viz., Candrabhāgā and Sindhu which join the western sea. (77. 108-13)
771. Mānasa—L.—No. 820.
772. ,, —L.—No. 1022.
772a. ,, —L.—No. 1178.
773. Mānasa—L.—No. 470.
774. ,, —Mt.—752.
775. ,, —Mt.—No. 1027.
776. ,, —Vr.—No. 1107.
777. ,, —Vr.—No.
778. ,, —Vr.—No. 826.
778a. Mandagā—Rv.—No. 130.
779. Mandākinī ?—Rv.—King Purūravas enjoyed with Uravasī at the following places : Caitraratha, bank (of the river) Mandākinī, spacious (city of) Alakā, Nandana forest, foot of Gandhamādana mountain, Summit of Meru, Uttara-Kuru and Kalāpagrāma. (91. 6-8)
780. Mandākinī—Rv.—Nos. 470, 130.
780a. ,, —L.—No. 469.
781. Mandara—Mt.—The Mahāpuruṣa created by Śiva was like the Mandara. (30. 130)
782. Mandara—Mt.—The following mountains are to the east of (Aruṇoda lake ?) or of Mandara ? :—Śītānta, Kumuñja, Suvīra, Vikaṅka, Maniśīla, Vṛṣabha, Mahānīla, Rucaka, Sabiṇdu, Mandara (?), Veṇumat, Sumedha [Gha and Ṅa : Samedha], and Niṣadha. (36. 17-20)
783. Mandara—Mt.—No. 819.
784. ,, —Mt.—No. 816.
784a. ,, — ? —It shakes at the movements of Kārtavīrya's arms. (94. 33)
785. ,, —Mt.—Nos. 1022, 130, 437, 674.
786. Maṇīcaka—Vr.—Nos. 1099, 1100.
787. Maṇimat—Mt.—It is inhabited by the Garuḍas. (69. 333)
788. Maṇiparvata—Mt.—No. 1022.
789. Maṇiśaila—Mt.—No. 168.
790. Maṇiśīla—Mt.—No. 782.
791. Maṇitaṭā—Rv.—No. 108.
792. Maṇivaprā—Rv.—No. 108.

793. Maṇivarta--Cy ?—Descendants of Hiraṇyakaśipu are called the residents of Maṇivarta.
794. Mañjamas—Ja.—No. 569.
795. Manojavā—Rv.—No. 606.
796. Manonuga—Vr.—No. 606.
797. Manuga—Vr. ?—No. 608.
798. Mānuṣī—Rv.—No. 569.
799. Māṭhara—F.—This holy forest is inhabited by Siddhas and Cāraṇas. (77. 33)
800. Mathurā—Cy.—The Nāgas (i.e. Nāga kings) will rule in the beautiful city of Mathurā. (99. 383)
801. Mathurā—Cy.—No. 696.
802. Mātsyas—Ja.—No. 470.
803. Mattakāsikas—Ja.—No. 569.
804. Mātuluṅga—St.—No. 1268.
805. Maunikas—Ja.—No. 130.
806. Mayūra—Mt.—No. 106.
807. Mayūrabarhavarṇa—Mt.—No. 818.
808. Meghā—Rv.—No. 108.
809. Meghaśaila—Mt.—No. 713.
810. Mekalā— ?—In Mekalā there will be seven kings. (99. 375)
811. ,, — ?—No. 888.
812. Meru—Mt.—The following varṣa mountains are described (in the Vāyu Purāṇa) :—Himavat, Hemakūṭa, Niṣadha, Meru, Nīla [Ga : Nila], Śveta, and Śṛṅgavat (?) [Kha, Ga, Gha and Ṅa : Śṛṅgin]. (1. 85)
813. Meru—Mt.—Sāvarṇa and other Manus reside on it. (1. 23)
814. ,, —Mt.—In a heavenly and holy cave of Meru mountain Śiva will reside with Viṣṇu in the 28th dvāpara in the Siddhakṣetra by name Kāyārohaṇa. Śiva's incarnation at this time will be known as Nakulin [Ga, Gha and Ṅa : Lakulin]. (23. 221)
815. Meru—Mt.—This is the *Īśvarī māyā* of the universe and this is the Meru mountain known as Devaloka. (24. 86)
816. Meru—Mt. ?—Meru's wife was Dhāraṇī, daughter of the Barhiṣad Pitṛs. She gave birth to a son Mandara and to three daughters. This happened in the Svāyambhuva Manvantara. (30. 30-35)
817. Meru—Mt.—In former times the shining peak of Meru was known throughout the three worlds. It was known as Sāvitra. On its one side dwelt the daughter of the lord of mountains (i.e. Himavat). It was here that the Ādityas, Vasus, the two Aśvins, the best of physicians, Vaiśravaṇa, the king of the Guhyakas, the lord of the Yakṣas and resident of Kailāsa, the great Muni Uśanas, the sages with Sanatkumāra being the foremost amongst them, Aṅgiras and others, the Devarṣis, the Gandharva Viśvāvasu, Nārada and Parvata and the various

gaṇas of Apsarasas dwelt. It is here that Mahādeva, the lord of the *paśus* (beasts) is worshipped by the Vidyādharas, Siddhas, Bhūtas, Rākśasas and Pisācas. Here it is that the lord of Nāndin dwells, with his shining śūla, served by the best of rivers (i.e. Gaṅgā) which is the source of water for all the tīrthas. (30. 81-93)

817a. Meru—Mt.—Due to the terrible howling of the Rudras the Meru mountain began to shake. (30. 145)

818. Meru—Mt.—(Continued from No. 435). On the east it is white, hence its *brāhmaṇya*; on the south it is yellow, hence its *vaiśyatva*; on the west it is black, hence its *śūdratā*; on the north it is red, hence its *kṣattratā*. Nīla, Śvetaśṛṅga, Hiraṇmaya (?), Mayūrabarhavarṇa, Śātakaumbha and Śṛṅgavat are the names of its ranges (?). It is in the centre of Ilāvṛta (varṣa ?) which surrounds it (?). It is 9000 yojanas in extent (*vistīrṇaḥ*). In the centre of the Meru mountain is a smokeless fire. It is (compared to or called ?) the southern portion of the sacrificial altar. There are seven varṣa mountains (equal in extent to ?) Jambūdvīpa. They are: Nīla, Niṣadha, Śveta, Hemakūṭa, Himavat, Śṛṅgavat and (Meru ?). The varṣas defined by them are: the Bhārata-varṣa (defined by Himavat), Kiṁpuruṣa (defined by Hemakūṭa), Harivarṣa (defined by the Niṣadha and Hemakūṭa mountains), Ilāvṛta (defined by Meru), Ramyaka defined by Nīla), Hiraṇmaya (defined by Śveta), and Kuru (defined by Śṛṅgavat). The Ilāvṛta varṣa is in the centre with three varṣas to its north and the rest three varṣas to its south. This Ilāvṛta varṣa is to the south of Nīla mountain and to the north of the Niṣadha mountain. To the east is the Mālyavat mountain and to the west, the Gandhamādana mountain [Kha omits information on Gandhamādana]. The Meru is the greatest in this chain of mountains. If the earth is like a lotus the Meru is its petal....Here Devas, Gandharvas, Uragas, Rākṣasas and Apsarasas reside. To its four sides are the following four deśas:—Bhadrāśva, Bharata, Ketumāla, and Uttara-Kurus... Here is a sabhā of Brahmā known as Manovatī throughout the three worlds. Here Iśāna, the lord of Śrī, and Indra have their dwellings. Here is a garden created by Jāmbunada (river ?). The great sabhā of Hutāśa, known as Tejovatī, is also situated here on the second *antaraṭaṭa*. On the third antaraṭaṭa is a great sabhā of Vaivasvata; on the fourth, that of the lord of Nairṛtya; on the fifth, those of Vaivasvata and Varuṇa, the lord of the sea; on the sixth, that of Vāyu; on the seventh, that of the lord of the Nakṣatras and on the eighth, that of Iśāna. (34. 16-93)

819. Meru—Mt.—To the east (of Meru) are the mountains Jaṭhara and Devakūṭa touching (?) the Nīla in the north and the Niṣadha in the south. The Kailāsa and the Himavat are to the south and north respectively (?) extending east-west. Of Meru there are four great pādas (ranges?) which are responsible for the stability of the earth. It is 10,000 yojanas in extent. Devas, Gandharva and Yakṣas [Kha, Ga and Gha omit mention of Yakṣas] dwell here...... To the east is the Mandara, to the south the Gandhamādana, to the west the Vipula and to the north the Supārśva. Yakṣas, Gandharvas, Siddhas and Cāraṇas dwell on all these mountains. On the summit of Mandara is a great Keturāṭ tree known by the name Bhadrāśva. The dvīpa known by the name Bhadrāśva is called after the name of this tree......(cf. No. 436). On the summit of the Vipula mountain (in the west) grows a great Aśvattha tree. Formerly, on the occasion of the "churning of the ocean", the party of the Daityas had been defeated. To celebrate this victory of the Devas, Sahasrākṣa (i.e. Indra) garlanded, as a form of worship (?), this great Aśvattha tree. This garland (*mālā*) still adorns the tree (Ketu) and thus is the dvīpa called Ketumāla-dvīpa after these two words. On the summit of the Supārśva mountain grows a great Nyagrodha tree attended by Siddhas and Cāraṇas. This is the tree worshipped by (?) the Uttara-Kurus. Here dwell the seven Kurus, the Sanatkumāras, i.e. the seven mind-born sons of Brahman. The dvīpa (in which this Supārśva mountain is) is called after them. (35. 8 ff.)

820. Meru—Mt.—To the south of the Mānasa lake, i.e. also to the south of the Meru mountain, are the following mountains : Ri(or Tṛi ?)-śikhara, Śiśira [Gha : Śikhara], Kaliṅga, Pataṅga, Rucaka, Tāmrābha [Gha and Ṅa : Tāmrābhra], Viśākha, Śvetodara, Samūla, Viṣadhāra, Ratnadhāra, Ekaśṛṅga (?) Mahāmūla (?), Gajaśaila, Piśācaka, Kailāsa and Himavat. (36. 21–5)

821. Meru—Mt.—The network of mountains (*girijāla*) of Meru is called Siddhaloka. Its centre (?) is the same as svarga. (41. 81–2)

822. Meru—Mt.—The earth is spread from the (central) mountain Meru to all the directions. (42. 79)

823. Meru—Mt.—To the west of Meru is the mountain Gandhamādana, to the north is the Nīla, to the south, the Niṣadha and to the east, the Mālyavat mountains. To the south of Nīla and to the north of Niṣadha is situated the Mahāmeru, the centre of all these mountain chains. To the south of Meru and to the north of Niṣadha is a big Jambū tree, named Sudarśana, touching the sky. The *vanaspati* (vegetation ?) in Jambūdvīpa is known after it. The local people enjoy the fruits and juice of this

tree and are free from old age...... The thirty three yajñīya Suras dwell on the Meru. (46. 17-32)

824. Meru—Mt.—To the west of Meru is a lake whence the river Jāmbunadī flows. (47. 65-6)

825. Meru—Mt.—Meru forms the centre of the earth. (50. 68-70)

826. Meru—Mt.—The following are the cities of Lokapālas in the astronomical sphere (?) :—To the east of Meru, on the head (? *mūrdhani*) of Mānasa, is the city (?) of Māhendrī. To the south of Meru, on the head of Mānasa, is the city of Vaivasvata Yama called Saṁyamana; in the same manner to the west is the city of Varuṇa named Sukhā ; and to the north, the city of Soma named Vibhāvarī. Thus, on the northern surface (*pṛṣṭha*) of the Mānasa, the Lokapālas dwell to protect the world and to uphold the dharma. The following is a chart which explains the direction of the movements of the sun in reference to these cities referred to above :—When the sun is at the zenith from Amarāvatī it is *udaya* [Gha gives a reading which it is difficult to make out] in Saṁyamana, and it is midnight [Ṅa gives an unconstruable reading] at Sukhā (?). When it is midnight at Vibhā (i.e. Vibhāvarī) it is sun-set at Māhendrī. It is then *aparāhṇa* in south-east, *pūrvahaṇa* in the south, *apararātra* in the Uttarāpatha, and *pūrvarātra* in north-east. If it is mid-day at Sukhā then it is rising sun at Vibhāvarī, the city of Soma [before referring to Vibhāvarī Kha introduces a long passage]. It is mid-night at Amarāvatī when the sun sets on the city of Yama. If it is mid-day at Vibhā [Kha and Gha : Vibhāvarī], the city of Soma, then it is rising sun at Amarāvatī, mid-night at Saṁyamana and sunset at the city of Varuṇa. (50. 88 ff.)

827. Meru—Mt.—Once upon a time the sages convened a meeting on the Meru mountain and they resolved that whosoever would not be present (at the next meeting) within the period of seven nights he shall be inflicted with the sin of the murder of a Brahmin (*brahmavadhyā*). It so happened that Vaiśaṁpāyana and his followers were not present at this meeting and thus he was inflicted with that sin. This incident led to the division of the Yajurveda. (61. 12 ff.)

828. Meru—Mt.—To the north of all is the Meru. (50. 108)

828a. Meru—Mt.—Dakṣa's grandsons practised penance on the Meru. (100. 25-6)

829. Meru—Mt.—The sun wanders about the summit of Meru and circumambulates it. It is the cakra (circle) of all the astronomical bodies (*jyotiṣām*). (52. 98-9)

830. Meru—Mt.—The gods had assembled on the Meru and after the incident of Śiva's drinking of poison (i.e. the Kālakūṭa) they dispersed. (54. 101)

831. Meru—Mt.—In the pṛthvī-dohana incident, Meru "milked" the earth; Himavat was the calf (*vatsa*) and Śaila was the vessel (*pātra*). (62. 190)

832. Meru—Mt.—Manu is still residing on this lovely mountain. (84. 82)

833. Meru—Mt.—Raivata practised penance on the summit of the Meru [Kha and Gha omit this]. (86. 29)

834. Meru—Mt.—Nos. 27, 106, 418, 779.

835. Meru—Mt.—Nos. 394, 435.

836. Mīnas—P. ?— Mīnā was a daughter of Ṛṣā (a Piśācī ?). Her progeny is known as the Maina gaṇa. (69. 292-4)

837. Mithilā—Cy.—Nemi was a son of Ikṣvāku. He became *videha* due to the curse of Vasiṣṭha. The son of Nemi was Mithi. He was born through the churning of araṇī (*araṇyāṁ mathyamānāyāṁ*) and hence his name Mithi. He was also called Janaka because of his *janana*. The city of Mithilā was called after his name [This last sentence is omitted in Kha and Gha] (89. 1-6)

838. Mithilā—Cy.—No. 267.

839. Mleccha—P.—The Pārthivas, Mlecchas and the irreligious Vṛṣalas were annihilated by Pramiti at the end of the Kali age. After accomplishing this, Pramiti perished voluntarily in the region between the Gaṅgā and the Yamunā rivers. (58. 88-90)

840. Mleccha—P.—They too make offerings to Pitṛs as do the four varṇas. (83. 110-2)

841. Mleccha—P.—Turvasu, son of king Yayāti, did not accede to the request of his father regarding the exchange of his youth for his father's old age. Yayāti then cursed him that he would be a fool amongst the Mlecchas who follow the habits of beasts (*paśudharmeṣu mleccheṣu*). (93. 42-4)

842. Mlecchas—P.—When this yuga will come to an end there will be born Kalki of Parāśara (gotra ?) and who will be known as Viṣṇuyaśas. Yājñavalkya will lead him. This Kalki will raise an army composed of armed vipras (i.e. Brahmins) and will proceed to annihilate the following impious (peoples) :-Udīcyas, Madhyadeśas, Vindhyas, Aparāntikas, Dākṣiṇātyas, Draviḍas, Siṁhalas, Gāndhāras, Pāradas, Palhavas, Yavanas, Śakas, Tuṣāras, Barbaras, Pulindas, Daradas, Khasas, Lampakas [Kha, Ga and Gha : Lampākas], Andhrakas, Rudras and Kirātas. With a discuss (as his weapon ?) he will also annihilate the Mlecchas. (98. 103-9)

843. Mlecchas—P.—Pracetas was a descendant of Gandhāra (cf. No. 291). He had a hundred sons who were, all of them, kings. They inhabited in the north and became the rulers of the rāṣṭras of the Mlecchas (*Mleccha-rāṣṭrādhipāḥ sarve*). (99. 11-2)

844. Mlecchas—P.—At the end of the Kali age, the kings will be (practically speaking) Yavanas in matters of dharma and artha and kāma; they will not be consecrated as kings and the evil effects of the age (yuga) will affect them. The offences regarding the murder of women and children will often take place. The janapadas will follow the customs (*ācārāḥ*) of the Mlecchas. The irreligious Pāṣaṇḍas and the Mlecchas will at last be annihilated by Kalki. Thus the word 'nṛpa' (i.e. king) will be heard no more and anarchy, pestilence and disease will follow suit...The Aryas and the Mlecchas will fly to forests. (99. 388-404)

845. Mlecchas—P.—They dwell on the Kailāsa with Yakṣas and Gandharvas. (41. 46)

846. Mlecchas—P.—Nos. 27, 130, 437.

847. Modaka—Vr.—Nos. 1099, 1100.

848. Mṛgakāntā—Rv.—No. 1278A.

849. Mudgalas—P.—One of the fifteen pakṣas of Aṅgirasas. (65. 107)

850. Muditā—Rv.—No. 989.

851. Mukuñja—Mt.—No. 1022.

852. Mukuṭa—Mt.—The habitations of the Pannagas are on the Mukuṭa mountain. (39. 62)

853. Mukuṭa—Mt.—Nos. 27, 1179.

854. Mūlikas—Ja.—No. 130.

855. ,, —Ja.—Cf. No.

856. Muṇḍas— —No. 130.

857. Muṇḍapṛṣṭha— ?—The tīrtha named Kanakanandi is to the north of Muṇḍapṛṣṭha. (77. 105)

858. Muni—D.—No. 608.

859. ,, —Vr.—No. 606.

860. Mūṣikas—Ja.—No. 130.

861. Nāga—Cy.—Nirvaktra, son of Adhisāmakṛṣṇa [Kha, Gha and Ṅa: Adhisīmakṛṣṇa], will desert the city of Nāga (?)—which was flooded by the river Gaṅga—and will establish himself in Kauśāmbī. (99. 271)

862. Nāga—Mt.—No. 713.

863. Nāgadeśa—D.—No. 437.

864. Nāgadvīpa—Dv.—No. 130.

865. Nāgapadī—Rv.—No. 108.

866. Nāgaśaila—Mt.—Nos. 106, 519.

867. Nāgavana—F.—The region defined by (?) Kauśikī [Kha and Kh : Kauśilyā], the sea, the river Gaṅgā and the Añjana mountain is the Nāgavana. (Another interpretation might be that Nāgavana is to the east of Añjana). (69. 238)

868. Naimiṣa—F.—The sages who started the sacrificial session at Kurukṣetra are called Naimiṣāraṇya-gocarāḥ. (1. 14–5)

869. Naimiṣa—D.—The sages started the sacrificial session at Naimiṣa. This holy deśa is so called because the axle (*nimi*) of the wheel of dharma broke here (*viśīryate*). (1. 183–5)

870. Naimiṣa— ?—When the rolling axle of the wheel of dharma broke here the place was called Naimiṣa and was revered by sages. (2. 8)

871. Naimiṣa— ?—Holy for śrāddha. (77. 93)

872. ,, —Here Śiva will reside in 24th dvāpara ?. (23. 206)

873. Nairṇikas—Ja.—No. 130.

874. Naiṣadha—Vr.—No. 434.

875. Naiṣadhas— ?—No. 597.

876. Nalakālikas—Ja.—No. 130.

877. Nalini—Rv.—No. 470.

878. Nandā—Rv.—No. 469.

879. ,, —Rv.—No. 1100.

880. Nandana—F.—No. 779.

881. Nandinī—Rv.—No. 569.

882. Nārada—Mt.—It is sub-merged in a sea in the west. (47. 74)

883. ,, —Mt.—No. 989.

884. Narmadā—Rv.—Havyavāhana (i.e. Agni) loved her. (29. 13)

885. ,, —Rv.—Narmadā, the best of rivers, was the daughter of Pitṛs. The river is holy for śraddha purposes. (29. 32)

886. Narmadā—Rv.—Sukālas were a class of Pitṛs (of Vasiṣṭha ?). They were worshipped by śūdras. Their mental daughter (*mānasī kanyā*) was Narmadā, the best of rivers. Narmadā was also the wife of Purukutsa and the mother of Trasadasyu. The river Narmadā flows to the Dakṣiṇāpatha. (73. 46–50)

887. Narmadā—Rv.—Kārtavīrya Arjuna had trampled on the region about the river Narmadā. (94. 28)

888. Narmadā—Rv.—King Jyāmagha took up a bow and entered a dense forest about the marshy tracts carved by the river Narmadā (Narmadānūpa) [Kha, Ga and Ka : Narmadāṁ nṛpa]. The word Mekalā also occurs along with Narmadā but it is difficult to make out its significance]. The king also went to the mountain Ṛkṣavanta (or Ṛkṣavat) and entered the Śuktimanī (or Śuktimatī river ?). (95. 30–31)

889. Narmadā—Rv.—No. 130[2].

890. Nāsikya—Ja.—(No. 130). [Ka : Nāsika].

891. Navarāṣṭra—Rg.—King Uśīnara, a descendant of Turvasu, had five wives, viz. Mṛgā [Kha : Nṛgā], Kṛmi, Navā, Darvā and Dṛṣadvātī. The sons of these wives respectively were : Mṛga, Kṛmi, Nava, Suvrata and Śibi. The territorial possessions of these sons respectively were : Yaudheya, city of Kṛmilā, Navarāṣṭra, Ambaṣṭhā (city ?) [Kha : Vṛṣṭhā] and Śivapura. (99. 18–27)

892. Nīla ?—Mt.—The varṣaparvata Nīla is described in the Purāṇa. (1. 85)

893. Nīla :—Mt.—Siddhas and Brahmarṣis dwell on the Nīla mountain. (46. 34)

894. Nīla—Mt.—The Payoda lake is situated on this mountain. The rivers Payodā and Puṇḍarīkā flow from that lake. (47. 66–7)

895. Nīla ?—Mt.—Nos. 105, 108, 713, 818[3], 819, 823.

896. ,, —Vr.—No. 434.

897. Nīla-Maulayas—Ja.—(No. 108) [Ka : Nīlaśaileyas].

898. Nīlamukhas—Ja.—No. 470.

899. Nīlotpalā—Rv.—No. 130.

900. Nirbandhyā—Rv.—(No. 130). [Gha : Nirvindhyā].

901. Niṣādas—P.—Ekalavya was brought up by the Niṣādas and hence the (region) Niṣada [Ga and Ka : Naiṣadha] etc. was so called (?). (96. 187)

902. Niṣādas—P.—Nos. 470, 576.

903. Niṣadha—Mt. This varṣa parvata is described in the Purāṇa (1. 85)

904. Niṣadha—Mt.—To the north of Niṣadha and Devaśaila mountains the whole surface of the earth is rocky without any trace of vegetation. A portion of this surface is under water...(37. 28–9)

905. Niṣadha—Mt.—On the central summit of the mount Niṣadha is a temple (? āyatana) of Viṣṇu attended by sages, Siddhas, Yakṣas, Gandharvas, and Apsarasas. On another summit in the vicinity is situated a beautiful city of the Rākṣasas named Ulaṅghis [Ṅa : Ulandhis]. To its south is another city the entrance to which is through a cave. On the western summit are situated various cities of Devas, Dānavas and Nāgas [Ka : Bhāgas]. Here is a Somastone (somaśilā) where Soma (i.e. Moon) comes very often. It is here that the sages, Kinnaras and Gandharvas worship Soma, the lord of Tārā. On the northern summit is the place of Brahman, the lord of Suras, who is worshipped by Yakṣas, Gandharvas and Dānavas. Here is also a temple of Fire worshipped by Siddhas and Cāraṇas. (41. 48–61)

906. Niṣadha—Mt.—The Nāgas, viz., Śeṣa, Vāsuki, Takṣaka, etc. dwell on the Niṣadha mountain. (46. 34)

907. Niṣadha—Mt.—On the Niṣadha mountain is the Viṣnupada lake. (47. 64)

908. Niṣadha—Mt.—Nos. 435, 782, 818³, 819, 823, 569.

909. Niṣadha—Rg.—Nos.—597, 901.

910. Niṣadhas—Ja.—The Maṇidhānyajas will rule the following janapadas : Niṣadhas, Yadukas, Śaiśītas and Kālatopakas. (99. 384)

911. Niṣadhas—Ja.—No. 130.

912. Niṣadhā—Rv.—No. 130.

913. Niścīrā—Rv.—Nos. 989, 130.

913a. Niṣpāpā—Rv.—No. 989.

914. Nivṛtti—Rv.—No. 1108.

915. Oṁkārapavana— ? —Holy for śrāddha purposes.

915a. Pahlavas—P.—They were annihilated by Pramiti at the end of the Kali age. (58. 82)

916. Pahlavas—D.—Nos. 130, 345.

917. Pahnavas—Ja.—Nos. 130, 470 [In 130 Kha : Pahlavas].

918. Pālapañjara—Mt.—Holy for śrāddha purposes. (77. 37)

919. Palāśā—Rv.—No. 569.

920. Palāśinī—Rv.—No. 130.

921. Palhavas—P.—No. 842.

922. Pampā—Rv.—No. 108.

923. Paṁpāvatī—Rv.—No. 108.

924. Pañcakūṭa—Mt.—The Dānavas, the enemies of the Devas, dwell on the Paṇcakūṭa mountain. (39. 53)

925. Pañcakūṭa—Mt.—No. 964.

926. Pañcāla— Rg.—Nila, an ancestor of Pṛṣata [Gha reads differently] was a king of Pañcāla. He was killed by king Kṛta, who was a compiler of the twenty-four Sāma-Saṁhitās. (99. 189-92)

927. Pañcalas—Rg.—Rikṣa, a descendant of Nīla, had five sons, viz., Mudgala, Śṛñjaya [Kha : Sañjaya. Ṅa : Sṛñjaya], Bṛhadiṣu, Vikrānta (?) and Kāmpilya [Ka : Kampilya] [Ṅa omits the reference to these five sons]. For the protection of the five (? cf. *pañcānāṁ*) the father said to his sons, "These are the five prosperous janapadas ; protect them." It is thus that the Pāñcālas [Kha and Gha : Pañcālas] are so called. [This last sentence is omitted in Ṅa]. (99. 195-8)

928. Pāñcālas—Ja.—No. 130.

929. Pañcālas—Ja.—No. 470.

930. Pañcavana—F.—The holy Pañcavana is inhabited by pious people. In it is situated the tīrtha named Pāṇḍuviśālā. (77. 99)

931. Pañcavarṇā—Rv.—No. 108.

932. Pāṇḍara—Mt.—No. 1179.

933. Paṇḍāraka—F.—Holy for śrāddha [Kha : Piṇḍāraka]. (77. 37)

934. Pāṇḍukula—Rg.—In Pāṇḍukula, by the sea-shore (*samudrānte*), it is meritorious to perform śrāddha. (77. 37)
935. Pāṇḍura—Mt.—On the Pāṇḍura mountain is situated the city of Vidyādharas. (39. 60)
936. Pāṇḍura—Mt.—Nos. 130, 611.
937. Pāṇḍuviśālā—Ti.—No. 930.
938. Pāṇḍyas—Ja.—King Janāpīḍa was a descendant of Turvasu. Pāṇḍya was one of his four sons. His janapada was the Pāṇḍyas. (99. 5-6)
939. Pāṇḍyas—Ja.—No. 130.
940. Pānītoyā—Rv.—No. 1108 [Gha : Yānītoyā].
941. Pārā (?)—Rv.—No. 130 [Gha and Ṅa : Pārā].
942. Parācakas—Ja.—No. 108
943. Pāradas—P.—They were annihilated by Pramiti at the end of the Kali age. (58. 82)
944. Pāradas—P.—Nos. 345, 842.
945. Pāradas—Ja.—No. 470
946. Parakṣaras—Ja.—No. 130 [Gh. and Ṅa : Paraskaras].
947. Pārijāta—Mt.—No. 1179 [Ka Pāripātra].
948. ,, —Mt.—No. 27.
949. Paritas—D.—No. 130.
950. Parivāyas—Ja.—No. 108.
951. Pāriyātra—Mt.—No. 130².
952. Parṇamāla—Mt.—One of the mountains inhabited by Garuḍas. (69. 330-3)
953. Pārthivas—P. ?—No. 839.
954. Pārvatīyas—P.—They were annihilated by Pramiti at the end of the Kali age. (58. 81)
955. Pāṣaṇḍas—P.— Do. Do.
956. Pāṣaṇḍas—P.—In the Kali age the Śūdra Kings patronize the Pāṣaṇḍas. (58. 40)
957. Pāṣaṇḍas—P.—No. 844.
958. Pātākā—Rv.—No. 108.
959. Pātāla—Rg.—In sea, mountains, sky and Pātāla (i.e. the underworld ?) untraceable are the ways of Cakravartins. (57. 79-80)
960. Pātāla—Rg.—The Asuras in Pātāla were frightened when the sea trembled at the movements of the arms of Kārtavīrya Arjuna. (94. 30)
961. Pātāla—Rg.—Viṣṇu, in the form of Śaṁvartakānala went to the sea in Pātāla and drank oblations (in the form of the water of the sea ?). (97. 18)
962. Pātāla—Rg.—The Asuras, after having been defeated by the Devas, told Kāvya that they might go to Pātāla. (97. 99)

963. Pātāla—Rg.—When Bali was vanquished by Vāmana, the whole of the Virocana-kula entered Pātāla. (98. 86.)

964. Pātāla—Rg.—At the time of the Deluge (*pralaya*) all the creatures in the Pātāla and in the oceans come to the surface of the earth and are destroyed. (100. 153)

965. Pātāla—No. 1048.

966. Pātaṁdhama—Mt.—No. 130.

967. Pataṅga—Mt.—Nos. 31, 820, 1302, 1340.

968. Paunikas—Ja.—No. 130

969. Pauras ?—Ja.—No. 569.

970. Pavanapura—Cy.—No. 1423

971. Pāvanī—Rv.—No. 470.

972. Pavitrā—Rv.—No. 674.

973. Payoda—L.—No. 894.

974. Payodā—Rv.—No. 894.

975. Payoṣṇī—Rv.—No. 130.

976. Pīḍikas—D.—Nos. 130 [Gha and Na : Cūḍikas].

977. Pīnas—D.—No. 130.

978. Piṅgala—Mt.—No. 1179 [Gha : Piñjara].

979. Piñjara—Mt.—No. 27.

980. Pippalā—Rv.—No. 130.

981. Piśācaka—Mt.—On the Piśācaka mountain is a great mansion (*bhavana*) of Kubera attended by Yakṣas and Gandharvas. (39. 57)

982. Piśācaka—Mt.—Nos. 820.

983. Piśācikā—Rv.—No. 130.

984. Piśaṅga—Mt.—No. 470.

985. Pittalas—Ja.—No. 569.

986. Pīvara—D.—No. 608.

987. Pīvarī—Rv.—No. 569.

988. Plakṣadvīpa—Dv. Medhātithi, the lord of Plakṣadvīpa, had seven sons, viz., Śāntabhaya, Śiśira, Sukhodaya [Ga, Gha and Ka : Sukhodadha], Ānanda [Kha and Gha : Ānalda], Dhruva, Kṣemaka and Śiva. Their respective varṣas are called after their names. In Plakṣadvīpa the people observe the rules of varṇāśrama. In Plakṣadvīpa and Śākadvīpa and in the other dvīpas (i.e. ?) the varṇāśrama is followed. (34. 31–6)

989. Plakṣadvīpa—Dv.—The Plakṣadvīpa is twice in area to Jambūdvīpa. It encircles the sea named Lavaṇodaka. The janapadas here are holy and the people live a long life without any fear of famine, pestilence and old age. The seven mountains in this dvīpa are : the first is the Gomedaka mountain, after which the Gomedaka varṣa is so called, the second mountain is Candra

where the two Asvins planted trees for obtaining amṛta; the third is the Nārada mountain where Nārada and Parvata were born; the fourth is the Dundubhi mountain where in former times the Suras beat a drum (the reference to Śālmala here is inexplicable); the fifth is the Somaka mountain where in former times the Devas placed amṛta and Garutmat forced it away for the sake of his mother; the sixth is the Sumanas (also called Ṛṣabha), mountain where Varāha killed Hiraṇyākṣa; and the seventh is the Vaibhrāja mountain so called because of its lustre.

The seven varṣas in this dvīpa are :—The Gomeda is the first varṣa also known by the name Śāntabhaya, [Ka : Śāntamaya] : of Candra the varṣa is Śikhara, of Nārada Sukhodaya, of Dundubhi Ānanda, of Somaka Śiva, of Ṛsabha Kṣemaka, and of Vaibhrāja Dhruva. Here the Devas, Gandharvas, Siddhas and the Cāraṇas rejoice.
The corresponding seven rivers in these seven varṣas are : Anutaptā, Sutaptā, Niṣpāpā, Muditā, Kratu, Amṛtā and Sukṛtā. Thus is the river Gaṅgā there with her seven courses (?). These rivers have their own numerous tributaries and they flow (towards the region ?) where the rain falls. The following janapadas drink the waters of these rivers: Śubhas (?), Śāntavahas, Pram das, Śivas, Ānandas, Dhruvas and the Kṣemakas. They follow the varṇāśrama, are ever healthy and free from any disease and fear. Here the yugas are not obtained and the conditions are always as in the Tretā age. The people enjoy a life of 5000 years. There is a great Plakṣa tree in this dvīpa whence it has derived its name. This tree is worshipped. (49. 1-28)

990. Plakṣa—Dv.—Nos. 433, 1108.

991. Plakṣapraśravaṇa— ?—Holy for śrāddha. (77. 67)

992. Plakṣatīrtha— ?—No. 666.

993. Prabhañjanā—Rv.—No. 569.

994. Prabhākara—Vr.—Nos. 673, 674.

995. Prabhāsa—Tī.—In the 27th dvāpara Śiva will be a *dvija* named Somaśarman who will reside at the Prabhāsa tīrtha. (23. 214–5)

996. Prabhāsa—Tī. ?—Holy for śrāddha purposes. It was situated near the sea (? cf. *mahodadhu*). It is mentioned along with Puṣkara which was also holy for śraddha. (77. 40)

997. Prabhāsa—Tī.—Having gone to the Preta mountain one should perform śraddha in Prabhāsa. (82. 20)

998. Prācyas—P.—They were annihilated by Pramiti at the end of the Kali age. (58. 81)

999. Prācyas— ?—Ālambira and others were the foremost among the Carakas (i.e. a branch of the Black Yajurvedins). (61. 9-10)

1000. Prāgyotiṣas—D.—No. 130.

1001. Pramodas—Ja.—No. 989.

1002. Prāṇa ?—Mt.—The Prāṇa (?) mountain was sub-merged in the northern sea. (47. 73)

1003. Prasthalas—D.—No. 130.

1004. Pratīcyas—P. ?—They were annihilated by Pramiti at the end of the Kali age. (58. 81)

1005. Pratiṣṭhāna ?—Tī.—One, who listens to the story of Pratiṣṭhāna, the holy place of Śatakratu (i.e. Indra), will not be affected by any evils. (The place appears to have some connection with king Raji). (92. 99)

1005a. Pratiṣṭhāna ?—Cy.—No. 1009.

1006. Pravaṅgas—D.—No. 130.

1007. Prāvaraka—Vr.—No. 606.

1008. Pravijayas ?—D.—No. 130.

1009. Prayāga—Cy.—King Aila Purūravas ruled in Prayāga, or Pratiṣṭhāna [Ka : Pratiṣṭhānta] on the northern banks of the river Yamunā. (91. 50)

1010. Prayāga—Tī.—Śrāddha should be performed in Prayāga on the banks of the Bhāgīrathī river. (77. 92)

1011. Prayāga—Cy. ?—Nos. 667, 708.

1012. Preta—Mt.—No. 9,7.

1013. Puleyas—Ja.—No. 1:0.

1014. Pulindas—P. ?—Theirs is the land of sin where śrāddha should not be performed. (78. 69-70)

1015. Pulindas—P. ?—No. 842.

1016. Pulindas—Ja.—Nos. 130, 470.

1017. Puṇḍarīka—Ti.—Holy for śrāddha. (77. 55.)

1018. Puṇḍarikā—Rv.—No. 606.

1019. Puṇḍarika—Mt.—No. 606.

1020. Puṇḍras—Ja.—Puṇḍra was one of the five sons of king Bali. His janapada was called the Puṇḍras. (99. 34)

1021. Puṇḍras—Cy.—No. 369.

1022. Puṇyodā—Rv.—Sòma is the fountain-head of all the waters of the sky. The river Puṇyodā has its source here. With its course guided by the wind it swiftly circumambulates the mountain Meru before it falls on its four northern peaks. From the sky to the Meru its course is of sixty yojanas. From the Meru it has four courses flowing towards the four directions. The eastern course circumvents the Mandara mountain and joins the Aruṇoda lake when it is called Ambaranadī. Then it falls on the Śītānta mountain, a habitat of the Siddhas. Here the course is called Sītā. Then flowing along the Mukuñja, Sumañjasa, Mālyavat, Vaikaṅka, Maṇiparvata and Ṛṣabha mountains it falls on the Jaṭhara mountain whence flowing along the Devakūṭa mountain it waters the Bhadrāśva dvīpa and joins the eastern sea. The southern course crosses the Gandhamādana mountain and waters the Gandhamādana forest. Here this course is called Alakanandā which later joins the northern Mānasa lake. It then flows along the Triśikhara, Kaliṅga, Rucaka, Niṣadha, Tāmrābha, Śvetodara, Sumūla, Vasudhāra, Hemakūṭa, Devaśṛṅga, Piśācaka, Pañcakūṭa and Kailāsa mountains. Then it falls on the Himavat mountain [Gha omits this sentence]. From the Himavat it pours into the southern sea. This river is supported by the god Śaṁkara and that is why it is considered as the holy river Gaṅgā. (42. 1-40)

1023. Puṇyodā—Rv.—Nos. 108, 569.

1024. Purikā— ? —Śiśuka, (a king of Aṅga dynasty ?) will be ruling in Purikā. (99. 370)

1025. Pūrṇadarvas—D.—No. 130.

1026. Puśkalā—Rv.—No. 569.

1027. Puśkara—Dv.—This seventh dvīpa encircles the Kśīroda sea. It is twice in area to Śākadvīpa. There is only one great mountain in this dvīpa and that is the Mānasa. There are only two janapadas in this dvīpa, viz., Mahāvīta and Dhātakīkhaṇḍa. The people live a life of 10,000 years. Here there is equality in all respects. The varnāśrama, the vārtās, cattle-breeding, trade and commerce, the three vidyās and daṇḍa-nīti are not obtained in this dvīpa. The sea named Svādūdaka (Sweet-water) surrounds this dvīpa. (49. 104-22)

1028. Puṣkara— ? —When the sun passes over the centre of Puṣkara one third of the earth is traversed (by the sun) in one muhūrta (?). (50. 119)

1029. Puṣkara— ? —Kaśyapa once performed an aśvamedha in Puṣkara where gods, sages and the Gandharvas were present. (67. 53)

1030. Puṣkara— ? —No. 996.

1031. ,, —Mt.—No. 106.

1031a. ,, —Dv.—Nos. 433, 237.

1032. Puṣkarāvatī—Cy.—No. 290.

1033. Puṣpagi—Mt.—No. 130.

1034. Puṣpajāti—Rv.—No. 130.

1035. Puṣpaka—Mt.—No. 509.

1036. ,, —Mt.—Munis dwell on the Puṣpaka mountain. (39. 62)

1037. Puṣpavat—Mt.—No. 674.

1038. Raibhyas—P. ?—They were called after Raibhya, the grandson of Kaśyapa. (70. 25-8)

1039. Raivataka—Mt.—No. 130.

1040. Rājīvakokilas—Ja.—No. 569.

1041. Rākṣasas—Ja.—No. 470.

1042. Ramaṇaka—Vr.—The Ramaṇaka varṣa is to the south of Śveta and to the north of Nīla mountains. The people here are white (in complexion ?) and are handsome in appearance. They drink the juice of the fruits of a big Nyagrodha tree, also called Rohiṇa (i.e. ?). These people live a life of 10500 years. (45. 1-5.)

1043. Ramaṭas—D.—No. 130.

1044. Ramyaka—Vr.—No. 434.

1045. Randhrakarakas—Ja.—No. 470.

1046. Rasātala—Rg. ?—Lord Hari, in his Vārāha form, entered Rasātala to lift up the earth. (6. 15)

1047. Rasātala—Rg. ?—Hari lay on the ocean-bed in Rasātala. (25. 33)

1048. Rasātala—Rg. ?—It is 10,000 (square ?) yojanas in area. Its seven (sub-divisions ?) are : Atala, Sutala, Vitala, Gabhastala, Mahātala, Śrītala and Pātāla. The first has a black (soil ?), the second white, the third red, the fourth yellow, the fifth like that of sugar (?), the sixth rocky and the seventh golden. In the first are the abodes of Namuci, the lord of Asuras, of Mahānāda and Kabandha. Here are also cities of Śaṅkukarṇa, Niṣkulāda, Dhanaṁjaya, Kālīya, Nāga and of Kalasa. In the second are the cities of Daityas such as Mahājambha, Hayagrīva Kṛṣṇa, Nikumbha, Saṅkha, Gomukha, Nīla, Megh, Krathana, etc. and of Nāgas such as Kambala, Takṣaka, etc. In the third are the cities of Prahlāda, Anuhlāda, Tāraka, Śiśumāra, Cyavana, Khara, etc. In the fourth are the cities of Kālanemi, Gajakarṇa, Sumālin, Vainateya, etc. In the fifth are the cities of Virocana, Hiraṇyākṣa, Mahāmegha, etc. In the sixth are the cities of Kesarin, Puloman, Mahiṣa, Nāga Vāsuki, etc. In the seventh are the cities of Bali, Mucukunda, etc. (50. 9 ff.)

1049. Rasātala—Rg.—The liar (*mithyāvādī*) king entered Rasātala. (57. 109)

1050. Rasātala—Rg. ?—While offering prayers to Śiva, Dakṣa also pays homage to those who dwell in Rasātala. (30. 281)

1051. Rasātala—Rg. ?—After being defeated by the Devas, the Asuras proposed to their preceptor Kāvya that they should retire to Rasātala. (97. 95) (98. 46)

1052. Rasātala—Rg. ?—Defeated by the Devas, the Asuras entered into the Rasātala. (98. 68)

1053. Rasātala—Rg. ?—The vicious kings in Rasātala were annihilated by Kṛṣṇa, an avatāra of Viṣṇu. (98. 102)

1054. Rasātala—Rg. ?—Having scorched the earth the Saṁvartaka fire soaked (*aśoṣayat*) the Rasātala. (100. 157)
1055. Rathītaras—P. ?—One of the fifteen pakṣas of Aṅgirasas. (65. 106)
1056. Ratnadhāra—Mt.—No. 584.
1057. Ratnadhātu—Mt.—The seven hermitages of the seven sages are situated on the Ratnadhātu mountain. (39. 45)
1058. Ratnāvatī—Rv.—No. 256.
1059. Rātri—Rv.—No. 606.
1060. Ṛkṣa—Mt.—130.
1061. Ṛkṣavat—Mt.—Kṛṣṇa started search for Prasena and went so far as the Ṛkṣavat and Vindhya mountains where he found the dead body of Prasena. (96. 36-40)
1062. Ṛkṣavat—Mt.—No. 888.
1063. Rohakas—Ja.—No. 470.
1064. Rohita—D.—No.
1065. Rokalas—Ja.—No. 130.
1066. Ṛṣabha—Mt.—This mountain is sub-merged in the eastern sea. (47. 72)
1067 Ṛṣabha—Mt.—No. 1022.
1068. Ṛṣabhā—Rv.—No. 569.
1069. Ṛśīkā—Rv.—No. 130.
1070. Ṛṣīkas—Ja.—No. 470.
1071. Ṛṣīka ?—Rg.—In the valleys and mountains at the extremity of Ṛṣīka people will take shelter at the end of the Kali age. (99. 403)
1072. Ṛtukulyā—Rv.—No. 130.
1073. Rucaka—Mt.—Nos. 782, 1022.
1074. Rudra—Mt.—No. 11179.
1075. Rudras—P. ?—No.
1076. Rudravaṭa—F. ?—At the end of the Kali age Śiva will reside in the holy Rudravaṭa [Kha : Rodravana]. (23. 212).
1077. Ruṣā—Rv.—No. 569.
1078. Ruṣāṇas—Ja.—No. 470.
1079. Śabala—F.—No. 566.
1080. Śabaras—P. ?—Their country is the land of sin where śrāddha ought not to be performed. (78. 69-70)
1081. Sabindu—Mt.—No. 782.
1082. Saddūhukas—P. ?—No. 470.
1083. Śāḍvala—F.—Saṁjñā, wife of Vivasvat practised penance in the Śāḍvala [Ka and Ga : Śādvala] forest. (84. 68)
1084. Sahacaiṣīkas—Ja.—No. 130.
1085. Sahasraśikhara—Mt.—The city of the Daityas is situated on the Sahasraśikhara mountain. (39. 61)
1086. Sahasraśikhara—Mt.—This mountain is inhabited by the Garutmats. (69. 333)

1087. Sahasraśikhara—Mt.—Nos. 27, 644, 1179.
1088. Sahotkacas—Ja.—No.—569.
1089. Sahya—Mt.—No. 130[2].
1090. Śailoda—L.—No. 470.
1091. Śailodā—Rv.—No. 470.
1092. Saindhavas—Ja.—No. 470.
1093. Śaiśītas—Ja.—No. 910.
1094. Saivāla—Mt.—No. 108.
1095. Saivālas—Ja.—No. 108.
1096. Śaivālinī—Rv.—No. 108.
1097. Sajāṅgalas—Ja.—No. 130.
1098. Śakas—P.—Nos. 130, 345, 470, 842.
1099. Śākadvīpa—Dv.—Havya, lord of Śākadvīpa, had the following seven sons : Jalada, Kumāra, Sukumāra, Maṇīcaka [Ṅa : Maṇīvaya], Vasumoda, Sumodāka [Kha, Ga and Gha : Samodāka; Ṅa : Samaudāka] and Mahādruma. Their respective varṣas were : Jalada, Kumāra, Sukumāra, Maṇīcaka, Vasumodaka, Modāka and Mahādruma. (33. 16–20)

1100. Śākadvīpa—Dv.—This dvīpa is twice in area to the Krauñcadvīpa and it encircles the Dadhimaṇḍodaka sea. The people here live a long life and there is no fear of famine, pestilence and old age for them. The seven mountains in this dvīpa are as follows : The first is the Meru mountain extending towards the east and is also called Udaya. Here Devas, sages and Gandharvas reside. Here the clouds rise and there is rainfall. The second is the Jaladhāra mountain where the rain-god (Vāsava) is always active in the rainy season. The third is the Raivataka mountain whence is seen (?) the nakṣatra Revatī. Then comes the Śyāma mountain whence the people had become black (*śyāmatvam āpannāḥ*). Then come the Asta, Āmbikeya [Kha, Gha and Ṅa : Ambikāyā], Ramya which is also called Keśari. The corresponding varṣas are : Jalada, Sukumāra, Kaumāra, Maṇīcaka, Kusumottara, Modāka and Mahādruma. At the centre of this dvīpa is a great Śāka tree which is an object of worship. With it the Devas, Gandharvas, Siddhas and Cāraṇas sport. The seven rivers in this dvīpa are : Sukumārī also known as Anutaptā, Kumārī, Nandā, Śivetikā [Kha and Ṅa : Śivenikā] also known as Tridivā, Ikṣu, Dhenukā and (?). These rivers have their own numerous tributaries which flow towards the region where the rains fall. There are many cities and prosperous janapadas in this dvīpa which is surrounded by the Kṣīroda sea. Here the varṇāśrama system works smoothly, the people being free from vices, such as, greed, anger, etc. Here taxation and laws do not exist. (49. 72–104)

1101. Śākadvīpa—Dv.—No. 433.
1102. Śākamuṇḍas—Ja.—No. 108.
1103. Śākavatī—Rv.—No. 569.
1104. Sāketu—Rg. ?—No. 708.
1105. Śākhāvatī—Rv.—No. 108.
1106. Śālagrāma—Cy. ?—Holy for śrāddha purposes. (77. 88)
1107. Śālma—Dv.—Vapuṣmat, the lord of Śālma (i.e. Śālmala) dvīpa, had the following seven sons : Śveta, Harita, Jīmūta, Rohita, Vaidyuta, Mānasa and Suprabha. The territories (assigned to them ?) were called after their respective names. (33. 28–31)
1108. Śālmala—Dv.—The third dvīpa named Śālmala is twice in area to Plakṣadvīpa. It circumvents the Ikṣurasodaka sea. The seven mountains in this dvīpa are : Kumuda, Unnata, Balāhaka, Droṇa, Kaṅka (wrongly mentioned as the tenth) Mahiṣa and Kakudmat. The corresponding seven varṣas are : Śveta, Lohita, Jīmūta, Harita, Vaidyuta, Mānasa and Suprabha. The rivers in this dvīpa are : Pāṇītoyā, Vitṛṇā, Candrā, Śukrā, Vimocanī and Nivṛtti. This dvīpa is named after a great *śāl.nali* tree in it. The Suroda sea surrounds this dvīpa. (49. 28–45)
1109. Śālmaladvīpa—Dv.—It is inhabited by the Garutmats. (69. 332)
1110. ,, —Dv.—Nos. 229, 433, 674.
1111. Śālvas—Ja.—No. 130.
1112. Samāheyas—P. ?—No. 130.
1113. Saṁbhavaktras—Ja.—No. 108.
1114. Samudramālā—Rv.—No. 569.
1115. Samūla—Mt.—Nos. 147, 820.
1116. Saṁyamana—Cy.—No. 826.
1117. Saṁdhyā—Rv.—No. 606.
1118. Śaṅkhadvīpa—Dv.—No. 437.
1119. Śaṅkhagiri—Mt.—No. 337.
1120. Saṅkhakūṭa—Mt.—No. 106
1121. Śaṅkhākyas—Ja.—No. 108.
1122. Śaṅkhanāgā.—Rv.—No. 437.
1123. Śaṅkukūṭa—Mt.—Nos. 713, 1473.
1124. Śāṅkṛtikas—P. ?—One of the fifteen pakṣas of Aṅgirasas. (65. 106–8)
1125. Śāntabhaya—Vr.—No. 988.
1126. Saṁtati—Rv.—No. 674.
1127. Śāntavahas—Ja.—No. 989.
1128. Śāntī—Rv.—No. 1278.
1129. Sarasa—Mt.—No. 27.
1130. Sarasvatī—Rv.—Agni loved her [Omitted in Ṅa]. (29. 12–4)
1131. ,, —Rv.—Nos. 130, 143, 1320
1132. ,, —Mt. ?—No. 385.

1133. Śaravaṇa—F.—Nos. 380, 469. (29. 12-4)
1134. Sarayū—Rv.—Agni loved her [Omitted in Ṅa].
1135. ,, —Rv.—Nos. 130, 470.
1136. Sarvamūlikas—Ja.—No. 470.
1137. Sasurasa—Mt.—Nos. 130.
1138. Śatadru—Rv.—Agni loved her [Omitted in Ṅa]. (29. 12-4)
1139. ,, —Rv.—No. 130.
1140. Śātakaumbha—Mt.—No. 818.
1141. Śatapatheśvaras—Ja.—No. 130.
1142. Śataśṛṅga—Mt.—The Yakṣas have their cities on this mountain. (39. 54)
1143. Śataśṛṅga—Mt.—The Garutmats dwell on the Śataśṛṅga mountain. (69. 333)
1144. Śataśṛṅga—Mt.—Nos. 106, 713.
1145. Ṣaṭsuras—Ja.—No. 130.
1146. Satīrā—Rv.—No. 130.
1147. Saumya—Rg.—No. 130.
1148. Sauvīras—Ja.—Nos. 108, 130.
1149. Sāvitra—Mt.—No. 817.
1150. Sāyana—L.—No. 370 [Kha : Akṣada].
1151. Setukas—Ja.—No. 130.
1152. Siddhakṣetra—Tī. ?—Holy for śrāddha. (77. 80)
1153. ,, —Tī. ?—Nos. 22, 392, 814, 1155.
1154. Sīgaṇas—Ja.—No. 470.
1155. Śikhaṇḍin—Mt.—In the 18th dvāpara, Śiva will be known as Śikhaṇḍin and he will reside with his four sons in the Siddhakṣetra in the Śikhaṇḍin mountain on the summit of the Himavat. (23. 181-3)
1156. Śikhara—Vr.—No. 989.
1157. Śikhi—Mt.—Nos. 27, 1268.
1157a. Śikhimālā—Rv.—No. 569.
1158. Śikhiśaila—Mt.—No. 1179.
1159. Śilāśinī—Rv.—No. 108.
1160. Siṁhalas—P.—They were annihilated by Pramiti at the end of the Kali age. (58. 82)
1161. Siṁhalas—No. 842.
1162. Sindhu—Rv.—In the land to the north of the river Sindhu the āśramadharma does not prevail and there śrāddha should not be performed. (78. 23)
1163. Sindhu—Rv.—The region to the north of the river Sindhu is a land of sin. The virtuous evade contact with its inhabitants. Here śrāddha ought not to be performed. (78. 69-70)
1164. Sindhu—Rv.—Nos. 130², 470, 770.
1165. Sindhus—D.—No. 130.

1166. Sindhumaru—Rg.—No. 470.

1167. Śiprā—Rv.—No. 130 [Gha and Ṅa : Kṣiprā].

1168. Sirindhras—D.—No. 470.

1169. Śiśira—Mt.—No. 820.

1170. ,, —Vr.—No. 988.

1171. Śiśoccaya—Mt.—This mountain is sub-merged in the northern sea. (47. 73)

1172. Sītā—Rv.—Agni loved her [Omitted in Ṅa]. (29. 12–4)

1171. ,, —Rv.—Nos. 1022, 470.

1173a. ,, —Rv.—No. 108.

1174. Sītānta—Mt.—This mountain is inhabited by Yakṣas, Kinnaras and Gandharvas. In it is a pleasure-garden (Krīḍāvana) of Mahendra. This garden or forest (?) is also known as Pārijātavana. There is always spring-time in this forest. To the east of Sītānta is the Kumuñja (or Kumuda) mountain on which are situated the eight cities of the Dānavas. (39. 1–29)

1175. Sitānta—Mt.—Nos. 655, 782, 1022, 1461.

1176. Siterajā—Rv.—No. 130.

1177. Śitibāhu—Rv.—No. 130 [Ga, Gha and Ṅa : Śiyudeva].

1178. Śītoda—L.—The four great lakes are : Aruṇoda in the east, Mānasa in the south, Śītoda in the west and Mahābhadra in the north. (36. 15–7)

1179. Śītoda—L.—To the west of this lake are the following mountains : Suvakṣas, Śikhiśaila, Kāla (?), Vaidūrya [Kha and Ṅa : Vaiḍūrya], Kapila, Piṅgala [Gha : Piñjara], Rudra, Surasa, Kumuda, Madhumat, Añjana, Mukuṭa, Kṛṣṇa, Pāṇḍara, Sahasraśikhara (?), Pārijāta [Ka : Pāripātra] and Triśṛṅga. (36. 26–9)

1180. Sitoda—L.—No. 27.

1181. Śiva—Vr.—Nos. 988, 989.

1182. Śivas—Ja.—No. 989.

1183. Śivā—Rv.—No. 674.

1184. Śivapauras—Ja.—No. 470.

1185. Śivapura—Cy.—No. 891.

1186. Śivetikā—Rv.—No. 1100.

1187. Skandamālā—Rv.—No. 108.

1188. Sodakas—Ja.—No. 108.

1189. Somaka—Mt.—This mountain is sub-merged in the western sea. (47. 74)

1190. Somaka—Mt.—No. 989.

1191. Somāvarttā—Rv.—No. 108.

1192. Soṇa—Rv.—No. 130.

1193. Sopasaṅgas—Ja.—No. 108.

1194. Śravaṇas—Ja.—No. 569.

1195. Śrāvastī—Cy.—Śrāvasta was a son of Yuvanāśva, a descendant of Ikṣvāku. This Śrāvasta founded the city of Śrāvastī. (88. 26-7)
1196. Śrāvastī—Cy.—No. 599.
1197. Śrī—Mt.—The Candratīrtha is inhabited by the virtuous. In this tīrtha, in Kumārī, at the source of the river Kāverī, in tīrthas on the Śrīparvata and on the Vaikṛta mountain, śrāddha should be performed. [Ka, Ga, Gha and Ṅa omits this information]. (77. 28)
1198. Śrī—Mt.—No. 130.
1199. ,, —F.—No. 146.
1200. ,, —L.—No. 146.
1201. Srīrāṣṭra—Rg.—It will be ruled over by one Kanaka [Kha, Ga and Na : Srīrājya]. (99. 387)
1202. Śrītala—Rg.—No. 1048.
1203. Śṛṅgasāhva—Mt.—No. 406.
1204. Śṛṅgavat—Mt.—It is described in the Purāṇa [Kha, Ga, Gha and Ṅa : Śṛṅgin]. (1. 85)
1205. Śṛṅgavat—Mt.—The Pitṛs live on the Śṛṅgavat mountain. (46. 35)
1206 ,, —Mt.—No. 818^3.
1207. ,, —Vr.—(No. 434). [Kha and Ṅa : Śṛṅgavāta].
1208. Śroṇī—Rv.—No. 130.
1209. Stanapas—D.—(No. 130). [Ga : Stanakas ; Gha : Stanasas].
1210. Stāvakas—Ja.—No. 569.
1211. Śubhā—Rv.—No. 569.
1212. Śubhas—Ja.—No. 989.
1213. Subhaumas—Ja.—No. 108.
1214 Sūcidarbhas—Ja.—No. 705.
1215 Śuddhas—Ja.—No. 108.
1216 Śūdras—D.—No. 130.
1217.—Suhmas—Ja.—Suhma was one of the five sons of king Bali, a descendant of Yayāti. His janapada was known as the Suhmas [Ka : Suhlakas]. (99. 33)
1218. Sujarakas—D.—No. 130.
1219. Sukāmas—Ja.—No. 108.
1220. Śukanadī—Rv.—No. 569.
1221. Sukeśa—Mt.—Inhabited by the Gaṛutmats.
1222. Sukhā—Cy.—No. 826.
1223. Sukhodaya—Vr.—Nos. 988, 989.
1224. Śukhā—Rv.—No. 1108.
1225. Sukṛtā—Rv.—No. 989.
1226. Śuktimat—Mt.—No. 130^2.
1227. Śuktimatī—Rv.—(No. 130). [Ṅa : Muktimatī].
1228. Sukumāra—Vr.—Nos. 1099, 1100.
1229. Ṣukumārī—Rv.—Nos. 130, 1100.

1230. Śūlikas—P.—They were annihilated by Pramiti at the end of the Kali age. (58. 83)
1231. Sumanas—Mt.—No. 989.
1232. Sumaṅgalas—Ja.—No. 108.
1232a. Sumañjas—Mt.—No. 1022.
1233. Sumaulas—Ja.—No.—569.
1234. Sumedha—Mt.—Between the Veṇumat and Sumedha mountains is an extensive valley (?). (37. 26-7)
1235. Sumedha—Mt.—Ādityas, Vasus, Rudras and the two Āśvins have their dwellings on this mountain. Here the Siddhas have built houses (*sthānāni*) for the gods where Yakṣas, Gandharvas and Kinnaras are always engaged in worship. (39. 48-50)
1236. Sumedha—Mt.—No. 882.
1237. Sumedhā—Rv.—No. 569
1238. Sumeru—Mt.—The Mahāpuruṣa created by Śiva was like the Sumeru. (30. 130)
1239. Sumeru—Mt.—Svayaṁbhu 'churned' the earth with Sumeru as the calf (*vatsa*). (8. 148)
1240. Sumeru— ?—No. 434.
1241. Sumūla—Mt.—No. 1022.
1242. Sumūlā—Rv.—No. 569.
1243. Sumūrdhajas—Ja.—No. 108. [Gha : Sumūlajas].
1244. Sunāga—Mt.—Here the Daityas have their dwellings. (39. 36)
1245. Sunaga—Mt.—No. 106.
1246 Śunakāsas—Ja.—No. 569.
1247. Śunāmukhas—Ja.—No. 470.
1248. Sunandana—F.—No. 1422.
1249. Sunandanas—Ja. ?—No. 108.
1250. Sunāsa—Cy.—No. 229.
1251. Supakṣa—Mt.—Vaivasvata, Soma, Vāyu and the lord of the Nāgas have their dwellings on the Supakṣa mountain. (39. 63)
1252. Supakṣa—Mt.—No. 27.
1253. Supārśva—Mt.—Nos. 106, 819.
1254. Suprabha—D.—No. 1107.
1255 ,, —Vr.—No. 1108.
1256. Supratīka—F.—To the north of the Vindhya and to the south of the river Gaṅgā is the forest of Supratīka. (69. 239)
1257. Suprayogā—Rv.—No. 130.
1258. Surālas—Ja.—No. 130.
1259. Surasa—Mt.—No. 1179.
1260. Surasā—Rv.—No. 108.
1261. Śūrasenas—Ja.—No. 130.
1262. Surāṣṭras—Ja.—No. 130.
1263. Surāvatī—Rv.—No. 108.

1263a. Surecakas—Ja.—No. 569.

1264. Sūrpākāras—Ja.—No. 130.

1265. Sūryakānta—Mt.—Nos. 180, 660.

1266. Sutala—Rg.—No. 1048.

1267. Sutaptā—Rv.—No. 989.

1268. Suvakṣas—Mt.—Between the Suvakṣas and Śikhi mountains is a rocky tract covering about a hundred yojanas. At its centre is a fire-place which is thirty yojanas in extent. Here the lord of Fire is always active. The Mātuluṅgasthalī [Ṅa : Mātṛluṅgasthalī] which covers ten yojanas is also situated here with the hermitage of Bṛhaspati in it. (38. 37-44)

1269. Suvakṣas—Mt.—No. 1179.

1270. Suvaprā—Rv.—Nos. 108, 569.

1271. Suvarṇā—Rv.—Nos. 108, 569.

1272. Suvarṇakaṭakas—Ja.—No. 569.

1273. Suvīra—No. 782.

1274. Svairathākāra—Vr.—Nos. 673, 674.

1275. Svapārśva—Mt.—No. 819.

1276. Svarṇavedī— ?—Holy for śrāddha. (77. 95)

1277. Śveta—Mt.—This varṣa-parvata is described in the Purāṇa. (1. 85)

1278. Śveta—Mt.—The Daityas and the Dānavas dwell here. (46. 35)

1278a. ,, —Mt.—On the Śveta mountain is the Uttaramānasa lake whence flow the rivers: Jyotsnā, Mṛgakāntā, Śāntī [Kha : Śaptā and Mādhvī. (47. 67-71)

1279. Śveta—Mt.—Nos. 27, 106, 406, 818², 1042.

1280. ,, —Vr.—Nos. 434, 1107, 1108.

1281. Śvetas—Ja.—No. 569.

1282. Śvetāṅgas—Ja.—No. 569.

1283. Śvetaśṛṅga—Mt.—No. 818.

1284. Śvetavarṇa—Mt.—No. 108.

1285. Śvetodara—Mt.—On this mountain is the city of Sunābha, son of Garuḍa. (39. 56)

1286. Śvetodara—Mt.—Nos. 820, 1022.

1287. Śyāmā—Rv.—No. 569.

1288. Śyāma—Mt.—No. 1100

1289. Takṣaśilā—Cy.—No. 290.

1290. Tāla—F.—This forest is situated along the bank of the river Sukhā between the Mahānīla and Kumuñja mountains. It is 50 × 30 yojanas in area. Here dwells Airāvata, the lord of elephants. (37. 22-5)

1291. Tālajaṅghas—P.—No. 345.

1292. Tāmaliptas—Ja.—No. 470.

1293. Tamasā—Rv.—No. 130.

1294. Tāmasas—D.—No. 130.
1295. Tāmasī—Rv.—No. 569.
1296. Tampākas—Ja.—No. 470.
1297. Tāmrābha—Mt.—On it is the city of Kādraveya Takṣaka. (39. 54)
1298. ,, —Mt.—Nos. 820, 1022.
1299. Tāmraliptas—P ?—The Maṇidhānyajas will rule over the Tāmraliptas together with the sea (cf. *Tāmraliptān sasāgarān*). (99. 385-6)
1300. Tāmraliptakas—Ja.—No. 130.
1301. Tāmraparṇī—Rv.—No. 332.
1302. Tāmravarṇa—Mt.—Between the Tāmravarṇa and Pataṅga mountains there is a holy lake inhabited by the Devas, Dānavas and Uragas. In the centre of this lake (?) is a janapada hundred yojanas in extent. The great city of the Vidyādharas is situated here where Puloman, the lord of the Vidyādharas dwells. (38. 8-17)
1303. Tāmravarṇī—Rv.—No. 130 [Tamravarṇā].
1304. ,, —Rg.—No. 130.
1305. Tanapas—Ja.—No. 108.
1306. Taṅgaṇas—D.—No. 130².
1307. ,, —Ja.—No. 470.
1308. Tāpasas—Ja.—No. 130.
1309. Tāpī—Rv.—No. 130.
1310 Tatsukhas—Ja.—No. 569.
1311. Tilaṅgas—Ja.—No. 130.
1312. Tomaras—D.—No. 130.
1313. ,, —P. ?—No. 470.
1314. Tosalas—P.—No. 130.
1315. Toyā—Rv.—No. 130.
1316. Traipuras—P.—No. 130.
1316a. Traiśaṅkava—D.—This deśa is a taboo for śraddha purposes. It is to the north of the Mahānadī and to the south of Kaikaṭa (i.e. ?). (78. 22)
1317. Tridivā—Rv.—No. 130².
1318. Trigartas—D.—No. 130.
1319. Trikaku—H.—No. 470.
1319a. Trikūṭa—Mt.—No. 437.
1320. Triplakṣa—Tī.—Śrāddha should be performed in the Vyāsa tīrtha on the banks of the river Sarasvatī and in the Triplakṣa (also on the banks of the Sarasvatī ?). [Ka reads Brahmakṣetra for Triplakṣa]. (77. 67)
1321. Trisāmā—Rv.—No. 130.
1322. Triśikhara—Mt.—No. 820, 1022.

1323. Triśṛṅga—Mt.—On this northern mountain is a great city graced by the three temples of the three chief gods, viz., Viṣṇu, Brahmā and Śiva worshipped by the Daityas, Dānavas, Gandharvas, Yakṣas, Rākṣasas and Paunagas. The cities of the Yakṣas, Gandharvas and Nāgas are also situated on this mountain. (41. 62–5)

1324. Triśṛṅga—Mt.—Nos. 106, 1179.

1325. Tumburas—P.—Nos. 130, 576.

1326. Tumuras—P.—No. 130.

1327. Tuṇḍikeras—P.—No. 130.

1328. Tuṅgabhadrā—Rv.—No. 130.

1329. Turasitas—D.—No. 130. [Gha and Ṅa : Turaminas].

1330. Tuṣāras—P.—They were annihilated by Pramiti at the end of the Kali age. (58. 83)

1331. Tuṣāras—P.—No. 842.

1332. ,, —D. No. 130.

1333. ,, —Ja.—No. 470.

1334. Udaya ?—Mt.—No. 1100.

1335. Udbhida--Vr.—Nos. 673, 674.

1336. Udbhidas—Ja.—No. 130.

1337. Udīcyas—P.—In connection with the distribution of the śākhās of the Yajurveda Śyāmāyani was the foremost amongst the Udīcyas. (61. 8)

1338. Udīcyas—P.—They were annihilated by Pramiti at the end of the Kali age. (58. 81)

1339. Udīcyas—P.—No. 842.

1340. Udumbara—F.—This forest is situated between the Śiśira and Pataṅga mountains. Here the Siddhas, Yakṣas, Gandharvas, Kinnaras, Uragas and Vidyādharas have their dwellings. The hermitage of Kardama, the Prajāpati, is also seen in this forest which covers an area of about 100 yojanas. (38. 1–7)

1341. Ujjanta—Mt.—On this holy mountain is an abode of Yogeśvara and a hermitage of Vasiṣṭha. (77. 52)

1342. Umātuṅga—H.—Holy for śrāddha. (77.82)

1343. Umāvana—F.—King Sudyumna happened to enter Umāvana while he was out for hunting and he was immediately converted into a female. (85. 27–8)

1344. Umāvana—F.--No. 469.

1345. Unnata—Mt.—No. 1108.

1346. Uraḥsaṁkīrṇabhaumakas ?—Ja.—No. 108.

1347. Ūrdhvamarus—Ja.—No. 470.

1348. Uṣṇa—D.—No. 608.

1349. ,, —Vr.—No. 606.

1350. Uṣṭrakarṇas—Ja.—No. 470.

1351. Utakacas—Ja.—No. 569.
1352. Utkala—Rg.—King Sudyumna had three sons, viz., Utakala, Gaya and Vinatāśva. Of these Utkala had Utkalarāṣṭra and Gaya the city of Gayā. (85. 18-9)
1353. Utkalas—P.—No. 130.
1354. Uttamārṇas—Ja.—No. 130.
1355. Uttarakurus—Rg.—Nos. 106, 180, 779, 818, 819.
1356. Uttaramānasa—L.—No. 1278a.
1357. Vācāṅgas—Ja.—No. 569.
1358. Vadātis—Ja.—No. 470.
1359. Vāḍavas—P. ?—No. 1322.
1360. Vāhā—Rv.—No. 569.
1361. Vāhas—Ja.—No. 569.
1362. Vāhakas—P. ?—A class of Bhūmirākṣasas. (69. 184)
1362a Vāhlīkas—D.—No. 130.
1363 Vaibhrāja—F.—It is to the west of (?) and the Nandana forest is to the south of (?). (36. 11)
1364. Vaibhrāja—F.—No. 470.
1365. ,, —Mt.—No. 989.
1366. Vaidarbhas—Ja.—No. 130.
1367. Vaideśa—Rg.—Bhūtinanda, the fifth king of a Nāga dynasty will rule in Vaideśa [Gha reads vaṁśa thus dispensing with a geographical name]. (99. 366–8)
1368. Vaidūrya—Mt.—Nos. 27, 1179.
1369. Vaidyuta—H.—No. 470.
1370. ,, —Mt.—No. 130.
1371. ,, —Vr.—Nos. 1107, 1108.
1372. Vaihāra—Mt.—No. 130.
1373. Vaikaṅka -Mt.—Birds, the enemies of the Pannagas, dwell on the Vaikaṅka mountain. Sugrīva is their chief. (39. 41)
1374. Vaikaṅka—Mt.—No. 1022.
1375. Vaikṛta—Mt.—No. 1197.
1376. Vainakas—P. ?—A class of bhūmi-rākṣasas. (69. 184)
1377. Vaiṇī—Rv.—No. 130.
1378. Vaitaraṇī—Rv.—Holy for śrāddha. (77. 95)
1378. ,, —Rv.—No. 130.
1379. Vajraka—Mt.—On the Vajraka mountain dwell the Nīlaka Rākṣasas. (39. 30–1)
1380. Vakra—Mt.—This mountain is sub-merged in the southern sea. (47. 75)
1380a. Vaktrā—Rv.—No. 108.
1381. Vakulas—Ja. ?—No. 569.
1382. Vāmanaka—Mt.—No. 606.
1383. Vāmodā—Rv.—No. 108.

1384. Vanamālā—Rv.—No. 108.
1385. Vanapātakas—Ja.—No. 569.
1386. Vanāsagajabhūmikas—Ja.—No. 569.
1387. Vanavāsikas—Mt.—No. 130.
1388. Vaṅgas—Ja.—Vaṅga was one of the five sons of king Bali, a descendant of Yayāti. His janapada was known as the Vaṅgas. (99. 33)
1389. Vaṅgas—Rg.—There the people will fly at the end of the Kali age. (99. 402)
1390. Vaṅgas.—Ja.—Nos. 470, 569².
1391. Vāṅgas—Ja.—No. 569.
1392. Vaṅgeyas—Ja.—No. 130.
1393. Vañjulā—Rv.—No. 130.
1394. Vaṁśadharā—Rv.—No. 130.
1395. Vapuṣmatī—Rv.—No. 108.
1396. Varāha—Mt.—This mountain is sub-merged in the western sea. (39. 74)
1397. Varāha—Mt.—Nos. 106, 437.
1398. Vārāhas—Ja.—No. 108.
1399. Varāhadvīpa—Dv.—No. 437.
1400. Vārāhī—Rv.—No. 437.
1401. Vārāṇasī—Tī. ?—Śiva in his Lāṅgalin incarnation will reside in Vārāṇasī. (23. 198)
1402. Vārāṇasī—Cy.—Śraddha should be performed in the city of Vārāṇasī. (77. 93)
1403. Vārāṇasī—Cy.—The following is the story of how this siddhakṣetra happened to be cursed by Nikumbha :—The royal sage Divodāsa was in former times ruling over this prosperous city. It so happened that at this very time Maheśvara was recently married and was residing with his father-in-law. Menā, however, disliked him and passed adverse comments about his behaviour to her daughter (cf. *mama pārśve tu anācāras tava bhartā maheśvaraḥ daridraḥ sarva eva iha akliṣṭaṁ laḍate' naghe*). The wife of Śiva took offence at this statement and pressed upon her husband to shift to their own place. (It appears Śiva had no such fixed place of residence.) Śiva thought for some time over the matter and commanded his attendant Gaṇeśa Kṣemaka to render desolate the city of Vārāṇasī. Nikumbha (i.e. Kṣemaka) appeared before the barber named Maṅkana in his dreams and directed him to instal his (i.e. of Gaṇeśvara Kṣemaka) image at (or outside) the gates of the city. Since that time this Gaṇeśvara became an object of worship especially for women who desired male progeny. King Divodāsa, as he had no son, asked his wife to offer worship to the deity;

but all her efforts were in vain at which the king got wild and cursing the deity as bhūtaṁ (note neuter) destroyed the place of worship (cf. *sthānaṁ Gaṇapates tasya nāśayāmāsa*). Thus did Nikumbha curse the city to become desolate. The king deserted the city and founded another city on the river Gomatī...Śiva now resided with his wife in this deserted city... After the effect of the curse was over, Alarka, the king of Kāśi, who was a descendant of Divodāsa, took possession of the city after annihilating the Rākṣasa Kṣemaka. (92. 24–68)

1404. Vārāṇasī—Cy.—Bhadraśreṇya was king of Vāranasī. (94. 6)

1405. ,, —Rv.—No. 325.

1406. Vāraṇāvata—Rv.—No. 267.

1407. Varapas—Ja.—No. 470.

1408. Varas—Ja.—No. 130.

1409. Vardhamāna—Mt.—No. 569.

1410. Varṇamālāgra—Mt.—(No. 108). [Ṅa : Varṇamālā.]

1411. Varṇāśā—Rv.—No. 130.

1412. Varuṇa—Rg.—No. 130.

1413. Vasudhāra—Mt.—The Vasus have their eight mansions (āyatanāni) on the Vasudhāra mountain. (39. 44)

1414. Vasudhāra—Mt.—Nos. 147, 584, 1022.

1415. Vasumatī—Rv.—No. 108.

1416. Vasumodaka—Vr.—No. 1099.

1417. Vāṭadhānas—D.—(No. 130). [Ka : Vādhadhānas.]

1418. Vātaraṁhas—Ja.—(No. 108). [Gha and Ṅa : Vātaraṅgas.]

1419. Vatsa—Mt.—No. 106.

1420. Vatsas—Ja.—No. 130.

1421. Vatsakas—Ja.—No. 108.

1422. Vāyupura—Cy.—Formerly Brahmā founded the Brahmakṣetra, the same as Kurukṣetra [Gha does not mention Kurukṣetra]. Here gods, sages and munis dwell. Once Brahmā inquired of the inhabitants whether anybody amongst them had seen the Vāyu-devatā. The sages answered in the negative. While they were thus deliberating they happened to see the Vāyupura. This city was inhabited by 18000 dvījas and 36000 Śūdras under the leadership of Matariśvan who declared to them : "You are my devotees and shall be known after my name (i.e. the city founded by them will be called Vāyupura). There will be eleven gotras amongst you." [From this sentence onwards Kha omits the remaining portion of the chapter]. Here is a tank which relieves one from all the miseries of life. This tīrtha is famous throughout the world. Here was Hanumat born. Here doth Rudra dwell and it was here that Vāyu installed an image (?) of Vāḍāditya [Kha : Vāyaḍāditya]. This Vāḍāditya is none else that Sūrya. Here are the four Kuṇḍas (or tanks), viz., Sūryakuṇḍa, Brahmakuṇḍa, Rudrakuṇḍa and Harikuṇḍa. Nine fortifications (*durgaḥ*) protect this Kṣetra. The customs of the Vāḍavas (i.e. the people of this Kṣetra) are manifold. There are many resting-houses (*dharmaśālās*) in this Kṣetra, which is situated on the banks of the river Ṙatnāvatī which in the Kali age is called Dṛṣadvatī. The forest Sunandava is situated in the vicinity of this Kṣetra. [This whole passage is omitted in Kha, Ga and Ṅa]. (59. 107 ff.)

1423. Vāyupura—Cy.—Yājñavalkya and his disciples incurred the sin of *brahmahatyā* (murder of a Brahmin). They approached Brahmā for this purpose. Brahmā advised them to go to Pavanapura, to worship the god Vālukeśvara and the eleven Rudras and to have a bath in the four tanks there and that their sin would thus be dissolved immediately. The sages did accordingly and merged themselves into the Sūrya-maṇḍala. Since that time this city of Vāyu is regarded holy. Here was Hanumat born of Añjanī. (60. 67 ff.)

1424. Vedaśīrṣa—Mt.—No. 385.
1425. Vedasmṛti—Rv.—No. 130.
1426. Vedavatī—Rv.—No. 130.
1427. Veṇumat—Mt.—On it are the three cities of Vidyādharas. (39. 37)
1428. Veṇumat—Mt.—Nos. 782, 1234.
1429. Veṇumaṇḍala—Vr.—Nos, 673, 674.
1430. Veṇyā—Ṙv.—No. 130. [Gha : Venva.
1431. Vetālī—Rv.—No. 108.
1432. Vetravatī—Rv.—No. 130.
1433. Vibhāvarī—Cy.—No. 826.
1434. Videha—Rg.—King Rukmakavaca established his two sons Parigha and Hari in Videha. (95. 28)
1435. Videhas—D.—No. 130.
1436. Vidiśā—Rv.—No. 130.
1437. Vidrumoccaya—Mt.—No. 674.
1438. Vidyādharas—Ja.—No. 470.
1439. Vihas—Ja.—No. 569.
1440. Vijayasthalas—Ja.—No. 108.
1441. Vikaṅka—Mt.—Nos. 168, 782.
1442. Vikīrṇā— Rv.—No. 569.
1443. Vimocinī—Rv.—No. 1108.
1444. Vinaśana—Tī. ?—Holy for śrāddha. (77. 67)
1445. Vindhya—Mt.—In the vicinity of this mountain Viśvāmitra managed Triśaṅku's entry into the heaven. [Omitted in Ka, Ga, Gha and Ṅa]. (88. 113)
1446. Vindhya—Mt.—Nos. 64, 130, 236, 470, 576, 599, 1061, 1256.
1447. Vindhyas—P. ?—No. 842.
1448. Vindhyamūlīkas.—Ja.—No. 130.
1449. Vipāśā—Rv.—Agni loved her. [Omitted in Ṅa]. (29. 14)

1450 Vipāśā—Rv.—No. 130^2.
1451. Vipula—Mt.—No. 819.
1452. Virāja—Mt.—No. 713.
1453. Vīrudha—Mt.—No. 106.
1454. Viṣadhāra—Mt.—No. 820.
1455. Viśākha—Mt.—There is a mansion of Guha on this mountain. (39. 55)
1456 Viśākha—Mt.—Nos. 31, 820.
1457. Viśālā—Cy.—Tṛṇabindu had a son named Viśāla who founded the city of Viśālā. (86. 15-7)
1458 Viśāla—Mt.—No. 569.
1459. Viśālā—Rv.—No. 569.
1460. Visarjayas—Ja.—No. 470.
1461. Viṣṇupada—Mt.—King Dharmaratha drank soma with Śakra [Gha : Śukra] in a sacrifice performed on the Viṣṇupada mountain [Ga omits this]. (99. 102)
1462. Viṣṇupada—Mt.—No. 937.
1463. Viṣṇupadī—Rv.—No. 108 [Ga, Gha and Ṅa : Viṣṇupadā].
1464. Vitastā—Rv.—Agni loved her [Omitted in Ṅa]. (29. 13)
1465. ,, —Rv.—No. 130.
1466. Vitala—Rg. ?—No. 1048.
1467. Vītihotras—Ja.—No. 130.
1468. Vitṛṇā—Rv.—No. 1108.
1469. Vivarṇas—Ja.—No. 470.
1470. Vrajakas—Ja.—No. 108.
1471. Vṛkas—Ja.—No. 130.
1472. Vṛṣa—Mt.—No. 106.
1473. Vṛṣabha—Mt.—Between the Vṛṣabha and Śaṅkukūṭa mountains is the Parūṣakasthalī. There Kinnaras and Uragas drink the juice of Parūṣaka (plants). (38. 63-5)
1474. Vṛṣabha—Mt.—Nos. 713, 782.
1475. Vṛṣadarbhas—Ja.—No. 705.
1476. Vṛṣalas—P. ?—No. 839.
1477. Vṛtraghnī—Rv.—No. 130.
1478. Vyāsatīrtha—Tī.—Śrāddha should be performed at Vyāsatīrtha on the bank of the river Sarasvatī. (77. 67)
1479. Vyāsatīrtha—Tī.—Holy for śrāddha. (77. 78)
1480. Yadukas—Ja.—No. 910.
1481. Yakṣas—Ja.—No. 470.
1482. Yamadvīpa—Dv.—No. 437.
1483. Yamunā—Rv.—Agni loved her. (29. 13)
1484. ,, —Rv.—Its source is holy for śrāddha purposes. (77. 69)
1485. ,, —Rv.—Yamunā, the best of rivers, was sister of Tvaṣṭṛ. (84. 84)
1486. ,, —Rv.—Nos. 130, 307, 308, 1009.
1487. Yavanas—P.—They were annihilated by Pramiti at the end of the Kali age. (58. 82)
1488. Yavanas—P.—Nos. 130^2, 345, 842, 844.
1489. Yavasas—Ja.—No. 470.
1490. Yaudheya—Rg.—No. 891
1491. Yuj.—Mt.—No. 130.
1492. Yūthas—Ja.—No. 569.

APPENDIX B

I

ON PLACES OF PILGRIMAGE

In the Vedic literature we find water as a great purifying agent,[1] washing off the sin of the evil-doer and the great sanctity of the water of a river is often mentioned in the ṚV. But in the Vedas we hear nothing of tīrthas or holy places of pilgrimage. The Jātakas mentioned four *titthas* named Gayā, Timbaru, Doṇa and Bāhukā.[2] Payāga (Prayāga) is also mentioned as a tittha for bathing.[3] The Buddhist Suttas state that Lord Buddha told Ānanda, " there are these four places, Ānanda, which the believing man should visit with reverence and awe". They are the places where Buddha was born, where Buddha attained to the supreme and perfect insight, where the kingdom of righteousness was set on foot by the Tathāgata and where Buddha passed away ; and " they, Ānanda, who shall die while they, with believing heart, are journeying on such pilgrimage, shall be reborn after death, when the body shall dissolve in the happy realms of heaven."[4] The Jaina Sūtras refer to holy bathing-places and they also mention separate places near rivers, marshes or ponds, where a monk or nun was not to ease nature.[5] Kauṭilya mentions tīrtha, sabhā, śālā, etc., as places where the king's agents were advised to do propoganda in favour of the king.[6] Thus, it appears that in the days of Kauṭilya, people often assembled at tirthas. In the Manusmṛti, however, pilgrimage as understood now does not appear to be popular for he regards visits to Ganges and Kurukṣetra as comparatively unimportant.[7] The Mbh. is replete with references to holy places or tīrthas and we find in that great epic the celebrated heroes or sages of tradition visiting holy spots or tīrthas almost as if on a holy campaign. There is a whole subparvan in the Āraṇyaka Book of the Mbh. devoted to the topic of tīrtha-yātrā (visiting places of pilgrimage).[8] Thus it would appear that in the period represented by the great epic the institution of pilgrimage had become well-known and popular. The Buddha-Carita of Aśvaghoṣa is familiar with separate bathing-places.[9] He is more than familiar with pilgrimages when he utters through Buddha's mouth : "The water that has been touched by the virtuous, that is the spot, if you wish for a sacred spot on the earth ; therefore I count as a place of pilgrimage only the virtues of a virtuous man".[10] In the questions of King Milinda we find sacred places familiarly mentioned.[11] In the Institutes of Viṣṇu are mentioned tīrthas called Puṣkaras

1. Keith, *Religion and Philosophy of the Veda*, (*HOS*. 32). In the Vedas we find the river Sarasvatī as holy and certain regions as previleged, cf. *ERE*. 10. 24.
2. Fausböll's edition, 5. 388 G 199.
3. *Ibid*, 6. 198. G 857.
4. *SBE*. 11. 90-91.
5. *SBE*. 45. 56 ; 22. 182.
6. P. 22.
7. *ERE*. 10. 24.
8. T. S. Shejwalkar, *BDCRI*. 5. 205 ff.
9. *SBE*. 49 (i), p. 8, 22.
10. *Ibid*. 74.
11. *Ibid*. 35. 139.

which confer eternal bliss on the giver in śrāddha. Equally fruitful is the efficacy of the muttering of prayers, offering of burnt oblations and practice of austerities at such places. Mere bathing in Puṣkara means purification of sin.[12] The work also contains a list of tīrthas belonging mostly to the Deccan. This list, however, is considered to be a later addition to the text.[13] The Viṣṇu-smṛti further says that by visiting tīrthas some minor offenders[14] become pure and that visiting places of pilgrimage is a duty, among others, common to all the castes.[15] He enjoins that ferrymen and officials at toll-offices should not levy toll on one about to visit a place of pilgrimage and asks them to restore it if it had been already levied.[16] He further adds that even the company of one purified by visiting a place of pilgrimage is itself sanctifying.[17] Thus it would appear that by the time of the compilation of this work places of pilgrimage have grown all over the country.

It appears that the institution of pilgrimage was first started by the Buddhists and this appears more probable when we consider the references of the Manu-smṛti in this connection. Later on, however, it had become common to all religions and by the time of the Institutes of Viṣṇu, it had become an established institution even with the Brahmins. The Brahmins seem to have developed the Buddist institution of pilgrimage on the lines of their institutions. The Buddhists regarded as holy the places connected with the life of Buddha, while the Brahmins knowing the sanctity of the river and the efficacy of bathing in its water enlarged the sacredness by developing the great institution of pilgrimage. The impulse to travel was already there when Indra (in Ait. Br. vii, 5) said to Hariścandra "There is no happiness for him who does not travel; living in the society of men, the best man often becomes a sinner; for Indra is the friend of the traveller. Therefore wander".[18]

In the Vāyu we often find references to tīrthas as situated on river-banks and the sanctity of the river-water is often mentioned in its geographical chapters. The peculiarity of the Vāyu information is that it associates the tīrthas mostly in connection with the śrāddha ceremonies and occasionally with the incarnations of the gods Viṣṇu and Śiva. The only clear reference to tirtha or holy place of pilgrimage in the genealogical lists occurs in connection with king Gādhi, father of the famous Viśvāmitra. But this reference occurs in the course of a narration which is undoubtedly a myth, pure and simple. This is really very significant as compared with the evidence of epic on the matter. As compared with the information of the Viṣṇu-smṛti our Purāṇa does not appear to be very elaborate.

---

12. *SBE*. 7. 256 ff. 13. See Jolly, *Introduction*, p. xxx. 14. *SBE*. 7. 135.
15. *Ibid*. 13. 16. *Ibid*. 36. 17. *Ibid*. 254. 18. *ERE*. 10. 24.

II

TĪRTHAS OR PLACES OF PILGRIMAGE

Tīrthas are occasionally glorified in the Purāṇa. It is said that even a sinner—if he is a believer—is bereft of his sin if he pays a visit to tīrthas, what then of a man of virtues ?[1] Such a person escapes his fets in chauldron and hell and finds a way to heaven and ultimately achieves mokṣa.[2] But there is an addenda that dhyāna (meditation) is the best tīrtha.[3] Gayā is said to be such a tīrtha that those in hell go to heaven and those in heaven achieve mokṣa by offering *piṇḍas* there. Many more are the merits of this tīrtha.[4] For the purposes of achieving mokṣa and for a place in heaven, gifts at tīrthas are recommended to be particularly meritorious.[5]

A tīrtha is a place where gods come down on the earth on certain occasions. The Brahma-kṣetra (i.e. the same as Kurukṣetra or Vāyupura) was founded by Brahmā and here gods, sages and munis dwell.[6] It is said that at the end of a yuga Viṣṇu is born as man in Brahmakṣetra.[7] Śiva too "will have" his incarnations at tīrthas. We are again told that in the two tīrthas of Śālagrāma and Kāśyapa (?) Dharma is actually seen in person.[8]

The sanctity of the tīrthas is indicated by the fact that they are places where men are purified of their sins. Yājñavalkya was responsible for the death of a Brahmin Devamitra Śākalya and thus he and his disciples were affected by the sin of brahmanicide (*brahma-hatyā*). But they were purified of this sin by a bath in the four tanks at Vāyupura.[9] The sacredness of the tīrthas, however, is more pronounced in the performance of śrāddha there. The śrāddha chapters of the Purāṇa are very eloquent on the merits of śrāddha performances at tīrthas and most of the tīrthas included in the appendix are found mentioned in the Purāṇa mostly for this very reason.

The tīrthas are shown situated on the river-banks and in some cases on the tops of the mountains. The Vyāsatīrtha was situated on the banks of the river Saraswatī.[10] The river Vārāhī is said to be streaming along holy tīrthas[11] and rivers are frequently described in the geographical chapters as containing holy waters due to tīrthas. For instance the river Gaṅgā "is the best of rivers and is the source of waters for

---

1. *Cf. tīrthāni anusarandhīraḥ śraddadhāno jitendriyaḥ kṛta-pāpaś ca śudhyeta kiṁ punaḥ śubha-karma-kṛt* ; 77. 125.
2. Cf. 77. 126.
3. Cf. *dhyānaṁ tīrthaparaṁ*, 77. 128.
4. Cf. No. 321 App.
5. Cf. 83. 102–5.
6. Cf. No. 1422 App. A for details.
7. Cf. No. 151 App. A.
8. *Sākṣāt* 77. 87–91.
9. For details cf. No. 1423 App. A.
10. See No. 1482 App.
11. Cf. *puṇya-tīrtha-taraṁgiṇī* 48. 39.

all the tīrthas".[12] The great tīrtha of Vāyusthāna (i.e. Vāyupura) is said to be situated on the banks of the river Ratnāvatī, which in this Kali age is known as the Dṛsadvatī.[13] We are told that by having a bath at the Kanakanandi tīrtha one goes to heaven.[14] In the Kośalā (tīrtha ?) there is a pond or well (vāpī) and by bathing here one is said to go to heaven.[15] It is unnecessary to mention the names of rivers whose waters are described in the geographical chapters as simply holy.

In the only reference to tīrtha in the genealogical portion of the Purāṇa, King Gādhi, on his way to holy places of pilgrimage, arrived at the hermitage of the Bhārgava Ṛcīka who was his son-in-law. This reference occurs in connection with the story which purports to narrate the birth of Jamadgani with the lustre of a Kṣatriya and of Viśvāmitra with the lustre of a Brahmin due to transfer of *Carus*, apparently unknowingly, which were meant by the sage Ṛcīka for his own wife and for his mother-in-law for the purpose of begetting a son.[16]

---

12. Cf. No. 297 App.
13. Cf. No. 1422 App. A ; cf. also Nos. 686, 1197, 297, App. A.
14. No. 504 App. 15. No. 601 App. 16. 91. 67 ff.

INDEX

[This Index does not include the names of Ornaments (pp. 88-9 and 208-10), Food-Preparations (pp. 91 and 211), Musical Instruments (pp. 98-9 and 217-8), Weapons (pp. 102-6 and 224-9), Plants (pp. 108-13 and 231-7), Animals (pp. 114-20 and 238-40), and of Places and Tribes (pp. 241-332), which are already alphabetically arranged and discussed in the Chapters concerned and in the Appendix A.]

ERRATA et CORRIGENDA

Page	Line	For	Read
11	3	*symantaka*	*syamantaka*
22	8	(*ṛṣanti mahat*)	(*ṛṣanti*) *mahat*
27	12	state	state is
43	33	Śādhyas	Sādhyas
43	39	*bhārgavo*	*Bhārgavo*
68	8	ś āddha	śrāddha
79	21	kroṣa	krośa
81	31	end	and
88	16	Śūras	Suras
100	6	and	(to be omitted)
101	33	mysterious reference to the chariot	reference to tl e mysterious chariot
101	38	inexhaustive	inexhaustible
155	33	Hari Vaṁśa	Harivaṁśa
171	34	Ṣamiti	Samiti
185	19	Upanīteśvara	Upamiteśvara
199	28	it and	and it
213	7	Dealer	dealer
214	1	Paruṣaka	Parūṣaka
215	23	The	(ii) The
215	30	The	(iii) The
231	17	given	discussed
261	34	Ganges	Jumna
263 } 265 } ff.	1	Identification of	Alphabetical list of